Guysborough
Sketches and Essays

Revised Edition

By A. C. JOST

GUYSBOROUGH, NOVA SCOTIA 2009

ISBN: 978-1-4269-1336-5 (sc)
ISBN: 978-1-4269-1874-2 (dj)

*Our mission is to efficiently provide the world's finest, most comprehensive
book publishing service, enabling every author to experience success.
To find out how to publish your book, your way, and have it available
worldwide, visit us online at www.trafford.com*

Trafford rev. 9/16/2009

 www.trafford.com

North America & international
toll-free: 1 888 232 4444 (USA & Canada)
phone: 250 383 6864 ♦ fax: 812 355 4082

Acknowledgements

About the Author

Dr. Arthur Cranswick Jost was born in Guysborough, Nova Scotia, in 1874 the son of Burton and Sarah (Norris) Jost. After completing high school at the county academy, he received a Bachelor of Arts degree from Acadia University . He then attended McGill Medical School. Graduating in 1897, he practiced briefly at Advocate and Neil's Harbour, Nova Scotia, before establishing himself back in Guysborough by 1901. He remained there until 1916 when he went overseas as a Medical Officer with the 64th Battalion of the Canadian Army. He left the army with the rank of Lieutenant Colonel. Dr. Jost then served as provincial health officer until 1929 and later occupied a similar post with the State of Deleware until his retirement in 1940. Returning to Guysborough in 1943, he was active in the Canadian Legion, Board of Trade, the Masonic Lodge, Order of the Eastern Star and once served as Vice-chairman of the Canadian Red Cross Society.

Dr. Jost was married twice. His first wife, Victoria Martin, died while he was serving in Europe. His second wife, Delene Bastian Reed, died just four days before the death of his youngest son, Squadron Leader Burton N. Jost, who was killed in action in Holland during the second World War .

Dr. Jost is best remembered today as the author of this book. For the last sixty years it has been regarded as the most authoritative account of the history of Guysborough County. The reader should be made aware that it was not written as a continuous narrative, but as a group of non interlinking essays. As Jost himself says in his introduction to Genealogies "more complete genealogies may in the future be completed". Some new information has therefore been incorporated into this section of the book to make the family histories more accurate.

Contents

Foreword

NOVA SCOTIA, the wharf of the Dominion, juts out from the North American continental mass as if it had been intended to be the point of approach or departure for all travelling on the North Trans-Atlantic sea lanes.

Guysborough County is the very pierhead. Excepting a slice of Labrador, the rocky promontory ending in Canso extends farthest to the east of any portion of the North American mainland. Only those barren Labrador shores, the islands of Newfoundland and Cape Breton, lying to the north and east, and the death trap of the Sable Island sands, more nearly approach the shores of Europe. It is little to be wondered at, therefore, that, in the days when the interest of all Europe was being directed to the newly discovered lands overseas, the story of discovery would refer many times and at length to Nova Scotia and to Canso. Like a gigantic finger that point beckoned to the traveller westward bound, as it pointed to the one eastbound the way to Europe and to home. The widely flaring mouth of Chedabucto Bay, of which Canso and the long promontory on which it stands forms the southern shore, stands open, as if to welcome the travel weary comer. We know of some who entered that gateway in the early years and of their aims, intents and purposes as they steered their ways into its protected waters. Some, engaged in discovery, came to replenish their supplies of fuel and water. Some came to take advantage of the fabulously rich fishery or to establish contact with Indians desiring trade. Some came on errands not so peaceful, either sent by their governments to ravage and destroy, or doing so on their own initiatives. Some came on errands of mercy, genuinely desirous of carrying to the benighted or the indifferent the message which represented to them more, perhaps, than life itself. Some came seeking refuge from persecution, some place which promised surcease from the hatreds which had made life unendurable for them elsewhere.

The earlier history of the County is built around the deeds of the first of these classes, the explorer, the fisherman and the trader. Its later and more modern history commences after the arrival of the refugee laden transports, bearing to their new homes the human debris of the Revolutionary War, the remnants of battalions of fighting men, their wives and families, the patriots who put honour above price, the persecuted fleeing from an implacable and venomous hatred.

Then, first it became necessary to make some territorial division of the hitherto undivided areas of the Province, in order to permit the machinery of government the better to function. A line was laid out across the long axis of the Province from the waters of the Atlantic Ocean on the south to those of the Gulf of St. Lawrence on the north, and so the County of Sydney came into being, with its two Districts, the Upper and the Lower. In time, this arrangement became inadequate. Then a line lengthways of the axis made the County of Antigonish of the Upper, and the County of Guysborough of the Lower, District. Then, at a time still later, when the upper end of the northerly drawn line had been swung to the west to the point where the County lines of Halifax, Pictou and Colchester Counties cornered, the limits of the County as they now are were set. Its greatest length from Cape Canso to its opposite upper corner is about ninety miles; its greatest width is about one-third that distance.

Its thirty miles of width may be considered as consisting of two zones, differing widely in their physical characteristics. Stretching the entire length of the area, along its seaward exposure, and for a width of about ten miles, is the region of rock and barren, scrubby spruce and fir, lake, morass and savannah,

1

which is characteristic of much of Nova Scotia's Atlantic seaboard. Here the geologist may revel over almost every indication of glacial action of which he can conceive, moraines, drumlins, eskers, boar's backs, and striae innumerable. Where glacial erosion has sheared away the mountain tops and exposed the deeper strata, the miner seeks the gold bearing leads which have in the past so contributed to the Provincial wealth. Here are the deeply cut harbours, long deep and narrow channels which shelter the boats of the inshore fishing fleets and give the County a shoreline, vastly greater than its point-to-point length. Nor does the evidence of erosion and deposit limit itself only to the area above the tide marks. Almost as far as the eye can reach to seaward, breakers reveal the extent and the number of the off-shore ledges, or islands, sometimes fir clad, give additional evidence of glacial action.

In the twenty miles of width which lies along the County's northern border, one sees a geological picture entirely different. Here are the timber and farm lands which form the County's forest and agricultural wealth. Here are the valley troughs of the St. Mary's and other rivers and the hills still clothed with forests, or, if cleared, forming the pasture lands which nourish the herds of cattle and flocks of sheep. It is a smiling land, with its long valley vistas, its rolling hills, its glimpses of snug farm houses nestling among the trees, its purling brooks, its fields rippling in the summer breeze, or, in autumn, its roads bordered with everlasting and goldenrod and its slopes resplendent in yellow and scarlet and crimson and gold. Well content it seems, that the days of its turbulent early history have passed.

THE INDIANS

The area now included in Guysborough County was one of relatively large importance during the period when the Micmacs held sway. It was a portion of one of the five districts into which their territory was divided. Not the least of its importance arose from the fact that through it, as through a covered way, led the road which connected the headquarters of the tribe with the rest of its sprawling territory. That territory included all of the Province of Nova Scotia, the Province of Prince Edward Island and the Gulf Coast of New Brunswick to, or beyond Gaspe. Micmac headquarters was on Cape Breton Island, far removed from their hated enemies, the Iroquois and the Eskimos. From the first of these, the Iroquois, the lands of the Malecites, who occupied the rest of New Brunswick, formed as it were a buffer state. From the second the wide expanse of the mouth of the St. Lawrence River gave protection. At one time indeed the whole area may have been Eskimo territory, but these had gradually been pushed back north of the St. Lawrence, though occasional raiding parties had made their way into the Micmac grounds as late as the early days of French occupation.

The district of which Guysborough County made a part was called by them ESKEGAWAGIK, their "Skin Drying Place", the place to which they resorted to prepare the skins on which so much of their comfort depended. Teeming with game, almost as far removed from the Iroquois and Eskimo as was Cape Breton itself, with extremes of cold much less than were to be found on the island of Cape Breton and the exposed western shore of the Gulf of St. Lawrence, it was one of their favored districts.

The French priests, our best authorities, tell us that the tribe did not number more than thirty-five hundred, so that there were many square miles for the head of each family. Tribal custom allotted to each family its area, nor are we ever told that friction developed over rival claims. The ancestors of the Indians living in the County today may have been given their hunting rights under this arrangement some hundreds of years ago.

The most compelling necessity under which an Indian lived was that of providing food for himself, his family and community. During the winter months, game, either trapped or killed in their yards in the snow, was the main source of supply. During this time the families were as a rule scattered, each in his own area, engaged in keeping themselves in food and in procuring furs for use or barter. As the spring months came on, food became more plentiful in places other than the deep forests. Fish became more abundant, filling the brooks and rivers in countless thousands as they obeyed the urge to spawn. Birds, especially seabirds, were nesting by the thousands on the islands and beaches. Berries were commencing to ripen. Accordingly, the winter home of the Indian was abandoned, usually given up for some selected locality on the bank of a river or brook near the sea, possibly within reach of a trader. What with game, fish, seals, eggs and berries there was a different menu for almost every month of the year.

The Micmacs were not included among the Indian tribes which depended largely on agriculture. After the opportunities for trading became regular and constant, even the little done in former times became curtailed. Cultivating even the most meagre plot interfered seriously with the Indian's freedom of movement, since it meant that he must be at a certain place at a certain time, to sow the seed and to reap the harvest. Freeing the Indian of this necessity was one result brought about by the advent of the trader. On the other hand, from the trader were procured axes immeasurably superior to the

3

stone ones formerly in use, guns and ammunition, fishing equipment and easily portable cooking utensils. The task of procuring food and of defence against the winter's cold became much easier.

It should not be forgotten that the Micmac territory afforded some of the best opportunities for the establishment of fishing industries to be found on the Atlantic seaboard. It attracted fishing vessels from Europe by the scores or even by the hundreds long before any attempt at permanent settlement was made. The Micmacs had been longer and more heavily exposed to European influence than almost any of the Indian tribes and were probably the richest in goods of European manufacture. The old French priests who knew both the Micmacs and the Indians of the interior are quite explicit and positive in their statements that the former enjoyed a measure of prosperity far exceeding that experienced by the Indians of the St. Lawrence River. But, if this trade had contributed to their physical profit, it may have had other and very harmful results. Those with whom the Indians had been brought into contact were by no means the best of their respective nations; in fact they may have been exactly the opposite. Thus, deteriorating influences had been at work, which the priest, however sincere he may have been, could do little to offset. As the old customs were lost, some of the old qualities disappeared. What had become of the old forensic or oratorical ability which had occasioned comment by the earliest of the French visitors who could appreciate these gifts? The cruel blood-thirstiness which is supposed to be characteristic of Indians in general never seems to have been a Micmac trait. There are few, if any, recorded instances of wanton slaughter, of the torture of prisoners or of cruelty to captives. The story of the bloodshed at Grand Pre, at Dartmouth and at Canso, all so-called Indian outrages, might perhaps be far better described as outrages into the perpetration of which the Micmacs had been coaxed or cajoled by the French. Any one gets the impression that it became increasingly difficult for the French to induce them to undertake or to participate in such deeds of violence, and, once French encouragement became inoperative, those instances of terrorism instantly ceased. In Nova Scotian history there are more instances of outrages inflicted on the Indians than of outrages inflicted by them. Their records of the treatment of crews shipwrecked on the coast seem particularly creditable, and one would be a cynic, who would say that discreditable instances are not known, only because the evidence had been destroyed. Some innate toughness of fibre saved them from being ruthlessly exterminated, as was their allied tribe, the Beothuks of Newfoundland, and to the possession of this quality they have owed their continued existence. Once the hatchet had been buried, an event which had taken place a number of years before the large influx of English settlers into the County, the Indians showed no desire to renew hostilities, and were never under any circumstances dangerous neighbours. Rather they were as they still are, somewhat pathetic figures, hopelessly caught up in the vortices of forces from which they were and still are not able to extricate themselves.

A group of people so nomadic in their habits would not be long in establishing for themselves a number of well known travel routes, and one of the best known of these, one of the trunk roads, extended almost the entire length of Guysborough County. It perhaps can be best traced if we consider ourselves placed at St. Peters, in the Island of Cape Breton, the easiest point of entrance to or exit from the Bras D'Or Lakes, on the shores of which was the headquarters of the tribe. From this point, the traveller west bound in his canoe, entered at once the sheltered waters of St. Peter's Bay and Lennox Passage. From the western end of this latter three routes diverged. If his inclination or desire so led him he could turn to the right, thread the narrow Strait of Canso to its northern extremity, and then, changing his course to the west, follow the shore line of the Gulf, past Tracadie and Antigonish, around Cape George, beyond Merigomish and Pictou, till he came to that route, which, turning north, continued to follow the shore of the Gulf, until Tantramar and the Isthmus of Chignecto ushered him out of the Province. Or, if he so desired, he could turn sharply to his left, around Isle Madame, and thence, weather conditions permitting, take the ocean jump to Canso, from which point, the entire south shore of Nova Scotia lay before him, broken at frequent intervals by harbours or rivers which afforded him access to inland camping sites.

What was, however, the most important route lay directly before him. Crossing the Strait of Canso and following closely the north shore of Chedabucto Bay, it was possible for him to enter the two-mile estuary of Salmon River, and at the head of tide water, the river itself. This River and a series of lakes could be followed or traversed for about twenty miles, to a height of land where a group of rivers or streams took origin. To the right or northward at a distance of about five miles were the headwaters of the South River, emptying its waters into Antigonish harbour and the Gulf. South at approximately the same distance were the headwaters of the Country Harbour River, finding the Atlantic under the shadows of Cape Mocodome. A little distance beyond were the streams entering the Atlantic at Port Hilford. Immediately in front of him and about ten miles distant were the eastern branches of St. Mary's River. These could be followed to their junction with the West River of St. Mary's, which would take him directly to the sea, or the West River could be entered and ascended for about thirty miles. About mid-distance to the north were the lakes or streams from which the East River of Pictou took its source. At the end, near the point where the Counties of Guysborough, Halifax, Pictou and Colchester now corner, was the height of the watershed which gave rise to a group of waterways. To the south were the lakes from which the Sheet Harbour River arises. To the southwest were the headwaters of the Musquodoboit River. West of the traveller were the origins of the Stewiacke. Entry on the latter gave him access immediately to the waters of Minas Basin, from which any of the routes of the western end of the Province could be reached. In his passage down the Stewiacke, he was following a portion of the canoe route from Halifax to Annapolis. He would here follow or cross the winter route of land travel, that, for example, which had been taken by the force of French and Indians which wrote in blood the story of the attack on Noble's sleeping forces at Grand Pre.

This route, taking advantage of the valleys of the Salmon, the St. Mary's and the Stewiacke Rivers, was an important one in the Micmac travel system. Nicholas Denys appreciated its importance, when he selected two points on it, Chedabucto and St. Peter's, as sites for his fishing and trading establishments, as did the Trading Company of Acadia, which at a later date occupied the old stand at Chedabucto. Villebon also may have done so, when he reported so favourably to his home Government in 1699 on the desirability of strongly holding Chedabucto as a trading centre. While primarily a canoe route, the route of land travel probably followed it quite closely, but taking advantage of the nearby hardwood ridges, in order to avoid the more impenetrable growths of the river valleys. It was by this road that Indians asserted their ability to send a message from Canso to Port Royal in six days, a distance of about two hundred and forty miles as the crow flies. In order to have done this, they must have been able to travel at a much faster rate than was possible across country from Port Royal to LaHave, which they were able to do in two days and a half. The latter distance in a straight line is not more than seventy miles.

But trunk roads were perhaps the Micmac's minor interest. All around him lay the opportunities for indulging himself in his desire to be on the move. His home was any place where he at any time happened to be. A travel trip was nothing for which provision must long be made. He could be on the road anywhere at any time at a few hours notice, taking all his possessions with him. Any river capable of bearing his canoe could beckon him; any hillside free from obstruction to travel was a road. And the effect of exposure to European influence but increased if anything the Micmac's urge and ability to travel. There were more bargain counters where he might dispose of his furs, with, unfortunately, more opportunities of his procuring the firewater, which his lately awakened thirst so craved. Life was easier by reason of his better weapons and equipment. No longer was it necessary for him to arrange his route of travel so as to be able to encamp near one of the cumbersome and ungainly wooden vessels, roughly cut out of a tree trunk, which, prior to his obtaining easily portable cooking vessels, determined very often his stopping places. Thus, the times of the late French occupation, were the Micmac's most prosperous days.

Before the coming of the European, the Indian may have killed game for the killing's sake, but with his crude weapons he could not deplete the fur bearers or the animals he needed for food. His need for furs was limited to the small quantity required for his comfort or for barter with his own race. There was game in abundance. After the traders came, all the fur which the Indian could procure could easily be disposed of, and, after better weapons had been provided, great and wasteful inroads were made on the game. We are told that on at least one occasion the stench of the carcasses of moose killed only for their hides, could be smelt by the crews of passing vessels. At the time of the English occupation the effect of this wastefulness was commencing to be felt seriously.

Then, too, the Micmac was finding that it was difficult for him to adjust himself to the conditions brought about by the disappearance of the French sovereignty. He had been friends with the French for nearly two hundred years; he had adopted their religion and had maintained an alliance which the English could not shake. The French had made themselves at home in the Micmac wigwams and had even taken Indian women for their wives. But now the French were gone, and the Micmac was little more than a hunted outcast in his own land, with but recently a price upon his head, and the scalps of his women and .. children drying in a Halifax Government office. One wonders that they survived at all. That they did so was largely because they buried their animosity to the English more quickly than did the English to them. Had they continued to resist, the tribe would almost assuredly have met the same fate as did the Beothuks in Newfoundland.

It seems somewhat remarkable that, taking into consideration the important place in the Indian territory which the area now included in Guysborough County had, and the presence within its borders or such a large group as to have justified the giving of the name, Indian Harbour, to one of their resorts, there have been found so few evidences of Indian occupation, as shown by artifacts and other Indian remains. An occasional arrow head or axe has been discovered, but, possibly from lack of interest or of careful search, evidences of Indian occupation have been rather infrequently found. One of the most interesting finds was made but several years ago, near the mouth of Salmon River, on the old travel route which has been referred to. The river breaks out into the Bay at the northern end of a long gravel beach, the northern side of the entrance to the estuary being formed by a clay knoll, now quite rapidly being eroded. This erosion, several years ago, brought into view a copper pot, seamless and in a fair state of preservation. It contained some bones, a portion of the skull and some of the long bones of what had apparently been a young woman, fragments of hair and fur, beads and wampum. Here had taken place, apparently some time in the seventeenth century, the final act of the long ritual which formed a Micmac burial ceremony. Soon after a death, following a crude embalming or the removal of the flesh from the bones, the remains were wrapped in furs. This fur-wrapped bundle was either kept in one of the wigwams or it was placed in some hidden spot where it would be safe from molestation. The possessions of the decedent were sometimes burnt, in order that there might be no hard feelings among those to whom otherwise they might have been passed, on the plea of unequal or unfair distribution. It might be some months before the final act of disposal took place. The time for that having come around, the bones were buried, in some secret place, often on an island, in order that enemies might not be able to treat them with disrespect. There is an old Canso record of European sailors having defiled Indian graves, stealing the furs in which bodies had been placed, and also one account of the death penalty having been inflicted on one member of the tribe, who had made known to visitors the place where bodies, wrapped in furs, might be found.

If the settlers arriving in 1784 anticipated hostility from the Indians residing in the area—as they well might have done—it was not long before it became abundantly clear that the anticipations were baseless. Those coming from Carolina may have actually seen the results of Indian fighting in the Southern States and may have dreaded the possibility of finding their Micmac neighbours as bloodthirsty and cruel as those with whose deeds they had become acquainted. The old settlers, those already occupying their little homesteads, knew the Indians much better, and Captain Hadley at least could bear personal testimony of their kindly consideration and assistance to seamen who had been wrecked near their camping grounds. It therefore was not long till their harmlessness was thoroughly appreciated, and though the Indians were never welcomed in the growing settlement, it was not because of the fact that they were considered dangerous. Their inquisitiveness and possibly their acquisitiveness, the latter possibly the result of their communistic ideas of property, prompted the newcomers to keep them at arm's length. One quick-witted woman on one occasion is said to have very speedily brought about their instant departure from her home by informing them that an individual ill in the house had small pox, a European disease they had already learned to dread. Perhaps on both sides was there the wish, more or less concealed, that all but the wholly necessary contact was to be dispensed with, and on that basis the relations between the new and the old occupants of the land was maintained.

7

INDIAN NAMES IN GUYSBOROUGH COUNTY

The County of Guysborough comprises a large portion of the old Micmac district called by them ESKEGAWAGIK, which was made up of the entire coast line of Nova Scotia from the Strait of Canso to Halifax. This was the nearest of the districts or subdivisions to the Island of Cape Breton, on which was the tribal headquarters. The meaning of the name is the place "where skins are dried", and the indications are that the area was one of the Micmac's common hunting resorts. Moreover, the county was traversed lengthwise by one of their old travel routes, the inner and protected route used by them in travel to and from the Island of Cape Breton. It would be remarkable if many place-names in the County did not hark back to the County's original inhabitants.

That many of these names have been preserved for us is due almost wholly to the labours of Dr. Silas T. Rand and Dr. W. F. Ganong. One of these admirably supplements the other. One, the philologist, has delved deeply in the study of the language itself and has compiled a dictionary. The other, versed in much of the Micmac language and in those of the allied tribes, has made exhaustive studies of the place-names themselves. We are thus permitted to profit from the happy combination of the labours of the philologist and the research worker.

There is a relatively short list of names of Indian origin which are still in use and some of these have been quite materially altered from their original form.

CANSO.

A number of variations of this word occur. It is one of the oldest, if not the oldest place-name in the story of the entire continent. It was Canso or some variation of that word from the very first of the recorded history of the New World. The variations have been numerous, both in the French and the English periods. The word has not always referred to the same place. Sometimes the Cape of Canso replaces the name of Canso as a harbour. In some of the first maps what is now called the Chedabucto Bay appears as the Bay of Canso. For many years the existence of a passage between Cape Breton and Nova Scotia had been overlooked. It was not unnatural that, the Bay being so named, the Strait also should bear the name, and other names, the Passage Courant and the Passage de Fronsac, be superseded. Thus as Cape, Harbour, Bay or Strait the name Canso appears on almost all the old maps or charts.

In LesCarbot's map of 1609 the word is written CAMPSEAU, the Harbour, the Bay and the Strait being so designated. In Champlain's Voyages and maps from 1613 to 1632 the word appears as CANCEAU or oftener as CAMPSEAU, the Harbour, the Bay and the Strait being again referred to. In that of 1632 the spelling is CANCEAU for the Harbour and Strait and CAMPSEAU for the Bay. Father Biard in the Jesuit Relations used the words CAMPSEAU and CAMPSEAUX; DeLaet in 1630 used CAMSEAU. Creuxius in 1664 used the Latin form CAMPSEIUM for both Bay and Strait. Denys, thoroughly acquainted with the entire area, used the word CAMPSEAUX. DuVal in 1677 used CAMSEAU for the Strait, CANZEAU for the Harbour, Jumeau in 1685 used CANCEAU, applied only to the Cape. In the De Meulles-Franquelin map of 1686 the word appears as CAMCEAUX, again for the Cape alone. Belin in 1744 used the spelling CANCEAU. The English map made by Moll in 1715 used the word CANSEAUX to the Strait and Morris in 1749 first used the spelling CANSO. Haliburton as late as 1829 used the

9

word CANSEAU.

There is a difference of opinion between Rand and Ganong in connection with the root words involved. Both agree that an Indian word meaning "cliff" is concerned, but they disagree as to another root component. Rand's idea is that the intention is to describe something opposite or away from the place itself; Ganong's that it describe something opposite or away from the speaker. Rand's opinion therefore is that the word means a place opposite cliffs; Ganong's that it means a place beyond cliffs.

From an entirely topographical point of view there is reason for the acceptance of Prof. Ganong's opinion. It can not be said that, looking outwards from Canso town or harbour, there faces the observer such an array of cliffs or mountains as would justify the assertion that Canso lay facing or opposite them. On the other hand, an observer, viewing the southern shore of. Chedabucto Bay from any point near its head or along its northern shore, could easily appreciate the fact that there was a place which might be considered as being beyond the rather formidable array of steep and broken hillsides which form the southern shore of the bay. At the head of the Bay it is known that a well known old Indian travel route emerged; to any traveller along that route the reason for the name is easily understandable.

The actual Micmac word from which the name Canso is taken is said to be KAMSOK or CAMSOK, this being a contraction from the complete word, KAMSOKOOCHECH, which Dr. Rand (in Prof. Ganong's opinion somewhat erroneously) defines as Little Canso, and applies to White Haven. Here again, there seems to be reason for Prof. Ganong's disagreement, for one little understands why White Haven, which could hold many Cansos, rightfully could be considered as a "little" Canso. It may be, however, that the place called by the Indians KAMSOKOOCHECH or Little Canso was not White Haven but one of the smaller coves or harbours nearer Canso itself.

The opinion of these students must be considered very conclusive, even in the face of those who have at one time or another advanced other definitions for the word. One such suggestion is that the name is a corruption of a word signifying goose, in allusion to the presence in nearby waters of large flocks of these migrants. But these are migrants, little likely to be found in large numbers at any time of the year when sailors from European waters were also present. There is, too, a very mythical sailor named Canse, whose name has been attached to the place, but so tenuously that little conviction accompanies the assertion. Both of these suggestions are interesting, however, in that they carry the attempt to name the place to an early Portuguese occupancy or visitation, some time in the earliest years of the sixteenth century.

TRACADIE.

It is but to be expected that, under conditions of a somewhat limited vocabulary, coupled with a marked tendency for Indian place-names to be descriptive of some physical feature or striking peculiarity, the same name should given to several communities, if in each of those places those features or peculiarities were prominent. This probably explains the fact that there were no fewer than four Tracadies in the area over which the Micmacs held sway. In one at least, Guys-borough County can be considered as being concerned.

There is little doubt, either of the Indian derivation or of the adequacy of the description. Both Dr. Rand and Dr. Ganong are of the opinion that the name means the "place where the Indians were accustomed to reside." The actual word from which the name Tracadie is taken is said to be TULUKADIK, and its meaning is "dwelling place".

10

CHEDABUCTO.

This is one of the names which has been changed very little from the original Indian form. That is SEDABOOKTOOK and its meaning is "running far back", in allusion to the length of the harbour, nearly ten miles from the head of tide to the harbour entrance. Both the description and the explanation appear to be adequate. The name is to be found on maps appearing after the middle of the seventeenth century or after Nicholas Denys' book and map had been issued.

It seems to have taken the geographers some little time definitely to fix its location. The name first appears on Nicholas Denys' map, and he was, so far as is known, the founder of the settlement, though it may easily be that by no means was he the first person to have used the harbour as a base for fishing operations. There is more or less resemblance between Chebucto, Chedabucto and possibly Richibucto, and it may be that geographers after Denys found this resemblance more or less confusing. The DeMuelles Map of 1686 correctly places and names both the Bay of Chedabucto and the Fort of Chedabucto. It, however, places another Chedabucto on the Atlantic coastline, west of Halifax, between the harbour or bay called the Bay de Muelles (which seems to be Halifax Harbour) and Mirliguaiche, this second Chedabucto corresponding in position with St. Margaret's Bay. Here it appears that an error was made due to the resemblance of the names Chebucto and Chedabucto. In a map of the Vissher collection dated about 1700, there is an error in the siting of what is intended presumably to be the fort or settlement, since it is placed near the northern, not the southern, extremity of the Strait of Canso. In LaHontan's map of the year 1715, there is not even an indentation corresponding to Chedabucto Bay lying between Canso and the Strait of Canso, while there is both a Chedabucto and a Sibucto (intended probably for Chebucto) located in New Brunswick north of the Isthmus of Chignecto. La Hontan, had, it will be remembered, little or no personal knowledge of Acadie, his fields of duty having been in those countries attainable through the St. Lawrence River, or in Newfoundland. Moll seems to have followed the lead given by LeHontan. Chabert's map of 1750 does not name Chedabucto at all, though in his text he speaks of the Bay and of the harbour lying at the head of the bay.

Nor does it seem likely that, in view of the agreement between the two authorities as respects the meaning of the word, consideration should be given to the fact, that according to the local Indians, the words Chedabucto and Chebucto are related, one referring to the place where the fire ended, the other to the place where the fire stopped, these having been given after a fire had raged along the coast many years ago.

MOCODOME.

Cape Mocodome is a noted geographical feature near the entrance to Country Harbour. The word in the Micmac language is MKUDOMK, and the meaning is the "haunt or home of the black-backed gull". It was in the first place applied not to the Cape, but to the Island lying not far from the entrance to the St. Mary's River. The island is now known as Goose Island, though it is thought to be the same one as that to which Champlain gave the name Isle Verte, or Green Island. What is now called Green Island is one lying to the east of the one named by Champlain, situated near the Isaac's Harbour entrance. It appears on maps as early at least as those to be found in the Vissher collection, the date of which is about 1700.

11

POMQUET

The Indian form of this word is POGUMKEK. Several meanings have been given, one of which, that it is the place of dry sand, is at least the more understandable.

There has been given to us in far greater number the Indian names for places, which, re-christened, are now known to us under a different nomenclature. These include almost all the prominent geographical features of the County.

The Strait of Canso, the Passage Courant of Champlain and the Passage de Fronsac of later French geographers, was known to the Indians as TAOOEG-UNAK, signifying a "passage" or "way". Port Mulgrave was to the Indian WOLUMKWAKAGUNUCHK, or "the lobster ground". Pirate Cove was called TESOGWODE, meaning "the place of flakes", this being one of the few places of which we know in which a hint is given of the antiquity of the name. It must have been of comparatively late origin, after the use of the Cove by some now unknown European fisherman. To the little island near the Cape Breton shore not far from the southern entrance of the Strait was given the name APAGWIT, the same name as had been given to Prince Edward Island, and recognizable as Abegweit, still in use. It means "lying on the water". The point of land called Red Head, also near the entrance of the Strait, was called WIP-KOOGWEIIK, the explanation of the name not being given.

In Chedabucto Bay, Queensport was called WEDONIK, meaning "having a mouth" and to another locality near it had been given the name WEDONE-JECH, another name not translated. Fox Island was called SEBELOG-WOKUN, meaning "the place where skins are stretched", and also WOKWIS-WAMUNEGOO, the present English name being but a translation of the latter. Along the Atlantic coast there was a CAMSOGOOCHECH or "little Canso" supposed to be White Haven, though it may have been one of the smaller coves or harbours between White Haven and Canso. Port Felix went by the name of WOLUNKAK, meaning the "scooped out place". Cole Harbour was known as WONPAAK, or the "place of still water", having reference either to the harbour itself or the river a short distance above salt water. The name for Tor Bay is interesting, in that apparently the Indians mistook the name, very often pronounced Tar Bay. In giving that place a name, the attempt was made to translate that word into Micmac, the word UPKOOAKADIK resulting, the meaning of which is "the place for pitch or tar". This is another instance of a name being given at a comparatively recent date, since Tor Bay is of comparatively recent naming. New Harbour was called OKOBOOGWEK, meaning "a foaming tideway", which does not seem entirely appropriate. Its dark brackish water, lighter in weight than sea water, seems to gather froth or foam very rapidly. That place was also called ANSAAKW, meaning "a solitary rock", which may have referred to the large rock lying in the upper reaches of the harbour, not far from the entrance of the river into the harbour. Country Harbour was another place of two names, one, ANUKWAKADE, meaning "the place for flounders", and the other MOOLABOOGWEK, meaning "deeply gullied out". The first may have been intended for one of the coves along the harbour shore; the second admirably describes the sunken valley of the harbour itself. Indian Harbour was called UTKOGUNAAKADE, meaning "the place of autumn fishery". Wine Harbour had two names, one, PULAMKEEGUNUCHK, meaning "an outlet through the sand", the other PELUMKEAGUNECH, meaning "the fish spawning place". Liscomb Harbour was called MEGADAWIK, meaning the "place of eel fishery", and Marie Joseph went by the name of KULOKWEJOOK, or "the sculpin ground". Thus the names have been preserved of almost every one of the prominent harbours along the coast line.

To a lake said to have been near Canso, (but which might easily have been the Loon Lake near Lundy) which was much frequented by loons, was given the name KWEMOOAKADIK meaning "a place where loons are to be found", a description for which many Nova Scotia lakes could qualify. A hill near Country Harbour was called WEESIK, indicating that near there was "the home of the beaver".

Perhaps of special interest are the names of a number of points along the travel route which ran westward, connecting Salmon River with the head waters of the Stewiacke and Musquodoboit Rivers. Salmon River itself was called ANASAAK, meaning "a solitary rock" the appropriateness of which is not understood, but which may have referred to the Salmon Hole above the New Harbour road. The first lake on the string, now called Chisholm's Lake or O'Neal's lake was called OSOOGOMUSOOGWEDAMK, meaning "a ford or wading across place". The second one, Miller's lake, was called MIL-PAACHK, meaning "the place of many coves", an entirely adequate description, as one who has almost been lost on it can testify. The third one, now called DesBarres Lake, was known as UTKOSKWAACHK, meaning "the twin girls", in memory possibly of some long forgotten incident occurring in the vicinity. The fourth, now called the Beaver Dam Lake, was called CLOOCHEOW-PAACHK , meaning "the cross shaped lake", a very adequate description. The fifth, or Lyon's Lake was known by the name of NEMCHENOKPAACHK or "the cross wise lying lake". In this instance the description is not said to be very accurate. The sixth lake, now called Round Lake, was called NOOGOOMKU-BAAK, indicating "the place of fine white sand", and this description is said to be very correct. The seventh, known locally as the Three Cornered Lake, was called MTABESWAAKADE, meaning "the place for horned pouts or catfish". The forks of the St. Mary's River was called NIMNOGUN, or "the black birch tree", and the St. Mary's (though this may have been intended for another stream than the River now so called) was NABOOSAKUNUK, or "a bead string". Possibly this was intended to call to mind a long past accident or incident which had taken place on its banks.

THE NORSE

From the time when first he came into possession of a vessel of his own, and could therefore please his fancy as to his sailings, either for pleasure or profit, Bjarne Herjulfson had spent each alternate winter at home in Iceland with his father.

The engagement had been kept during the winter of 984. The spring saw Bjarne again on the move. Now the fall of 986 had come around and it was time for him to start homeward for the usual winter visit. But, behold, when Bjarne arrived in Iceland, his father was not there. Eric Thorwaldson had in the meantime returned to Iceland from Greenland, discovered by him in the course of his three-year outlawry from his Iceland home, bringing such enthusiastic reports of the wonders and advantages of the newly found land, that he had had little trouble in inducing a number of his old time associates to experience these advantages for themselves. Bjarne's father was one of those so charmed by Eric's glowing account that he had undertaken to substitute the comforts of Iceland for the novelties of Greenland. Now, what was Bjarne to do? He decided quickly. Since Herjulf, the father, had gone to Greenland, Bjarne, the son, must follow him, if the two-year engagement was to be kept.

Instead of Greenland, experienced navigator though he was, Bjarne's landfall, after he had left Iceland and the long northerly gale had subsided, was far to the south, believed in fact to be some place in the vicinity of Cape Cod. So he sailed north. He coasted for several days along a low shore to his left, and only after many days was his haven in Greenland reached. Thus was the biennial tryst kept. The important news he brought to the Greenland settlers was that on at least two of the lands which he had seen there was an abundance of timber, something sorely needed both in Greenland and Iceland.

RESEN 1605

Ed. Note: The 1605 Resen Map (Copenhagen, Kongelige Bibliotek) shows Viking sites in North America. Dr. Jost is incorrect in thinking Markland is Nova Scotia, it is Labrador and Vinland is Newfoundland.

This was the inducement which led Lief, son of Eric, to endeavour to backtrack Bjarne's route. He did so, discovering Helluland (now Newfoundland) and Markland (now Nova Scotia) and finally Vinland, wintering there in the year 1001. Tales of other adventures he had to tell when he arrived home, sufficient to fire the imagination of Thorwald, his brother. But Thorwald, the unfortunate, died, the victim of an Indian arrow, though not without there having been named two additional localities in the newly discovered wonder-land, Keelness, where had been erected on a prominent headland the old keel which it had been necessary to remove from his ship, and Crossness, where took place the fatal attack by the Indians. Then Thorstein,. Thorwald's brother, sailed, intending to bring back Thorwald's body for interment in consecrated ground, but was driven far off his course by adverse winds. But next, Thorfin Karlsefni won through, with his ship load of persons intending to settle, but prevented in this by the hostility of the Indians. When he came back to Iceland, he reported the finding of Thorwald's old keel, and thereafter the path was so well known that Freydis, Lief's half sister, could and did follow it.

So runs one commentator's version of the old Sagas, with perhaps as many versions as there are commentators, but after these voyages the curtain drops. Were there more voyages, more navigators? Nansen thinks so, in fact so many of them that their voyages became commonplace as were the trips to the Baltic. Some portion of the North American coast seems to have been visited as late as 1 342, but the details of the many voyages probably made in the whole period of about three hundred and fifty years are lacking.

And so it is now impossible to do more than hazard a guess as to the circumstances under which some one of a crew of a Norse vessel, presumably some time in the 11th century, failed to carry with him when he returned to his vessel—if indeed he returned at all—the axe with which he had been felling timber on a Cole Harbour hillside. There may have been only an accident, since many a lumberman has inadvertently mislaid his axe. There may have been a tragedy, Indian arrows ending the axe-man's labours, and possibly not his alone but those of all his associates. Only the axe remains to tell the tale, with its Runic markings on the blade, its wooden handle long since disappeared, its once keen edge now dulled by eight hundred years of exposure to the elements.

It is said to have been found lying near the surface of the ground by a fisherman-farmer tilling his land about the year 1880. The spot where it was found was a sandy knoll east of the Cole Harbour entrance and the unusual appearance and rather odd shape of the find at once attracted attention. It was taken to the home of the finder, and though conjecture was often made concerning its origin and history, no effort was made to examine it carefully. In the year 1936, an itinerant prospector, who had made himself nearby a rough shelter in which to live while engaged in the task of searching for mineral specimens, happened to visit the home where the axe was still preserved. He was shown it and his curiosity was aroused. He received permission to take it with him to his shanty to examine at his leisure. There it was placed in a container of kerosene oil, with the idea of removing some of the rust and corrosion. Then an accident occurred. The shanty in some way caught fire and was burned to the ground. In the ruins the axe was found, and it was seen that the heat and the oil had removed much of the heavily caked accretion. On the sides of the blade were a number of peculiar marks, very prominent on the left side, much more corroded and less distinguishable on the right.

The axe is now about one pound and twelve ounces in weight. The width of the blade is somewhat more than double the width of the poll. Its depth from poll to edge is approximately double the width of the edge. On the inner side a tang projects, probably intended to re-enforce the handle. The Professor of Physical Metallurgy of Harvard University reports that it is very primitive manufacture and that it consists of an extremely high quality of steel. The markings on it are said to be of two distinct types. Olaf Strandwold, an expert on the subject of old Norse runes, has deciphered both. The upper one was driven deeply into the steel in the process of manufacture, and this rune, he thinks, is the name of the maker. The other markings consist of a series of semi-circles, with straight lines and dots, the semi-circles being seven in number, the whole being "secret runes" which Mr. Strandwold has had little difficulty in translating. According to him the inscription reads,—"Engr engraved this for Aelu", Engr being the name of the craftsman, Aelu the name of the original owner of the axe. He has not been able to decipher the rune on the other side of the blade.

The axe is now in the possession of a gentleman living in Hartford, Conn., and its discovery has been hailed as very convincing proof of the presence of Norsemen in Nova Scotia, some time in the 11th Century, the runes conforming with other known specimens of that date.

Whether that conclusion is entirely justified or not it is difficult to say. It would be justified, if we knew that the axe had been in the possession of none other than Norsemen, previous to the time of its discovery on the Cole Harbour hillside. But could it not have been brought here by some European trader, himself ignorant of its value, but thoroughly aware that even the gatherings from European junk heaps might be very profitably exchanged with the Indians for furs? How can it now be told who carried this interesting relic across the Atlantic?

Or, is the presence of the axe to be considered as a link in the chain of evidence, corroborative of the opinion which has been expressed, that Keelness, where Thorvald's discarded keel was later seen by Karlsefni, was no other than one of the Guysborough County headlands? The answer to the question may be in the negative, a most decided and vociferous negative on the part of some of the commentators, though at least one of them has expressed the opinion that Keelness was one of the prominences on the Eastern Nova Scotia coast line. But the Norse Sagas present much the same opportunity for differences of opinion respecting elucidation and exegesis as does the Bible, and the intolerance to adverse opinion which the theologian exhibits is not greater than that displayed by the Norse commentator.

So, though we may accept the statement that a Norse axe was found on a Cole Harbour hill, all else is lost in a haze of doubt and uncertainty.

PORT SAVALET

If old Captain Savalet, in the fall of the year 1607, after the visit of Champ-lain and LesCarbot to his fishing establishment in the New World, succeeded in piloting safely his laden schooner into his Basque home port, he had ended his eighty-fourth Trans-Atlantic voyage. That surely was a record to be commented upon, and one which up to that period few or none had surpassed. Surely, too, the explorers were entirely justified in doing what they could to perpetuate the memory of the worthy old pioneer, by giving his name to the hitherto unnamed little port, the occupant of which had extended to them a greatly appreciated hospitality. True, the benefit was not entirely one-sided, since in return it had been possible for the visitors to make a little more secure the tenure of the temporary occupant to the little port which he had made the base of his fishing operations. There is something very creditable to both parties in the story of the incident, not only to those who were engaged in one of the first attempts to acquaint themselves with the potentialities for settlement which the—to them—New World afforded, but as well to him whom the newcomers were not slow in recognizing as one who had already done in practice much that they were planning to do in the future, but of which they yet knew only the theory. They were amateurs in discovery, and must have recognized in him one capable of being to them a very Mentor, one little vocal perhaps, but none the less qualified by an experience far exceeding their own, an experience worthy both of comment and acknowledgement. What would one not give for a full account of that experience.

But, though both Champlain and LesCarbot intended as much as lay in their power to perpetuate the memory of one whose record was even to them a notable one, an unkind history has almost entirely annulled the effort. The little port was one which, though chosen probably from many sites by Savalet for his own particular requirements, did not have those advantages or qualifications which were required in the new order of things which the explorers were desirous of bringing about.

Perhaps its very size was against it, though that size suited most admirably Captain Savalet's requirements. Perhaps it was tucked away so safely among the reefs and rocks of the broken shore line, as to be too inaccessible. Perhaps it was too far removed from protection in the troublous times which were ahead. Canso, the pierhead of the Continent, was but a short distance to the eastward, and was already a point of rendezvous for craft westbound, as it was the point of departure for those returning home. Perhaps Port Savalet suffered from the propinquity of its more prominent neighbour. For it was to come about that, though some of the places visited and named by the exploring group were to retain those names and remain for all time more or less identifiable, to Port Savalet such a future was denied, and the very whereabouts of the little harbour where the hearty hospitality had been given and accepted, is now a matter of doubt.

The comments made by Champlain and LesCarbot deserve reproduction in their entirety. From these reports we get almost the only information now available concerning the port. Champlain's narrative tells of the stages of the voyage by which Isle Verte had been reached and then proceeds,—

> "Thence we went to- a place where there is an inlet with two or three islands and a very good harbour, distant three leagues from Isle Verte. We passed also by several islands near and in a line with each other

which we named the Isles Rangèes, and which are distant six or seven leagues from Isle Verte. Afterwards we passed by another bay, containing several islands and proceeded to a place where we found a vessel engaged in fishing between some islands and distant four leagues from the Isles Rangèes. This place we named Savalette the name of the master of the vessel engaged in fishing, a Basque, who entertained us bountifully and was very glad to see us since there were some savages there who purposed some harm to him, which we prevented. Leaving this place, we arrived at Canso, distant six leagues from the port of Savalette."

LesCarbot gives us much more detail. He, accompanying Champlain, was giving his version of their stage-by-stage travels along the coast, bound to Canso, from which place the united expedition was to return to France.

"Finally, we arrived within four leagues of Canso, at a harbour where a fine old fisherman from St. Jean De Luz, named Captain Savalet, was fishing. He received us with every possible courtesy, and inasmuch as this harbour, which though small is excellent, has no name, I have given it on my map the name of Savalet. The worthy old man told us that that voyage was his forty-second to these parts, and one must remember that these Newfoundlanders make but one a year. He was wondrous content with his fishing, and told us that he caught daily a good fifty crowns worth of cod and that his voyage was worth to him about ten thousand francs. He had sixteen men in his employ and his vessel was of eighty tons burden and was able to carry one hundred thousand dry fish. He was at times troubled by the savages encamped there who too boldly and impudently went on board his ship, and carried off what they listed. To stop this, he threatened them that we would come and put them, one and all, to the sword, if they did him any injury. This frightened them, and they did not do him so much harm as they otherwise would have done. . . . Now the courtesy of this man extended not only to ourselves, but also to all of our party who passed the harbour for it was the port of call in going and coming to Port Royal. But some of those who went to fetch us behaved worse than the savages, and conducted themselves towards him as the gendarme does to the peasant; of which I heard with great regret. There we spent four days on account of the contrary wind."

It is of interest, also, to note the comments which Nicholas Denys makes of his portion of the coast line.

"From River Sainte Marie to the Cape of Campseaux there is a good ten leagues. Having made four or five leagues along the coast, one comes to a bay where there are rocks. There is no refuge here save for boats. About three leagues out there are islands where one or two vessels can anchor, but with little safety. Here they make their fishery and dry their fish upon the islands where there is not much woods. From the bay, continuing the route along the coast, there are only high lands and rocks without refuge."

The accounts of Champlain and LesCarbot supplement themselves very nicely, picturing for us not only Savalet and his retreat, but as well the individuals who tell the stories. Champlain, careful, precise and laconic, contents himself with the statement that at the time of the visit, Savalet was met, his hospitality was thoroughly appreciated and that some little return was given him for that hospitality. Those facts were sufficiently noteworthy in his opinion to justify the perpetuation of the memory of the incident by attaching Savalet's name to the hitherto unnamed locality. Possibly jealous even then of his coming reputation as a cartographer, he did not intend to sully that reputation by making any statement which he was not in a position to fully substantiate, but contented himself with a bald statement of the facts with which he was personally acquainted and for which he could vouch. If Savalet made to him any reference to a very lengthy period of connection with the Atlantic fisheries, Champlain, with no opportunity for deciding for himself the accuracy of the claim, did not accept the responsibility of passing it on to posterity. On the other hand, LesCarbot, the poet and man of imagination, as prolix and verbose as Champlain was precise and reticent, scented at once the human interest to be attached to Savalet's tale, and did not hesitate to pass it on to his readers, without, apparently, concerning himself greatly with its accuracy. Champlain may have had more experience with the "brassbound" men of the sea, who are "splendaciously mendacious" when ashore, and may have listened to the story with his tongue in his cheek. But most of LesCarbot's readers would like to believe it and would be of the opinion that, if Savalet told the truth, his record deserves recognition, and that, if he did not tell the truth, he also deserves recognition, though for an entirely different reason.

There are several things which will be immediately noted with these accounts. The first of these is the differences in the estimates of the distances involved. LesCarbot estimates the distances from Savalet to Canso to be four leagues; Champlain estimates it to be six. A French league, it will be remembered, is supposed to be equivalent to three English miles, or to be more exact, a little over two and two thirds miles. Denys estimates the whole distance from St. Mary's River to Canso to be about ten leagues: Champlain estimates it to be sixteen or seventeen. The means of computing distances, if any were available at all, were rudimentary and individual opinions could and did vary widely. But Champlain's estimates, as we shall see, were seldom far wrong, and in respect of them a great deal of reliance can be placed. A second thing is the accentuation of the island features of the harbour, and that this is done by Champlain, the correct and precise. He says plainly that the site of the fishery was "between some islands". LesCarbot only says that the harbour was "small but excellent". And Denys, on whose statements in this connection a great deal of reliance ought to be placed, says specifically that there were islands in the bay where vessels had been accustomed to "make their fishery and dry their fish upon the islands"; A minor point is the difference in the spelling of the name, and perhaps in this connection LesCarbot's rendering is the more correct. LesCarbot uses the shorter form, Champlain the longer one, and from them later writers have taken their cues.

It is perhaps hopeless to expect that much information could be gained from the maps of the period. It seems somewhat strange that, though Champlain referred to the port in his text, he did not attempt to locate it on the map which accompanied that text. It may be that other cartographers took their cues from him, and hesitated to put the name on their maps, though one would think that they gladly would have done so, and placed names wherever possible along a coast line where names were few. In LesCarbot's map, the name Savalet appears as one of the only three named points along the entire coast of Acadie, Canseau and LeHeve being the other two. On this map, the relative positions of Savalet and Canso are suggestive. Canso, dignified by the rough representation of a building, in recognition of a status somewhat more assured, is situated behind some islands lying to the east of an indentation, intended to represent a harbour of considerable extent. LeHeve is also given the credit of having so established itself as to merit the notation of a building. Not so was Savalet, situated not far from the western border of the bay shown to be to the west of Canso. The distance of Savalet from the western shore of this bay, and of Canso from the eastern shore of it, is approximately the same, The information intended to be conveyed apparently is, that if the bay in question is supposed to represent White Haven, the port of Savalet was west of, and nearly the same distance from it, as Canso was to the east. Denys does not name Savalet in his text at all. His map names and locates the Bay of Canso, the Cape of Canso, the River St. Mary's and the Bay of Islands, while, between the River St. Mary's and Canso are the letters "P deSte", which presumably are intended to be considered as a contracted form of Port De Savalette. The name does not appear either in the text or on the map of LaHontan. In one of the maps of the Vissher Collection, prepared about 1700, one notes the name of Port de Savalette, Isles Rangèes, Muckdome, (a variation of Mocodome, the cape lying to the west of Country Harbour) Isle Verte, (located at the entrance of the St. Mary's River) the Bay of All Islands, Sainte Helaine, and Sesambre, these being given in order from east to west. The similarity of names suggests that very great reliance has been given to Champlain's account of the coastline. The name does not appear on the Coronelli map of the year 1689, this map being said to be one of the best of the time. It is not shown on any of the maps of the "English Pilot" of the year 1698. Villebon, reporting to the government in Paris in Oct. 1699, does not mention Port Savalet, though his report is of interest in that it estimates distances between ports in that area. According to him, the distance across the Bay of Islands is twenty leagues; from St. Mary's to Mocodome is 6 leagues; from Mocodome to Tarbe (Torbay) is 5 leagues; thence to Martingo. (White Haven) 4 leagues and thence to Canso also 4 leagues. But mapmaking was in its infancy; the exact siting of any particular locality was difficult or impossible and estimates largely took the place of actual measurements. Gradually, successive map makers, probably unable through any effort of their own actually to identify any particular spot as the one to which a particular name was to be given, solved the problem by omitting the name altogether, and not for many years has the attempt been made to carry into effect the laudable effort to perpetuate the name of one of France's little known pioneers.

This is the more to be noted, since a number of the names which appear in the narrative still remain in common use, though some have been slightly altered. Thus, St. Marguerite has become St. Margaret. Sesambre is now known as Sambro. It seems to be the commonly accepted opinion that Port St. Helaine is now known as Petpeswick, the use of the old name having disappeared entirely. The Bay of Islands is not now recognized as a bay, and the use of that name is now little followed. It was supposed to represent that long portion of the coast line, studded with islands, rocks and shoals, which extends from the vicinity of Clam Harbour in Halifax County on the west to Liscomb Island on the east. It is to be noted that Champlain does not give the measurement, either of the distance from Port St. Helaine to the western side of the Bay of Island. or the distance of its eastern border, near Liscomb Island, to St. Mary's River. The River St. Mary's still remains identifiable, though it is the opinion that the island near its entrance to which he gave the name of Isle Verte or Green Island, is not the island now so called. Champlain's Isle Verte is supposed to be the island now called Goose Island, and the present Green Island, lying not far from the entrance of Country Harbour, does not figure at all in Champlain's narrative, unless it is one of the first of the chain of Islands to which he gave the name of Isles Rangèes. These are supposed to be the group of islands lying east of the Isaac's Harbour entrance, which help to form the harbours of Drum Head, Seal and Coddle's Harbour. Canso is quite identifiable, the name having had, however, a number of variations. The body of water which Champlain describes as an "inlet with two or three islands" between Isle Verte and the Isles Rangèes is probably the entrance to Country and Isaac's Harbour; this bay which contains some islands must be Tor Bay.

Tor Bay is a rather prominent geographical feature of the Atlantic shoreline of Guysborough County. It was recognized as a bay at least as early as 1699, in Villebon's report, though spelt Tarbe. It is the body of water between Berry Head on the west and the point of land which forms the west side of White Haven on the east. Berry Head may be a corruption of the name Barry Head which appears on some of the DesBarres charts. The distance between these two points is approximately 7 miles. Opening off from the bay are a number of harbours, usually where rivers or brooks make access to the sea. From west to east, these are Tor Bay Basin, tucked away under the protection of Berry Head, the landing place of one of the first Trans-Atlantic cables, but now long vacated as a cable station, Larry's River, which place marks the most western reach of the Bay, Charlo's Cove, Cole Harbour and Port Felix, the latter closely approaching White Haven, so that a short boat canal connects the two waters. Ail these form safe harbours for fishing craft and small vessels. Berry Head may be the old Norsemen's Keelness, and the finding of an old Norse axe at Cole Harbour has caused interesting speculations of the possible presence of Norsemen many hundred years ago.

While the waters of the bay are for the most part deep, there are several rocky islands which the navigator must shun. In addition and much nearer the shoreline there are islands near Charlo's Cove, which help to form its protection, a cluster of islands about two miles off shore from the mouth of Cole Harbour and wooded glacial drumlins which form the seaward side of Port Felix Harbour. The cluster of islands off Cole Harbour is called the Sugar Islands, the name said to have been given many years ago after the wrecking in its vicinity of a sugar laden craft. The existence of so many fishing villages, ringing the shores of the bay, give evidence of the richness of its waters in fish life.

We can rely, it has been said, a great deal on Champlain's estimate of distances. In his work of charting the coasts of the new world, he had examined that portion of the coast line between LaHeve and Port Royal in May and June of the year 1604. According to the estimate then made, the distance from LaHeve to the entrance of Annapolis Basin was about 61 leagues. The scaled distance between the two points is about two hundred miles. His is therefore an under-estimate, though it can be shown that this under-estimate is very evenly distributed, there being relatively the same error in every estimate. The coast between LaHeve and Canso was examined in August, 1607, and the distances between points considered recognizable are here given.

It will be seen that there is again the same tendency to under estimate the distances. With the exception of the Isles Rangèes these points can be recognized within quite close limits. It is very difficult for us to select any definite place in the Rangèes chain as that from which Champlain's measurements ended or began. Nor can we tell how many islands he includes in the chain. The total length of it may be two of Champlain's leagues. The greatest error, it will be seen, is between that chain and Savalet. If Champlain measured to the western end of the chain and from its eastern end, two leagues additional might have to be added to his measurements. This would greatly reduce the error. But there seems to be one deduction which must be quite evident. Champlain's measurements would not carry him so far to the eastward as is White Haven, but only a relatively short distance past Berry Head, and that therefore Savalet was in Tor Bay.

Champlain's Estimates

	Leagues	Miles	Scaled Miles
From LaHave to St. Margaret	8	21	23
From St. Margaret to Petpeswick	7	19	18
From Sambro to Petpeswick	8	21	24
From Petpeswick to west side of Bay of Islands..	Not Given		15
Across the Bay of Islands	14 to 15	38 to 41	48
From west side of Bay of Islands to St. Mary	Not Given		6
From. St. Mary to Isles Rangèes	6 to 7	16 to 19	16
From Isle Rangèes to Savalet	4	11	18*
From Savalet to Canso	6	16	17*

* Note. Savalet considered to be the Sugar Islands.

Some corroboration to this view is given in the statement which Denys makes. He says that the bay, from islands in which fishing operations had been carried on, was about half the distance between Canso and St. Mary's. In this estimate he is quite incorrect, if we consider Tor Bay as the bay to which he refers, but the error would be magnified very much indeed, if the bay and the fishing places were as far to the east as White Haven. White Haven is only about one fifth of the distance between Canso and St. Mary's, and it seems impossible for Denys to have made such an error as to say that it was about midway between those points.. The farther west one goes across Tor Bay, the less Denys' error is.

To some extent at least it is possible for us to know what must have been the general characteristics of the place Captain Savalet had selected as offering tc him the greatest number of advantages and therefore to be preferred by him to any seen during his long and varied experience. Proximity of suitable fishing grounds was of major importance. There must be good fishing banks from which fish in large numbers were to be obtained. The shorter the distance between the fishing grounds and the place where the curing operations were to be carried on the better. The fishing season was relatively short; the labour of catching and curing a full cargo great. Naturally islands were likely to be nearer the fishing grounds than was any point on the mainland and advantage must be taken of all the working hours it was possible to crowd into a day. Safety from interference by the Indians who might be unpleasant neighbours was greatly to be desired. For this reason also an island site had its advantages. It will be remembered that even one hundred years later, the fishing sites which had been, and were being used, were those on the outer sides of the islands which, formed Canso Harbour, and not on the mainland, the site of the present town. To Savalet, the fisherman, Indians might be nuisances to be avoided, whereas, had he been a trader, as was Rossignol, their neighbourhood was to be sought. But it should also be remembered that the difference in the treatment given to Savalet and that given to the unfortunate Rossignol was largely due to the fact that Savalet, the fisherman, was not encroaching on any monopoly, as was Rossignol, the trader. A suitable beach where the fish might be spread to dry and cure was greatly to be desired. It was an advantage if this beach was very close to the mooring ground, the safe and protected nook where the vessel was laid up during the fishing operations, these being usually carried out from boats and not from the vessel itself. If such a site could be found as permitted the vessel to be moored directly to the beach, it was an advantage, since then the construction of a pier or wharf would not be necessary, nor would it be necessary to build huts for the crew or sheds for the protection of the drying fish, the vessel itself serving these purposes. Water and fuel were necessities, as well as material to be used in the construction of drying flakes. A plot of ground suitable for a garden was desirable. The technique of the fishery divided the men into two groups, the fishing group, who, in small boats, repaired daily to the fishing grounds and caught their loads, and a shore party. This shore party was headed by the doctor or the cook, and their duties were those of seeing after the curing of the fish, distributing them daily to the curing flakes or spreading them, on the beach, looking after the garden, obtaining fresh water and meat, preparing the food and attending to all the work which presented itself on shore. Captain Savalet was thoroughly acquainted with the techniques of the industry, so carefully described by Denys, and probably had helped to develop it.

For he, it will be remembered, was of the class of fishermen called by Denys the "sedentary fishermen", there being a distinction made between these and the fishermen who carried on their fishing, operations from the vessel itself, taking the load home to France to cure. The "sedentary fisherman" prepared his fish for market before he set out for France. This involved larger crews and more organization, and explains why it was that Captain Savalet, in his small craft, had a larger crew, for example, than is to be found on a Lunenburg banker of much greater tonnage. There can be no doubt of the classification in which Savalet is to be placed.

The opinion that Port Savalet was an island port has already been expressed. Champlain's wording is that Captain Savalet was "fishing between islands." This certainly does not mean that the place where the fish were actually being caught was between islands, and that he was carrying the fish to another place, presumably on the mainland, to be cured. The fish were actually being caught on fishing banks offshore, out to sea as far as it was safe to send the small boats,, and were thence taken to a place "between islands", where the curing was being done, and which place was hence the headquarters of the whole fishing operations. Here the vessel was laid up while her lading was being prepared. Here the shore crew was at work on the task curing the fish. Here was Captain Savalet himself, directing the operations of both those who caught

25

the fish and those who prepared them. This must be the meaning of Champlain's phrase, and also that of Denys, when he tells us that it had been customary for some French fishermen to "make their fishery and dry their fish upon the islands" of the bay.

What are the places, one of which might be that secluded little harbour which the explorers visited so many years ago and which impressed them so favourably? At one time or another or by one observer or another a number of places have been suggested. In the list of these, and naming them in order from west to east, one should consider Country Harbour, the islands near Drum Head and Seal and Coddle's Harbours, islands in Tor Bay, either those near Charlo's Cove, the Sugar Islands near Cole Harbour or the islands forming the harbour of Port Felix, White Haven and some cove or harbours lying east of White Haven in the vicinity of what is now known as Raspberry Cove.

Country Harbour has been suggested and in fact has been said to be old Port Savalet in a semi-official publication issued by one of the Nova Scotia Government Departments. It is extremely difficult to find any justification for this opinion, Country Harbour is not a small harbour, but one of the most commodious along the entire coast line, rivalling that of Halifax in size and safety. But it is not among islands, though Green Island is not far from its entrance. And there is no doubt but that Port Savalet was east of the Isles Rangèes, and all the evidence seems to be that these were the group of islands off Drum Head and Seal and Coddle's Harbours. If Country Harbour were Port Savalet, or if Port Savalet were one of the coves or protected portions of that large harbour, the Isles Rangèes and Isle Verte must have been well up in that stretch of coast line which is thought to be the Bay of Islands, which would put. them west of the St. Mary's River, and Champlain must have been in error indeed. Country Harbour is at least forty miles from Canso, but Port Savalet was sixteen, if we take Champlain's estimate, or twelve if we take LesCarbot's. And, if we accept the opinion that Port Savalet was Country Harbour, it is quite impossible for us to identify the bay and inlet referred to by Champlain as having been passed after Isle Verte had been left behind, and every one of Champlain's measurements east of St. Margaret must have been seriously in error.

The Drum Head, and Seal and Coddle's Harbour group of islands, though undoubtedly they might have provided sites which would have suited Captain Savalet's purposes, can not be considered as meeting fully the description. If it did, where were the Isles Rangèes? It is impossible to make much of an error in the identification of the St. Mary's River, which seems to be a point almost as surely fixed as is Canso itself. There are no islands between this group and the St. Mary's River, which can be considered as meeting Champlain's description of islands in a row, which prompted him to select that name. It is true that the bay which Champlain passed before coming to Port Savalet from the Isles Rangèes, might have been the entrance to Country and Isaac's Harbours, but if so, there are again mote errors in Champlain's estimates of distances than we have elsewhere found.

A quite similar argument can be found against the Raspberry Cove site, though here there is involved a large under-estimation of the distance from the Isles Rangèes. Champlain's estimate of this distance is about eleven miles, where actually it is over twenty. It hardly seems possible that he could so have underestimated this distance, especially as this means an over-estimation of the distance to Canso. In some ways the description might tally. Raspberry Cove is small, almost diminutive in size, secluded and out-of-the-way. There is lacking a sand beach, but flat stretches of bare granite might have provided places for the curing flakes. It is little more than a slit, or a series of slits, in the granite shore line, so clean and sharp that at places vessels can be moored directly to the shore as to a wharf. Behind it are the granite barrens which give the whole coast its forbidding aspect. The name indicates that there is to be found in its vicinity in abundance the berries noted by Champlain as having been found so plentiful on the Canso islands and which were so greatly enjoyed.

White Haven itself has been suggested, and by no less an authority than one of the translators of Champlain's text, although, in an opinion expressed after its publication, a site not in White Haven but near it is said to be more likely. There are certainly among the many coves to be found on its rocky uneven shores some places which might have provided almost all of Captain Savalet's requirements. But, how can this harbour, in which a whole navy could find shelter, be described as being very small? On LesCarbot's map, Port Savalet appears to be approximately the same distance to the west of a large indentation which might be White Haven, as Canso was to the east. And why the stressing of the island features, and the express statement that Captain Savalet was fishing "between islands", if any place on the mainland were Port Savalet?

Mainly by exclusion, therefore, we arrive at the decision that Port Savalet must have been among the islands near Port Felix, in the Sugar Island group, or in those near Charlo's Cove. Of these, the little harbour which is to be found within the protecting circle of the Sugar Islands most nearly satisfies the description. The Port Felix Islands face the settlement on the mainland to seaward, as do the Charlo's Cove group. A fishing establishment located on their landward shores would be described quite incorrectly if it was said that it was "between islands". On the other hand, the description is accurate, concise and correct, if it is used of the harbour in the Sugar Island group. The other single isolated islands would give no anchorage or protection.

There remains only Denys' disparaging comment that they could be used with little safety. However, it is natural that Denys would rate their qualifications very low indeed, since he was more interested in localities which provided room for much larger establishments than the modest one of Captain Savalet's, which could hold out hopes of developing a lucrative trade with the Indians, and which had capabilities for agricultural development so that eventually self supporting communities might be in existence. And one thinks that he personally never could have visited the port, or he would not have described it as being three leagues to sea. Actually, the group is only several miles from the nearest point on the mainland. The distance could be nine or ten miles, only if measured from the extreme western end of the bay, at Larry's River.

Five islands with some rocks and outlying reefs make up the group of the Sugar Islands. As one approaches from the landward side, one sees two tree clad islets almost connected by a gravel bar, which projects from the one on the right, so as nearly to connect the two. The local names for these are Pond Island, that one on the right, and Tanner's Island, that on the left. The height of Pond Island is made up of an eroding clay bank, on which there is a stand of thickly set spruce and fir, of scrubby dimensions, with in places open barren. Tanner's Island gives one more the impression of a rocky outcrop, in the crevices of which trees have found lodgment. No break in the growth of trees is to be seen on Tanner's Island, which in this respect differs from Pond Island. They are separated from each other by a distance of about five hundred yards, but somewhat more than half of this is taken up by a bar of gravel and shingle, about fifty yards in width, and somewhat curved inward at the extremity, which juts out from Pond Island. An under water shoal makes out from the end of this bar, still more to narrow the gap between the two, and prevents other than small boats under favourable tidal conditions from entering the harbour.

Standing on the bar and looking seaward, one sees directly in front and about five hundred yards away a densely wooded island, relatively of the same size and height as Pond and Tanner's Islands. This island is known as Dort's Island, and the space between it and the gravel bar is the anchorage. Dort's Island is separated from Tanner's Island by a channel of sufficient depth to allow entrance of a vessel, though narrowed by a ledge of rock which rises above the surface on the Tanner's Island side of the channel. One can see directly out the channel to sea from the bar, the direction being somewhat south of east. On the right of Dort's Island two other islands can be seen, both lower in height than the other three, though apparently of about the same superficial extent. The nearer one is Gooseberry Island; the one farther in the distance is Cook's Island. They are not wooded as are the other three and the water in the area between them and Dort's Island is shoal. From the eastern end of Cook's Island a long reef projects, which helps to protect the channel and Dort's Island. The group of three islands, Dort's, Gooseberry and Cook's, with the reef and shoals connecting them, forms a complete protection to the roadstead from all southerly and westerly winds, and, joining up with Pond and Tanner's Islands, makes an almost complete encirclement of the anchorage. Pond Island has received its name from the presence on it of a lagoon or pond of brackish or salt water. The portion of the island not covered by trees shows the characteristic growth commonly seen on the barrens of the mainland, moss and blueberry bushes and bracken. Here the sea birds nest in large numbers. On this island, near the base of the gravel bar, is to be found a projecting ledge of rock, on which the names of fishermen have been carved. The name of the Sugar Islands has been given to the group since the publication of the DesBarres Charts, as on these they appear to have been called the Camp Islands. One wonders whose camp it was which led to the naming.

The harbour in the group is known to the local French who for years have fished in the neighbouring waters as L'Hopital, for, they say, — "Where can a man be safe, if not in a hospital"? Other fishermen from Canso and even from Chedabucto Bay have in years gone by made the little nook the scene of their fishing attempts. Might not a careful search give evidence of an occupation far ante-dating theirs?

And have any of these transients ever realized, that they might have been visited many times by the wraith of that fine old gentleman from St. Jean de Luz, who very gladly, if he could, would show them his methods of business when last he occupied that fishing stand, would discuss ground tackle and equipment, fishing banks and weather signs, and who might give them many valuable tips from his fund of experience, gathered over three hundred years ago.

(NOTE: A plaque designed to commemorate the memory of Capt. Savalet's little port was erected within sight of the Sugar Islands during the summer of 1949, by the Historic Sites and Monuments Board.)

28

CHEDABUCTO

Many years elapsed, even after several detailed accounts of French exploration and settlement had appeared, before the name of Chedabucto Bay appears in the literature. By no means does this mean that there had not been visitors to the harbour or the Bay and that fishermen, seeking suitable locations for their fishing stands, had not pried into its coves and protected waters. Indeed, the opinion is held that the record of the Bay having been visited can be traced back to the earliest of the Portuguese explorations, and that it was the "Sweet Water Bay" of Joao Alvares Fagundes who entered it in June, 1520. If it was, it is doubtful if there can not be claimed for it the honor of its being one of the first places to be visited and named on the mainland of Nova Scotia. The Portuguese mariners who landed there to fill their depleted water casks, and named the Bay from that incident, may have been among the first individuals, after the Norsemen, to set foot on the Canadian mainland.

But that was long before Chedabucto came into being, except perhaps as a camping ground for the aboriginal Indian. The years passed. Champlain and LesCarbot came, making a landfall on the Atlantic coast line of Acadia, and providing for us a most completely detailed description of the shoreline from Canso to New England, along which they coasted. Even they made but vague references to the Bay which, from the rocky promontory ending in the Canso islands, stretched to the west and north. Champlain refers to it, and was aware that a passage, called by him the Passage Courant, separated the mainland from Cape Breton Island, but the Bay was to him nameless. Another quarter century was to elapse before Chedabucto became a geographical entity.

The interval was not without incident in Acadie. Argall broke up the French settlement at Port Royal. The attempt made by Sir William Alexander to establish a Scotch colony followed and failed. Then came the Treaty of St. Germain in 1632 which gave Acadie back to France. That opened the way again for French colonization and Razilly availed himself of the opportunity. With Razilly were three men, whose actions for some years were to make Nova Scotian history. There was Charnisay D'Aulnay, Razilly's cousin, far-seeing, energetic and determined, the recipient of certain privileges over a large portion of the tremendous area over which Razilly could claim overlordship. There was La-Tour, with already some claims which could not be denied, with sufficient adroitness to have been able to deal for his own advantage with French and Scot, English and New Englander, who was to divide with D'Aulnay certain of Razilly's rights in all that portion of his grant west of Canso. Finally there was Nicholas Denys, too intent on business to be a good courtier, with little education except that gained by experience, honest, honourable, hardworking, little disposed to fight, if a solution of a problem could be found by peaceful means, and asking only for himself that he be permitted to carry out the plans he had in mind. He had been given by Razilly the control of the large sub-district which extended west and north of Canso to Bay Chaleur, and included the islands as well as the shores of the Gulf of St. Lawrence. There had been received from the French authorities a confirmation of this division of authority.

However it may have been with the others, it does not seem that this was Denys' first experience in the New World. While he himself says little about it, there are indications that he knew from experience much about the district in the development of which he was interested. If, of the three, D'Aulnay was the greatest colonizer, Denys was the greatest fisherman, and his outlook was that of one who, aware of the richness of the teeming waters, looked to the sea for his wealth. Indian trading and colonization were for him but incidentals to that main purpose and aim, to be developed only to the extent that they made possible his reaping greater and greater harvests from the sea.

His settlements, Chedabucto, St. Peters, St. Anns, Miscou and Nepisiguit, all appear to have been chosen from the point of view of suitability for the development of the fishing industry, subsidiary being both agriculture and Indian trade. Nor was the evangelization of the Indians one of the purposes near to his heart. The presence of the priest in his settlements, one surmises, was something rather more tolerated than welcomed.

Chedabucto's story is for many years the story of Nicholas Denys. It is indeed a checkered one. There were periods of relative success, when, undisturbed by the internecine feuds which were raging around him, Denys was free to carry out without interference the plans which he had in mind. But there were also times when he was caught up in the maelstrom of conflicting interests and quarrels, and suffered heavily before extrication was possible. When Denys prospered, Chedabucto prospered, as it suffered with him in his periods of loss. We can follow best the story of the settlement by tracing the doings of its founder.

Razilly died in 1635, willing his concessions to his brother. The new proprietor seemed disposed for a time to continue the old arrangement under which the three, D'Aulnay, LaTour and Denys, had been given rights in the vast grant, but soon sold out his interests to D'Aulnay. Immediately D'Aulnay and La-Tour commenced their quarrel, and Denys also felt the weight of D'Aulnay's displeasure, finding himself dispossessed of the result of his work near Rossignol, where he had established himself, seemingly with Razilly's consent. This occurred soon after the year 1636.

We then for some years lose sight entirely of Denys. It seems safe to assume that he was continuing to fish and to trade at some of the harbours in his large concession, perhaps making arrangements for financing himself more plentifully, in order to open up establishments of a more permanent character. When next we do hear of him, it is in connection with a fishing business being carried on at Miscou, near the northern limits of his grant. This was about the year 1645, and here it was that, a short time later, D'Aulnay's displeasure again caught up with him and resulted in the closure of his business and his removal from Miscou.

Thereafter, for a time, he seems to have directed his attention to the southern portion of his concession, even though doing so meant his being brought into closer relationship with his determined enemy, D'Aulnay. That he dared to do so, indicates not only his belief in the justness of his claim, but also at least a measure of support from the home authorities. There does not seem to be any doubt but that his claim to the island of Cape Breton was an entirely valid one, and one perhaps little disputed. Chedabucto may have been debatable ground, owing to the deep indentation which the bay makes to the westward after the point of the cape at Canso had been passed. Miscou, lying deep in the Gulf of St. Lawrence had always had the reputation of being for some reason an unhealthy station, scurvy being an almost constant scourge. It well may be that on this account, among others, the decision was arrived at to develop his southern holdings, and the commencement of the occupation of Chedabucto probably dates from about this period.

The site presented many advantages, although it was situated within thirty-miles of the extreme southern limit of his district. We can very easily imagine him when first he stood on the little promontory on which his fort later was built and looked out over the prospect which lay before him. Directly south the view was limited by the forest clad slopes of the high ground which ended at Canso, thirty miles eastward. To his right, in front of him and on his left was water; on his right a cove which promised shelter and anchorage for his vessels, in front the Chedabucto Bay, to his left, the water of the Bay and the Harbour, as safe and secluded as the Indian name, "running far back" signified. The height of land on which he stood perfectly commanded the harbour entrance. Here were beaches ample for the cure of the fish, to be found in abundance on the nearby fishing grounds. Hidden behind a steep point of land directly in front of him was the mouth of the little river which formed the chief highway of Indian travel connecting the Indian settlements on the mainland with the headquarters of their confederacy on the Island of Cape Breton. Behind him was the unbroken forest, with every indication of there being found land suitable for tillage and for gardening. A short stockade behind him across the point of land on which he stood would make his fort as difficult to assault from the rear as it was from the sea. There are few fairer prospects than that which lay before him as he examined the suitability of the locality for settlement, and later comers were to appreciate the soundness or his judgment.

This was some time about the year 1650. He had lost his Rossignol establishment in 1636 and had been driven from Miscou in 1647. Was this attempt to re-establish himself to be a failure? It was, if Madam D'Aulnay could compass it. She, attempting to salvage what she could of the estate after D'Aulnay's death, brought to the task vindictiveness as great as her late husband's, even though she may have lacked some of his abilities. Denys was never a believer in physical combat and might have resisted, but when next we know of him in 1651, he was a prisoner in her hands and being delivered to the French authorities in Quebec for punishment.

There, Madame D'Aulnay was unable to prove the justness of her claim, and before the end of the year, Denys was at Nepesiguit, one of his stations on the Gulf Shore. His return the following year to St. Peters and Chedabucto brought him within reach of another determined enemy. This was LeBorgne, to whom D'Aulnay had been heavily indebted, and who now claimed D'Aulnay's concessions in Acadie in recompense for the debt. History has given to him a somewhat dubious reputation, and in his treatment of Madame D'Aulnay he is said to have been harsh, if not actually dishonest. Harsh also Denys must have considered him, when he found that he must suffer again the indignity of arrest and transportation, this time to Port Royal.

Effecting his release he went as soon as possible to France for a re-examination of the terms of his concession and if possible for redress. In the latter he failed, but in respect of the former, his attempt was entirely successful. He returned to his district, as Lieut.-Governor of the whole Gulf Coast, including the Islands, and especially Newfoundland, which had not hitherto been included in the limits of his concession. At last he appeared to be in a position to carry out fully his plans for the development of his fishing

31

establishments.

But the whole of Acadie was only a pawn in a much larger game, and the very year, 1654, which saw Denys' prospects brighten also saw the slender hold which France had on Acadie threatened by Sedgewick, whose attack on Port Royal was successful. Though Port Royal fell, the French settlements on Cape Breton and at Chedabucto were not molested, and, encouraged by the freedom from attack, the development of Chedabucto went quietly on. It is permissible to assume that some of the French dispossessed at Port Royal, found shelter at Chedabucto, and if so, its inhabitants now included a number of women and children. Father DeLyonne made it the headquarters of his Indian mission in 1657, and continued to do so till his death in 1662. Now for a time Chedabucto was the most important settlement which remained in French occupancy throughout the whole of the mainland of Acadie. There were still some French near Port Royal, but over these flew the English flag. There were said to have been four at Cape Sable, and a few more fishing from LaHave and Canso. Chedabucto thus represented for a time all that there was of French government and authority in Acadie.

Denys himself has told us that about this time at Chedabucto he had about one hundred and twenty men in his employ, that there were thirty arpents (about 20 acres) of land cleared and that most of it was in crops. There were two buildings, each of about 60 feet in length, and another was ready to be raised. These were of wood, probably within an encircling palisade. How many guns there were or whether it was prepared to resist other than Indian attack is not told us. This was of importance, since unfortunately a time of trial was approaching.

For now LaGiraudiere and his brother DuBay appeared upon the scene. In some way these had succeeded in getting from the home authorities some kind of a concession for a portion of the eastern coast of Acadie from Canso and extending at least as far as St. Mary's. According to Denys, it had been obtained after LaGiraudiere had represented that Canso was the cape now known as Cape George, beyond the northern entrance of the Strait of Canso. La-Giraudiere's concession was for privileges south or west of Cape Canso, and if that cape was Cape George, Chedabucto was outside of the territory considered to belong to Denys, since his concession was for that extent of country lying north of Cape Canso and extending to Gaspe.

Presumably acting under authority, LaGiraudiere established his fort on the St. Mary's River, at a point not far from where the town of Sherbrooke now stands. With this as a foothold, he undertook to expand, casting covetous eyes particularly at Chedabucto. As Denys tells the story, LaGiraudiere left France very early in the spring of 1667, having with him about a hundred and twenty men. He arrived in Canso ahead of the vessel sent out by Denys, and when that vessel arrived, seized it. Denys, as a result, found himself unable to keep his bargains with the men, also numbering about 100, whom he had brought out for the summer fishery, and was consequently forced to allow these to go to other fishermen, who could maintain them, give them work during the summer, and take them back to France in the fall. But, while he could, he kept some of them in Chedabucto, attempting, even at a time so late, to fortify the place so that its seizure by force might be prevented, if LaGiraudiere attacked. He did attack, but the attack was unsuccessful, owing to the measure of preparation. He had no intention of giving up the struggle though. He knew that St. Peters was ill prepared to resist an attempt made to capture it, with no more than five or six men to protect it, and a sudden attack on it placed it in LaGiraudiere's possession. Then DuBay was sent to Denys, with the proposition that St. Peters would be returned if Chedabucto were handed over in exchange. Then the matter was to be submitted to the home authorities for decision.

Denys could do nothing but consent to this arrangement. He went to France in the winter of 1678, and had little or no difficulty in having his side of the contention sustained. Chedabucto was returned to him, but the decision quite failed in reimbursing him for the loss of the profits of one year's operations, for the advances he had made to a large number of men, and for his expenses in contesting LaGiraudiere's claim. One thing he gained. Both LaGiraudiere and his brother remained in France, leaving Huret in charge of the St. Mary's fort, quite impotent for future harm.

Made secure in his holdings Denys returned to St. Peters and Chedabucto; the Treaty of Breda became operative and France again ruled at Port Royal. In the winter of that year came the crowning misfortune. At St. Peters was located his largest warehouse, stored with goods for trade or awaiting shipment to France. On a winter night that storehouse went up in flames. Thereafter there was no recovery, no chance of fighting, off the growing pressure of debts. At a low ebb, too, was Chedabucto's lot, till new faces appeared upon the scene.

As was to be expected, the return of the French to Port Royal and the new regime brought many changes. There was a new Governor. A new Company, the Trading Company of Acadie, came into existence. At its head was the Marquis of Chevry; what might be called the acting managerial position went to Bergier, a Huguenot from New Rochelle, who, it seems, had had some experience at LaHave, and was more or less acquainted with the problems to be met. Three Paris merchants, Gautier, Boucher and DeMantes were the other members interested. On Feb. 28, 1682, the king of France signed their concession, and with commendable industry, the Company set to work. Bergier came immediately to Chedabucto, plans concerning which seemed to bulk large with the new Company. Chedabucto appeared to be safer from attack than was Port Royal, and it was much nearer the sea route of travel from Acadie to Quebec. At the start, it seemed the intention that Chedabucto was to be developed less as a fishing station than as an agricultural one. Within two years, Bergier was able to report that crops of wheat, rye, barley and vegetables had been gathered and that vines and fruit trees had been planted. Reliance seemed to be placed on other of the Company's stations for the development of the fisheries.

But all was not entirely plain sailing with the Company. Its concessions had been given it, subject to the condition that French persons actually in possession were not to be disturbed. LaValliere, formerly Lieut, du Roy, who had married Denys' daughter, had given concessions to some English vessels to fish along the coast, and these were clamouring that the terms of their licenses be kept. Other English vessels were fishing without licenses and interfering with the Company's monopoly. Friction arose. Captain Carter of Salem seized six French sloops in which Bergier was interested. In return, eight English vessels were taken, their loads confiscated and the captains sent to France. Here, those who had LaValliere's licenses were released but the others suffered the loss of their belongings. A party of English sailors even endeavoured to try out the resisting power of the new Chedabucto fortifications but they were driven off. But La-Valliere lost favour and his position, and Bergier took his place, thus more closely-linking the Company and the Government, with perhaps more profit accruing to the Company than to the Government.

Ail the time, however, progress was taking place at Chedabucto. A chapel was built, named St. Louis of Chedabucto, for St. Louis seemed to be the patron saint of the fort. A mill for the sawing of lumber was erected. A few families came and settled in the vicinity. Then a small body of troops under M. De La Boulais was sent. This was in 1686. In the following year, still more supplies were sent out, and an Engineer officer, M. Pasquine, was sent to lay out more effective fortifications. So a fossa or ditch was made around the point on which the Fort lay, palisades were erected and barracks built. A map prepared about this time showed the fort on the point of land at the entrance of the harbour, a little cluster of settler's houses on the sloping hillside several hundreds of yards north of the fort, and a group of Indian tents somewhat farther north, near where the town of Guysborough is now located. The little settlement was making headway.

Indeed, so much headway had been made, that a watchful piratical group operating, it is said, out of Boston, took notice, observed that the fort was no: being very strongly held and decided that a considerable amount of loot might be gathered at comparatively little cost. According to the French account, the leader of this party was called Ouillesse, which one may with justification translate into Williams, but the English accounts give the name of the pirate leader as Captain Peterson, while hints are given that Sir Edmund Andres lurked somewhere behind the scenes. The French also say that, previous to the visit, several New England fishermen, posing as shipwrecked seamen, and awaiting the opportunity of being transported home, had visited the fort and for about six weeks had been the recipients of French hospitality.

The Company had already that spring lost one vessel, the first supply ship leaving France to bring to the fort its necessities and trade-goods. The French naval vessel whose duty was the protection of the fisheries had been greatly delayed. Leaving Rochelle on May 2nd, her passage to Port Royal was not completed till July 16th. Warned at Port Royal of the danger from there being a pirate on the coast, she sailed as soon as possible for Canso, but before she arrived the blow had fallen. An English man of war was supposed to be in the neighbourhood, but may not have been very solicitous in the protection of French interests.

The Strait of Canso was the first place visited by the unwelcome intruder. Here was met Sieur De Castine's vessel, bound from Quebec for his settlement in Maine. She was a large bark, with a cargo estimated as being worth five hundred pounds. From her crew, the pirates obtained information of the recent arrival of the French supply ship at Canso. Taking pilots from Castine's vessel the pirates proceeded to Canso, and at ten o'clock that night approached the unsuspecting French vessel lying at anchor. No persons could be seen on board, and the pirates gained her deck unmolested. Not till after a pistol had been fired by Peterson was there any sign of life. Then the Captain came on deck, carrying a cane, thinking that the disturbance was caused by his own crew. He was seized and the men captured as they appeared on deck, apparently without the firing of another shot. The French vessel was one of about three hundred tons, mounting a number of guns and carrying a crew of about twenty-five men.

Next morning, there arrived a boat from Chedabucto, carrying the Governor and others, anxious to greet the incoming vessel for whose coming they had impatiently waited so long. The doctor from the pirate ship and one of the crew, were out in a small craft examining the harbour. They met the French boat, immediately opening fire on it. The occupants asked for quarter and were taken. Thus provided with pilots for Chedabucto, the pirate vessel that night sailed thither. The soldiers, about fifteen in number, were surprised in their sleep, and the fort became an easy prey. It was found to be about one hundred feet square, with a bastion for big guns, and several wooden storehouses and other edifices. There was much booty, considering the fact that the stores were depleted, and had not been replaced after the year's operations. There were a number of chests of trade goods, and arms, and what was very much to their taste, the pirates found a good supply of wines and brandy. On the Governor's urgent intercession, and the plea that the occupants of the fort would be defenceless against Indian attack if the guns in the bastion were spiked, these were not damaged. The raiders helped themselves liberally to the stores, but did not take all there was in the warehouses.

Either at Chedabucto or in Canso on their return thither, they fell in with another small vessel of about thirty tons bound for Port Royal from Quebec. There too, they heard of there being in a near by harbour a ketch which was being used by some French fishermen, but which had been captured from the English several years previously. They sent to get her and ordered that she be tent home to New England, for, said this righteous pirate, "these French rogues have nothing to do with other people's vessels." Then, burning their own old vessel, they departed in the large newly acquired one for the Gold Coast, having about one hundred men, an ample quantity of guns and ammunition and much wine and brandy.

Thus fell the fort on Aug. 9th, 1688. Menneval at Port Royal as well as the fishing company at Chedabucto has been hard hit. Menneval, in reporting the incident, urgently asks that more supplies be sent, "because there is nothing here."

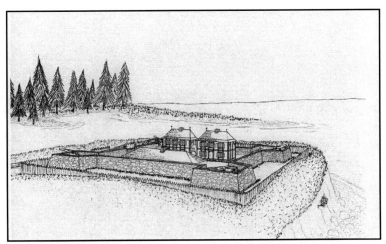

Fort St. Louis à Chedabuctou on Fort Point, 1690.

35

Little is recorded for the year 1689. Presumably there was better success in getting the supply vessel safely across and the company may have succeeded in making up some of the loss. But, if Chedabucto was progressing, the affairs of the French in Canada were not, and in desperation Frontenac was being ordered to return to Quebec, again to take command. His instructions outlined an attack which was to be made during the summer on New England, and for which he was to endeavour to bring about the co-operation of the French land and sea forces. A French war vessel was to carry him and Callieres to Chedabucto, from which place they were to go to Quebec, in a trading vessel. When his arrangements at Quebec had been completed, Frontenac was to notify the commander of the French naval vessel at Chedabucto and ask him to hold himself in readiness for a descent on the New England coast. Nothing came of the plan, for the vessel carrying Frontenac was fifty-two days in making the passage, reaching Chedabucto only on Sept. 12th, entirely too late for any action that year. Frontenac could remain but a short time, for he was needed in Quebec, for which place he sailed on Sept. 19th. There is little doubt that Chedabucto fully appreciated the honour of the visit of one so high in office and of such outstanding reputation. Assuredly the utmost resources of the little settlement were strained to do honour to the occasion.

The next was another year, and now the English were ready and struck the first blow. Phipps appeared in front of Port Royal on Saturday, May 10th 1690, with a demand for its surrender. This was obtained the following day, and within ten days the demolitions had been completed and his victorious troops were homeward bound. Captain Cyprian Southack had been one of his captains of transports. In the harbour had been found a brigantine, the *Supply*, which had been an English vessel but captured and now in French possession. Now, recaptured, a Board of Enquiry placed her value as 105 pounds; she was given over to Southack who was discharged from his position under Phipps, loaded with the necessary number of troops and sent to mop up what remained of the French possessions at LaHave and Chedabucto. Captain Alden was with him, and also, it seems, the notorious and elusive Basset.

There were from twelve to fifteen French soldiers in Chedabucto under Lieut. DeMontorgueil. His own report of the incident is in existence as well as reports from other sources. He was expecting an attack, and says that he was at work overseeing some repairs to the palisades when Alden's two ships were sighted coming up the Bay. Next morning one was anchored near the entrance to Cook's Cove. Most of the day was spent in getting the men ashore. Firing between the attackers and defenders occurred for about six hours. There were several summons for surrender, to which no attention was paid. Little damage seems to have been done to either side; on that of the French, because the cover was ample, on the side of the English, since Alden knew that Montorgueil's position was untenable and thought it useless to sacrifice his men. Finally, some of the attackers, creeping along the shore under the protection of the bank which shielded them from the defender's fire, reached a storehouse which encroached upon or formed a part of the enclosure. Entering it, they found some wet powder. The building was of wooden construction with a heavily thatched roof. With the wet powder they made flares with which the roof was set on fire. This made its way rapidly to the fort it-self, and conditions became desperate within the stockade. Again summoned to surrender, Montorgueil refused and continued to refuse till terms had been granted him. He demanded security and Alden sent his seal, cautioning him that it might be necessary, since the attackers had in their ranks some

Huguenots determined to give no quarter. The terms of surrender included repatriation to Placentia, and made provision for a Nazarene friar as well as for the soldiers themselves. Then the little band marched out, with arms in their hands, drum beating and matches lit, one officer, about a dozen soldiers and one friar.

Southack, a dutiful son writing an interested father, gives a more picturesque account. "On the third day of June I arrived at Canso in the afternoon and the 4th I put 50 men into my tender with myself and left my Lieutenant with my ship at Canso, so I made sail for Shebuctor Fort which being several leagues from my ship. But 4 o'clock in the morning I landed my men and they fired a gun to alarm the Indians and at 5 o'clock in the morning I came within great gun shot of the fort so they fired eight great guns at me and three patareroes coming over a sandy bank and when we came to their bridge, which was within pistol shot of the fort, no more than one man at a time could get over, so they made at the fort at once and they killed me two men and wounded me six. We fought them for about six hours and they beat us off from the fort but about pistol shot of the fort we got into a great house where I found four barrels of powder and we made fireballs and we made up again to the trenches and there got in myself and several men so the great guns could not hurt us and we hove several balls into the fort and at last the house of the guard was set on fire and then the governor struck the flag and he with the soldiers and the priests came out and in half an hour the fort blew with the powder and the grenadoes that were in it. I was five days demolishing of it which the Governor now informs me stood the French King 3000 sterling within these two years which was built of stone and plaster of Paris and trenched around."

So fell Fort Chedabucto on June 5th, 1690, if we accept Southack's account or the 13th, if we take the reports of others. The settlers were not interfered with, though Alden reports their presence.

Five soldiers were soon sent from some Depot, (presumably Placentia) which probably could ill afford to spare them, for the protection of the sixty French who still clung to their little holdings. But Phipps failed to take Quebec. The French soldiers had to be sent elsewhere in 1691 and the settlers, without protection, must leave. The census of 1693 does not indicate that a single one was left in that year in the Chedabucto area.

The Treaty of Ryswick (Sept. 20, 1697) returned Nova Scotia to France, but Chedabucto, in the relatively short period between that date and 1710, when Annapolis finally became a British possession, had no part in the French renaissance. Finally, in 1713, the Treaty of Utrecht gave all of Nova Scotia proper to England, and so, Chedabucto, which had been the scene of Denys' labours and disappointments, on which Bergier had set such high hopes, which for a time had been the seat of French government in Acadie and as such was the only place on which an Upper Canadian Governor had ever set foot, finally passed into British ownership.

THE COMING OF THE PRIEST

Religion crossed the Atlantic slowly. The lure of the wealth to be obtained from the fur trade and the fishery was a more compelling magnet, but even that did not for generations produce much result. It is a remarkable fact that one hundred years slipped by without the potentialities of Columbus's discoveries having been appreciated to the full in Europe.

There are shadowy evidences of fishing voyages made during the first ten years of the sixteenth century. Shortly after the close of the century, writers of the Jesuit Relations estimate that 500 ships, representing a number of nationalities, were yearly engaged in fishing and trading, most of these vessels making use of the facilities which were afforded by the harbours in or near the Gulf of St. Lawrence. Only at the end of that century were plans made which brought to these shores the priest and the minister as well as the trader and the fisherman. Then — strange combination — arrived two Jesuit priests under the protection of a Calvinist explorer, to whom we are indebted for the first detailed information given us of the Nova Scotia coast. As might be expected, to woman's insistence and persistence must be given the credit for the presence of the priests among the members of the expedition.

We hear little of the part played in this programme by those of DeMont's entourage whose religious beliefs more closely coincided with his own. The Jesuits, Pierre Biard and Ennemond Masse, to whose presence had been given a grudging consent, left more records. Their first visit to America served but little more than to give them some knowledge of the nature of the task they had undertaken and to welcome Membertou into the fold, thus preparing a basis for the friendship of the French and Indian which was to play such an important part in the story of Nova Scotia. Their second was brought to a tragic end by Argall's raid in 1613; at their third attempt, their paths had been diverted to the larger opportunities afforded by Quebec.

Recollets then undertook the task of opening a mission field in Nova Scotia, but met with so little success that they returned to Quebec in 1624. Again the Jesuits took up the task, and between 1625 and 1634 had so established themselves as to be able to extend their field from Quebec and the St. Lawrence to include Gaspe and Nova Scotia. This position had been gained in the face of discouragements, losses, even death itself. The Jesuit Relations of the year 1629 tells most vividly the tragic story of one of the first wrecks of which we have record on the Canso headlands. Father Charles Lallement, arriving in Canada in 1625, had almost immediately been asked to return to France for supplies. One or two abortive attempts had been made by him to return to Quebec, bringing with him not only the supplies which were so greatly needed, but a very welcome re-enforcement of workers for the field. Finally, in the spring of 1629, they got safely away on the return voyage. In the vessel were Father Charles Lallement, Father De Vieuxpont, Father Noyrot and his two nephews and Brother Louis.

Disaster met them as they neared Canso, a south-east gale against which it was impossible for them to make an offing. Father Lallement, who apparently was in the cabin of the ship with Louis when the vessel struck, made his way to the deck where he found Father Noyrot. They joined each other in their devotions, and had just completed them when a wave swept over the vessel, carrying Father Noyrot with it. Father Noyrot disappeared. Although

Father Lallement was severely injured by floating wreckage, he was able to maintain himself, till a second wave carried him off the wreck, with a plank which he Was able to seize. It was then nine o'clock and dark, but the plank, tied to the wreck in some way, kept him up till he was able to see some others on what remained of the mast, floating in the water and still attached to the ship. He was able to make his way there and found some of the surviving sailors, who eventually were able to assist him, badly battered, to the shore. Father De Vieuxpont had also escaped; of the others, there was no sign. They passed the night in the protection of some trees or bushes on shore, there being only seven survivors of the twenty-four passengers and crew.

Next morning they found that the portion of the shore on which they were was a semi-detached island from which they were able to get to the mainland. Searching the shore they were able to get a few articles of clothing, some food, materials with which to make a fire, and a few tools. On the fourth day thereafter, while engaged in making a kind of a make-shift boat in which it was the intention to travel along the coast, one of the party saw a passing fisherman and was able to attract his attention. The fisherman took them to his vessel, where they met with a kindly reception and the promise of being carried back to France when the fishing trip was concluded. Staying there the balance of the month of August and the month of September, the return trip to France was undertaken, hurriedly, since an Indian messenger had brought them word that an early visit from an English vessel, bent on attack, was expected. Father De Vieuxpont remained, going with the messenger to the French settlement at St. Anne's or Sydney, but Father Lallement returned to France. His troubles were not yet over, for while approaching the French coast, the vessel was completely wrecked with a total loss of all its hard earned cargo.

It is impossible to identify now the place of the wreck at Canso. The fisherman to whom they were indebted for their rescue, was fishing from some harbour or cove about one and a half leagues (five or six miles), from the scene of the disaster. It does not seem that this harbour was that of Canso itself, with only one fishing craft making its headquarters there. The wreck probably took place on one of the islands west of Canso, and the fishermen might have been fishing from Savalet's abandoned little retreat.

But it required more than incidents such as these to deter those who had the salvation of the new world in mind. In spite of losses, in 1634, the parent establishment in Quebec considered itself able to send Julian Perault and Charles Turgis to the Gaspe coast and to Nova Scotia. The records thereafter give us the names of many who laboured from time to time, taking up the work of those whom death had removed or welcome enforcements, as the burden of the work increased. There are several, however, whose connection with Chedabucto was sustained for a period which served actually to identify them with its story.

The evangelization of the Souriquois or Micmacs was a most important portion of the missionary effort being carried on by the Jesuits who had made Quebec their headquarters. These Indians had for their tribal grounds the entire Province of Nova Scotia including the Island of Cape Breton, and much of New Brunswick, especially that portion of the coastline along the upper portion of the Chignecto Bay and the Gulf of St. Lawrence as far north as Gaspe. In a number of ways, their situation was relatively a favourable one. The interposition of the Maleseets, the next tribe to the west, between them and the hated Iroquis contributed largely to their safety from attack by that malevolent group. The Micmacs and the Maleseets were closely allied tribes, the relationship between them being one of peace, not of war. The Micmacs had only one feud which never ceased, this being with the Eskimos. As late as the Jesuit Relations of the years 1659-60, a report is made of a descent by the Eskimos in their kayaks on Micmac territory, the invaders having made the crossing of the River St. Lawrence.

Moreover, the Indians of the Gaspesia district, a district considered as extending the whole distance from Canso to Gaspe, and corresponding roughly to the territory which Nicholas Denys claimed on the authority of a Royal grant, had for many years been in touch with visiting Europeans. It is said that about five hundred ships were then coming yearly to the Gulf, bringing crews probably themselves fruitful prospects for missionary enterprise. The Gaspesia field was one therefore which was characterized by the presence of a more tractable and peaceful group than were many of the western districts, with a European infiltration which was considerably greater than that which had yet reached the western Indians, even though that infiltration may have contributed a good deal to the Indians potential detriment.

It never seems to have acted in any way towards the severance of the ties of friendship between the French and the Indians or to the establishment of better relations with the English.

The total number of Indians in the district was not supposed to have been more than 3500 or 4000, these being the figures made by the missionaries, though it is possible that in the enumeration consideration was given only to the fighting strength of the tribe. At least during some of the time in question, the headquarters of the confederacy was considered to be on some portion of the Bras D'Or Lakes in the island of Cape Breton, and this was the most thickly settled portion of the district. At a somewhat earlier period, old Membertou, residing at St. Mary's Bay, near Port Royal, was one of the most noted of the tribal chiefs.

The headquarters of the mission, however, was usually considered as being at Miscou, one of Nicholas Denys' fishing stations. Here was a fairly well established settlement, somewhat removed from the internecine strife which was so interfering with the development of Acadie. It, however, had a sinister reputation on account of the unusual amount of sickness which seemed to prevail there. Scurvy was a constant menace, and took heavy toll in the first few years of permanent occupation. From this place as a centre, however, other outlying fields of missionary effort were supplied and Chedabucto in due time received attention.

The particular priest whose name was most commonly associated with Chedabucto was Rev. Martin DeLyonne. (DeLionne, DeLyonnes.) Born in Paris on May 13, 1614, he entered the Jesuit novitiate at Nancy on Dec. 8, 1629. He studied at Pont a Mousson from 1631 till 1634; at Rome from 1638 till 1642, the intervening years being occupied by instructorships at Sens and Charlesville. Having spent the last years of his novitiate at Rouen, he joined the Canadian mission in 1643.

His intention on arriving at Quebec was to proceed westward for duty among the Hurons, but those plans were altered by the circumstance of the illness in Miscou of Father Dolbeau, one of the members of the mission who had been only about a year on the field, sent there to assist Father Andre Richard. Father Dolbeau, ill of scurvy, and his place taken by Father

DeLyonne, died on his way back to France, in his search for treatment.

Father DeLyonne narrowly escaped the same fate. He himself became ill, so ill that from May till September of the year 1644, his recovery appeared doubtful. The temper of the man can be judged by his refusal to return to France for treatment though urged to do so, with the comment made by him that he preferred to die in Canada than in France. Recovering, the Relations tells us that "he seemed to bury the disease, for since that time it has not appeared in Miscou." This would appear to be a remarkable result of constancy and a more correct diet.

The Relations of 1646-47 tells of another incident. An Eskimo, captured in a fight about ten years previously, became ill and unable to care for himself, was due to receive very short shrift from his Micmac master. Father DeLyonne prevented the immediate murder of the slave and carried him to his own home, caring for him so effectually — doubtless as a result of the experience which he had himself painfully acquired — that a recovery was entered upon. This was interrupted by the return of the slave to his old master, whereupon the illness returned, and again the threat of death hovered closely. Again Father DeLyonne interceded, again he took the patient to a hut specially built in the courtyard of the priest's quarters and cared for him till a recovery was brought about. So complete was convalescence this time, that the patient was able to stock the communal larder with no fewer than a dozen moose during the next fall hunting season.

Thereafter, for a period of years, Father DeLyonne's duty seems to have required his presence at times at other portions of the missionary field than the Gaspesia district. It would appear that he passed the winter of 1647-48 in Tadoussac, going to Quebec in July of the latter year and sailing for France on September 23rd. He seems to have returned the following spring direct to Miscou, probably on some vessel engaged in the fisheries. However, in the fall of the year 1649 he was again in Quebec, having arrived there on Captain Poulet's vessel on September 7th. In 1650, he was for a time at Sillery (in February) and on the 3rd of May left for Tadoussac and Miscou, but returned to Quebec again on July 5th. He again sailed for France on September 21st of that year with Captain Ferrier.

There was delay in his getting away from Rochelle the following year on his return to the field, the vessel not leaving France till July 16th. Owing to the unfavourable weather it was not till the 14th of October that he arrived in Quebec. He sailed again for home on the 17th of November, an extremely late date on which to attempt an ocean passage. A violent storm was experienced, during which the ballast shifted, nearly bringing about the loss of the vessel, a fate which befell a sister ship which was accompanying them. But their difficulties were not yet over, for when almost in the home waters, their vessel was pillaged near the Isle of Re. This was on Christmas eve. In a letter informing his superiors of his experiences, he regrets the loss for the effect it will have on the continuance of the mission, since in view of this misfortune those who had formerly supported it would not now be able to contribute, and the savages having "nothing but faith and Christianity for their sole wealth".

Arriving again at Quebec on Aug. 31st, 1652, it was necessary for him to set out again on a return passage on October 21, the vessel being said this time to contain a very valuable cargo of fur. The passage to Quebec was completed again on Aug. 6th, 1653.

During the following years there were other visits to France and other incidents and escapes to add to the toll of his experiences. In 1656, planning on getting back to Quebec by a vessel sailing from Rochelle, a fortunate accident prevented his arrival in the city till after the vessels had sailed. He was thus saved the unpleasant experience of capture by the Spaniards, who stripped the vessel of the supplies she was carrying.

About this time, Nicholas Denys was entering upon his period of greatest prosperity, an interval all too brief, before came the misfortunes which clouded his latter days. His difficulties with Madame D'Aulnay and Le Borgne had been composed, his claims upheld and the honour given him of the Governorship of the entire coast line from Canso to the St. Lawrence, including the island of Newfoundland. After a number of years of strife with rival claimants, the way now appeared open for him to develop his establishments and Chedabucto and St. Peters had made headway. Chedabucto had been passed by when, under Cromwell's orders in 1654, the French settlements in Acadie had been raided.

Both of Denys' establishments were on the old Indian travel route which connected the island of Cape Breton with the main land, one on the direct route through central Acadie and the other on the same one, but after it had been joined by that route which passed southerly through the Strait of Canso. The threat of embroilment with La Giraudiers from his station on the St. Mary's River may have been impending, but for the present the prospects appeared bright for the gathering of the profits for which Denys had so long striven but which had heretofore been denied him. These were the conditions at Chedabucto about 1657, when we find Father DeLyonne stationed in that portion of the Gaspesia mission.

His part in the history of the settlement was not destined to extend over many years. We hear little of the details of his actions from 1657 till 1660. When we do hear, already his career was drawing to a close.

The fall of 1660 had been a sickly season, scurvy being again rife. Father DeLyonne's unremitting zeal wrought to his own disadvantage, and ,he himself became ill. A call came to him to see some one needing his care at some little distance from the settlement. This was in January and ice covered the brooks and rivers, but not so safely as to prevent his breaking through and becoming thoroughly soaked on his way to answer the call. He hastened onward and though suffering from the effects of the mishap gave what aid it was within his power to give. On his return to the fort, his illness became rapidly worse and death came speedily. He died on January 16th, 1661, and another of his brotherhood had laid down his life in order that others might profit. His place in the mission was taken by Father Andre Richard, who, however, remained only till some time in 1662.

The writer remembers in early boyhood seeing a skull which had become exposed through an erosion of the clayey headland on which the old fort was located. The place was on that side of the headland looking south and somewhat west over the waters of the harbour entrance and die nearby cove, neatly at the western limits of some dimly traceable outworks. Doubtless many persons had died in the years of Denys' occupancy and that of the Bergier Company and it may well have been that at that spot the burials had taken place. If so, a clue might be given as to the spot where sleeps this faithful servant of his Master.

Thereafter we know little of the missionary work being carried on in Chedabucto. Nicholas Denys' days of dispute and losses were approaching. LaGiraudiere laid claim to Chedabucto and though Denys' contention as to ownership was upheld, the losses he met with as the result of the seizure and in defence of his rights were heavy. The crowning misfortune, the loss of his storehouse at St. Peters by fire in the winter of 1668, determined his removal entirely to what was left of his holdings on the Gulf.

Doubtless there may still be found in some repository the reports of the missions and the later visits of priests, but with the cessation of regular printings of the Jesuit Relations, little definitely is now known of these. Under the Trading Company of Acadia from 1682 till 1690 Chedabucto was developed into a much more important centre than it had been at any time during its occupancy by Denys. There was a chapel, St. Louis of Chedabucto, within the protective limits of the fort; quite a sum of money had been spent on its fortification and it was considered as being of such importance as to justify the continued presence of a small section from the very limited number of regular troops stationed in the Province.

But the period of French domination was drawing to a close. Port Royal fell to Phipps in 1690, and Captain Southack was sent to bring about the reduction of Chedabucto. Lieut. de Montorgeuil, largely outnumbered, made a spirited defence, a defence so determined that when the little garrison of a dozen men was allowed to march from the fort with drum beating and matches lit, he had been able to extract the promise that not the soldiers alone, but also the "Nazarene Friar" making the fort his headquarters, should be sent to Placentia. Then Chedabucto, either as a colonizing, a trading or fishing centre or a centre of missionary effort, no longer existed.

Reference has been made to the death by drowning of Father Noyrot at Canso and his burial on one of the Canso islands, and also to Father DeLyorme, buried at Chedabucto. Somewhere on the Guysborough shore of the Strait of Mulgrave there sleeps another priest who gave up his life in the performance of his duty. Father Trouve, whose station was at Beaubasin, had come to Canso on a mission some time in the early spring of 1704. While there, he heard that an inroad had been made on his home station and that his early return was advisable. He set out immediately on his return. The perils of a crossing from Canso to Mulgrave in the early spring by a frail Indian canoe surely need no amplification. That far, however, he succeeded in getting, but there he became sick, possibly the result of over-exposure. He could get no farther, and with only his Indian boatmen to assist him, in a few days passed away, "heart broken and worn out with fatigue", in the language of the record. So three at least of the old French priests gave up their lives in the prosecution of their duties, within the limits of the County.

A PROBLEM IN GOVERNMENT

St. Ovide and Vaudreuil, the French Governors at Louisbourg and Quebec, had a problem on their hands. It was not a national problem, for questions of national policy were often decided for them. But, since the outcome of national undertakings often depended for success on the way in which individuals performed their allotted tasks, it was a portion of their duties as governors to see that each individual under them was playing his part in the national scheme. The problem they were facing was what to do about young Petitpas.

The incident which brought about the correspondence between the two was the direct result of the seizure of a number of English fishing boats and vessels at Canso by Indians, acting in all probability with the French authorities knowing well of the intended attack and covertly assisting. The English had promptly rallied and sent vessels and men to the harbours lying to the westward, where the booty had been carried. The Indians had been forced to pay dearly for the damage done. A number of them were killed. Several of the vessels and boats had been recaptured. Some such retaliation as that was to have been expected but it could hardly have been foreseen that one of the persons most active in carrying out the punitive effort was a Frenchman. But so it was. Nor was there any doubt about the part played by this Frenchman. Having boarded one of the captured vessels and finding some Indians on her, he had attacked instantly and viciously, cutting the head off one who was vainly trying to throw himself overboard to swim to safety. This Frenchman, the elder Pettipas, was plainly a man to be reckoned with.

This was not the first time his actions had caused comment. It would have been difficult for him to have been defined as a good Frenchman, that is, one who was always responsive to patriotic appeals. There had been evidences of that in the war lately over. He was altogether too friendly with the English, too ready to receive from them a favour. And receiving a favour meant that there also was a readiness to give one, which might be awkward in the struggle which was taking place between the two crowns. Now his siding with the English in their attack on the Indians was the more to be unexpected, since his first wife had been an Indian woman.

In point of fact that was one of the first evidences that Petitpas was a man little given to be guided by advice or the opinion of authority. He, a Port Royal man, knew that the taking of Indian wives and the adulteration of French blood had been frowned upon, though it is true that the teaching at Port Royal had been ill received by some of those responsible in other settlements for the maintenance of French authority. La Tour and Baron De Castine, for example, were not unfavourable to contracting alliances with the Indians, but Port Royal had not encouraged the practice. That Petitpas had gone beyond the pale indicated that he was a man of determination, not easily moved by argument or remonstrance, though possibly in no way actually culpable. The fact that, his first wife being dead and French spouses being then more easily obtained, he had on his second venture married a French woman, to an extent atoned for his first refusal to heed advice. Now it was being proven that there was something in the argument that intermarriage with the Indians was capable of bringing about troublesome complications.

Petitpas, the younger, was one of the fruits of the first marriage. He had been brought up more as an Indian than a white child, and had early learned to speak Micmac, much better than any interpreter could, says the record. The father naturally thought very highly of him, and in discussing his future with some of his. English friends, the suggestion had been made that the boy be sent to Boston with them, when they were returning at the close of a year's fishing operations, and there an effort be made to secure for him some education. That had been done. For three years the boy had remained in New England. A bright intelligent young man, he had turned out to be, with a command of Micmac obtained from his mother, of French from his father and step-mother, and of English from his New England hosts. Few indeed had these qualifications. It ought to be possible to put them to some good use.

His English friends had thought so. While the New England Indians were not Micmacs, there were related dialects used by members of the Algonquin tribes, the mastery of which would not be difficult to one versed in Micmac. There was also a dearth of material from which Indian missionaries could be made. The French had profited greatly from the presence among Indian tribes of priests who had labouriously acquainted themselves with the languages of their hosts. New England might well take a lesson from this, and endeavour to do some Indian evangelization for political purposes. Petitpas might be the very person for whom search was being made. There was no doubt concerning his qualifications for the role.

The plan did not work out. Perhaps the father was a better Catholic than he was a Frenchman and the severance of the religious ties represented a step which he was little disposed to take, though the national ones had been sacrificed without demur. It seemed better to have the young man brought home, accepting gratefully the three years of maintenance and education, but withdrawing when the course of action, perhaps lightly entered upon, threatened to lead to complications.

The young man came home, probably quite unaware of the intentness with which his actions were being followed. He re-joined his family in Isle Royale, whither they had gone after leaving Port Royal, and where his father returned each year after the termination of the fishing season at Canso. There, he was under the immediate observation of St. Ovide, who was keeping himself aware of what was taking place.

The situation was one to be handled with delicacy and finesse. It was not desired to do anything still farther to weaken the ties which bound the older Petitpas to France. There was even a possibility that careful management of the situation might cause him to re-trace his steps and again place himself wholeheartedly on the French side in the struggle which was looming up. The offer of an education at Quebec or Montreal might so serve, appealing to the father's sense of pride and interest in his son's welfare. But in the meantime, it was necessary that the breach be not more widened. So St. Ovide took the young man under some kind of a protective custody, and on a pretext, sent him to Quebec.

There, the Governor introduced him to the Bishop. At the Seminary which had already been established, the young man would be received, and given the advantage of whatever facilities there were for education. The course of training was such as would open up the way to the priesthood and possibly later to a mission. This was the opportunity now available to him if he desired to take it. There was no doubt but that the two making the offer, the Governor

46

and the Bishop, desired that the offer be accepted.

The young man did not hesitate. If he had entertained any such idea when he left Isle Royale, something had in the interval occurred which made the prospect of being a black robe unendurable. The salt was in his blood. The memory of his experience on the sea was too vivid and alluring. The sea was to be his profession and the only training he would accept was that which would help him realize his ambition of commanding a vessel. He would be a navigator, not a priest.

The proposal thus summarily rejected, there remained little for the Governor and the Bishop to do. It was not in the best interest of France that the recalcitrant be allowed to return to Isle Royale, for access to Boston was there too easy. Even retaining him in Quebec was not desirable, for it was little more difficult for a determined man to get to Boston from Quebec, than it was from Isle Royale. It was safest to send him to France, thus placing the whole Atlantic between him and the possibility of the English becoming possessed of his services. So Vaudreuil's despatch to the Council of Marine ends,—"As it was as easy for this young man to return to Boston from this place as from Isle Royale, we have considered it expedient to send him to France in *La Chameau.*" Thus was France's interest best served.

Is this the end of the story? Does not a lifted corner of the curtain afford us another glimpse of this poor unfortunate, whose value lay in his command of the Micmac and other languages? Of the means by which he escaped from the threat of being carried to France in *La Chameau* we have no information. But in some way he must have done so, for the record stands, that Barthelemi Petitpas, the Indian interpreter, again got into the hands of the New Englanders, and was held in New England forcibly till he died, in spite of all the efforts made to bring about his return to Canada, in exchange for English prisoners.

Thus always have and ever will private interests suffer when public issues are at stake.

THREE REMARKABLE MEN

They were three remarkable men whom Razilly had gathered together, when, in 1632, with them as his assistants, he undertook the task of opening up Acadie for France. Perhaps, instead of three there may have been four, the fourth being Razilly himself, for he must have been a man of unusual ability to drive three other such men in harness. Each had ability; each was an individualist; and they differed from each other as widely as the poles. Each, too, has left his imprint on all that followed them in the story of the French settlement of Acadie. Under Razilly's guidance and direction one sees evidence of a collaboration without friction or strife. His guiding hand lost, that collaboration disappeared, as it became possible for each to act in accordance with his own ability, ambition method and purpose. Perhaps there was one quality which all possessed to a degree approaching equivalency, that of persistence, persistence which never flagged, never halted and which could bide its time. That persistence in the end brought to each at least some qualified reward, some measure of success during a period, possibly indeed brief. Its effect, however, persists to some extent, even to this day.

It was but natural that Razilly, on his arrival in Acadie, should pay respect to Charles LaTour's rights, which had never been wholly annulled. That arrival meant, for LaTour, the end of many years of marooning, he being one of the few Frenchmen who were left in Acadie after the collapse of DeMont's unfortunate expedition. Staying, whether of his own will or through compulsion, he had found a home among, the Indians on the southern coast of the Province, living with them, to all intents becoming one of them. The years passed, and if, in the long interval before Razilly's arrival, LaTour as much as saw another late comer from France, it was only one of the crew of some visiting fishing vessel. Claiming as he did a concession from the French Court, the tendency for him to ally himself or even to fraternize with the American fishermen who were disposed to deny his right, was easily curbed. Nor could he have remained and lived among the Indians unless he had succeeded in establishing with them a friendship which must have been based upon esteem and regard. It was not a purchased regard, since he had lost all opportunity of purchase. Deprived of all means of communicating with his countrymen in France, unable to obtain the trade goods which might have been used to purchase a friendship, he still very evidently was able to instill into the minds of the Indians a genuine and sincere liking which was his only safeguard during many years. May we not consider that the effects were so far reaching that all Frenchmen profited therefrom, and that from it grew and developed that traditional friendship between the Indian and the French which persisted unbroken for so many years. Without that friendship, lasting and unassailable, the course of history might have been very different in Acadie in the following years. Difficult and arduous though La-Tour's years of absence from France might have been, they were well worth while from the French viewpoint, to have achieved such a result.

Might not another of his qualities have been developed during his long sojourn with his Indian friends? Force he manifestly could not use with them, though doubtless there were many occasions when there were ends which he desired to achieve. Was it then that he learned his methods of indirect approach, and gained the knowledge that there were many ways in which differences might be composed, other than by a resort to physical means? He had been content to break off the conflict with D'Aulnay, even after the death of his wife and the slaughter of his men, confident that another day would come when it would be his turn. In the meantime, "to day to thee, tomorrow to me" was to him no idle saying, for he had learned to bide his time and seek another solution. That solution came when D'Aulnay suddenly died, and he was then not slow in again pressing his claims. But D'Aulnay's widow gave evidence of being no less energetic in her defence of what she considered her rights than was D'Aulnay himself. Who, perhaps, but LaTour would have seen that the most satisfactory way of ending that difference was to be gained by the marriage of the two claimants? Never for him were disputes to be settled by methods so crude as were involved in physical combat, when methods of diplomacy and discussion would in the end be equally effective. At the same time, this attitude of mind could not have been accompanied by cowardice. No person, without a high degree of physical courage could have succeeded in gaining or in keeping the esteem of the Indians, in whose code that virtue stood pre-eminent. Who can doubt but that, when attacked by D'Aulnay, LaTour, with his Indian friends might have completely crippled D'Aulnay's plans for the colonization of the area? Or, what would have become of D'Aulnay's plans, if LaTour, with his known powers of persuasion had sought the intervention of the New Englanders in his behalf? But, if the idea of the internecine strife of Frenchman with Frenchman was repugnant to him, equally or more repugnant was the idea of making an appeal to a common enemy. Better, far better, was the policy of biding his time and of submitting to what seemed to be inevitable in the present, in the hope that in the future, other conditions would present themselves.

So we must picture to ourselves LaTour to be a man in possession of all the qualities which were needed to cement firmly to him and to France the friendship of his Indian associates, a man of persistence, holding on through long and possibly dangerous years to what he considered to be his rights of possession, a patriotic man, since throughout those years when his services to the New Englanders might have cost France dear he had never forgotten that he was a Frenchman, and owed to France his firm allegiance, and withal, adaptable, diplomatic, and in possession of qualities which commanded the respect and liking of Indian and Frenchman and New Englander.

What was his weakness? It arose from the possession of those very qualities which served to unite the French and the Indians. It is but creditable to him that he was as staunch a friend of the Indian as the Indian was of him. It is not discreditable that he may have condoned in his family or among his associates the sealing of that friendship by marriage. But not in that way was a colony to be built up. Acadie, if it was to be a New France was to be an Acadie of French, not of mixed blood. Acadie, to become rooted, to grow, to flourish, must be a French Acadie.

Razilly's venture, to be successful, must largely pay its own way. The profit principle bulked very large in any attempts at colonization. There was need of some kind of a technical expert, preferably one who had some experience on the ground, who knew that locality, and if he did not know the methods could develop them. This seems to have been the part which Nicholas Denys was to play and to explain his place in the group. He was then 35 years of age. It is not known definitely that he had previously visited the New World, but there is every evidence that he felt himself quite at home in several of the harbours, knew the ones which best suited the different profit making ventures and was acquainted with many of the details of technique, which up to that time had been developed. No one can read his book, that was written many years later, without knowing how thoroughly the technique of everything relating to the fishing industry had been acquired. We first know of him in connection with a sedentary fishing undertaking at Rossignol. The war between France and Spain brought that to a close. Next year the transportation of timber to France was attempted, only to be brought to an end by D'Aulnay. Far to the north he went to escape from D'Aulnay, where at Miscou was a promising site for a fishing establishment. He seemed to know each nook and cranny in the miles of coastline, the advantages and disadvantages of each for some phase of business from which profit might be extracted. Here was a suitable location for a fishing venture. There was an Indian travel route, and a good opportunity for Indian trade. While much of this information may have come to him after his connection with Razilly had been brought about, it seems that at least the rudiments of that knowledge had been his even before Razilly's appearance on the scene.

The picture which we get of him is that of a great, simple souled big-hearted, generous, honest but indomitable man, whom adversity could not discourage and success could not spoil. LaTour may have known what it was to suffer reverses and his transition from being a refugee among the Indians contrasts sharply with the most successful periods of his later life, but he was never called upon to undergo what Denys suffered. The latter's experiences ran the gamut from the dungeons of Quebec and Port Royal to the position as Royal Governor of almost all the Atlantic seaboard. He was attacked in turn by D'Aulnay, his widow, Leborgne and LaGiraudiere, and from the losses which he suffered from these attacks he never recovered. One of the singularities connected with his experience of persecution was that on every occasion those who attacked him were of his own race and possibly his old associates or at least acquaintances. For thirteen years he was the Governor of his area, while Nova Scotia was being claimed by the English, but we read of no interference which he ever suffered during that time from them. On every occasion in which he was able to bring his case to the attention of the home authorities, his claims were upheld, though on no occasion was he indemnified for the losses to which he had been put. His forts or places of business were apparently as indefensible as his peace-loving disposition was sincere. In his fifty or more years of extremes in Acadie, we know of no instance of bloodshed in which he was in any way directly responsible or which occurred in any of his establishments. And, when adversity came to those who in a number of instances had wronged him cruelly, it was to him that application was immediately made for assistance, an assistance always generously given. He sheltered some of LeBorgne's entourage when they fell upon evil days. Though LaGiraudiere, without a shadow of right had caused him grievous loss, he freely maintained all of these under Huret, La-Giraudiere's lieutenant, after they had succeeded in escaping the surprise attack made by Basset on the fort on the St. Mary's River. He suffered reverses of every kind, loss in most instances caused by those who should have been his friends, but no reverse embittered him, and after every loss, a brave effort was made to recoup himself. He may not have been as some have said he was, a beggar on the streets of Paris, but his strength of character might have enabled him even to bear that adversity. And in all the lists of France's pioneers there are few or none to compare with him. He was not a colonizer, though undoubtedly he served to open up several of the harbours in the Gulf of St. Lawrence for permanent French occupancy. He may not have been militantly religious, though priests always found shelter and a place to prosecute their callings in the establishments which he controlled. These may be defects, but they were defects well compensated for by a nobility of character to which few have attained.

What were his limitations? More than by anything else, Denys had been impressed by the fabulous wealth of the fisheries. He envisaged a New France composed of a number of what he called "Sedentary Fishing establishments" situated at intervals along the coast line. To his thought colonization was but an adjunct to the maintenance of these establishments, and with sufficient of these functioning, the future of New France was assured. Events were to prove how fallacious this opinion was.

From both LaTour and Denys, D'Aulnay differed as the daylight does from the dark. Where LaTour was diplomatic and suave, D'Aulnay was impulsive and dogmatic. Where Denys was a peace-lover, D'Aulnay was bellicose and belligerent. Where LaTour would have temporized and delayed, D'Aulnay demanded instant action. Where Denys was kindhearted and humane, D'Aulnay did not scruple at deed of violence, with which his name still reeks. Where La Tour inspired liking and Denys' career demanded esteem and regard, if, among any but his immediate family, D'Aulnay was liked, esteemed or highly regarded, the fact has been skillfully obscured by his contemporaries.

Yet, withal, D'Aulnay left an imprint on events immeasurably greater than did the others. It was given to him more to shape the future of the French in Acadie than to any other of the early French explorers and colonizers.

Undoubtedly he saw farther into the future than did his two associates. With a grasp of affairs much more statesmanlike, he realized that if a New France was to be born in Acadie, the idea of LaTour that it might be reared upon a basis, part French and part Indian, and the prescription of Denys, that the establishment of a series of sedentary fishing centres at intervals along the coast would perpetuate the French regime, were equally erroneous. He knew, either instinctively or from observation that the preservation of the purity of the French blood in Acadie was vital. He knew, moreover, that the future of Acadie depended on the development of its agricultural resources more than it did upon the development of its fisheries. He knew that could he develop at Port Royal and in its vicinity a well-rooted colony, capable from year to year or from time to time of casting off aggregations of its members to establish other prosperous farming sections, the path to a permanent future might be opened up.

Toward that end he worked, in the short time it was given to him to work, and fortunate it was for France that along that line development took place. Once definitely started, the movement gathered weight, for there was behind it the remarkable reservoir of French fecundity which soon demanded outlets. From Port Royal the excess population spread swiftly from locality to locality along the shores of the Bay of Fundy, Minas Basin and Chignecto Bay, a population as French as was France itself. The rapid population growth was a phenomenon which was to affect the entire course of history in Acadie, and the aftermath of its effects have by no means yet disappeared. Thus was D'Aulnay's opinion justified.

WILMOT TOWNSHIP

The Township of Wilmot is comprised of the extreme eastern end of Nova Scotia proper. Its northern boundary is the southern line of the Township of Guysborough and the waters of Chedabucto Bay. Eastward and southward are the waters of the Atlantic. Its western boundaries are formed by the eastern limits of the Township of Guysborough and by St. Mary's Municipality.

These, at least are the limits of the Township as they are delineated in the map accompanying Haliburton's Historical and Statistical Account of Nova Scotia,. At the present time, neither the Townships of Wilmot nor that of Guysborough can be considered as geographical or administrative entities. The eastern boundary of St. Mary's Municipality does not now pass as it then did east of the settlements on the east side of Country Harbour, but reaches the Atlantic at a point some miles to the west. The town of Wilmot, from which the Township got its name, died at its birth, and was almost if not quite a town without a resident. To all intents, the Township enjoys but a shadowy existence, the very fact of it ever having been formed known to but few.

No portion of the Province, however, has a history of earlier discovery than have some of the lands included in the Township; none has had a more checkered history or has passed through greater vicissitudes. Micmac and Souriquois, Portuguese and French, English and Colonials flit across the scene. There are stories of bloodshed and violence, raids and reprisals, 'Man's inhumanity to man' in many different aspects. There are, too a different series of pictures, those of hardy and brave pioneers, fraternizing with their kin born under a different flag, ardently endeavoring to work and thrive, but too often the sport of those who made them pawns in the game of empire. There are pictures of harried exiles, being chased relentlessly from one temporary resting place to another. There are glimpses of such motley throngs as can be gathered together, if the lure of easily acquired riches entices. There are stories of disaster and ship wreck relieved by unlocked for heroism, or accompanied by the most sordid selfishness. Lastly, there is a story of development, when, the fires of war and discord having ceased their ravages or been transferred to other regions, an era of progress has been entered upon, subject only to the limitations of changing economic conditions, or marking stages of advancement in our common history. If stories such as these make history, surely the Township of Wilmot has claims which must be recognised.

The sea forms most of the boundaries of the Township. From Queensport (old Crow Harbour) on Chedabucto Bay eastward to the numerous rocky islets which form the harbour of Canso, and thence south and west to the head of what is now called Isaac's Harbour, the coast line, if measured in such a way as to follow the sinuosities of the shore, will measure many times the length of the straight lines connecting the points. Its landward borders are without exception in the barren wastes which are a distinguishing feature of the Atlantic coast counties of Nova Scotia.   Even to this day what settlements there are fringe the indentations of its harbours and coves, or depend on the proximity of the sea for their raison d'etre.

Bleak, rocky and uninviting, its acres of barrens, interspersed thickly with lakes, offer no inducement to the agriculturist. In earlier years, an unthrifty forest growth may have covered many acres of what are now uninviting barrens, or have hidden under its shade the boulders and rocks which devastating fires have now laid bare. But there are miles upon miles where there is barely sufficient soil over the bedrock to nourish the most stunted of vegetable growths and occasional peat bogs, with their fringes of scrubby spruce. One does not see how these could greatly have altered.

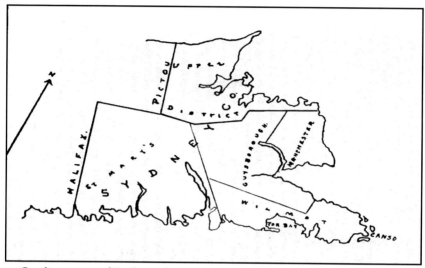

Outline map of Sydney County showing division into Townships

Without a doubt the district was quite well known to the Souriquois or Micmac, the original inhabitants. The territory between Canso and Halifax was the Eskegawaage district (in English, the Skin dressing place) of the loosely knit Micmac confederacy, and was one of their most thickly settled districts. One of the routes of travel, the inland route, by which communication was maintained between the Indians of the island of Cape Breton and those of the mainland, parallel at but a few miles distance much of the northern border of the Town-ship. Even yet, within its borders there are hunting grounds, allotted according to the tribal custom to individuals, probably descended from those who several hundred years ago enjoyed the same privileges. It was possible for these nomads to reach the extreme end of the point at Canso, either by coasting along the southern shore of Chedabucto Bay, or, on the Atlantic shore, by threading the waterways protected by the outlying ledges and islands, crossing the harbours, or in places, portaging across the narrow necks of land which separated one harbour from another. To this day the fisherman do likewise, making use of portages or boat canals to avoid rounding the headlands, exposed to the full force of the Atlantic.

It was not the richness of the forest or the land which was the attraction, which was drawing thither visitants from across the sea, when we get our first clear picture of the district. Nature had most profusely lavished its wealth in the seas which washed its shores, and this was being eagerly sought after at the time when our first authentic records of the district begin.

If Chedabucto Bay, entered upon in June 1520, was the Fresh Water

54

Bay of Jao DaFagundes or the Bahia de la Ensenada (Bay with the Cove) which Stephen Gomez named in 1524; the credit of discovery, withheld from the Norsemen from our failure to identify the points visited by them, goes to the Portuguese or the Spaniard. Even by the first of these, Basque fishermen had been met with along the Cape Breton coast, and one must conclude that these or other fishermen were by no means strangers to the rocky harbours, during the many years which elapsed between Fagundes' visit and our next record, though unfortunately any evidences of their presence have been long since obliterated. For our first authentic information concerning any portion of the area, we must wait for Les Carbot's description and the information obtained from Champlain. But already Canso at least was a well known point, the circumstances connected with the naming of which had long since passed into oblivion. Micmac and Portuguese, Spaniard and French have at various times been credited with its naming, and the correct solution of the mystery may never be brought to light. For the present we can do little but accept Dr. Ganong's explanation that the words signify, in Micmac, 'beyond the frowning cliffs'. One acquainted with its geographical features does not readily accept Dr. Rand's version 'opposite the frowning cliffs', but sees in the first a vivid picture of the low lying Canso islands beyond the cliffs which are so prominent on the south shore of Chedabucto Bay. DeMont's expedition of settlement left the shores of France in March 1604, and Canso, according to Champlain, was the appointed rendezvous, if, during the long passage his ships became separated. They did so, and the one in which Poutrincourt and LesCarbot sailed made a landfall far to the west. The other vessel visited Canso, finding there four Basque fishermen engaged in their occupation or in trading with the Indians. These poor unfortunates met with very harsh treatment at the hands of their countrymen, and the incident is the first of a long series of stories of oppression and suffering with which we shall have to deal. Without a doubt these or others of their kind were no strangers to the Shores and of that fact both LesCarbot and Champlain are witnesses.

If Chedabucto Bay, entered upon in June 1520, was the Fresh Water Bay of Jao DaFagundes or the Bahia de la Ensenada (Bay with the Cove) which Stephen Gomez named in 1524; the credit of discovery, withheld from the Norsemen from our failure to identify the points visited by them, goes to the Portuguese or the Spaniard. Even by the first of these, Basque fishermen had been met with along the Cape Breton coast, and one must conclude that these or other fishermen were by no means strangers to the rocky harbours, during the many years which elapsed between Fagundes' visit and our next record, though unfortunately any evidences of their presence have been long since obliterated. For our first authentic information concerning any portion of the area, we must wait for Les Carbot's description and the information obtained from Champlain. But already Canso at least was a well known point, the circumstances connected with the naming of which had long since passed into oblivion. Micmac and Portuguese, Spaniard and French have at various times been credited with its naming, and the correct solution of the mystery may never be brought to light. For the present we can do little but accept Dr. Ganong's explanation that the words signify, in Micmac, 'beyond the frowning cliffs'. One acquainted with its geographical features does not readily accept Dr. Rand's version 'opposite the frowning cliffs', but sees in the first a vivid picture of the low lying Canso islands beyond the cliffs which are so prominent on the south shore of Chedabucto Bay. DeMont's expedition of settlement left the shores of France in March 1604, and Canso, according to Champlain, was the appointed rendezvous, if, during the long passage his ships became separated. They did so, and the one in which Poutrincourt and LesCarbot sailed made a landfall far to the west. The other vessel visited Canso, finding there four Basque fishermen engaged in their occupation or in trading with the Indians. These poor unfortunates met with very harsh treatment at the hands of their countrymen, and the incident is the first of a long series of stories of oppression and suffering with which we shall have to deal. Without a doubt these or others of their kind were no strangers to the Shores and of that fact both LesCarbot and Champlain are witnesses. Both these navigators left descriptions of the coast line and of a number of their ports of call, and refer to meeting Basques or Bretons in several localities. LesCarbot's account is the more complete and well repays the telling. His narrative is a running account of each day's proceedings and the experiences met with, given in fairly full detail, and at times with much flowery embellishment. It is corroborated in the essential points by Champlain, though the two sometimes do not agree in their estimates of distances. Again in the fall of 1607, the party rendezvoused in Canso, preparing for the long journey home. LesCarbot's description that Canso 'is a small harbour amid seven or eight islands where ships can lie in shelter from the winds, and there is a bay more than ten leagues deep and three broad', is one of the first definite pictures of it which we have.

From DeMont's expedition to the time of Raziily a number of years elapsed. Springing from it, after the death of the leader, was the division of his grant among his three lieutenants, Nicholas Denys, LaTour and D'Aulnay. East and north of Cape Canso to Gaspe lay Denys' concession, while D'Aulnay's included the portion west of that first named point. At least Denys appears to have made earnest efforts to develop his grant, but the strength of the three claimants was wasted in fratricidal contests, which resulted finally in their disappearance and the new apportionment of the territory.

During the progress of the struggles, others, little recking of ownership, had been making use of the advantages for fishing which the coast afforded. There were well established lines of procedure followed by these visitors, (for visitors they were, coming to their chosen locality early in the spring, procuring their catch and returning homeward in the fall) and one has only to read Denys' description of the fishery to know how well established the industry was. The construction and rigging of boats, the methods of catching and curing fish, the customs of the fishermen during their stay on the grounds, the construction of staging and wharves, all are dealt with in his exhaustive work with a marvellous minuteness. Further we are given by him some information concerning the location of the settlements, which information has for us quite an amount of interest.

There can be little doubt but that the islands forming the eastern side of Canso harbour were then much more largely occupied than they are at present. Self protection may have had something to do with this, and also the fact that these islands afforded more beaches on which fish might be cured. It was then the custom for the first comer in the spring to select for himself the most desirable location, and to apportion to the later arrivals the grounds to be occupied by them. The first comer was for the year the 'Admiral' of the port, and Denys tells in a most graphic way of the efforts to secure that coveted position. His description of the port is as follows, 'Campseaux is a harbour which has at least three leagues of depth, and from the Cape ,(Campseaux) commences the entrance of the great Bay of Saint Laurent. The harbour is

56

composed only of a number of islands. There is a large one of about four leagues in circumference where there are streams and springs. It is covered with rather fine trees but the greater part of them are only firs which is a convenience to the fishermen for making their stages, of which I shall speak in the proper place. This island is in the midst of the others, and forms two harbours; one is for the Admiral, or the first ship to arrive, and this is the nearest to the entrance from the side towards the sea. The anchorage for the ship is between two islands, where it lies in safety. The other harbour is for the Vice-Admiral and is on the other side of the island, where the ships are not under such good shelter. These two places have gravel beaches.

From that description, there can be little doubt but that the location of choice, the Admiral's harbour, was the cove made by the islands now known as Grassy, George's and Piscataqui islands, opposite the site of the present town of Canso, or the old site of the town plot of Wilmot. The Vice-Admiral's harbour was on the other side of George's Island, where up till quite recent years fishing lots were laid off and in more or less demand. At the present time, they are in little if any use.

Fifty or more years elapsed before the veil was lifted on Canso. The Province changed hands a number of times, or at least Port Royal did, and the fate of the only settled town and the seat of government determined the destiny of the remainder of the area. It is interesting to know, however, that though elsewhere strife reigned, in Canso we get another picture, one which shows us French and English fishermen, freely fraternizing in friendly rivalry, little disposed to take part in the strifes of their overlords. French methods apparently were better than were those used by the English; the presence of the French had a restraining influence on the Indian and common dangers prompted a mutual understanding and appreciation.

During all the period little of a definite character is to be observed in the development of the area., as evidenced by actual settlement. Apparently the advantages of its location were fully appreciated, but the times were too disturbed for permanent settlement. But yearly, in spite of the dangers of navigation or of capture, a few hardy fishermen, French, English or Colonial, when the times were propitious, ventured to run all the risks for the purpose of procuring a catch. The coast was becoming better known; a number of harbours were being given names which have present day flavour, and some of the old names were dropping out of use and being forgotten.

The conquest of Port Royal in 1710 and the Treaty which followed prepared the way for many changes. This peace, the Treaty of Utrecht, acknowledged the English ownership of Nova Scotia, "in such ample manner and form that the subjects of the Most Christian King shall be hereafter excluded from all kinds of fishing in the said seas and bays and other places on the coast of Nova Scotia, that is to say, on those which lie towards the east within thirty leagues beginning from the Island called Sable, inclusively, and thence stretching along towards the southwest". The debatable ground had been removed to localities more remote from the settlements along the Massachusetts coast. Henceforth Nova Scotia ports were destined to be the outposts along the newly formed borders and a new line of contact had been formed.

Annapolis, captured from the French before the close of the war, was made the seat of the English government. It was the only fortified place in

Nova Scotia; it was within easy reach of the English settlements along the Massachusetts coast, from which help in case of emergency must first be sought. Its position in the Bay of Fundy sheltered it to some extent from attacks which might be launched against it from the Island of Cape Breton, still retained by the French. In addition, its climate and the possibilities of agriculture it afforded were more likely to appeal to settlers than were the settlements along the eastern shore, where fishing formed the main source of wealth.

At the same time, the location of the capital at a point so out of the ordinary line of travel was not satisfactory. 'Not one sloop in a thousand years would come to Annapolis unless sent', says Phillips. As well as being the capital, it (Annapolis) was the only port of customs entry, and since no fisherman would go there to enter, no duties were collected.

Unsuitable though Annapolis was, it can not be said that Canso should have been selected as the seat of government. It offered no inducements to the agriculturist; it was far removed from points from which help might be secured; the dangers of a rocky uncharted coast must have contributed to its isolation, and the proximity of the French in Cape Breton was a constant menace, for it was the very point of contact of the jarring races.

A few years saw the French occupation of Cape Breton buttressed upon Louisbourg, founded to support that interest. The terms of the Treaty of Utrecht had confirmed them in their possession, not only of the Island of Cape Breton, but of all islands in the estuary of the St. Lawrence River. According to the French contention, the Strait of Canso, the passage now known as the Tittle, and the waters of Canso harbour itself might be regarded as mouths of the St. Lawrence, and granting this, the islands forming the eastern shore of Canso Harbour belonged to France, though the mainland might be conceded to be in the possession of the English. Far fetched as this contention appears to be, at least it gave a basis for the French demands of ownership, and was only finally disposed of when the sovereignty of France was definitely limited by treaty to the barren islets of the St. Pierre and Miquelon group.

Once settled in the new seat of government at Annapolis Royal, it was not long before representations of the value to the English of the Canso fisheries were sent home to the Government overseas. Caulfield, in a report to the Board of Trade in 1715 says that 'Canso has the richest fisheries, and that New England alone, mostly from the eastern shore, takes in one season above 100,000 kentalls of fish over and above what our inhabitants take and sell to our merchants'. From the west coast of England, from Spain and Portugal, from New England, in spite of the dangers presented by the rocky uncharted coast, braving the perils of the deep to be met and overcome in vessels which today would appear unwieldy and unsafe, venturesome fishermen were coming to Canso in gradually increasing numbers. Caulfield 'recommended particularly' its value, and his reports bear frequent reference to the necessity for a hearty interest in its welfare and the need of active steps being taken to prevent French encroachment. In 1716, he informs the Lords of Trade that he "is creditably informed that the French take most of their fish at Canso and along the eastern Nova Scotian coast and urges that a ship of war be stationed there to prevent this".

It seems doubtful if this, the official attitude, can be considered as expressive of the sentiments of those, both French and English, who were actually in occupation. A common interest and a common danger seems to have drawn together for mutual protection all who sought the harbour. There is authority both French and English for considering that the relationship between the members of the different races was on the whole very friendly. There can be little doubt but that there was little local friction, and of this Vaughan, a former Governor of New Hampshire, who visited there in 1717, bears witness. "All was peaceable and quiet, the French and English fishing in all friendship and love." That this was not idle talk is substantiated on the French side, for it is known that, in the following year, when they were ordered by their Governor, St. Ovide, to retire from the disputed territory, they refused to do so, because, it was affirmed, their absence would expose the English who remained to greater danger of attack by the Indians. So side by side they worked away, and if the French were interlopers at Canso, there is no doubt but that the English were outside their own sphere when they fished, as they did, from Petite DeGrat or other places in Isle Madame.

It is regrettable that such an idyllic state could not long continue.

That it could not was decreed apparently by those high in authority. While the busy fisherfolk were interested only in procuring their ladings, and at this task were labouring in harmony side by side, their leaders were playing the game for dominion, zealously guarding the possession of territory held, or instituting reprisal where injury had been inflicted. It seems in this case that it was as a result of an English order that the peace on the frontier was disturbed.

Captain Smart of H.M.S. *Squirrel* was deputed by the Council of Massachusetts to protect the rights of the English at Canso, where it had been reported they were being threatened. English fishermen at various harbours along the south coast of Nova Scotia had been molested by the Indians, and the pretext was made that these were allies of the French. Whatever the pretext, the incident was the first of many such, which, carried on first by one side and then by the other, finally brought about an open rupture. Captain Smart arrived in Canso on Sept. 6, 1718, and sailed the following day to Louisbourg with a summons to the Governor to have the French occupants ordered home. On the 14th he returned to Canso, and a few days after, every French vessel had been seized, their cargoes taken and all the French property was on its way to Boston. The amount of the loss incurred is said to have been 200,000 livres.

Most of this was sustained by M. DeHirriberry, a merchant of St. Jean de Luz, and many are the documents which tell of his long fight for justice. Visits to Boston and London, with conferences and correspondence lengthened out over many years, obtained for him only a partial recompense, and before the matter was finally settled, counter reprisal had followed reprisal till settlements of the conflicting claims had become impossible.

Meanwhile, other steps were being taken to protect the English interest. Governor Phillips was in Canso in the summer of 1718, and doubtless as a result of the personal knowledge then obtained, it was decided that additional protection for the English residents was desirable. A company of his reorganized Regiment was on this account detailed for duty there, and from this time till the capture of the blockhouse by DuVivier in 1744, the presence of some soldiers aided in its protection. For the first years they were not in Canso continuously, but returned to winter in the fort at Annapolis.

From the very interesting chart 'most humbly dedicated and presented' by Captain Cyprian Southack to Governor Phillips about this rime, we are given the opportunity of picturing quite clearly the sites of a number of the establishments. There are inaccuracies without a doubt, but in the main the chart is little less valuable. Piscataqui, George's and Grassy Islands are represented as being one island called Canso Island, the narrow passage way between the latter two being ignored. The cove which was the old "Admiral's Harbour" is well marked, anchorages are therein noted, with depths of from two to four fathoms, and the sites of several fishing stages are given. Of these, Messrs. Hall and Henshaw's establishment is located at the extreme head of the cove, while on the point of what is now Grassy Island, two more are situated. Immediately behind these two are placed several houses, noted as belonging to "French Intruders". On the seaward side of the beach connecting Grassy and George's Island another stage is located. No less than seven more are placed on the western side of George's Island, in coves or protected by the outlying rocks and ledges. On these islands lying to seaward other stages and houses are marked, and it is to be noted that several of them apparently have a growth of trees. The note "French intruder" is liberally scattered over the seaward side of the main island, and a number of houses are placed there, especially along its southeastern shore. Especially noticeable is the size of what is now but a beach covered at high tide, Burying or Grave Island. Apparently then it was of some size, for on it was located the only fortification marked on the chart. Light House Island is marked as being occupied by the French, as is also Durell's Island. On the mainland only one house and stage is marked, this one, well down the harbour, below Burying Island, being noted as being a French house and stage. Altogether eighteen stages are noted, and a larger number of houses. The map allows us to identify quite well both the Admiral's and the Vice-.Admiral's harbours, referred to by Denys a number of years before, and is, perhaps, doubly interesting on that account.

The story of the happenings which were of moment in the history of the settlement can for a number of years be read in the mass of correspondence to be found in the records. Incidents in connection with it are frequently referred to in the Governor's Commission Book, in his Letter Book, and in other correspondence. Commissions as Justices of the Peace were given to Peter Proudie, Gyles Hall and Thomas Richards in 1719, and in letters of that or later years, instructions are given them, information respecting the doings of the French in Cape Breton is asked for, and notice is given that the Government expects an account of the ships, boats and men fishing from the port, with the quantity of fish taken. About the same time commissions in a company of militia to be raised among the fishermen were given to a number of prominent residents. How necessary protection was is intimated in the account of the seizing of the sloop *William* in the year 1719, by a Spanish privateer, which brought home to Governor Armstrong the insecure tenure of property in the troublous times. While proceeding from Canso to New England, the sloop, commanded by Captain Joseph Cole was captured and taken to Martinique. A letter from Capt. B. Young, refers to King George's Island, (the present name George's Island being evidently a contraction of this) for he recommends that a fort he built for the protection of the port. His duties on a vessel guarding the coast placed him in possession of first hand information, and in fact it seems to have been he who for a number of years reported on the trade of the harbour. During that year 96 sail of English and 200 of French 'made their voyages'.

The year 1720 is noteworthy as being that during which a raid on the

English establishments, doubtless in reprisal for the losses occasioned by Captain Thomas Smart, was made. The news of it was received in Annapolis on Aug. 27th, which tells us very plainly how far removed from assistance the settlement was.

During the night of Aug. 7th, a force of French and Indians made a sudden attack, killing three and driving the remainder from their huts or stages into their boats. Next night their fish were put on board the French vessels which had aided in the attack, while the captured merchandise became the spoil of the Indians. Some vessels were also captured, and the amount of the loss, it was estimated, was 20,000 pounds. In an itemised account of these, Capt. John Richards is said to have lost over 3000 pounds, while Capt. John Vernon, Hall and Henshaw and Capt. John Calley each lost over 1000 pounds.

The English, however, quickly rallied from the surprise. A sloop luckily arrived next day. Armed with the authority of Thomas Richards, the Justice of the Peace, a hastily organized attempt was made to secure some of the stolen property. Six or seven small French vessels were captured, containing more or less of the English goods, some prisoners were taken, a vessel was sent to Annapolis with requests for assistance, and a Mr. Henshaw of Boston, temporarily in Canso on business, was sent to Louisbourg with a complaint to the authorities. Meeting with no satisfaction, on the pretext that the Indians were the sole offenders, Mr. Henshaw took his prisoners to Annapolis, where they were handed over to Governor Phillips. The following is the record of the Council Minutes which refer to these prisoners. "Jeannice Souhare, Martin DeMolve, belonging to Captain Philibert D'Habilene, commander of a French ship at Nirichaw (Arichat), Jannice de Candos, belonging to Nicholas Petitpas fishing at Petit de Grat, Martin Dixipare, belonging to Martin De La Border, fishing at Petit De Gratz, Francois Pitrel, belonging to John Harenbourg fishing at the same place, five French fishermen who were taken a robbing the English at Canso, were sent for in before the Board, and examined. They all declared they were commanded by their masters to do what they did."

Aroused to action by the outrage, steps were taken at once to prevent repetition of it. Henshaw returned to Canso, having been given a Commission as Justice of the Peace and also one as Captain of Militia in a Company to be raised there. Representations urging prompt action were sent to the Home Government, and it was requested that 200 men be stationed in Canso to erect fortifications, 100 of whom were to be a permanent garrison. Governor Phillip's letter of Sept. 27th says, "In my humble opinion, the Man of War upon the station of New England should have attended the fishery at Canso in the season, according to the orders which were sent upon my application when at London; why she has lain all summer at Boston Harbour I can't guess, unless she waited for the relief which was said to be coming. It is certain that, had she been at Canso, that loss to the King had not happened". Major Paul Mascarene, in his 'Description of Nova Scotia' made out for the Lords of Trade the same year, called attention to the raid, and added his voice to those calling for better protection to the thriving industry. His estimate, that were it not for the interruption of fishing caused by it, 20,000 quintals of dry fish would have been exported, throws some light upon the extent of the fishery being carried on at the time.

To such strong pleas for succor, an answer was forthcoming, and the fall of the year saw a strong detachment of soldiers, with Major Armstrong in command, installed in a fort erected by the fishermen, and under orders to defend the place till spring. Lieut.-Governor Armstrong was empowered to allot beaches for fishing and stations and plots for gardens, the arrangements made by him being subject to Phillip's approval at a later date. A Lieut. Jephson was one of the officers sent to Canso at this time, for a reason which might appear strange. He had been under arrest at Annapolis for some time, on account of debt, but sufficient officers to hold a Court martial could never be gathered together. Now he was sent to Canso, being more likely to save money there and thus escape from the clutches of the law.

Major Armstrong returned to Annapolis soon after, taking with him two prisoners accused of murder, the loss of life having occurred under circumstances which prove the extent of the fear which the recent raid had engendered in the minds of the residents, and the constant apprehension lest another similar raid be undertaken. The defence in the case admitted that the person shot had come to his death by reason of shots, fired by the accused parties, these thinking that he was one of another band of French, coming to attack the place. That the defence was held to be a reasonable one is proved by the fact that bonds were accepted that the accused persons would present themselves for trial, when called upon to do so.

Bad luck followed the attempt to secure the place from attack during the fall and ensuing winter. The vessel containing equipment and stores was wrecked on Grand Manan, no lives being lost, but the cargo, gathered together with so much effort and so difficult to replace, becoming impossible of salvage. Hearing this, Major Armstrong was sent with another supply, which cargo arrived safely. Major Armstrong remained in Canso all the ensuing winter.

It would thus appear that the year 1720 was the first year that the permanent establishment of an English garrison in Canso was attempted. Up to this time, the summer months alone had seen life and activity along its shores, 'for each succeeding fall had witnessed the deeply laden ships of the fishing fleet sail homeward, leaving the scene of their labours to its pristine solitude or at most peopled by a very few of the most hardy of their class, undeterred by the dangers and isolation of their exposed situation. The amount of protection so slowly furnished after requests reiterated during each succeeding year, must yet have been inadequate, but it appears to have been sufficient to encourage more permanent settling, and from that time the number of families gradually increased till the muttering of approaching war became so ominous that safety was sought by flight. In the meantime, the assistance, meagre as it was, was thankfully appreciated and did much to allay the apprehension of Indian attacks.

To the little fort was given the name of Fort Phillips, doubtless in honour of the Governor. Of its equipment we know little, but it seems that it was the custom for the guns to be taken from the vessels and placed in earthworks onshore, the better to repel attack. Over two hundred and fifty pounds had been collected from the fishermen and given to Major Armstrong to provide for its construction. We have a description of it as a palisaded structure on a point of beach which had a view of the main harbour, but which was liable to be overflowed at high tide and which was, moreover, commanded by an eminence nearby. Without a doubt it was on George's Island. If one pictures it as a rough stockade sufficient to give shelter from musketry attack, but little likely to withstand an attack from heavier guns, one is probably not much in error.

Attack from the Indians was apparently most dreaded. It is now somewhat incomprehensible that a body of persons so few in numbers could so have overawed the settlers. What purports to have been censuses made during 1721 and 1722 places the numbers of the Indian fighting men in the whole of Nova Scotia as few hundreds only. Knowing the present day Indian, we are quite unprepared to reconcile the boldness, ability and determination of the old Micmac with the present day absence of these qualities. They had captured trading vessels in the Bay of Fundy and in the harbours along the south coast, armed though these vessels were. They had manned these vessels, and with them cruising among the fishing fleets on the Banks, spread consternation and dismay. They were capable of fighting with the utmost determination, on one occasion fifteen of them holding at bay for two hours a sloop attacked by Phillip's schooner, manned by sixty men. Ten of the fifteen escaped, and the heads of the remainder were brought to be placed on the pickets of the fort at Canso.

In the spring of 1721, hearing of an Indian gathering at Antigonish and fearful of its purpose, Major Armstrong sent post haste to Governor Phillip at Annapolis for stores. The reply reassures Armstrong that the gathering is but for the usual Easter feast. He informs him also that stores are being sent, but instructs him not to proceed with any active fortification till more definite orders are received from England. "So that you may content yourself with that fort which the fishery have erected at their cost which I hear is very defensible, and in case it wants any strengthening and necessary conveniences, there is no doubt but that these people will be easily persuaded to do it, since it is for their own defense." It also tells Armstrong that Phillips expects to be in Canso in six weeks, as Capt. Durell is to call for him in a man of war.

His visit, however, was somewhat delayed. It was not till the middle of August that he left Annapolis, arriving in Canso about the 5th or 6th of September. Again misfortune followed the vessel engaged in the transportation of stores. It was wrecked on Tusket Island, and the stores lost, though the lives of the crew were saved.

Soon after, writing from Canso to the Lords of Trade, Phillips informs them that it was a very agreeable surprise to him to find Canso in such a flourishing condition. "It would have been broken up had he not sent a detachment there, which detachment had lately been strengthened by the addition of two companies moved thither from Placentia". He further dwells upon the importance of the place and asks that it be made a free port for four or five years. 'My arrival here gave a general joy, being taken as good presage of the Government's intention to assert its rights, and to confirm the opinion more, I have determined to pass a bad winter here, without the necessaries of life, which hinder me being more particular to Your Lordship, my papers being left at Annapolis Royal'. 'In the meantime I have made disposition of small plots of ground and little rocks and islands in the harbour, for the conveniency of the fishery, which I have promised to confirm.' In this letter he complains to the Lords of Trade against their decision that no lands be granted to settlers, without being first surveyed, and certain areas reserved to the Crown. As no surveyor had been sent out, this amounted to making it impossible for the settler to acquire title to lands, except in case of lands granted provisionally, and subject to later confirmation, such as those to which he refers. Not till a much later date was it possible for an intending settler to get a satisfactory title.

Phillip's complaint that he must stay in Canso for the winter without 'the necessaries of life' was perhaps well grounded, but it is doubtful if his situation at Canso was more arduous than it would have been at Annapolis. We know from his old accounts the general run of prices for provisions, etc., about that time, and we know that these were being carried freely to Louisbourg from the New England ports, at least during the summer. A sheep could then be purchased for a pound, a hog cost a little more. A barrel of beef cost about three pounds, and we know he paid a pound for two dozen poultry. Two hundred weight of bread or ten bushels of Indian corn cost two and a half pounds. Rum and liquors were extremely cheap. Boards cost from two to four pounds per thousand feet, nails from a shilling to two shillings and six pence a pound. He paid from four to six shillings a day for labour.

Among these accounts, perhaps the most interesting item to be seen is one of ten pounds for cutting timber for building a church. This item is contained in his accounts for the period between Nov. 28th, 1720 and Sept. 5th, 1721, and the church probably was the first Protestant church constructed in Canada. At Annapolis the old French chapel was in use. It would be interesting indeed if we but knew the site of this building.

We are told too of the amount of trade being carried on during the year. The first vessel had arrived on Mar. 22nd, the last in July. The total number was 83 with crews numbering 602. Most came from Boston, Piscataqua, Salem and Barnstable. About 21,000 quintals of fish had been, caught, in addition to what was called a 'vast quantity' exported to Jamaica.

Soon after this broke out the long threatened Indian war between the English Colonists and the Indians. (Lovewell's War.) which kept the border in a turmoil for three years. The Micmacs and the Malecites of Nova Scotia and New Brunswick made common cause with their kindred along the Maine frontier, and a bloody war resulted, accompanied with all the needless cruelty usually seen in struggles of such a nature. Nova Scotia bore its proportion, sharing the dangers of the outbreak in common with the other settlements along the New England coast. Hibbert Newton, the Collector of Customs at Annapolis and later at Canso, was one of the passengers on a vessel captured at Passamaquoddy upon the outbreak of hostilities. For his release Lieut-Governor Doucette contributed by arranging for his ransom, after capturing twenty three Indians who were held as hostages. The Indians succeeded in taking trading vessels in the Bay of Fundy and captured eighteen fishing vessels in harbours along the Nova Scotian coast. Governor Phillips, writing from Canso to the Board of Trade on Sept. 19th, 1722, gives the following account, - "By this time we were in the middle of the fishery, and the harbour full of ships awaiting their loading, when fresh advices carne that the Indians were cruising about the Banks with the sloops they had captured, assisted by prisoners they had taken whom they compelled to serve as mariners, and gave out that they intended to attack this place with all their strength, which alarmed the people to that degree bringing to their mind the suffering of two years ago, and being very disheartened to find that no measures had been taken this year for the security of the place, from which they judged my representations to have had no weight with the Government at home, and their misfortunes to proceed from my want of interest, that they were upon breaking up and each man to shift for himself. To prevent this, I assembled the harbour and prevailed with them to concur with me in fitting and manning two sloops to protect the fishery, re-enforcing them each with a detachment of the garrison and an officer." One of these sloops was commanded by John Elliot of Boston, and the other by John Robin-son of Cape Ann. "Elliot, as he was ranging the coast, espied seven vessels in a harbour called Winnipeg (or Winipang) and, concealing all his men except four or five, until he came near to one of the vessels, which had about forty Indians on board, who were in expectation of another prize falling into their hands. As soon as they were within hearing, they hoisted their pendants and called out, "Strike, English dogs, and come aboard, for you are all prisoners", Elliot answered that he would make all the haste he could. Finding that he made no' attempt to escape, they began to fear a Tartar, and cut their cable, with intent to run ashore, but he was too quick for them and immediately clapped them aboard. For about half an hour, they made a brave resistance, but at length some of them jumping into the hold, Elliot threw his hand grenades after them, which made such havoc that all who remained alive took to the water, where they were a fair mark for the English shot. Five only reached the shore. Elliot received three bad wounds and several of his men were wounded and one killed. Seven vessels with several hundred quintals of fish and fifteen of the captives were recovered. They had sent many of the prisoners away, and nine they had killed in cold blood. Robinson retook two vessels and killed several of the enemy. Five other vessels had been carried up the Bay above the harbour of Malagash, and they were thus out of his reach, and he had not men sufficient to land, the enemy being very numerous". The prisoners from these vessels were subsequently ransomed by Captain Blinn, however, so that in Phillip's words, "in three weeks I had retook all the vessels and prisoners except four". In another letter he says that the result of the lesson had been so salutary, "that we in Canso are now easy and quiet as if there were not an Indian in the country, so that the business of the place will conclude with success". Among the trophies of the victory which Elliot and Robinson brought home from their cruise was the head of an Indian Chief, who had but three weeks before been with his band at Canso, where he had received presents from Phillips on behalf of the English Government in token of amity and goodwill. The head of this chief with five others were placed upon the pickets of the fort at Canso.

During the following year, 1723, the Indian outrages were again continued, Canso being surprised. The scene of this attempt was Durell's Island, the unfortunate victims being a Captain Watson, two other men, a woman and a child.

In the year 1724 Canso escaped Indian attack, though in its vicinity there were several outrages. A party of eight Malecites captured an English schooner three miles off the land near Mocodome. (Country Harbour). A prize captured from the French on which a crew of eight men with two guns had been placed by Major Cosby, and which had been sent by him to intercept French vessels carrying on illicit trade between the Island of Cape Breton and the mainland, was captured in the Strait of Canso, five men being killed and the remainder being taken prisoners.

But from this time on the Indian war, though still waged along the Massachusetts border, was not so vigorously prosecuted in Nova Scotia, which was comparatively out of the range of active hostilities. Gradually the Micmacs allowed the quarrel to drop, many of them coming to terms, the rough handling they had received/having taught them that severe measures would be taken in reprisal for injuries inflicted by them. Finally, the capture of the Indian stronghold at Norridgewoak in August of this year prepared the way for a peace which was concluded in the fall of 1725, a peace in which the Micmacs of

Nova Scotia were interested, and in the conference leading up to which, Major Mascarene and Hibbert Newton were the Nova Scotian representatives.

This put an end to any organized contest both along the New England border and in Nova Scotia, though isolated instances of murder and outrage committed by the Indians, supposedly at French instigation, were met with, were always dreaded, and in no place more than in the community which had already suffered so severely.

A description of Canso by Governor Phillips in November, 1724, informed the Lords of Trade that there had been erected a small fort at his own expense, with a battery for twelve guns. Three guns were then mounted and the fort was garrisoned by four companies of his regiment. In addition, to protect the shipping more effectually, guns were taken from the arriving vessels and placed in the battery. Major Alexander Cosby was the commanding officer of the battery. It apparently was situated on the eminence which we are told overlooked in 1721 the first location. It overlooked, we are told, "two other coves on the Great Island and the whole of the main harbour". It has an easy and gradual ascent, but was as yet (1721) full of stumps of trees and uncleared, except for the places where some few inhabitants had settled and where the garrison was fixed.

Amid the pictures of danger and bloodshed a wholly different picture of the local government of the place is afforded us in the rules drawn up to be observed in the community. Most of the inhabitants were New Englanders, and had brought with them that peculiar complex, the New England conscience. We believe they were arrant smugglers, but they did not permit Sabbath breaking. A church was one of the first necessities, but they decorated their fort palings with the heads of their enemies, if they could get them. They were far from the restraints of a normal society, but any one could be called on to explain why he was not at home after nine o'clock at night.

Withal, in their New England homes, they had experienced the advantages of community organization, and even under the conditions imposed by life in an outpost far from their homes, they were disposed to introduce in Canso some of the features of community government with which they were so well acquainted.

In order that the rules now drawn up should be observed, a committee of fifteen persons, including the magistrates, was appointed to enforce them. Was it by some premonition that they were dated July 4th? The year was 1724.

"Article 1. That special respect shall be had to the laws of Great Britain for the trying and determining any matter or cause depending between one man and another.

"Article 2. That drunkenness, slandering, quarrelling, Sabbath breaking and the like be heard and tried before one single Justice of the Peace.

"Article 3. That all debts contracted not exceeding forty shillings shall be determined before one Justice of the Peace.

"Article 4. That all matters of controversy, whether occasioned by the non-performance of contract, trespassing on another's man's land or lands, right or rights, cutting down or removing settled bounds, shall be decided by five at least of those appointed, one of whom to be a Justice of the Peace.

"Article 5. That the said persons shall meet weekly on Tuesdays at five of the clock in the afternoon, five at a time, alternately at the house of Mt. Parrott and Ginning's and Captain Wright's, and for default of not appearing shall suffer the penalty of ten shillings, unless good reason be shewed to the contrary.

"Article 6. That the complainer's grievance shall be in writing with his name affixed to it.

"Article 7. That the plaintiff or complainant shall be obliged to pay all damages and charges that may arise by his failing to prove the complaints which at any time he may exhibit.

"Article 8. That no complaint or plea that may be made, (criminal cast excepted) shall obligate the defendant to answer within twenty-four hours notice, and that he shall be notified by a man under oath.

"Article 9. That no commander or owner of vessels or shipping or shoreman shall be obliged to pay any debts contracted by their men, without their leave or approbation.

"Article 10. That two taverns be allowed in Canso, (Fort Hill excepted) the one at Captain Thomas Wright's, and the other at "William Austin's, and that no other person or persons shall presume to set up or keep an inn without license of the Commander in Chief or penalty of five pounds for each offense.

"Article 11. That the inn holder take special care that every person in his house repair home, to their quarters at or before the hour of nine at nigh:, on penalty of ten shillings for the inn holder or five shillings for the person so offending.

"Article 12. That the necessary charges for trying any action or cause be first paid out of the fines or forfeitures as may be thought proper by the person appointed, and the overplus, (if any be) to be disposed of at the discretion of the Commander in Chief.

"Article 13. That any man neglecting his duty either as a sailor, shore-man or fisherman, to the detriment of those he is concerned with, shall be liable to pay the damages as shall be made to appear against him.

"Article 14. That no crew shall break up their voyage or voyages contrary to their contract or agreement, without the consent of their owner, shoreman or major part interested in their voyage.

"Article 15. That owners and shoremen on penalty of damages sustained shall be obliged to supply their vessels with all the necessarys for the good of their voyages, if to be had in the place.

"Article 16. That there be seven or eight judicious men chosen and sworn to decide any differences that may arise between buyer and seller of fish, concerning cullage, which men are to be chosen by said persons appointed to inspect such affairs, and the buyer and seller are to pay their equal share in culling and cullage to the culler.

"Article 17. That when power has been given to several persons by the Commander in Chief to regulate and keep a strict watch, it is ordered by the authority aforesaid that the watch be set at night at places appointed, and that every person shall repair to their own place of abode on penalty of being apprehended and taken up by the watch, or at least complained of to some Justice of the Peace, who shall fine him or them according to discretion, and the watch shall examine and know the persons they may see after the hour of nine and if they will not answer and stand by first, second or third calling and give an account or themselves, they shall be counted as enemies and treated accordingly. All merchant vessels are required to keep watch and pass the word."

It would appear that Canso profited much from the prospect of the cessation of the Indian war. Lieut. - Governor Armstrong, returning from England, arrived in Canso on the 29th of May, 1725, and appears to have made it his headquarters for some time after that date. There is evidence to prove that Canso was thought to be the most important English settlement in Nova Scotia. Up to August of that year 198 vessels had fished from that port, or had departed, laden with fish for foreign markets. Meetings of the Council -were held there, Armstrong, Mascarene, Hibbert Newton and Shirreff being noted as being present at a Council Meeting held in that month, in which it was determined to send Newton to Louisbourg to protest against the continuance of French intrigues with the Indians. Writing to the Secretary of State on Sept. 5th, Armstrong again urges the necessity for more adequate protection. Under his inducements, the inhabitants had built several blockhouses for protection, at their own expense. He further says, "it being very demonstrable, from the great concourse of English subjects here, that this is the principal seat of Government, I intend to bring Major Paul Mascarene, Hibbert Newton, William Skene and William Shirreff, Esquires, Gentlemen of the Council of Annapolis Royal, down to this place in order to have a quorum. The inhabitants (of Nova Scotia) are all French except one or two families at Annapolis Royal. Canso is the only settlement on the coast. Its inhabitants amount to 49 families. The New England people trade in the cod fishery to the extent of 150,000 pounds yearly, New England Currency, yet they are under the disadvantage of taking their fish home 150 leagues to cure it, from which necessity settlers on the coast would be free."

Additional proofs of the prosperity of the community are found in the 19 allotments of land for fishing rooms made during the year. No. 1 is a Large island made over to Captain Durell and Co. Cyprian Southack had a peninsula 1740 by 1620 feet in measurement; Captain Edward How had 1100 by 500 feet on How's Island. Bunking Wentworth had one of 121 by 400' feet, and also another on what is called Wentworth's point, this one being 1180 by 580 feet. No. 43, given to Samuel Bassett and Samuel Butler was a high head of land with a low beach, the same being formerly called Petipas' Head, now Bellenden Head, in memento mori of Lieut. John Bellenden being descended iron a noble family and buried there. Dr. Cuthbert had 272 feet front on Topsham's cove. Sir Thomas Bury and Richard's room was a small island 920 feet long and 270 feet broad.

Many of these names recur time and again in the story of Canso or the Province. Captain Durell was Thomas Durell, and he is spoken of foe some years before the appearance of another Durell, whose name constantly occurs in the story of events between the years 1743 and 1766. This latter was Philip Durell, commissioned Captain in the Royal Navy in 1742, and passing through the successive grades to become Rear Admiral of the Red in 1759 and Vice Admiral of the Blue in 1762. He was present at both sieges of Louisbourg and died in Halifax while in command of the North American Station in 1766, being buried under St. Paul's Church. The island forming the northern shore of Canso Harbour and separated from the mainland by the narrow Tickle is still called Durell's Island.

Cyprian Southack's was also a well known name in the story of the period, rand to him we are indebted for a chart which has already been referred to. He was for some years one of the members of the Council, as was also Edward How. That persons so identified with the industrial life of the Province, (though at this time How was not a Councillor) should also be so closely connected with its government, throws an interesting sidelight on the condition of affairs at this time.

In accordance with Governor Armstrong's instructions, Hibbert Newton. who had been Collector of Customs at Annapolis, was this year moved to Canso, a Deputy Collector being appointed in his place in Annapolis, From this time Newton appears to have been a resident of Canso, till, it being thought to be untenable in the event of re-opened hostilities between France and England it became necessary for the Government to seek asylum in a place not so vulnerable. His position was not a sinecure. Illicit trading was being carried on openly and its volume had assumed large proportions. It was being carried on in the face of a helplessness to prevent it, on the part of both the French and English local authorities, — if indeed there was not on their parts a certain amount of connivance. It was being carried on so openly that it could hardly be called smuggling. Newton himself has described the procedure. Vessels cleared from New England ostensibly for Newfoundland with cargoes of lumber, bricks, livestock and flour, which cargoes, however, never reached that destination, bur were exchanged or sold. Return cargoes consisted of French brandy, wine, iron, sailcloth, rum and molasses. An occasional variation of this was the exchange of the whole or a part of the season's catch of fish at the English fishing ports for the above mentioned French commodities. Several ports in the vicinity of Canso in time earned a notoriety as being rendezvous where this exchange was being carried on. There seem to have been regular depots of this trade at Petit de Grat on the east of Canso, and at the old port called Martingot (now Whitehead) on the west. There is no intimation that the governing authorities of the Province had allowed themselves to become active participants in the business, though officials in both Louisbourg and New England ports can with difficulty be cleared of a charge of complicity or connivance. Utter inability to control it was rather the attitude of the Nova Scotian authorities, though doubtless they made what attempts their very limited resources permitted.

An entry worthy of note, casting as it does an interesting sidelight on the methods by which justice was administered and the forms of punishment meted out to offenders at that time, is to be found in the Council records of this year. As the offense was committed in Canso, though the trial took place in Annapolis, the incident requires no apology for the telling. Robert Nichols, a servant of Lieut.-Governor Armstrong's, according to the Council record, was found guilty of attempted assault on the person of the Lieut.-Governor, which offense was evidently a very flagrant example of lese majeste and one which called for a punishment fitting the crime. Owing to the fact that there was no other Court of Judicature in the Province, the Council had perforce to deal with the case, and did so, with the result that the unfortunate wight was condemned to, "Sitt upon a Gallowes three days, half an hour each day, with a Rope about thy Neck and a Paper upon your Breast, Whereon shall be Writt in Capital Letters, AUDACIOUS VILLAIN, and afterwards thou are to be whipt at a Cart's tail from the prison up to the uppermost house of the Cape, and from thence back again to the Prison house, Receiving each hundred paces five stripes Upon your bare Back with a Catt of Nine tails, and then thou art to be turned over for a soldier".   One wonders if he became a good soldier.

The year 1726 appears to have brought a continuation of Canso's prosperity. Some friction developed in connection with Customs dues, now levied for the first time. The residents, of whom Armstrong writes, "an angel from Heaven could, not please or govern these fishermen", objected to the imposition of a tax of Six shillings and Eight pence made by the Naval Officer on each vessel in port. A cental of a quintal of fish yearly for each fisherman had been charged for some time, probably from the time the first grants were provisionally made, but this additional burden was greatly resented. When we remember that from Armstrong's own admission, the fishermen had built forts for their own protection, and were at their own expense as militiamen when manning the forts, we can not help thinking that they had a certain amount of right on their side. At the same time, the Government was at a great expense keeping a portion of the regiment stationed there, the cost being estimated at about 15,000 pounds a year, towards the payment of which the Province returned little in taxes or imposts. We shall see later a statement of the total revenue of Nova Scotia, and shall appreciate that the money being spent by the Home Government for its protection gave very small and inadequate returns.

Nine companies of infantry comprised the garrison during this year, the largest garrison in Nova Scotia. The necessity for fortification was still being urgently though fruitlessly presented to the Lords of Trade. Armstrong himself remained in Canso most of the year, though he spent the winter in Annapolis.

On June 11, 1727 King George the First died, news being brought to Canso about the first of August, being thence transmitted to Annapolis, where it was received on Sept. 7th, Captain Cavalley, who commanded the Canso detachment having forwarded it.

Embers of the Indian conflict still continued to flare up at intervals, and some did so this year. Canso itself escaped, probably by reason of the fact that there were soldiers in sufficient numbers to make extremely hazardous any attack, but outlying ports were made scenes of outrages. At both Jeddore and Liscomb there were murders, which kept the eastern shore on the qui vive.

During the following winter, that of 1728, Canso itself was threatened by a large body of Indians, who had collected for the purpose of making a descent upon the inhabitants, but fearful of the result, and mindful of the retribution which Elliot and Robinson had exacted, the attack was not delivered. Governor Philipps himself spent the summer there, arriving from England about the end of June, 1729 in H.M.S. Rose, Captain Wellar, and proceeded to Annapolis at the end of the fishing season. His report to the Duke of Newcastle, dated Oct. 2nd, again calls attention to the importance of the place, and the necessity for taking additional measures to safeguard the industry, there so advantageously located. He had found there about 250 vessels, and from 1500 to 2000 men employed in catching and preparing their cargo. "Many families would settle here if they saw the commencement of a fortification for their protection, which till then they look upon as very precarious in regard to the numbers and strength of the enemy in case of a rupture at any time with France and the near neighborhood of Cape Breton." This year's records contain the grant of a fishing station from Governor Philipps to William Mooney of Marblehead.

The summer of 1730 was also spent by Governor Philipps in Canso, and again we find a report of the same tenor as those of former years. "Canso, (which is the envy and rival of Cape Breton in the fishery) will be sure to be the first attacked, which will take them no more than six or seven hours to march and possess it; but I am only the watchman to call and point out the danger, it's Your Grace to get it prevented". He also says that the returns of the fish carried to markets yearly from Canso bring 30,000 to 40,000 pounds increase in the home duties, "If so, is it not losing a sheep, according to the proverb, when one third of the year's income only laid out in fortification will put it out of danger". One answer at least had been given to repeated requests, for during this year a surveyor arrived, though the. result of his presence is not seen for some years.

In the meantime, some preparation for the protection of the inhabitants was all the more necessary, since there seemed to be very good prospects of the arrival in Nova Scotia of settlers from England or the Palatinate, as the result of the efforts being put forth by Thomas Coram or of the Hintzes, father and son. From one cause or another, this expected addition to the population did not take place. Other colonies offered superior inducements, or the negotiations fell through, so that neither Annapolis nor Canso, both places having been named as destinations for the settlers, profited by their presence. In the light of future events, their choice of homes elsewhere was perhaps fortunate for these settlers.

The year 1731 appears to have been comparatively uneventful, so far as Canso was concerned. Governor Philipps visited it on his way to England. The fisheries that year were very successful, there being more fish in the fall than ships to take them to market. Lieut.-Governor Cosby was this year successful in getting a grant of land, the quit rent being two shillings six pence a year. The plot changed hands the following year, being transferred to Edward How, and its description as contained in the Minutes of Council is interesting. It is, - "a plott of Ground, situate on ye North side of ye Hill of Canso, butted and Bounded on the Southwest side upon Doctor Elliot's grounds, and on the Northeast side by John Lumasses Ground, with Pallasadoes, being in front one hundred and thirty feet, reaching along northeast and southwest, ranging back to the sea northerly, with a wharf into ye pond. The whole being environed with Pallasadoes".

This is one of a number of references to the 'Hill of Canso', and to the 'Pond'. The riddle of their whereabouts can perhaps be read if the pond is taken to be what has already been called the Admiral's harbour among the islands. The Hill of Canso must therefore have been a portion of Grassy Island, and the location of this lot must have been east of the fort. If this supposition is correct up till this time there has not been any reference to any settlement on the mainland side of the harbour.

In the records of the following, year, more detailed information is given concerning the settlement and from it we can see that it has passed the heyday of its prosperity. The thunder clouds were banking, and safer sites for homes and industries were being sought. Governor Philipps, on whose authority the estimate was made, says that the quantity of fish exported was 60,000 to 70,000 quintals, the markets being Spain, Portugal and the Straits of Gibraltar. The claim of the French that Canso belonged to them was noted, and the state of the garrison, posted there without a defensible structure was commented upon. From this letter we obtain the information that the total revenue of the Colony was about 30 pounds a year, this sum being derived from the rentals of the Canso fishing plots, on the basis of a quintal of fish paid yearly by each proprietor. But the number of English families was decreasing yearly, owing to the impossibility of obtaining title to lands.

In addition to the other branches of the fishing industry reference is made about this time to quite a prosperous whaling industry, which had its headquarters in the settlement. Sloops fitted out in New England were reported to have been successful, seventy sloops bringing in fourteen whales, the presence of one hundred other sloops deeply laden with the results of their catch being recorded.

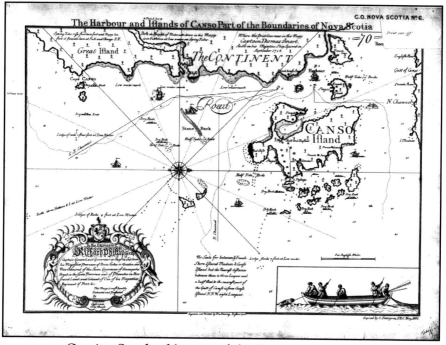

Cyprian Southack's map of the Canso Islands, 1720

A representation made in 1734 of the state of the Province in case of war with France deals quite fully with the condition and prospects of Canso. "Just at the doors of the Cape Breton French and much coveted by them, it is most advantageously situated for the whale and cod fishery, and has recently made a considerable figure in these two great branches of trade. It lies naked and defenseless, without so much as a barrack to lodge the four companies of Col. Philipp's Regiment stationed there for its defence, or storehouses, except the hasty erections put up from time to time by the commanders, assisted by the fishermen. If taken by the French, its loss would seriously affect not only Nova Scotia but New England, New York and the other plantations, for British subjects resort thither from all parts. As it is the only place in the Province which can be said to have been frequented all along by British subjects, its loss

72

would very much affect the traders, and strengthen the French, and enable them to do more damage along the coast with their privateers. At the first declaration of war, the French and Indians will fall upon Canso and besiege this place by land. Canso is, in a word, in a more deplorable state and condition than Annapolis Royal, and several families have already retired from it".

In fact, the high tide of Canso's prosperity had passed. Those versed in the signs of the times could plainly discern that the calm which had been enjoyed would shortly be broken. The period of peace was felt to have been but a breathing spell in the contest, a rest before the deadly grapple which must decide the ownership of the new world, and that period of peace was drawing to a close. The English population was retiring from the place over which it was known the storm would break, and the French, encouraged by the absence of the English pressed their claims of possession with more insistence. In 1735, 39 French boats had resumed fishing operations from stands on the outer islands of Canso, under permission to that effect from the Governor of Louisbourg. Still, in the fall, after his summer visit Governor Philipps was able to report a fairly successful year, 30,000 or 40,000 quintals of fish having been exported and a profitable whale fishery having been carried on. No fortifications had been erected, however, and the place was still in a defenceless condition. Nor had its unpreparedness escaped the eyes of the French, who were even then looking forward to the time when the outbreak of hostilities would allow them a pretext for the seizure of the coveted spot. DuVivier, in a report to his home government, informed them that with 100 men from the garrison of Louisbourg and arms and ammunition to distribute among the inhabitants, he would pledge his head to make a conquest of all that part of North America, including Canso.

From this time on, less and less mention is made of it with each succeeding year. Nova Scotia appeared to be slipping back to its old ownership. The English, numerically outnumbered, the disparity becoming yearly greater, appeared to be shrinking from the blow they knew must soon fall. There are records of grants of land to Christopher Aldridge and Edward How; Francis Cogswell was made a justice of the Peace in 1738; other appointments were made in 1740; reiterated comment on its lack of defence was sent home to the Board of Trade; Hibbert Newton was made a grant of one acre and two perches of land on Canso Hill in 1740, but two months later war was declared between England and Spain, and everyone knew the blow was due. But three or four families wintered there in the winters following 1740 though it is safe to assume that the French were not backward in taking the places of the retiring English.

News that the final break had occurred arrived first in Louisbourg, being received on May 3rd, 1744. To DuVivier was given the command of the attacking party, and his arrangements were quickly made. Captain Patrick Heron, who commanded the garrison had under him a force of about 120 men, and there was in the harbour a small guard sloop. There were inadequate defences, if any existed at all. DuVivier had with him on his arrival about 350 men, soldiers from the garrison and sailors from the ships at Louisbourg. Defence was little more than a gesture, for Canso fell bloodlessly, the capitulation being signed on May 24th. The soldiers and sailors taken were to be prisoners of war for one year, and the women and children were to be sent to Boston as soon as possible. The settlement was looted and burned and Canso had again changed ownership. It is not without interest to know that two months afterwards, in England was signed the authority for the erection of a sod fort for defence, the home government being ignorant that they then had no place to defend.

The seizure of Canso by DuVivier was criticised by the French themselves as a bad stroke, in that it served most effectually to arouse the English, who otherwise might not have attempted reprisals. The loss of Annapolis might have been borne with more or less equanimity, but that of Canso, the headquarters of the fishing industry, could not be accepted in so philosophical a manner. So expressed himself the 'Habitant of Louisbourg', possibly wise after the event, and whether this opinion was correct or not the burning blockhouse at Canso was a signal for the renewal of the conflict in the new world, during the course of which the plan conceived in Massachusetts for the capture of Louisbourg was consummated.

Most interesting are the steps by which this plan was worked out, its conception in the minds of persons who were considered dreamers, its gradual unfolding till victory crowned the seemingly fool-hardy attempt. It was a "triumph of the utterly absurd, of the patently impossible and vain", which is of moment to us, however, mainly so far as the story of Canso is concerned. And Canso was connected in many ways. In the first place, much of the information on which the plans were based, information of the strength of the garrison, the condition of the defences and other particulars, without knowledge of which the fantastic orders given the commander of the forces could not have been drawn up, was obtained from former residents of Canso who had been carried to Louisbourg and from thence paroled to their homes in Massachusetts. Without that accurate and recent information it is possible that the attack might not have been made. Aided by it the Massachusetts government had an advantage which it was not slow to use. In the second place, Canso was the place most suitable as a rendezvous for the combined militia and naval forces which were to make the attack.

William Pepperell, whose home at Kittery was within sight of the Piscataqua River, was given the command of the combined militia of Massachusetts, Connecticut, New Hampshire and Rhode Island which was to constitute the land force, the other States having refused assistance. With this force and a set of instructions which probably are without a parallel in history, the expedition started and achieved a success equalling Governor Shirley's most roseate imaginings.

Comment as one may on the instructions, we are thankful for them and to several diarists, at least one of whom is unknown by name, for some light they give concerning Canso. Read them, and judge for yourselves.

"Sir, —

The officers and men intended for the expedition against the French settlements on Cape Breton, under your command, being embarked and the necessary artillery, ammunition, provisions, etc. shipped for the purpose, you are hereby directed to repair on board the *Snow Shirley Galley*, Captain John Rouse Commander and to proceed with the said vessels and forces, wind and weather permitting, to Canso, which place it is absolutely necessary should be appointed a rendezvous for the fleet. On your arrival there, you are to order two companies, consisting of forty men each with the proper officers, on shore, to take possession of the place and keep it, appointing one of the two captains commandant of the whole; which party is to have

74

orders without delay to land, and erect a blockhouse frame, on the hill of Canso, where the old one stood, and hoist English colours upon it; enclosing it with pickets and pallisadoes, so that the sides of the square may extend about one hundred feet, for which it is presumed there are garden pickets enough left standing. This party is to plant there eight nine pounders, for the security of the harbour; and build a sod battery where it shall be judged most convenient; keeping stores, etc., in the blockhouse, or some shed or other conveniency, built for that purpose, within the pickets; and must have necessary tools left with them; as also a carpenter or two or a mason, if none among themselves, to build a chimney and other conveniences. And Captain Donahew and Captain Becket, with their vessels, to attend them; who are to have directions, to follow from time to time the commandant's orders, unless countermanded by yourself, after which they have been, with an additional party of two hundred men more, and the transports they are on board of, to St. Peter's, on the Island of Cape Breton, and destroyed that settlement, which additional party, having completed your orders, at St. Peter's, are to join the fleet at Chappeaurouge Bay, to which place you are to proceed, with the fleet from Canso, in order to attack the town of Louisbourg, which it is thought may be surprised, if they have no advice of your coming. To prevent this, Captain Donahew and Captain Becket are gone before you, to cruise from Cape Canso to Whitehead and thereabouts; that no shallop or other vessel either fishing or fowling, may be on the coast to discover the approach of your fleet, and escape with intelligence; and if you have good reason to think that you are hitherto undiscovered, and you prosecute the design of surprise; to effect it, your proceedings from Canso must be such as to time your arrival at Chappeaurogue Bay, about nine of the clock in the evening, or sooner or later; When the transports are discharged at Chappeaurouge Bay, at which it will be proper to detain them as long as they can lay at safety; and it is necessary for them to put out of the bay, they must have your orders to repair to Canso; there to lay up in the pond for your further commands; and there they must be under the inspection of a cruise, who must cruize in such a manner, as to be sometime off the harbour of Louisbourg with the others; and as the wind permit go there to look at them, I have ordered hooks and lines, etc., to Canso to be put on board the cruisers there, that they may in their frequent voyages back and forth take care to supply the camp with fresh fish, which will help the provisions."

Such are some of the instructions. From the diarists and the reports sent back by Pepperell, we can trace the arrivals, and are given a fairly accurate idea of the trend of events during this noted period in Canso's history. On Wednesday, March 27th, the Rev. Joseph Emerson, one of the diarists, arrived, after a twelve days' passage. By that time, it was expected that the whole fleet would have arrived, but only two sloops had done so, entering the port on the 25th. Of one of these, Captain David Donahew was the commander. Ill fated Donahew, who was to learn the lesson that when it came to stratagems and ambuscades and the waging of a war of wits, his wily opponent, the Micmac, was well able to look after himself. Emerson's diary tells us rather unctuously that Donahew had captured three Indians in the harbour of Owl's Head on his way to Canso, having decoyed them aboard by what he calls the "stratagem" of

75

hoisting a French flag. Read now from the diary of an unknown author of the fate of the same Donahew but a few weeks later. Unless, indeed the diarist's information was as faulty as his spelling, Donahew did not realise that he was engaged in a game at which two could play. "July 8, Monday, Vessell came in with soriful News, Viz, they was in the gut of Canso, and seven Indins made sins as if they wanted to come on bord, and said Donnehew went to goo on shoor he and the rest of his offsirs and when they came at the shoor their appeared 2 hundred Indins and fired upon them and destroyed them they was chiefly ofsers the number being 12, and after they had barbeusly butchrd them they burnt their bodys to aschies".

Emerson went on shore on the 27th and 29th, to view the ruins, "a melancholy desolation". Somewhat slowly the transports came straggling along. Seventeen had arrived by the second day of April. On the fourth the one bearing Peppereil entered the harbour, with about twenty others in company. By the eleventh of the month, all had arrived but three, though some store ships were still at Country Harbour or Island Harbour. On these was the frame for the Canso block house and artillery and ammunition, the need of which was great, if an immediate attack was to be made upon Louisbourg. There was little which could be done to hurry them along. However, the coast to the eastward was still blocked by ice, which helped to keep the threatened fort in a state of isolation, preventing friend from embarking as well as foe from landing. Till this ice was removed by favourable winds no progress was possible.

The store ships arrived very soon after the tenth. Preparations for clearing the site of the building and getting things in readiness must have been proceeding apace. By the fifteenth of the month the block house frame had been landed and was so far advanced in erection that an English flag could be shown, and since this day was the birthday of His Royal Highness, Prince William, the fort was duly christened Fort Prince William..

Admiral Warren's squadron arrived on the 22nd, but hastily departed to take up station off the entrance of the harbour of Louisbourg, to intercept any vessel bringing assistance. The minor expedition against St. Peter's was duly carried out, not in a way which Peppereil considered commendable, but with a modified measure of success. His efforts at maintaining secrecy of his presence at Canso, very necessary if he had any hopes of surprising the garrison, were apparently meeting with some success. The French inhabitants of Petit DeGrat noticed the unusual stir off Cape Breton, it it true, and sent a boat with two French and one Indian occupant to endeavour to find out the reason. The two Frenchmen were captured, though the Indian escaped, but his story failed to carry conviction to the Louisbourg garrison, even if they heard it.

Occupied in drill and the duties of observation and protection, the month no doubt passed slowly. There was much ice on the coast, and there must have been much discomfort if a backward spring and cramped quarters could cause it, but of it, no complaint has come down to us. Slowly the days passed. No doubt the review which we are told was held on Canso hill helped to break the monotony, and was therefore more welcomed than dreaded. Occasionally a prize was taken. One of these, brought in on the 17th of the month, had 5 hundred "hogsitts of rum and sum melasoes, whereon was a cownsil of war hild on the 18 day, to see if our men could not keep sum of the rum and other for the suport of the fleet." We have another little vignette of one Sunday during the stay, with zealous sergeants and officers endeavouring

76

to instruct their ill trained men in the rudiments of drill in one field of the picture, while in another, Major Moody, the enthusiastic bur long-winded chaplain is endeavouring to deliver his discourse to a number, who perhaps, preferred even a sermon to drill,

However, the day came when the ice had disappeared. Preparations were quickly made, and on April 29th, the transports left the harbour. For a month all had been hurry and bustle, now there was left only a little rearguard of seventy men under the command of Captain Cutter, who remained to man the fort, and protect any empty transports which might be sent back from Louisbourg.

Before many weeks had passed, Louisbourg had fallen, and with it for a time-collapsed the effective French resistance in Nova Scotia. Canso does not appear to have profited by this, in so far as resettling is concerned. Probably the remembrance of its recent destruction was too vivid, its isolation yet too complete, :to induce any to remain long so far from aid. In a few years, had tranquillity been restored, some might have attempted it, but those few years saw, not the banishment of the French from Cape Breton, — which hope had actuated the Massachusetts colonists in their attack upon Louisbourg —but a return to the old territorial limits. Again Canso was a border settlement, one side of its harbour grudgingly conceded to the English, while the other was claimed by the French. The commissions of the new Governor of Louisbourg named the Canso Islands as a portion of the territory over which his governmental power was to be exercised.

On the other hand, the English were little if any stronger in Nova Scotia than they were before the outbreak of war in 1744. Annapolis was far away, and even after the settlement of Halifax in 1749, the new colonists had all they could do to maintain a precarious footing within their entrenchments, and succor and support could be given to no one far removed from the infant settlement. The French and Indians were not slow in taking advantage of this weakness. Twenty Englishmen were captured at Canso by them in August, 1749. Some of them were settlers. who had been drawn from Halifax by the prospect of procuring hay from the abandoned clearings, for which there was a market at Halifax, and others being members of the crews of New England vessels, who were again attempting to carry on fishing operations from their well known haunts. The inability of the English to maintain their rights tempted still more encroachment, till in 1751 the French were occupying the islands almost as far west as White Haven. In 1752, two English vessels with their crews were captured and taken to St. Peters, and it was necessary to arrange ransom ere the return of the crews could be secured. In 1754, the proposition advanced by LeLoutre, that the entire eastern end of Nova Scotia be given over as an Indian reserve, had at least this of justification behind it, that throughout that area the English appeared powerless to maintain their sovereignty.

Then, after several years, came the second capture of Louisbourg, and the conflict on the Plains of Abraham, and all smaller issues were disposed of, when the larger were settled. A new condition immediately arose. Heretofore, there had been not far removed a powerful force, both ready and willing to expend itself in efforts to make the tenure of Canso by the English as unpleasant as possible. This force had been dissipated, leaving only some scattered remnants of its instruments, powerless of themselves to prevent the development of the Province by the English, now firmly settled in undisputed possession. Nova Scotia was at last ready for English settlement, and Canso was not forgotten in the scheme for the development of the Province.

This scheme called for preparation for settlers being made by the laying off of town plots in various parts of the Province, in places where the number of settlers justified it, or where former experience had proved that settlement was either possible or desirable. Canso, with its record of having been for hundreds of years one of the most frequented fishing ports of the continent, came under the latter classification. Its attractive power over those for whom fishing was the means of support was fully appreciated. It was felt too that this attraction should be made use of, to draw thitherward a desirable class of settlers.

There does not appear to have been any residents in 1763, when an official return of the population of the' Province passes Canso by unnoticed. By the following year, however, 150 French had gathered there, either scattered parties who had escaped deportation by hiding in the woods, or unfortunates who had in various ways found their way back to the land of their childhood. Memory of the old friction was yet too bitter, and tolerance had not replaced persecution, so it was felt that their presence was undesirable, and they were rather incontinently herded off to St. Pierre or elsewhere. Then, in order to prepare the way for an English settlement, a town plot was laid off, a measure which it was hoped would induce permanent settling by persons whose presence was acceptable, rather than the reverse.

The town plot, called Wilmot, after the then Lieut.-Governor of the Province, was on the western or mainland side of the harbour, and south of much of the business portion of the present town. Directly across from it was Burying Island, now rapidly disappearing, the 'pond' in which the Louisbourg transports of 1745 were laid up, and the pallisadoes of the old English entrenchments on Grassy Island. Four streets paralleling the water front were provided for, which streets were intersected by others at right angles in such a way as to form blocks, each block containing six town lots. Altogether there appears to have been eighteen such blocks. The depth of the town plot was about 60 rods; the length, from a reserved watering place on the north to its southern corner on the shore of a pond separated by a beach from tide water, was about 120 rods. South of the plot was a reserved area of about thirteen acres intended to provide for overflow, if the town showed a disposition to extend beyond the set limits.

Alas, such a time did not come. Governor Wilmot reported his action in thus laying off the new town to the Home authorities in several of his messages; progress was reported in the Local Legislature; provision was made for its representation in the House when a certain number of tax-payers were resident within its limits; each succeeding summer doubtless saw its harbour thronged with the visiting fishing fleets, its beaches enlivened with crews at work in the preparation of their catch for the distant market; already in 1764 Johnathan Binney was deputed to proceed thither from Halifax as the local Collector of Customs, for the convenience of the fishermen, but no record of the transfer of a single town lot has come down to us. We must conclude, therefor, that the occupation of the place was only such an occupation as was necessary to enable the crews of the fishing fleets to procure and prepare their catches, and that the fall months witnessed their departure as they did that of the migratory fowl. The town of Wilmot was duly brought into being, but died at its birth, and is now only a historical memory..

Two years after this birth and death, what might be called the natural development of the town of Canso commenced. To Joseph Woodmas of Halifax was then given (in 1766) a grant of a tract of 198 acres of land, north of the Wilmot Town plot, and extending along the Tittle. In 1767, Admiral Lord Colville was given or claimed to have been given some land in the vicinity, though the lot is not mentioned in a special memorandum prepared by Surveyor General Morris in 1822. In 1770, Enoch Rust obtained his first allotment, one of 72 acres South of the area reserved for town expansion. In 1773 David Munro obtained 50 acres between Woodmas' grant and the town plot of Wilmot. In 1774 William Lovegrove obtained 189 acres in the rear of the town plot, and also, it seems, 11 acres, which was a portion of the town plot itself. Evidently, therefor, a community was growing. It is a matter of record that Johnathan Binney went there each year in connection with the customs, collecting the fees and receiving remunerations for his services, though doing so in such a way as to call forth unpleasant comment and even persecution from the hand of Governor Legge. But that is another story, not here intruding itself upon us. What has been discoverable of the others whose names have been mentioned deserves first consideration, us some of them at least have earned the distinction of being for a time at least.. actual settlers and residents in Canso.

Concerning Woodmas, little has been secured except what is contained in several reference works. An intimation that he was so situated from a financial point of view as to be able to come to the aid of the impecunious Province In time of need is contained in the Provincial reports of the year 1760, in which year he had advanced the Province eight hundred and fifty pounds 'for the poor'. In the following year he was returned as member for Annapolis County at the Third General Assembly, though his record as a legislator is marred by an altercation with the Speaker, which little comported with the dignity of either of the disputants. His name was submitted for a vacant Councillorship by the Lords of Trade to the King in 1763, though the recommendation was not, for some reason, accepted. His grant of land in Canso was received in 1767, and some recognition of his having been in favor with the powers at Halifax is seen in his having been appointed Receiver of Quit Rents, Fines and Escheats in 1768. The amount of salary attached to the position was small, and not so imposing as the title, but other commissions appeared to have been given him from time to time, doubtless as became a person well disposed to the coterie in whose hands were the reins of government. He was sent to St. Pierre in 1769 to report on the activities of the French on their last remaining bit of territory in North America, and the Governor received somewhat more than an earful, for having incurred the expense.

A few years before this, in 1759, the light house on Sambro had been built. The maintenance of this light, the first lighthouse built in Nova Scotia, was provided for by the imposition of a tax of six pence a ton on all vessels entering Halifax harbour, which, under ordinary circumstances, resulted in gathering in sufficient funds to permit the payment of expenses incurred in the lighthouse, and left a balance of about forty pounds a year for the contractor. The position of Light-keeper was given to Woodmas in 1769, who thus added another title to those of which he was the possessor. But paying quit rents was very unpopular. and commissions resulting from these payments were brought to a point where they were practically non-existent. The receipts from the shipping either were not sufficient to pay the light house bills or were diverted to other purposes, and there came a night, or in fact several of them, when the unlighted lamps of Sambro Sight house bore unmistakable evidence of the fact that he, who had once come to the assistance of the Province when bills for the poor were to be met, had himself joined that very social, class which once had profited from his beneficence. He was unable to buy oil for his light, and of what use is an unlighted beacon. It became necessary that someone else attempt that which Woodmas had failed to perform, and not long after that, Woodmas, apparently relinquishing all his high sounding but lean positions, returned to England. Though he had been given a grant of land at Canso, he does not seem at any time to have been a resident. He may have had business connections there, but the very fact of his having official positions at Halifax practically precludes the possibility of his being in Canso except for short intervals, if at all.

Enoch Rust was, as we have seen, the second person to whom a grant was given. From one source or another there seems to be quite a little information gatherable concerning this old pioneer and resident, some at least of which does not depict him as a character altogether admirable. There does not seem to be any doubt but that he came originally from New England, and had been attracted to Nova Scotia and Canso especially by the near lying fisheries. At least it is known that he returned to New England after many years spent in Nova Scotia. His property, or some of it, eventually came into the possession of Patrick Lannigan, and in the deed which conveyed it, Rust's address is said to be Boston. The date of this deed is 1803, and the land conveyed is a block of about 70 acres. Rust is described as being formerly of Canso. Old plans note the location of his fishing establishment near the southern end of a beach separating tidal water from a small pond or lake on the western shore of the harbour, not far from the entrance. Lannigan's stores were at a later date on the northern end of this beach, and the whole of it was included in the 13 acres reserved for town expansion, south of the town plot. The entrance to what has been referred to as the *pond* in Pepperell's instructions was directly across the harbour.

Rust appears to have been connected with Canso in an active way from at least the time the grant was obtained (1770) till after 1781. Was he one of those on whom John Paul Jones wrought such havoc in 1776? According to Jones' account, no one was spared in the cleanup then made.

The story of his connection with Canso, as it has been discovered is as follows: His grant was obtained in 1770. His name is given among those who took the state oath at Halifax on June 5, 1775, this oath being required from all 'persons in trade, coming into this Province to become inhabitants from any part of America', in accordance with the Order in Council of May 6th of that yeat. He was a Justice of the Peace, apparently at Halifax, though it may have been for the County of Halifax, (which at that time included Canso) in 1780. Finally, in 1803, when his Canso land was deeded to Patrick Lannigan, he is said to be a resident of Boston.

During his stay in Canso he had at least one visitor, who gives an account of him, and this is not a flattering one. Ensign S. W. Prentiss left Quebec on the 17th of November, 1780, bound with despatches from Governor Haldimand to General Clinton at New York. His vessel was wrecked near what is now known as Judique on Dec. 5th, some lives being lost. Prentiss undertook with a few of the survivors to obtain help for the remainder, and, ignorant of the fact that help might have been obtained quite easily by

80

travelling south through die Strait of Canso, directed the course of the party around the northern extremity of the Island of Cape Breton in quest of it. After weeks of hardship, he won through, and sent the much needed help by volunteers from an Indian encampment which he was fortunate enough to find near Sydney. Then, his despatches still undelivered, he pressed on his way to Halifax. He arrived in Canso on the 27th of April, 1781, there meeting Rust. According to Prentiss' story, Rust was hand in glove with the Americans whose depredations had been severe along this coast, so much so, in fact, that Prentiss considered his precious despatches in danger. A brother-in-law of Rust's was, according to Prentiss' story, the captain of an eighteen gun privateer which made Canso its headquarters. Prentiss' stay in Canso was therefore short. Early on the 28th of April he left, without acquainting Rust, and eventually arrived in Halifax, where his troubles were practically over. In his account of the arduous winter trip, he strongly recommends having a man-of-war stationed at Canso during the succeeding summer, in order to keep the privateers in check.

One would like to think that Rust was not so despicable a character as he is pictured to be in this account. We must remember that his position at Canso was an exposed one. It had already suffered from an incursion or raid, and was not in a position to defend itself against another one. It may have been necessary for Rust to adopt an attitude very different from that which his liking would have preferred, even, perhaps, to have rendered a grudging assistance as the price of safety of himself and his belongings. It may have been, too, that Prentiss' jealous care over the precious despatches, which had cost some men their lives and many more unbelievable hardships, led him to conjure dangers where few or none existed. How could conduct, such as Rust's is said to have been, have escaped the observation of the Halifax Customs officials, who had had Canso under their supervision for a number of years? Possibly, each of these men, Rust and Prentiss, had his own trials, and was endeavouring to the best of his ability and in the manner which seemed to him the wisest, to acquit himself in the way in which he thought duty lay. The third grant was one given to David Munro, and this is a name very-familiar, in Canso and the vicinity. This does not seem to have been the ancestor of the many families of the same name now residing in the Whitehead district. The name of William Lovegrove is the last on the old return of Surveyor General Morris dated 1822. He seems to have moved to Canso from Halifax, in which place he had been an officer in one of the Masonic Lodges. There is in the Archives a very voluminous correspondence concerning him in connection with a series of legal difficulties into which unfortunately he was drawn. Apparently he had moved to Canso about 1764, his house being on Lot No. 1, of Block A of the town plot. Considering that one of his fences was an encroachment, Johnathan Binney and another resident, John Peart, tore it down, thus exposing his crops to damage. A commission of arbitrators decided in Lovegrove's favour, on the ground that he had suffered damage, but expressed the opinion that he had not a legal claim on the land which he had fenced. A remonstrance against the award brought Lovegrove into difficulties with the judges of the Supreme Court, whom he was held to have insulted. Altogether he had a most unpleasant time of it. He seems to have returned to Halifax about 1774, ant! Jo have been given a grant of property in settlement of some claim for services rendered during the. time he lived in Canso. About the time of his legal difficulties, he had a wife and ten children.

In addition to these names which are on Surveyor-General Morris' list, that of Admiral Lord Colville may perhaps be added. It is known that to him

81

were given at one time or another a number of grants of land in various portions of the Province, most of which were later escheated. There is on record an interesting agreement referring to his Canso land, which perhaps deserves transcription.

"License is hereby given to Mr. George Smith of Halifax, merchant, to occupy and improve that division of land at Canso on Canso Hill known and called by the letter 'C, supposed to contain about six acres, and which was granted to me the Second Instant by the Commander in Chief and the Council of Nova Scotia, and all persons are hereby forbid to cut hay or otherwise make use of the said land without my order in writing or permission from Mr. Smith, except the Commanders of any of His Majesty's ships which may happen to be in Canso, to whom I do hereby give leave to make such improvement in gardens or enclosures as may suit their convenience whilst they remain on that station. This License is only to be in force during pleasure. In witness whereof, I have hereunto set my hand and seal at Halifax this 12 day of July 1766."

We shall later have to refer to Mr. Smith at a very trying time in his career.

As has been seen, quite an interval of time separated the first of these grants, given in 1766, from the last dated about 1774, and tracing them and outlining something of what is known concerning grantees has led us far afield, so far at least as a record of events in their chronological order is concerned. During the interval which had elapsed between these years, not the least interesting period of Canso's history had passed, namely, that period when it, in common with other ports along the eastern shore of Nova Scotia, afforded refuge to bands of French Acadians, on whom the events of 1755 had wrought such hardship. Let us call to mind briefly the conditions, and the reason will be obvious why Canso and the eastern portion of Nova Scotia was regarded by these poor unfortunates as localities offering them relatively the best prospect of immunity from persecution.

Halifax was becoming yearly more able to defend itself. The western portion of the Province from which the French Acadians had been driven was being settled by persons attracted to the vacant clearings from Halifax or the New England States. East of Halifax, the Province was yet almost closed to the English. Cornwallis had not been able to carry out that portion of his instructions which directed him to make a settlement of about five hundred English at Whitehead, and the entire eastern shore was almost wholly given over to the Indians. Here these were in practical control, and that they were by no means a despicable foe there had been many and bloody proofs. The Acadians who had been placed upon the transports had been scattered almost to the four winds of heaven. The States along the Atlantic and the Gulf of Mexico, the Islands of the West Indies, England and France saw the human wreckage cast upon their shores. Now they were attempting to return, while those who had been driven to the woods, to the haunts of their Indian friends, were plucking up courage to take up again, if possible, a life more in line with their traditions and their former habits of living. The Island of Cape Breton seemed to many of them a locality of comparative safety, and thitherward at this time, many were groping their way. Could they but reach Cape Breton or Chedabucto or other localities on the shore of the Strait of Canso, they would have the eastern Indians between them and Halifax, and these seemed to be the strongest available bulwark.

According to the Provincial Census of 1763, there were no Acadians at Canso in that year. The fourteen or eighteen families at Chedabucto about that time seemed to have been overlooked, however, so that it is possible that some escaped enumeration at Canso. By the following year, however, about one hundred and fifty had gathered in Canso, but on threat of removal, these seemed to have passed over to Isle Madame. Their places were soon taken by new arrivals, who appear to have succeeded in getting back to Nova Scotia from St. Pierre and Miquelon, for in 1767 there were altogether in Canso 519 persons, of whom 276 were Catholic, and 197 of these were Acadians. Those living in Chedabucto were reported as having been removed in 1764, and seem to have been in St. Pierre in 1767.

Meanwhile, the restrictions limiting their choice of residence were gradually becoming lightened. Already provision had been made for limited numbers of Acadian families to be settled in townships where the English residents were sufficiently numerous to overawe the small number of Acadians permitted to remain in each district, but Canso was not on this list of districts, possibly because of the nearness of Indian support. The concession, however, resulted in their gradual withdrawal, possibly under more or less pressure, to other communities, so that the number in Canso does not appear to have increased. Not all the bitterness had disappeared and any settlement preponderantly French was not encouraged, so that even as late as 1774, French settlers from Jersey to the number of about 150, were given to understand that Canso was not a portion of Nova Scotia in which their presence could be tolerated. With these hints or the threats of more forcible removal, they moved elsewhere, and the settlement oi the now existing French communities in Guysborough County does not appear to have progressed very far till after 1784. Time settled the difficulty by degrees, but another matter was arising which appeared to become more vexing as time passed, and here again Canso was more or less in the lime light.

Very soon after the year 1763, the commencement of a very vigorous illicit trade was observable, which from small beginnings became of the greatest importance, and was in fact one aspect of that great schism, which, if we believe one school of historians, resulted, when efforts were made to control it, in the break with the New England States, and the War of Independence. From the reasons which we have seen, a population, more or less disaffected, was gradually collecting in the sheltered harbours along the entire coast line from Canso to Bay Chaleur, and these were not at all averse to bartering or selling to the crews of French vessels from St. Pierre and Miquelon, or vessels ostensibly fishing from the New England or European ports, or passing vessels engaged in the Quebec trade, the produce which they were able to collect for the purpose, receiving in exchange therefor either money or goods on which no duty was paid. Canso was a noted fishing pore, frequented, at least during the summer months, by vessels from New England, for the crews of which a dollar was a dollar, whether obtained by legitimate means or by the evasion of a customs regulation. In addition to these, others were continually passing and calling on their way through the Strait of Canso to their ultimate destinations in the River and Gulf of St. Lawrence. Some of these may have had perfectly legitimate errands, but if we believe the stories of the extent to which this illicit trade was carried on, we must realise that very few of these traders hesitated over the honesty of any process by which profits were obtained. Frequently, then as now, the contraband appears to have been liquor, and then as now, taking part in such a traffic brought it about that the participants scrupled little at the observation of a number of the moral laws, and eventually became a class of daring and dangerous semi-outlaws, carrying on a mixture of trading, smuggling and privateering, as inclination prompted, opportunity offered or the prospect of gain allured. Brandy and other European commodities were exchanged for furs and peltry or the produce of the fisheries, or at a little later date for coal from the Cape Breton coal fields. It can be readily understood that exact data can not be found of the extent of the trade, but no doubt of its presence can exist.

Canso unfortunately developed a more or less unenviable notoriety as one of the outposts of rather unsavory reputation. To this period probably dates the suggestive naming of the 'Rogues Roost', a little harbour among the Canso islands. Johnathan Binney, the Customs Collector at Canso, in whose district was included at the time all of the island of Cape Breton, writing to Governor Legge on June 27, 1774, tells that five topsail vessels and two large schooners had arrived from Jersey with crews to carry on the cod fishery. Besides, 'here is forty shallop; owned and employed in the coal (sic) fishery by the French Acadians of this Province'. 'It is very necessary that one of His Majesty's armed vessels should be stationed at this port, as some of the people here are very disorderly, and many vessels from different parts of this continent come into this district, the masters of which break bulk and take on board goods contrary to the acts of trade.' 'I fear I shall be a great sufferer in farming the Imports and Excise for the Island of Cape Breton, and the district unless I have some assistance from the Government.'

What was the size of the community about this time? Quite minute and accurate are the reports which are obtainable for the year 1767. There was in that year a total population of 519 persons, of whom 152 were females. So (at as origin was concerned, 197 were given as of Acadian descent, and of the remainder 130 were English, 112 Irish and 73 American. There were 10 oxen, 15 young cattle and 20 swine, so that agriculture occupied a very minor place in the industry of the community. What was the nature of the industry mainly carried on was sufficiently indicated by the return of 75 boats and 12 schooners, the crews or owners of which had been successful to the extent of having prepared fos market 13,372 quintals of dry fish, 250 barrels of mackerel and salmon and 150 barrels of oil. It is specifically stated in the return that many of the boats and vessels belong to New England, and that many of the people retire there or to the island of Jersey for the winter after the fishing was over. It is unnecessary to say that the 242 persons who were said to be of English or Irish descent were not of necessity Nova Scotians. In fact, the number of persons living in the community throughout the year can be much more accurately judged from a consideration of the live stock owned, and if this is taken as a criterion, it is doubtful if the autumn exodus did not almost depopulate the little settlement. However, it seems that a settlement was in existence and that growth was taking place, which growth might soon have given Canso an assured standing among the more important Nova Scotian settlements, had not a few years later another incident occurred which again scattered its inhabitants, and for a time made progress impossible.

The friction between the colonists in New England and the home Government developed sufficient intensity in 1776 to light up the Revolutionary War, The strength of its protection made the prospect of an attack on Halifax one net to be lightly undertaken. The outlying ports were much more vulnerable, and this vulnerability did not long escape the observation of the naval forces which fought the American battles on the high seas or committed depredations among the defenceless Nova Scotian fisherfolk. Without fortification or garrison and beyond the reach of assistance from Halifax, having in its population a number of persons on whom the yoke of British attachment sat but lightly, John Paul Jones — a Basset with a vocabulary, since at this stage of his career it seems difficult to accord to him a position little if any higher than that of many a freebooter or privateer who had been a source of annoyance to the authorities at Halifax — saw the opportunity of inflicting serious damage with a minimum of danger.

He entered the harbour on Sept. 22, 1776 and when he left again a few days later there was little left of the prosperous fisheries of Canso and Isle Madame, it appears that not a musket shot was fired in the defence of either place. His stores replenished, his crews augmented, laden with his ill-gotten plunder and satisfied because there had been no 'inhumanity', Jones scuttled away, fearful lest the *Dawson* Brig, which he informs his correspondent was only about 15 leagues away, might intercept him. A German U boat could hardly have done a neater job.

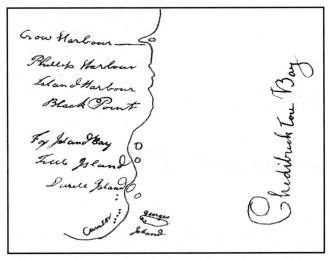

Ed. Note: 1783 map showing the location of nine houses at Canso. (By the surveyors Meighan and Mcdonalds from the estate of the late Lord Charles Montague, NS Archives).

We have seen that some time in the year 1766 Lord Colville had given to George Smith a merchant of Halifax, licence to use a portion of his grant on Canso Hill as a fishing station. In the years which had elapsed up to the time of the foray made by Jones, Smith had succeeded in building up an extensive business, and he was one of the great losers by reason of the raid. Precisely as a French attack one hundred and fifty years before had brought about the cessation for a time of all business activities, so this wanton act destroyed for the time being an industry which was assuming very material proportions. In a despatch to the Home Government in 1779, Lieut.-Governor Hughes stated that 50,000 pounds a year had been lost to the British Government as a result of the activities of the American cruisers, and much of this loss was due to the destruction of the Canso fisheries. We must wonder little if, during the War of Independence, no return to its pre-war prosperity was brought about. For nearly ten years the blight or John Paul Jones's effectual raiding hung over the blasted settlement.

The war of independence came to an end. The United Empire Loyalists, driven from their homes in the States by a persecution as bitter as that which it had been the lot of the unfortunate Acadian French to endure, had arrived to augment Nova Scotia's population and lay the foundation for her prosperity. At the head of the Chedabucto Bay, at the southern extremity of the Strait of Canso, at County Harbour on the Atlantic littoral, these Loyalists settlements had sprung up. Canso was passed by. A locality which promised so little in the way of agricultural possibilities did not appeal to the disbanded soldier or the gentry which largely made up the Loyalist ranks. It was still a rendezvous for fishermen, and a port of call of passing vessels. John Peart, Lovegrove's old antagonist, had retired to Chedabucto, to be one of the 'nine old settlers' ekeing out a living near Denys' old fort, when the settlers from New York and the Montagu Corps came to settle in its vicinity. Another one of the same group was using one of the deserted stands in the summer, returning to his more sheltered home at the head of the Bay on the approach of winter. Alas, for him, William Callahan, the trip to the fishing grounds was made once too often, and was but the preliminary for a voyage from which no return was possible. But in the gain in population which the Province was enjoying, Canso had no place. We look in vain for evidences of the growth elsewhere springing up in the Province.

Thus, Colonel Landeman, a visitor in 1797, tells us that there was at that time but one settler, when the captain of his ship, short of food and water, hazarded an entrance in search of these necessities. An ox was procurable from this settler if the price was given, but to be obtained it must first be found in the wilderness of barrens. A number of the crew, armed with guns, were sent to sweep the countryside, and did it effectually in time, while Landeman occupied himself in the interval by almost filling the boat with lobsters, which be impaled with the ramrod of his gun in pools along the shore.

The years passed. The War of 1812 came and passed quickly. At the close of the war, a vessel arrived in the harbour, on its way to or from Quebec. To the mind of the captain the advantages the location afforded were greater than those of his home community, Chester, more advanced though the latter war in many respects. There were in Canso but five residents. Patrick Lannigan was carrying on a business near the location of the old establishment which Enoch Rust had built up. John Munro, an O'Hara, a Fitzgerald, and Lewis M. Uloth were the others present, one at least being the former member of a regiment which had been disbanded in the neighborhood. The decision to cast in his lot with the five was quickly made.

His wife and family, then consisting of 8 children were moved from

Chester an the spring of 1813, and with the arrival of that family a new era in the history of Canso may be said to have commenced.

Meanwhile, what was occurring, or what was the process of development in the other harbours along the lengthy coastline of the Township?

Commencing with the shores west and north of Canso, along the fifteen mile strip bordering on Chedabucto Bay, there is no record of settlement till after the arrival of the Loyalists in 1784 or 1785. Nicholas Denys had written of the. coast about the middle of the seventeenth century and had described the harbour of Queensport (the name decided on to replace the ineuphonious one, Crow Harbour) in such a way as easily to permit of its identification. One may surmise that Phillip's Harbour was so named after Governor Phillipps, but there seems to be no authority for the claim, though undoubtedly the name antedates the arrival of the Loyalists. Fox Island had been named on the charts at as early a date as that of Montressor's in 1768. Mr. Smith refers to damage done to his stages at Crow Harbour at the time of the Jones raid in 1776, but of any occupation other than temporary occupation during the fishing season there are no traces.

The western border of the Wilmot township here linked up with the eastern limits of the Township of Guysborough, the lands immediately contiguous thereto being those granted to the members of the disbanded 60th Regiment. In 1764 James Sterling and Nichol Bower had grants of land included within the limits of the Wilmot Township, but apparently no settlement resulted. The exposure oi the coast, open to the sweep of the north winds over Chedabucto Bay, was not a pleasant one. Only near the heads of some of the coves were there fringes of land suitable for settlement, the interior being largely rocky and barren, worthless from the agriculturist's or lumberman's point of view. Harbour protection was only relatively good, and that against winds from some quarters only.

It appears that the larger fishing firms at an early date obtained control of the beaches, charging rentals for fishing sites to those who later came to take advantage of the almost fabulous richness of the fisheries.

How plentiful fish were, especially mackerel, in the proper season, almost passes belief. Haliburton tells vividly of the catches, so enormous that often the fish could not be made use of. Seines were then used to a very great extent, and it was not unusual for the weight of the fish to make recovery of the seine impossible. Little was the distinction then made as to who owned the seine for all dipped from it to the extent of their capabilities of curing the catch. The name, Waterloo Beach, given to one of the beaches is said to date back to the time when often the rotting fish lay in piles upon the shore. Exorbitant rates were, however, often charged for fishing stands, which practice on more than one occasion led to quarrelling and disorder.

It is to be expected that in such temporary communities of roving individuals, a tendency towards departure from ordinary conventions might be observed. Readers of Haliburton will remember one of his stories referring to this locality which, he says, was based upon the belief, freely expressed and put into practice, chat absence on the part of one of the members of a marriage contract for over one year justified the other one in seeking another alliance. One must hesitate at raking Haliburton, when in a story telling mood, as an historical authority, but at the same time one must admit that the reputation

87

of the district as a law abiding community was on more than one occasion sadly smirched. Riots resulting in serious damage, it not to property at least to heads, on one or more occasions required government intervention for control, the pretext of the difficulty being the injustice of the extortionate rentals. An extension of a bitter religious quarrel between Catholic and Protestant at Canso is supposed to account for at least one murderous affray, when on April 8, 1823 George Lamb, John MacKenzie, and Alexander and George Smith lost their lives.

The development of the district has been in the main, however, affected to the greatest extent by altering economic conditions, associated with the prosperity or the reverse of the fishing industry. The disappearance of the tremendous schools of mackerel which formerly thronged the waters, the growth and decline of the lobster industry, the interdiction of supplying other than Canadian fishermen with bait and ice, and more recently still the decline of the inshore fishing, these are the conditions which have affected in largest measure the growth and development of the district.

Today, a thinly settled population, living frugally and law abidingly, still attempts to wrest a livelihood from the adjacent waters, which, in progressively greater degree from year to year, seem reluctant to furnish the harvest sought, and the depression which this is causing and which is facing so many of the fishing communities of the Province bids fair to render doubtful the continuing prosperity and growth of the district.

The story of the settlement and development of the miles of seaboard between Canso and Isaac's Harbour is much longer in the telling as the settlements are more numerous. The extremely irregular nature of the coast line is such that in the distance of about thirty Of forty miles as the crow flies are to be found a great number of coves and harbours, which being in close proximity to good fishing grounds, have tempted occupation by fishermen. Rocks and islands innumerable, ledges and shoals stretching in places miles seaward, assist in breaking the force of the Atlantic, affording shelter for the fishing or coasting craft, or adding to the difficulties of pilotage for those to whom the coast is relatively unknown. Many there are who have experienced the dangers of navigation along this ledge-sewn coast. The wreck history of the coast line of which Canso is the extreme point is well worth the telling and may some time be attempted.

Reference has been made to several places named by the old French navigators or appearing for a time on their charts. It is well worth while to identify some of these, piecing out information from the old records concerning places which were the landmarks of the earliest visitants. On this coast was old Port Savalet, mentioned and quite fully described by both Champlain and Lescarbot as early as 1608, a little harbour in Torbay, the existence of which has been forgotten. The Isles Rangèes of these authors are supposed to be the series of islands forming the outer aspects of the harbours of Drum Head and Seal and Coddle's Harbours. Torbay seems to have been first referred to as Tarbe, in 1699 by Villebon. The boiling breakers ("giant combers crashing cream-crested against gray granite") which foamed around one white granite headland early earned for it the name of Tete Blanche, with which the English name White Head has established direct continuity. Old port Martingot or Havre des Martingots is noted as early as 1656 and on many maps thereafter till at least 1780. Its identification as White Haven presents no difficulties, nor does the recognition of Cape Mocodome. placed on the old French maps at a date almost as early as Port Savalet. In this case the name has been transferred to the Cape from a nearby island on which the black backed gulls nested in numbers.

These are some of the old French names of the era before the English occupancy. The French pioneers having been ousted, some of these names have disappeared, and others have been added — of a present day flavour. Country Harbour is referred to by Captain Young as early as 1720, and at that time the name of Isaac's Harbour seems to have been given to what is now called Raspberry Harbour. The Isaac's Harbour of today seems to be of much more recent naming. When Catherine's River (now New Harbour) and Port Hinchinbrook (now Isaac's Harbour) were first so called it is difficult to say. The former is said to have been so called after Catherine Barss, the first white child born in the settlement, which event took place in 1808, but this may not be the case. The naming of Port Hinchinbrook probably is connected with the naval vessel *Hinchinbrook*, which for a time was stationed on the coast. The same name was given to a Cape Breton harbour, and this may account for its having fallen into disuse. It brings to our minds Hinchinbrook Castle, the home of the Earl of Sandwich, Admiral of the fleet at the time of Samuel Pepys, and Carlyle's account of the purchase of the estate from Sir Robert Cromwell, the "Golden Knight", father of Oliver.

Does Cole Harbour owe its name to the Captain Cole, whose sloop the *William*, had been captured by a Spanish privateer in or near Canso in 1719? Charlo's Cove is said to have been so named after the first French Acadian settler. It is possible that that settlement, and one of the other French communities, Larry's River or Port Felix, (the old name for which was Molasses Harbour) antedated any of the English settlements along that entire coast line. Larry's River is said to have been so-called after Larry Keating, it being his winter headquarters when engaged in hunting and trapping. Not only has his name been perpetuated in the settlement, but almost without exception in every French family, one or more Larrys still help to keep his memory green.

There is no record of any settlement on these many miles of coast line till after the opening up of the Province to Loyalist refugees. There seems to be proof that no persons were living there in the early winter of 1780, when a number of the crew of the *Freemason* perished miserably of starvation. In December of the same year, Benjamin Marsden led his men along the shore from the vicinity of Canso to what was later the limits of the Township, before he met the Indians who gave him shelter and food.

It seems that not till twenty or more years after Marsden's enforced wanderings was there a permanently located white settler. The first actual record which has been discovered is that of settlement in New Harbour in 1806, though it seems very likely that in the interval the French settlements on the shores of Torbay had been founded.

In that year, James Barss, (Bears) after moving from Port Latour or Barrington to Manchester, made still another migration, and located in New Harbour. He was joined in 1808 by James Sangster from Manchester. Charles Nickerson from Sambro, and Isaac O'Hara soon came to add their numbers to these pioneers and the list was later added to by the arrival of the Luddingtons and Hulls. Today these are the names to be found in the community.

James Sangster, born in Ireland in 1777, was the oldest son of Joseph Sangster, of Scotch ancestry, then serving in an English regiment. Sent out to

America about the close of the war, he was given lands in Manchester (Guysborough) with the Associated Department of the Army and Navy in 1784. A second son had been born to Joseph Sangster and his wife (Margaret Mann) on the Transport which brought them to America, and to this son was given as one of his names the name of the transport in which they were being carried. That name, *Minerva*, is still handed on among the members of the family living in New Harbour. A third son was born within a year after their arrival in Guysborough.

Within the year, too, the father was drowned. His burial place is said to be on the western shore of the Narrows of Milford Haven above the present bridge. The widow later married Edward Kergan.

James Sangster was married to Eunice Leet in 1799, and there were four children when the move to New Harbour was made. The place selected for his home was on the west side of the River, near the Narrows, where at present there is a bridge.

The Luddingtons are descendants of another member of the Associated Departments above referred to. The Hulls trace their descent from Samuel Hull of Connecticut, who, with the Leets, were settlers on the Hallowell Grant.

White Head appears to have been next in the order of settlement. Thither came Moses Cahoon from Queens County about the year 1818. Thomas Munro and wife, Mr. and Mrs. John Munro and Mr. and Mrs. Robert Spears, all from Shelburne arrived a little later, and the Demings with four children, the Coffins and the McDuffs followed. Other early arrivals, perhaps earlier than some above mentioned were the Dollivers (Should this be Taliaferros?) from whom Dolliver's Cove gets its name, and the Travers, whose name is perpetuated in Travers Point.

The first settler of Isaac's Harbour, near the western border of the Township was a coloured man, Isaac Webb, who had moved thither from Shelburne. According to local tradition, the harbour was named after him, the older name, Port Hinchinbrook, being supplanted. We have already called attention to the fact that the same name appears on maps of a much earlier date, but that it seems to have been given to a harbour a number of miles to the eastward.

Simon Giffin, also from Shelburne, was the first white settler, arriving in 1832. To accompany him came very soon his brother Ira and two MacMillan brothers, John and Allan. These returned to Louis Head, Shelburne, in the spring of 1833, for the brides who were to undertake the task of home building in the remote little settlement, and with the party came John Latham and Duncan MacMillan, all truly pioneers, who lived to see the full fruition of their work in the growth and development of the district.

This has been in merest outline a story of first beginnings. The growth of Canso, of which growth the unique position it now holds as a cable centre, is a factor, Whitehaven's brief dream of glory, when, after Captain Owen's Reports in 1846, it appeared that the decision had been arrived at that it more than any other Nova Scotian port seemed a suitable terminal for the much discussed inter-colonial system of railways, Torbay's brief prominence, when as Port Faraday, the site selected by Mr. George Von Chauvin was made the landing place of the Direct Cable Company's transatlantic lines, none of these can be considered as coming within the scope of such a story. Barred too are the stories of disaster and peril of which there- have been many instances along the wreck strewn coast. Even the story of the Saladin, cast away near the entrance of Isaac's Harbour, concerning the details of which, few incidents occurring in the Province have had more chronicles, must be passed over. Nevertheless, if there has been sufficient for a time to fix our interest, to direct some attention to a section of our Province than which few have more of interest or romance, to encourage in us that desire for knowledge of our home land which is the basis of patriotism or love of country.. its purpose shall have been amply fulfilled.

Appendix

CAPITULATION OF CANSO

Nous, Capitaine D'Infanterie deatche de la Marine, Commandant des batiments et troupes pour l'Expedition de Canso, par ordre de Mons'r Du Quesnel, Capitaine de vaisseau du Roy, Chev'lr de L'Ordre Royal et Miiitaire de St. Louis, Commandant de L'Isle Royale et adjacentes, suis convenu, avec Mons'r Patrick Heron, capitaine de compagnie du Regiment de Mons'r Phillips, commandant a Canso, qu'en meyen qu' il se rend a moy ce vingt quatrieme jour de Mai, mil sept cent quarante quatre, prisonier de guerre avec tout sa garrison tant hommes que femes pour an un, que je lui promet que tout ce que luy appartiendra et a la dit garrison leur restera et sera charge dans la goulette du S. Jean Bastrick, la quelle je feray conduire a Louisbourg, et qu'en surplus je lui promet de faire tout mes efforts aupres de Mons'r Du Quesnel pour l'engager a accorder aux dames des officiers de cette dit garnison la liberte de s'en retourner avec ce qu'eles auront judgeront apropes aussitot mon arrive a Louisbourg dans la dit goulette du dite Sr. Brastrick, et je m'engage de plus de faire reconduire le dit garnison a la nouvelle Angleterre ou a Annapolis Royal au bout d'un an, ainsy que les dames des officiers et leurs enfants en cas que Mons. Du Quesnel ne leur accorde pas ta permission de s'en retourner plutot estant bien entendu que Mons. George Royal, Lieutenant de vaisseau du Roy d'Angleterre, commandant de Batteau du Roy La Marie, avec son equipage des memes droits.que la dit batteau en dependance au meyen de qucy Mons'r Patrick Heron me remet la place avec armes, artilleries et munitions de querre.

A Canso a bord du succez ce   Signed   Duvivier

24 Mai, 1744

THE REFUGEE FRENCH AT CHEDABUCTO

In the many years which had elapsed since the time of Nicholas Denys and his successors, the importance of Chedabucto had declined very markedly. The old travel route, proximity to which had determined its selection as a suitable site for a trading establishment, seems to have been less used as time passed; it had not the advantage of nearness to the fishing grounds which other places afforded; it offered but limited areas of the meadow or marsh land which the French agriculturist loved.

On this account, its name is absent from the census rolls of the early 18th century, such for instance as that of the year 1714, or as in the census of 1731, it was joined with Canso in the statement that an estimated number of persons lived in the two places. It is then to be surmised that Canso was the more populous. Neither place seems to figure at all in the census of 1737.

This information from French sources receives corroboration from the only extant English source, namely, the report of judge Morris about the year 1755, in which no mention is made of any French settlement east of Cobequid. (Truro.)

Following the expulsion of the Acadians in the latter year, and the escape to sanctuaries with their Indian friends of many who had escaped the dragnet prepared for them by Lawrence, its secluded position, far from the English seat of government at Halifax, and separated from it by leagues of wilderness, almost entirely given over to the Micmac, offered a relative tranquillity which was accepted with much thankfulness by some families, who there found for a time more or less freedom from persecution.

Writing in the year 1764, Judge Morris says that fourteen families had there found a temporary resting place, but we can not tell the year concerning which he writes. These families had not more than five acres of cleared land, and fishing in the summer and boat building for their compatriots in the island of Cape Breton is said to have been their sources of livelihood. Since we are told that these boats were supplied especially to the fishermen of Louisbourg the presence of the boat builders at Chedabucto earlier than 1758 is evident.

For how long before 1758 families were living there it does not seem possible to say. We do know that as early as 1745 the forests near Denys' old clearings were sources of supply for Louisbourg's fuel and wood, and that the easily accessible deposits of limestone had been remembered in connection with the demand for that commodity to be used in the construction of the Louisbourg fortifications. The prosecution of these industries may have been carried on by the crews of the visiting vessels, but it appears to be more reasonable to think that a few families were occupying the settlement redolent of the memories of Nicholas Denys and the scene of DeMontorgeuil's spirited defence.

After the tragic events of 1755 the numbers of families increased, until the number given by Judge Morris had been materially exceeded. As harried wild fowl, relentlessly pursued by numerous and merciless hunters, flit wearily from cover to cover, the Acadians were vainly seeking rest and safety from a merciless pursuit. Chedabucto was thus for a time a refuge around which the hunted were circling or in which they were resting, till the gradually increasing number disclosing the hiding place, another flitting became necessary. Abbe

Casgrain tells us that it is a tradition of one of the families of our western French Acadians that their ancestor passed the most heart-breaking of those years of terror in sanctuary among the hills bordering the Strait of Canso, and he, though his name is not among those whom we know to have been there, may have been one who for a time found a measure of respite in the seclusion which Chedabucto afforded. If not he, at least others were there of whom we have knowledge, cowed, terrified and disheartened, eking out a miserable existence in some precarious manner, and hourly expecting a renewal of their persecutions. If driven from thence, what refuge was open to them? Many, from their homes in the west of the Province, had traversed almost the entire length of the Province, had crossed the narrow seas to Prince Edward Island or to Cape Breton, and, when driven from thence, had found shelter in Chedabucto. Failing this, no portion of Nova Scotia could promise safety, and St. Pierre was their only refuge.

While in St. Pierre a census was taken, from which it is possible to obtain their names, ages, and the numbers in each family, and which permits, too, when taken into consideration with other censuses, especially that of 1752, some knowledge being obtained of their wanderings before Chedabucto, and later St. Pierre, was reached. The names of the refugees are as follows,—

Louis LeMal, his wife Marie Cormier and five children.

Widow Arseneau.

Pierre Arseneau and his wife Theophiste Bourgeois.

Francois Cormier, his wife Marie Bourgeois and five children.

Pierre Cormier, his wife Modeste Cyr and one child.

Jean Cormier, his wife Modeste Vigneau and one child.

Joseph Cormier, his wife Anne Vigneau and three children.

Jean Cormier, his wife Roze Vigneau Maurice and two children.

Joseph Cormier, his wife Marie Vigneau Maurice and three children,

Joseph Vigneau, his wife Catherine Arseneau and six children.

Jean Cyr, his wife Marguarite Dugas and two children.

Joseph Bourgeois, his wife Marguarite Hebert and three children.

Jacques Sire, his wife Angeline Dugas and two children.

Joseph Vigneau, his wife Madeline Sire and two children.

Joseph Boudrot, his wife Marguarite Chaisson and seven children.

Widower Joseph Landry with three others in the family.

Charles Boudrot, his wife Madeline Chaisson and three children.

Widow Isabelle Chaisson and one child.

Jacques Chaisson, his wife Marie Arseneau and two children.

Pierre Gautreau, his wife Elisabeth Terriau and five children.

Joseph Melancon, his wife Anne Hebert and one child.

Pierre Richard, his wife Marguarite LeBlanc and one child.

Toissant Blanchard, his wife Angelique Bertrand and five children.

Jean Bertrand, his wife Marguarite Blanchard and three children.

Joseph Vigneau and his wife Catherine Arseneau had been living with their seven children at Port Toulouse in the Island of Cape Breton in 1752. He had been there fourteen years, and both he and his wife had been born in Acadie, the birthplace of his wife being Port Royal. Joseph Boudrot and his wife Marguarite Chaisson and one child had lived at Etang des Berges in Prince Edward island, having been there since some time in 1750. His wife was born in Acadie, while his birthplace was in the island of Cape Breton. Joseph Landry, with his wife Marie Breau, had lived at River Inhabitants with three children. Both were Acadia born, she having been born in Minas, and they had moved to Cape Breton in 1751. Jacques Chaisson and his wife Marie Arseneau had lived at Etang des Berges with nine children, having moved there in 1750. Both he and his wife were Acadia born. Pierre Gautreau and Elisabeth Terriau had lived in Anse a Pinet in Prince Edward Island with ten. children, having moved there in 1750 and both were Acadia born. Those residing in Prince Edward Island in 1752 were probably included among the numbers driven thence in 1758 or 1759, and had sought refuge in Chedabucto after dispossession from their Island homes. In some cases their farms on the Island in 1752 were stocked in such a way as would be a credit to a present day farmer.

The conjecture may be advanced that the Cormiers were among those whose residence in Chedabucto had antedated that of the 1758 refugees. There was not a family of that name among all those enumerated either in Cape Breton or Prince Edward Island, and the name was an uncommon one in the Acadian censuses. On the other hand, Bourgeois, Blanchard, Richard and Melancon were names frequently met with on the rolls of the French districts in the Annapolis Valley, and from thence, after devious wanderings the shelter which secluded Chedabucto afforded had been sought by the families bearing that name.

In 1764 or 1765 another stage in their wanderings commenced. St. Pierre became now their only place of refuge, and thitherward they made their way. They found the islands crowded with fugitives, unable to procure a livelihood except by fishing, for the barren rock had no soil for the tilling. These, among whose rustic homes dire want had never stalked, were now forced to accept from she French nation a scanty if an ungrudged charity. In 1767 the French government, unwilling longer to maintain the refugees by grants of assistance and desirous of relieving the too great congestion, ordered that the number of families which would be permitted to remain was limited to thirty or forty. To the rest, a choice was offered of passports to return to Nova Scotia or free passage to France in French ships to be sent out for the purpose. About a thousand accepted the latter offer, but two hundred or more preferred to make another attempt to regain their Nova Scotian homes. Among these were the number amounting to about 150 who landed in Canso in 1767.

They found that conditions had changed quite materially in their absence. A different spirit was in evidence; there was a disposition to accept their presence under conditions which, though degrading, were supportable, and these conditions were accepted. There is no evidence of their remaining long in Canso, nor in fact was Canso on the list of places in which even a limited number was permitted to remain, and by the year 1771 they had succeeded in rejoining their compatriots in the western settlements of Nova Scotia or in unfrequented portions of Cape Breton. The French settlements now to be found in Guysborough County appear to date from a time much later than 1771.

In what part of Chedabucto did these refugees find a temporary shelter? Tradition tells of the French cross, indicating an old cemetery, still erect near Cutler's Cove when the Loyalists first arrived, and of the ruins of French cellars on the hillside above. Possibly the evidences of French occupancy, said to have been found at the head of tide water at the Interval, ruins of cellars, one or two old forges and the omnipresent willow trees, mean that at that place some of them had found for a time a retreat. Here the meadows of the river valley would recall to them some of their more prosperous days, while perhaps the forges rang, as the iron for the boats to be sold at Louisbourg was being shaped. Only conjecture is possible, but the fleeting glimpse of the number and composition of the refugee settlement is not the less interesting.

PIRACY, SMUGGLING AND MARTINGOT

Piracy is said to be the second oldest of the world's professions. It moulded largely the entire world history of the 17th century. It appealed to everyone who desired to make wealth quickly, there being no stock exchanges. Every European nation had its rovers, sailing up and down the seas, preying on the defenceless. There was ready disposal for everything which a pirate could seize; cargoes of merchandise to merchants eager to buy at less than usually current prices, men to the galleys, to slavery or for impressment to make up for the wastage of crews. The result of successful piracy brought wealth to many,, though more suffered. Once the wealth had been obtained, it might reasonably be expected that honours would follow, a forgetful world not prying too closely into antecedents. Scratch a pirate and you might find an eminently respectable-citizen, or public servant.

The extent to which the evil so widely distributed affected the history of the new world can hardly be fully estimated. Many pirates were discoverers, though st was little to their interests to be very explicit concerning their haunts, their places of business or their doings when on their cruises. The exploits of some diverted to their home ports the streams of the world's wealth, intended for other channels. Some, if the need arose, placing their experiences and qualifications it their country's service, won for themselves justifications which include now their being recognised as among the greatest of their country's defenders. For, it times, it was almost impossible to draw a line between the pirate, the privateers-man and the naval officer. Was Drake a pirate? Some of his doings were almost. as far removed from the pale of legitimate warfare as were some of the feats of the buccaneers. Was, at a later date, John Paul Jones a pirate? He was following the best piratical procedure when he wiped out the fisheries at Arichat and Canso, taking full advantage of the state of utter defenselessness of these unprotected fishing settlements, making a leisurely job of destroying vessels and buildings, taking men and leaving destruction and misery in his wake. The Nova Scotian families who still keep among their family papers the records of their unsuccessful attempts to be reimbursed for their losses, may have placed him in a category very different from that in which he is placed by an Annapolis Academy graduate.

Especially did the fisherman, who perilously made his way from the European coast, feel the effect of the widely spread piratical practices. He, simple-minded man, was trying to make an honest living for himself, often in a craft so small that, as one of them has left on record, he could wash in the sea while standing on the main deck. He could not afford either the armament or the crew necessary for his protection, and when in the fall, heavily laden, he attempted to make his lumbering way homeward, had no more chance of escaping a pirate vessel, intent an chase, speedy and well manned, than has the sparrow that of evading the hawk. It is said that one of the principal reasons which were advanced for the establishment of fishing companies and the replacement of the smaller individual fishermen by Company owned craft was that the Companies would probably be able to build larger vessels, man them more heavily and so protect themselves against the roving pirate. Business bad elsewhere, where the pirate roamed for loot, there were always the Newfoundland, the Gulf of St. Lawrence and the Bank fleets which could be attacked. And this was the more frequently done, since the pirates considered these fleets their recruiting ground.

The records during the earlier years are full of the descents made on the Newfoundland coast of whole fleets of piratical vessels, intent on taking booty, stripping the Vessels of guns and ammunition for their needs, and impressing men. The choice of joining the pirate or of walking the plank was in reality no choice. So, a captured vessel usually had to reconcile itself to losing its crew and of giving up its stores, and there were none to stop the practice. From a port on the west coast of Ireland, English, French, Dutch and Portuguese pirates, Algier rovers and Salee men, were accustomed to swoop down on the fishing fleets. If the fish were wanted and a sale ready, they were taken. If the pirates wanted men, they took every sixth man of the crew of the fisherman. If they wanted provisions, they took them, loudly extolling their clemency if the amount taken was only four-fifths of that which was in the fisherman's store-room. If they wanted guns and ammunition, these were taken, and thus equipped and manned, the pirate was then prepared to sail for those travel routes where pieces of eight and more easily portable loot was to be obtained. In the absence of banking arrangements, in any unladen vessel on the high seas there was in the captain's custody either the gold in pieces of eight which had been received for the sale of her load, or that which was to be used for the purchase of the material in quest of which the voyage was being made. If laden, there were places where her load could be sold at great profit, if it cost no more than the labour of transporting it from the hold of the captured vessel, and cities and towns were clamouring for the privilege of thus obtaining expensive goods at bargain prices. So, laden or unladen, she was in danger of capture. The wonder is that legitimate business was able to exist at all, under the devastating losses daily being inflicted upon it.

There are described as being three distinct phases of the piratical wave which involved the new world in the 17th and 18th centuries. In the first, there was that phase when the individual element largely predominated, that is, when any individual of any nationality who could in any way procure the necessary equipment, might set himself up in the business, and levy tribute upon any and all of those whom he could in safety attack. If he made a noteworthy success, he might be able soon to retire and possibly entirely to rehabilitate himself in the eyes of those who might have been following his career with looks more or less askance. Thus, the English rovers, who brought fame and money to England at the expense of Spain. Thus, Captain Mainwaring, described as being the greatest of them all, was declared by a court as having "committed no great wrong", was made Warden of the Cinque Ports and an English M.P. So, many others could be found, sailing under one flag or another, actuated solely by individual greed, either working alone or, if necessary, banding together to attack larger prey. Especially were the Banks and the Newfoundland fishing fleets the grounds from which recruits were obtained during this phase. Determined English action, after years during which her shipping had paid tribute to Barbary pirates, Dutch Beggars of the Sea and others of their kind, at last brought this phase to a close.

About the time that this was taking place, a new piratical phase was developing. Spain claimed the entire right of trade with Central and Southern America. The native tribes were being stripped of their golden stores and Spanish galleons were busy in transporting homeward the spoils of the continent. The richness of the booty which the Spaniard had uncovered drew the eyes of the world to their convoys, and it became appreciated that the Spanish ships were very vulnerable to the attack of a speedy and active foe. The Spaniards had driven from San Domingo a number of French settlers who had been engaged there in the slaughter of wild cattle and the sale of salted meat and skins. Driven from the "boucans" where they had been accustomed to work, these outcasts turned their attentions to the treasure ships passing homeward, laden with the loot of the Americas. Under suitable leadership, the boldest of attacks were made upon the treasure convoys or even on the Spaniard's strongholds themselves, and that so successfully, that from all the world recruits to the buccaneers came flowing in. It was a system of organized piracy, originally aimed only at the Spaniard. It inflicted on them losses of almost unbelievable extent. The buccaneer crews worked under definite agreements, on signed articles and with the protection of a kind of compensation for injuries. The northern seas little felt the effect of the lawlessness, but the desperate nature of the struggles of attack and defene made the buccaneers of the Spanish Main notorious. They were at last forced to cease operation by the combined naval fleets of England and France, but only after years of hard fighting around and among the little known harbors and keys of the West Indies.

The disappearance of the buccaneers about the close of the 17th century was followed by a recrudescence of piratical undertakings which was of more moment to the northern colonist. Largely contributing towards the development of the movement was the passage of laws by England intended to control navigation and trading. The English Navigation Laws of 1696 attempted to do much as had been attempted by the Spanish laws of earlier date, that is, force all the purchases by the colonists to be made through their home ports. The goods which had followed the established procedure became scarce and prices rose. It thus became more profitable to handle the goods the sale of which it was intended to restrict. But of much greater importance was the fact that these laws came to be considered as encroachments on personal liberty, and as such, demanded not compliance but evasion. In addition to the added profits now to be made from the handling of the interdicted articles, the principle that interference with trade should not be tolerated by free men could now be used in justification. The pirate could actually salve his conscience by the assertion that his conduct was being actuated by a high degree of moral virtue.

Piracy, in prosecution of a principle, became popular. State governments actually vied between themselves in their attempts to lure to their ports persons who were engaged in piratical undertakings, and to procure for their citizens supplies of goods which could be sold at prices lower than was possible, if the Navigation Laws were being complied with. New York attempted to induce pirates being outfitted in Providence to make New York, not Providence, their headquarters, and in a similar way Boston made overtures to crews sailing from Philadelphia. New York especially took part in these attempts to evade the laws. Here were several business firms engaged entirely in procuring from pirate ports in the Red Sea the loot taken by pirates in East Indian waters. Two of its Governors in succession were known to have given commissions to pirates, including Capt. Kidd. Thomas Pound, sailing from Boston, after being sentenced to death for piratical practises, was saved through the influence of the Governor, and eventually obtained a commission in the Royal Navy. A number of Every's men, after his arrival from the far east, where he was known to have been engaged in piracy, found safety and protection in Philadelphia, where they were admitted to be proteges of the Deputy Governor. But that all the Colonies were not equally involved is apparent, since an armed force sent out by the Governor of Virginia brought to an end the depredations of Teach or Bluebeard, who was operating with the connivance or support of the Governor of North Carolina.

It is but to be expected that, with piracy so widespread and the northern fishing fleets so unprotected, there should be preserved some records of piratical exploits in the waters bathing the shores of Guysborough County. Undoubtedly the Canso fishing fleets suffered in common with all the North Atlantic fleets during that phase of piracy when their haunts were being combed for recruits or were considered the most promising ground for impressments, but, if so, little positive proof has come down to us. There was, however, one outrage concerning which quite full details are known, there being accounts of it in both the French and the English literature. This was the attack made in the early part of August, 1688, on Chedabucto, then being occupied by the Trading Company of Acadie as the headquarters of their operations. The very complete reports which are to be found give us a very vivid picture of piratical methods and make us wonder that any persons at all might be found ready to undertake any work of settlement or development if the results of their labours could be destroyed almost overnight by these enemies of society.

The visit paid by John Paul Jones to Canso and Arichat in 1776 may not be classed by some as a piratical raid, since it is said that he acted under commission from an existing government. The two exploits were very similar, however, in respect of the damage which was inflicted, the wantonness of attack on a wholly unprepared and unsuspecting group of fishermen, and even in the comments made by the perpetrators. The patterns of the two attacks were almost identical.

In addition to these two quite well documented events, one incident of a much more shadowy authenticity has come down to us in a traditionary way, and one place name in the County harks back to the time when the pirates were swarming, or is tinged with the flavour of an incident in which they were concerned.

The place is Pirate Cove, on the southern side of the Strait of Canso, said to have earned its name by the fact that a pirate vessel, being pursued up the Strait by a vessel of the British Navy, here hauled itself under the lee of a little island, which there forms a diminutive harbour, where it remained snugly concealed, while its pursuer passed on its way up the Strait. There may be no actual basis for the tale, and if it occurred at all, it must have been prior to 1750, for Pirate Cove seems to be identical with the Anse au Forban, which is the French name, and which appears at least as early as Chabert's Map of 1750.

Smuggling and piracy were very different matters. One could be a smuggler, successful, prosperous and respected, as such, since he was not breaking any moral law. All that was broken by the smuggler was a man-made restriction, none of the ten commandments being in anyway involved. An occupation which carried with it a spice of danger and the opportunity of matching wits with one's opponent, which did not involve running counter to at least the major moral precepts, which in its prosecution gave evidence of a certain amount of individual initiative in thinking, which gave opportunity for self-commiseration in the event of interference on the grounds of having suffered for a principle, which had little difficulty in finding a supporting clientele and one withal which promised very large remuneration and an easy road to competence, is one which it is difficult to keep from being entered upon, or if developed, is difficult to control. The New England colonists gave

100

many proofs of this. They took up the practise very willingly and easily. The French observer who predicted that the loss of the Colonies by Great Britain would follow within a very short time after the disappearance of French dominion in the New World, based his opinion on the belief that the smuggling which the colonist was doing with the French possessions was of the nature of a safety valve, which, if not existent, would allow other and more dangerous forces gradually to appear and develop, with the result which would probably be disastrous to the continuance of British rule. Events were to prove the correctness of the prediction.

Nor need it be expected that anywhere there is to be found information in great detail telling us of the smuggling operations and operations in contravention of the trade laws. From the very nature of the traffic, secrecy respecting place and procedure was essential, a secrecy involving the participants on both sides of the transactions. There remains only the knowledge, more or less nebulous and indistinct, that Martingot, a harbour now as humdrum as any of the little fishing communities which dot the coast line, and now known as White Haven, had the dubious reputation of being a favoured meeting place for those engaged in the traffic. Here, cargoes of bread, flour, Indian corn, sugar, molasses, rum and tar might be sold or exchanged for European brandy, wine, clothing or fish ready for the market. These latter could be taken to the West Indies and there exchanged for sugar, or for the molasses which was so essential for the manufacture of rum in the New England distilleries. If French molasses was obtained, it might be purchased for one-fifth of the cost asked for English molasses purchased under the restrictions of the English trade laws. Rum was one of the basic articles of trade, considered necessary both where fish were being caught or in Africa where slaves were to be obtained.

Its connection with this trade gave to Martingot a kind of sinister prominence. The name had first appeared on maps dating from the latter part of the seventeenth century. For example, it is found on the De Muelles Map of 1686, and it is referred to as late as the work of Chabert in 1750. Its period of greatest prominence was that period during which France was endeavouring to buttress its waning power in North America.

So Louisbourg arose, intended to be a fortress of such strength as to insure for France the control of the Gulf of St. Lawrence and its colonial empire on that river, the gateway to the continent. Ice free and open the year around, its site had been determined upon in preference to that of St. Anns, even though the latter was in some respects more defensible. Actual construction commenced about 1720 and proceeded apace. Over six million dollars eventually passed from the grudging coffers of Paris in furtherance of that idea.

Here was an opportunity for the disposal of his excess materials which the New Englander, a born trader, was not long in discovering. Some lumber, rock and lime could be procured locally, but much else was needed which he could supply, and that even though the French restrictions against trade were as strict as those of England herself. With a ready market for what he could bring, and the opportunity of obtaining in exchange commodities at a price which was said to have been but one-fifth of that which he would have to pay had they been secured through the regular channels of trade, the profits to be obtained were so large as to be irresistible. Neither French nor English home Governments could prevent the traffic from being carried on, and it may have gone on to some extent with the connivance of the local authorities. The seat of English Government was at Annapolis Royal, far remote from Martingot and about all the Governor there could do was to write letters to the home Government, informing them of the extent to which the trade had developed, and ask for some means with which to attempt its control. At Canso, but a short distance from Martingot, there were a few soldiers, but they were ill supplied even with barracks, or at times, with their pay. The Government sloop, which was intended for the protection of the fisheries and to prevent illegal trading was often not in commission at all, since there was no money for the pay of her crew. So the trade went on undisturbed. At one time in Boston, five of the leading merchants, John Hancock among them, were under indictment for engaging in the practise, and had been fined, but this made little difference in the volume of the traffic. It is said that at times New England rum flowed so freely in Nova Scotia that, if one desired it, he could get drunk for a sou.

It was halted temporarily for several years, when the New Englander, who had helped indirectly in the construction of Louisbourg, changed his tactics and undertook the destruction of what had been to some extent his handiwork. When Louisbourg was handed back to the French after its first capture in 1745 and the work of reconstruction began, the traffic was again renewed, to cease only after the capture both of Louisbourg and Quebec. Then Martingot, absolved and re-christened, faced life anew.

A RAID

It was time to consider the formation of a navy. The war had been going on for some time and little or nothing had been done to hamper the sea operations of the foe. What engagements had taken place had been minor ones, but sufficient, it was thought, to prove that fighters could be developed from those who had been willing to accept privateering commissions from the State Governments or from Washington himself, and also sufficient to engender the hope that the strangle hold which England had on the sea might be loosened.

So Congress thought and took action on Dec. 13th, 1775, deciding that 'a fleet to consist of thirteen ships was to be made ready for sea. On the 22nd of the month appeared the list of the four ships already available, with the names of the Commander-in-Chief and the four Captains selected to command. First on the list of the First Lieutenants, published at the same time, was that of John Paul Jones, and he it was, acting as First Lieutenant of the *Alfred*, who first broke out the American flag on an American war vessel.

The first naval engagement, which occurred early in the year 1776, was not one calculated to arouse much enthusiasm. A British frigate of 24 guns was met off Block Island by the two American vessels, the *Alfred* and the *Columbus*, the one mounting 30, the other 28 guns. Garnering no credit, at least Jones, who, as Lieutenant was in charge of the lower deck batteries of the *Alfred*, was not one of those on whom the responsibility for, failure could be placed. After the court martials were over, we find Jones with a Commission as Captain of the 12-gun *Providence* as of the date May 10th, 1776, buttressed by a Congressional Commission as Captain in the Navy as of Aug. 8th of the same year. A few days later came orders for him to undertake his first independent cruise against the enemy, unhampered by any restrictive suggestions as to locality or method.

Here now was his chance.. He was then 29 years of age, and, in the number of years he had been following the sea, had had a variety of experiences. His qualifications to command a naval vessel do not appear to be impressive. As an apprentice to a merchant engaged in the American trade, he had his first seagoing experience before the age of thirteen, crossing the Atlantic, and, before returning home, spending some time with his brother in Fredericksburg, Virginia. There may have followed some experience as a midshipman in the Royal Navy, a position obtained through the influence of the Earl of Queensbury, a friend of Lord Selkirk, his father's employer, but soon relinquished. Then followed a number of trips as an officer on a slaver and later, his captaincy of the *John*, engaged in the West Indies trade. The death of a sailor, Mungo Maxwell, shortly after he had been flogged, first brought Jones into conflict with British maritime law, from which an escape was made through the intercession of friends. The captaincy of his own vessel, the *Betsy*, and his setting himself up in his own business at Tobago, followed. But another sailor was killed, and Jones' explanation that the unfortunate man had accidentally impaled himself on Jones' sword, seemed so inadequate that his most ardent friends counselled flight. This was successfully accomplished, but vessel and property had to be abandoned, a loss little recompensed by the acquisition of an additional name, so that John Paul, gardener's son of Kirkcudbright, Scotland, became John Paul Jones of North Carolina. That during the next two years, he was one of a band of North Carolina pirates, preying on all sea-going commerce, whether of friend or foe, his own admissions furnish the proof. His commission as Captain of the American Navy came opportunely, and it was now his responsibility to prove his merit. Although, in his correspondence, he says that he had inherited a sufficiency of riches, his biographer hastens to add that these riches were the gifts of nature, and had not come from his gardener father. Not the least of these gifts was his readiness with the pen, with the use of which he was as familiar as he was with the better known instruments of his profession, and to it we are indebted for much of the information which has come down to us.

His opportunity having arrived, and a chance for rehabilitation, where now was he to go? It might not be well to attempt a voyage to the West Indies, since, though he was now a naval officer, he might not be protected from trial under the old warrant if he was so unfortunate as to meet with a reverse. He was still a British subject, and in fact never became an American citizen during his whole career. It would be better for him to go northward, towards the Nova Scotian coast, up to the present not so greatly harried and the nearest shore in English possession.

But Halifax itself could not be attacked, and near that port hovered the English fleet, with the vessels of which his twelve-gun craft, manned by but seventy men, could not expect to cope. The Nova Scotian ports west of Halifax had already been seriously harried and were learning the means of self-protection. Blockhouses were being built and an alarm brought groups of defenders becoming increasingly better able to look after themselves. These ports, too, were themselves now fitting out privateers which were earning the reputation of being well able to give a good account of themselves in any rough and tumble contest in which they were forced to engage. The inhabitants of these harbours were themselves of New England origin and a story goes that a leader of a band of visiting desperadoes, knocking for admission at the doorway of a Nova Scotian fisherman's house, beheld, when the door opened, the face of his own grandmother, who, with tongue and broom convinced him that his safest refuge was the deck of his vessel. War or no war, she did not intend to take any nonsense from one whom she had more than once across her lap. So, west of Halifax, there was little to be gained, and that little might be expensive.

It was different east of Halifax. The only port was Canso, many miles from Halifax, the only place from which help might be obtained. It had not yet been attacked, and its occupants, accustomed to scatter to their homes in the fall at the close of the fishing season, had not had the incentive to prepare those defensive points which they would have prepared had they been permanent residents. Little or nothing had been done to keep in repairs the blockhouse, built by the New Englanders themselves at the first taking of Louisbourg. Although a Town Plot had been laid off in 1764, the fishing establishments were still scattered among the coves and beaches of the outer islands. A number of those using the fishing stands might be expected to be at heart American sympathisers and it was doubtful if there was even an irate grandmother to be feared. If the cruisers from Halifax could be evaded or avoided, the prospects appeared favourable for the infliction of heavy damages with comparatively little danger of meeting with serious or expensive opposition.

Here is the report, written off Sable Island on Sept. 30, 1776. "The 19th, I made the Island of Sable, and on the 20th, being between it and the main, I met with an English Frigate, with a merchant ship under her convoy.

104

I had hove to, to give my people an opportunity of taking fish, when the frigate came in sight directly to windward, and was so good natured as to save me the trouble of chasing him, by bearing down, the instant he discovered us. When we came within cannon shot, I made sail to try his speed. Quartering and finding that I had the advantage, I shortened sail to give him a wild goose chase and tempt him to throw away powder and shot. Accordingly, a curious mock engagement was maintained between us for eight hours, until night, with her sable curtains, put an end to this famous exploit of English knight-errantry. . . . We saw him, next morning, standing to the westward, and it is not unlikely, that he told his friends at Halifax, what a trimming he gave to the 'rebel privateer' which he found infesting the coast.

"That night, I was off Canso harbour, and sent my boat in to gain information. On the morning of the 22nd, I anchored in the harbour, and before night, got off a sufficiency of wood and water. Here I recruited several men, and finding three English schooners in the harbour, we that night burned one, sunk another and, in the morning, carried off the third, which we had loaded with what fish we had found in the other two.

At Canso, I received information of nine sail of ships, brigs and schooners, in the harbour of Narrow Shock (Arichat) and Peter de Great (Petit de Grat), at a small distance from each other, in the Island of Madame, on the east side of the Bay of Canso. These I determined to take or destroy; and to do it effectually, having brought a shallop for the purpose from Canso, I despatched her with twenty-five armed men to Narrow Shock, while my boat went, well manned and armed, to Peter de Great; and I kept off and on with the sloop, to keep them in awe in both places. The expedition succeeded to my wish. So effectual was this surprise and so general the panic, that numbers yielded to a handful, without opposition, and never was bloodless victory more complete. As the ships that were unloaded were all unrigged, I had recourse to an expedient for despatch. I promised to leave the late proprietors vessels sufficient to carry them home to the Island of Jersey, on condition that they immediately fitted out and rigged such of the rest as might be required. This condition was readily complied with, and they assisted my people with unremitting application, till the business was completed. But the evening of the 25th brought with it a violent gale of wind, with rain, which obliged me to anchor in the entrance of Narrow Shock, where I rode it out, with both anchors and whole cables ahead. Two of our prizes, the ship *Alexander* and the *Sea Flower*, had come out before the gale began. The ship anchored under a point, and rode it out; but the schooner, after anchoring, drove, and ran ashore. She was a valuable prize, but, as I could not get her off, I next day ordered her to be set on fire. The schooner, *Ebenezer*, taken at Canso was driven on a reef of sunken rocks, and there totally lost; the people having with difficulty saved themselves on a raft. Toward noon of the 26th, the gale began to abate. The ship *Adventure* being unrigged, and almost empty, I ordered her to be burned. I put to sea in the afternoon with the brigantine *Kingston Packet*, and being joined by the *Alexander*, went off Peter de Great. I had sent an officer around in

105

a shallop to order the vessels in that harbour to meet me in the offing, and he now joined me in the brigantine *Success*, and informed me that Mr. Gallagher (the officer who had commanded the party in that harbour) had left it in the beginning of the gale with the brigantine *Defense*, and taken with him my boat and all the people. I am unwilling to believe that this was done with an evil intention. I rather think he concluded the boat and the people necessary to assist the vessel getting out, the navigation being difficult and the wind at that time infavourable; and when the gale began, I knew it was impossible for them to return.

Thus weakened, I could attempt nothing more. With one of our brigs and the sloop, I could have scoured the coast and secured the destruction of a large boat fleet which was loading near Louisbourg, with the savages only to protect them.

The fishery at Canso and at Madame is effectually destroyed. Out of twelve sail which I took there, I only left two small schooners and one small brig, to convey a number of unfortunate men, not short of three hundred, across the Western Ocean. Had I gone further, I should have stood chargeable with inhumanity.

In my ticklish situation it would have been madness to lose a moment. I therefore hastened to the southward, to convey my prizes out of harm's way, the *Damano* Brig having been within fifteen leagues of the scene of action during the whole time."

This is the story of the incident as told by one of the persons who figured in it most prominently. It seems unfortunate that any reference was made at all to 'knight-errantry' or 'humanity'. The 'knight-errantry' of attacking and ruining defenceless fishermen, wholly unable to protect themselves, can not be highly extolled, nor can the "humanity" of the outrage. It was as wanton and affected as little the course of the conflict as did the German U-boat sinkings of Bank fishermen in the first world war.

It is to be noted that the account of the meeting with the English frigate, the *Milford*, as reported to the Secretary of the Navy, differs quite materially from the account which Jones has given of the incident in his other writings, the other account presenting the action in a much more favourable light. According to this version, the frigate was met under such circumstances "that it was impossible to avoid an engagement", and that a running fight took place, from which Jones was able to disengage himself only by sailing his lighter and shallower vessel over "flats" (possibly the Sable Island bars) too shoal for the passage of the larger craft.

From the standpoint of Jones and his American superiors, the raid was considered a most satisfactory one, a most outstanding success. Sixteen vessels had been made prizes, in addition to those destroyed, and much damage had been done without the loss of a single man and almost without the firing of a shot. In fact, his vessel was more heavily manned at the end than at the start of the cruise. So successful was it indeed that the determination was arrived at immediately to return to the same vicinity to sweep up any crumbs which might have been left, and especially to break up the coal carrying fleet engaged in transporting coal from several Cape Breton harbours.

Accordingly, early in November Jones again sailed eastward. Again prizes were captured and again damage was done at much the same places. A ship from Ireland loaded with stores was run ashore and burned. Warehouses used in the whale fishery and for the protection of fish in the process of cure were destroyed. Again the English man-of-war was successfully evaded and again the settlements attacked were unable to put up any resistance. The attack on the coal fleet was not made, because, Jones tells us, the northern Cape Breton harbours were already ice bound, something extremely unlikely at that season of the year. Again on the way home the *Milford* frigate was met and again she was evaded by a successful night manoeuvre. There was havoc indeed at Canso, Arichat and Petit de Grat when the second visit had ended.

There are still preserved in the family of descendants of George Smith, one of the Canso merchants and one of the heaviest losers, copies of the claims for damages made in his attempts at seeking reimbursement for his loss. On the Cape Breton side, the Jersey fishing firms were heavily involved and probably lost more than did Smith. These were the persons whom Jones reports as having been left with craft not sufficient to carry them in safety to the homes across the ocean, when the fishing season had come to an end for the year. The Smith claim, interesting in its detail, impresses on us the fact that little transportable was overlooked.

"Sundry Losses sustained in the Harbour of Canso in Nova Scotia the Twenty Second of September 1776 by George Smith, Merchant.

The ship *John*, lying in said Harbour burnt by John Paul Jones Commander of the first vessel Commissioned by Congress, called the *Providence*, mounting sixteen guns and seventy five men.

1500 Quintals of codfish part burnt in the ship and part destroyed on shore and carried away by said Jones and his men	Lbs.	900
Schooner *Two Brothers* (a new vessel of seventy five tons) run on shore and burnt		500
Her cargo, consisting of salt, bread, flour, Pork, Rum and Molasses being put on board to collect fish		450
All the dry goods and provision in his stores carried away and otherwise destroyed.		600
His Stages at Crow Harbour, near Canso where for many years he carried on a considerable Macraill Fishery, his seines, boats and other necessary materials entirely destroyed and five hundred bbls of Macraill carried away		1000
Damages done to his wharves, stages and stores at Canso and cattle carried away by the rebels		<u>350</u>
	Lbs.	3800

Himself made a prisoner, his house plundered, his wearing apparel, Books and paper taken away."

And so, at heavy cost to Smith and the Jersey fishermen and others who suffered losses at Canso and Isle Madame, Jones laid the foundation of his reputation. His step now firmly placed on the ladder of advancement, he went upward to the larger destinies which were before him. Not again was it to be the fate of any Nova Scotian port to suffer so severely and undeservedly, perhaps because more effective measures in protection were thereafter taken by the British fleet engaged in patrolling duties, perhaps because the Nova Scotians themselves were making rapid progress in the art of self protection. Privateering was a game at which two could play, and when the Nova Scotians learned how to play it they played it well. But the loss of the Canso fishermen was to some extent England's gain. Nova Scotians generally regarded it as one of the list of outrages which assisted the authorities in Halifax in their efforts at keeping a somewhat disaffected population firm in its allegiance to the British Crown. The Canso outrage was one of the incidents which made it impossible for Nova Scotia to become the Fourteenth State, and thus Jones, by his successful looting, contributed towards the formation of a Province.

THREE SHIPWRECKS

Do events happen in series of threes? He who believes that they do might find extenuation for the belief in the three shipwrecks which occurred in a space of two years, some act in connection with which had taken place at or near Canso. Their tragedy or their drama are equalled by that of but few similar events in the history of Nova Scotia.

In February, 1780, the *Freemason* went ashore near White Haven. How many, if any, of the crew were lost at the time of the wreck is not known, but nineteen men succeeded in getting safely ashore. Three of these were ultimately rescued at Canso; all the others perished. Since the scene of the wreck was within twenty miles as the crow flies from Canso, it seems obvious that the deaths could not have occurred as a result of the hardships attendant only upon the exertions of traversing a distance so short. We are not told when the survivors were found. Was it in April, by the first of the fishermen who arrived to take part in the spring and summer fishing? Had the unfortunate men been prowling for some weeks among the fishing huts, deserted in the winter after John Paul Jones' destructive raid, and awaiting the assistance which was so slow in coming? Possibly they had been unable to get to the islands on which were most of the fishing huts. Could they have done so, they might have found, not only shelter, but sufficient sustenance to have tided them over the weeks when disease, exposure and starvation were thinning their numbers so rapidly. It is said that the few who survived did so only because they had fed upon the bodies of their fallen comrades. No other similar incident has been recorded in Nova Scotian history.

Several months later Canso had another visitor, Lieut. Prentiss, carrying despatches from Quebec to New York. His vessel had been cast ashore near Port Hood late in the fall of the year 1780. Following some entirely unknown reasoning, he became convinced that his way to safety, with those who survived the wreck, lay in their turning north and not south in the hunt for assistance. South was the Strait of Canso, protected waters and possibly safety on Isle Madame. West there was help at Pictou, could he have crossed the Strait. North were scores of miles of inhospitable, forbidding and uninhabited shore line. In the end, he got through, and friendly Indians, met near Sydney, helped him to get to Canso, still fearful of the fate of his precious despatches.

Then on Dec. 19, 1781, Benjamin Marsden, with his crew of seven men, got safely ashore from the wreck of his vessel, the *Brittania*, at some place which could not have been far west of the entrance to Canso harbour. Driven from Marblehead, Mass., he had been one of the first of those who had succeeded in getting to Halifax and thus of escaping from the mob tyrannies of an infuriated Massachusetts populace. He could not long have resided in Marblehead, without knowing something of the ways of the sea and a seafaring life, so naturally, that future seemed to open up before him. He soon found an outlet for his energy and a means of making a living when he became the captain of a little coaster engaged in a carrying trade between Halifax and other Nova Scotian ports. Earlier in the month he had left Annapolis Royal for Halifax. A storm drove him far to the east. His longboat was lost. Provisions ran low, exhausted on a trip the length of which had far exceeded all expectations. When, after being driven off shore, he succeeded again in reaching land, his vessel struck in waters entirely unknown to him. All he or his crew knew or thought they knew was that they were near Canso, how near they did not know. All their efforts at getting the vessel off failed. Finally they determined to leave her. All got safely ashore, taking with them the ship's dog, a Newfoundlander, which had been called Tiger. They took with them all the provisions which were left on the brig, a pitifully small supply. They had two pieces of beef, eleven ducks and fowls, about five pounds of flour which they had made up into hard dumplings, four gallons of boiled rice and a few potatoes. They seemingly had no firearms of any description and thus were not able to kill any game birds or animals, if these were met. Nor had they any means of taking fish from the brooks or rivers they must cross. Probably they had arranged to take some extra clothing, and it may be some canvas or tarpaulin for shelter.

Fortunate indeed they were that they had succeeded in getting to the mainland from their vessel. Had she struck on Andrew's Island, where the *Cedar Grove* was wrecked, or White Island or Dover Island, it would have been impossible for them to have reached the mainland and all must quickly have perished, since their provisions were not sufficient for more than a few days. It is difficult to say just where they succeeded in landing. However, it must have been either in Glasgow Harbour, about three miles from Canso, or Andrew's Passage, between Andrew's Island and the mainland and but a few miles farther away, or in Dover Bay, several miles still farther to the westward. The farther west it was, the more remarkable it is that it took them five days of travel to get to White Haven.

How little equipped for the journey they were is very apparent. They knew nothing of the country, and how to take advantage of the short cuts which might save them miles of travel. They must grope their way from point to point, quite ignorant of what was ahead, wearily travelling miles to find that in the end little progress had been made. For they must keep near the sea, close to which was the only chance of finding evidence of occupation. Winter was on them, and they knew that ice and snow must soon impede their progress. Could they have realized that their progress was to be so slow, that in nine days of travel, from the 19th till the 29th, they had succeeded in shortening the distance to Halifax by only about twenty-five miles?

The shore line along this portion of the coast is broken and rocky, almost beyond description. The land is for the most part rough, granite barren, rather low in elevation, covered with moss, blueberry bushes and other low shrubs. Here and there are to be found bogs and peaty swamps, with occasional soaks and swampy watercourses, fringed with scrubby spruce. Coves may cut deeply between the rocky headlands, so deeply and irregularly that in one place a short "Haulover" makes unnecessary miles of travel around a far projecting headland. Not knowing of such a place as this, Marsden and his men may have spent a whole day of tedious travel, only to find themselves at the end of the day but several hundred yards from the point which they had left in the morning.

Why, without attempting to reach Canso at all, did the party set out immediately to get to Halifax? Apparently, no thought of seeking aid in Canso was entertained, though the place of the wreck must have been much nearer Canso than was the *Freemason's* resting place. If they landed at Glasgow Harbour, Canso was only several miles away, though hidden from them by Glasgow Head. It is understandable why Chedabucto was not sought, for Marsden may not have known that any persons were passing the winter there.

110

Did he refuse to think of going to Canso, having heard in gossip from some of his seafaring associates the story of the men of the *Freemason*? He would certainly know of the havoc wrought there by John Paul Jones. We can not now tell the grounds on which the decision was based; all we know is that immediately on landing he and his men started on their long tramp west. This was on Wednesday, Dec. 19th, possibly in the afternoon of that short day. That evening they ate their first meal on shore, a meal which accounted for about one-fifth of their supply of food.

The following day, Thursday, was a wet snowy day, making travel slow and disagreeable, as they pushed their way through the snow laden scrubby undergrowth. The night was also unpleasant, the rain and snow dripping on their still wet clothing. On Friday, it turned very cold, but they were able to continue on their route, as they did on Saturday, the 22nd.

On Sunday morning they made a discovery, finding about four ounces of chocolate among their supplies, which was appreciated as an addition to their breakfast menu. But they were beginning more to realize the hopelessness of their situation. The prospects looked black indeed. Their noon meal consisted of a small piece of beef and a quarter of a dumpling. But shortly they made another find, an Indian hut in which was a quantity of dried moose meat, a shallop hidden nearby and her sails. These seemed to be fit for use. They might be extremely useful.

This find seems to have taken place in one of the coves along that stretch of the shoreline which lies between Port Howe and Raspberry Cove, possibly at the latter place. It is a slit or series of slits in the granite foreshore, several miles to the east of the entrance to White Haven. For this place, White Haven, must be the wide bay of which Marsden tells in his travel note for Monday. With the exception of Dover Bay — but surely that is too near Canso to be reached now after four days of travel — it is the first body of water which could be described as a bay, lying west of Canso harbour. If they had reached Raspberry Cove, they might have been about fifteen miles from Canso as the crow flies, and had reached

a point about twelve miles nearer their destination in the four days. How far they had walked is an entirely different matter.

The afternoon of Sunday and the morning of Monday were spent in getting ready for the new way of travel. Then, on Monday afternoon they crossed the wide bay, camping soon after they reached the western shore of it. This must have been somewhere near Dolliver's Cove. It represented by far the best day's progress yet made. At the same rate as that of former days, they would have been a week in travelling around the deeply indented shores of White Haven, one arm of which is nearer to Chedabucto Bay than it is to the Atlantic.

The next day there was an entirely different story. They did not know that by entering White Haven and taking advantage of a short portage or "haulover", the head of Port Felix harbour could have been safely and quickly reached. Had they gone that way, their stop would not have been on' an island the following night, where they nearly met with disaster. Ignorant of this route, they must take the long passage outside of Flying Point, exposed to the full sweep of the Atlantic, surely no very safe undertaking for an overcrowded little boat. Rounding Flying Point would bring them into Tor Bay, the whole shoreline of which would now be presented to them, ending at Berry Head, which is the western confine of the Bay. If they were to continue to use the boat in their travel, they must round Berry Head, on their way west. That they did not attempt to cross the Bay means that they were being disappointed in their expectations of using the boat safely and advantageously. Instead, they were content to turn shoreward, apparently seeking the first land they could safely reach.

This was an island, probably one of the islands which form the eastern shore of Port Felix harbour and here they passed the next night, narrowly escaping disaster and nearly losing the boat. And so Tuesday, the 25th was passed, truly, as the record goes, a dismal Christmas Day. The next day they set out again, striking westward towards and along the northern shore of Tor Bay. They crossed a narrow arm of the sea, which must be Cole Harbour, and there, shaken by their experience in the leaky and unfit boat, decided to abandon it, and resume their way on the shore. Here, in a different geological formation, travel along the shore was much more easy. The shoreline was much more regular, and from any elevated position the route which they must follow could be quite readily seen. The remainder of Wednesday, Dec. 26th, after they had left the boat, and the whole of Thursday, Dec. 27th, was spent in their slow progress. It would appear that they had reached by that time some place in the vicinity of what is now Charlo's Cove. But hunger was pressing them, for most of their food had been consumed. That night they killed the dog, Tiger, expecting that he would keep the party going for two days more.

When, next morning, the morning of the 28th, the time arrived for them to resume their march, Marsden found himself so lame that it was impossible for him to keep up with the others. Quickly he made his decision. He must stay. The others must keep on. If they stayed or even if they remained only for one or more days, in the hope that then he could proceed with them the chances of all being helped would be seriously lessened. If they, leaving him, found help, they might be able to return to him in time. This was the only chance and Marsden insisted that they take it, both for his sake and their own. They demurred but there was no budging Marsden from the decision he had made. He would make himself as comfortable as possible and wait, and, since they might need it more than he, he gave to them some of the provisions which might have been considered as his share of what was left. So, reluctantly, they left him, and Marsden was left for what the future might bring to him.

He lay in some hastily improvised shelter Friday and Saturday. He was alone and helpless. With each succeeding hour he must have thought that his chances of relief were becoming fewer and fewer. He dared not now attempt to follow the others. Help might be on the way to him. If he moved away from the place where he had been left, that help might not be able to get to him. There was nothing he could do but wait, starving and freezing, for an ending which could not now be long delayed.

Then, when perhaps all hope had gone, the help did arrive. His mate, with two Indians, arrived on Sunday, Dec. 29th, and his long vigil was over. The party, diminished in numbers by the absence of their leader, had struggled onward on Friday, reaching some place near the head of the bay. Saturday morning came, and with it tragedy. They had come to a stream or river which it was necessary to ford. This must have been Larry's River, the first stream after leaving Canso which could not be easily crossed by wading in waters no more than waist deep. Even here, a passage might have been safely effected, had the river been followed farther up from its entrance into the sea. It may have been that, where it entered into the harbour, some ice had made, which tempted John Boyd, one of the crew, to try the crossing. In the attempt he perished, all efforts to save him being ineffectual. Soon thereafter, dogs were heard baying in the nearby woods, and the sound was recognized as evidence of Indians on the trail of game. The party succeeded in finding the Indians and were immediately treated with every consideration and kindness. They were taken to the camp of their hosts, and as soon as possible, the mate, with two of the Indians, went. in search of Marsden, whom they quickly found. Thus was Marsden snatched from the very jaws of death. With the assistance of the Indians he was able to get to their huts that day, Sunday, Dec. 29th, there to receive every kindness and attention which could be given him.

It was some time before Marsden and the re-united party could proceed farther, hot till Jan. 9th. Then two Indians were sent to carry the news of the ship wreck and rescue to Halifax. Marsden himself on the same day started with his Indian host for the larger settlement at Country Harbour. We do not know at what part of the River this Indian settlement was located, but in all probability it was at or above the point where the river enters the harbour, perhaps twenty or twenty-five miles in a straight line from Larry's River. Travel was leisurely, possibly on account of storms and bad weather, almost sure to be experienced at that time of the year. Undoubtedly his Indian guide and host, Michael, thoroughly conversant with the country to be crossed and the route to be followed, took the easiest and best road. By that time there must have been ice on the lakes and rivers, and the route may have been up the New Harbour River, across Ocean Lake and thence to Country Harbour. Why he was not taken at once across country to Chedabucto, which may have been nearer than Country Harbour, we are not told. Possibly the Indians themselves were not then aware that there were any white persons living at Chedabucto during the winter months. Leaving on the 9th, the party did not arrive at Country Harbour till the 15th of the month. They built themselves a hut, and, fed and cared for by the Indians, remained there till February had passed.

By that time, Marsden had found that in Chedabucto was a white settler, who might be able to get him to Halifax more quickly than was possible by the land route on foot. Accordingly, his Indian friends took him through the woods to Chedabucto. This must have been a tiring snowshoe trip, if Marsden and his men were not accustomed to this form of Indian travel. With Joseph Hadley, five weeks were passed. By that time, April had come, spring was well on the way, the sea and harbours were becoming free from ice, and travel by boat to Halifax was possible. The boat was not a large one, one used by Hadley in his fishing or coasting operations, and accommodations for so many persons, in addition to the crew, were very insufficient. But, though they could neither "walk, stand or sit", and though successfully piloting such a craft through the dangerous waters was a task from which many present-day navigators would shrink, Halifax was reached in safety, the passage taking ten days.

So, Marsden, by his sacrificial insistence that the safety of the other members of his little party should not be jeopardised had contributed not only to their rescue but to his own. All had not escaped but that any had done so may have largely depended upon his renunciation of what chances he might have had in order that the chances of the others might not be imperilled. Such renunciations, whenever and wherever made, are the decisions of heroes.

CANSO AND THE CODFISHERY

When, within a few years after the discovery of the New World, it became evident that fish in almost countless numbers were to be obtained from certain of the waters which washed its shores, the European nations were not slow in taking advantage of the opportunity thus held out to them.

One little understands the importance of the discovery, if one thinks only in terms of the fishing industry of today. Then, there had not yet arrived such conditions of comfort or security that the largest part of the energies of all people of all nations could be diverted towards the procurement of non-essentials. Every nation arid every individual in every nation was constantly nearer the bread line than is the case today. The procurement of food even in sufficient quantities to prevent starvation, was then a task more difficult, more pressing and more immediate than now. That requirement was a compelling necessity and when it became known that, especially in the waters of the northern part of the continent, food could be procured in quantities almost unbelievable, little time was lost in applying that knowledge. The cod was specifically the fish which was most sought, its flesh containing protein in large amounts, without such an excess of fat as made the curing difficult or expensive. Justly known as the "beefsteak of the sea", the ease with which it could be obtained promptly drew the fishing fleets of all nations to the teeming banks. Soon vessels of all sizes, Portuguese, Spanish, French and English, numbering scores or even hundreds, were braving the dangers of Transatlantic passage for the purpose of procuring their ladings of the food which Europe needed.

After nearly two hundred years, or about the time of the early years of the eighteenth century, a condition more or less stabilized had been brought about. The Portuguese and the Spaniard had almost been driven from the area. France and England were engaged in a desperate struggle for ownership. By this time, the technique of the industry had become well established. From Labrador and the Gulf were being obtained the small, uniformly sized fish, which, lightly cured with high grade salt, were fit for the high class trade of Spain and the Mediterranean, the Catholic countries where fast days and Lent were being strictly observed. The French had largely monopolized the bank fisheries, where large sized cod, heavily salted, were obtained for additional curing at home and sale in the domestic market. From Nova Scotia was being obtained a fish, which might be still larger, since the largest fish were being found nearer the southern limits of its distribution, not so well cured as was the northern catch, but still being sought in large quantities as cheap food for the slave labor on the West Indian sugar and other plantations. The volume of this whole industry reached very impressive figures.

To but a relatively small extent was trade being carried on by outright purchase. Disposal by barter, the exchange of product for product, was rather the accepted procedure. So it had been brought about that the fishing industry, centering on the new world sources of supply, became one support in a tripod, on which a large part of the structure of the trade of European nations was being borne. There may have been variations in the procedures being followed, occasioned by a number of circumstances, the kind of fish caught, its cure, the articles to be exchanged for it, national laws respecting trade and navigation, and the dangers of interference by vessels of other nationalities, but in respect of every nation, their whole trade, both internal and foreign, came to be concerned very largely with the fishing industry. Thus interference with the fishing industry, on account of the ramifications of the barter system, was capable of very seriously discommoding the whole system of both foreign and internal trade.

The vessels engaged in the business came to the fishing grounds manned and equipped for the form of fishing which was to be undertaken. A certain amount of the catch was taken home for the domestic markets. The balance was carried to that market best suited for its disposal in accordance with its quality. There it was exchanged for locally procured products, goods from the Mediterranean storehouses, if the destination was Europe, sugar, molasses, salt and other commodities, if disposal took place in the West Indies. Since the New Englander was a born trader, intent on making his profit wherever business could be done, he too followed the same routine, catching or procuring his fish in exchange for flour, lumber, sugar and rum, and carrying it usually to the West Indies, and procuring for it his lading of salt, sugar and the molasses, so necessary for his distilleries. In each instance, the success of the whole venture depended on the results of the fishermen's catch. Of the three steps in the process of the routine, that formed by the fishing industry was by no means the least important, when there is considered all the elements concerned. These involved ship building, the manufacture of equipment, of packages in which the fish were marketed, supplies for the fishermen and the finding of personnel for the work. Persons so trained were eagerly being sought after by all the navies of the world.

As the hold of the French on Acadie became gradually loosened and the English gained in strength, the important place in the traffic which England took and was able to keep gradually increased. After 1713 the mainland of Nova Scotia passed into English ownership and the French were driven to the more northern fisheries and to the banks for their supplies. And so it came about that the opportunities for the trade which the English possessed increased. This increased trade centred in Canso, not only in so far as England was concerned, but also for New England, which had no intention of being barred from a traffic which had been found so lucrative. Canso became the depot or headquarters on which was based one branch of the three way traffic, both of England and New England. This amounted to a very considerable proportion of the total foreign trade of both.

This is the explanation of Canso's outstanding place in the trade system for the whole period of English occupancy, from the Treaty of Utrecht until the whole French colonial system collapsed in 1763. For a number of years no other place in North America approached it in importance and during some of them, it returned the only profit which England received on her colonial expenditures in the New World.

But was there not something more than profit? The struggle for trade supremacy had been accompanied by the passage of trade and navigation laws on the part of all the nations which were concerned, which were intended to direct all the trade into their own trade channels, and to deny these channels to the ships of other nations. In some cases there were subsidies which had been given to serve the same purpose. These navigation laws were the cause of bitter resentment. In some cases they produced effects as harmful to friend as to foe. For example, the New England trader was as great a sufferer in respect of some of the supplies he needed as was the trader of a different nationality. In respect of some of the commodities he needed, the laws meant that the New England trader must purchase supplies at a price five times as great as that he would have to pay in outside markets. It was impossible to enforce these laws, and the result was the development of a system of illegal trading, paralleling that being legally carried on, and almost approaching it in amount. In the many years of its existence this illegal trade became thoroughly organized. It brought into existence large groups devoted to the task of a law evasion and encouraged disrespect for all laws. It can hardly be denied that the attempts at the repression of this illegal trade were of moment in the precipitation of the final break between England and her colonies in America.

And how remarkable it is that, on that finger of land pointing Europe ward and within fifteen miles of each other, there should have developed the two communities, Canso, which was the hub or centre of a trade entirely legitimate, some ramifications of which involved almost every community where the English language was spoken, and Martingot, a depot of the contraband trade, little less wide flung.

THE NINE OLD SETTLERS

An old official French chart dated 1780 notes the existence of a settlement at the head of Chedabucto Bay to which the name of Milford was given, and thence, Milford Haven became almost automatically the name of the adjacent harbour. The settlement was on the hillside which looks directly down the whole length of the Bay, with, on the one side Cook's Cove and on the other what is now known as Back Cove, into which the brook, called by the French the Beaver Brook, empties. The sloping hillside was an entirely suitable farming site, with opportunities for the protection of boats and fishing stands in the coves which hemmed it in.

With the possible exception of Canso, this little settlement, previous to the arrival of the Loyalists, represented the largest grouping of the English east of what is now Halifax County. Canso was doubtless more populous in the summer months, after the influx of the fishermen who made its famous waters their fishing ground, but on the authority of Colonel Landmann of the Royal Engineers, there was but one permanent settler in Canso as late as the year 1797. When Milford was first occupied it is now impossible to say, and when its hardy folk first decided on remaining for the winter after the termination of the fishing season one can now only conjecture. We know little more than of its existence, an isolated and out of the way little community, where a hardy group of courageous men and women were content to work and to live.

The arrival of the first of the Loyalists in early May of the year 1784 was for this group a momentous occasion. It may have been viewed by them with more or less misgiving, as they remembered the tenuous nature of the claims they had on the lands on which they had made their homes. It was for them indeed a happy decision, the one that their claims were to be recognised and legalized. In due course the issuance of the grant on Oct. 18th, 1787, confirmed their rights. The grant was made out in the names of John and Elias Cook and the Callahan brothers, and intended to transfer to them 1807 acres. Actually in some way they seemed to have received 100 acres more than the acreage named in the grant.

Nine families were referred to in the grant, but that number did not fully represent the whole population of the little community. There was a tenth family, that of the patriarch, the Mentor and Nestor of the group. His lands had been reserved for him, even prior to the issuance of the Hallowell grant in 1765, though the grant was not actually made till Oct. 1, 1784. The land it conveyed to him was a block which included the east side of the harbour entrance, extended up the harbour for about two miles and along the north shore of Chedabucto Bay for a distance of four miles, the area being 1500 acres. This individual was Captain Joseph Hadley, and beyond a doubt to his influence was due the presence of a number of persons who went to make up the group of nine, the Pre-Loyalist settlers of Guysborough County.

There is no doubt but that he was a member of that Hadley or Headley family in which was one of the original settlers of Liverpool, after the departure of the Acadians. Tradition tells us that in that family was a captain of one of the transports which carried the troops which shattered the French power at Louisbourg, and that while engaged in that duty information respecting Chedabucto had been gained. The reservation of land on the shore of the bay had been made for him in recognition of the services then rendered.

119

What was the date of his first occupancy of his holdings, and the first year-round stay in what must have been an isolated place indeed during the long winter months? There is a record in the Liverpool files of the marriage of a son, John, to Elizabeth, the daughter of Henry and Elizabeth Yoing, on March 12th 1767, and also of the birth of a daughter, Ruth, to this couple on Jan. 1st 1768. This birth is said in the records to have taken place in Milford Haven, the child being born posthumously, the father having been lost at sea, while on his way from Milford Haven to Liverpool. This would seem to indicate that already in 1768 the permanency of winter occupation had been gained for the little settlement. The first winter of which we know surely that Captain Joseph Hadley was at Chedabucto was that of the year 1781, and Benjamin Marsden had reason to be thankful for that.

Marsden had been wrecked near Canso in the early December of the year 1781, having been blown by a storm far to the east of Halifax, his destination. Ignorant of the country, he and his men decided that there was nothing else to be done but to try and get to Halifax, by following the coast line, and set out on their long tramp. After some days of travel, Marsden could go no farther, and was left by his men, who, however, soon after met some Indians. With these the mate returned to search for Marsden and found and rescued him. When it was possible for him to travel, Marsden was taken by his Indians friends through the woods to Chedabucto, where he spent some weeks with Joseph Hadley, before passage to Halifax was possible.

Whether the Joseph Hadley who settled in Chedabucto was the son or the nephew of the Liverpool Joseph can not now be told. The widow of the Liverpool Joseph married Simeon Perkins, the Liverpool diarist; the wife of the Chedabucto Joseph pre-deceased him, he thereafter marrying Esther Atwater, the widow of one of the Hallowell grant settlers. Very interesting is the way in which marriage ties bound the members of the little settlement together. One of Joseph's daughters was married to John Godfrey; Diana, another daughter was married to William Callahan and Robert Callahan was married to the widow of William Hadley. One of the Pearts was joined to this family group, by reason of his having married into the Godfrey family, so that the Hadleys, Godfreys, Callahans and Pearts formed a closely connected and related group.

The land which was given to the 'nine old settlers' was made up of two blocks or divisions. The site on the hillside overlooking the Bay was divided into a number of long narrow strips, the whole area involved being about 550 acres. To each of the nine was given one of these long blocks which gave a sea or cove frontage. In the rear another area was laid off, the area of which was 1356 acres, and this was so divided that it contained the balance of the allotment due to each of the parties concerned.

Name	Front Lands	Back Lands
Isaiah Horton.	61	146
John Godfrey's Heirs.	48	102
Elias Cook.	61	139
John Ingersoll.	48	102
Robert Callahan.	61	139
John Cook.	91	209
N. Toby.	61	139

120

Godfrey Peart.	72	278
William Callahan. (Heirs.)	48	102
	551	1356

Total 1907.

The front lots filled in much of the space between the land included in the Binney Grant, which took in an area near the mouth of Salmon River, and the southern border of the Guysborough Town plot. Commencing on the south, the first lot, which took in the southern side of Cook's Cove was given to Isaiah Horton. Next to him on the north and including the head of that Cove was the area given to John and Elias Cook. Toby was given the next block, which in-eluded the northern side of the Cove. Next in order were the lots given to Robert Callahan, the heirs of John Godfrey, William Callahan, Godfrey Peart and finally John Ingersol. The land of the latter included the south side of Back Cove.

It has been possible to obtain some information respecting almost all of the individuals here named. Readers of Patterson's History of Pictou County will remember the comments made by that author on Isaiah Horton, living near Pictou when the Scottish settlers arrived. While it is not now possible to say definitely, it is probable that he had arrived in Nova Scotia from Pennsylvania, being one of the settlers shepherded thither by Anthony Wayne, employed for that purpose by the company of which Benjamin Franklin was a member. When he removed from Pictou and the cause of his removal are not now known, but it is known that when the lines became sharply drawn between England and the colonies to the south, several families who had moved to Pictou County from the States, desired to return, finding the presence of the intensely loyal Scotch uncongenial. The family was a large one, and the number was added to after its arrival in Chedabucto.

The Cook brothers are said to have come from Beverly, Massachusetts, and fantastic indeed are the family traditions respecting the circumstances of their presence in Nova Scotia. The story involves a love match frowned upon by unrelenting parents, a running away from home as a member of one of the fishing crews engaged in fishing off the Canso Banks, a ship wreck and salvation by the Indians and the enforced presence of the rescued in an Indian wigwam during the winter months, of sickness among the Indians, and their gratitude for the assistance which they received from the visitor, of return home to find that objections to the union had been withdrawn, the marriage and the return to the scene of the winter's sojourn. They were a prolific group and now their name is legion. There was another of the same name who was granted land in the vicinity, but so far as can be ascertained his stay was a short one, and all the persons of that name residing in the eastern end of the County are descended from these two brothers. It has not been possible to connect them with the Cook who was one of the early arrivals at Plymouth and a Pilgrim Father, but that may yet be done.

Little has been found respecting Nathaniel Toby, the next in order and whose land took in the north side of Cook's Cove. No record has been found or his death, but his wife died in April 1816, aged 95 years. There are records of a family of but one, a boy grown to manhood, since he married in 1784. The property is still in the possession of a member of the family of the same name, three houses having been built on it and successively occupied.

The Callahans, without a doubt, accompanied Joseph Hadley in his removal from Liverpool, NS and the two families were closely connected by marriage. Robert Callahan was married on Nov. 10th, 1782 to the widow of William Hadley, who before marriage was Jane Gordon, he being her third husband. William Callahan, who, according to the wording of the grant was Robert's brother, was married to Diana Hadley and there was one child. The father was drowned at Canso in the summer of 1784, being pulled out of boat by the rude killick used as a mooring, and the grant of land was made out in the name of the widow. She later married John Morgan, and since all the Callahans now in the County are descended from the son born of the marriage to William Callahan, and all the Morgans from the children born after her marriage to John Morgan, her descendants, if all rose up at one time to call her blessed, could certainly make a very respectable volume of sound. It would seem that Robert Callahan returned to Liverpool after some years residence in the County, and left no descendants.

It is not known when John Godfrey, to whose heirs the land was given, died. The widow's name was Bethiah, and there was a family quite well grown up. The marriages of seven children are on record. It is thought that the John Godfrey who married Ruth, the daughter of Joseph Hadley was one of the older sons. He was lost on a voyage to Barcelona. One of the saddest tragedies of the early days of the settlement involved this family. A daughter, Hannah, had married William Sealey, an officer of the 60th Regiment, he, with Augustus Fricke, being the only officers of that unit who came to Chedabucto. A child was born, and on a Sunday morning, Oct. 22, 1785, father, mother, child and the nurse, left their home to come up to church by boat. Some accident occurred in the swirling tides of the harbour mouth and all were drowned. In all probability the Godfrey family belonged to the same family as the noted privateersman who was given a commission in the Royal Navy in recognition of his valuable sea services. Only within quite recent years has the name become extinct in the County.

The block of land given to Godfrey Peart was a large one, and it may have been the intention that it be divided between him and his brother, since both of them were in the community. It would appear that the two, Godfrey and John, were the sons of a Peart — whose name is variously given as Thomas and John— who, soon after 1764 was living in Canso, and who had become embroiled in some legal difficulties with William Lovegrove over a matter dealing with a right of way. He is said to have been an officer on a privateer, and his wife, a Miss Wheaton, first was met by him, after he had captured the vessel in which she was a passenger. Her re-capture and return to her parents is said to have been requested of no less an individual than John Paul Jones himself, when he was hovering in the offing, intent on damage, but his crews wholly failed to recognise, in the decrepit old woman, sitting by the fireside, smoking her pipe, her clothing in rags and her face begrimed with ashes, the young lady whom they were seeking. Thereafter, she accompanied her husband in his cruise, till more peaceful times had come. The family is, moreover, said to have been connected in some way with the Cribbens, which name is well known in connection with another noted privateer of that time. To go back still farther and connect the name with Transatlantic enterprises of times far earlier, the name is said to be found among those of the crew of Cabot's vessel, in his voyage of some hundreds of years ago.

The last name, that of Ingersoll, is that of the only individual of whom little or nothing is known. His land was on the shore of what is now called Back Cove, though it has been called both Ingersoll's Cove and French Cove. Old maps give the name of Ingersoll's Lake to the body of water on the height of land between the Salmon River Valley and the Atlantic shore, now more familiarly called Donahue's Lake. Was this lake named after Ingersoll, who in some of his wanderings, might have visited its shores? If so, one would get the impression that he was a landsman, a hunter or trapper, rather than a fisherman. If not, there has been left no record of his presence.

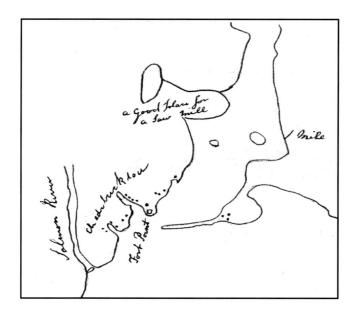

Editor's Note: Information uncovered since Dr. Jost published this book suggests there were other pre-loyalist settlers than the ones mentioned in the book. This 1783 map by the surveyors Meighan and Mcdonalds (from the estate of the late Lord Charles Montague, NS Archives), shows eighteen houses around the harbour entrance. Among these settlers were David Smith, Andrew Leet, Matthew Hawley and Daniel Bigsby. There may have also been a Benjamin Bowden. The Liverpool, NS, records state, "June 11, 1776, Capt. Boden and family sail to Chedabucto Bay with view of living there". He married widow Ruth Godfrey (daughter of Joseph Hadley) and built one of the first business establishments in the area. Another pre-loyalist settler may have been John Morgan whose sawmill was producing lumber by 1784 when the Loyalists arrived, suggesting an earlier date for its establishment. James Lodge, the first Sheriff of Guysborough, recorded that he had "payed Morgan for lumber sawn 3/8" for panels for the house he was building in that year".

One thing is very prominent in connection with this group. It is, that among the whole ten families, there was but one in which there was not some member, destined to play a part — often a most important part — in whatever activity was going on. To a great extent they were responsible for what the settlement has ultimately become. In business, in the religious field, in the political arena and in every civic or social activity, they have been prominent. They have helped to make the town, even the County and the Province, what it is. Scores of the descendants of the families are living in the County today; scores, have moved out of the County and the Province, good citizens all, wherever they have been. The total number of their descendants now can be counted by the hundreds, after the hundred and sixty years which have elapsed since the group was officially recognised. It has been one of Nova Scotia's misfortunes that she has been able to retain but a proportion of those born within her limits, and since in such an exodus, a certain amount of selection must always be present, other Provinces and States have profited from what was Nova Scotia's loss. It is very doubtful if, among the hundreds who made up the ranks of the Duke of Cumberland's Regiment, or the 60th Battalion or the Associated Departments, there can be selected nine families from each unit who have had larger roles to play in the development of the County or the Province. All honour, then, to Guysborough's "nine old settlers" and their worthy patriarch.

THE DUKE OF CUMBERLAND'S REGIMENT

British aversion to the maintenance of a standing army led to great difficulties when, war having perhaps suddenly been declared, it became necessary quickly to augment the forces in the field.

Such an emergency arose when the Revolutionary War broke out. England soon thereafter found herself in conflict not with the United States alone, but as well with France and, later, Spain. The need for more regiments became pressing. Recourse must be had to the system under which wealthy private individuals were encouraged to undertake the responsibility of recruiting men for regiments not on the regular establishment. The Duke of Cumberland's Regiment, also called the Montague Corps, was a Regiment so brought into being.

The person assuming the responsibility of forming a Regiment was accorded certain privileges. One of these was the permission for him to name a certain number or all of the officers. He also received certain expenses, though there were some which he himself had to pay. He must have the ranks full in four months. The system was not without its disadvantages. One was that "raising men for rank" was objectionable, in that in some instances, commissions had been given to individuals quite unqualified to receive them, the recipients of the favours, sometimes inefficient and untrained, being made senior to, and therefore entitled to command, officers of many years of experience in the regular army.

Persuasion, on recruiting trips made through districts where men were likely to be found, often was all that was necessary to fill the ranks, especially if an adequate bounty was paid the new soldier. This bounty was at first three pounds, though later it was increased to three pounds and three shillings. Men could also be impressed, and any young man who could be classed as a smuggler or an idle and disorderly person, was very apt to find out that his movements for the next few years were to be governed not by himself, but by some regimental officer. Able-bodied men, between 18 and 45 years of age, and of a certain height were the class sought after.

After the regiment had been in the field for some time, and its numbers had become depleted by battle or other losses, two courses were open. The few remaining privates might be "drafted" to another Regiment, a course, which was sometimes sorely resented and at times had resulted in mutinous outbreaks, and in which event the officers usually returned home to commence another recruiting campaign, or, if the end of the war was in sight, the whole Regiment was disbanded. In the latter case, the members of the unit were often encouraged by grants of land, to become settlers in some new areas then being opened up. This was the choice of the Regiment we are considering.

Of all the newly formed Regiments none more enjoyed the prestige of close connection with the Royal family than did the Duke of Cumberland's Regiment. William Augustus, who held the title from 1726 till his death in 1765, and who was the third son of King George the Second, had made the name a household word in England after his defeat of the forces of the Pretender at Culloden in 1745 and the ruthless measures the rafter taken to quell the rebellion. He had fought at Dettingen and Fontenoy and had been Captain General of the British forces on the Continent. He had favored and encouraged the idea of forming Highland Regiments for fighting England's battles, and had been particularly instrumental in the formation of Lovat's or Fraser's Highlanders, under Simon Fraser, who later brought the 71st Regiment into being.

The Duke of Cumberland who held the title at the time of the war with the Colonies was Henry Frederick, son of Fredrick, Prince of Wales, and the brother of King George the Third. He held the title from the time of its revival in 1766, after the death of William Augustus, till his own death which occurred in 1790. The title was revived again in 1799 and given to Ernst Augustus, who became King of Hanover, on the accession of Queen Victoria to the throne of England in 1837.

In command of the Regiment in the field was a member of one of the most distinguished families of the English nobility. Lord Charles Greville Montague was the son of Robert, the third Duke of Manchester. He was born in 1741 and in 1765 married Elizabeth, the daughter of James Bulmer. He and his bride arrived in Charleston on June 12th 1766, to take over the duties of Governor, which were being vacated by Thomas Boone. Esq. Their first child was born in October 1766, and duly christened George Charles on April 27th, 1767, with much pomp and ceremony, the grandfather, the Duke of Manchester being one of the Godfathers. The knowledge of the conditions in Carolina gained by Lord Charles while Governor, his acquaintance with the portions of the State likely to furnish recruits for the Regiment it was desired to form and the prestige of his name all were doubtless useful in drawing men to the colours. It is little surprising that in the ranks the Scottish elements of the Carolina population was largely represented, and also that the unit was often called the Montague Corps.

After Culloden there had been an exodus of Scotch, many of whom settled in the Southern States, and though some of them had been active in the interests of Prince Charlie, they showed little disposition to assist the Continentals. Even Flora MacDonald was one of those who had moved to America. A regiment with which Lord Charles was connected, and which moreover had as its Colonel the follower of the Duke who had opened the ranks of the British army to accept Scotch recruits, was not likely to be forgotten when men were needed.

There has been preserved some correspondence between Lord Montague and a former acquaintance in the days of his Governorship. In a letter from Charleston dated Feb. 9th, 1781, Lord Montague writes to General Moultrie, arranging for an interview. The correspondence is continued on March 11th, and the suggestion is made that General Moultrie join Lord Montague in Jamaica, Lord Montague offering to quit in General Moultrie's favor, the Colonelcy "in the Regiment I am going to command". General Moultrie, then a prisoner of war, replied, quite grandiloquently refusing the offer, and the correspondence has been published as an evidence that at least one American patriot refused to listen to the British wiles.

The date of the correspondence is of interest, since, if the Regiment here referred to is the Duke of Cumberland's Regiment, here is implied that it was then in the process of being recruited, and that this was taking place while the final stages of active hostilities were rapidly drawing near. It may never have been possible completely to fill the ranks of the two battalions of which the Regiment was composed. When the peace negotiations had been completed and the time for the disbanding of the Regiment arrived, these two battalions were in Jamaica. Those of the officers who had been given British commissions and who were Americans found themselves excluded from the terms of the amnesty, and were refused permission to return to the United States. For these and for the men of the unit who desired to be given lands in Nova Scotia, Lord Montague was very desirous of providing assistance to the fullest extent. Finally, two ship loads were collected and left Jamaica in the transports, the *Argo* and the *Industry*. The one hundred and twenty who were in the *Argo* arrived in Halifax on Dec. 13th, 1783, and Lord Montague, in reporting their arrival to Governor Parr, estimated that about three hundred would have to be provided for. The *Industry* was detained and had to put in to Havana before continuing her voyage.

It is said that place was found for some of the men during the winter in hastily erected huts and cabooses taken from the transports and set up along Hollis and Granville Streets, near where the Province building now stands. A letter also refers to Lord Montague being with some of his men, living in huts with them about five miles from the city. It does not require much imagination to picture to one's self that the winter must have seemed long to these men and that the coming of spring was anxiously awaited.

Meanwhile, the decision had to be made concerning the portion of the Province in which they were to be located. It is known that Major F.W.W. DesBarres, whose duties as Surveyor had made him acquainted with some of the area bordering on the Strait of Canso, had spoken highly of the land to be found to the eastward. It is impossible to say at this time when the decision was made and lands were selected near Chedabucto. There is, however, in existence an old tracing or map of the area, not drawn to any scale, quite inaccurate as regards many of the features represented, but very evidently prepared by some person who had made a careful examination of the whole area from Canso to the head of the Milford Haven River. Brooks suitable for mill sites are marked, distances are roughly given and comments made on the country. What makes it of special interest is there is on the back the names of two Lieutenants of the Duke of Cumberland's Regiment, Lieutenants MacDonald and Bryan Meighan. Could they have gone there in the dead of winter, following an old Indian route along the Stewiacke or the Musquodoboit River till the St. Mary's River could be reached and thence to Chedabucto? Or had the map been prepared for them by some person to whom they had applied for information? It is now impossible to say.

But there was one thing concerning which the evidence seems to be very clear and that was that Lord Montague was taking the heartiest interest in the welfare of his men, sharing with them the hardships they were forced to undergo and doing everything that was in his power for their benefit. There even seems to be authority for the statement, that the better to forward their interests be made the long trip to Quebec to consult with those higher in authority than the Halifax officials. If he went, since it was winter, he must have gone overland, by one of the old Indian routes, up the St. John River valley, a formidable snowshoe trip even for one accustomed to that method of travel. It is said that it was the hardships of this trip which helped so to weaken him, that, when ill, disease quickly overcame him. Serving to discredit the tale, there is the fact that no one could have gone to Quebec and returned in the space of time that Lord Montague was known to have been in Halifax before his death. Presumably he arrived in Halifax Harbour on Dec. 13th, 1783, with those of his men who came in the Argo, and his death occurred on Feb. 3rd, 1784, a little more than six weeks afterwards. His Majesty's mail, that same year, took nearly three months to make the round trip and it. does not seem possible for Lord Montague to have done it in six weeks. He may, however, have been one of a party, possibly including as well Lieutenants MacDonald and Meighan, who visited Chedabucto, in order to see for himself the lands on which his men were considering settlement. A putrid sore throat is said to have been the actual cause of his death. One of the oldest of the historic churches of Halifax is still proud to do honour to his memory.

The winter passed. Early in May the time for their setting out on the final stage of their journey arrived. But the number who went on board the transport *Content* on the 12th or 13th of May was very much diminished from those whom the two transports had brought only a few months previously. Lord Montague had then estimated them to number about three hundred; those who were mustered on June 20th at Chedabucto were but one hundred and forty-nine. About twenty-five had preferred to go to Shelburne, where eventually was to go one of the officers at least, Captain Gideon White, a descendant of one of the first white children born in America to one of the Mayflower colonists.

The extent to which the reduction in numbers which had taken place was due to disease it is now impossible to say, but, if one of the officers died, it seems impossible that the rank and file could have escaped unscathed. Indeed, it would be almost of the nature of a miracle, if these men, accustomed all their lives to the mild Carolinian climate and recently living in Jamaica, could have been brought almost in mid-winter to Nova Scotia, there to be exposed to the rigours of a Canadian winter, and had not paid a heavy toll of suffering and disease. Whatever the cause, either deaths or a slackening of the determination to settle in Nova Scotia, we find that only about half of those who had arrived in December decided on continuing to Chedabucto in early May. The defection applied both to officers and men. The senior officer now present was Captain R. F. Brownrigg. Lord Montague was gone and Major Bulmer, his brother-in-law, seems to have returned to England, nor need it be considered surprising if his interest in the welfare of the men of the unit fell far below that shown by his superior officer. The officers in the group were now three captains, two lieutenants, one ensign, an adjutant and a surgeon. There were six sergeants, and 13 other non-commissioned officers, twelve bandsmen, drummers and filers, and one hundred and twelve other ranks, making a total of one hundred and forty-nine. There were only nine women, the wives of officers and privates, and five children, three over ten years of age and two under. There were ten servants of officers, of whom two were women. It was almost a womanless Eden which was to be formed far to the east. In one of Lord Montague's first letters to Governor Parr, dated as early as March 14, 1783, he had spoken of the impossibility of the men of his unit being permitted to return to Carolina, and asked to be remembered in any disposition of lands made in Nova Scotia, "so that our children might have the advantage of British Government". Alas, the children yet existed only in Lord Montague's hopes for the future.

In due course, the transport *Content*, leaving Halifax on May 12th or 13th, arrived at Chedabucto on May 16th. Carefully the line of the channel, leading around the long sand bar which almost completely closes the harbour mouth was threaded, perhaps under the pilotage of one of the local fishermen. There had been passed a cluster of rude houses on the hillside facing directly down the bay and the newcomers were to find that in that little settlement (called Milford on an old French chart of the year 1780) was the largest collection of residents, all Pre-Loyalists, on the Atlantic shoreline east of Halifax County. On the left as they entered the harbour were the ruins of the old French fortifications, now rapidly going to decay. Beyond these was a sloping hillside, facing the east and forming the site of the present town, and on which there was still some evidences of former occupancy. It is said that in a cove at the upper end of the harbour was still in position an old French cross. On the right near the harbour entrance was the home of the first English settler, Captain Joseph Hadley, with his fishing stand in a nearby cove. With the exception of what clearings he may have made and what was in evidence of the former French occupants, there was no break in the uninterrupted forest, which, to right and left, to the extreme limit of tide water, nearly ten miles away, clothed the steep hillsides.

The work of unloading the transport, getting the settlers and their supplies on shore and the location of grants commenced at once. The decision was made to locate the town on the sloping hillside, north of the old French fort. Here was the only site available, as Joseph Hadley's grant and one made to Benjamin Hallowell occupied the entire eastern side of the harbour for a distance of about four miles. The Surveyor Extraordinary, John Nutting, whom Amos Chapman assisted, had orders to give the Duke of Cumberland's Regiment locations between the grants given to Hallowell and one which had been given to Dr. Boyd of the 84th Regiment at the head of tide water. A block of one thousand acres was to be given to a field officer; a subaltern was to get five hundred acres; the apportionment for a non-commissioned officer was two hundred acres and a private was to be given one hundred. There were to be fifty acres additional for each woman or child in the family.

It was not long before very much friction developed. The area on the riverside was altogether too small to satisfy the needs of all. Naturally, each person wanted some location within reach, and that was impossible to arrange. Other groups were now arriving, the Associated Departments of the Army and Navy, the 60th Regiment and that hapless group, the Augustine Loyalists. All were clamouring for sites and few or none could be satisfied. Finally, it became necessary for Kichard Morris to be sent down from Halifax to straighten out the surveyor's troubles. As the claims of the Duke of Cumberland's men were finally settled, their lands were in three blocks. On the north side of Milford Haven, extending the whole length of the river bank from the Hallowell grant to the head of tidewater was a narrow range of lots, comprising in all 2,656 acres. Immediately east of the Hallowell grant, and including what remained of the north side of Chedabucto Bay was the second block of 10,110 acres. On the shores of the Strait of Canso, north of the lands given to the St. Augustine Loyalists and extending almost, as far north as Pirate Harbour was a third block of 6,800 acres. It is to be noted that on the plan showing this survey, the town was called, not Guysborough but Manchester, the date being March 5, 1788. In order to appreciate how much of a shuffle bad been made when the areas were finally decided upon, it is only necessary to say that the area of the first block had dwindled from 7,400 acres to 2,656, that of the second block had increased from 6,000 to 10,110 acres, and that of the third had risen from 2,850 to 6,800 acres. And, strangest thing of all, apparently no place had been found for allotments for either Lord Montague or Major Bulmer. Lord Montague was given a town block (N 4 in tlie South East Division) but Major Bulmer was not even that fortunate.

In the meantime the town had been laid out. From a central parade, streets led off in such a way as to form four quadrants or divisions. The Northwest and the Southwest Divisions were those away from the harbour; the Southeast Division most nearly approached the harbour entrance and the Northeast Division occupied the remainder of the harbour frontage. Men from the Duke of Cumberland's Regiment and those from the 60th Regiment were allotted almost the entire Southeast Division.

Thus was brought about an almost impossible situation. The very nearest of the farm blocks was five miles from the town plot and the majority of them were from fifteen to twenty-five miles away. If the man could build on his town lot, and maintain himself, well and good, but his land, deep in the forest, was of little use to him. If he must make a living on his farm "lot, his town lot was almost an encumbrance.

It need not be surprising, therefore, that, though they were first on the ground, few or none of the members of the Regiment remained on their town lots. And, as their voice in the management of the town's affairs became less and less, that of those who were desirous of honouring the memory of Sir Guy Carleton became greater, till finally they succeeded in supplanting entirely the name of Manchester for the town, substituting for it the name of the deserted and defunct settlement on the shores of Port Mouton.

It has been said that there were few women in this group of the new arrivals. Nor was there an excess of these among those who very shortly arrived to commence the task of home building. What was it that prompted this group to take the last action which is to be found concerning them in the literature? For years the British Government had fed and clothed them. It was still rationing them and giving them land. Had the Regiment been so sympathetically treated that it seemed that even wives might now be obtainable on indent? Or was it the work of some wag or some notoriety-seeker? Whatever the explanation, the request went in, a request for English women to become the homemakers and helpmeets for those who were engaged in carving out for themselves homes in the wilderness, and if the request were not granted, it may have been because the indent was not made out on the proper form.

So, womenless and forlorn, condemned to the solitude of their isolated farm lots, and deprived of the privilege of honouring their dead leader, the Duke of Cumberland's Regiment passes from the literature. Even the officers, with their larger land grants and presumably better qualifications, found that fate had stacked the cards against them, and, with the men, took part in the exodus. Though Captain Gideon White may have been in the settlement a short time, he preferred the opportunities which Shelburne afforded, and there his descendants are still to be found. His title to the Manchester lands had been lost in 1800. Captain R. F. Brownrigg soon moved to Mirimachi, and references to him will be found in the Winslow Papers. No reference has been found which tells of the presence of Captain Ralph Cunningham, another of the senior officers. In all likelihood, he was of that Cunningham family the members of which had been so prominent on the British side, in the bitter partisan fighting which took place in the Carolinas. It has not been possible to connect him with any of that name now living in Guysborough and Antigonish Counties, most of whom were descended from the three brothers, John, Richard and Michael, whose shipwreck on Sable Island about 1769 was a rude introduction to their careers in the Canadian colonies. Captain William Graham is said to have moved to Ontario in 1794. It is interesting to note that

130

his original unit seems to have been the 22nd Regiment and no explanation has been given for his having drawn lands with the Duke of Cumberland's Regiment. He was a prominent member of a Regimental Masonic Lodge, and a demit signed by him is still preserved. Lieut. Bryan Meighan was married to Letitia Wheaton in 1790, according to an entry in the Town Clerk's book, but in 1793 was in Antigonish, having sold his lands in 1787. It is said that the Hon. Mr. Meighan, who for some years controlled the destinies of the Conservative party, is a descendant of Lieut. Meighan. Lieut. Angus MacDonald sold his lands in 1786, getting for them one hundred and ninety pounds, a good bargain, considering that in a number of cases the lands were actually given away. Ensign Barret's lands were sold for taxes in 1800, after he had been absent for some years. There are records of the birth of five children to Dr. and Mrs. John MacPherson, the last in 1791, after which nothing is known of the family. It has not been possible to connect him with any of that name now in the County. It will thus be seen that even the officers of the Duke of Cumberland's Regiment had little part in the development of the town or the county.

What should be considered as Guysborough's Natal Day? What, indeed but May 16th, for shorn as the men of the Montague Corps were of the privilege of naming the town, no one can question their priority of arrival.

THE BRITISH LEGION

Some of the bitterest fighting which occurred in the War of Independence took place in the Carolinas. For many years there had been friction and the lines between the parties had been very early drawn. It is the claim of the Carolinians that the first bloodshed of the struggle took place there, antedating Lexington and Bunker Hill. While, during several years, the pitched battles were almost always decided in the favor of the British, the Continentals could hot thereby be prevented from carrying on a relentless guerilla warfare, the resulting losses constituting a severe drain on the strength of the British forces. In this guerilla warfare, Carolinian fought Carolinian and British fought Continental to the death, and quarter was sometimes not asked for or given. Raid and reprisal followed quickly and the evenness of the contending forces kept the issue long in doubt.

A unit which on the British side took one of the most prominent parts was the British Legion, sometimes called the Tarleton Legion, in recognition of the outstanding genius for leadership displayed by its commanding officer. He, Banastre Tarleton, born in Liverpool, England, and a law student in London when the war broke out, obtained by purchase a commission as Cornet in the Light Dragoons and left England as one of the officers accompanying Cornwallis. He arrived at Cape Fear on May 3, 1776 and took part in the unsuccessful attempt to capture Charleston. Sent thereafter to Staten Island, Clinton's army joined that of Lord Howe, and Tarleton took part in the engagements which followed. These included the battle of White Plains and the captures of Forts Washington and Lee. Trenton, Brunswick and Princeton followed, and after July 1777, when the scene of operations had been shifted to the Chesapeake, the battles of Brandywine and Germantown. Promotions came rapidly, and when he was sent back to New York in the summer of 1778, he found that he had been selected for the command of the Legion then in process of formation, Lord Cathcart being the Colonel and Tarleton the Lieutenant-Colonel. It was not a large unit, its strength never much exceeding three hundred men, and it consisted of a cavalry section, numbering about two hundred, an infantry section, smaller in numbers, with a three pounder gun. It was recruited in New York, from Loyalists of that State, and was there organised and partially trained. Many were to know of its deeds under Tarleton's leadership, and with this unit as his special instrument, Tarleton was to establish a record excelled by but few of those taking part in the contest. Clad in their short green jackets with black collars and cuffs, cross belts, white buckskin breeches and black boots, its natty soldiers were to become the most hated and feared of all the contestants in the southern field of operations.

Sent from New York to Georgia, Tarleton lost all his horses in the prolonged and stormy passage. The infantry of the Legion were employed during the successful defense of Savannah in October, 1779, under Major Cochrane, its Commander, while Tarleton set himself to the task of rehorsing his cavalrymen. This could be done only with difficulty in Georgia but by one successful raid after another mounts were eventually obtained. When General Clinton disembarked at St. John's Island to attempt again the reduction of Charleston early in the year 1780, a request was made to General Prevost at Georgia for assistance. The Legion was one of the corps sent for this duty, being a part of General Patterson's command. They proceeded north, pausing on the way to break up a party of American militia, killing and capturing about 50, and soon Tarleton was able to get the horses he desired. Lieut.-Governor Bee's plantation on the Edisto supplied some, but General Huger and Col. Washington of the defending forces supplied most. In a surprise attack and with the assistance of some of Ferguson's Corps, Tarleton completely routed a body of Continentals, capturing about two hundred horses, forty-two wagons, ammunition and supplies. This action at Monck's Corner, about thirty miles northwest of Charleston, was one of the first of Tarleton's lightning like strokes, and in this particular instance, since by it the last remaining avenue of approach and assistance to Charleston was cut, the downfall of the city was greatly hastened. Tarleton's losses were quite negligible, though those of the American's were very heavy, including Major Venier of the Pulaski Legion killed with many others. This blow was immediately followed up by another one on Col. White at Lenud's Ferry on the Santee River, his force being broken up and fifty or sixty more horses obtained.

Co. Banastre Tarleton

Charleston fell on May 12th, and on the 18th Cornwallis commenced his march to Camden. On the 27th, Tarleton was ordered with 40 of the 17th Dragoons, 130 of the Legion and 100 mounted infantry to watch Cornwallis' right flank from Georgetown. Finding that General Buford was in that vicinity, he gave chase, eventually catching up with him on the 29th near the North Carolina line. On this occasion his force covered 154 miles in twenty-four hours. Buford had about 350 Continental infantry and some horses, but was immediately attacked. The Americans lost 113 killed, 150 so badly wounded as to be paroled on the ground and 53 prisoners able to march. The British loss was but 5 killed and 14 wounded. On this raid General Sumter's home was destroyed. The scene of the action was in the vicinity of Waxhaw.

On August 5th, the infantry of the Legion was in action at Hanging Rock, losing its commanding officer, Captain McCulloch and about twenty men. The battle of Camden followed closely, and General Gate's complete defeat was brought about, very largely by the timely charge of the Legion cavalry. The Continental army was completely destroyed and Gates himself escaped with difficulty. This action left Tarleton free to pay his attention to General Sumter, who, in command of the American cavalry, had been acting independently. On August 17th, Sumter was surprised, with a loss of 150 men and officers killed and all his supplies. This action took place on the Wateree River, and for a time brought to an end all the organized resistance in South Carolina.

Tarleton himself being ill, his second in command led Cornwallis's army into Charlotte, North Carolina, on Sept. 8th, and was wounded in following up the retreating Americans. A month later, the disaster inflicted on Ferguson, who was acting on the left wing of the army, and who was isolated and severely defeated at King's Mountain, necessitated the retirement of Cornwallis from Charlotte and his taking up quarters at Wynnesboro. Here, reinforcements under General Leslie were gladly welcomed.

Meanwhile, Marion and Sumter, the Continental irregulars, were resuming operations. Marion was driven by Tarleton to hiding in the impenetrable swamps, his knowledge of which had earned for him the title of the "Old Swamp Fox". Sumter, "the Gamecock", with sufficient numbers behind him, could strike back, as Tarleton found at Blackstock on November 8th. Here, Tarleton, with but 100 cavalry and 180 infantry did not hesitate to attack 1,000 of the Carolinian militia in fortified position. As was to be expected, the attack was costly to the attacker, but as the result of the action the Americans withdrew.

Cow Pens, fought early in 1781, also cost him heavily, again the result of his impetuosity and scorn of the fighting qualities of the irregulars.

The losses replaced, in February, with his cavalry alone, he dispersed and put to flight a force of three or four hundred Continentals at Tarrant's House, and on March 2nd took the measure of an equal number of Lee's Legion, dispersing and scattering them. On March 6th, the battle of Guildorn Court House was fought, near the Virginia State line, and Tarleton's charge on the enemy's left wing put the Continental army to flight, with the loss of their artillery. The victory was achieved, however, only at such a cost that Cornwallis considered that his retirement, first to Hillsborough and later to Wilmington on the sea coast, was necessary. In this engagement, Tarleton was himself wounded, but not so severely as to compel him to be absent from his command for a protracted period.

The stay of Cornwallis in Wilmigton was not prolonged. Arriving on April 7, 1781, he left on April 25th, with what reinforcements he had been able to secure, persisting in what was to be a fateful attempt to establish himself in Virginia. The movement appears to have been made entirely on the initiative of Cornwallis himself, without consultation with the Commander-in-Chief, and it was destined to have far reaching results. The Virginia line was crossed near Halifax, North Carolina, and by May 20th, Petersburg had been reached, and a junction effected with the British forces under General Phillips which had been operating along the Chesapeake. Under Cornwallis there were now to be found all the British forces in that entire field of operations, and around them the continentals were gathering. The summer was spent in marching and counter marching in Virginia, with neither side able to inflict a telling blow or permitting itself to be caught at a disadvantage by its opponent. Tarleton found these conditions unfavorable to the carrying out of the kind of warfare which was his forte, and during the period was able to carry out only one of his characteristic exploits. With a small force, he made his way to Charlotteville, north and west of Richmond, capturing seven members of the Virginia Assembly, narrowly failing in the capture of Jefferson at Monticello, but destroying 1,000 firelocks, 400 barrels of powder and other military supplies. In this raid, he covered a distance of seventy-four miles in twenty-four hours.

Around Cornwallis the Continentals were swarming. A success at sea gave the French fleet temporary control of the Chesapeake, and permitted the junction of the French and the Continental forces. Yorktown was the result, when Cornwallis, with but 7,000 men, found himself surrounded by 17,000, the combined strength of the united French and Continental army and naval units. His disaster to all intents brought about the termination of the war. During some of the final stages of the conflict, Tarleton had been in command of the British detachment lying directly opposite Yorktown at Gloucester on the eastern shore of the York River. When Yorktown fell, the military career of the British Legion came to an end.

Its strength, as reported by General Washington, when finall the terms of the capitulation became effective, was on Lieut.-Col., six Captains, eight Lieutenants, three Ensigns and Cornets, six Quartermasters, one Surgeon, seventeen Sergeants, seven Drummers and one hundred and ninety-two Privates, a total of two hundred and forty-one, all ranks. In the Return, no mention is made of the arm of the service, mounted or unmounted, to which these belonged.

Tarleton, on parole, proceeded to England as soon as possible, where his book, dealing with the campaign, was issued. Several times thereafter returned to Parliament, eventually he became a Lieut.-General of the army and a Knight Commander of Bath. He died on Jan. 25th, 1833.

It is difficult to say to what extent the personnel of the Legion had changed during its two years of service in the south. The recruits of which it had originally been composed were New York Loyalists, and it may not have been easily possible to keep the ranks filled up from that source. Its greatest recorded strength, as given on Aug. 15th, 1780 by Tarleton himself, consisted of a Lieut.-Colonel, nine officers, a medical officer and one hundred and seventy-one other ranks in the cavalry section, with eight officers and one hundred and eighteen other ranks in the infantry, a total of three hundred and eight. At the time of the surrender, its strength was two hundred and forty-one, all ranks, not a great reduction for two years of almost constant fighting.

136

With the exception of the losses at Blackstock and Cow Pens, its battle losses had not been severe, it being remarkable how much had been accomplished with so little loss of men. Sickness especially malaria, and, it is said, yellow fever, had at times been very prevalent, and Tarleton himself had suffered from it. One seems to be justified in the opinion that there must have been at Yorktown a considerable percentage of the original members of the unit, and that the others consisted of Carolina Loyalists who had been recruited to make up deficiencies. This was therefore, in all probability, the composition of the Legion, when, sent to New York, they awaited with what patience they could muster, the news of the disposition which was to be made of them, when hostilities had terminated.

When next we hear of the Legion, it, or what was left of it, was at Port Mouton. Colonel Tarleton was not with it, having gone to England, engaged in the preparation of his book on the story of the Southern Campaign. It was not alone, but formed a portion of a group of about one thousand persons, the senior military officer with them being Lt.-Col. Molleson, who has been Wagon Master General of the British forces in New York. So far as it has been able to determine, there were in the thousand about seven hundred who had been in the Commissary Departments at New York, or had been connected with some naval units. The remaining three hundred or more belonged to fighting units, especially the Legion and the 71st Regiment. The Legion men probably outnumbered the men of the 71st by over two to one.

Among those who had been in the Commissary Departments there was a large number of women and children. There was also a large number of slaves or servants, some of whom had been owned by the members of the units individually, and some who were seemingly Departmental property. This was a distinction without much difference, since all became free on arriving in the Province. Very few women and children accompanied the men of the Legion and the 71st, these units being about as womanless as was the Montague Corps. A certain amount of building materials and supplies had been obtained and there was no doubt respecting Col. Molleson's solicitude for the welfare of the group. It is impossible at this time to determine how it was that Port Mouton had been selected as their destination when they left New York, since it is one of the most unfavorable sites for settlement along the entire Nova Scotian coast line. Almost utterly unadapted for agriculture, a meager living from what might be wrested from the sea was the most which could be looked for and for that the new arrivals were wholly unprepared. But they were not far from Shelburne, which was growing rapidly, and the thriving settlement of Liverpool was less than a score ot miles away. The nearness to assistance was almost the only favorable feature. something which was denied to many whose destinations were more isolated and remote.

They landed from the transports in November, 1783. Hastily, rude houses were constructed, while in the intervals between the tasks of fending off starvation and keeping themselves from freezing, the possibilities of the development of a permanent settlement were examined. There was but one conclusion which could be arrived at. Guysborough, the name they had given the settlement in honor of Sir Guy Carleton, could offer to no one a reasonable prospect as a place for making a livelihood. Rocky, barren and uninviting, with the most meager agricultural possibilities, its scanty soil among the granite boulders allowing sustenance for nothing but scrubby spruce and the barren loving berries, the utter unsuitability of the location was all too quickly apparent.

The winter was a bad one. Starvation was narrowly averted. A number became ill and died. Fortunately, game was to be had and this was a welcome addition to their fare, without which they might not have survived. Then, in the spring, attempts were made to have allotted to them a more suitable site, Col. Molleson actively interesting himself in the endeavor.

The crowning misfortune very quickly came. In their rude efforts at erecting homes for themselves and providing themselves with firewood, trees had been cut down close to the dwellings, and a great fire hazard had in ignorance been allowed to develop. It was spring, and even hardship had not stifled the house cleaning urge of at least one of the women. Some rubbish in her door yard invited a match. The fire immediately got out of control. It spread so rapidly that nothing could be done to arrest its progress. The terrified settlers were driven to the waters of the harbour to save their lives. One person was not so fortunate as to be able to escape and perished. Even their few head of live stock could not escape. Their little, rude houses with everything they contained disappeared one after the other. There was saved literally and only what few clothes the settlers were wearing, all their food having been destroyed. They would have starved, had it not been possible to get some food from some of the nearby settlements.

Small wonder it was that the decision to leave Port Mouton, and that quickly, was made. Fishing vessels from nearby Liverpool or other ports, were immediately pressed into service to act as transports to take most of the poor unfortunates to Halifax. Little more than a handful remained in that County, and few or none of these were members of Col. Molleson's own group, the Commissary Departments. Perhaps acting under his advice, this group joined in Halifax some who were going eastward to Chedabucto, forming for this purpose the group which is known as the Associated Departments of the Army and Navy. It may, too, have been that to his influence was due the fact that these persons maintained some cohesion and were not so badly disrupted as were the members of the fighting units, to whom the staff officer, Col. Molleson, might have been a somewhat alien figure.

These fighting men, the members of the British Legion and the 71st Regiment, eventually broke up into three distinct groups. One portion of them, convinced though they might have been that the Port Mouton site offered opportunities for home building few and meager indeed, were not convinced that in the immediately surrounding neighborhood conditions were so unfavorable that a future more or less assured could not be theirs. Members of this group decided upon staying, if not on, at least in the vicinity of, the original site. To these in course of time, land grants were issued and the County records still preserve for us their names, and the sizes of their grants. Almost without exception these were Legion men.

This group consists of a total of 102 grantees and they were given all told a total of 20,250 acres.

Number of Persons	Sizes of Grant	Total
1	1,050 Acres	1,050
1	750	750
2	650	1,300

3	600	1,800
2	550	1,100
1	350	350
3	300	900
5	250	1,250
21	200	4,200
9	150	1,350
_52_	100	_5,200_
102 Grantees		20,250 Acres

Several of the grants were made to women, probably the widows of men who had died since leaving New York.

At least a proportion of these remained either on the lands received by them under the grant, or on lands obtained by occupancy, exchange or sale in other portions of what is now Queen's County and there many of their descendants are still to be found.

Of those whose decision it was that they would continue their search for suitable home making sites elsewhere than on the inhospitable shores of Port Mouton, two groups can be followed. One group, made aware that lands suitable for agriculture were to be had in the valley of the St. John River or of some of the other rivers emptying into the Bay of Fundy, attached themselves to individuals seeking there to obtain home sites. Captain Nehemiah Marks, first commissioned by Sir Guy Carleton as Captain in a Corps of Armed Boatmen, and later holding commissioned rank in King's Own Maryland Loyalists, was interesting himself in procuring land in the vicinity of Passamaquoddy on the Bay of Fundy shore. A number of the Legion, after, it is said holding a camp "election" in which doubtless this and other projects were discussed, decided in favor of attaching themselves to the group which Captain Marks was gathering around him. It consisted of a number of persons who had been in the British service in transport or other naval duties, of members of the British Legion who had been dissatisfied with their original allotments at Port Mouton and of a number of persons who had been connected with the 71st Regiment.

Thus was formed a group called the Port Mouton Association, which succeeded in getting away quickly from their ruined holdings, and arrived at the selected location on the Schoodiac (now the St. Croix) River on May 26th, 1784. There they formed a settlement which was named by them Morristown, presumably in honor of the Surveyor-General of Nova Scotia. The settlement, afterwards became known as, and still goes by the name of, St. Stephen.

In the grant which was eventually given them 106 parcels of land were allotted, these being the lots which today make up the town of St. Stephen. It is difficult to say with exactness how many of the recipients of these lots were Legion members. There are records of at least twelve stated to have been in service on the Despatch Boats, *Miranda* and *Neptune*, and there are several known to have been members of the 71st Regiment. Possibly, too, other Regiments were represented.

It is interesting to know that there are persons still living in St. Stephen who trace their ancestry to persons born during the long-to-be-remembered winter which their parents spent in hastily improvised shelters in Port Mouton.

Still a third group of the Legion members, convinced with the others that Port Mouton presented them with but inadequate prospects in their quests for permanent home sites, placed their reliance on the guidance which Colonel Molleson seemed able and willing to provide.

He it was, seemingly, who directed the attention of the Legion members to the settlements being opened up in Eastern Nova Scotia. Here, on the shores of Chedabucto Bay and the Strait of Canso, settlers were being placed, while at Country Harbour, not many miles away, a number of Regiments from both North and South Carolina were being given land.

It is impossible now to say exactly how many there were in the Legion who determined to throw in their lots with those of Colonel Molleson's special proteges, but since about two hundred of a total of three hundred or less of the two units, the Legion and the 71st Regiment, are accounted for as having remained in Port Mouton or of accompanying Captain Marks to St. Stephen, the number .going to Chedabucto could not have exceeded several score. Colonel Molleson took with him to the new location six hundred and ninety-five persons, almost the exact number of persons said to have arrived at Port Mouton from the Commissary Department alone. Unfortunately, the Guysborough County records do not tell of the military service of many of the individuals to whom land was given, except where it is necessary to identify one of two individuals of the same name but of a different service, and not a single instance is to be found where a person is named as having belonged to the Legion.

Thus it was that the ranks of the Legion were shattered, never again to be re-assembled. Both Nova Scotia and New Brunswick gained, but the Legion as a group was no more. Time had ruthlessly effected what Sumter, the "Gamecock" or Marion, the "Swamp Fox" could never achieve. Few units which had participated in the bitter struggle had finer records of service or had gained more battle honours. Ought we not to be justified in expecting that the qualities which had earned those distinctions would contribute towards attaining an equal predominance in the arts of peace?

But, in the meantime, as proof of their presence in Port Mouton, there remained little more than a small group of neglected graves on a bleak and barren Nova Scotia hillside.

APPENDIX I.

Dress of Legion. Short round light green jacket, black collar and cuffs, with variety button-holes. In 1780, green jackets, white waistcoats and breeches. Cavalry, plush breeches. Drummers, green waistcoats and breeches. It was intended to wear the waistcoats with their sleeves during the campaign and to add sleeves to the shell or outer coat to be worn over the waistcoat in winter. "Green is without comparison the best color for light troops with dark accoutrements, and, if put on in the spring, by autumn it nearly fades with the leaves, preserving the characteristics of being scarcely discernible at a distance".

Although Lieut.-Col. Tarleton, when he prepared his book, "The History of the Campaigns of 1780 and 1781 in the Southern Provinces of North America", may not have produced a masterpiece worthy of becoming a Staff College textbook, he did succeed in arousing thoroughly the ire of one of his former companions in the field, and was to find that, even as his military operations had detractors, so also had his literary efforts. The book itself is one of six chapters, each dealing with one distinct phase of the fighting which ended at Yorktown, each chapter being followed by an Appendix which is made up or copies of documents, orders and despatches supporting the material found in the text.

Its appearance was followed in 1787 by a volume written by Roderick McKenzie, a Lieutenant in the 71st Regiment, who prepared and published his book, under the name of "Strictures on Lieut.-Col. Tarleton's History". It took the form of a number of letters addressed to Lord Rawdon, A.D.C. to the King. Instances are given when Tarleton's headlong leadership resulted in severe loss without compensating advantage. He cites as an example one occasion when the Legion attacked a British detachment in a night assault, Major Ferguson, one of the foremost of the British officers of irregulars, being beset by three of Tarleton's men, and would certainly have been killed had his voice not been recognized by an officer of the Legion Cavalry. Major Ferguson, whose right arm had been made useless as a result of an injury sustained some time before, had learned to defend himself with his sword in his left hand, but would have been bayoneted had not, by a lucky accident, his call for help been heard. Another instance, in McKenzie's opinion was the costly reverse at Blackstock, when Tarleton attacked precipitously, not asking the opinion of several experienced officers, such as Majors MacArthur and Newmarsh of the 71st, both of whom, McKenzie says, had commissions before Tarleton was born. Similarly, the heavy losses at Cowpens were the direct result of his precipitancy in attack, and could have been avoided. It was in this engagement that the 71st suffered so severely, losing their Commanding Officer by capture. Especially galling to McKenzie, however, was Tarleton's disregard or actual belittling of the work done by any unit other than his own, or by any other officer, however meritorious. The loss of a Legion horse, apparently bulked larger in Tarleton's estimation than the loss of any number of officers or men, no matter how capable they were or how nobly they had done their duty. Finally, says McKenzie, the History was written with a professional experience "so limited as scarcely to exceed the duration of a butterfly's existence".

If Tarleton had his detractors, he also had his friends. Two years later, the Hon. George Hanger, fourth Baron of Coleraine, took up the cudgels. He describes himself as having been a Major in the Legion Cavalry, and says that he wrote entirely without the knowledge or consent of Tarleton. He had left the Legion, from Charlotte, the victim of an attack of yellow fever, he being the only one who survived from a convoy of the sick being sent down to Wilmington. His book is entitled "An Address to the Army" and is written with a venom which the author makes no attempt to conceal. The incident in connection with Major Ferguson was one of the accidents almost inseparable from night operations. A night attack had been planned with Tarleton and Ferguson to attack from different directions. The Continentals, warned, had fled from the encampment; Ferguson then came and, unknown to Tarleton, occupied the ground, the Legion not knowing when it arrived, of the change. Blackstock was a British victory, since Sumner was wounded and the enemy was forced to retreat across the Tiger River, Tarleton retaining the ground of battle. He reminds McKenzie, whom he continually refers to as the "Stricturist", that Tarleton had received his first promotion to Major of Brigade from Sir William Erskine of the. 71st, and refers to his valuable work in the north, before he had been sent to the Carolinas. Especially resentful of the remark about the butterfly, he refers to "certain gnats which lodge themselves in the posteriors of the finest horses, which do not, however, prevent them from running". Reserving comment on the judgment displayed in making such a remark, we may respect the loyalty to a friend, considered to be unfairly attacked, which evidently inspires it.

THE SEVENTY FIRST REGIMENT

The victor at Culloden was one of the first of those to advise that the formation of Highland Regiments would not only put in the ranks of the English armies men equal or superior to any to be found on the European battle fronts, but might also serve to remove temporarily persons who might, otherwise, become very troublesome.

The Black Watch, Loudon's Highlanders, Montgomery's Highlanders and Fraser's were formed between 1739 and 1757. Between 1757 and 1766 no less than eleven more regiments were recruited. The 71st was the eighth on this list. It might almost be considered the reincarnation of Fraser's Highlanders, which, formed in 1757, had been disbanded in 1763, when for a time there was peace in Europe. Col. Simon Fraser had recruited it and now, when again the necessity for raising men for England's armies arose, he was no less prompt in action than he had before been. Within several weeks 2,340 men had been gathered together at Stirling for their march to Glasgow, where the battalions were to be formed. In addition to Fraser, now a Major General in the English army, and also head of the Fraser Clan, there were no fewer than six chiefs of Clans and two sons of chiefs, besides chieftains and sons of chieftains among the officers. If such a person brought into the Regiment with him 100 men, he was eligible for a captaincy; if he brought 20 or 30, he might be given rank as subaltern.

The arms were a musket and bayonet, a basket hiked broadsword, pistol and dirk. Needless to say it was a kilted regiment. The only black mark ever placed against the 71st Regiment was caused when some of its men were drafted to a non-kilted unit. Then they mutinied; lives were lost in the ensuing struggle before they were overpowered. Court martialed, they were sentenced to death, a sentence immediately annulled in proof of the justness of their complaint. The Black Watch and the 71st Regiment were the only two Highland regiments ever entitled to wear the red heckle in their feather bonnets. Major-General Simon Fraser was their Colonel, the Battalion Lieut.- Colonels were Sir James Erskine and Angus Campbell.

Formed into two Battalions in Glasgow, almost immediately they were sent to America. Becoming separated from the other transports in the long voyage, one of the vessels carrying about five hundred men and officers, one or whom was Lieut.-Col. Campbell, the officer commanding the battalion, sailed into Boston harbour, not knowing that the port had been evacuated by the British. It was attacked by an American privateer, and an unfortunate shot carried away the rudder. The vessel then drifted ashore under the guns of a revolutionary Battery. Major Menzies, one of the battalion officers, was killed and the remainder were taken prisoner, including Colonel Campbell.

The remaining members of the Regiment arrived at New York on July 21,1776, and joined General Howe's army at Staten Island. There it was formed into a small brigade of three battalions, with a grenadier division. The first engagement was at the battle of Brooklyn, the total loss of killed and wounded being fourteen. There was some desultory skirmishing during the winter months and in the spring the Regiment was sent to the Chesapeake. It took part in the skirmishing at Cooche's Bridge, where first the American flag was displayed in battle, and shortly after in the Battle of Brandywine. In the fall, the Regiment was sent to New York. There it received a reinforcement of two hundred men. The Regiment was in action at the successful attack on Fort Montgomery on October 6, 1778.

Selected to be one of the Regiments included in the army being sent to the Southern Area, the 71st sailed from New York on November 27, 1778 and arrived off Savannah on December 27th. Colonel Campbell, who had been exchanged, was again at the head of his men. . The transports immediately crossed the bar and prepared for disembarkation.

This bade fair to be a difficult operation, since it involved making a landing in the face of opposition by the Continentals, long forewarned of the attack. The total British force consisted of about 3000 men, of which the Scotch battalions numbered about 1300. Collected for the defense of Savannah was a Continental force under General Howe, who had not been able, however, to concentrate all his forces to repel the attack. On the morning of the 29th the landing was attempted, a body of light infantry with the First Battalion of the 71st heading the attack. A foothold was gained at Girardeau's Plantation, about two miles below the city of Savannah, from which point a narrow causeway, bordered by ditches, led across the swamp and rice fields to the higher ground on which the city was located. The Highlanders advanced to meet a hail of fire at the end of the narrow passage way, Captain Cameron, who commanded the attack, falling, and several others being killed and wounded. Little deterred by this, the Highlanders pressed the attack; the Continentals broke and fled and the way was prepared for the landing of the remainder of the troops.

The Continental army was drawn up in a very strong position in front of the city, with morasses and swamps protecting both flanks, and the only route of approach being a narrow road leading to the Continental center. Col. Campbell, however, had discovered that a road which led to the rear of the Continental position had been left undefended. Dividing his force, he awaited till the arrival into position of the flanking force and then delivered his attack. Assaulted both from the front and rear, the result of the conflict was not long in doubt. The Continental forces retreated, losing all their artillery and baggage, their flight taking them through the City of Savannah, which was immediately occupied by the British. At a loss of but seven killed and nineteen wounded the British had caused casualties amounting to about five hundred and fifty in killed and captured and had completely dispersed the defending force. The initial success of the 71st Regiment had a large part to play in this result.

Equally effective was their action in March 1779, when next, except for outpost actions, the major forces of the contestants were engaged. Col. Campbell undertook to prevent the junction of two bodies of Continentals which would have resulted in about 8000 troops being gathered into one striking force, a total far outnumbering the British forces in the field, by attacking Colonel Ashe, commanding one of the Continental armies. The First Battalion of the 71st, led by Major MacPherson, here comprised one of the units engaged in carrying out a frontal attack, while the Second Battalion had been ordered to seek out the rear of the Continental position. Again the British loss was slight, only sixteen killed and wounded, while two hundred of the Continentals were captured. One hundred and fifty were killed or drowned in their flight, all their arms, artillery and baggage being lost. This action at Brier Creek quite effectually ended for a time all organized opposition in Georgia, and the advantage thus gained was maintained till the end of the war.

As one of the more immediate results, General Prevost, who now commanded all the British forces, decided to make the attempt to capture Charleston, South Carolina, and arrived before that city on May 11th, his total force numbering about 3600 men. Negotiations for the surrender of the city were actually in progress when the presence of large reenforcements of Continental troops made Prevost's withdrawal necessary. The retirement to Savannah was made in safety, there being but one engagement of note, that of the battle of Stono Ferry, a rearguard action, which took place on June 19th, and in which the First Battalion of the 71st Regiment took a prominent part. Two of its companies, engaged in advanced positions, lost all their officers and of the men only eleven regained their unit. A Regiment of Hessians broke, and only the exertions of the remaining companies of the 71st Battalion prevented the infliction of a defeat on the small British force. Finally, the Continentals retired, having lost over one hundred and fifty men, while the loss of the British was twenty-six officers and men killed and about one hundred wounded. Much of the loss was sustained by the 71st Battalion, the Commanding Officer of which, Lt.-Col. John Maitland, commanded on this occasion the entire British detachment.

The return of the British troops to Savannah was timely. Count D'Estaing, Commander of the French fleet had temporarily gained an ascendency in the South Atlantic, and somewhat unexpectedly appeared off the Georgia coast. Effecting a junction with the Continental troops, there were made available for an attack on Savannah about 7000 men in the combined French and Continental armies and navy, to resist which but 2500 British troops could be mustered. The city was under attack from September 23rd till October 8th, when an attempt to storm the British breastworks was made. It was nearly successful, and the Spring Hill Redoubt, the possession of which was necessary for a successful British defense, was on the point of capture, when Col. Maitland made a counterattack and regained the breastwork, on which already the French and Carolinian flags had been displayed. This resulted in the siege being raised. The French and Continental losses totalled over 1200 men in killed and wounded, in comparison with which the British loss of 120 men was insignificant. On the 71st Regiment fell most of the brunt of the defense, and Col. Maitland, though even then fatally ill, himself took a prominent place in all that transpired. The siege was lifted on October 19th, and Col. Maitland died but six days after. Lt.-Col. John Maitland, brother of the Earl of Lauderdale and himself a member of the British Parliament, was one of the highest type of British officers. He had already gained for himself an outstanding reputation and was considered one of the best officers engaged in the field. His untimely loss may have seriously affected the whole subsequent course of events in this area of the conflict.

Early in the year 1780, Sir Henry Clinton, then Commander-in-Chief, at New York, determined to make another attempt at the capture of Charleston. He, with a new army gathered together for the purpose, left New York on December 26, 1779, but it was not till February 11th that the transports arrived at a point about thirty miles below Charleston, storms having dispersed the fleet and caused serious losses of material and equipment. Lord Cornwallis, who accompanied the Commander-in-Chief, desired from General Prevost in Georgia the presence of all the troops who now could be spared from Georgia, and in response to the request,

General Patterson was sent with all the forces not required for the maintenance of the peace in that State. Included in the troops thus transferred were the two Battalions of the 71st, now under the command of Major McArthur, who, leaving Savannah about the middle of March, effected a junction with the force attacking Charleston on March 25th. From that time onward the fortunes of the 71st were those of Cornwallis.

Charleston fell on May 12, 1780, and on the 18th Cornwallis set out to extend the circle of British occupancy. The Commander-in-Chief having returned to New York with a number of the Regiments used in the reduction of Charleston, there were left to Cornwallis only about 4000 men to maintain order in the Carolinas. This necessitated the dispersion of his relatively small force into small groups, scattered throughout the wide area it was desired to enclose within his sphere of influence. But then commenced and rapidly gained in strength and effectiveness the bitter guerilla warfare, the constant attrition from which, in the absence of reinforcements to make up the losses, greatly weakened and eventually brought to naught the British effort. The encounters between the larger groups always without exception were British victories, especially where the British regulars were involved, but still the guerilla warfare kept on, fought bitterly, often without the giving or the asking of quarter, and from the losses of which Cornwallis sought vainly to escape. Tarleton, with his British Legion, ranged far and wide, and though he became the most effective of the British raiders, he could not break up the numerous and increasing small aggregations always alert to harass the outlying posts.

According to Cornwallis' plan, the two battalions of the 71st were first sent to Cheraw, near the North Carolina border, there making use of the Parish church of St. David's as a barracks. The Highlanders stood the climate very badly and there was much sickness. Some of the most noted of the partisan leaders were operating in that vicinity, cutting off foraging parties and waylaying convoys. The Regiments were ordered from that place on the arrival of the Continental armies under General Gates, and, effecting a junction with the main body of troops under Lord Cornwallis, were placed in reserve when the opposing forces met at the battle of Camden. This was a most disastrous engagement for the Continentals, 2000 men being killed and captured at a British loss of only about 300, and, being followed by Tarleton's success at Fishing Creek, for a time eased the pressure on the British. Still, losses in outpost engagements and sickness were so heavy that on August 15th of that year, there were but 144 men fit for duty in the First and 110 in the Second Battalion of the 71st Regiment, of over a thousand of which it had shortly consisted. Enabled after the battle of Camden to cross the line into North Carolina, Charlotte was occupied by Cornwallis, but Ferguson's disastrous defeat at King's Mountain, although his troops were entirely locally raised recruits, necessitated a withdrawal to Wynnesborough. Soon after, it was the misfortune of the 71st Regiment to be included in the force under Tarleton which General Morgan met at Cowpens on January 17, 1781, near the Carolina line.   In this the Regiment met its most disastrous experience of the war.

Tarleton's force consisted in large part of his own Corps, the British Legion, and the 71st Regiment, and therefore must be considered as among the best troops in Lord Cornwallis' command. Tarleton himself has minimized the effect of the engagement, but it must be considered as the most severe repulse which up till that time had been inflicted upon the British regular army. The losses were over one hundred men killed and from four to five hundred taken prisoners, included among the latter being Major McArthur, Commanding

Officer of the 71st Regiment. This officer expressed the opinion that the reverse was due to Tarleton's impetuousness and his disregard for the fighting qualities of his opponents, the criticism being the first intimation of the differences of opinion between Tarleton and the officers of the 71st, differences which became greatly embittered when Tarleton, in his story of the Campaign, made comments which at least one of the officers of the 71st considered derogatory to them. Whatever the cause of the defeat, the result was serious, being one of the contributing factors, which, after the battle of Guilford, forced Cornwallis to retire to Wilmington, North Carolina, for supplies and reenforcements. With these reenforcements, Cornwallis set out from Wilmington for Virginia on April 29, 1781, effecting a junction with the British troops in that area under General Arnold on May 20th, at Petersburg. The Continental armies became heavily reenforced, and a French naval success placed them temporally in command of the Chesapeake Bay and its contributaries. Finally, hemmed in at Yorktown and outnumbered by nearly ten thousand men, Cornwallis was forced to surrender, the 71st Regiment being one of the units thus forced to lay down its arms. It had lost during the siege 10 killed, 22 wounded and 11 missing. Its place in the battle line was on the extreme left of the British position, where the British line came out to the waters of the York River. Its Commanding Officer at this time was Lieut.-Col. Duncan MacPherson; its Senior Major Patrick Campbell. Its strength was 1 Lieut.-Col., 1 Major, 1 Captain, 11 Lieutenants, 4 Ensigns and Cornets, 1 Quartermaster, 1 Surgeon, 1 Surgeon's Mate, 28 Sergeants, 9 Drummers and 242 men, a total of 300 men. It had lost over 1500 men in the years of fighting between Savannah and Yorktown.

Sent to New York under the terms of the surrender at Yorktown, the Regiment was later returned to Scotland and disbanded at Perth in 1783. It is said, that though special inducements were many times held out to the Highlanders to desert, not a desertion took place during its service in America. Major MacArthur, captured at Cow Pens, was afterwards exchanged, serving to the end of the St. Augustine evacuations, and made Brigadier General by Carleton.

The 71st Regiment now on the British Army list is not connected in any way with the old 71st, whose course has been here followed, but was formed from the old 73rd Regiment.

It seems difficult to explain the presence of some members of the 71st Regiment in the group of settlers which was brought first to Port Mouton and later to Chedabucto, after the evacuation of New York. Nor is it easy to tell how many there were. Most of the men were mustered out at Perth, in Scotland in 1783 and the Regiment was disbanded. It is possible that those who came to Nova Scotia consisted of persons who, having been detained in hospitals or as prisoners of war and on that account unable to rejoin the unit before it sailed for Scotland, had asked for the opportunity of obtaining lands in Nova Scotia in preference to returning home. If there were any officers, they were but in the lower ranks. It is fitting that their futures seem to have been bound up with those of the British Legion, for the two units had fought side by side in almost every engagement in the southern field of operations. Though the officers of the Legion and the 71st Regiment may have had their differences, there seems never to have been anything but the heartiest comradeship between the men. Whatever the explanation may have been, it seems a matter beyond doubt that a number of men of the 71st Regiment were among those who had passed a disagreeable winter at Port Mouton, and participated in the misfortune which in the spring befell the whole group.

Then, when it was decided to leave Port Mouton, there can be no doubt but that the men of the 71st divided themselves into two groups. One group accompanied Captain Marks to St. Stephen; the other Col. Molleson to Chedabucto, being accompanied in each instance by a number of men of the Legion. It seems that none of the 71st remained in Queens County.

How many of the members of the 71st were given lands at Guysborough? This it now seems impossible to say. The unit to which the grant was eventually made out was the Associated Departments of the Army and Navy, brought into existence for the express purpose of including a number of persons not otherwise provided for and who were eligible for assistance and the receipt of lands. In the records of this Department are very few comments on the history of any individual before his becoming one of the Departmental protegees and these were made only when it became necessary to distinguish one individual from another of the same name but belonging originally to a different unit. Thus, only respecting John Stewart (called Esquire, but the recipient of 550 acres, which indicates the holding of some commissioned rank) Andrew MacNeil, John MacDonald, Malcolm MacIntyre and John MacKay are there any definite statements made which indicates that they had seen service with the 71st. Altogether there were several score with names which one can readily distinguish as Scotch, but how many of these had been soldiers in the 71st it is impossible to say. A common obscurity engulfs both the members of the 71st and the British Legion, their comrades in arms. Largely outnumbered in the heterogenous mixture of refugees and their holdings scattered widely, there was not possible such a grouping as would lead to the formation of any settlement distinctly Scotch in characteristics, and not only the language but even the traditions have been forgotten. Undoubtedly there are now living in the County many persons whose forefathers once proudly marched under the banners of the 71st Regiment, but in few or no instances is definite documentary proof of the fact to be obtained.

THE ASSOCIATED DEPARTMENTS OF THE
ARMY AND NAVY

It was a little after mid-June and again transports were slowly making their way up Chedabucto Bay, laden with settlers, a little disillusioned, perhaps, but still intent on another attempt at home building. Cautiously they approached the crooked and narrow harbour mouth, threading their way between the nets of the fishermen, whose little log huts could be seen in the clearings on the hillside, in front of which the vessels must pass. It was the time of the mackerel run, and the fabulously rich harvests of the sea must be garnered in their proper seasons, even though the routine of years was being greatly disturbed by other events.

With the incoming tide the vessels entered the harbour, passing on their left the old French fort and on their right the fishing stand of Captain Joseph Had-ley, and moved to an anchorage. This certainly looked better than Port Mouton, and the work which had been done by the men of the Duke of Cumberland Regiment, which had arrived less than a month previously, seemed to bring to the newcomers a greeting and a welcome.

It is easy to picture to one's self the view which the watchers on the transport saw spread before them. There were evidences of building operations, huts and houses in all stages of construction, the commencement of wharves and piers, the little tents on the hillside, where the woodsmen's axes were busily swinging, the temporary structures on Helpman's Island, where supplies were being stored and the contents of the transports placed in safe keeping. Already the outline of the town was taking shape. Streets were being laid off, and land was being cleared. Advantage having been taken of the clearings from which the French had been driven, some attempts at cultivation might already be seen. Deep in the woods, the surveyors were laying out their lines, setting off the blocks for distribution and engaged in the multifarious tasks which must be done for the needs of a community in the process of its birth.

To most, if not to all those on the transports, this was no new experience, but one with the details of which they were well acquainted. When last, however, they had gone through this routine on the rocky shores of Port Mouton, winter was rapidly approaching, and that threat permitted no leisurely action or delay. Now the long summer was on its way, short enough indeed for all that was to be done, but allowing somewhat more leisurely and thorough construction. But there was one great difference. Whereas in Port Mouton the newcomers had been able to approach their task of home building in possession of some comforts which they had been able to amass during the weary months in New York, these had all disappeared in that disastrous fire the memory of which was still so vivid. But they had indomitable spirits, a leader who had proved that he had their interests at heart, and had succeeded in equipping themselves again with some of the materials which they knew were most needed. Governmental bounty would provide them with the food they required for some months, and they trusted to their strong arms and their stout hearts to see them through whatever they must now face.

They were persons of most diverse antecedents and experiences who now were gazing about them and attempting to gauge what their future was to be. There were trim troopers of the British Legion, in their white breeches, now perhaps dingy and worn, and their green tunics, selected so that the color would turn with the leaves as fall approached". There were men of the 71st Regiment, in their swinging kilts and their regimental tartans. There were men from the inshore naval units, boatmen and pilots as distinctively clad. There were members of the Commissary Department and the odds and ends of headquarter staffs and employees. There were women, an unusually large proportion of them in contrast with the few who had come with the Duke of Cumberland's Regiment. Children were also present in quite large numbers. There were negroes, lately slaves, now not a help but rather an encumbrance, since, freed automatically on their arrival in Nova Scotia, they but made extra mouths for their former masters to feed, without their being able to do the work which now must be performed. There were others, servants, and these too were likely to be but additional burdens in the approaching period when each man must fend for himself, and find that the task of maintaining himself and his immediate family was as much or more than many of them could do. One hundred and seven negro men, sixty-nine negro women, fifty negro children, of whom thirty-nine were under ten years of age, and twenty-four negro servants made a total of two hundred and fifty negroes in the transports slowing making their way to their respective mooring places. This was a very large proportion of the total of six hundred and ninety-five, which the transports carried. The whites numbered two hundred and seventy-five men, the wives, sixty-five, and the children, eighty-five, of whom sixty-two were under ten.

There had been little in common in the services of the various units, which made up the whole group. The Duke of Cumberland's Regiment, already on the ground, had been in garrison duty at Jamaica. These, all Carolinians, were separated from the other Carolina settlers at Country Harbour by about forty miles of untrodden forest. The British Legion, recruited in New York, had fought from Georgia northward to Virginia, taking part in every engagement rill Yorktown put an end to the fighting. Very similar had been the experience of the 71st Regiment, in the active fighting which had seen their strength dwindle from two thousand strong to a few more than three hundred. The members of the Commissary Departments had been at New York, in the more sheltered employment of headquarters. Now a common future faced them all, and experiences which might make greater demands on their fortitude and endurance than any thing they had yet met.

Over some of the other units the newcomers had at least one advantage, the knowledge that there was one who was determined that those who looked to him as their leader should have every opportunity it was possible to secure. Even before the disastrous Port Mouton fire he had been actively engaged in endeavoring to procure for those under him a better site, convinced that Port Mouton could offer them few opportunities. He had succeeded up to the present, not only in holding his group together, but apparently in inducing some men from Other units to throw in their lots with him. His rank gave him access to persons whose ear could not be easily reached by men of the line; of his energy and his interest in the welfare of those under him no one could doubt. This man was Colonel Molleson, formerly Wagon Master General at New York.

Undoubtedly persons from the Commissary Department formed the largest unit in the group. It seems doubtful if the men of the British Legion combined with those of the 71st numbered as many as three hundred when they arrived at Port Mouton. About one hundred had stayed in the vicinity and eventually were given lands. Approximately one hundred more went to St. Stephen. Allowing for the defections of some others, which under the circumstances would not be surprising, it may be that not more than a couple of score of the Legion and the 71st came to Chedabucto. Credit for service in the Legion is not given to a single person in the Guysborough records; for service in the 71st it is given to but five, one of whom was an officer.

The grant which conveyed their lands to the Associated Department of the Army and Navy, for this was the official designation of the group, was made out in the name, of Nathan Hubbill and two hundred and seventy-five others. There seems to have been an unusually high percentage of persons of commissioned rank. Colonel Molleson was given eleven hundred acres; Major Colin Campbell received one thousand and Dr. Boggs nine hundred. Other large areas were nine hundred acres to John Grant; seven hundred and fifty to Hugh Hugh, (from whom Sir Sam Hughes was descended) and Nathan Hubbill; seven hundred to John Curtis and William Gibson; six hundred and fifty to John Stewart; six hundred to Thomas Cutler and Peter Stark; five hundred and fifty to John Stewart of the 71st Regiment and James Henderson and five hundred to James Wyatt, William Campbell, (later Sir William Campbell, Chief Justice of Upper Canada) and John Clark. A private received one hundred acres. A noncommissioned officer might receive three times that much. In addition, each person received a town lot, and to some were given water lots.

Few places offer natural advantages in excess of those to be found on the hill side on which the town was laid off. This work was proceeding when the Associated Departments arrived, and already the infant town had been christened New Manchester. It extended along the western side of the harbour a distance of roughly a mile, its depth being somewhat less. Its southern border was the reserved land on which had stood the old French fort; its northern limit a grant of land made to Johnathan Binney. He, astute man, with influential connections at Halifax, had long before assured for himself some holdings in a place so promising and had obtained a grant of land at the mouth of the Salmon River and also one at the head of the landlocked harbour. His line interfered with the regularity of the town plot in such a way that the lines making up the northern and the southern limits of the town were not parallel, but converged as they approached the harbour. Four Town Divisions are grouped at the corners of the central parade, and the total number of town lots provided for was far in excess of the needs of all the incoming settlers. The Duke of Cumberland's Regiment almost without exception, were given the lots in the South-East Division, that Division most nearly approaching the harbour mouth. The Associated Department's lots were in the North-East Division, farther up the harbour. When, at a date still later the men of the 60th Regiment arrived, town lots were given them in the South-East Division. Thus the two Divisions fronting on the harbour were quite completely filled up. A few lots in the South-West Division, which abutted on the old French Cove were drawn, but some of those making up the North-West Division were distributed. Behind the town plot was a common in rear of the common were a large number of five-acre blocks, intended to be given to the negroes; in rear of these again, commenced the Front Division of the Back Lands.

Three large blocks of land were laid off, one forming the Front Lands, so-called, and two the Back Lands. It was the intention that each person be given a lot, both of the Front Lands and the Back Lands, approximately in the ratio of thirty acres in the first to seventy in the second. The lots in the Front Lands numbered two hundred and fourteen, and included about twelve thousand acres. These Front Lands commenced above the Binney Grant and extended up the southern and western side of the Haven and around the Interval. . In the rear of the Front Lands were set off the Back Land blocks, one of about twenty thousand, the other of over twelve thousand acres, to be divided up among two hundred and twenty persons. It will be seen that there are some discrepancies in the numbers, two hundred and fourteen in the one case and two hundred and twenty in the other, but this figure, with the number of the men of the 60th Regiment, make up the total who are covered by the Hubbill grant. A few received blocks of the Front Lands whose names did not appear as having been given Back Lands and some were given their allotments of farm lands who did not receive town lots.

From the method of distribution which was followed this was the situation which developed.

Those persons of the Associated Departments not included in the 60th Regiment, if they did not choose to live on their farm lots, but remained in the town, were within a very short distance of much of their Front lands, which moreover, were easy of access, since they were on the same side of the harbour and river. The nearest of the Duke of Cumberland's lands were at least five miles away from the town lots and were separated from them by the river or harbour, quite unbridgeable at that time. Most of their lands were still farther away, lying deep in almost impenetrable woods, and attainable much more easily from the Strait of Canso than from the Milford Haven side. The nearest of the 60th Regiment lands was at least five miles away, and with those also communication was made difficult by the estuary of the Salmon River. From that point, their lands stretched away in a long line, down the south shore of the bay ending about fifteen miles away. These two units, therefore, must choose whether they would develop their farm lands at the expense of their town lots, or the reverse, and the problem was decided in different ways. Most of the men of the Duke of Cumberland's Regiment left their holdings altogether. The men of the 60th, their lands being utterly unsuitable for development into farms, looked to the sea, the teeming waters of which fronted their lands, for a livelihood. The town was developed by the Associated Departments, less the 60th Regiment, and as this influence grew and the influence of the others declined, the name first given the town, Manchester or New Manchester, was gradually replaced by that name for which the Associated Departments were the sponsors. Thus Guysborough came into being, though the Township of Manchester, situated on the eastern side of the harbour, across from the town, retained its name, a name still in use.

Several of the reservations made deserve noting. It was but natural that the site of the old French fort, commanding as completely as it did the harbour entrance, should be one of these, although it was not long before permission to use two and a half acres of this was obtained, till such time as it was required for fortification. Both of the islands in the harbour were reserved, Helpman's Island (now called the Little Island) and Hog Island (now called Big Island). Shadowy tales come down to us that on the former a number of the newcomers first erected their temporary shelters'; to be used while their homes on their lots were being constructed. The unpleasant attention of Indian visitors, never dangerous but acquisitive and inquisitive, was thus most easily avoided. Reserved also was the point of land then called Smith's Point, — having once been granted to an individual of that name, — which forms the northern side of the harbour, and is now a part of the Belmont estate. In the town plot itself, the central Parade or Grand Square as it was called, was not granted and there also was an un-granted market situated about the center of the water front. At least as late as 1832, there was yearly appointed by the town an individual to take care of the market lot. The market was on what is now called Muller's Cove, after a member of the 60th Regiment, and if Colonel Molleson wished to go to the market, he had to walk but the length of a town block, while Lord Montague would have found it necessary to walk only across the front of two lots. Colonel Molleson's lot was a corner one on the center of the Grand Square; Lord Montague's about where the late E. C. Peart used to live.

From the start, the relations of the persons of the different units as between themselves, and of the newcomers with the old settlers, appear to have been entirely amicable. If there was any friction or discontent, no evidence of it appears in the records. The claims of the old settlers had been recognized and legalized; several of them in some way became the owners of town lots. Among them there were several marriageable young women, and if this were a fault, it was one which there were a number of young men among the newcomers able and willing to rectify. A young lieutenant of the 60th married one of the Godfrey daughters. "There goes Mrs. William Campbell", is said to have been the remark of young William Campbell of the Associated Departments, when first he saw Hannah Hadley, then said to have been but a bare footed girl, in the midst of her father's fishing flake on the beach, nor are we told that in after years, either Sir William Campbell, Chief Justice of Upper Canada or Lady Campbell repented of a decision so quickly made. Nor did Captain Joseph Hadley object, for it was not long before from his quite ample fifteen hundred acres, he had given a block of two hundred to the young couple, in proof of his "love and affection". The newcomers and the old may have had their differences in the legislative halls at Halifax; here there seemed to be understanding and appreciation. There were very great differences in the agricultural possibilities of the farm lands, both of the lots in the same large block and of the blocks themselves. The Hallowell Grant settlers had by far the best land from an agricultural point of view, next to them in value being the land given to the Duke of Cumberland's men. There was some very excellent land given to the Associated Departments, but a great deal of it was suitable for no more than lumbering. In the thousands of acres given to the 60th Regiment, it can hardly be said that there was one lot of uniformly good tillable land. Luck and not a neighhor was blamed for an unfortunate drawing and illwill or differences have left no traces in the accounts which have come down to us.

Not that there were no delays and inconveniences and interferences with the smooth progress of events. A surveyor, Mr. Morris, had to be sent down from Halifax to settle some surveying dispute in which the Duke of Cumberland's Regiment men were concerned. There was a long delay in connection with some of the plans, said to have been lost at sea, while being taken to Halifax for approval. Grants giving title to the town and water lots were not received till the year 1790, and there seems to be evidence both that the designation and numbering of some lots had been changed and that two separate drawings took place. But, that there ever was in New Manchester a repetition of the Port Mouton experience and another catastrophic fire loss, as one would understand from his story of the town as given by Haliburton in his History of Nova Scotia, has not been chronicled in any account elsewhere found. Though Haliburton may be most meticulously accurate in most of his statements, it seems that here the oracle was in error, the loss to which he refers taking place at Port Mouton and not on the shores of Milford Haven. Nor is the statement correct that thereafter the town was nearly deserted for some years. In connection with this event, Hollingsworth writing in 1786, only two years after the fire, is a better authority than Haliburton writing in 1829.

In quite marked contrast with some of the other units, a number of those having commissioned rank in the Associated Departments remained and had a large part to play in the development and progress of the town and the County. By no means did all remain. William Gibson sold most of his lands in 1785 and John Curtis his front lands in 1786. John Clark, whose name, with those of Thomas Cutler and James Henderson, appears on the list included in the Massachusetts Banishment Act, left no record of occupancy. What became of Henderson is doubtful. Major Colin Campbell may not have remained. Both of the Stewarts had gone by 1792. There is no comment on the presence of Colonel Molleson in the settlement, after his success in bringing about the removal from Port Mouton, but there is no doubt of his continued interest and his friendship with those who did remain. He himself is said to have returned to England though members of his family are said later to have visited Guysborough and renewed the old acquaintanceships. One of the first children born in the new town was a son of Thomas Cutler's, to whom the name of Robert Molleson was given, and thereafter Molleson is a kind of family name. The Grants remained as did the Cutlers, and in later years, if anything took place in the County in which "King" Cutler was not interested and in some way involved, one may be sure it was of very minor importance. More stayed for a time, in preparation for experiences in wider fields. William Campbell remained, studied law with Thomas Cutler, became the member for the County and Attorney General for the Island of Cape Breton and finally Chief Justice of Upper Canada. Dr. Boggs also remained for a time only, removing to Halifax, where he had a prominent position in the professional life of that city. James Wyatt, after opening up a business in Guysborough, moved to Halifax, as did Peter Stark. No record is found of Hubbill after 1792. He had married Honor Hierlihy and in that year their last child born in Guysborough was baptised. Altogether, this record is very different from that of the other units, and can leave no doubt but that the members of the Associated Department largely guided the destinies of the town and left their imprint on all that there occurred. The Rev. Peter De La Roche reported in a letter in 1788 that there were two hundred and twenty-five families then living in Guysborough and ninety-nine living in Manchester; there can be little doubt but that most of these had come with the Associated Departments.

There were some persons whose connection with any of the named units can not be traced. For instance, there was the family of James Lodge, who himself, as well as members of his family, had been given town lots. He and a certain William Armstrong had probably been attracted there by business prospects which were considered promising, and Lodge at least had a kind of meteoric career. He was the first Sheriff; he was the agent for the Hallowell estate. He owned Beechcroft, seemingly carved out of that Estate, and grants of land at Salmon River, as well as a license to use Smith's Point. But it may be that his business ventures were characterised more by energy than by good judgment. For the making of potash, large bottle necked cast iron retorts were obtained at great expense, but these were landed and permitted to rust to destruction unused on the shore. Cutting timber for lumber was attempted and a huge windmill was supposed to furnish the motive power. But the windmill

154

was not finished and the frame blew down. A vessel, the building of which was commenced at Salmon River, could not be launched and eventually rotted to pieces on the stocks, unchristened except for the name "Lodge's Folly". Finally, all his holdings, the Smith Point establishment, Beechcroft and the brig *Guysborough* were mortgaged for a thousand years at a rental of one barleycorn a year, and both Lodge and Armstrong disappear.

It is not now possible to determine what in each instance was the reason which induced these persons, roving and up to this time unattached, to throw in their lots with the builders of the new settlement. Their trades, businesses or professions may have brought some, as for instance the Morrises and the Scotts, and at a later date the Taylors, all said to have come in their capacities as surveyors. Morgan, who married Diana Hadley after the death of her first husband, is said to have been a Welsh millwright, and one of the first mills in which he was interested is said to have been on the Hadley property, on a brook east of the old Stiles Hart place. We are not told what the business was, other than that it was secular and not connected with the ministry, that brought Peter De LaRoche to the town in 1786. But he found the field ripening to the harvest, and threw himself so vigorously into the task of baptising the many who requested it, performing the ceremony one hundred and forty-six times between July 23rd and August 9th, that, when it was considered that a minister could be supported, he was asked to accept the position. So Christ Church came into being and on July 6th 1787, he entered into the pastorate, as the copperplate script of Augustus Fricke, the ex-Adjutant of the 60th Regiment, informs us. It also tells us that he lodged at the house of Benjamin Elliott, Vintner, so the town had so progressed that a vintner could be maintained, though one must wonder what he found to buy "one half so precious as the goods he sold". What brought the unfortunate Bixby or Bigsby, ancestor of a family but recently extinct, we do not know. The terse record "frozen to death on Birch Island" (supposed to be another name for the Big Island) completes his own story in 1788, and chronicles the first of many such deaths. Alas, there were too many such and of drownings, perhaps understandable if we remember that probably there were few of the settlers who were accustomed to the use of boats, now the only means of transportation and travel. The dangerous eddies of the harbour mouth, Salmon River and the Narrows all took their toll.

But in spite of such incidents, drawn by one magnet or another, the settlers arrived and undertook the task of home building. The Town and County of Guysborough thus came into being.

THE SIXTIETH REGIMENT

The war clouds were again gathering. England, which had already drawn upon every source of supply to meet the call for reenforcements for her armies, must prepare anew for the shock of battle. She must again call upon her old reserves in order to expand her scanty forces or must discover new sources from which to obtain the regiments on which her safety depended.

So, when it was suggested that in the new world sufficient man power to keep in the field four battalions of one thousand men each was to be found among the aliens from Europe who had there found shelter, action was not long delayed. The new Regiment, it was planned, would be something of the nature of a foreign legion. The recruits would be largely from those colonists of German or Swiss descent who had cast in their lot with the English among the dangers of the new world. Many of these were not wholly unacquainted with military training. Many had had experience in border warfare, and would be the more valuable on that account. They would be taught a simple drill, would be lightly equipped, would be mobile and would be trained especially to take part in the open style of fighting at which their probable adversaries, the French and Indians of the frontier, were adepts. General Braddock's defeat had amply demonstrated the uselessness of the soldier trained according to the European ideas under the attack of the skulking Indian or woodsman. The new regiment would be used largely if not wholly in the new world, against the French and the Indians, who were a constant menace on the border, but whose attacks would doubtless be made with redoubled intensity when war had been declared.

There was one objection, that of language. The British army, from its own training cadres, could not supply the officers qualified in languages to lead the alien troops. There were on the Continent, however, many Protestants with the necessary qualifications for the junior, and in fact for many of the senior ranks, who would gladly serve, if provision could be made for the employment of other than British officers in the commissioned grades.

However distasteful this might have been under ordinary circumstances conditions now were not those which permitted much procrastination or delay, and the decision was quickly reached. In December 1755, the orders for the equipping and raising of the Regiment were given, and the Royal Americans came into existence. A special Act of Parliament permitted the employment of Swiss or German officers, who were not British subjects. What loss of prestige the Regiment might suffer on this account was counter-balanced by making the Commander-in-Chief of the forces in America the Colonel-in-Chief of the Regiment. About 81,000 pounds were voted for the expenses of the Regiment. The enabling Act received the assent of Parliament in January 1756, though not before Pitt had denounced the arrangement, demanding that none but British soldiers be permitted the privilege of fighting Britain's battles.

The Earl of Loudon, then Commander-in-Chief, was made Colonel of the Regiment. It was first numbered the 62nd, but the following year it became the 50th, The uniform was red, with blue facings, made more resplendent with white lace and two blue stripes.

Thus the services of four thousand additional defenders were added to

Britain's forces, at a most critical period in her history, and thus were taken the first steps in the formation of a Regiment which since that time has upheld the military traditions of the service on many a stricken field.

It was not long awaiting its baptism of fire. Almost from the time of its formation its battle records commence. The reverse at Ticonderoga was followed shortly by the successful attack and capture of Fort Frontenac, in both of which actions the 1st and 4th Battalions of the Regiment took part. It participated in the capture of Fort Du Quesne, thus striking a blow at the French tenure of the new world which was never successfully countered. The 2nd and 3rd Battalions were present both at the capture of Louisbourg in 1758, the battle on the Plains of Abraham and the taking of Quebec in 1759, and the capture of Montreal, the final victory of the war, in 1760. At the battle of Montmorency Falls these Battalions so distinguished themselves as to obtain from General Wolfe himself permission to use the motto the Regiment still displays, 'Celer et Audax'. These were the Battalions which for a time were stationed in Halifax.

At a date still later, to the unit was given the responsibility of garrisoning the western frontier, no mean task, when Pontiac's treacherous and determined effort to oust the English from the hunting grounds of the Indian Confederacy was made. The successful defense of Forts Pitt and Detroit foiled Pontiac's attempt, and at Bushy Run, the most noteworthy instance of a defeat by an English body of troops fighting according to the accepted methods of Indian warfare, was prepared the way for his defeat and England's undisturbed possession of the vast territory west of the Alleghenys.

With the coming of peace, the 3rd and 4th Battalions were disbanded. Recruited as all its men had been from the American colonies, the presence of the Regiment in those colonies during the troublous times antedating the War of Independence was not considered desirable, especially since there was ample work for it in the conquest and protection of the West Indies. When, however, it became necessary to meet the situation arising from the threatened outbreak of hostilities with the colonies, there was added to the Regiment a large accession of strength, the 3rd and 4th Battalions being again formed, but recruited now in the Isle of Wight, where was the Regimental Depot.

After a period of service in the West Indies, the different Battalions or portions of them were gradually drawn into the struggle on the mainland. The 4th Battalion took part in the expedition to Georgia, was present at the siege and capture of Fort Sunbury, and, with the 3rd Battalion, also fought in Florida in 1778. In 1779 the 4th Battalion was at Briar's Creek, Hudson Ferry and the Siege of Savannah. In 1780 it took part in the siege of Fort Mobile and the defense of Baton Rouge. In 1781, the 3rd Battalion was at Hobkirk's Hill and some of it was at the capture of Fort George on the West Coast of Florida by the Spaniards. Finally, some members of the Regiment were present at the surrender at York Town, the deciding engagement of the conflict.

With the close of the War of Independence the Regiment had already passed through 18 years of a most eventful career. There had been in the period several changes in the Colonelcy. James, Earl of Loudon had been followed in turn by James Abercromby, Jeffrey Amherst, the Hon. Thomas Gage, and still later by Lord Amherst. Other distinguished officers during the period were the two brothers, Augustine and Marc Prevost, who commanded the 3rd and 4th Battalions during the bitter fighting in Georgia and the

Carolines. In the Prevost family is still preserved the colours of a Carolina Regiment captured by units of his battalion by the latter officer. One name which perhaps is of special interest to us is that of J. F. W. DesBarres.

DesBarres is said to have been born in Paris in 1722. He was of Swiss; descent, and joined the Regiment under the special inducements offered to foreign Protestants who had the requisite engineering training. His Lieutenant's Commission was dated 22nd of February, 1756; his commission as Captain, 23 Sept., 1775. Those who remember the story of the DesBarres family will remember the family tradition, apparently accepted by Henry J. Morgan, that the officer in whose arms Wolfe fell when he received his death wound on the Plains of Abraham was this DesBarres, afterwards the author of the Atlantic Neptune, the Surveyor of the North Atlantic littoral and the Lieutenant-Governor of Cape Breton. He died in Halifax at Poplar Grove on 27th of October, 1824. His descendants and the descendants of members of the disbanded 3rd and 4th Battalions of his old Regiment now fraternise in Guysborough County after art interval of nearly a century and a half.

While the story of the Regiment so far as the history of Guysborough County is concerned, centres around the battalions disbanded at the close of the War of Independence, its later history well repays attention. It was again made a four battalion Regiment in 1788, and took part in a large number of engagements in the West Indies. In 1797 the 5th Battalion was raised and became a special Corps of Riflemen. A 6th Battalion was added in 1799. Some of these were in every engagement of note in the Peninsular War, others being scattered from Dominica to the Cape of Good Hope. The 7th and 8th Battalions were added in 1813. In 1815 the whole Regiment adopted the green uniform of riflemen, and, when reduced again to two battalion strength, changed its name to the Duke of York's Own Rifle Corps. He was Colonel for 30 years. After his death in 1827 the Duke of Cambridge followed in the appointment. In 1830 the Regiment became the King's Royal Rifle Corps.

India and South Africa were next the scenes of the Regiment's exploits. Forty-one all ranks, with seven women and thirteen children were among the heroes of the Birkenhead in 1852. Throughout the whole of the Indian Mutiny, especially at the siege and taking of Delhi, some of its units fought, as also in China in 1860. The 1st Battalion took part in the Red River Rebellion in 1870. Detachments from it were present in Quebec in 1871, when the Union British Flag was lowered from the standard to give way to the flag of the Dominion, as they had been in 1759 when the British flag was first raised in that place. It was represented at Kabul, Kandahar, and the engagements of the Afghan War, also at the Zulu War and the First Boer War. Tel el Kebir and the Nile Expedition, Chitral and the wreck of the *Warren Hastings* were incidents in its history, with, still later, Ladysmith, its defense and relief, Talana Hill, Spion Kop and the long drawn out Great Boer War. A Regimental history refers to it as,—"a Corps whose battle honors are unequalled in number, and whose reputation for courage and discipline is unsurpassed in the annals of the British Army".

Possibly it is because of the relatively large number of persons in the battalions disbanded in 1783 whose names indicated German origin that they are sometimes referred to as Hessians. Some of the individuals may have been Hessians, but the regiment or any battalion of it was by no means one to which that term may rightly be applied.

Precisely as in the last war all Germans became eventually to be called Huns, so in the Revolutionary War the term, Hessian, was used in a more or less opprobrious way and was applied to all troops hired by England from the lesser German principalities. Six German rulers made use of this opportunity of filling their coffers. Hesse-Cassel and Hesse-Hanau supplied most of the troops, but their ruler was not alone in earning for himself the unsavory reputation of selling his men to the English. Actually, the first completed contract was made with Charles First, Duke of Brunswick, this being dated Jan. 9, 1776. Landgrave Frederick of Hesse-Cassel and his son William of Hesse-Hanau followed, sent most of the troops and drove a harder bargain for doing so.

The agreements provided for the cash payment of thirty crowns (about seven pounds) per man supplied, with the payment of a cash subsidy for each year of the war and for a varying time thereafter. The princes undertook to supply the deficiency made up by desertion and sickness, unless there was an unusual outbreak of disease or extremely heavy losses in battle or siege. The blood money clause, considered peculiarly barbaric even in those rude times, provided that if any man were killed in the service, an additional amount, approximately seven pounds, was to be paid, this amount being intended for the families of the men killed, but the princes have not been exonerated from the unpleasant charge of having themselves pocketed the amount. Three wounded men were to be paid for at the rate of one man killed. This blood money clause was not in the Anspach agreement. England was to pay all the troops at the rate usually paid to her own armies. If extremely heavy losses were met, England must make them good, and must bear the expense of procuring recruits to re-establish the contingents.

The total cost to the British Government has never been given out. It is known that the amount paid exceeded 1,770,000 pounds sterling, beyond the pay of the soldiers and expenses other than for recruiting and equipment.

The number of men brought out under these agreements were as follows,—

Brunswick		5,723
Hesse-Cassel		16,992
Hesse-Hanau		2,422
Anspach-Bayreuth		2,553
Waldeck		1,225
Anhalt-Zerbat		1,160
	Total	29,875

Of these 17,313 returned. It is estimated that 6,354 died of disease or accident, about 1,200 were killed in action or died of wounds, and there were about 5,000 desertions. This latter seems a large number especially when we remember that the difference of language made detection relatively easy, but it must be borne in mind that Congress made special overtures with promises of rewards and lands to any German who would desert. If an officer did so, and brought forty men with him, the reward promised was a grant of 800 acres of land and a number of livestock. The Duke of Brunswick sent instructions that those of his men who were guilty of crime or disorderly conduct and those unfit for military duty were to be left in America.

The distinctively German units were not numbered but were called after their commanding officers or "chefs". Their sick were to remain as much as possible under the care of their own surgeons, though British hospitals were to be open for them. The English government was to pay the expenses incurred in bringing back to a port on the Elbe or the Weser the wounded who were not fit for further service.

These were the conditions under which whole German regiments were obtained from the rulers of a number of the lesser German States. In addition to these, arrangements were made under which the British government was permitted to open recruiting offices for several of their own regiments at certain places en "he Rhine. One ventures to suggest—though no evidence of it has been discovered—that the 60th Regiment, which was known most closely to resemble a foreign legion, would be selected by a number of the Germans as the Regiment in the ranks of which they would prefer to serve. This possibly explains the presence of such a large number of aliens in the ranks of the battalion, and also their eligibility for land grants at the termination of the war.

The 3rd and 4th battalions of the Regiment which it had been decided to disband, arrived in Halifax from New York in September, 1783. It has not been possible to secure a nominal roll of the battalions as they then were, for the purpose of ascertaining how many of these eventually took advantage of the land grants offered them, nor has any information been obtained of the conditions under which the winter was passed in Halifax. It is possible that here many of the members of the units took their discharges and disappeared. In December, however, the number was added to by the arrival of another party who had set out from Plymouth, England, in the *Prince of Orange* transport, and who had been driven off the Nova Scotia coast in November. A letter now in the Archives written by Augustus Fricke from Falmouth and dated January 22, 1784, tells of his arrival there on December 8th in a most distressed condition, and begging assistance for himself and those who were with him. Another memorial dated 31st March, 1785, gives more details, and also asks that consideration be given to their claims for arrearages dating from that time. This memorial is signed by Augustus Fricke, Lewis Hulsman, Adam Uloth, Christian Wendell, Casper Rheinhold and one other, all of whom appeared to have belonged to the draft, and all of whom received lands at Chedabucto.

For some reason the men of the 60th Regiment were detained in Halifax a longer time than were others who there passed the winter and who were to be their neighbors in Guysborough County. The Montague Corps and the Associated Departments were sent away in May 1784, but not till several months later did the members of the battalions of the 60th leave Halifax. Whatever their numbers had been on their arrival in Halifax in the preceding fall, and even with those who had come from Plymouth to join the battalion, they numbered only 133 when they were mustered in Halifax by William Shaw, Muster Master on July 17, 1784. There were then 76 men, 34 women, 12 children under and 7 children over the age of ten years, with 4 servants.

Probably a short time after that they set sail for their new homes. In the party were two officers, Augustus Fricke, who was the Adjutant of the 3rd Battalion, and William Sealy, a Lieutenant.

161

Arriving in Guysborough, at that time called Chedabucto or Manchester, they found that considerable progress had been made in preparing for the new settlement. Already tents and huts and other rude habitations were arising on the hillside lying open to their view, on Nicholas Denys' old clearings near the harbor mouth, at the site of the old Indian encampment near Cutler's Cove and on the smaller of the two islets in the harbor. The clearing of land was doubtless proceeding apace, and from the shipping in the harbor lumber and supplies of all kinds were being unladen. To the south, near or beyond the harbor entrance, glimpses might be caught of the homes of some of the nine pre-Loyalist settlers, the little group of which the Hadley family from Liverpool was the nucleus. Surveying and clearing of the town site was proceeding rapidly, though not for several years were the allotments actually made, owing to the loss of the surveyor's records by shipwreck on the way to Halifax, and the necessity of repeating the work.

When the town was laid off, the planning was done in such a way, that, radiating from a central ungranted parade, lots formed four town Divisions. Of these, the North-east and the South-west Divisions were bounded by the waters of the harbor. Streets separated the divisions into areas, to each of which a block letter was given, and these in turn divided into lots of approximately 65 by 155 feet in size. There were from six to twenty of these lots in each area of which a letter served as designation.

When lots were assigned to the members of the 60th Regiment, they found them to have been given in the South-east division, in many ways, the choicest of any in the whole plot. Immediately in front of them was the harbor, wholly protected from the waters of the bay by a sandy beach or bar which almost completely closes the harbor entrance. South of them was the eminence overlooking the narrow harbor mouth, on which was yet traceable the old French fortifications of Denys and his successors. If we accept the evidence of an old French map of the year 1744, the ground they occupied was that on which the old French settlement had been located.

Their larger lots, however, did not at any place impinge upon the area comprising the town plot. These commenced beyond the old, Binney grant at Salmon River, and stretched in a long line along the southern shore of Chedabucto Bay towards Crow Harbour, (now Queensport), where they abutted on the Finucane grant. Lot No. 1 was nearly fifteen miles away from the town plot, and Lot 59 was about five miles away.

If they were to live on their town lots, their other lands were of little value to them. Without a doubt, many could not afford to do other than to attempt at once to make for themselves a living, and hence, relatively few remained in the town. Their lands facing as they did the waters of the bay, teeming with fish, offered some prospects of providing a means of livelihood. The shore line here was in many places precipitous, falling steeply to the water's edge, with the scanty soil characteristics of granitic formations or of glacial denudation. Only in a few places were there breaks in the shore line which offered shelter for boats. The whole littoral was exposed to the sweep of north or east winds. Nothing but small boats could be used, boats so small that they could easily be drawn up beyond reach of the waves. From the rough shore line their lands extended back through a thin growth of stunted spruce to the wholly barren upland, strewn with granite boulders. Only in few places was it possible to find land suitable for tilling.

It speaks well for the quality and determination of the group, that a very fair percentage of them remained to become identified with the growth and progress of the County.

It will be seen that even the larger lots were not of a very great area, only the amount, in fact, usually given to privates or non-commissioned officers. Sealy and Fricke were the only officers. Fricke obtained his land in due time, but when Sealy was to have received his apportionment, not only his life, but the lives of all his family had been blotted out in a tragic accident, which must have saddened unutterably the hearts of his neighbors and friends. His wife was a Miss Hannah Godfrey, thought to be the daughter of one of the nine pre-Loyalist settlers, who were living in Chedabucto before the new influx of settlers commenced. It would appear that they were living on the Godfrey land, not far outside the harbor mouth. A child was born to the couple in March, 1785. On the morning of October 23rd of the same year, Sealy, with his wife and child and the Nurse, Martha Gottfrey, left by boat to attend the Sabbath morning service in the settlement. Some accident occurred and all were drowned.

From the records which still exist, it is quite easy to follow the story of those who remained for any length of time on their town lots, or who remained in town, as opposed to those who moved very soon to their other lands. Perhaps the one of all who left the deepest mark in the memory of the community was the doctor, Ludovic Joppy, who for many years attended to the professional needs of the whole countryside. He was not a regimental surgeon, in point of fact on one nominal roll he is named as a sergeant. He received 250 acres of land, as did others of that rank. Drs. John McPherson and James Boggs who were surgeons of other units, received from 600 to 800 acres each. These quite soon were lost sight of or moved away from the settlement, but Joppy remained. His home eventually was made on the eastern side of the harbour, among the Montague Corp., and those who settled on the Hallowell grant. The dates of the deaths of both Joppy and his wife are unknown, but his estate was administered on in July, 1817. Since his wife was not one of the administrators, she may have predeceased him. It is said that he is one of those who are buried on the private burying ground on the old Hadley property. He left no family. A cove on the western side of the harbour is still among the older persons referred to as Joppy's Cove and there comes down to us echoes of the doings of the good little man, as, riding his mare Lively, he made his rounds among the ailing of the community. It is of interest to note that in the records of the Court of General Sessions for the year 1803, Dr. Joppy was named as Health Officer for the area.

Readers of the writings of Joseph Howe may remember his 'Eastern Rambles' and the account of his visit to Guysborough. In the issue of the Nova Scotian of August 4, 1831, is a short account of his stay in the old tavern kept by Christian Muller, whom Howe recommends to those who are curious as to the details of the Seven Years War, and insufficiently acquainted with the merits of Frederick the Great. At least one of Mullet's experiences soon after his arrival in Chedabucto and before his life had assumed the placid and pastoral quality which Howe noted, must have made this old German think that with the cessation of his war service, the moments when for him life or death hung in the balance were by no means at an end. Early in 1785, he with several men was engaged in the transportation of supplies from Halifax, and if the story is correct in all its details, there it no doubt but that anxiously indeed his arrival with them was awaited. He arrived in time, but he brought no supplies with him, but a tale of mutiny, marooning and narrowly averted death. His men had seized the vessel, and after placing him on an island on the eastern shore had gone, to sell their booty in some Massachusetts port. The long arm of the law reached them, however, and they were in time brought back to Halifax to give an account of their actions. The final stage of the tragedy was played on the shores of St. George's Island in September of the same year, when two of the mutineers were hanged. It is said that the scene of Muller's enforced marooning was somewhere among the Jeddore islands.

His name, in a somewhat altered form, is still attached to a prominent landmark on the waterfront of the town, on the shore of which his home was built. He was one of the members of the battalions who married in Halifax, while awaiting transportation to his grant, his wife's name being Ann Francheville. He had no family, but there lived with them a brother or nephew of Mrs. Muller's, named John George Francheville, from whom are descended the families now bearing that surname. Both Muller and his wife lived to a round old age, he dying in March, 1841, aged 90, while Mrs. Muller lived until August, 1846. She was 82 years old at the time of her death. For many years Muller was the Sheriff of the County, when as the County of Sydney, its confines included all the eastern portion of Nova Scotia.

Another member of this group will be remembered by those who have had occasion to examine the records of Christ Church. Such persons could not but have been struck with the sedulous care with which the first records were kept, and have noted the name of the Vestry Clerk, Augustus Fricke. With copperplate writing and with the text embellished here and there with appropriate Latin quotations, these old records do infinite credit to their maker. It is hoped that they still are in existence. Few persons in this day and generation could produce their like, or give evidence of the possession of artistic and literary abilities of a higher order. His connection with the story of Guysborough was not of long duration. During the period he was one of its residents, he too, held several positions of relative prominence in connection with the affairs of the County.

These are some of the 60th Regiment settlers who did not betake themselves to their out-of-town allotments, but became residents of the town which sprang up where the residential lots were located. The large majority quite soon moved to their larger grants on the shores of Chedabucto Bay, and there their descendants still live. One is struck with the fact that the numbers who remained in the County constituted a very large percentage, in contrast with the members of some of the other regimental units. Possibly their long stay in Halifax had weeded out very effectually all the fainter hearted; possibly they were better colonizing material; possibly the fact that there was a large number of married men, accounts for this. In this latter respect this unit contrasts most sharply with the Montague Corps, very few of whom brought wives. This latter Corps petitioned the home Government that wives be sent out to them from England, but found that match-making was not considered within the purview of the Colonial Department. The result was that many of them moved away, leaving little trace of their presence in the County.

There is still another reason why the 60th Regiment settlers may have made a better showing as regards the number of them who remained on their places than did the other units. The 60th Regiment lands were almost wholly unfitted for agriculture, except for scattered patches here and there among the granite boulders. The waters of Chedabucto Bay, however, bounded their lands, and these waters teemed with fish. A few miles to the east of their limits was Fox Island, where the mackerel fishery was of a richness which almost exceeded belief. Few of their numbers could have been expert fishermen, but one did not have to be an expert in order to procure at least sufficient fish to keep one's self from starving. It took a much longer time and much more preparation before one could clear his land, however fit for cultivation it was, and be independent on an allotment in a better agricultural district. Many quailed before the slower and more tedious task, and moved away to seek other conditions. The members of the 60th Regiment stayed on, and while opulence or even comfort was in many cases denied them, they at least never found conditions so unbearable that migration or removal became for them a necessity.

Drab enough to many would appear to be the story of these settlers since that time. One pictures to one's self the steps by which they painfully made their way, the erection of log huts and the development of the little clearings, though indeed there were many lots on which there could be found between the precipitous shore line and the granite barrens not sufficient level land for even the tiniest of farms. Some were more fortunate, and found little patches suitable for their needs, where here and there brooks had through long years made their way down the hillside and deposit miniature deltas at the base. Especially near the head of the bay is the shore line precipitous, almost unclimbable, so that road building was no easy task. A road from Guysborough to Crow Harbour was ordered to be laid out in 1805. It was to cost no more than 60 pounds. It has been impossible to determine when the first road was made to traverse the length of the district. The first obtainable reference is to a bridge which was made over a brook at Half Way Cove, in 1800, which bridge was to cost no more than three pounds. Some kind of a road, costing no more than 60 pounds was built in 1805, but not till 1824 was there a road passable for carriages through the district and on to Canso.

Shelter having been obtained and paths or roads completed, the erection of the first church was undertaken, a little chapel in the parish of which Christ Church in Guysborough was the centre. Here, on land said to have been donated by William Bedford, was built the first of the churches, the present being the fourth which have successively been called the Dutch Churches. Around it are clustered many of the graves of the pioneers, their days of warfare over, the harbour gained at last. Other denominations gradually obtained foothold; schools followed, but slow and tedious indeed must have been the progress. Ever down the hillside from the little houses strung along the heights, the waters of Chedabucto Bay, mirror-like in calm or a heaving and seething cauldron when the east wind brings into it the surges of the Atlantic, have provided at times a begrudged and reluctant, at times a plentiful harvest, gathered however, not without an infinitude of forethought and labour and toil. Nor has the toll been always so easily paid, for the sea has claimed many of those who in their childhood days, watched from a vantage point in safety the riot of the waves, or marvelled at the cloud-flecked mirror below them.

But since the sea is what it is, these hardy and simple folk have persisted, have contributed the toil, braved the danger and paid the price, have learned if not to love, at least to endure without complaining, their existences so drab. They early learned how to construct for themselves their tiny boats, from the product of the nearby forest. The handicraft of the boat-builder may be observed in the fittings and furniture of their homes. Their wants for many years were of the simplest description, and few indeed were the calls on the factory or the shop. Knitting their own nets in the winter evenings, fashioning the rude 'killicks' which served as boat or net moorings, constructing their own lobster pots or other fishing equipment, tending their gardens or cultivating the sterile soil, they have passed their self-contained and peaceable existence.

Gradually around the homes have expanded the little clearings, where carefully tended gardens or none too fertile farms have given employment to those agriculturally inclined, or for those who shunned the period of enforced idleness when the harvest cf the sea could not be gathered.

And so we find them to this day, though the advent of the motor boat and the failure of the fish to return to the inshore grounds have of late complicated their heretofore simple lives.

Patient and peaceable and painstaking, they have led their harmless existences, and if at times some have rebelled at the monotony and the toil, they have done so under circumstances which call for sympathy, not criticism. So we understand why one old patriarch, whose sea experiences go back over eighty years since first he accompanied his father to the nets in the offing, rebelled at last against hauling the ungainly 'killick', and impetuously putting off in his little boat rowed ten miles to the nearest blacksmith, accustomed to the forging of iron anchors. Here he loudly declared his intention no longer of fishing with the aid of the old contrivances. Henceforward for him, none other than the forged anchor was to be used. His 'killick' days were over.

We can forgive them if we can not chronicle that from this little group have arisen some whose names have become household words in our Province or Dominion, some perchance whose diction has held audiences spellbound, whose legal talent has earned for them the respect and admiration of their equals, whose skill in treatment has made them to be honored among their fellows, whose attainments in the arts or sciences have contributed to the accumulations of an appreciative world. For them the simpler homelier attainments, the skill to man their frail craft, in which, to use their own homely expression, they feel themselves to be "as safe as in God's pocket". These belong not to the intelligentsia or the aristocracy of our Province, but are of those whom God must have loved most, in Lincoln's apt epigram, since He made so many of them.

Mention has been made of the old 'Dutch' Church. Strange transposition or miscalling that is, the result of a process of mind comparable possibly to that indicated in a Halifax experience, where again a Church is connected. Strange though it is, it is almost the only intimation apart from the foreign flavor of the names diat indicates the alien origin of the population. Years of residence under conditions which have permitted access into all the homes, and a more or less intimate acquaintance with the majority of the people have failed to elicit one story or one tradition of the home across the Rhine. There is not only no German spoken, but, within the memory of the oldest inhabitant, there never was a time when German was in use. There is no German book, there are no German traditions. The last member of the regiments died at a time well within the memory of persons now living. One remarkably intelligent and well-informed old gentleman, born in 1822 and dying but a few years ago, could give no information connected in any way with the fatherland, or could tell of no incident which served as a link connecting his ancestors with their original nationality.

Very shortly after their arrival, it appears that communication with their old homes ceased, and the old ties were soon completely severed. It seems that no other families or individuals at any time came from Germany, to throw in their lots with their friends and relatives here, as for instance did the three Jamieson brothers, who moved to the vicinity as a result of accounts sent home by John Jamieson, a Scotch sergeant in one of the battalions. There has been much, intermarriage with persons of other blood, but there must be many who are of undiluted German stock.

Nor is there discoverable any semblance of a tradition based on connection with any specified military unit. One might expect that remembrance of connection with a unit so prominent in military annals as the Royal American Regiment or the King's Own Rifle Corps might have been preserved. History tells us of the martial achievements of their comrades in arms, but these having doffed their accoutrements of war, gave or give no evidence of any desire again to don them. Possibly we would all be the happier, could we, as easily as they, condone or accept the substitution of the plow-share for the sword, the reaping-hook for the spear.

167

THE HALLOWELL GRANT SETTLERS

There was land to be had for little more than the asking. Why not ask for some?

And ask he did, this far-seeing Commissioner of the Customs in Boston, and, what is more to the point, the asking was successful. Why should it not be in his case, if any requests were being favorably received by the rather complacent body of men then comprising His Majesty's Council at Halifax? It was anxious to do everything possible to procure colonists for Nova Scotia, and if a request came, as come it did, from some eminently respectable individual, favorably known in the official circles of his own community, with connections the most irreproachable, and a position quite well assured among the favored few who, to a great extent comprised the governing class of the day, there was every reason why it should be favorably received.

And so Benjamin Hallowell was given a grant of land in the eastern portion of Nova Scotia proper, in what is now Guysborough County.

The long struggle with the French had ended in the loss of all their lands on the mainland of the North American continent. There were those who at the time may not have looked with a great deal of favor on the idea of possessing land in Nova Scotia, with its solitude practically unbroken, except along the courses of the tidal rivers whose meadows had attracted the French, or around some of the harbours of its rocky uncharted coast, within easy reach of which were the fishing grounds which had proved mines of wealth to both new and old country fishermen for scores of years. But Hallowell had had some personal acquaintance with it, and had perhaps not found it quite so desolate or uninviting a country as many persons pictured it. One son, at least, had been born in Halifax. Possibly the father's idea was to secure some portion of that terra incognita for that son, and if this was the plan, then we shall see that it was blessed with quite as large a measure of fulfilment as are many plans made in this world of disappointment. Others were applying for lands in the areas from which the French had been driven, but not so Hallowell. Assuredly he possessed information derived from a trustworthy source that not in those portions of Nova Scotia alone were there lands which were most suitable for settlement, choice uplands where lumbering or farming operations might be profitably carried on, or locations adjacent to the fishing settlements. So on October 22, 1765, the necessary formalities having been proceeded with, Hallowell became the possessor of a grant of 20,000 acres of land, situated on the north side of Chedabucto Bay and along the eastern shore of Milford Haven, this being in what is now the district of Manchester.

He would have seen far, far into the future to have been able to recognise those names. No County subdivisions existed east of Halifax. Not for twenty years was the eastern portion of the Province set apart in a County separate and distinct from Halifax County, and the first one so set-off,—Sydney County— comprised much of what is now included in both Guysborough and Antigonish Counties. Could he have seen these and other changes which the years were to bring, doubtless he would have thanked the informant for the correct information given and acted upon, and congratulated himself upon the foresight displayed in his getting his share of the spoils of the victor.

But just for the present, there were other things to consider. There were multifarious duties connected with a quite responsible official position. There were growing evidences that these ditties might be attended with unpopularity or persecution or still worse trials, as one measure after another, put in force by the authorities at home, served to increase the rapidly growing friction between the official Class with which he was connected, and the stubborn-tempered colonists in whose government he was assisting. True, his connection with this governing class was such as to make his own position quite secure, so far as help which they might give was concerned. Sir William Pepperell, the Winslows, the Boylstons, the Adams, each and all members of influential families, were some of those with whom he was connected by ties of friendship or intermarriage, but in spite of the comforting assurances derived from a knowledge of this support, one can not but feel that there must have been periods when he would have greatly welcomed some evidence of a higher degree of statesmanship at home or a greater tractability in the colonial population.

These considerations were doubtless sufficient of themselves to make impossible at the time any attempt at colonising his grant, especially so, perhaps, when to them were added the responsibilities of looking after a rapidly growing family. Eventually, there were no less than fourteen, who must be settled in life, and for whom plans must be made. Possibly, even at that time the sturdy Benjamin, Junior, born at Halifax in 1760, was intended for the Navy, for he was on active service long before most boys of his age had quit school, there to lay the foundation of a career, which even among the fighting sea captains of that day, was a notable one. Another son was destined for a very different sphere in life. For him, the tamer excitements to be found in the marts of trade, in travel and study, and finally a leisured retirement were in store, a future which was the result of a combination of the restrictions which a delicate constitution imposed and the advantages which the timely inheritance of a fortune made possible. But, separated though these two brothers were in constitution, in disposition and career, though apparently they had little in common but a common parentage, though it was their peculiar destiny that each would die, beating names distinct and different both from that of the other and from that of the parent, they eventually had one thing in common, namely, the ownership of the grant of land which their father's foresight had procured for them in the wilderness of eastern Nova Scotia.

Their concern in the property, however, did not commence till many years had elapsed from the time the grant was first made, and when one remembers that the father occupied a Customs position in the city of Boston at the outbreak of the War of Independence, one is quite prepared to conjecture that the intervening period would be one fraught with excitement and danger and changed circumstances. Probably little of personal animus underlay the intense unpopularity in which Hallowell found himself, an unpopularity evidenced by his being pursued by 160 men on horseback through Cambridge to Boston in 1774, and public indignation may have been rather against the official than against the man, but feeling ran high, and early in the conflict, it became necessary for him to seek his own safety and the safety of his family in flight. A voyage of six days, after a period spent cooped up in most cramped quarters in a victualling ship bound for Halifax,—quarters occupied by no less than 37 unfortunates like himself and family—saw them safe in Halifax harbor some time in April, 1776. In July of the same year they were able to continue their voyage to London, where the reunited members of the family found a home. Reunited they now were, for though Benjamin, Junior, was at that time on naval duty, Ward, his brother, had preceded the other members of the family to London, for had he not been sent in January of the same year, by no less distinguished a messenger than Sir William Pepperell himself, "Nicky's little spoon, your can and a pair of tongs", which family mementos, were, we must suppose, duly received. Here the family, or some of them, remained for some years. In a letter dated February 27, 1785, Hallowell announced his intention of returning to Halifax as early as possible that spring, to look after his Nova Scotia property. Whether or not he did so is not known, but it is known that he was able to revisit the scenes of his old trials and tribulations in Boston in 1796, and was there received with great hospitality. He died in York, (now Toronto) in 1799, at the home of his son-in-law, Chief Justice John Elmsley, at the age of 75. A Township in Ontario, the grant of which he had received in addition to his holdings in Nova Scotia, perpetuates his name and memory.

Let us now follow the sons in their widely separated careers. Benjamin, named after the father, was born as has been stated in Halifax in 1760. He joined the navy at an early age, and after a career which seems to be more a romanticist's imaginings than actual history, died about 1834. His naval experience was one long succession of hard fighting and brilliant achievement, in a period when fighting was plentiful and when he must indeed have been noteworthy to have merited singling out from among the crowd of sea captains, the lustre of whose doings is not yet dimmed. Read what Fitchett says about him,— "He fought in American waters under Sir Samuel Hood as a very youthful Lieutenant; cruised for sweltering months on the African coast; shared with Nelson in the sieges of Calvi and Bastia; commanded a 74 in that miserable scratching match under Hotham, called the fight off Hyeres; saw the battle of Cape St. Vincent from the British flagship's quarterdeck; took part in sieges, in desperate frigate actions, in yet more desperate boat attacks; was shipwrecked; was captured; played a shining part in the great fight of the Nile; tasted the bitterness of defeat in the second expedition to Egypt under General Fraser; and knew a still more bitter disgust by missing the great Armageddon of Trafalgar, his ship, the *Tigre*, being one of the little known squadron detached to Gibraltar under Louis just before Villeneuve came lumbering out of Cadiz to his doom. This surely makes up a very gallant and stirring record!" It does, and when to it is added the fact of his known intimate connection with Lord Nelson in a friendship which ended only when death came, Hallowell seems to occupy a pinnacle which none but he could hope to attain. The absurd physical contrast between the two has been noted, Hallowell, a gigantic figure, of athletic build and proportions, with a face indicative of humour and good nature; Nelson, small in stature, maimed of body and scarred of face. Between the two there was the firmest of friendships dating back to Calvi, where they had shared common dangers and duties in an alternating command of the batteries, and which was born of mutual understanding and respect. The intimate understanding which existed between the two is perhaps both the reason and the justification for Hallowell's having presented Lord Nelson with the coffin, which ever afterwards Nelson carried with him and in which he was eventually laid to rest, a coffin made from the mainmast of *L'Orient*, blown up at the battle of the Nile. Hallowell, in his ship, the *Swiftsure*, had contributed largely to the disaster, and his ship's carpenter, having secured the mast, made therefrom the coffin, which was sent to Nelson with the following inletter,—

"Sir —

I have taken the liberty of presenting you with a coffin, made from the mainmast of *L' Orient*, that, when you have finished your military career in this world, you may be buried in one of your trophies. But that this period may be far distant is the earnest wish of

Your sincere friend,

BENJAMIN HALLOWELL"

In the year 1828, about the time of his retirement from the Navy, through the death of his cousin, Hallowell fell heir to the estate of the Carews of Beddington, on the condition of assuming the Carew name and arms, and bearing this name, he died in 1834.

The other brother had a very different career. Born in 1749, his maternal uncle, Nicholas Boylston, prevailed on his parents to permit his taking the name Ward Nicholas Boylston on his having attained his twenty-first birthday, having promised to leave him very considerable estates in Boston. Of a sickly constitution, the active and dangerous life selected by his younger brother was barred to him. From 1773 till 1800 his life was spent in travel in Europe, and in residence in England. Returning then to Boston, the remainder of his life was spent in that vicinity. He died in Roxbury, Mass., in 1828. Boylston Street in Boston was so named after some member of the family whose name he-took, and Harvard University was largely a recipient of his beneficence.

Whether or not Benjamin Hallowell, Senior, visited Halifax in 1785, for the purpose of pressing his claims of ownership to the properties he had been granted in 1765, is not known. There is ample evidence in his letters to Edward Winslow, written during his stay in London, that he was greatly interested in the retention of them, and that he realized their value. He quotes Major DesBarres, the Surveyor (afterwards Lieut.-Governor of the Island of Cape Breton) as authority for the statement that his grants contained some land as good as was to be found in Nova Scotia; he is aware that his actual claim on the lands is but slight, inasmuch as the terms of the grant had not been complied with, but in spite of this he wishes that some arrangement might be entered into which would give him another chance of undertaking' their development.

And how, one might well ask, could he have proceeded with this development at a time when other and weightier matters, even life and' death, hung in the balance? Family ties had been snapped in the struggle. His wife's family, she being a connection of John Quincy Adams, supplied some of the warmest supporters to the cause of the Revolution. Hallowell had escaped with his life, being more fortunate than many of. his intimates, but he had undoubtedly lost in fortune and in friends, and this loss must have made it impossible for him to have complied with the terms under which the grant had been obtained. The presentation of these facts was probably the deciding factor in favor of the retention of the grants by him, for retain them he did, though the ownership was almost immediately passed over by him to his two sons, the Admiral and Ward Nicholas Boylston.

The block of land of 20,000 acres extent situated in Guysborough County well deserved any reasonable eifort made to keep it in possession. It included some miles of the north shore of Chedabucto Bay (called Gegabucto

Bay in Hallowell's correspondence) and some three or more miles of the east side of Milford Haven, which stretches practically at right angles from the head of this Bay. The extreme point where the two waters join was not included in this area, for it had been reserved from a date earlier than 1765 for Joseph Hadley, said to have been a captain of transports at the first taking of Louisbourg in 1745. Hadley had been resident on his land for some years in 1784, and accordingly was able to claim actual possession and improvement in support of his ownership, and his presence helped to enhance, in a way, the value of Hallowell's property. The latter needed settlement only in order to transform it into a most valuable holding. The fishing privileges of the north shore of Chedabucto Bay were most valuable; the land was of the best; there was plainly in view a most valuable outcrop of limestone which was early made use of by the arriving settlers, the presence of which, in fact, had been reported to the home government in Paris, long before the English possession of Nova Scotia. The adjacent country was rapidly filling up. Large grants had been made to the Associated Departments of the Army and Navy and to the remnants of the Corps named after the ill-fated Lord Montague, and the settlers on these lands had already during May and June of the year 1784 landed from the transports and commenced hewing homes for themselves out of the wilderness.

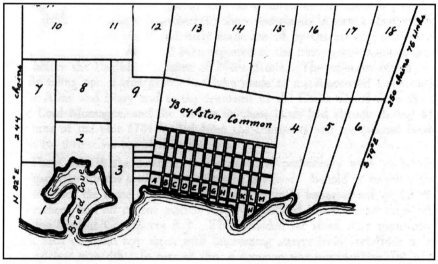

Plan of Portion of Hallowell Grant, showing plan of Town of Boylston

There was, in the meantime, very necessary preliminary work to be done in preparation for the settlers who might be obtained. Behold at length a town plot, to which the name of Boylston had been given in honor of one of the owning brothers, laid off on the eastern shore of Milford Haven about three miles from the head of Chedabucto Bay. This provided for about sixty town lots or blocks each of about five acres, with intervening streets from forty-four to one hundred feet in width. In rear of this, a common was provided for, the whole area of the town plot and common being 576 acres. The remainder of the grant was divided up into farm lots of varying size, but averaging about 150 acres. Richard Morris, the Deputy Surveyor of the Province, duly completed this task; everything was now in readiness for the settlers, and they arrived some time during the summer of 1786.

The settlers who were secured differed widely from those whose presence in the vicinity was of several years duration. The Carolinas and New York had been the homes of most of the first arrivals, before their enforced removal from the States. They were a heterogenous mixture of sailors and soldiers, of members of headquarters staffs and slave owners, of masters and servants, of persons from die most varied walks of life and of die greatest diversity of social standing. The efforts of Hallowell and Boylston to get settlers had evidently been directed towards an altogether different source of supply. The New England States, especially Connecticut, were drawn upon for the settlers of the Hallowell grant, who thus represented a strain of immigrants from a totally different source and of different capabilities. The first or older settlers included in their midst many absolutely unaccustomed to the life of the pioneer or the backwoodsman, and to diem die new situation presented difficulties which were insurmountable. Accordingly, many moved elsewhere, or made the most ineffectual attempts at procuring satisfactory living conditions.

The New England Colonists, as they are frequently called in the County records of the time, appear to have been much more adaptable or capable. True, not all remained. Some evidently returned to the States, or removed to other portions of the Province, but all who remained undoubtedly made good, some of them to a remarkable degree, and have left their imprint on the life, not only of the community in which they first settled, and in which many of their descendants still live, but on that of many communities in Nova Scotia and Cape Breton, now peopled by descendants of this stock.

The deeds which gave the new settlers the possession of their land are two in number, dated August I, 1787. They were not signed by the owners of the property themselves, but by Col. Edmund Fanning, the Lieut.-Governor of Nova Scotia, in his capacity as attorney for the owners. One of these deeds though signed by only seventeen, gives to each of eighteen persons whose names are on the document a farm block of about 150 acres for the named consideration, five shillings and the subscription to the following conditions. They were to pay sixpence sterling rent per hundred acres yearly; they were to cultivate three acres of each hundred, and to build a good framed house at least 12 by 16 feet thereon, with a good brick or stone chimney, and reside constantly therein with their families for seven years. The other deed gives to the same persons a lot in the town of Boylston. The consideration is the same. The conditions are the yearly rent of one barley corn and two shillings sterling, the latter to be paid to a Town Clerk to be appointed by Hallowell, "the sums to be by said Town Clerk applied to the purpose of sinking wells, buying pumps, erecting schools, and marketplaces and other public uses". This deed gives the name of the eighteenth settler, the full list being as follows,—

Mansfield Munson.	David Smith.
Andrew Leet.	Ira Atwater.
Gideon Bryant.	Samuel Hull.
Willis Stillman.	William Atwater.

Aaron Andrews.	Theophilus Yale.
Isaac Andrews.	Josiah Hart.
David Scranton.	William Atwater, Jr.
Matthew Hawley.	Moses Hull.
Walter Munson.	Ebenezer Merriman.

On the first of these deeds, though eighteen is the number repeatedly referred to, there are but seventeen signatures, Walter Munson's name being missing. Hallowell's address is said to be in the Parish of Marylebone in the County of Middlesex, Great Britain.

Only in respect to some of these eighteen persons is information now obtainable. Walter Munson, Hawley, Merriman, Stillman and Bryant appear not to have remained long in Nova Scotia, or at least in the vicinity of their first abode, for no record of their stay has come down to us. Mansfield Munson remained for some time, for there is a baptismal record of one child, born in 1787, after which his name is no longer seen. Theophilus Yale remained for a longer period, the last of three children baptised having been born in 1793. Retiring from his land, it was given to Colin McNair. The Hulls who arrived were father and son. Moses, the father, returned to the States after some years residence in Nova Scotia, but did not long survive his removal from the Province. The son, Samuel, married Sarah Ingram (Ingrahara) and was the father of a family of at least nine children. The eldest of this family accompanied or followed other settlers moving to the Margaree district about the year 1809. To others, the Hulls or their descendants now living in Guysborough County can trace descent. One daughter, Elizabeth, was a member of the family party of Hulls, who are said to have come from some portion of Connecticut, and it is conjectured that other members of the family remained in the States, for it was with these that Moses, the father, died. Elizabeth Hull married Stephen Pyle, in 1797, and from that union are descended the Pyles of Boylston and New York.

Many families of Leets are yet to be found in the vicinity. Six children accompanied Andrew Leet, and Submit, his wife, when they arrived in Nova Scotia, of whom five married and left descendants. The Andrews, Aaron and Isaac, appear to have been brothers, probably unmarried at the time of their arrival. Aaron married Charlotte Grant in 1793. Isaac's wife is said to have been named Lydia Potter. Both had descendants, some of whom are now living in the County.

The Atwater family, three in number, were another party who left the home of the free for a home still freer. These, too, have left many descendants, whose history is traceable in the Atwater Genealogy.

David Scranton was accompanied by his wife and one child when he came to Nova Scotia, bringing, it is said, some at least of the other settlers with him. He was a sailor, and the captain of his own little seventy ton sloop, the *Nancy*, in the intervals when farming did not occupy his attention. His acquaintance with Chedabucto Bay dated to a stay made in its waters, during the course of a trading voyage made to Quebec, and so favorable was the impression then received, that, the war being over, he left the States for the purpose of taking up a home in Nova Scotia. With him came some, if not all, the other settlers. For a number of years after his arrival, he continued to follow both his chosen vocations, farming his land, or, when freight offered and the prospects of trading allured, hieing forth in his sloop on freighting or trading voyages. He could trace his descent through Abraham, his father, Samuel, his grandfather and Thomas his great-grandfather to John Scranton, the first settler in Guilford, Connecticut, who moved to Connecticut from Guilford, England, in 1639.

David was twice married, the first wife being Phoebe Curtis of Durham, Conn. His second wife, Lorian Strong, and his infant daughter Sarah, born in 1786, accompanied him to Nova Scotia. He died on the 5th of March, 1838, and at the time of his death, four of his ten children, thirty-four out of thirty-nine grandchildren and thirty-two out of thirty-five great grandchildren, born before his death, were still living.

Not all of these were in Guysborough County, however, for this was one of the families whose members formed the group who went to make new homes for themselves in die Margaree district about the year 1809. The Margaree family altered their names to some extent, eventually, and are now known as Crantons.

Josiah Hart was a descendant of the fourth generation from Stephen Hart, born in 1605 in Braintree, Essex, England, who moved to Hartford, Conn., in 1635. With Josiah came his wife, Lydia Moss, and at least nine children, born between 1766 and 1782. The fourth son, Irad, moved to Margaree in 1809, and is the ancestor of the Harts now living in the Island of Cape Breton. Other members of the family married, and gave their names to numerous descendants, some in Guysborough County, and some in many other Nova Scotian communities, many of whom played a very prominent part in the development of the Province, in whatever paths of life their vocations have called them.

There still remains one, who is somewhat of a mystery, namely, David Smith. A person of that name, whose address was said to have been Truro, Mass., was given a deed by Joseph Hadley of enough land for a wharfing and business site in 1784. Is this the same David Smith? Most if not all the other settlers appear to have come from Connecticut. Was he a link between the Massachusetts owner or part owner and the Connecticut settlers? This seems to be a plausible conjecture, but for its accuracy no evidence can be adduced. After this one entry, he seems to drop entirely from observation, for no record of him or a family can be unearthed.

Mention has been made of the fact that about the year 1809 several of the persons whose parents moved to Guysborough County as members of the Hallowell group of settlers, removed to Margaree or to other portions of the Island of Cape Breton. This offshoot from the Guysborough settlement included members of the Harts, Hulls and Scranton families, as well as other persons descended from those arriving in Guysborough with other units. The Crowdis were of this connection, David Crowdis, the first settler, being one of the Associated Department of the Army and Navy. It is thought that the Ingrams (Ingrahams) were of this group, though little record of their presence in Guysborough, or their inclusion in any of the units there disbanded is to be found, none in fact, except that contained in the Marriage Register of Christ Church. It would appear that the Harts took a prominent part, if not in fact a leading part, in this little migration, which, if it was Guysborough's loss was a gain on the part of the Island of Cape Breton, and the whole incident of this exodus, especially if there is also taken into consideration a corresponding movement under which members of the Hughes family, (the ancestor of Sir Samuel Hughes) and also members of the Aikins family moved to Ontario, has more than a little interest attached to it. Without a doubt, had there been no Hallowell settlers, there would have been a much smaller contingent leaving Guysborough for Cape Breton, and since the latter place to no small measure has profited by the presence of these persons, we are justified in stating that Hallo-well's work in the development of his Guysborough property had results which extended to the Island of Cape Breton to a measure almost equalling that produced in the immediate vicinity of the property in which he was interested.

Col. Edmund Farming's connection with the property was terminated in 1787, James Lodge being made the attorney on July 27th of that year. Lodge was at this time a prominent business man in the newly settled town of Manchester or Guysborough, at a little later date was the Sheriff for the County, and in addition to acting as agents for Hallowell and Boylston, appears to have acted in a like capacity for at least one other English claimant for a Nova Scotian estate. Col. Fanning's removal from Nova Scotia to Prince Edward Island, of which Province he was made Lieut.-Governor in 1786, was probably the reason the change was made, though there is a little discrepancy in the dates of the first deeds and the date of Lodge's power of attorney, which is not clear. It is of interest that this power of attorney, which was signed at Chichester in the County of Sussex, England, gave to Lodge the power to take or sell 'Houses, Plantations, Lands, Hereditaments, Negroes, live and dead stock', etc., which is one of the first or only mention made of negroes as property, (except, indeed, the bills of sale of several of these poor unfortunates) to be found in the Guysborough records.

There are few changes to be noted during the period in which Lodge was the Attorney. William Nixon, a trader living in Guysborough, was given a deed for a block of 150 acres, and a block of sixty acres was divided among seven of the persons named in the first deeds. In addition to these transfers, Lodge deeded to his own son an estate of 750 acres, called Beechcroft, on which was Lodge's residence. Though Lodge was to meet with serious business reverses at a period a little later than this, the reason he relinquished the position can not now be told. Relinquish it he did, after a short tenure of office, so that on August 25, 1788, three prominent Guysborough persons were appointed in his stead.

These persons were Thomas Cutler, afterwards Custos Rotulorum, Member for the County in the Provincial Assembly and business man, John Stuart, the Registrar of Deeds, and James Wyatt, a prominent fish merchant.

During the next few years a number of deeds are recorded, among which are the following,—

172 acres given to	John McMaster	in	1790
150 " " "	Godfrey Peart		1791
150	Richard Morris		1791
150	Tyrus Hart		1791

150	Titus Luddington	1791
150	Alex Cummings	1791
150	Malcolm McIntyre	1791
150	Alex Henderson	1791
150	Irad Hart	1792
150	Tyrus Hart	1792
150	Peter McGregor	1792
160	William MacIntosh	1792
150	Edward Kergan	1792
280	R. M. Cutler	1793
150	Aaron Andrews	1793

These names did not indicate the accession of new families to the community, differing thus in a very marked way from the list which was before given. Godfrey Peart was a descendant of one of the 'nine old settlers', who had made their homes in Guysborough before the arrival of the Loyalists, and who probably had moved to Chedabucto from Liverpool some time between 1780 and 1784. Morris, Cummings, McIntyre, Henderson, McGregor, Macintosh and Kergan were members of the Associated Departments of the Army and Navy who had received other apportionments with that unit in the distribution of lands which took place after their arrival in 1784. The Harts and the Andrews had both received portions of the Hallowell land by former deeds. R. M. Cutler was the son of Thomas Cutler, one of the attorneys, and was at this time only nine years old. Luddington seems to have figured in other deeds of property, under which a change of ownership took place, so that of all on the list, only one, John McMaster, seems to be a new name in the history of the settlement.

In the year 1794, a supplementary power of attorney was given by Hallowell to Stuart and Cutler, Wyatt having in the interval returned to Halifax. Complaints had evidently been made that the old authority restricted the attorneys in their endeavors to comply with the instructions given in private letters, and it was the intention of the second instrument to make good the defects of the first. Reference is made to the fact that thirty-four lots had been conveyed away by Hallowell previous to November 1793, which number corresponds with that above given, exclusive of Beechcroft. Instructions were given to sell ten or fifteen more lots and one-fifth of the blocks in the town of Boylston. This power of attorney was executed in London, being attested to by Paul LeMesurier, Mayor of London, at the Manor House.

In accordance with these instructions, lots were sold to the following pet-sons,—

150 acres deeded to	John Peart	in	1794
150		Lee Hart		1795
113		Wm. Frederick Pape		1795

110	John Stuart	1795
90	Thomas Cutler	1796
150	Lewis Hulsman	1795
188	Wm McCarty	1795
186	Alex. McKay	1795
140	John Conrad Demas	1795
100	Robert Carr	1795
150	James Bruce	1795

Of these, the land deeded to Lee Hart was the same block which had previously been deeded to Gideon Bryant, it being evident that Bryant had not complied with the terms of his agreement. Peart was another descendant or was one of the 'nine old settlers'. Pape and Hulsman had been given lands in 1784 with others of the 60th Regiment. Stuart, Cutler, McKay, Demas and Carr were among those whose names are included in the list of the Associated Departments of the Army and Navy, and McCarty and Bruce were members of the Montague Corps, (The Duke of Cumberland's Regiment) who had been given lands in Manchester. Lee Hart was another descendant of Josiah Hart, so that again this list does not indicate that successful efforts had been made to induce settlers to move in from outside districts or counties, in order to take up land.

And surely it is very excusable if for a period of years after this, there is no information of Hallowell's active interest in the property. These were indeed stirring times with him. He certainly had done everything in his power, everything that it was reasonable to expect that a man could do, to encourage the development of his land. The years which had elapsed since his taking over the direction of it had not been idle years for him. Possibly he was discouraged at the meagre results of his efforts, possibly it was a sheer impossibility for him to continue to combine the oversight of this faraway encumbrance with what was undoubtedly the main object of his life, namely to fight and beat Old England's enemies, wherever they were to be found. Not always did he beat, but at all events, he tried to do so, with very much the same tenacity of purpose which we think can be traced in his efforts with his Nova Scotian lands. But see how full were the next few years in his life, and wonder not that for a time at least his thoughts were fully occupied.

In 1795 he was present in his frigate, the *Lowestoft* in the fight off Genoa under Hotham. There, he had been forced to endure for nearly an hour the broadsides of the great French seventy-four, the wind having failed and made his escape impossible. Hallowell, finding this to be the case, sent all the crew of his frigate below, but the man at the wheel, and then, with his lieutenant, paced up and down his quarterdeck, while the broadsides of the enemy, to which little reply could be made, were hurtling through his rigging or sweeping his decks. A change of wind permitted his drawing away, very much bedraggled, but fortunate to have escaped so well as that.

He was promoted the same year, and given the command of the *Courageuse*. While her commander it became necessary for him to attend a court martial, leaving his ship for the purpose. The time was December, 1796,

179

the place the Bay of Gibraltar. A sudden storm came up. His ship was torn from her moorings. To escape her falling into the hand of Villeneuve's fleet, the officer in command steered towards the Barbary coast, on which the ship was driven during the night. Of the 600 officers and men on board, only 129 escaped, those few having scrambled to safety along the insecure bridge made by the mainmast of the ship, which, in falling, landed on the rocks, high up on the shore.

Thus losing a seventy-four, he was given a frigate, the *Lively*, which he commanded till transferred to the *Swiftsure*, under the flag of Nelson himself. In her, he took part in the chase of Bruey's fleet across the Mediterranean, and the discovery in Aboukir Bay. Far to the rear when the French fleet was first sighted, it was after dark when the *Swiftsure* was able to join the fight. Hallowell had given the sternest orders that not till each ship had anchored in her place in the line, her sails been clewed up and he had given the word, was a shot to be fired. His ship was struck and holed seriously in passing the fort, and went into action with the pumps going and four feet of water in the hold. Joining the fight, she passed the *Bellerophon*, going out of action disabled after an unequal contest with the gigantic *L'Orient* of nearly double her guns, and the *Tonnant*. Hallowell promptly took the place in line which had been vacated by the *Bellerophon*, dropped anchor, clewed up his sails, and then from a distance of 200 yards, opened fire on the *L'Orient* and the *Franklin*. For an hour he fought. Then the French ship caught fire. Soon it became evident that she must blow up. Hallowell suddenly closed his ports and awaited the shock. It came, showering his vessel with burning fragments. Nine men escaped from the *L'Orient*, picked up by Hallowell, than whom, none of the British fleet fought more nobly that day.

After refitting his ship, she was detailed to guard the Egyptian coast while Nelson sailed for Naples. In March 1799, Hallowell joined Nelson at Palermo, and then took part in the siege of St. Elmo, and later the same year operated with him in the Italian coast.

But this stern fighting did not always have the ending that Hallowell wished. In 1801 he found himself in the *Swiftsure* in the midst of a French squadron composed of four ships, equal in size or larger than his own, and a frigate. He fought till fighting was no longer possible, and then surrendered, and thus it came about that the ship which is inseparably connected with Hallowell's fame flew the French flag in the contest off Trafalgar. It took bitter fighting by her old comrades in the English fighting line, before she was restored to English ownership at the close of that eventful day.

The cessation of hostilities which the Peace of Amiens brought about in 1802 released Hallowell from his parole. The interval had seen him honorably acquitted for the loss of his ship, and soon after hostilities broke out again he was cruising on the African coast in the *Argo*. Transferred to the *Tigre*, his ship joined Nelson's squadron and chased Villeneuve's to the West Indies and back. He missed Trafalgar, his ship having been detailed for some detached duty at Gibraltar, just before Villeneuve quitted Cadiz. He was one of the few officers who returned from General Fraser's expedition to the Nile with a creditable record, and, had others performed their tasks in the way Hallowell performed his, the result might have been vastly different. In 1809 his ship was one of the English squadron which was the cause of the destruction of three of the finest men-of-war remaining to the French after Trafalgar. In the same year, his boats led in the boat attack in the Bay of Rosas, which resulted in the capture or destruction of eleven French ships, under the guns of the French forts and in spite of the musketry of the defending troops.

In 1812 he was in the *Malta*, perhaps the finest eighty gun ship afloat, and while serving in her in the Mediterranean, one of the next incidents in the story of the Hallowell grant was enacted. For some reason or other not now discoverable, it had become necessary or advisable to change the personnel of the attorneys, so a deed was drawn up on October 27, 1813, appointing Benjamin Vaughn and John Merrick of Hallowell, Maine, and Foster Coffin of Boston, his attorneys. Vaughn was probably a family connection, either of Benjamin Hallowell, Senior, or of Robert Hallowell, the Admiral's uncle. Merrick is unknown at this time; Coffin was in all probability a member of the family which had given so many members to the Loyalist cause, and which included among others the General John Coffin who died, a Loyalist refugee, near St. John, N. B. Under the provisions of this agreement, Vaughn appointed Lieut. John Elmsley his substitute attorney. The document is stated to have been made out by 'Sir Benjamin Hallowell, Rear Admiral, now serving in the Mediterranean, and Ann his wife', and was witnessed by Capt. Charles Adams of H.M.S. *Invincible*, and Arch Murray, Purser of H.M.S. *Malta*.

Again, for a period of years, no record is to be found. There is a reference to a grant, made in September 1807, of 6000 acres conveyed to Rear Admiral Hallowell and Ward Nicholas Boylston, which grant was probably made to confirm them in the title to the balance of the original lot, all of which had not been distributed. As the years passed away, the joint owners evidently found it desirable to divide the balance of this undisposed land between themselves. Partition deeds were accordingly prepared, Hallowell's share of the whole being one third. This partition took place about 1826, and in the same year a deed from Hallowell to Boylston conveyed to the latter all of Hallowell's interest in the third which the partition deeds had given him. Thus Hallowell's connection with the property ceased.

Two years after, the estate of the Carews of Beddington fell to him, a welcome gift, since his retiring allowance was not a large one. Though, as he states, it might have done him more good had it come to him before he became "old and crank", it was doubtlessly thankfully received and heartily enjoyed during the period of life which remained to him. Six years of the restful quiet of a fine old English manor house were his before the end came in 1834.

In the meantime, Boylston was proceeding with the full direction and control of the property made necessary by Hallowell's withdrawal. R. M. Cutler, a son of Thomas Cutler, was appointed attorney on April 13, 1827. Boylston, too, was approaching the end of his allotted span. It was fitting that his last act in connection with it was one quite in keeping with the record which one or both owners had consistently maintained, one evidencing a genuine desire for the well being of the community, for whose existence they doubtless held themselves responsible. In August 1827, a town lot in Boylston was conveyed, a free gift to the inhabitants, in order to assist their efforts to provide for the education of their children. He died in 1828, at his home in Roxbury, Mass.

His Executors,—and the name of at least one of them will compel attention —were John Quincy Adams, Nathaniel Curtis and the widow, Alicia Boylston. In the days when it was the custom for a person to choose the executors of his will from among the most trustworthy of his friends, he must himself have been a person worthy of note who could aspire to the honour of having as an executor the President of the United States. This was the position that John Quincy Adams, the sixth President, was holding in 1828, which was the date of Boylston's death. Surely, in his own way, Boylston must have possessed qualities or attainments which in other spheres of action might have secured for him a position as assured as was that of his brother. What changes a comparatively few years had wrought! It was not long since Boylston's father had quitted Boston, a refugee, his life endangered, his property sequestrated. See now the son, reposing in the confidence of the head of the very nation which had been founded as the successful result of a resistance to the authority to which the father owed and gave allegiance.

R. M. Cutler was again made the attorney for the estate by these executors, and by him the last transfers of property were made. The fast recorded one seems to be one which was made in 1834. With it, the story of the Hallowell grant, as obtained in the records of Guysborough County, is complete.

THE ST. AUGUSTINE LOYALISTS

Lured by the hope of finding that spring, the waters of which would confer upon him everlasting youth, and presumably eternal happiness and content, Ponce de Leon, sailing from Porto Rico in 1512, entered the harbour, later to be known as St. Augustine. The spring was not found; the gift of eternal youth, of perpetual happiness and bliss was denied him. Instead, there had been placed upon the pages of history the first notices of that locality which to art extent probably not surpassed by any in the New World, was to witness scenes of misery, suffering, unhappiness and death.

Other places, as it, were to experience battle and siege and the cruelty of the conqueror. Other places were to know the refinements of Indian ruthlessness and the horrors of Indian revenge. Other places were to be ravaged by swaggering pirates and cutthroats or to be sacked in international strife. At other sea ports slave laden ships were to arrive and their cargoes were to be scattered, after the obscenities and indecencies of the slave block. Other places were to be selected as sites for the reception of prisoners and parolees and to know the miseries of the captive. All of these were to be St. Augustine's lot, with the added experience, of concentrated and venomous religious hates and cruelties reminiscent of the Spanish Inquisition. Blessed by nature though it was, man was to make it, not a place of happiness but one of misery and suffering, not an Eden of bliss but a place the name of which was for years to reek with the memories of man's inhumanity to man.

Hate eventually colonized it, laying the foundations of what is the oldest city in America, the hate being that of the Spanish Catholic, resentful of the French Huguenot's attempt to escape from the persecutions of the old world and to make for himself a new home across the Atlantic. The massacre of these French at the St. John's River by the Spaniards marching from St. Augustine in the early years of its settlement was one of the first expressions of that hate.

The slaughter of the French, "not as Frenchmen, but as Lutherans", immediately invited reprisals, duly undertaken by De Gourges, who slew several hundreds of the Spanish, "not as Spaniards, but as traitors, robbers and murderers." Sir Francis Drake sacked it in 1586; Captain John Davis in 1665. The coming of the English under Oglethorpe to Georgia in 1732 was the signal for more fighting, for disputes over boundaries and for raids and counter raids. One writer has said that during the first Spanish occupancy, the town of St. Augustine had been so often burnt, (though not on these attempts had the Fort always been captured) that it became as easily lit as a cigar. Such was its history till the British occupancy after the year 1763.

The treaty of Paris brought this about, and the English immediately attempted to consolidate their position. For administrative purposes, the whole district was divided into East Florida, with its center at St. Augustine, and West Florida centering about Pensacola. A number of English settlers were brought over, and since these were in no way concerned in the quarrel between the northern colonies and the mother country, their sentiment was continuously and unhesitatingly Loyalist, the only disorder being when John Adams and other revolutionaries were being hanged in effigy. Since the colony was in peace and prosperous, it became one to which the persecuted Loyalists of the Carolinas and Georgia made their way, and it received, it is said, over

7000 of population from those sources. Almost its only war activities were due to its being the recruiting ground of the Florida Rangers and those resulting from the necessity for the protection of its borders, against raiders from Georgia. Moreover, it was being so strongly held by the British, that St. Augustine was considered to be a place to which could be sent for detention as prisoners or parolees a number of persons from the Carolinas or elsewhere who were considered hostile to the British interests. Thus, Cornwallis sent a number of persons from South Carolina to the parole camp or the dungeons of St. Augustine, after the battle of Camden.

The years between 1776 and 1781 are said to have represented the high tide of Florida's prosperity. There was little or no division of sentiment in the population on those questions so bitterly being contested to the north. The Indians were as a rule friendly to the British. Its settlers were accustomed to making livelihoods for themselves, and were living under conditions with which they were quite well acquainted. There was ready sale for their products which the war to the north had prevented from getting access to the English markets. If what we are told is correct, during those years more progress and prosperity were experienced than had taken place during the whole period of the Spanish occupancy. This happy conditions was destined not to be long maintained.

England, then fighting almost all of Europe, had among its foes the Spaniards, who still resented the loss of Florida, exchanged for Havana at the peace conference of 1763. In 1781 the time seemed opportune for them to endeavor to recapture it, and a blow struck at Pensacola, was, through an accident unfavorable to the British defenders, successful. With the loss of Pensacola went the loss of West Florida, so that there remained in the British control only East Florida, including St. Augustine. Then in the fall of the year came Yorktown, the surrender of the bulk of the British forces then in the field, and, virtually, the end of the war. There remained for the Americans only the mopping up process. The Carolinas were over run; Augusta was lost and finally orders were received by Governor Wright in Savannah to prepare for the evacuation of that city. This was carried out in July 1782, though strongly protested against by Governor Wright. The British regulars were sent to New York and Col. Brown with what remained of his unit were sent to St. Augustine. But, though the British resistance in Georgia had thus disappeared, there seemed to be little evidence of a desire to carry on the mopping up process across the Florida border, and no intimation that the British occupation of Florida was to be disputed. Apparently the Florida settlers, refugees from the Carolinas and Georgia; were not to be molested, and could look forward to an undisturbed possession, under British rule of the lands where they had found and were maintaining freedom from persecution.

But, in England's long history there are many instances where she has treated her own with a measure of severity or ruthlessness as great as she has meted out to her enemies, instances where the best interests of her own have been sacrificed for some national benefit, actual or imaginary, sometimes to placate a nation for the time being dubiously friendly, at other times without even that motive to explain the action. The Florida refugees had established for themselves and for England a community in which there was less discontent and disaffection with the home government than there was in any portion of North America, except possibly Ontario and Quebec. Here at least was a place where a Loyalist was not in constant danger of insult, injury, persecution or perhaps death and where his property was not in peril of confiscation. The condition had been achieved not without suffering and loss, on the part of those who had finally succeeded in crossing the State borders, and not without fighting, strife and bloodshed as the protection of those borders had been maintained. In many instances refugees had reached safety having lost all their possessions, barely arriving in Florida with their lives. From seven to eight thousand persons in due course had settled there, driven out of the Carolinas and Georgia, and had formed a number of communities, entirely loyal, quite untouched by any suspicion of disaffection or revolt, and determined to remain so. So impossible did it seem for any disloyal sentiment to gain headway, that to Florida for guarding and safe keeping had been sent the prisoners and disaffected from other States.

Imagine, then, the consternation with which these persons heard in 1783 that in the peace which had been prepared, the privilege of their remaining as British citizens in Florida had been denied them. Florida had been exchanged for the Bahama Islands. England undertook to remove from Florida within eighteen months, those of her colonists who desired to leave. The dubious safety of a West Indian island, the hardships of beginning life anew in some far remote and unknown Canadian Province, the transfer of their allegiances to Spain, or their throwing themselves on the mercy of those who had ousted them from their possessions in other States were the choices allowed them.

Britain's bargain thus uprooted a number of prosperous and growing settlements and drove from their homes about seven or eight thousand men, women and children, most of whom had already suffered severely for their adherence to their Loyalist opinions, who had proved their value as colonists and who now found themselves consigned anew to the task of hunting for themselves some spot where safety and the opportunity of making a livelihood was to be permitted them. To many it meant a death sentence. The retention of Florida, thus given up for one of the minor West Indian islands, might have altered the whole course of history on this continent. It is doubtful if a worse bargain was made in the entire story of England's bargaining experience.

The three evacuation points in the Southern area were Savannah in Georgia, Charleston in South Carolina and St. Augustine in Florida. Some of the evacuees were passed through all three of these, shuttled from one to the other as plans changed. Thus, at Savannah, on July 2, 1782, there still remained about three thousand persons, two thousand white and one thousand colored, all those who could do so having already gone. The Governor of Georgia protested strongly against the evacuation but was overruled. Some of these persons, mainly those belonging to some of the fighting units, went to New York. These were mostly the garrison troops. The South Carolina Royalists, King's Carolina Rangers, Royal North Carolina Regiment and North Carolina Highlanders were first sent to Savannah, and after a time, returned to St. Augustine. The East Florida Rangers arrived at St. Augustine, it is said, without first having been sent to Charleston.

This meant that there was an addition of about ten thousand persons to the population of St. Augustine, of all three places the least able to care for such an influx. The evacuation authorities could with difficulty maintain order. The seven or eight thousand persons who had been maintaining themselves only with some difficulty, had to care for an influx of ten to twelve thousand persons, a large number of whom were colored, and all of whom had had their sense of moral values blunted by years of lawlessness and strife. Food was scarce and became more expensive. There was not enough housing for the incomers. The few who had succeeded in making a living for themselves saw the values of their properties deteriorate under the rapidly rising living costs. Since all were to go, there were none to buy, properties and slaves were lost, values disappeared and financial ruin was the lot common to all. Had the Officer in charge of the evacuation been less able, the situation might have got entirely out of hand. This officer was Major MacArthur, formerly of the 71st Regiment and captured at Cowpens, but exchanged and again on duty. Carleton thought so highly of his ability and the results he brought about that he promoted him to the rank of Major General.

Eventually about seventeen or eighteen thousand persons passed through the St. Augustine evacuation center. It is possible to trace about ten thousand of these, the rest disappearing, literally to the four winds. About three thousand went to the Bahamas. Jamaica took about one thousand. At least three thousand, possibly many more, went to unoccupied portions of the lower Mississippi Valley. About eight hundred and eighty came to Nova Scotia, seven hundred and twenty-five white and one hundred and fifty-five colored. There remained at the end of the process only about four hundred and fifty persons content to transfer their allegiance to the incoming Spaniard.

The first transports for Nova Scotia left St. Augustine on October 28, 1783, with part of the officers and men of the South Carolina Loyalists and the King's Carolina Rangers. From time to time other parties were sent out, as shipping became available. St. Mary's Bay and Stormont in Guysborough County were the destinations of most. At this latter place there were ultimately grouped members from at least three of the military units which had been recruited among the loyal residents of the Carolinas and Georgia. These units were the King's Carolina Rangers, the Royal North Carolina Regiment and the South Carolina Regiment. Other vessels left in April, June and October, 1784. Long before that time, those whose duties were to take charge in Halifax of the thousands of incoming Loyalists must have become pretty well steeled to the appearance of human misery, as ship after ship unloaded its distressed cargo and sailed away for more. Of all the arrivals, history has recorded that the group of about two hundred and sixty, both white and colored, which arrived in Halifax from St. Augustine on July 29, 1784, in the Argo, was the most pitiable, their poverty and distress the greatest. It is well that there were no more, to face the disappointments and disillusionments of Mount Misery in Stormont or sufferings, hardships and privations on the shores of the Strait of Canso. And one is tempted to think that, if there were some who here decided on leaving the transports and not proceeding to the Strait of Canso, they made a decision which was fortunate indeed for themselves.

In the absence of definite information, it would not be surprising to know that in this group there was a larger proportion of women and children than there were in many of the arriving groups. These settlers represented a complete section of an uprooted population, a section entirely different from many composed only of soldiers and their families. If it numbered two hundred and sixty on its arrival in Halifax, an idea of the extent to which it soon dwindled through deaths and removals, is gained from knowing that, when at last the long awaited grants were made out, there were but forty-eight heads of families named as being given lands.

The extent to which the members of this group had war records in the conflict now brought to a close it is difficult to say. Florida had been the recruiting ground of the Florida Rangers, which, under the command of Colonel Thomas Browne, had been in the field almost from the commencement of hostilities. When Savannah was evacuated by the British on July 2, 1782, Col. Browne, with what remained of his unit, was sent to St. Augustine. But the numbers who went north were small, only several hundred, and this is much smaller than the number which at one time or another during the years of war, had been in the ranks of the Rangers. Browne has stated that he recruited over 1,000 men, for the units with which he was from time to time connected. Credit for service in any particular unit is not given in any of the existing Guysborough records, nor is any rank, either commissioned or noncommissioned, referred to. Browne's name does not figure in the grant, nor the name of any commissioned officer. Perhaps to this is due some of the hardships which the settlers were to undergo. A forceful officer might have been able to secure for the settlers somewhat more favorable treatment, and that Browne had been such a forceful officer none can deny.

He had made himself one of the most feared and hated of all the officers who fought on the British side in Georgia. A Scotchman and an Indian trader near Augusta before the opening of hostilities, he had been one of the very first victims of Revolutionary mob rule in the State. In the year 1775, having made a remark in ridicule of the leaders of the growing opposition to British rule, he had been arrested, tarred and feathered and driven in a cart drawn by mules around the streets of Augusta. It is also said that, in the additional effort to make him recant his statement, his feet had been stripped and exposed to a fire. A few months later he was to appear at the head of the Rangers, which he had raised in Florida, and from that time till the end of the war, there was no more determined or ruthless fighter in the field. During most of the war, he commanded the British forces in Augusta, a post which he held successfully till 1781. Captured when the city at last fell to the Continentals, he was exchanged and again appeared at the head of his command. He was in Savannah when the evacuation of that city was ordered in 1782. It is said that he died in one of the islands of the West Indies, after a lengthy and honorable career.

The distressed shipload brought in to Halifax Harbour on the Argo have been called the St. Augustine Loyalists. It will be seen that they comprise a group—fortunately a very small one—entirely different from any of the thousands who were moving northward, now that victory had crowned the banners of the Revolutionaries, The other could be divided into two classes. In the first group were the military men whose regiments were being disbanded and whose services were no longer required by England in her armies. Many of these were married and there were a number of children. In the second class were the civilians, whose property had been confiscated and who had been proscribed and banished by the action of the American authorities. The St. Augustine Loyalists belonged to neither one of these groups. They were Loyalists, or had been Loyalists, when they fled from the Carolinas or Georgia to Florida, but now they were something more, made refugees by England's own action. Their status more nearly approached that of the deported Acadian French, who had been driven from Nova Scotia about thirty years previously. But even in comparison with these there was an important distinction. The necessity for national or provincial security could be argued in extenuation of the removal of the French, an alien population, giving little promise of assimilation with their neighbors. The St. Augustine Loyalists had been almost as ruthlessly uprooted, though they were not aliens, but the staunchest of England's supporters, sacrificed for a fancied national advantage.

This being the case, it may reasonably be expected that their status might have been recognized, and that some preferential treatment might have been given them. What actually occurred was this, that difficult though the lots of the Loyalists were, it is probable that none, as a group, suffered the hardships and privations which these were called upon to face.

One does not have far to seek for the reasons. Lack of leadership was probably one. There seems to have been no person with the rank equivalent to that of a commissioned officer, who might have had either the intention or the ability to procure for them the opportunities for which surely they had a right to ask. A forceful leader might have done much, might have assisted them in selecting their lands at some more favorable place. Colonel Molleson had done this for the British Legion, after it became plainly apparent that the first site given the Legion was entirely unsuitable. Lord Charles Greville Montague was another officer who had shown his interest in the future of the corps with which he had been connected. The St. Augustine Loyalists sadly lacked the assistance which such a leadership might have given. Then they formed a small group, unimportant so far as size went, hampered by a degree of poverty which had marked them out among the thousands of arrivals. Their small size limited the weight of any protest they might make; their poverty limited the equipment which they were able to gather, for their comfort or even for their survival. Undoubtedly, the earlier arrivals had selected the choicest sites and what remained for the late comers were sites which others had passed by. The slaves which were brought with them, but added to their burdens, hindrances rather than helps in the tasks so different from those which were routine on a southern plantation. The site might have been used to very good advantage by a group of persons accustomed to reaping the harvest of the sea, but this was far from being the means by which they had been accustomed to make their livelihoods. And, once they had accepted and entered upon their lands, communication with Halifax was so difficult, that there was little prospect that any application for another site would be given consideration. So far as is known, not a single individual from the whole of the county met the members of the Commission appointed to consider Loyalists' claims after the war was over.

It is not now possible to say who it was who was responsible for the selection of the lands to which they were sent. It does not seem reasonable to suppose that any persons from the group itself did so. It is quite likely that the first view any of them had of the sight of their future homes was that which they obtained from the deck of the transport which brought them from Halifax. In order for one or more appointed to act for them to have been able to visit the site for the purpose of preparing a report upon its suitability, it is likely that a vessel must have been sent from Halifax for that express purpose, something quite improbable indeed.

What were the thoughts of these settlers when first grouped together on the deck of the transport, they were shown the land to which their destiny had led them? They had coasted along the eastern shore of the Province, rounded the rocky group which forms the Canso Islands, crossed the flaring mouth of Chedabucto Bay, at length to anchor within the southern reach of the Strait of Canso. Ahead of them was the deeply cut passageway of the Strait, its upper end hidden in the folds of the hills. On the right were the wooded shores of Cape Breton Island, mile upon uncounted mile of untouched forest growth. Much the same prospect presented itself on their left, though there the ground rose more sharply than it did on the Cape Breton side. It was autumn, and the densely wooded hardwood ridges were masses of color, bringing into relief the dark greens of the spruces and firs. Did their thoughts carry them back over the years of buffetings, of their searchings for peace and security? The hillside, densely wooded from crest almost to high water mark, seemed to have decked itself in colors in honor of their arrival. Did the very difference in aspect bring to their minds their Florida homes?

Eventually there was laid out for them a tract of 8,450 acres, though not for several years were the surveyors through with their work and the grant signed. Forty-eight persons were named in the grant. The negroes did not receive lands. The names of several widows are to be found on the list of grantees, though how long these had been widows it is difficult to say. Their husbands may have died on the passage up from Florida, or during the interval between their arrival and the completion of the grant. Most of the lots were of one hundred acre size, long narrow lots, extending from the shore line up over the hill. The largest block was one of four hundred and fifty acres, conforming in size with the area usually given to a noncommissioned officer with a wife and family, and fifty acres less than what was usually given to a regimental ensign, the lowest commissioned rank. There was no town plot, nor were any lots corresponding to town lots given out.

Naturally they would be interested in any evidences of former occupation of the lands now coming into their possession and also of the whereabouts of their neighbors. Of the first there was little or none. At Pirate Harbour, further up the Strait, there may have been some remains of a temporary fishing camp, since its Indian name, "the place of Flakes" seems to indicate its use by fishermen, probably during the French regime. It is a tradition in one of the families of the Acadian French, that, several members of the family who had escaped the English dragnet, had lived for several years in the woods, at some place along the shore of the Strait. So far as is known, these are the only two hints of occupancy by other than the Indians, prior to the incoming settlers. Of their neighbors, they would certainly know that a large number of persons had preceded them and were building homes and settlements at Guysborough and Manchester at the head of Chedabucto Bay. Nearly twenty miles of untrodden wilderness separated the St. Augustine group from these other settlers, while the distance by boat was much greater, involving, as it did, the distance down the Strait and the whole length of Chedabucto Bay. Across the Strait of Canso, the nearest settlement was at Arichat in Isle Madame, the old French fishing station, well satisfied with the coming of peace, since this brought to it an assurance that a repetition of John Paul Jones' disastrous raid, at least for a time, was not again to be dreaded. There were probably a few families at Canso, sharing with the "nine old settlers" of Guysborough, the distinction of being the only white persons living in the County, when the Loyalist-laden transports commenced to land their cargoes.

The transport dumped its load on the narrow beach and sailed away. There was much to be done. Already it was fall, and very few days remained for the work which must be done before winter had the settlers in its grip. Shelters had to be constructed hastily, homes for the settlers themselves and protection for the winter's supplies. Was it realized that structures which would have been adequate in their old southern homes would be of little use in the winter now rapidly approaching? Had the settlers any conception of the rigorousness of that winter and what suffering it was capable of bringing to them?

There is little or no detail of the experience. Even tradition does not provide many clues. It is not known how many perished from cold, disease or starvation. Only one story seems to be well authenticated, having been told so frequently that one must accept it as true. In the desperate situation in which they found themselves as spring approached, some of the men resolved to seek aid from Arichat. The Strait was filled with ice, solidly packed by the tides for the time being, but a dangerous and untrustworthy bridge indeed. It sufficed, however, to allow them to travel all the way to Arichat, where a supply of potatoes was obtained which enabled them to ward off starvation, till other supplies could be secured. Thus aided, the survivors won through what must have been an unforgettable winter. The story of the later development of the settlement is another tale.

A NAMING AND A MAN

When new settlements are springing into being almost over night, one foresees that the quest for suitable names would occupy much attention. Can anything be then more natural or more laudable than, that he whose name was written large in all the doings attendant upon the very existence of the settlement should not be overlooked?

So there was a Guysborough Township in the western portion of the Province of Nova Scotia, now almost forgotten, and a Guysborough Town and later a Guysborough County far to the east. Another appeared in Ontario. And there were Carletons, either alone or as Port Carleton, which, if they did not intend to honor the individual, served to bring into remembrance the family. There were Dorchesters, when additional honors had been given to Sir Guy; there were others, as Maria, in honor of his wife; Effingham, after his father-in-law; Strabane, in honor of his birthplace; Claremont, in memory of the Irish fortress of which he had been made Governor; Rothes or Rothesays, in honor of the Earl of Rothes, in whose Regiment the foundations of Carleton's military career had been laid; and Basingstoke, to perpetuate the memory of the place to which he retired, after his eventful and honorable period of public service had been completed. More than forty places arose, the naming of which serves to remind us of Sir Guy Carleton, Lord Dorchester, surely proof beyond cavil that his name was for years a household word throughout the length and breadth of the land, for whose very existence and survival he deserves a large mead of credit.

Guy Carleton was born in Strabane, Ireland, in the autumn of 1724. His father, Lt.-Col. Christopher Carleton, was descended from a family whose deeds for England had won in recognition the title of Viscount Dorchester and an honored grave in Westminster Abbey. When but 14 years of age, the father died, the mother marrying the second time the Rev. Thomas Skelton, under whose guidance and direction young Guy's education was carried out. The profession of his father, that of arms, was his choice, and his introduction to military life followed upon his being made an Ensign in the Earl of Rothe's Regiment in 1742, at the age of eighteen. Three years later he was made a Lieutenant, and with that rank his Continental experience began. In 1747 he was at Bergen of Zoom, cutting his way to safety through the same gate, where later his son, George, Lt.-Col. of the 44th Regiment, was to be killed in 1811, carrying the same sword which his father had used over sixty years before at the same place.

When a Captain, in 1756, he was selected, on the recommendation of General Wolfe, to be sent to the Continent again when the Seven Years War broke out. Here he served under Prince Ferdinand of Brunswick, experiencing the varied fortunes of the British which marked the early stages of the war. Then Wolfe, Carleton, Amherst, Boscawen and Saunders were laying the foundations of the careers which were to be rounded to fullness on the banks of the St. Lawrence.

Recalled from the Continent in 1758, he found himself to be one of the officers selected by Wolfe to take part in the final attempt to oust the French from North America. But at this selection, King George demurred. Carleton at some time had made some remarks derogatory to the Hanoverian troops, King George's special proteges, and this had not been forgotten. But Wolfe insisted and would not be denied. The outcome was that Carleton accompanied Wolfe to Halifax on the General's personal staff, performing his duties so satisfactorily, that within a month after the fall of Louisbourg a promotion to the rank of Lt.-Colonel was given him.

The winter of that year saw Carleton in Halifax on garrison duty, while Wolfe was in England, desiring above all things that the opportunity of serving his country be again given him. With avidity, therefore, he accepted the offer of the command of the troops to be sent to attack. Quebec, though he would have preferred duty on the Continent. This time, Pitt took care of the objections again raised in opposition to Carleton's employment and the friends and comrades in arms sailed together. To King George's credit it can be said that never again was there any evidence of hostility, and Carleton from this time on had no firmer friend.

At Quebec, Carleton's actions were again of moment, paving the way for the final result. His duty of protecting the fleet during the dangerous passage of the Traverse, below the lower end of the Island of Orleans and the mainland, was efficiently carried out. He commanded at Point Aux Trembles, twenty miles above Quebec, when sixty prisoners were captured. At the battle on the Plains of Abraham he commanded a Corps of Grenadiers and was wounded. Wolfe, alas, was no more.

The winter of 1759-60 was spent in Quebec on garrison duty. The spring months saw the desperate attempt of De Levis to oust the British from the fortress, and its failure. Then, England's need for soldiers drew him across the Atlantic for service at the attack on Port Andrew. There, though again wounded, he was given the rank of Major-General on the field. He served during the siege of Belle Isle and its taking in June of that year, and was given the rank of Colonel in the Army in 1762. Thereafter, accompanying Lord Albemarle to Cuba, for what was to be the successful attack on Havana, he commanded the party which captured Morro Hill, making the taking of Morro Castle possible. The cessation of the war was brought about by the peace of 1763. Carleton had risen from Ensign to Colonel during the period.

The appointment in 1766 as Commander-in-Chief and Governor of the Canadian Provinces ended the humdrum experience of garrison duty, but welcome though this might have been, he might well have paused before accepting the new position. No one, perhaps, more than he, knew its difficulties. In Quebec were from sixty to seventy thousand French who had become British subjects under the provisions of the Treaty of 1763. Their tradition during a hundred years had been one of hostility to England. Their religion, since they were almost without an exception Roman Catholic, was one almost proscribed in England. Even then there were either audible or palpable the indistinct rumbles of the coming conflict with the colonies to the south. Fresh in the minds, both of the English and the French, were the memories of what had occurred in Nova Scotia, which had resulted in the Acadian French being scattered over the Atlantic seaboard, an act of unsurpassable cruelty in the minds of one group, as in the minds of the other group, it was at least proof of a shameful incapacity for government. Was it possible for anyone, in the short period for preparation which he might have, to overcome the traditions of a century, to make British citizens of those whose every instinct was one of hostility to the British Crown, and firmly to establish the British supremacy among a people differing in religion, in race, in custom, in laws and in thought?

One cannot step to follow the steps by which the transformation was wrought, but carried out it was, a very triumph of the "perfectly absurd, the utterly impossible and vain". Step by step the stings of defeat were mollified and soothed. Step by step confidence in Carleton's fairness, justice, patience and inherent kindness was built up. Step by step concessions were wrung from the home Government, which were prompted by a sense of justice and of goodwill, which could not but meet the approbation of all, French and English, Protestant and Catholic. In vain was the clamor of the older, the English colonies, jealous of their presumably favored positions, and resentful of the favors given to the newest addition to the family. In the midst of factional disputes, with an embittered and hostile population on the one hand and on the other a group almost as unreasonable in their insistence upon what they considered their rights, hampered by extremists both in Canada and England, Carleton slowly but surely made his way. The French Catholic was made to feel as secure in the exercise of his religion as was the English Protestant. Justice was as free to the one as to the other. His arms, wrested from him after the defeat on the Plains of Abraham, were given back to him, willingly received for protection against any common enemy. His legal rights were assured to him, and his customs were respected. The Test Act was removed and the halls of Legislature made open to him. So were the foundations for the development of a national life in understanding and good will well and truly laid.

But other matters than affairs of state and national policy occupied Carleton's attention during this period. He went to England in 1770. He was then forty-six years of age and a busy and eventful life had given him few opportunities for the development of a family life. Lady Anne Howard, the daughter of Lord Effingham, was his first choice. But, she, alas, preferred Christopher Carleton, Colonel Carleton's nephew and Aide-de-camp, and refused Sir Guy's offer of marriage. Very indignantly, Lady Maria, Lady Anne's sister, when she heard that Guy's offer had been spurned, gave Lady Anne a piece of her mind, and declared that she had refused a man who was too good for her. Carleton, made aware of this, became interested in the younger daughter, with the result that they were married on May 22, 1772. Although Lady Maria was but nineteen years old, less than half as old as her husband, the union has been described as an ideal one, and no shadow of discontent or regret marred the companionship destined to last for many years. Nine children were born to the couple, of which seven were boys. No fewer than six of these ultimately died in the King's service, five in the army and one in the navy. Little wonder it is that the desire of the seventh to enter the army was more than Lady Maria could willingly consent to, and eventually he became a clergyman. A promotion to the rank of Major-General was a very acceptable present on the occasion of Colonel Carleton's marriage.

Carleton returned to his Canadian post of duty in 1774, having in the interval been instrumental in the preparation and passage of the Quebec Act, which was finally accepted by the British Parliament. On the provisions of this Act, not only his own future but the future of all Canada was to be determined, and the testing time was swiftly approaching. A few days before he landed, representatives from a number of the American colonies met at Philadelphia and about six weeks later the Declaration of Independence was accepted so that the break had finally come. Almost as the Quebec Act was going into effect, on May 1st, 1775, the firing at Lexington widened the breach between England and the southern colonies. Then, before Carleton could muster even the little forces which were at his disposal to protect Canada, the taking of

Forts Ticonderoga and Crown Point proved that in addition to the campaign of persuasion already entered upon by Congress to lure the French from their allegiance, Carleton must be prepared to repel actual attack. Soon St. Johns was occupied by Congressional troops. Then Montreal was taken, and Three Rivers submitted. Only the fortress at Quebec, in all Upper Canada, withstood.

Carleton had early hastened to Montreal on the outbreak of hostilities. His return to Quebec was made under the greatest of difficulties and he narrowly escaped capture. Now he must organize the defence of Canada, and attack, he knew, was the surest defence. But soon Montgomery was at the doors of Quebec and the fate of Canada was hanging in the balance. But he, unfortunate man, died before the guns of Bairnfair's batteries and four hundred and twenty-six of Arnold's men were captured by a lucky stroke. Then in May, the coming of the King's ships forced the closing of the siege and the remnants of the attackers hurried homeward. With them went the temporary occupants of Montreal, and Canada was cleared of all the invaders, who left even more rapidly than they had come. And, wonderful though it be, the presumably disaffected French, who had been wooed so carefully and from whose help so much had been expected, had actually helped in speeding the unwelcome guests.

But Carleton wished more. The Continentals controlled Lake Champlain with a flotilla of sixteen vessels mounting a hundred guns and carrying about seven hundred men. Carleton resolved to attack these. But he must first build his boats and his vessels, in many cases in sections so that they could be carried to the launching place, must obtain and train his crews, must painfully collect and transport his supplies, must drag boats and equipment up the rapids to within striking distance. A three masted vessel was built in a little over a month. By prodigies of effort the work progressed and in October he was ready. The story is soon told. The result of a vicious attack which lasted for only three days, resulted in the capture or sinking of all the Continental fleet but three vessels, with the second in command and a Brigadier-General taken prisoners, the evacuation of Crown Point, and the Lake being entirely in possession of the British. This opened the way for the attack to be made through New York during the following year.

The year had been a good one for him. He had been given a knighthood for his defence of Quebec. The invaders had been completely routed. His policy had been vindicated, for his French friends had helped to contribute to the result. Next year he hoped for still greater things.

But Lord George Germain thought otherwise. Family or political influence had raised him to the position of principal Secretary of State for American Affairs, in spite of his having been court martialed for cowardice on the field. He was now Carleton's superior officer, and Carleton had been one of the officers who had appeared against him at the court martial. He had already attempted to have Carleton removed from his position. Now Carleton found himself being censured for not having attacked Ticonderoga. Most of his troops were removed from his command and he himself was superseded, General Burgoyne having been placed in charge of the operations of the ensuing year.

Carleton's resignation immediately followed and he returned to England. That King George did not consider the charge of incapacity seriously was proved by his immediately being given the appointment of the

Governorship of Claremont, which carried with it a pension of a thousand pounds for life, but for the four years, while matters in America were going from bad to worse, he was denied the opportunity of service.

In 1782 a change came. The very day which saw Germain relinquish his office saw Carleton made Commander-in-Chief of the British forces in America. Yorktown had to all intents ended the fighting. Though the Commander-in-Chief, his duties were more those of a Peace Commissioner. In that capacity it fell to his lot to gather up the wreckage of the long drawn out war, return the troops to duty elsewhere or to disband the Regiments, to relieve as much as possible the distresses of those who throughout the war had been faithful to the British cause and whom a victorious and enraged populace were persecuting with venomous hatred, to collect those desirous of leaving the country and find suitable locations for them, to provision those who were starving, and to gather up the broken debris of the fight, humans as well as material. There were about 35,000 persons for whom it was necessary to provide. They were scattered along the Atlantic seaboard from New York to St. Augustine, persecuted, deprived of their possessions, homeless and the objects of an unreasoning and implacable hatred. Slowly the task proceeded. As transportation became available, they were moved to the places of their selection. The large majority went to Canada and there commenced life anew. But of all that great throng of the broken and the dispirited, the poverty stricken, starving and persecuted, there were none whom Carleton's ministrations did not reach and assist.

The evacuation of New York occurred in the fall of 1783. One must think that the weary task was ended with feelings of relief. With the last remnants of his staff and the sweepings of the unfortunates of all nationalities and creeds and colors, who during the many years had been faithful to the British cause, Carleton went first to Halifax and later to England. He remained in retirement till 1786 when again there was need for his services. Canada again needed him. On April 17th of that year he was appointed Governor of Quebec. In August he was made Lord Dorchester and in October he was sworn in at Quebec as the Governor-General of Canada.

That post he occupied for about ten years when he requested permission to resign. Consent being finally given, he sailed for home with his family, but, as if Canada was reluctant to allow him to depart, shipwreck on the island of Anticosti delayed the final severance. The party made its way to Halifax, whence another vessel of the navy returned it to England. The appointment as Colonel of the 15th Dragoons, from which Regiment he was transferred to the 14th Dragoons in 1802, awaited him.   This was his last official appointment.

It was given to him to enjoy some years of quiet retirement, first at Kempshot near Basingstoke and at Stubbins near Maiden Head, before the end came suddenly on November 10, 1808. He had then attained the age of 84 years. His wife outlived him twenty-nine years.

In the naming both of the settlement at Port Mouton and that one on the shore of Chedabucto Bay in honor of the then Sir Guy Carleton, one sees the influence of Colonel Molleson, who had been one of the members of Sir Guy's staff in New York. Manchester the latter settlement was first named, in honor of the Duke of Manchester, father of Lord Charles Greville Montague, but as the members of the Montague Corps scattered and the influence of Col.

Molleson and his former associates gradually increased, the older name was superseded by that now in use.

Did Lord Dorchester ever visit the little settlement which had been so proud to do him honor? The late James S. MacDonald of Halifax insists that he did, quoting the authority of an article prepared by the Hon. Hezekiah Cogswell in the year 1854 which appeared in the British North American Post. The especial purpose of the visit was to acquaint himself with the progress being made in providing educational facilities for the children of the settlers, and the name of the teacher then employed was John Maxwell. The visit, he insists, was made while the H.M.S. *Dover* was being prepared to take his party back to England after the Anticosti wreck.

But according to Murdock, Lord Dorchester arrived in Halifax in the Earl of Moira on August 15th and sailed for England on the Dover on the 30th, arriving there on September 19th. Would it have been possible for him to have made the trip from Halifax to Guysborough and return in less than two weeks? It is doubtful if at that time there was even as much as a blazed trail between the two places.

If he did so, he was the first English Governor-General to visit the town, the last before him, and he French, being Frontenac in 1689.

THE POLITICAL HISTORY OF GUYSBOROUGH COUNTY

The Act which resulted in the delimitation of Sydney County, from one of the subdivisions of which Guysborough County was later formed, is Chapter Five of the Acts of 1784. The same Act provided for the representation of the County by two members, in the Local Legislature. Another Act of the same year provided for the establishment of a Court of Common Pleas, sitting the second Tuesdays of May and October later changed to the second Tuesdays of February and August.

Up to the year above given, the County of Halifax comprised almost the whole of the eastern half of Nova Scotia proper. Sydney County was declared to be that portion of the Province east of a line following the St. Mary's River from the sea to a point at or near the present location of the town of Sherbrooke, and from thence continued northerly in a compass course to the coast line on the Gulf of St. Lawrence. The name was chosen in honour of the then acting Secretary of State, Lord Sydney.

In the whole area east of Halifax, it was supposed that approximately 2,000 of the total Provincial population of 20,400, were settled. The session of the General Assembly which passed the Act referred to was the Seventh Session of the Fifth General Assembly, and, its duties having been completed early in December, 1784, it was dissolved in the October following, preparations being very shortly commenced for the election of representatives for the Sixth General Assembly.

For once, at least, the political trumpets failed to arouse any enthusiasm among those whose presence in the new County was of such short duration. More important and pressing problems were theirs at the time. They were too actively engaged in preparing shelters for themselves to give any time to any except the most pressing duties, so we need not be surprised to learn that, to two persons who had little or no connection in any way with the County, was given the political honour of being the County's first representatives. That, however, it aroused some interest, we know from the records of the House of Assembly. Anthony Stewart protested against some procedure, but the protest was not sustained.

So far as personality or prominence or ability was concerned, the County had little reason for adverse comment. J. M. Freke Bulkeley was the talented son of the Provincial Secretary of the Province, although the budding promise of a useful and honorable career was destined to be withered by an early death. Though young in years, he was most influentially connected, and he bade fair, by reason of those connections to be so placed as to be able most adequately to protect the County's interests. His colleague, also a young man, could boast of a descent no less noteworthy. His father was the Judge James Putnam, (a connection, by the way, of General Isaac Putnam's), who had the reputation of being one of the most distinguished lawyers in America, at the time when his adherence to the Loyalist cause resulted in his being driven, a refugee, to seek asylum in Nova Scotia. John Adams had been a student with Judge Putnam, and arose by the very cataclysm to which the latter owed his fall. He (Judge Putnam) was made a Judge of the Supreme Court of the Province of New Brunswick in 1784, and died a few years afterwards.

James Putnam, Jr., was therefore a descendant of a family as distinguished as was that of Bulkeley himself. A graduate of Harvard University in the year 1774, he was, at the time of his election to a seat as representative for Sydney County, a Barrack Master in Halifax. He became later in life an executor of the estate of the Duke of Kent, and moving to England, there died in 1838.

So far as the records of the Assembly go, there is little reason to think that Putnam at any time during the session bore his political honours other than lightly. We must remember that the Assembly of that time differed vastly in ideas, in construction and in importance from the institution with which we are acquainted today. It may be said that among the comparatively small number of the class who controlled the Provincial destinies, there were men abler on the platform and in administrative positions than is the average Nova Scotian of the present time. There was then no party system. There were only the 'ins' and the 'outs', the 'ins' of the time being the party of privilege who looked on the governing of the Province as a right or privilege peculiarly theirs. The commencement of a friction or clash between these members of the older governing cheque and the newer arrivals in the Province might be traced, but was not yet of importance. The late comers were perhaps no less able—possibly, since they were a selected group, they were more able—and they seemed to have treated the 'Bluenoses' (which name they gave to the older residents) with a certain amount of condescension, till their preponderance in numbers eventually handed over to them the control of the Province. There were a few sharp passages, and the debates over the impeachment of the Judges gave evidences of a division of opinion, but Murdoch characterizes the period as one of the halcyon periods of the Province 'when the only fancy line of division was owing to fretfulness of Lawyers who were unsuccessful in some of their litigated suits'.

It is to be surmised that the County, while these two members held their seats, had a representative in each of the classes above referred to. Both were born in the purple, so to speak, and could almost look on their admission to the governing class as theirs by right of birth. But Putnam, as one of the later arrivals, would probably sympathize more strongly with the sentiments of his late companions in misfortune, while Bulkeley, as instinctively, would be inclined to appreciate the viewpoints of the class with which he was intimately connected. We really have little definite knowledge concerning Putnam's attitude, for his name is to be found on few of the records of legislation of the time, and he appears to have borne lightly the burdens of his legislative position.

Bulkeley, however, early proved himself to be one of the most influential members of the House, leaving a very firm imprint upon the doings of the Assembly. His natural ability, added no doubt to the advantages of a prominent official connection, was the justification for his being appointed Provincial Secretary in 1792. Under any circumstances, when the time for the dissolution of the Assembly arrived in 1793, his position among the leaders of the members of the Assembly was an assured one. He died in 1796, much regretted, leaving behind him an honourable and creditable record, one which, no doubt, his Sydney County constituents had followed with interest and pride.

The election of 1793 determined that others than Bulkeley and Putnam, promising or highly connected though they were, were next to enjoy the honour of representing the County. At the election were returned two men, who unlike the former representatives, could claim to be a part and parcel of the movement which had resulted in the settlement, and was carrying on the development, of the County. To John Stuart and Thomas Cutler, both residents of Guysborough, was then given the support necessary to have placed in legislative positions two residents of the County, interested in its welfare by reason of every tie which could make the County's interest their own.

John Stuart, a member of the disbanded 71st Regiment, Registrar of Deeds for the County, then or at a later date one of the attorneys of Admiral Sir Benjamin Hallowell and his brother, was a prominent member of the colonising band to whose efforts the settlement of the County was largely due. To him, and to Thomas Cutler, an equally prominent member of the community, was thus given the honour of being the first of the County residents who represented the County in the deliberations of the Assembly.

So far as the drawing of party lines was concerned, little change seems to have taken place in the interval. We may assume, however, that both these men would favor, should the necessity for deciding arise, the newcomers rather than the old. So far as can be determined, there were in the whole County but a very limited number of persons, to whom the term 'bluenoses' in its original significance, could be applied. These could not have numbered fifteen heads of families in the year 1784, and while there may have been more in 1793, when Stuart and Cutler were returned, their numbers could not have greatly increased. Almost without exception the inhabitants of the entire County or at any rate the southern portion of it, in which both members lived, were refugees. Questions of privilege, and clashes over the qualifications of some of the holders, of responsible positions arose during the course of the Assembly debates, but these questions made the only line of cleavage yet discernible, though this cleavage was destined to become more distinct with the advancing years, and ultimately was to crystallize into the present party division.

For the present, the House of Assembly was serving the needs of a Province not so populous as are some of the Counties at the present time. Estimated as numbering about 20,000 in 1784, the population of the Province had not greatly increased in 1793, and the whole of Sydney County had not more population than some of the Municipal Districts of the present day. It was not the amount of sessional indemnity which at this time led men of rather exceptionable ability to offer themselves as candidates for legislative honours. The pay of the out of town members was ten shillings a day, those living in Halifax serving for nothing. The difficulties of travel to Halifax must have been a deterrent for those living at some distance from the capital, who were forced to proceed thither on horseback or by vessel. An election once obtained, the member continued to represent the County for a longer interval than now, for the life of a Parliament was seven years.

If at the time, there was little evidence of party friction, there were certainly occasions when the course of action to be followed by the Province was decided only after careful debate and consideration. France and England were at war. There was much uneasiness in the Province occasioned by its defenseless position, an uneasiness much justified by the constant danger of unwelcome visitations from lawless privateers. The militia was embodied on several occasions, and a position of constant watchfulness had to be maintained. Both the representatives were prominent members of the County Militia, and a letter is in existence from the Governor (Governor Wentworth) which proves the temper of the times, and the constant dread of the recurrence of disaffection among the Indian population. "By the Schooner *Friendship* I send you 50 lbs. gunpowder, 100 weight Shot, 100 lbs. lead, 200 flints, 100 yards baize, 20 blankets, 20 shirts, 20 coats, 20 trousers, 30 jackets and undervests, 20 yards blue cloth and 20 barrels of flour, all of which I beg you to distribute among the Indians." In addition, the purchase and distribution of 200 bushels of potatoes and 20 barrels of herring ss authorized. In return, they are expected "to be faithful to the King, and to take arms with us in case of invasion. All those that are in the district have so engaged. Major Monk will command them. If any man refuses this just testimony of loyalty and love to his country, whether Indian, Acadian, British or Blackman, let him depart to Old France, whither I will certainly send him, when his recusance is established."

The time for the elections of representatives for the Eighth Assembly came around, and brought about a change in the membership. Again the members chosen were from among those who were quite prominent in the Loyalist group, though for some reason or other the electorate did not see fit (if indeed the old ones offered) to return those who had formerly been honoured. Neither of the two new members, Joseph Marshall nor William Campbell, was present at the first meeting of the Assembly on February 20th, 1800. Indeed, one wonders little at this, when the difficulties and dangers of travel are considered. In the opening sessions of the Assembly the necessity of a road to connect Antigonish and Manchester with Halifax was commented upon. If, in order to attend the Assembly the members for the county were forced to proceed to Halifax by a vessel, running in the passage not only the dangers attendant upon a perilous winter sea voyage, but that of possible capture by a privateer, it were indeed marvelous had they been present.

Captain Joseph Marshall,—if we give him the rank by which he was referred to in the rolls of the Country Harbour settlers, his later rank of Lieut.-Colonel being that held in the County Militia,—was one of the members of this Assembly, he being the first of a number from the family, to be honoured from time to time by the County electorate.

Originally one of the settlers of Country Harbour with other members of the King's Carolina Rangers, lands totalling about 1,100 acres had been given to him. The difficulties of making a prosperous settlement in that locality were great, so that many sought homes elsewhere within a few years. Among those who left Country Harbour was Captain Marshall, who moved to Manchester some time about the year 1794. The regimental rolls refer to Captain and Mrs. Marshall, and one son, Joseph, (Joseph Henry) who is named among those under the age of ten years. Another son, John George, was born to them in 1786. The age of still a third son has not been found. The very outstanding ability which some members of this family possessed has been widely transmitted through some of the branches and evidenced in far wider fields. It was given to several of them to honour not only themselves but the County in their terms of office in the Local Legislature, and a great grandson, Sir John G. Bourinot is known still more widely.

So far as personal achievements go, still more can be said of the other representative, William Campbell, who then entered upon a career which was destined to lead him far. Already he had seen many vicissitudes of fortune. For some time he had been a prisoner with the Revolutionary forces. While the records do not so say, his original unit may have been the 71st Regiment. He had been given lands at Guysborough which totalled 500 acres, together with a town and water lot, and he is said then to have been a Quartermaster. He married shortly after arriving in Guysborough, and with his former comrades in arms, commenced the task of home building. Where he picked up his legal knowledge it is impossible to say, but he had some, and some assurance as well, if any credence at all is to be placed in the story of his first lawsuit, outside of the narrow sphere of Guysborough practice. There was need in Sydney, Cape Breton, of a legal opinion on some knotty question, and a vessel was sent to call at some of the neighboring settlements for a lawyer, Guysborough was reached in the search, and Campbell responded. He went to Sydney, settled the difficulty, and came back, not only the better off for a substantial fee and a free trip to his home, but having made so favorable an impression that a connection was established which was very valuable to him in later years. The steps by which he became Sir William Campbell, Chief Justice of Upper Canada can not here be followed.

If these gentlemen had any pronounced political leanings the record is silent. It has already been said that party government, as we now understand the terms, was largely a development of later years. There may still have been some friction between the later arrivals and the 'bluenoses' proper, and if so, the Sydney County representatives, if they followed the obvious course, probably lined up with their friends, whose experiences had been similar to their own. In place of party lines, differences of opinion were expressed over matters which would not now be considered worthy of inclusion in a party platform. There was a growing opposition to what was considered a clique at Halifax. But for the time being, and at least during the first session of the 8th Assembly, the war with France overshadowed other considerations, and minor differences remained submerged in the presence of what was of more moment.

This same year was memorable for at least one incident which deserves comment, namely a visit made to the town of Guysborough by the Lieut.-Governor of the Province.

It was not the first occasion on which the town had been visited by the King's representative. Governor Parr in the *Dido* had been there in 1788 and 1789. It has been an interesting speculation, a speculation decided affirmatively by at least one individual who has spent much time over the story of Sir Guy Carleton, whether this latter had been able to visit at any time the community linked in name so closely to him. So far as can be definitely stated, the speculation has little on which such an affirmative statement may be based, but no doubt exists of the presence of Sir John Wentworth in Guysborough in the year in question, and that while there he received 'addresses from the Magistrates and Clergy'.

From another source we are able to obtain the names of the Magistrates at the time, though to which of them fell the duty of preparing and delivering the address, history telleth not. John Stuart, the former member; Joseph Marshall, the present representative; T. W. Hierlihy of Antigonish, and Benjamin Ogden, we know were among the Justices of that year and possibly divided the duty .

There was no possibility of such a division among the clergy of the County for there was but one clergyman, so far as we know, in the County, namely the Rev. John Wingate Weeks, formerly Chaplain of the House of Assembly. One wishes there were some record of the visit, and some portrayal of the locality and the residents at the time. The sixteen years which had elapsed since its founding had doubtless been sufficient to make evident the progress towards a thrifty settlement brought about by unremitting toil. It does not require much effort of the imagination to conjure up the scene at the Court House, situated at the time on the steep slopes overlooking the cove now called Miller's Cove. And knowing something of what was taking place in the settlement at the time, one may safely hazard the conjecture that the visit of the Lieut.-Governor filled a large place in the local interest and conversation, till, a month later, the tale of the arrest, trial and hanging of a poor unfortunate for the theft of 20 pounds furnished a newer sensation.

Everyone was doubtless relieved the following year by the news of the peace with France, this removing as it did the shadow of danger which had been present for some time. Doubtless this freedom from the possibility of encroachment from outside encouraged criticisms of internal conditions, which in the opinion of many, were not as they should be. It is not surprising that one of the County members, Campbell, able as we know him to have been, energetic and fearless as later events proved, was not under these circumstances among the legislators who could be considered yielding and complacent, if a just cause for criticism offered. Campbell, as we have seen, was fitting himself for a much more prominent position than his opportunities at Guysborough opened up for him, and his ability and prominence brought him into collision with the ruling powers at Halifax in such a way as to make him a somewhat marked man. We have seen what is said to be the commencement of his connection with the Island of Cape Breton, and Governor Wentworth has added some details, in a comment indicative of some bitterness. He says,—"'The opposition has been increased by the addition of William Campbell, Esq., H.M. Attorney General, counsellor and coal contractor of the Island of Cape Breton, who has signalized himself in this reprehensible opposition". Cottnam Tonge was at this time the great cause of the Governor's disquiet, and apparently Campbell and Tonge were more or less kindred spirits in thinking that the Government would be little the worse for some close watching and criticism. It was therefore with something of relief that, Campbell's seat having been unoccupied for two Sessions in 1806, it was declared vacant, and, in the general election which followed the same year, a change of personnel was accepted with probably a fair degree of satisfaction.

The first Session of the Ninth Assembly sat on November 18, 1806. Captain Joseph Marshall was again returned, his colleague being Edward Irish, a resident of the Upper District of the County, now known as Antigonish County. He died before his term of office expired, and his seat was taken by Allen Chipman, at a later date one of the County Court Judges. Some irregularities committed during Chipman's election resulted in the seat being declared vacant, and, a new election being run, John Cunningham was declared elected. Mr. Cunningham was not sworn in till the latter part of 1808, so that the County, through one cause or another, was not fully represented during the first years of the Assembly.

The fact that at least two of these members, Edward Irish and John Cunningham, were residents of Antigonish, indicates the growing importance of the northern section of Sydney County, an importance considered sufficient to justify the division of the County into an Upper District, now closely conforming in boundaries with the County of Antigonish, and a Lower District, consisting of the remaining portion of the County, that facing upon the Atlantic.

It may here be advisable to give some information of these two men, the first representatives to be sent from the Upper District. Edward Irish was the son of Levi Irish and Hannah Church. The elder Irish was one of a band of American settlers, who, shortly after the expulsion of the Acadians, left their homes, enticed by what appeared to them the better prospects which Nova Scotia afforded. His home in Rhode Island had been in Little Compton, from which place he moved to Falmouth in Hants County. His family was a large one, some of the children being born in Little Compton and some in Nova Scotia, and his descendants have contributed their full share to the growth and development of the Province.

Edward Irish, whose wife was Mrs. Phillips, the widow of an officer, moved to Antigonish about the same time as did Richard Cunningham, the father of John Cunningham, their grants being a few miles distant from the present town of Antigonish, in the direction of the harbour. John Cunningham was married to Ruth Amelia Irish, a sister of Edward's, and there were other intermarriages which still more closely cemented the family connection. Descendants of Edward Irish, bearing the family name are still to be found in the County. He died in Halifax at a time when it was impossible for arrangements to be made for the transportation of the body to the plot on the family estate, and he is buried in St. Paul's cemetery in Halifax.

John Cunningham was the son of Richard Cunningham, who, with his two brothers, John and Michael, left their homes in Roscommon, Ireland, about 1769 for Nova Scotia. Their vessel was wrecked on Sable Island, but the brothers were saved and eventually were taken to Halifax. In October, 1785, he and his wife were given grants of land amounting to 1,700 acres near Antigonish. A very large number of the families of the Cunningham name now in the Province are descendants of Richard Cunningham, the other brothers having, it is said, died unmarried or moved out of the Province.

John, the eldest son of Richard Cunningham, was born in 1776 and died at his home in Antigonish in 1847. For some years before his death he had been Registrar of Deeds for the County of Antigonish.

From a party point of view, little can be said to have occurred during the Assembly which indicates party cleavage. Indeed, we have the authority of no less a person than Dr. Croke, Judge of the Admiralty and interim Administrator of the Government, during Sir George Prevost's absence, that "little or nothing whatever of party divisions prevails." There were differences of opinion, it is true, reflected in a number of Assembly divisions, but these arose mostly from questions of policy or interest having little relation to the fundamental principles underlying a party division. So far at least as Mr. Marshall is concerned, if the criterion afforded by the presence of his name in the Assembly divisions is accepted, he seems to have been somewhat steadfastly 'agin the Government'. How the other member was accustomed to support the ruling body can not now easily be determined. The County at least profited during the period as a result of the progress made in educational matters, for it was one in which provision was made for a grammar school. This was one of the last important measures provided for by that Assembly, which came to a close on August 14, 1811.

The Tenth Assembly meeting early in 1812 saw two new members representing the County. Both were young men, connected with or belonging to prominent county families, families which already had been represented in the Assembly chamber, and which at times still later, were to be similarly honoured. Unfortunately, one of them did not live long to carry on the connection personally, for he, John Ballaine, was drowned in Halifax Harbour on the day the first Session prorogued. His wife, a Miss Cutler, (daughter of Thomas Cutler, a former member and Custos Rotulorum), to whom he had been married but a few years, served to connect Ballaine, whose home originally was in Arichat, with one of the leading families of his adopted County. A daughter, only a few months old at the time of her father's death, lived to marry into the family, which, as we shall see, contributed largely in its personnel to the list of County representatives.

A more extended reference must be made to the second member, for he occupied during a long and eventful life a place in the history of the Province to which any County resident may point with pride. This representative was John G. Marshall.

In one of the several books which Marshall has written, he details at some length the circumstances under which he submitted his name for consideration by the County electorate. His law course at Halifax in the office of Lewis M. Wilkins was completed in 1808, and with his horse and outfit and four pounds of money given him by his father, the young lawyer left Halifax in search of a practice. Truro and Amherst were visited but no more than a guinea or two a week was there to be obtained. Pictou, however, appeared to promise more, and there he took his way, and presumably was successfully practising when the time came around for the elections to be held for the Tenth Assembly. Marshall's mother, some time previously, had suggested to him that he oppose his father in the contest about to take place, and the suggestion was carried out by a brother, who placed John's name before the electorate in opposition to that of his father, who had already been eleven years a representative. John G. Marshall and Ballaine opposed Joseph Marshall and a Mr. C, (so the account goes, this person being probably John Cunningham) and were so favorably received that the father and Mr. C. withdrew, Ballaine and John Marshall being elected. We are told that at least the father accepted the situation very philosophically and gracefully and that no unpleasantness resulted from a situation which had in it some unpleasant potentialities.

Once obtained, the seat was retained by Marshall with honour, till he was removed to a more responsible position, a position equally ably and honourably filled. An able lawyer, (for one of his books on legal subjects is still consulted), farseeing, (for his efforts at establishing a school system based on assessment antedated that of Sir Charles Tupper's day by many years), conscientious and fearless, (as anecdotes of his experiences while Chief Justice of the Court of Common Pleas of Cape Breton will show), a reformer, (for many years of his life and much of his money were spent in the most extended tours to both England and all parts of then known Canada in the advancement of temperance and world peace) Nova Scotia has few names which can be pointed to with more pride. He died in Halifax at the age of 84 at the home of his daughter, Mrs. William Black.

It is somewhat of a coincidence that, as the former Assembly had seen several changes in the County membership, so also, in this Assembly, several changes occurred. A seat was left vacant by John Ballaine's unfortunate and untimely death, on April 10, 1812. The steps by which Samuel Hood George was given the representation can not now be determined. George had been Provincial Secretary since 1808, and had left Halifax for England in 1812. He died there in June 1813, aged 24 years, surely a representative and Provincial Secretary of tender years or precocious ability. The seat again becoming vacant after George's death, it was contested for by John Cunningham, who had represented the County in a former Assembly, and Simon Fraser, the former being declared elected. Feeling evidently ran high between the opponents or the candidates, for several petitions against Cunningham's return were presented to the House. They were unsuccessful, and Mr. Cunningham completed the term of office, taking no doubt his full share of the worry and responsibility which must have been the lot of any or all of the members of that time. The Assembly had been largely a war Assembly. That with the United States had now terminated, but the European situation was ominous. During a large portion of the Assembly, the shipping and even the home ports of the unprotected Province were facing the necessity of resisting inroads of men of war or privateers which found them for a time an easy prey. The Province was learning most effectively to hit back, and even to enjoy doing so, but news of the battle of Waterloo was most heartily welcomed. Not till August 3rd were the full particulars of the fight known in Halifax.

Thereafter, problems associated with the development, rather than the protection, of the Province, could be considered. The building of light houses, the attraction of immigrants to the Province, extensions of the educational system, these were some of the matters occupying the attention of the Assembly during the remaining period of its existence. Before it was dissolved, the "Letters of Agricola" had made their appearance in the Provincial press, and with them, a new impetus to the progress of the Province had been received. The population of the whole Province was but 77,000, but the way appeared to be opening for growth and progress. Towards this total Sydney County contributed 6,991, a threefold increase in 30 years.

From a political point of view, the years had been too fully occupied with protective measures to permit of the amenities of party politics. Marshall himself has told us something of the way in which the business of government was carried on. The Assembly usually met at 10 A.M. and generally continued till 4 or 5 o'clock in the afternoon. "The public business, I can aver, was, in those days, diligently attended to and despatched. The Session continued, on an average, about ten weeks. The debates were conducted with far more courtesy and moderation than those of the parliaments of the present day. Rarely, indeed was there any personal bitterness, or asperity, rude epithets or severe accusations or unbecoming language."

The first Session of the Eleventh General Assembly met in Halifax on February 11, 1819. There was now a change in the personnel of the representatives, the new members being Robert Molleson Cutler and Thomas Dickson.

The former of these was the son of Thomas Cutler, a former representative, and at a later date represented the County in the Legislative Council. Tradition says that he was the first white child born in the new settlement at the head of the Chedabucto Bay, the date of his birth being October 9, 1784. He died in October, 1883, and the fact that he is still referred to as 'King' Cutler informs us of his prominence in the community.

Concerning Thomas Dickson, the information up to the present received has been scanty. He was the son of Charles Dickson, who moved from the States first to Kings County and later to Truro in his search for a new home. Thomas was one of three brothers to whom were given the distinctions of being representatives in the Assembly at the same time, the others representing the Townships of Truro and Onslow.

Born in 1788, he studied law in the office of S. G. W. Archibald in Halifax, and practised, there is reason to believe, at Pictou. There he married a Miss Sarah Ann Patterson, and there he died in 1857. It will be seen that this is not the only time he appeared before the electorate of the County with the request for their suffrages, though the means by which he had established a connection in the County has not been discovered.

If Thomas Miller is correct, there is at least one undertaking in bringing about which he was instrumental. This may appeal to that portion of the Nova Scotian population, which does not look askance at Samuel Johnson's definition of a certain very important food grain. To him, according to this historian, should be given the credit of causing to be erected the first mill in the Province in which oatmeal was prepared, prompted thereto by the recommendation of 'Agricola', one of his confreres in the Assembly chamber.

The life of the Assembly was of short duration. Shortly after the close of the second Session the death of King George Third necessitated, according to the political procedure of the time, the dissolution of the Assembly and the issuing of writs for a new general election.

With the Twelfth Assembly, Cutler's place was taken by John G. Marshall, while again Thomas Dickson was the other member. Four contestants had been in the field, Marshall, Dickson, John Steele and Col. S. Fraser. Fraser withdrew early in the progress of the election, the final results being that Marshall received 621 votes, Dickson 518, Steele 463, and Fraser, 398. Mr. Marshall's popularity in the poll at Guysborough is proved by the fact that of 280 votes polled in that section, he received 278.

The first Session of the Assembly opened in the latter part of 1820, (Murdoch and Haliburton not agreeing on the month) with Dickson present, Marshall being absent during the first few days of the Session. The election was petitioned against, but the Sheriff, David McQueen, was exonerated.

Marshall's connection with the political life of the Province was drawing to a close, on his being called to a new sphere of duty, but the reputation he had made as a farseeing and constructive statesman was not to be diminished by the events in which he then took part. It was in this Assembly that he made his sincere attempt to provide for better educational facilities for the children of the Province, and though the attempt failed, it was in spite of his forceful presentation of the favoring arguments and not from any lack of careful preparation of the details of the proposition. The public opinion of the Province had not yet been aroused to the importance of the matter, nor in fact, did it become so aroused till a much later date.

His appointment as Chief Justice of the Inferior Court of Common Pleas for the Island of Cape Breton was made in April, 1823, and early in 1824, he submitted the resignation of his seat in the Assembly, on account of the impossibility of his attendance at the Sessions.

The occasion of the vacancy in the representation of the County was seized by John Young (Agricola) as one favorable for his appeal to the electorate. His letters had brought him into prominence, and, with his known connection with the Provincial Agricultural Society, had made his name a household word. His friends had been attempting to secure for him a seat in the Legislature, and this attempt was to succeed. He was opposed at the polls by Mr. Steele, but succeeded in getting 354 votes to his opponents 218, the election being decided in his favour.

Again some irregularity had been committed in the course of the contest, and a petition was presented against his taking his seat. The report of the Committee appointed to investigate the matter was unfavorable to Young, not on account of his own action, but on account of the doings of the County Sheriff, and a new election was ordered.

In the press of the time appears an interesting letter which refers to an incident in connection with this election. The correspondent writes from his home in Musquodoboit, and the whole letter is worth perusal.

"In this remote district, we seldom see strangers, but for some days past we have had small straggling parties on their way from Manchester to Halifax to give evidence on the contested election between Mr. Steele and Mr. Young. The broken rear was brought up yesterday by an old man of the name of Burke, a remote relation of Bishop Burke, late of Halifax, a genuine, descendant of St. Patrick. This intrepid pedestrian bowed with the weight of eighty years, in the middle of winter and all alone, crossed the frightful wilds between Manchester and Musquodoboit. He carried his provisions with him, and pitched his tent in the woods. He halted in the settlement during the night, and reposed some time in an armchair, but was early on the road next morning, and seemed as anxious to finish his task as the devout Mussulman on a pilgrimage to the tomb of the Prophet.

His strongly marked features indicated great sincerity, and self devotion to the cause, and when he spoke of the election his countenance seemed to be lighted up with the fires of youth. All admired his zeal, but deeply lamented that the stormy politics of Manchester should have brought this time worn pilgrim so far from his home at this season of the year. The season has indeed been uncommonly mild, for had winter reigned with his usual severity, he would probably have shortened the careers of most of the electioneering pilgrims, and introduced them to the unseen world, where the din of politics and the noise of war are equally unknown."

Mr. Steele again opposed Mr. Young in the by-election, but was again defeated, and Mr. Young sat during the Session of 1826, the last Session of the Assembly.

The County had participated in several important events, during this period of rather disturbed representation. The extension of the Provincial Light house programme had brought it about that Cranberry Island, off Canso Harbour, was now the site of a lighthouse, maintained by a tax levied on all vessels coming to an anchor or passing through the Straits. The formation of the Agricultural Society, called the Guysborough and Manchester Farmer's Society, affiliated with the central Society at Halifax, somewhat antedated the period, the first meeting taking place at Guysborough on June 4, 1819, according to the Minute Book, still in existence, but throughout the period the Society was in active operation, and doubtless profited much from the personal attention to its programme which Agricola could give.

207

The county was opening up, and increasing greatly in population. The great Eastern Road, passing through Truro and Pictou to Antigonish, which point had been reached in 1818, was bringing the County into a measurable degree of communication with the rest of the Province. Not that travel by water was wholly superceded, for by this route, the Lieut.-Governor of the Province, Sir James Kempt, visited the shire town in September 1822, landing from the *Chebucto*, and being greeted with a salute from the Sherbrooke battery, and also one of seventeen guns for which Sheriff Christian Muller was given credit. His stay was not a long one, and by the time evening had arrived he and his party, convoyed by the local celebrities, had passed the forty mile stretch of doubtlessly execrable road leading to Antigonish, again to be met with the roar of cannon, and the cheers of enthusiastic townspeople.

The division of the Province into Judicial Districts also dated from this period, Judge Jared I. Chipman being appointed to preside over the Inferior Courts of Common Pleas for the area of which this County formed a part. Thus was commenced Judge Chipman's connection with the County, of which indistinct echoes are still to be heard.

In the elections for the Thirteenth Assembly, held in the summer of 1826, a three cornered contest was successfully passed by Mr. Young and Mr. Dickson, their opponent being a Mr, J. H. Hill. The final result stood as follows,— Mr. Young, 296 votes; Mr. Dickson, 241, and Mr. Hill 171.

The Assembly appears to have been an uninteresting one. The County was, however, progressing most rapidly in population and in importance. The census of the year 1827 gave evidence of the fact that it had almost doubled in population since the year 1817, the population gaining from 6,991 to 12,683. The growth of the St. Mary's district, set off as a Township in 1818, accounted quite largely for the increase, but not wholly, for other sections were prospering as well. The Hallowell grants in Antigonish County had been opened up for settlement. A prosperous trade in the shipping of cattle to Newfoundland was being built up. The efforts to increase the agricultural output of the County were not being wholly lost. Added to these, the fabulously rich fisheries of Chedabucto Bay and Canso were contributing to form a total of growth and prosperity to which the present day resident looks back with envy.

There was still great need of roads and easy connection with the remainder of the Province. The trunk post road lay far to the north of most of the settlements, and satisfactory progress had not been made with the extension of the road through Musquodoboit to the St. Mary's Valley. Burke and his political friends and enemies had little better than a blazed trail to follow when they started for Halifax on foot to participate in the election trial. The advocates of this more direct route were striving hard, occasionally breaking into the columns of the press in their endeavors to further the scheme. They could state no more than that, after its first opening nearly 25 years before, there were about fifteen miles just west of Guysborough and thirty miles through the St. Mary's Valley, which were kept open in winter and along which travel in what the correspondent calls "sled carriages" was possible.

The same individuals who had contested the 1826 elections were in the field for the elections preceding the Fourteenth Assembly, which met in its first Session in 1830. Again the contest was a three cornered one, and again Young and Dickson led the polls. The final voting took place in Antigonish, and when completed, showed that Young had been given 476 votes, Dickson

436 and Hill 355. Apparently the numbers of voters had approximately doubled, very fair evidence of the healthy growth which had taken place in the County, for it was then the third most populous of the nine counties in which the Province was at that time divided.

In a series of articles which appeared about this time in the Nova Scotian are to be found some very interesting notes of the prominent places in the County, which had been visited by the author, in collecting data for his 'Eastern Rambles'. Lochaber, already known to the reading public from the cut which had appeared in Moorson's 'Letters from Nova Scotia',—Sherbrooke, the site of a prosperous lumbering and shipbuilding industry, and Guysborough were visited during these 'Rambles', and are referred to in such a way as to leave no doubt in the mind of the reader that the traveller received of them the most favorable impressions. It is perhaps excusable if, concerning the latter place, his comment is quoted. He says,—"There are few places in the Province whose natural beauties and great commercial advantages are more agreeably blended".

In June, 1832, Jared I. Chipman, who had for a number of years filled the office of Judge of the Court of Common Pleas for the District of which the County was a part, died. His successor in the Judgeship was W. Q. Sawers. To him and to Martin I. Wilkins, who had been associated with him for the purpose, fell the duty of conducting an investigation into the Canso Riots, which, borne of religious misunderstandings, for a time focused the attention of the Province upon that remote fishing community.

Shortly after this, in the year 1835, the growth which had taken place in the eastern portion of the Province, coupled with the fact that its large area was being found to make problems of its legislative representation very difficult, justified the division of the County of Sydney into two separate and distinct counties. The division followed quite closely that of the old District divisions. The Upper District in this way became a separate County, and for a time retained the name which had formerly served to distinguish the whole. To the Lower District was given the name of Guysborough County, and thus this County came into being.

In the following year came the elections, those for the 15 th Assembly, and for this election a new group of candidates presented themselves. It is very apparent from the electoral letter sent out by Mr. Young, that, during at least the latter years of their representation of Sydney County, there had developed an appreciable degree of friction between himself and his colleague, Mr. Dickson, but these now fought out their differences before the electorate of Sydney County proper. In Guysborough County the candidates who presented themselves were Guysborough County residents, W. F. DesBarres and John J. Marshall being proposed for the eastern end of the County, while Hugh MacDonald was the nominee from the St. Mary's Township. These were the first of a series of Guysborough County residents, who for a number of years offered themselves for the positions under the control of the electorate, and who, in the positions they received, ably upheld the interests of the County, and proved their ability to take their places in the Legislature among the stalwarts of the political life of the time.

There does not appear yet to have been much if any party cleavage. Des-Barres, Marshall and McDonald were apparently all men more or less well known in their communities, with business or social connections which merited respect. Apparently they received support from the electorate, as individuals, rather than because they were the standard bearers of more or less distinct parties. W. F. DesBarres was a rising lawyer in the town of Guysborough, the son of J. W. F. DesBarres, who had been such a prominent figure in the early development of the Province. John J. Marshall was the son of Joseph H. Marshall and grandson of Col. Joseph Marshall, who had represented Sydney County in the Eighth and Ninth Assemblies, and the nephew of Judge John George Marshall, also one of the former representatives. They were connected through marriages into the Cutler family, and this connection earned for them some unpleasant comment in later times, when any combination savoring of a family compact became sure of being noted. In addition, this tie of relationship is noticeable, in view of the breach between them which later developed as the political lines became more sharply drawn. Hugh MacDonald, the St. Mary's representative, was doubtless as prominent in his own community as were DesBarres and Marshall in theirs, and how strong he was is proved by the result of the voting in the three cornered contest which followed.

Voting took place first in the eastern end of the County, and when the polls were opened in St. Mary's, DesBarres was leading his nearest opponent, Marshall, by a number of votes. MacDonald, however, was given every vote in his district, and DesBarres every vote but two, which resulted in Marshall's being at the foot of the poll. DesBarres' popularity is further attested by the fact, a fact which brought out comment in the press of the time, that though in this contest, the whole Provincial electorate expressed their resentment at the legal profession on account of some enactments of the Assembly just terminated, by rejecting at the polls a great majority of the lawyers seeking election, DesBarres, a member of that profession, was returned triumphantly. Moreover, before the Assembly had terminated, he had laid the foundation on which rested a long and prominent political career.

A period of the greatest moment in the history of the Province was developing. The trial of Joseph Howe for libel had taken place in 1835 and his entry into political life for the avowed purpose of procuring for the Province an adequate and responsible government followed shortly. Great questions were being fought out and decided. The House had among its members men of the most outstanding talent, attracted thither by the earnestness and ability with which the contest was waged.

The Assembly, however, is not one in which marked evidences of participation by the County's representatives on one side or the other was forthcoming. It is worth while, however, to quote two stanzas from a political effusion of the day, which serves to place quite accurately the positions occupied by the two representatives. McDonald's attitude in connection with the growing disfavour of a Government considered autocratic and unrepresentative evidently admitted of no doubt. Respecting DesBarres, not so clear cut a statement was then possible, and indeed it would appear that even Howe himself knew not at times how the issue would finally be determined. DesBarres' family connections were on the side stoutly opposed to Howe, but very evidently other influences were at work. But the time had not yet arrived when the fury with which the long drawn out political fight was waged forced every voter to indicate in an unmistakable way his political adherence.

MacDonald.

Although exposed to Tory hate

210

When an election comes again,
Think ye, a Tory candidate
Would dare oppose him then?

DesBarres.
Intentions pure, in timid men
O'er awed by stern official power
Sometimes avail but little, when
Arrives the trying hour.

Even before the end of that Assembly, the agitation for Reform had gained some tangible results. A reorganization of the Governmental Chambers had been brought about, and provision had been secured for a Legislative Council. In this Chamber the County was given representation in the person of Robert Molleson Cutler, the son of Thomas Cutler, who received his appointment in 1838.

The passing years of the Assembly brought varied fortune to the County. There is evidence of its participation in the growth of the Province, so far at least as some phases of industry are concerned, for lumbering and shipbuilding was proceeding apace in and around some of the County centres. The press of the time refers continually to the accessions to the shipbuilding of the Province which owed their origins to Guysborough County endeavor. On the agricultural side the impetus given the industry by Agricola showed signs of halting, and, in this connection there seemed lacking many of the advantages possessed by many of its sister counties. At best it does not appear as if it more than held its own in this particular, in comparison with the more favored communities, On the other hand, so far as the fishing industry was concerned, there were many evidences of a most distinct falling off, as the harvest of the sea became more grudgingly available. There was market only for fish of certain varieties and quality, and it was inevitable, if the experience of all history is trustworthy, that there could be not forever such abundance of fish as is referred to, for instance, in the pages of Haliburton's History. To such an extent had the catch fallen off, that in some of the fishing settlements there was well marked distress, and this distress showed no signs of abatement in succeeding years. The County was, moreover, still lacking in means of easy communication with the rest of the Province. Only in the closing years of this Assembly was sufficient assistance obtained to enable the completion of the great Eastern road to be carried out. This followed the old Wightman survey, through the Valley of the Musquo-doboit to the St. Mary's Valley and thence to Guysborough, and the construction was made possible through the provision of 3,800 pounds of Provincial assistance in the years 1839 and 1840.

When the time for the elections for the next Assembly came around, the same three candidates again appeared before the electorate. In the meantime, however, Marshall had become a much more prominent figure in County affairs, on account of his connection with a dispute which had arisen

211

between the Grand Jury of the County and the County Magistrates. This had gone to the extent of justifying, in the opinion of the Magistrates, the fining of the Jury for some dereliction of duty. A petition had been addressed to the House, and was there sustained by a resolution which laid down the principle that such an action was unconstitutional and a remission of the fines was secured. In this dispute Marshall took a very prominent part, and his success at the polls in the following contest has been considered to quite an extent to be the evidence of the approbation with which his action in the affair had been met. The election took place in October of the year 1840, being that for the Sixteenth Assembly, and in the three cornered contest MacDonald was at the foot of the polls.

Meanwhile the fight for responsible government was becoming hotter with each succeeding year. Elected members were being eagerly scrutinized for evidences of their support of one or the other party, now being well differentiated. Apparently the stand which DesBarres would take was favorable to the rapidly growing sentiment which demanded a more representative government, while Marshall's attitude would be that of opposition thereto. This did not prevent them both being pilloried in the Reformer press of the Province when an instance was desired of a county family compact or combination of persons to whom there had been apportioned an undue number of governmental favours. They are both named as members of what is called the *Cutler Compact* of Guysborough County, when among nineteen individuals were distributed no less than fifty-seven commissions, in addition to other local offices.

To a political incident which occurred at this time is due the naming of a road on the outskirts of the town of Guysborough, and the reasons for the naming may be worth the telling.

Not long after Lord Falkland's arrival in the Province, His Lordship undertook, as was the custom, a round of visits to the county seats, for the purpose of familiarizing himself with the more prominent localities under his supervision. The date on which he was to visit Guysborough was well known, and some supporters, in anticipation of his coming, had erected an arch across the street by which it was thought that he would enter the town. The morning came, and the vicinity of the arch was crowded with persons collected to watch the proceedings. From this place, which was on the top of a hill, could be seen a mile or more away the summit of another hill over which the Lieut-Governor's cavalcade must pass, but which was separated from it by an intervening elevation behind which for a time his course would be lost. In due time his carriages were seen passing over the distant slopes, to disappear in the intervening valley. All was excitement, waiting then his Lordship's very speedy arrival. The time passed. No more carriages came in sight. His Lordship and his retinue had disappeared. Finally the news was brought to the awaiting crowd that he had been conducted by a bypath to another road entering the town, and was even then at the Courthouse. To this bypath, now in daily use, is still given the name, Falkland Lane. It may be worth noting that on the morrow the arch was visited by his Lordship, that the address prepared for the occasion was duly given, and that then the equipages returned to Antigonish.

Whether or not the incident made or lost votes in the contest which shortly followed can not now with ease be determined. In this election,

212

DesBarres and Marshall were opposed by W. O. Heffernan and Hugh MacDonald. At one time in the course of the polling MacDonald led the polls, but the contest ended with the return of the old members.

But some change had occurred. There had been some crystallization of opinion, and there was now no difficulty in discerning the cleavage between the two representatives. From the first divisions, in this, the Seventeenth Assembly, DesBarres was to be found as consistently with the Reformers as was Marshall with the so-called Tories. It was Marshall who proposed the amendment to Howe's motion of want of confidence in the Executive Council. DesBarres opposed the amendment, and thereafter throughout the Assembly, their courses lay in different directions.

From the way in which during the Assembly each of these members strove for the advancement of the interests of the party which he supported, one must realize that each brought to the contest more than the average share of ability or talent. Their prominence in the debates of the day can be read on every page of the proceedings. Step by step the Reformers were winning their way, and the vigour of the attack was only equalled by the determination of the defense. The representatives of the County were divided, but to each of the contestants must be accorded full recognition of the ability which he brought into the fight.

One important advance made during this Assembly was a change which did away with the old method of voting, under which the polling of votes took place according to a schedule, in the course of which many polling districts were visited. The Act which provided for simultaneous polling became law in the early part of 1847, and under its provisions ten districts were named for the County of Guysborough. Hereafter at Guysborough, Manchester, Interval, Milford, Crow Harbour, Country Harbour, Canso, Sherbrooke, The Forks of St. Mary's and Marie Joseph, voting was to be conducted on the same day, thus allowing for a more satisfactory expression of opinion on the part of the voter, as well as expediting what had hitherto been a long drawn out and arduous performance.

Under these new conditions, the election of 1847 for the Eighteenth Assembly took place. Again the three contestants, DesBarres, and MacDonald on the Reform platform, and Marshall as the standard-bearer of the Tories, meet in the political arena. The Reform candidates headed the polls, on this occasion, this being the fourth time on which DesBarres had appealed with success to the electorate. It was not to be his last, for higher political honors were awaiting him, which, however, were not to be gained without another struggle. Early in the following year, when Howe was accorded the responsibility of leading the Government, it was seen that to DesBarres had been given a position as member of H. M. Executive Council of the Province, and a position in the Cabinet as Solicitor-General.

This necessitated another election, and again the irrepressible Marshall appeared in opposition. But DesBarres' strength was such that the opposition efforts were of little avail. In the counting up, it was found that DesBarres had received one vote more than double the number given to his opponent, a very surprising vote, in view of what the near future had in store.

213

Newsletters of the time throw some very interesting light on the conditions imposed on travellers, which in these days it is somewhat difficult to appreciate. On the Monday following Declaration Day, Mr. DesBarres, escorted by a number of his enthusiastic adherents on horseback and in sleighs—for the election had been held in February, 1848,—left for Halifax to take up the duties and responsibilities of his new position. His course lay up the Salmon River, to the St. Mary's Valley and from thence through the valley of the. Musquodoboit, along the line of the Eastern road which had been so long in the building. "The learned gentleman arrived in town on Sunday morning", the columns of the press inform us, or in other words after one week spent on the road. And this was probably very good time indeed for the long and tedious journey, a much shorter time, in fact, than would have been required had any unusual storms blocked up the little frequented roads. Little wonder the volume of travel to the outlying sections of the Province was so small as to be inconsiderable, and that the impulse of growing public opinion was long delayed in reaching from the centre to the circumference of the Province.

Marshall had been defeated in the election held in February or this year, 1848. It comes somewhat of a surprise to know that before the end of the year, he was back again in his accustomed seat. But so it was. DesBarres did not long remain in the Cabinet position to which his ability and legislative experience had elevated him. In November he was given the position of one of the Assistant Justices of the Supreme Court, in succession to Judge Hill, deceased, and for the vacancy in the House of Assembly, it became necessary that another representative be appointed. The Reform nomination went to E. H. Francheville, while Marshall promptly took up again his old position in opposition, and when the polls closed on December 14th, it was found that he had succeeded in overturning an adverse majority of 211 to one which exceeded that of his opponent by 23.

Thereafter, DesBarres' position on the Provincial Bench precluded his participation in political matters. A few years after receiving that appointment he removed his residence from Guysborough to Halifax, and there he died in June, 1885. He left a number of descendants some of whom still reside in the county for whose interests he had so zealously fought. It is a coincidence worth noting that his descendants commingle with those who trace their origin to members of the disbanded battalions of the 60th Royal American Regiment, the regiment to which Lieut.-Governor J. F. W. DesBarres had been posted as a lieutenant in 1756.

There can be no doubt concerning the bitterness with which the political battles were being fought in Guysborough County. Undoubtedly, Marshall was a bonny fighter, and indeed this is his reputation in the county to this day, when the old stories of the battles on the hustings are rehearsed to willing listeners. Undoubtedly, the candidates who were seeking the support of the electorate were able men, men who were not only capable of forming independent opinions but could ably defend those positions if need be. Moreover, they not only occupied prominent places in the political life of the day by reason of that ability, but their opinions were of weight because of the fact that they were the spokesmen of a County of much greater importance in the Province than the Guysborough County of today. We have seen that in the year 1827 the population of Sydney County was 12,760. That area in 1849 had increased in population to about 23,000, more than one-tenth of the

214

population of the whole Province. (It is now little more than a twentieth.) This was double the population of Cumberland County, it equalled the population of Pictou, and was half the total population of the whole Island of Cape Breton. The Province had been doing much more in the period than give an absorbed attention to politics. It was Nova Scotia's growing time, and no portion of the Province had grown more rapidly than Guysborough County.

It is moreover of interest to note that the old political cleavages were being obliterated and new ones were forming. Both DesBarres and Francheville had been pilloried in 1842 as members of the 'Cutler Family Compact', but this connection no longer existed. And we shall see the time when even Marshall, uncompromising supporter of Johnstone as he had always been, had no hesitancy in aligning himself with those who resented the enforced inclusion of Nova Scotia in the Confederation compact.

There was dawning too, another stage in the development of the Province, that stage in which railway construction was an active issue. Howe, the leader, and DesBarres, his lieutenant, had already been members of a Committee appointed to report on the possibilities of a Halifax-Windsor line. Then the larger project was mooted,—the connection of Nova Scotia with the central Canadian Provinces,—and to it, in a short time, all attention was devoted.

Almost from the inception of the railway movement, some ports in Guysborough County were carefully considered when terminal facilities were under discussion. As early as 1848 at least the route from Whitehead to the St. Mary's valley and from thence to Pictou and the isthmus of Chignecto was proposed, the Whitehead terminal having been strongly advocated by Captain W. F. W. Owen, R.N. and Naval Surveyor, as presenting advantages far beyond those of any other Nova Scotian harbour. His reports to His Excellency Sir William G. Colebrook, Lieut.-Governor of New Brunswick, are worth perusing, even at this date. That little result followed the publication of the report was probably due to the fact that it had been prepared at the instance of the New Brunswick government, not the government at Halifax, which was interested naturally and mainly in railroad construction from Halifax. But the agitation over the Guysborough Railroad carries us back at this time one hundred years at least.

Weil worthy of note during the 18th Assembly was the legislation from which by slow degrees has developed our present educational system. Under James W. Dawson, (later Sir James W.) as Superintendent of Education, a system calling for the appointment of County Commissioners of Education was introduced. The first Commissioners were Wentworth Taylor, William Walsh, Thomas Patterson, E. H. Francheville and Christopher Jost for the Guysborough Municipality and Rev. Alexander Campbell, Hugh MacDonald, Thomas Glencross, William McKeen, William Bent and Joseph Alexander for the Municipality of St. Mary's.

In preparation for the election preliminary to the 19th Assembly, the railroad issue bulked more largely than did any constructive school policy. The Guysborough County electorate were not at the time fully seized of the idea of railroad expenditure, and listened to John J. Marshall's opposition quite contentedly, and he was returned. . With him as his colleague was Stewart

Campbell. Opposing these were Hugh McDonald and W. O. Heffernan.

Of Hugh McDonald we have already known, and we recognise in him the reform candidate as uncompromising in his predelictions as was Marshall in his. Of W. O. Heffernan we shall later hear, since from that time his name is prominent in the political story of the County.

He was the son of Dennis Heffernan, an old naval surgeon, who had resided the beliefs of a number of the Reformers, enough of these crossed the floor of the House to enable a want of confidence motion to be passed, and the Assembly ended with the old opposition administering the Government. This was the Johnstone-Tupper administration of 1857-59. In this administration Marshall took the place of Campbell as Speaker of the House.

In the meantime, the railroad policy had fructified. On December 10, 1858, the road was completed between Halifax and Truro, and thus a certain amount of credit accrued to the party which had sponsored it. This was sufficient, but barely, to override the rancour of the religious quarrel, which had been fanned into a blaze during the 20th Assembly, and the next Assembly, elected or. May 12, 1859, saw the brief existence of the Johnstone-Tupper administration brought to a close. The test of strength occurred in the new House over the appointment of Speaker, Stewart Campbell being opposed by John C. Wade. Campbell was appointed, receiving 28 votes to his opponent's 25, and Mr. Johnstone's resignation and the formation of a new administration under Mr. Young followed.

We have seen that Campbell was returned for this Assembly, but he had not now with him as his colleague the redoubtable Marshall, who had on more than one occasion snatched victory from defeat. W. O. Heffernan was on this occasion the second County representative. The margin of strength between the two parties was extremely small, so small as quite effectively to paralyse any attempt at new or constructive legislation. There was a deadlock, and the tide of popular opinion was arising against that party which had done so much for Nova Scotia, but which had blundered so seriously on more than one occasion. In the face of an opposition so able and pugnacious these blunders had cost dear, and the Reform party was losing its hold over the Provincial electorate.

Meanwhile, the Province was progressing rapidly in growth and wealth. Its shipping thronged the seas, and each little community was a hive of industry. In this growth and progress Guysborough County was participating. The census taken about the middle of the life of the 21st Assembly indicated a gain of 2,100 in population in the ten year period, the figures being then 12,943. Moreover, in the same year, 1861, the discovery of gold was made in the County, in July at Goldenville, and a little later at Wine Harbour. Thirty years before it had been found in the sand near Isaac's Harbour, but the memory of the discovery was almost forgotten when the inquisitive neighbors of Nelson Nickerson, wondering at his unusual actions on the Goldenville barrens, set a watch on him, and at length discovered him, tracing him down by the sound of his hammer on the rocks. That party that day is said to have taken home with them four hundred dollars worth of gold, broken by them from the quartz drift found on the barrens. Other discoveries were soon made, and thereafter the development of the County for some years was determined by the progress made in the gold mining industry.

But, in the realm of politics, other things than gold mining were being talked about. The leader of the Government, Mr. Young, eldest son of Agricola, was appointed to the Bench. His mantle fell upon Mr. Howe, who had been Provincial Secretary. The extremely narrow margin by which Mr. Howe held sway—two at the outset and never larger—was a most effective deterrent to the introduction of new or contentious legislation and little more than a temporizing program could be considered.

The election of 1863 ended these doldrums, but now Johnstone was in the lead, although Guysborough County returned its old representatives, Stewart Campbell and Heffernan. But Johnstone became Judge in Equity. Charles Tupper was getting into his stride and assumed the leadership. Then, in 1864, apparently casually and with little comment, there was taken the first step in that road which was to lead Nova Scotia far.

Lord Durham, in his report submitted in 1839, has suggested a union of the Canadian Provinces. The progress of events in Upper Canada about this time were such as to remind the authorities that there might be something after all in the claim that advantages might accrue from this procedure. There was little sentiment in its favor in Nova Scotia, but in the minds of a number of persons there was shaping itself an opinion that closer relations between Nova Scotia, New Brunswick and Prince Edward Island could be brought about. A number of years previously they had formed one Governmental unit. Might not now that condition be with profit resumed? The matter was considered worthy of discussion, and so, in 1864, it was decided to hold a meeting of the representatives of the three Provinces to discuss Maritime Union, the meeting to be held in Charlottetown in 1865. The time for the meeting came around. But visitors came, who desired to broaden the field of discussion and the Quebec Conference resulted. Maritime Union was shelved for Dominion Union, and Nova Scotia found herself caught up in a maelstrom of circumstances from which extrication became impossible.

But though in connection with this matter a storm of disapproval was arising, in connection with another one, the desirability of some reform of the educational system, there was an unanimity. John G. Marshall had vainly fought for some such legislation, and its success at this time may well have been due in part to some of his pioneering work. Now the Province was ready for it, so ready that political friend and foe temporarily composed their differences for a mutual benefit. They were later to unite on another matter.

Of Guysborough County interest about this time was the legislation as a result of which much the present day limits of the County were set. The western line of the County was hereafter to be a line drawn from the south-east corner of Colchester County to a point at or near the Ecum Secum bridge, and from thence to the sea, this area making up the Thirteenth Electoral District.

Meanwhile, a storm of discontent over the provisions of the Confederation agreement was arising. The time for the expression of this discontent came around in 1867, when voting both for the Local and the newly formed Dominion Parliament was to take place. There was no doubt concerning the result. Only one Confederate, Dr. Tupper, weathered the storm and survived to represent the Province in the upper House, and only two obtained seats in the Local Legislature. Stewart Campbell became the first representative of the County in the Federal Parliament. The County returned as Anti-Confederates John A. Kirk and John J. Marshall, the latter becoming the Speaker. However, the events since Confederation make up another story.

NOTES ON SOME OLD TIME PRACTITIONERS

That portion of Nova Scotia contained within the limits of Guysborough County has much of historical interest. Canso, jutting far out into the Atlantic, was early a landmark to a number of the old explorers, a rendezvous or point of departure to many who visited or left behind them the shores of the new continent. The record of its first visitation by Europeans carries us back to some of the earliest chapters in the story of the new world.

From the time of the earliest settlements within the precincts of the County, there are references to medical practitioners or to medical practice which well repay collection. The glimpses we catch are at times fleeting and uncertain, especially those of the times of the pioneers of the earliest occupation, but the very vagueness has in it something of allure and of attraction.

The first settlement, if we exclude the claims of the Portuguese or Spaniards, appears to have been at Chedabucto, at the head of the Bay of the same name. Here was the site of the little fort, built by Nicholas Denys and occupied by him for a number of years, a period of alternating successes and reverses, which at last ended with the larger entries on the wrong side of the ledger.

He was in many ways the most remarkable of the old French pioneers of the 17th century. He was the first great publicity agent of North America, a firm believer in and a staunch advocate of the procedure which he calls "sedentary fishing', as opposed to the method of catching and salting fish for early and speedy removal to the home fishing ports in France. He argued strongly in favor of the establishment of fishing stations at selected places on the mainland of the continent, around which would gradually grow up communities more or less fitted to become centres of colonization. In every detail related to that method of carrying on the fishing industry he was thoroughly conversant, writing quite voluminously and with a wealth of description which we now accept with interest and thanks. And nothing which he writes appeals to us quite so strongly as that portion of his book in which he tells of the medical arrangements which must be made for such an undertaking, and the place which the doctor or surgeon had in a carefully planned enterprise.

We have indeed come far since the time when Denys wrote, if we consider our present position in the social fabric in comparison with that of less than three hundred years ago. Sometimes we comment harshly against the present day tendency to specialize in the different branches of medicine; evidently the time had not arrived in those days when the whole realm of medicine was not considered ample to occupy the time of one individual. Under Denys' scheme, the doctor had many and most diversified duties to perform.

He was the cook's helper, ready with the hot evening meal when the boats returned at nightfall deep laden from the fishing grounds. He was the gardener, who must have in satisfactory state of productivity the garden plots, the produce of which served as a welcome addition to the otherwise monotonous diet. He was moreover the purveyor and provider of the flesh of fowl or game. He had in his charge the boys or apprentices of the ship, and was

219

empowered if necessary to mete out to them such chastisement as their sometimes unruly conduct might have in justice earned. He Was the splitter at one of the tables, where the catch of the day was nightly cleaned and prepared for the process of cure, nor could these splitters rest from their labours till that catch had been wholly disposed of. He must take his place with the other shore men at the barrow during the day, carrying fish from the shed on the stage to dry on the flakes or on the beaches. And withal he might earn something beyond his share of the proceeds of the voyage by trimming the hair or shaving the beards of the others of the workmen, being privileged to charge for this service at a set tariff. All these duties were supplementary to those of looking after the sick or ailing or injured under his care, and hiving performed all to the satisfaction of his employer, he was permitted at the end of the voyage to retain the medicine chest with its depleted supplies, the chest which he was supposed to have bought and stocked with the proceeds of an advance payment made him when first he signed the articles and undertook to perform his onerous duties.

It is regrettable that Denys, having so carefully enumerated and outlined for us the doctor's tasks, did not in any of his writing preserve for a wondering posterity the names of some of those from whose services he had profited. This he has not done, but certainly he writes as one having authority, and we are quite sure that, could we have looked, about the year 1650, on some of the fishing ventures with which Denys was connected, we would have found some now unknown medical hero, bravely undertaking the multifarious tasks so carefully set down.

Almost equally unsatisfactory in some details are the medical references of a time nearly one hundred years later than Denys' appearance on these shores. Now the English were in possession of Canso, but it was debatable ground, the very point of contact of the two contesting races. The medical man was now in all probability a member of Governor Phillip's ragged, ill-paid and not remarkably efficient regiment. From about 1720 until Du Vivier's descent in 1744 the English doggedly held their Canso possessions. The settlement at that time was almost wholly on George's Island or the other islands across the harbour from the site of the present town, and the homes and stages were clustered around the wholly insufficient fortifications which guarded the little community. Who of all there were who were responsible for the health of the soldiers and the fishermen, we can not now tell, but history brings to us the name of one doctor who had some stake in the community, as evidenced by an old record of real estate transfers. This deed refers to a plot of ground occupied by some Dr. Elliott, the plot of ground being described as 'being surrounded with pallisadoes', but whether these pallisadoes were intended to ward off the always dangerous Indian, or to act as a deterrent to the midnight pilferer, is now to be settled by our imaginations. At any rate, we know that some Dr. Elliott was in Canso about the year 1731, and that his grounds were on the north side of the Hill of Canso, his land stretching down to the shore of the now little frequented cove on Grassy Island, not far from the site of the old fort.
And further deponent sayeth not.

Another blank of many years duration now interposes, and the curtain next lifts at the time when the eastern portion of Nova Scotia was receiving its quota of those who had fought and lost in the Revolutionary War. Now commences the story of the present day occupation, almost the first comers being the members of the regiments, which; after a winter in Halifax, were set down in several of the harbours of the County in May and June of the year 1784.

By far the larger number of these settlers were given land near the site of the town now called Guysborough, from which the County takes its name. Here about 1100 persons were placed, men, women and children. Of the whole number about one quarter were negroes. Later arrivals from Connecticut and from Halifax swelled the numbers of the white settlers.

Among those given land, there were at least three who had some medical qualifications. Two at least were regimental surgeons, Dr. James Boggs and Dr. James (or John) McPherson.

It is said that Dr. Boggs was born in Philadelphia, to which place, or to any portion of the revolted Colonies, his pronounced Tory leanings made it impossible for him to return at the end of the war. He may have held a Royal Commission as a surgeon in a battalion or regiment, by the acceptance of which he had forfeited his opportunities of returning, except under heavy penalties. At least for the purpose of being given land, he was included among the members of the Civil Departments of the Army and Navy, which were disbanded in Guysborough County. He received altogether about 900 acres, 216 of which were in the Front Division of Back Lands, and 684 in the Rear Division. His town lot was Lot No. 5 in Block Letter O of the South East Division, which is now a portion of the Francheville property.

He did not long remain in Guysborough, but moved to Halifax, where for many years he was a Regimental Surgeon. It does not appear that he was married at the time of his presence in Guysborough, for no reference is made to Mrs. Boggs, or any family in the departmental rolls which still exist. He sold his town plot to Thomas Cutler in 1801, but by that time had been in Halifax for several years. In many of *Occasional's Letters* references are made to Dr. Boggs, and his activities in Halifax, where he occupied for many years a very prominent position and where some of his descendants still live.

It is not now possible to verify the statement, but it is believed to be the case, that the old Church records of the town refer to the fact that some of the material used in the construction of the first church was obtained from Dr. Boggs, who, after purchasing it, sold it when his removal to Halifax was soon to be effected.

The second of these regimental surgeons was Dr. McPherson, who was the surgeon of the Duke of Cumberland's Regiment. In the Town Clerk's records his name is given as John, but on the rolls of the regiment he is called James. These rolls do not refer to' his wife, but he was able to induce some one to share his lot very soon after his arrival in his new home, being in this particular more fortunate than many of his regiment, who in vain petitioned the English government to send wives out to them from England. Five children were born to him and his wife, Anna, between 1785 and 1791, after which date no other record has been found of the family. It has not been possible to connect this regimental surgeon with any of the McPherson families who now live in the County.

The land which he was given was a block of 600 acres of woodland, and Lot No. 1 in Block Letter K of the South East division, a lot across the street from the land now owned by the estate of the late Lieut.-Governor Fraser.

221

The third person referred to was not a regimental surgeon, and in fact appears on the rolls of his Regiment, the 60th Royal Americans, as a sergeant. He is said to have been of German descent, his name appearing first on the rolls as Ludovic Joppe, and being later anglicized to Lewis William Joppy. The name of his wife Jane is also on the roll, but no mention is made, nor has any been found, of any family. Dr. McPherson is credited with having two servants, one of whom was a negro, but Joppy was not so fortunate.

He drew lands on the south shore of the Bay, his town lot being one overlooking the waters of what is now called Back Cove. He is said to have lived during most of his working life, however, among the settlers on the Hallowell Grant or the Duke of Cumberland's allotment, who were on the eastern side of the harbour. His was the task for many years of looking after the medical needs of the community, a task performed in such a way as to have earned for him the appreciation and gratefulness of all in the community. A cove on the western side of the harbour still is known among the older persons by his name, though why this is, it is impossible to say. It may have been that at this point he made it his custom to cross the harbour, when called over to the western side on duty. His description is incomplete, unless reference is made to his mare 'Lively' which for some reason has not achieved oblivion, and one pictures without much effort the worthy little man, with his little pony and his well stuffed saddle bags, on his rounds among the sick and ailing.

He is said to have been buried on the old Hadley place, near the harbour entrance, in a private burying ground belonging to that family. His estate was administered upon in July 1817, and it would appear that his wife predeceased him. The Church of England records make few or no references to him, and one surmises that among his predilections was a liking for Lutheran rather than Church of England beliefs.

It is worthy of note that in the year 1803 he was one of the Health Officers named by the Court of General Sessions of the County.

About the same time these settlers were being landed in Guysborough, a smaller group of about 300 were set down at Country Harbour, on the Atlantic coast, under the shadows of Cape Mocodome or the Micmac 'home of the black-backed gull'. This group was made up of the members of three regiments, the North Carolina Regiment, the King's Carolina Rangers and the Royal South Carolina Regiment. The first of these had on its roll the Captain McNeil, so frequently mentioned in the life of Dr. D. McNeil Parker, who was a descendant. On the roll of the Royal South Carolina Regiment was the name of Lieut. Daniel Cornwell or Cornwall, who for some years thereafter was the doctor of that community.

He was not married when lands were given him, but he had a menage of three negro slaves, whose names are duly set down, Joe, Bob and Binna. Not until 1787 was he able to induce any person to share his joys and sorrows, when he succeeded in obtaining the consent of Miss Sophia Honseal to leave her home in Halifax and bear with him the hardships of a pioneer. Miss Honseal was one of three daughters of the Rev. Bernard Honseal who married members of these Carolina Regiments and settled in Country Harbour. Seven children were born to the Doctor and his wife between 1789 and 1798, the names and dates of birth being given in the Town Clerk's book. There also is to be found the doctor's sheep mark, from which we infer that he did not rely wholly on his medical practise to feed his rapidly growing family.

He himself died intestate in 1808. One cannot help wonder what became of Mrs. Cornwall and her brood, but if 'sparrows do not fall to the ground', Mrs. Cornwall was duly looked after and protected.

About the same time Antigonish was being settled, and here Dr. Dennis Heffernan of the Navy seems for a time to have provided for the settlers the service which the military practitioners were taking upon themselves in the other places named. About 1792 however, it would appear that he moved to Guys-borough, for deeds of that date bear his name, and in one of the year 1795 his residence is said to be Manchester, which name was sometimes then applied to the town of Guysborough itself. Other records are the births of several children, including that of the son William Owen Heffernan, who in after years was one of the county representatives, and whose grave is to be seen just inside the entrance gates of Camp Hill cemetery. The residence now occupied by the DesBarres family is the house in which in former times William O. Heffernan lived. Little has been discovered of the practice carried on by Dr. Heffernan, and even the date of his death is unknown.

If Joppy and Heffernan divided the meagre practise between themselves for a time in the early years of the nineteenth century they were not long in undisputed possession of the field, the newcomer being John Frederick Augustus Stickles. Most of the references to him have been found in the Christ Church records, of which church he was for several years a vestryman. He was present in the town for at least the time between 1811 and 1816, after which he disappears and his place is taken by Dr. Henry Inch.

No references have been observed of Dr. Stickles' family. He owned at different times a number of lots in the town, the first he bought being that lot on which later Mr. McColl lived. This was bought in May, 1811 for twenty pounds.

One of the first references to Dr. Inch is the date of his marriage to Mary Patterson, a widow, whose name before marriage was Nixon. She was a daughter of William Nixon, who seems to have moved from Halifax to carry on some kind of a business, not long after the arrival of the first settlers. There is no record of any family. On the morning of January 28, 1828, Dr. Inch's body was found under circumstances which pointed conclusively to foul play. He had been run through with a sword, and had perished from exposure during the night. The scene of his death was the vicinity of the old market square near the head of Miller's Cove. An effort was made to discover the identity of the persons responsible for the murder, and several members of a very prominent family were arrested. It was not possible to secure a conviction. The whole story of the events leading up to the doctor's death has never been made known.

Even before Dr. Inch's death another doctor had arrived. This was Dr. William Russel Cantrell, of Irish birth and parentage, who had already been in the Province several years before moving to Guysborough. A romantic, perhaps wholly incorrect, story explains his presence in Nova Scotia after a runaway match with the daughter of a neighbor in Ireland. In the Acadian Recorder of July 10, 1819, will be found one of the first references to his presence in Nova Scotia, this being an advertisement informing the public that 'next Wednesday' there would be opened in the city of Halifax a Pharmaceutical and Chemical Laboratory under Dr. Cantrell of Dublin. Perhaps this venture did not meet with the success for which he hoped, and about the year 1821 he is to be found in Guysborough. In the interval or for a short time after his first practising in

Guysborough he is said to have been at Sydney.

His field of practice was a large one, extending over half the county, and including in his territory the settlements far away on the Atlantic shore. There were no such roads as we have and many of the settlements were reached by following poorly marked trails through miles of wilderness and barrens. Such was the road which the doctor took one morning in August 1838, to attend a call in New Harbour, over twenty miles from the shiretown. Near the place where this trail was crossed by a woodland brook his lifeless body was later found, and Cantrell's Lake and Brook and Pond are landmarks on the now existing road, built in after years along the line of the old trail. He was buried in Guysborough on September 2, 1838.

There was a family of one or more daughters, and a number of Dr. Cantrell's descendants are now living in the Province. Among them are some of the Blanchards from Truro, and the family of which the much lamented Mrs. A. I. Mader was a member.

There have been few opportunities of judging of the professional attainments of some of these old practitioners. From the old church records, a number of which refer to the cause of death, we can obtain some idea of the prevalent diseases, and cannot but help remark the frequent deaths from infections, especially scarlet fever and small pox. One is saddened by the number of deaths in child birth, and the great frequency of entries indicating deaths from exposure tells a vivid story of the hardships inseparable from the task of home building in the wilderness. Around Joppy's name there still linger kindly memories, echoes of gratefulness for sympathetic work well done. These have been for him an enduring monument, his only one, since no stone marks his grave. When, however, we come to the period during which Dr. Cantrell labored, there are contemporaneous documents which permit us to judge of the quality of the professional work of which he was capable and in the light of which he need not be ashamed.

In 1832 an outbreak of Asiatic Cholera threatened, the disease having appeared in Halifax and Quebec. The minutes of the County Board of Health are still in existence, and very complete; the description of the means taken to meet the emergency is very full. The first meeting of the Board was held on August 9, 1832, following instructions from the Central Board in Halifax. His Excellency's Commission appointing five members was read. The County was thereupon divided into a convenient number of districts, in each of which an Inspector was appointed. Provision had been made for the appointment of Health Wardens in these districts by the Court of General Sessions, and an early special meeting of this Court was requested. The Board then proceeded to draw up regulations dealing with the destruction of offal on and near the fishing stages and beaches. Provision was made for obtaining supplies of blankets and medicines which might be necessary, and for securing such buildings as might be required for hospital purposes at various places in the County. The action taken was promptly reported to the Central Board, and attention was called to what was supposed to be a source of great danger, namely, the great influx of fishermen which yearly took place to the noted fishing resorts of the County. Then, in anticipation of infection being introduced from coasting vessels, the Board set off in the various harbours quarantine areas, where all craft entering from infected ports must remain for the quarantine period.

That scare passed off, but in the summer of 1834 there was another alarm. The schooner *Dolphin* of Arichat arrived in port from Quebec with the following story. She had cleared from Quebec in company with the Schooner *John Wallace* of Guysborough on the 17th of July. Cholera was then present in Quebec. On the following day three of the crew of the *John Wallace* sickened and died, and on the 19th the pilot also passed away. The vessels kept company till the 24th of the month, when they parted, somewhere about the northern end of Prince Edward Island, four men then remaining alive on the *John Wallace*. This vessel, greatly undermanned, was wrecked on the Island, the crew escaping to shore, and no more deaths taking place.

Dr. Cantrell was ordered by the Board to investigate and report, and on the strength of his report the *Dolphin* was released from quarantine, no cases having occurred on board that vessel, and there having been no direct communication with the unfortunate *John Wallace*.

During this year Halifax became severely infected, and it became necessary to adopt protective measures against that port, all of which are set down. Shortly after, the disease having disappeared, the record ends, the whole being by no means a discreditable record, in accordance with the accepted practice of the time.

During the latter years of Dr. Cantrell's life his colleague in the field was Dr. Henry Elliott, who was present at least during the years 1835-36 and '37. This is of especial interest, since another physician of the same surname and family followed him between the years 1893 and 1900, and at the present time, has been followed by still a third of this well known medical family.

Dr. John Pyke (or Pike) followed Dr. Cantrell from 1839 to 1842, during which year he was succeeded by Dr. Edward Carritte, who, the Christ Church record somewhat unctuously remarks, took over not only the practice but the pew. Dr. Carritte died in Dartmouth in 1888, and his eulogy, said to have been from the pen of Dr. D. McN. Parker, gives us many details concerning his well filled life.

GOLD MINING IN GUYSBOROUGH COUNTY

The gold bearing measures of the Province form a wide belt which extends from Canso westward along the Atlantic seaboard nearly if not quite the entire length of the Province. In width the belt varies from ten to thirty-five miles. Countless ages ago were laid down the quartzites and slates of a bed which is supposed to have been at least three, and which may have been as much as eight miles, in thickness, sedimentary deposits dating back to Cambrian or Pre-Cambrian times. Later, these quartzites and slates were exposed to such forces of pressure and displacement as served to crumple the strata into folds or pleats, so that in few places are they yet to be found in the horizontal positions they once occupied. The crumpling has taken a quite definite pattern. Pressure in roughly a north and south direction has resulted in there being formed a number of folds, called anticlines or synclines, running generally in a line parallel to the long axis of the Province. The upper folds are the anticlines, the lower are the synclines. There are nine or ten of these anticlines, with an average distance of four miles between them, where the greatest width of the deposits is exposed. Pressure lengthwise of the axis of the Province has formed anticlines which intersect the others at a high angle, even approximating a right angle, the distance between these crests being about twenty-five miles. Where the two anticlines meet or cross, a "dome" is formed, and these are important, since in them most of the gold is to be found. Here, where the folding has been the greatest, there has been the most cracking and crevice formation. Quartz and gold have been deposited from their watery solutions, in such a way as completely to have filled these cracks, thus forming the leads, which average about six inches, but which vary from mere threads to several feet in width.

Forces other than compression have been at work through these ages. Faults have cut across the folds, displacing the layers vertically or laterally. Erosion has carried countless millions of tons to a lower level. Glacial action has sheared away the heights, so that mountain masses of from three to five miles in vertical height have completely disappeared. Thus has been formed the drift or float, the riddle of the origin of which is often unsolvable to the prospector.

The gold measures in Guysborough County form a rough triangle, the apex being near Canso, the base in St. Mary's Municipality, where the width of the belt approaches its maximum. In that thirty-five miles of width, there appear to have been no fewer than nine anticlines. Although numerous faults or slips have interfered with their direct continuity, a number of them can be traced for some miles. As one moves eastward the exposed measures become narrower, so that near the Whitehaven road, where they are last seen, only five anticlines can be traced. At Canso, the quartzites and slates have been completely sheared away, leaving exposed the granites, much older geological formations.

The finding of gold at Mooseland on the Tangier River in the summer of 1860 was the spark which set the settlements east of Halifax on fire. One of the next discoveries was at Wine Harbour in July of the same year, when gold was found in the sand near the Barachois, this being the first discovery in Guysborough County. Just a year later, Joseph Smith found the first sights in quartz, in what was later known as the Smith lead, and a rush of gold seekers invaded the district. The Earl of Mulgrave found 200 men at work, when he inspected the field that fall, and a number nearly double that when he reinspected it a year later. On August 26th, a picnic party from Sherbrooke included sharp eyed Miss Margery Macintosh as one of its members, as it spent some time on the barrens west of Sherbrooke. She saw some shining particles in a rock, and was sufficiently interested to carry the specimen home, where no one knew what it was. But the secretive Nelson Nickerson, who had spent some days at Tangier, had his ideas on the matter and was told by Miss Macintosh where she had picked up the rock. That was sufficient to make him start a search, the results of which he kept to himself, as did his family, though not without arousing the curiosity of some inquisitive neighbours.

The month passed, and September came, an important month in the story of gold discovery in Guysborough County. Now, however, the scene shifted to Isaac's Harbour, to which place Elias Cook had returned after having worked at Wine Harbour, where he had learned to recognize quartz. On the 14th of that month, J. Hynes, who had been working with Cook, turned in the first specimens, found on the Free Claim, and John Latham found sights on the Burke Lead.

Four days later, Nelson Nickerson's suspicious neighbors in Sherbrooke turned out en masse after the sound of his hammer as he broke up the quartz boulders had betrayed both his actions and his whereabouts. Two hundred of them gathered and the result of their first day of work is said to have netted them about $400.00. Country Harbour next joined in, J. Fraser having added that settlement to the list of places where gold was known to exist. Then, two Indians found the Mulgrave Lead on the east side of Isaac's Harbour; Freeman Hudson made his discovery at Country Harbour, and now the conflagration was burning briskly, never, since that time, having wholly been extinguished.

It was not long before other names were added to this list. The Lower Seal Harbour group of leads was worked about 1867; exploration and prospecting was done at Cochrane Hill in the following year. The Crow's Nest workings dated from about 1878; the Upper Seal Harbour developments, though prospected much earlier, can not be considered as having been of much importance till the discovery of the belt of leads to which his name was given by Harry Richardson in 1892. The last important find was that by Samuel D. Hudson in 1893, who added the Forest Hill group of leads to the list of well known producers in the County. In addition to these places, the presence of gold has been proven in a number of other localities. Thus at Half Island Cove and Queensport there are known to be deposits, discovered a number of years ago, though little has ever been done fully to determine their values. The find of but a few years ago, on the barrens south-west of Lundy, is the latest addition to the list.

The extent to which the Guysborough County gold fields have contributed to the gold production of the Province has been very noticeable. According to the tables which have appeared in Malcolm's report, which gives the figures from 1862 till 1907 or 1909, over 305,000 ounces from a total Provincial production of about 900,000 ounces came from the Guysborough County mines. In more recent years, the percentage has increased rather than diminished, as will be seen from the statistics of the industry which appear in the Reports of the Mines Department. According to these in the years between 1862 and 1942, inclusive, there have been mined in the Province 1,127,646 ounces of gold, of which total 415,433 have been raised from the Guysborough County mines, nearly 37 per cent. For the three years, 1939, 1940 and 1941 the figures are 32,555 ounces raised in the County out of a total of 65,447 for the entire Province. This is 49 per cent of the total Provincial yield. From Goldenville alone has been obtained almost one-fifth of all the gold the Province has produced.

One is struck with the remarkable richness of the Guysborough County fields, as evidenced by the reports for the period from 1862 till 1907. Wine Harbour had a production of over 4,000 ounces in 1864, a production never again reached. In its first year, 1862, it reported over two ounces of gold to each ton of quartz crushed. Country Harbour reported over two ounces to the ton in 1862, three to the ton in 1863 and two in 1864, while the total raised in 1865 was not surpassed till 1883. Goldenville reported over three ounces to the ton in 1862 and over two ounces in 1866. Its total of over 9,400 ounces raised in 1867 was not exceeded during the remainder of. the period.

This is all the more remarkable if one remembers the conditions under which mining was being carried on at that time. In the newly developing industry skilled management was as lacking as were skilled mining crews. The mining law was defective and the miner had to develop his properties under conditions which gave him only a minimum of opportunities. Little or nothing was known of the geological formations in the mining areas, for not till a number of years had elapsed was the miner able to take full advantage of the help which could be given him by competent geologists. There was not even a good explosive available since these were the days of black powder, and not for some years was dynamite used. Many newly formed companies lacked funds for developmental purposes and in some instances the small amount which was available was wasted on unnecessary construction and experimentation. The desire to declare large dividends very quickly diverted money which should have been spent in developmental or exploratory work. And if mining methods were wasteful, still more wasteful were in some instances the methods taken to extract the gold from the quartz. In some instances as much as 20 per cent of the gold escaped the crude milling processes. The Guysborough County fields could by no means escape all of these adverse conditions, which were affecting to their detriment every Nova Scotia area, and it is little to be wondered at if flush early years were followed by a reactionary period from which the industry made but a difficult and slow recovery.   The year 1874 was the. darkest of these first reactionary years.

It was not, however, the worst which the industry in the Province has met, for the curve of gold production has been an unusual one. After a peak of over 27,000 ounces in 1867 the figure dropped to somewhat over 9,000 ounces in 1874. Then followed a definite and sustained recovery which carried the figure to 31,000 ounces in 1898 and over 30,000 ounces in several shortly succeeding years. Then followed a decline, very regular and sustained, so that in 1921 the total amount of gold raised in the Province was but 378 ounces. From that low point the figures again improved very steadily and regularly, till another peak of over 28,000 ounces was reached in 1938. Since that time, war conditions have caused a rapid diminution of the figures, and that though the price of gold has greatly risen.

WINE HARBOUR.

Gold having first been found here near the Barachois in 1860, it was not long before a number of leads were discovered. In 1862 seven were being

229

worked, the Smith, the Middle lead, the Major Norton, the Barachois, the Halliday, the Wiscasset and the Gillespie. The Smith lead produced for a time 6 ounces of gold to the ton of ore crushed. On one occasion, from the Hattie lead, five tons of quartz gave 135 ounces of gold. Its average production over a period of some months was 3 ounces of gold per ton of ore, the Middle lead with 2 1/2 ounces coming a close second. In 1863 the district produced more gold than any other in the Province, and it continued to pay richly for several years. Its banner year for that period was 1864, when over 4,000 ounces of gold were raised.

The names of some of the earlier Companies are the Eldorado, the Orient, the Provincial, the Caledonia and the Glenelg. A few years later the Eureka, the Napier, the Globe, the Phoenix, the Gladstone, the New Eldorado, the Wine Harbour Goldmining Company .Guysborough Gold Mining Co., the Plough Lead Gold Mining Co., and the Wine Harbour Co. were active.

After 1864 the production of the field declined till in 1880 only 61 ounces were obtained. The Plough Lead Mining Co. was largely responsible for the rehabilitation of the field, but production never again greatly exceeded 2,000 ounces a year. In recent years the returns have been negligible, though during its productive period it contributed 42,727 ounces to the Provincial total.

COUNTRY HARBOUR.

Although gold had been discovered in Country Harbour in 1861, it was several years, not in fact till 1868, that much more than some prospecting and developmental work was carried on. Then a small crusher was built and several leads were worked. In 1889 a find of greater richness was reported, and after that the Mason belt and the Prince lead reported production for a number of years. The Companies which have been most active in that field were the Country Harbour Co., the Antigonish Co. and the Sydney Co. This last one was in existence as late as 1909.

This is another of the Guysborough fields which has made no returns during recent years. The total yield of the field was about 10,000 ounces, during those years in which active operations were carried on.

GOLDENVILLE.

Activity in the Sherbrooke or Goldenville district commenced in 1861. The mines shortly thereafter opened up have been the most productive of all in the Province having contributed about one-fifth of the total Provincial yield, during over seventy-five years of continuous operation.

Shortly after the initial discovery, seven leads were being profitably mined, the Cumminger, the Aitkins, the Hayden, the Drysdale, the MacKay, the Blue and the Hewitt. The names of some of the Companies concerned were Messrs. Cumminger &C Co., the New York and Sherbrooke Co., the Wellington, the Grape Vine, Messrs. Bayne and Hayden and Messrs. McClure & Co. This field early took the lead among the greatest producers of the Province, and as early as 1867 made a return of 9,463 ounces, which, obtained from 7,378 tons of ore crushed, represented a yield of over one and a quarter ounces per ton.

230

In 1869 there were nineteen Companies actively operating. The names of some of these were the Wellington, working on the Cumminger and Dewar leads, the Rockville, the New York and Sherbrooke, the Delta, the Crescent, the Stanley, the Dominion, the Palmerston, the Metropolitan, the Kingston and Sherbrooke, the Meridian, the Chicago, the Canada, the Wentworth, the Cobourg, the Woodbine and the Caledonia. In 1870, over 6,000 ounces of the total of over 7,000 ounces produced in the field, came from the four Companies, the Wellington, the Dominion, the New York and Sherbrooke and the Palmerston. In the following year the main producers were the Wellington, the Sherbrooke, the Dominion, the Palmerston, the Caledonia and the Wentworth, which brought up a total of over 5,750 ounces.

The years between 1870 and 1895 were years of very varying success. The year 1877, for example, was one of the good years, with a production of over 8,000 ounces from only a little more than that number of tons of ore, or at the rate of 19 pennyweights per ton. The production declined, so that the very low point of 119 ounces for the whole field was reached in 1891. That was the period of a reconstruction of some of the companies at work, the Palmerston and several others combining to form the Pactolus Company. From that slump a relatively rapid recovery was quickly made, possibly because there was now available for the guidance of the mining operators definite and scientific knowledge of the geology of die field. New companies then came into being, as for example the Stellarton Gold Mining Co., in 1894, the Springfield and the New Glasgow. In the year 1897 when Faribault was preparing his carefully drawn map of the area, the operating Companies were the Bluenose, the Sutherland, Stuart Hardman, the New Glasgow, and the Stellarton. A little later came the Royal Oak and the Nova Scotia and Mexican. The Bluenose Co. had been formed by the amalgamation of the Springfield, the Caledonia, the Woodbine and the Cobourg Companies, and was very active from this till at least 1905. The three Companies, the Blue Nose, the Royal Oak and the Nova Scotia and Mexican, were responsible for most of the gold mined during the '90s, though at the end of the period production had so far stopped that only 28 ounces were reported as the output in 1909. It was the Nova Scotia and Mexican which pioneered in the construction of a power plant on the Liscomb River, where a 33 foot fall gave promise of being sufficient to furnish power. The total production of all the companies between the years 1862 and 1909 inclusive, with what was obtained from the Crow's Nest and Cochrane Hill properties, was 158,703 ounces.

The extent to which the Goldenville anticlinal dome had been prospected and developed is evidenced by the fact that in 1912, fifty-five different leads had been discovered in a width of 1,200 feet on the north side of the dome, and fifty in a width of 500 feet on the side to the south.

Since 1909 and including the production of the mine for the year 1941, Goldenville alone has produced 51,230 ounces. In 1941, after which production ceased on account of war conditions, it returned over 4,150 ounces from 25,617 tons of ore crushed. Its total production in 80 years is 209,952 ounces.

ISAAC'S HARBOUR.

To Joseph Hynes and Allan MacMillan is due the credit for the discovery of the first gold-bearing quartz to be found in Isaac's Harbour. Three anticlines have been located in the District, though the presence of faults has greatly disturbed the continuity of the leads. The first leads to be mined were the Mulgrave, the Victoria, the Burke and the Fraser. All these were very rich in gold. The Mulgrave, which for a time averaged a production of over 1 1/2 ounces to the ton, showed in one pocket a valuation of over 5 to the ton. The Victoria has produced 1 ounce and 7 pennyweights, the Burke 2 ounces, and from the Fraser as much as 120 ounces has been taken from 40 tons of quartz mined. The Consolidated Mining Co., the United Mining Association and the Gallagher Mining Co. were the prominent producers of the earlier years. In the year 1884, the latter Company produced 2,212 ounces from 913 tons of quartz, and its total production was 5,034 ounces from 1,978 tons.

In 1887 the leads on Hurricane Island were opened up and produced over 2,000 ounces. About this time the North Star and the Rockland Co. were active, the former being on the west side of the harbour. The Skunk Den was opened up in 1891 and mined in 1893 by the Eureka Co. In 1898 the Hurricane Point Company, under the management of W. F. Fancy, and the Economy Mining and Milling Co., under C. F. Andrews, were the producers. Still later, the Gold Finch Co. produced in one year 846 ounces from 1,193 tons.

This is another area in which for the recent years, production has well nigh stopped, only 1,234 ounces being reported for the years 1939-42, inclusive. The total production of the whole field has been 34,636 ounces.

LOWER SEAL HARBOUR.

The story of the Lower Seal Harbour District is an unusual one. Very early, a line of very rich boulders was found on the barrens back of the settlement. It extended for a distance of about two miles, from the sea near Cook's Cove to the Seal Harbour Lake. The boulders were so rich that the name of the Golden Stair was given to the formation. Prospecting in the years 1867-68 and 69 failed to disclose the origin of the drift, nor did search for many years thereafter prove any more successful. In fact it was not till October, 1904, that the large auriferous belt was discovered, the explanation being given that this was an instance in which the gold quartz originated in a cross lead which ran parallel to and not across the line of drift. The belts which have been worked are the Dominion, the Slate and the John Bull, and the Companies which have been the most active are the Beaver Hat Co. and the Seal Harbour Co.. They were most active in the years 1904 to 1907. However, in the years 1939-41, 12,806 ounces were produced from a total of 235,000 tons of quartz crushed, and the total production of the field amounts to 33,940 ounces.

UPPER SEAL HARBOUR.

This District is situated north of the Isaac's Harbour District. After much fruitless prospecting, Harry Richardson, in 1892, located the wide belt of low grade ore which was later known as the Richardson belt. The story of the whole District is largely the story of the development of operations on that belt, from which over 50,000 ounces of gold have been obtained from 375,000 tons of quartz brought up. As many as sixty stamps have been required to crush the product mined. Considerable difficulty has been experienced in separating the gold of this belt from the impurities, largely arsenical, which accompany it, and much experimental work has been necessary in order to discover how best the separation can be brought about.

The Dolliver Mountain Mining Co., organized in 1901 under G. J. Partington, joined the Richardson Co. in work on this field, and, after a certain amount of Provincial assistance had been obtained, endeavored to sink a shaft through the top of the anticline to tap the other underlying leads. The results, however, did not meet the expectations, and the project came to a halt in 1905. Only 361 ounces were obtained from the field in the years 1939-42 inclusive, although the District, since first being opened up, has produced a total of 57,661 ounces of gold.

COCHRANE HILL.

This includes the Crow's Nest mine, placed on the same anticline. At Cochrane Hill the paying leads are on the Ross and the Mitchell belts, while at Crow's Nest the Stake, the Ross and the Belt leads are those which have been most worked. The first work was done at Cochrane Hill in 1868, the Crow's Nest workings being opened up about ten years later. The Companies which have been mainly concerned in these workings are the Cochrane Hill Co., Kirk and Co., and Cumminger and Co., while the managers have included A. H. McQuarrie and G. F. McNaughton. The ore from these mines has not graded so high as that found in a number of other fields and the District is not among the important ones of the Province. Production was stopped on these leads some time ago, though while operating they reported 1,192 ounces, obtained from 11,649 tons of ore crushed.

FOREST HILL.

Samuel D. Hudson and his brother found first good drift and, at a later time, June 1894, the leads known by the name of the Ophir and the Mill Shaft. Later, the Salmon River and the Schoolhouse leads were located, these being the most remunerative, at least in the earlier days of the workings. The Companies which have done the most work are the Modstock, working on the Ophir lead, the McConnell Co., the Phoenix and the Strathcona, W. J. Mcintosh, G. F. McNaughton and B. E. Paterson being some of the managers. The leads have been found to be well mineralized, yielding nearly 2 J/1 ounces to the ton in 1907, over 2 ounces in 1908 and about 1 1/2 ounces in 1909. Little work has been done in this area for some years and only about 54 ounces of gold has been procured in the years 1939-42 inclusive: That, while operating, the district was a good producer is evidenced by its having reported a total of about 25,000 ounces from 56,378 tons of quartz brought up in the relatively few years it was in operation.

MILLER LAKE.

Prospecting opened up the gold bearing leads at Miller Lake, about five miles from Ecum Secum in 1903. The Noughler, the Lone Cloud and the Mill leads are the ones on which most work has been done, the operating Companies having been the Miller Lake Gold Mining Co. and the Liscomb Falls Mining Co. The field is one of the minor ones, having produced only 178 ounces of gold in 1939-42, inclusive, that amount having been produced from 514 tons crushed, and its total production having been but 386 ounces from

991 tons brought up.

Almost without exception the work which has been done in the fields which have been referred to has been rock mining on well marked auriferous quartz leads. Washing for gold has been undertaken as a prospecting device, but, if we except the attempts made at Wine Harbour and Isaac's Harbour in the early days of the industry, alluvial mining has been both seldom attempted and very little lucrative.

What are the prospects for the future of the industry in the County? When one thinks of a settlement, such for example as Forest Hill, where at one time a prosperous little village was to be found, now without an inhabitant, its workers all drawn to other fields, mostly outside the Province, one sees little hope for its rehabilitation. On the other hand, it seems indisputable that there are localities which have never been carefully prospected and tested and it is known that there are fields which are by no means exhausted. At prices which today prevail, nearly $35,000,000.00 worth of gold has been raised in the Province, of which Guysborough County has contributed about 35 per cent. There may easily be that amount or much more securely hidden or resistant to the present day systems of mining and recovery. This seems to be the opinion of W. Malcom, writing in 1912, and it is doubtful if, in the years which have since passed, additional information has afforded grounds on which an adverse opinion can be safely based. If his opinion is correct, the future of the industry in Guysborough County may not be so dark as at present it appears to be, and especially is this the case if the price of gold is long maintained at the present level.

TELEGRAPH AND CABLE

A wave of telegraph line construction swept the country when it became evident that a revolutionary system of intercommunication had been discovered. Nova Scotia caught the fever. It voted in 1849 the sum of 4,000 pounds with which to construct a telegraph line from Halifax to Amherst. A New Brunswick fine connected Amherst with Calais; the Maine Telegraph Co. formed a link which connected Calais to Portland, and thus the network spreading rapidly over die United States was given a connection to Halifax. More construction took place. In 1855 a line was built from Antigonish to Canso, passing through Guysborough. Miss Margaret MacGregor, in an office in the residence of William Moir, was the first Guysborough operator and Miss Esther Taylor, in the old Bigelow house, held the same position in Canso. It is quite unlikely that either one of these persons could take a message by sound alone, but depended on instruments by which the message was recorded. The first operator who in 1847 declared his ability to read a message by sound alone was regarded as a prodigy whose performance was nothing short of miraculous.

Soon came a period of consolidation and amalgamation. The American Telegraph Co. gathered together a number of lines of the American system. Then, Nova Scotia decided to go out of the telegraph business, as had Congress in 1847 and as Great Britain has not yet done, and gave a fifty year lease of its lines to the American Telegraph Co. The Western Union Telegraph Co. had been incorporated in the State of New York in 1856. It had made a phenomenal growth and had become a popular speculative stock. In the year 1866, it bought out the American Telegraph Co., and thus linked Nova Scotia to its American network. It did more, since by this purchase it procured an interest in a cable, the construction of which was under consideration.

The Atlantic Cable Co. did the pioneer cable-laying across the Atlantic, but almost immediately ceased operation when its cable broke in 1865. Then the Anglo-American Co. came into existence and in 1866 its cable landed at Heart's Content, Newfoundland. A little later it raised the end of the cable broken in 1865, and also landed it at the same place, the European end being at Foilhummerum Bay, one of the inlets of Valencia Harbour. In 1872, the Anglo-American bought out a French cable which had been laid to St. Pierre from Brest, and which was continued from St. Pierre to Duxbury, Mass., so that, when at a later date it itself was absorbed by the Western Union, with its own cable equipment, the Western Union became the dominating line on the Atlantic. That was long, however, after it had landed any of its cables in Canso.

Now appears Cyrus Field again on the scene, wholly undeterred by the experiences through which he had passed while the cables of 1865 and 1866 were being laid. This time, however, he was connected with the Direct Cable Co., and not the Anglo-American.

Bold Cyrus Field, he says, says he,

I have a pretty notion,

That I can run a telegraph

Across the Atlantic Ocean.

235

And run it, he did, in fact, for the second time. On May 27, 1874, the Steamer *Faraday* appeared off Torbay and landed the shore end of a cable which it then proceeded to continue to Rye Beach, New Hampshire. It then returned to England, took on board the main cable, which from Ballinskelligs, Ireland, was to pass to Faraday, Nova Scotia. But there was an accident; the cable broke and nothing more could be done that year. The next was a new year. The broken cable was picked up, spliced and the landing made at Faraday on September 15, 1875. A few messages passed, but in twelve days, the cable broke about 320 miles from Faraday. It was repaired and working again on November 4, but it again broke about 128 miles from Faraday on December 10th. Repairs were completed on January 10, 1876, and the *Faraday* returned to England. She had immediately to return, as a break took place on the La Have Banks, between Faraday and Rye Beach. Repaired on March 1st, a break nearer Rye Beach occurred on March 26th. When this one was repaired on April 11th, the jinx of breaks appeared for a time to have been laid, and Guysborough County had its first really successful cable, with the little Cable Station of Faraday in Torbay placing it on the cable maps of the world.

F. H. Blanchford was the Engineer in charge until early in 1875 when his place was taken by C. W. Lundy, who had come from Madras to accept the position. He had come to the Direct from the Anglo-American, and, at Heart's Content had read the first flickering cable news message which had ever crossed the Atlantic. Associated with Mr. Blanchford were Fife Jamieson, the Electrician, and Baron O. VonDhyre, the contractor's representative. The operating staff at Faraday in 1874 consisted of C. H. Yell, F. W. Kevett, S. S. Dickinson, S. H. Fenn, J. Manley, G. R. Mockridge, J. Laing, J. Grant, F. B. Gerard, T. H. Chapman, G. W. Mitchell, W. West, and W. J. Brown. A Mr. Wilson and T. P. Hambling came in 1875. Oscar Peterson was the Mechanician and J. Collins the batteryman. The names of other operators who were on duty at Faraday at one time or another are Messrs. Dicketts, A. Foden, J. Lawson, F. Paget, F. Burstall, T. Waugh, G. Bain and T. Stevens. In addition to the connection with the United States by cable, there was a connection with the Western Union Telegraph Co. by a line which passed through Larry's River and Lundy to Guysborough. Charles Barss was in control of this land line. Needed repairs to this line were made by Hugh MacDonald, the lineman, who lived at Guysborough. and who worked on a number of the Western Union lines. He had worked on a line which crossed Newfoundland, and also on the Western Union line which ran from the Strait of Canso to Sydney.

In numbers that group of operators is not a large one, but these persons, in the years which have elapsed, have made cable history over the entire world. Even today, there is not in existence throughout the world, a single cable station in which some member of that group is not remembered for the part which he has played in the story of cable undertakings. Many transferred to other companies, where they have taken much more than a minor part in the development of the vast cable systems which today link the continents so effectively.

They are remembered in the county today for many other reasons. Almost all young men, they quickly made themselves known for their participation in every social activity being carried on in their vicinity. Although the station was over twenty miles from Guysborough, they were soon welcome visitors in the Guysborough homes. Many of them married young ladies from Guysborough or the neighbouring towns. So they left pleasant memories of their presence in the homes, in the churches and on the athletic fields.

A cable operator of those days had duties far more difficult and exacting than has a present day operator, especially in connection with the receipt of messages. There was then no satisfactory and easily operated receiving mechanism. In a darkened room two persons were constantly on duty. One, the reader, watched intently a small galvanometer mirror. If a message was coming in he saw flashes of light of varying length in the mirror, reading them as letters which he announced to the second individual who wrote them down. There was no system for recording or keeping a message as it came over the wire. The faint flashes of light, seen for an instant and then lost, could not be strengthened beyond a certain point, since, if too great an electric impulse was put into the wire, there was danger of its heating, which would cause the destruction of the insulation, and the ruination of the cable.

The hours on duty of the operator were hours of intense application, so intense that they could not be long sustained. And in spite of it, a speed of not more than fifteen words a minute was all that could be maintained. Speeds of twenty-five hundred words a minute are now very commonly reached. The life of one of the old cables may not have been more than seven years, since by that time the insulation had so deteriorated that it could not stand raising for repairs. Built at a cost of $2,000 a mile, the annual repair bill may be from half to a million dollars a year.

The Direct Cable Co. did not long have to itself the advantages of location which the Guysborough County harbours afforded. The Western Union, always a progressive and enterprising company, and one, too, which had little scruples in its competitive methods, decided to add more cables to its equipment. In February, 1881, it had effected an agreement with the Gould lines, the Atlantic and Pacific Telegraph Co. and the American Union Co., and thus the control of a cable which had been landed at Port Hastings. It, however, selected Canso as the landing place for the new cables, though some of the Port Hastings buildings, knocked down in sections and carried to Canso, were used in the construction of the Canso offices. The European landing was made at Penzance; the landing place on this side being at Dover Bay, the cable being thence trenched to the buildings located on the hill in Canso which overlooks the harbour. This was in 1881. It was necessary to secure staffs for the new lines, and but natural that the staffs of lines already in existence be canvassed in order to obtain trained personnel. So in time it came about that the Direct Cable Co. lost a number of its operators who had been on duty at Faraday. Mr. Gerard and Mr. Brown joined the Western Union staff at Canso; Mr. Mockridge its staff at Penzance, where its European shore line was. The Western Union had telegraph connection with its American network, and also cable connection with New York by a cable, the shore end of which was at Coney Island. C. B. Dunham was the first Western Union Superintendent in Canso, having control of the shore lines, while W. J. Brown, from the Direct Co., controlled the cables. The staff included John Fothergill, who as a telegraph operator at Hull, England, had read off his wire the first news of the battle of Alma. The whole staff in its various departments has numbered as high as forty, remaining near that figure for some years. At a later date, having then landed some of its cables at Sydney, the Canso staff were for a time moved there, there remaining in Canso only one operator in charge of the equipment. They, however, moved back to Canso after several years, and the Canso offices are again open.

Meantime another individual was commencing to make cable history. The Codstock lode in Virginia City, California, was pouring millions into the bank account of J. W. MacKay. He put one million of it into Postal Telegraph stock and was made its President. He became interested in cables and talked J. Gordon Bennett into forming a partnership with him. The partnership in two months became the Commercial Cable Co. It selected Dover Bay for the Canso landing place and a hillside overlooking Hazel Lake as the site of its offices and buildings for its staff. The site was about two miles from Canso, where were the offices of the Western Union. The cables were brought through lakes or trenches from Dover Bay to the Hill, a distance of about four miles.

Eventually there were at least seven cables which were brought into the offices at Hazel Hill. No. I, the North Cable, ran from Waterville to the Hill, through Dover Bay, as did also No. 2, the South cable. No. 3, a heavy duty cable, ran from Waterville to the Hill, but through Fox Island. No. 4 ran from Waterville to the Azores and thence to the Hill through Fox Island. No. 5 ran from Waterville to the Hill through Fox Island. Shore cables were Coney Island Nos. 1 and 2, one through Dover and the other through Fox Island, and there was also a cable to Rockport, Mass. From Waterville, in addition to its London connection, there was a connnection with Paris through Le Havre. Hazel Hill was not an originating office, messages passing through it, but not being accepted there for paid transmission. The first cables of this system were landed at Canso on July 19, 1884, and the line was ready for business on Christmas Day of that year.

Commercial Cable Company building in Hazel Hill, about two miles outside of the town of Canso.

The cable system being thus provided for, there remained to be considered the land line system. The Postal Telegraph Co., being still dominated by MacKay, made a contract with the C.P.R. Telegraph Co., the lines of which paralleled the C.P.R. railway system, which gave it a connection through to Westminster, B.C. The Commercial Cable Co. had already, through the Postal, access to all its American lines. Traffic agreements made by the Postal and the Commercial with the All-American Cable Co., eventually determined their connection with the International Telegraph and Telephone Co., which, absorbing the Postal in 1928, makes the International the world encircling organization of today.

Again there were staffs to be gathered together and again the offices of the Direct Cable Co. formed a recruiting ground. G. G. Ward left the Direct to become General Manager of the Commercial, and Mr. Burstal, Mr. Foden, Mr. Paget, Mr. Dickinson and Mr. Lawson all joined the Hazel Hill staff from Faraday. Mr. Hughes did the same after some duty in Cornwall.

The first operators on duty at Hazel Hill made their appearance sometime before messages were actually transmitted. They were Mr. Dickinson, the Superintendent, who had been Mr. Lundy's Assistant Manager at Faraday; Mr. Lawson, also from Faraday; Mr. J. Peters, from the French Atlantic at Sydney; B. W. Colley, from the French Atlantic at St. Pierre; A. G. Winterbotham, from the Western Union at Canso, and J. D. Gaines from the Anglo-American at Duxbury. Miss Minnie Selden was the first C.P.R. Telegraph operator in the office at Guysborough, her office being in the old Masonic building.

The coming of the new Company into the field was not without other incident. Competition between the various lines had cut the rate per word of a message from $9.75, the 1866 figure, down to 75 cents. The Commercial reduced it to 40 cents. The Western Union, not to be outdone, cut it to 25 cents, and when the Commercial met that figure, made an additional slash to 12 cents. But the Comstock millions made the Commercial able to hold its rate to 25 cents, and eventually the Western Union gave up the fight, and accepted that, the rate of today.

From the proximity of the two stations at Canso, they being but about two miles apart, arose some interesting situations. Since deadhead communication, not involving the payments of the commercial rates, was permitted, operators in Canso habitually chatted with their friends in London and New York. The London offices of the two cables were in buildings almost adjoining. A Commercial Cable Co. operator in Hazel Hill could give a message to his London friend, which, handed to a messenger, could almost instantly be in the Western Union office and on its way back to Canso. Thus, dinner and fishing and tennis engagements could be and habitually were made between Hazel Hill and Canso, though the messages travelled over three thousand miles each way to arrive at their destinations.

Again, a blizzard of frightful intensity completely demoralized all telegraphic communication to or from New York. But cable communication through Hazel Hill to London was possible, and from London the message could be sent, also through Hazel Hill, to Boston or elsewhere in the United States. Thus hundreds of messages were sent during the enforced isolation of the city, each message paying full cable charges each way from New York to London, since Hazel Hill was not an originating office and could receive no messages for pay.

The Western Union cables, opened for business in 1881, used, as did the Direct Cable Co., the old mirror system for the reception of its messages.

239

Already by the time the Commercial Cable Co. was opened for business a satisfactory recording system was available, ink flowing in a capillary tube, and being read as above or below an imaginary or "zero" line on a moving strip of paper. The Commercial used this system, though its operators, could, if need be, use also the mirror system. Later advances have made both of these systems out of date.

For several years, the three cable companies made use of the facilities which the Guysborough County harbours afforded. Then, the Direct Cable Co. made a change. Its shore ends were moved from Torbay to Halifax; its staff of operators was moved to that place, and almost immediately the little community, Faraday, was left without a single occupant. This was in the year 1887. One by one, its buildings were torn down or moved away, and today even their foundations are little discernible. But many memories of the existence of the company remain, these including that of the personal visit by Cyrus Field and of his being entertained by the Guysborough residents.

In the year 1900 there were 19 Trans-Atlantic cables in operation, scattered quite widely along the American Atlantic seaboard. More of these landed in the immediate vicinity of Canso than at any other single point on that seaboard. The temporary removal of the Western Union lines to Sydney may for a time have altered this condition, but likely much more to have altered it, was the proposal made at one time to move all the Commercial lines to the head of Chedabucto Bay. One spring every one of the lines of that Company which had been landed at Dover had been cut by the heavy ice. Mr. Dickinson, who had always been partial to a site farther up the Bay, but who had been over-ruled by Sir Alexander Siemens, the maker of the cable, again proposed the selection of a site near Cook's Cove. But at that time the Electric Light plant had just been completed and was in operation and the work was being done on the erection of a new office building. The Company considered that too much money was tied up in these new constructions to justify moving to the Cook's Cove location.

One of the most remarkable things in connection with the development of the now worldwide cable systems is its international aspect. The cables themselves were made by Germans, though the German, Sir Alexander Siemens, had his factory at Woolwich in England. The Americans first conceived the idea of so linking the hemispheres and it was American money which financed the companies. The English not only did the actual work of laying the cable, providing the ships which were necessary for this important task, but almost without exception operated every cable which was laid. Almost all cable operators were persons who had been rigidly trained in England, having met the tests which would have procured for them positions on the English governmental lines. Even in the largest offices, where both land lines and cables met, all the work connected with the cables was done by men trained in England, while Americans or Canadians were the land line operators. To some extent that distribution even today exists. Perhaps a still more remarkable fact is that the American ingenuity which had fashioned the instruments used in telegraph and land line work, was singularly sterile in the fashioning of instruments for cable offices. Here every instrument was the production of English inventors or scientists, with the possible exception of one, an instrument now in use in every cable office in the world, which was the invention of a member of a family which for many years lived in Canso.

SABLE ISLAND

Dark Isle of Mourning—aptly art thou named,
    For thou hast been the cause of many a tear
For deeds of treacherous strife too justly famed
    The Atlantic's charnel, desolate and drear.
If, for a moment rests the Muse's wing
    Where through the waves thy sandy wastes appear,
'Tist that She may one strain of horror sing,
    Wild as the dashing waves that tempests o'er thee fling.

                  J. Howe.

Seaward from the shores of Nova Scotia and Cape Breton for some hundreds of miles stretch the relatively shoal waters of the continental shelf, built up by the attrition through countless ages, of the nearby land. This shelf, perhaps better known as the Banks, is among the richest of the world's fishing grounds. Here are the submerged deltas of mighty prehistoric rivers, the product of glacial or other erosive action on the continental mass. Over much of it, the average depth of water is now from thirty to seventy fathoms. The bottom is composed of sand, pebbles, shells and corals. Only in one place does the bank extend to or above the water level. This is at Sable Island, about eighty-five miles from White Haven in Guysborough County. The island thus represents the extreme height reached by the heaped up sands of a bank which extends for two hundred miles east and west and nearly that same distance in a north and south direction.

The Island is a long narrow elevation, lying in a southeasterly direction from Canso or White Haven. It is now about twenty miles in length and approximately one mile in width, of a slight bow or crescent shape, with the concavity facing shoreward. At the ends the cusps continue the curve in bars, the total length of which exceeds the length of the island itself. The general direction, as one stands on the eastern end of the island and looks along the gradually curving crescent, is westerly. During heavy weather the sea breaks for nearly twenty miles on each of the bars which form the ends of the island, so that, by island and bars, has been formed an area of danger, nearly sixty miles in length though but two or more miles in width, roughly parallel to the Nova Scotian mainland. Many conditions have united to make of it a veritable marine death trap.

It is somewhat difficult to say how early it was in the story of the discovery of the American continent that this sinister reputation was acquired. Sir Humphrey Gilbert's loss,—if it was among its breakers that he met his fate— may have been among the first to have warned the mariners, groping their hesitant way along the coast line. Not the least terrifying to these hardy men must have been their doubt as to its exact location, a doubt which it took many years to remove. In cumbersome vessels, little able to make much headway to windward, with the crudest of instruments to aid them in their navigation, it is little wonder indeed if the terror of its shoals obsessed them, since, lacking a precise knowledge of its location, there was no safeguard against their vessel striking, even at a time when all seemed safe. As late as the middle of the Eighteenth century, when Chabert first definitely fixed its location, English, French and Dutch maps varied by as much as nine degrees in their longitudes of the eastern coast of North America and the Sable Island shoals. Different maps placed its position in latitudes as far apart as almost two full degrees. French maps placed it on a due north and south line from Louisbourg; English maps on a line south from Canso. Even Chabert, who sighted and verified the position of its western end in 1750, deducing its latitude and longitude from that of Martingot, (White Haven) had not been able even to estimate its length or size or the direction of its axis, since, after sighting its western end on a clear evening, a three day storm had drawn a curtain between him and it and driven him far seaward. The west end which he saw is, too, the part where erosion has most taken place, and the land which Chabert saw may now be a score or more of miles from the west end of today.

As it has been placed upon the modern charts, the situation of the Radio Station, which might be considered as the heart of the island, is but several miles south of. the point where the parallel of the 60th degree of west longitude cuts the 44th degree of north latitude. Its position, near the southern limit of the continental shelf brings it about that depths of over one thousand fathoms are to be found less than fifty miles to the south, although the greatest depth of water between the island and the mainland, a distance of about eighty-five miles, little exceeds one hundred fathoms. Fortunate indeed it is that the long axis of the island is parallel with the stream of ocean traffic to and from the Banks and Europe. Were it otherwise, the perils of navigation would be greatly increased.

The island consists of two long narrow ridges of sand, coming together at their ends, with an intervening valley throughout much of their lengths. On the outer sides of these the seas break. Much of the inner sides of these ridges form the shore of a long narrow lake, called Lake Wallace, now about eight miles in length, though formerly twice that long. There have been times when a small vessel could enter this lake by a natural channel, but the passage way has been subject to change or even to complete blocking as a result of storms.

The similarity of vegetation found on places so far removed from each other as Newfoundland. Sable Island and Cape Cod has led geologists to believe that, in one of the glacial periods, an immense glacier forced southeastward from the continental heights, ploughed up a bar which connected those three points. In later geological eras, portions of this bar were eroded and removed, Sable Island being the only portion yet remaining, and above tide level.

The tide range is that usually seen along the Nova Scotian coast, from four to six feet. As is common along any sandy bar, the water does not deepen gradually and evenly from low water mark. There is formed a series of sloughs with intervening bars over which the seas break heavily in bad weather. There may be as many as three such bars, with at places deep water in the intervening sloughs. On the south side of the island the water shoals more gradually than it does on the north, till the edge of the continental shelf is reached. Visiting vessels usually anchor a mile or more from shore on the north side. From such an anchorage with an offshore wind a landing can be made in good weather, but usually only in a surf boat.

The difficulty of navigation said to be peculiar to that portion of the coast is due largely to the strength of the ocean currents which may at any time be experienced. In fact, those currents may have been responsible largely for the deposition of the island itself, since it is said that wreckage or bodies may completely encircle the island several times before being cast ashore. Situated as it is on the fringe of the Gulf Stream, there passes it, inshore, the various branches of the great Arctic flow speeding southward along the Newfoundland shore and out the Cabot Strait. To the south and east is the Gulf Stream, hurrying Europe-ward. Fogs of a density little known elsewhere are experienced frequently and at any time of the year. These conditions, with the violent and little heralded storms which are but too frequent along the northern edge of the Gulf Stream combine to give the island its widely known designation as the graveyard of the Atlantic.

The island is at the present time entirely treeless. The highest ground is to be found near its eastern end, but this is not more than eighty feet above sea level. At its western end it rises not more than twenty feet above the level of the surrounding waste of waters. Over much of it there is no vegetation, nothing to hold in place the shifting sand dunes, but there are places where there is some coarse grass mixed with wild peas. In the long central valley and along the edges of the lake there is to be found in places a soil of black peaty texture capable of providing subsistence to some vegetable growth, and here and there some small ponds, the water of which, protected from the surrounding sea water by a somewhat impervious subsoil, may be fresh. Some birds such as wild ducks and sparrows are said to remain on the island during the entire year. In seasons of migration others visit and rest before renewing their journeys. Many seabirds nest in large numbers at certain portions of the island. Seals, both the common harbour seal and the larger Greenland seal are sometimes seen, though the latter variety does not remain throughout the year. Walruses, the catching of which was formerly an industry which brought temporary residents to the shores of the island, have entirely disappeared.

It is somewhat difficult to say to what extent design has been supplemented by accident in respect of some of the other life which is now to be found on the island. The commonly accepted version that cattle were first left there by Baron De Lery in the year 1518 is said to rest entirely upon the authority of Les Carbot, writing nearly a hundred years after the incident had occurred. Champlain, to whose statements as a rule more credence can be attached, makes no reference to Such a visit, but gives the credit for their presence on the island to some Portuguese whose names are unknown, but who placed the herds on the island in the year 1552, and the historian of Sir Humphrey Gilbert's expedition also makes the same statement, supplementing it with the information that hogs were landed there at the same time. Charlevoix seems inclined to the opinion that the accident of the shipwreck of a Spanish vessel at about that period was the better explanation of the mystery. However they got there, and regardless of the identity of the individuals who brought them, the fact remains, that the presence of cattle on the island from the time of Champlain till about the year 1700 was appreciated with thanksgiving by many luckless individuals whom chance threw upon its shores, even though the herds had, at times, severely suffered from the inroads made upon them by greedy visitors who slaughtered them only for their skins. They aided in keeping alive De La Roche's convict colonists and doubtless many more. John Rose, in 1633—forced to remain on the island for three months after his vessel had been wrecked, by the end of which time he had built a yawl

243

in which he was able to reach the mainland— reported the number of cattle then on the island as about 800. Within a few years the number had been cut to about 150, by Acadians, who, on the strength of Rose's report, had gone there for the purpose of collecting skins. About the last which is definitely known of them is the report coming from Bishop Saint Vallier, who says that there then were, at Beaubasin, cattle which had been brought some years since from Sable Island, which though wild when first brought ashore, were gradually becoming more tractable and profitable for their owners. This report was made after the visit of the Bishop in the year 1686.

The island has a past which is sinister and dark. Even at the present time, in spite of the safeguards which it has been possible to install, there are few places in navigable waters which are more dreaded. What its future will be it is difficult to forecast. This is the case, since there is no doubt but that changes are taking place on and about it which threaten its complete disappearance. According to the charts and plans made in the year 1775, the island was then about forty miles in length and two and a half in breadth. Another careful survey made about twenty-five years later indicated that there had been a diminution of total length amounting to about nine miles. The eastern end of the island had been extended about four miles, while thirteen miles of the western end of the island had become submerged. The island was then only about two miles in width. The earliest French writings refer to the presence on the island of many thickets of bushes and note the presence of trees, though these were not very numerous. The presence even yet of peaty soil near the center of the island indicates that there had been a time when there was much more vegetation than is now to be found, and the suggestion has been made that in the early days of discovery, its appearance was such as to make it seem that it would be a more suitable place for the planting of a small group of colonists than would be the mainland. The lake in the center which used to be about fifteen miles in length has shrunk to about eight miles, and the width of the island has also been halved. Particularly, the erosion has taken place along the length of the southern ridge which separates the lake from the seas. This, which was some time ago about a mile in width, in places, is now not more than one hundred yards wide, and the sea breaks over it in stormy weather. Even one hundred years ago, the height of the eastern end of the island was about two hundred feet, and there were several other hills as high as one hundred and fifty feet. The prevailing wind, which is westerly, seems to be bodily moving the whole island to the east, while at the same time it is leveling it at a rate which must be considered alarming. When first the island was made the site of a Government establishment, the opening into the lake was on the north side of the island. That opening was closed for many years thereafter, and an opening in the south side was formed by a furious gale in 1826. Two American vessels which had sought refuge in it were trapped inside in 1836 by a storm which closed up the entrance they had used. A number of changes in the sites of the lighthouses and stations have been necessary, as the sea has encroached upon and undermined their foundations. To what extent these changes will be progressive it is difficult to say.

Although the Island is situated but a short distance from the mainland of Nova Scotia it is not in any way under the control of the Nova Scotian government. Its status is that of a private possession of the former Department of Marine and Fisheries, or its successor in office, in whom is vested its complete control. It has latterly been the custom, at least locally, though there may not be actual authority for the procedure, for the senior individual in

244

charge to be called the Governor. From the harbours on the mainland it has not been difficult to procure persons thoroughly capable, of manning the life saving craft, and of being trained to handle the life saving equipment quickly and efficiently. In recent years, since the shore equipment has been motorized, since motors have largely replaced oars in the boats, and since the installation of directional and other radio apparatus, a class of personnel of greater technical ability has been required, but it has not been difficult to obtain for these services thoroughly proficient individuals. With constant communication with the mainland now possible, with frequent trips to the Island from the mainland of steamers engaged in the maintenance of the lighthouses and with the knowledge that if an emergency arises, help from the mainland can be procured in relatively few hours, the lot of the staff has been greatly improved from what it was when communication with the shore might not be possible for months. One has little difficulty in picturing the staff as a contented little group, happily engaged in their daily tasks and thoroughly alert to the importance of their duty of safeguarding the passing wayfarers of the deep. The predecessors of those now on duty literally have been able to save from an almost certain destruction hundreds of the crews and passengers of the unlucky craft driven on the Island's cruel bars. There is every reason for believing that the staff of today will no less ably and efficiently meet any emergency which may arise.

If one attempts to follow understandingly the story of the island from the time of its first appearance on the maps of the world till the present time, it will be seen that there are three separate and distinct phases or divisions into which that history very naturally divides itself. The first phase would include the story of its discovery, the gradual appreciation of its unique position as a menace to navigation, the harrowing tales of the very few individuals who lived to tell of their experiences after having been cast away upon its shores and the dark and sinister accounts of the lawless acts which finally compelled governmental action. This phase can be considered as having ended during the first years of the nineteenth century. During the second phase, after there had been placed on th island a number of men equipped for giving aid to those in distress, the number of wrecks was little if at all diminished, but there was this important difference, that almost in every instance the crews or passengers of the wrecked vessels were saved. This was the case for a number of years, even after lighthouses had been placed on the island, and various devices had been installed intended to warn the passing navigator of danger. Only in the third or final phase, when steam propelled vessels of greater maneuverability replaced the sail driven ones, when improved sounding apparatuses came into more general use, when radio systems could be used to warn vessels of their danger and when the passing navigators learned to avail themselves of the widely spread warnings of the approaching onset of storms and foul weather, has the number of wrecks greatly diminished.

Little is known of the early history of the island and its discovery. It has been suggested that Cabot may have seen it on his first homeward voyage, having mistaken the sandhills for the two islands which he reports. It has also been suggested that it is the island named Santa Cruz which was described by Herrara about the year 1505. If so, it was included in the grant given by the King of Portugal to Joam Alvarez Fagundez in 1521, and as such it makes its first appearance on a world map, that of Cabot's which is called the *Mappemonde*, supposed to date about the year 1544. A Portuguese navigator of the year 1546 first makes record of the characteristic physical feature, calling it the

I. de Sable, and an Italian one of the year 1548 refers to it as the Isella del Arena. Thereafter, possibly because of the sinister reputation it already was commencing to acquire, some attempt to establish its position is made on every map which appeared, though there are differences, both in respect of its outline and its distance and relative bearing from the main coast line. Champlain places it as an island triangular in shape and of approximately the correct bearing from Canso, but at a greater distance than is actually the case. Denys notes its presence as a long narrow island, curved, with its convexity towards the land but correctly located. According to him, however, it covets a much larger area than one expects to see, a length, for example, more than half as great as that of Prince Edward Island and of about half the width..

The first incident in its recorded history is supposed to have been the visit of Baton DeLery and his placing on the island a number of cattle. The date has been variously given as 1518 and 1508, possibly with the former as the one most generally accepted. It should be remarked, however, that doubts have been cast, not only on the date of the event, but on the event itself. Champlain, the accuracy of whose statements is almost universally conceded, gives an entirely different explanation to account for the presence on the island of those cattle. However, that they were there is an important factor on its next and undoubtedly correct breaking into the headlines of the news of the world.

Troilus du Mesgouez, Marquis De La Roche, received from the French court an authorization to undertake the settlement of the new world, and since volunteers to undertake with him the task which was in mind were not forthcoming, fifty or sixty convicts from different French prisons were turned over to him as the human element of the experiment. He is said to have left France in the year 1598 with his convicts in one ship, piloted by Chef D'Hotel, a Norman pilot of experience. Making his landfall at Sable Island, and knowing little of the potentialities for settlement of the land to which he proposed to sail, he decided on placing the convicts upon the island, while he went ahead to select a place on the mainland considered suitable for the establishment of a permanent settlement. Leaving therefore his settlers on Sable Island with a small supply of provisions and equipment, he sailed away towards the Nova Scotian coast. A storm came up and he was driven far to the east, so far in fact that it became impossible for him to return. He therefore made his way back to France, leaving the convicts to their fate. In France he met with other misfortunes, and for a number of years, an attempt to reach the abandoned unfortunates could not be made. At last, in the year 1603, Chef D'Hotel was sent to bring back to France any of the survivors who might be found. On his arrival on the twentieth of September, only eleven were found to have survived, the remainder having succumbed to disease, exposure, hardship and crime. They had succeeded in making for themselves some kind of a shelter from the elements and had subsisted on the flesh of seals and cattle which they had been able to kill, dressing themselves in the skins of the animals so obtained. Thus dressed, they were presented to the King of France on their return, their sufferings having gained for them a remission of their sentences.

Was it upon Sable Island that the *Delight,* the "Admiral" of Sir Humphrey Gilbert's little fleet was lost in 1598? The account that she was battered to pieces on those cruel bars before the eyes of the crews of the *Golden Hind* and the *Swallow* seems to be definite enough to carry conviction. Those crews themselves escaped so narrowly that they were not able to come to the assistance of the few members of the crew of the *Delight* who succeeded in leaving the doomed vessel in one of her boats. Fortunately a passing French vessel picked up this little remnant and it was eventually returned safely to England. It has, however, been a much debated question whether or not it was on Sable Island that the *Delight* was lost. If it was, to her must be given the dubious credit of being the first of the long list of hundreds of vessels known definitely to have come to grief on the island's bars and the few sailors who escaped the catastrophe were the first fortunate few who so narrowly approached death's portals and lived to tell of their experiences.

For some years thereafter little is known of what took place on the island. It undoubtedly was visited at intervals by persons who were drawn thither by the opportunities it afforded for the capture of seals and walrus and the collection of material from the increasing number of wrecks, as the opening up of the continent brought more and more vessels within the reach of its dangerous sandbars. All who could avoid it did so. Of those who could not do so, few returned to tell the tale of their experiences. John Rose, of Boston, was one of these few, after his vessel the *Mary and Jane* was lost there during the year 1633. After a stay of about three months, which he occupied in making from the wreckage of his vessel a small boat in which eventually he was able to get to the mainland and safety, the reports which he made were such as to result in several parties or individuals becoming so interested as even to attempt a settlement. He then estimated that there were about eight hundred cattle. Foxes were to be found in large numbers, including many of the highly prized black variety. Rose himself first piloted a party of seventeen prospective settlers there, and after his return to Boston, succeeded in organizing a company to return for the purpose of hunting. Again arriving, he found the French Acadians well established and in control of the island, with already the number of cattle so diminished that but one hundred and fifty were to be found. The absence of undergrowth in which game animals could take shelter, the disappearance of the walrus from Nova Scotian waters and the decimation of the herds of cattle soon discouraged more visitors and thereafter for many years few indeed were those who landed willingly upon its inhospitable shores.

But all were not so fortunate as was Rose. Its reefs and bars continued to take their annual toll. With no assistance from persons on the shore, few indeed of those whose vessels once struck reached land in safety. If they did so, it was but to substitute for a death among the surges, a death still more horrible to contemplate, for their chances of removal by a passing vessel were few in the extreme. There are only too many proofs of such experiences, the later discovery of an extemporized shelter, a few articles of clothing, a tattered flag, some rude utensils and both human and animal bones, telling the tale of suffering and death.

One is quite justified in thinking that an appreciation of these conditions was one of the reasons for the next appearance of information about the island in the governmental records. It may safely be assumed that the losses of life and property which had taken place on its shores had been commented upon freely in Massachusetts, from whence came such a large proportion of the fishing fleet which sought its lading on the surrounding banks. We might expect, too, that humanitarian interests, rather than interests of profit, would weigh heavily with the Rev. Andrew LeMercier, the pastor of a French Protestant church in Boston, when he conceived the idea of applying to the Nova Scotia government for the grant of the island in March, 1738, for the purpose of settlement. Indeed, the proof of such humanitarian interest is plainly manifest, in that, even though he never succeeded in making much headway with his attempts to place settlers on the island, he did succeed in placing there again a number of domestic animals, sending numbers of them on more than one occasion. One respects also his business qualifications and quite agrees with him in his contention that, considering the difficulties which would have to be faced by his settlers, it would not seem quite reasonable for the government to expect him to pay the quit rent of a penny an acre, which usually was the monetary consideration on which a grant was issued. It is a sad commentary on human nature that the reverend gentleman found that not only had he to make headway against the natural disadvantages of the island, but that he had to protect himself against the depredations and losses inflicted upon him by occasional lawless crews of visiting fishing vessels, who stole his cattle and his goods. Nor were these replaced, even after advertisements had appeared in the Boston papers. The net results which he experienced may not have been very satisfying, but it is known that for a time some persons induced by him to settle on the island, did so, temporarily occupying quarters, probably rude and uncomfortable, indeed. It is also known that through their presence on the island a number of persons escaped death, whose vessels the far reaching sand bars had claimed as their prey. The horses to be found on the island today are the descendants of those placed there by Mr. LeMercier. The cattle have long since disappeared.

The years rolled on and when next reference is made to it, on its bars had occurred a number of disasters which conceivably may have altered the whole trend of events in the New World and determined the future destiny of North America. The fight for the control of Canada was being bitterly fought out between France and England. France, determined to maintain her sovereignty, made a supreme effort forever to settle the question, placing upon D'Anville the responsibility of sweeping away all the English claims of discovery and ownership. One of the largest fleets of the period was equipped to oust the British from all the disputed territory. Of that mighty fleet no fewer than four ships of the line and a transport went to their doom on the Sable Island bars, and if from their crews a single individual was saved except a few survivors from the *Legere*, transport, history has not recorded it. This occurred on September 14, 1746, and was one of rhe shattering blows which forever dimmed the high hopes of France and brought to naught one of her greatest efforts.

Reference has already been made to the fact that up to this time there existed among those most often engaged in the prosecution of their designs in the New World but a very hazy idea of the exact location of the island. It is reasonable that France, so lately the victim of this ignorance, and determined that ignorance should be dispelled, used this as the argument justifying the sending out of Chabert in the summer of 1750 to determine accurately the position of a number of landmarks along the Nova Scotian coastline. From his landfall at Louisbourg, his first expedition was directed towards Sable Island. That one failed and it was not till the 5th of July of the following year, that as evening fell, he caught to the southeast, his first glimpse of the island and the seas breaking on its western bar. But that was all he was fated to see. He was able to deduce its latitude from that of Martingot (Whitehaven) as 44 degrees and 6 minutes, but a heavy blow came up during the night. For three days he endeavoured to beat back to its vicinity. Then he was forced to give up the attempt and sail for Louisbourg. He estimated that the distance of the west end of the island from the southwest point of the large island of Martingot (probably White Island) as being twenty-five and a third leagues.

Again for a time there is a break in our information concerning the island. Several persons headed by a Michael Flannigan asked for permission to stay on the island in 1774. During the Revolutionary War, the Revolutionary authorities, quite well aware that their own shipping stood to profit most by any arrangements made to succour persons in distress on it, enjoined their fleet and privateers to respect any vessel which might be engaged in carrying there provisions or supplies. John Paul Jones, on the occasion of his descent on Canso, had a rendezvous near it, and on one occasion, is said to have used his superior knowledge of the island's bars, when being pursued by a heavier English frigate, to effect his escape, crossing the bar in his lighter vessel at a point where he knew his heavier and deeper opponent could not follow. An individual, Jesse Lawrence, in the year 1788 resided there, engaged in the seal fishery and presumably made there a livelihood, sheltering his vessel in the central lake, then accessible from the sea, till lawless visitors destroyed his home and forced him to return to the mainland.

A more interesting effort, one not actuated by ideas of personal profit but entirely by humanitarian motives dates from that same year, and it is rather remarkable that it again originated in New England. Governor Hancock of Massachusetts had acquired, or was thought in New England to have done so, some claim to the island, presumably by lease. The Boston Humane Society became interested and appointed a Committee to consider what action might be taken, giving due consideration to the fact that anything which might be done would involve what might be thought to be an intrusion into what was alien territory. The report of the Committee, signed by Thomas Russell, the Chairman, was in due course received. It dwelt shortly on the purpose which had called the Society into being. It referred to the fact that the Society had been instrumental in the construction of a number of small houses for the protection of persons cast ashore along the coastline near Boston Harbour. It suggested that similar structures might be erected on Sable Island or that families might be induced to settle there. The size of the island was such, however, as to require the construction of so many houses or the settling of so many families that the funds of the Society were utterly inadequate to permit the Committee to make a recommendation for the adoption of either one of those procedures. Mr. Russell then went on to say that as Governor Hancock was largely concerned in the ownership of the island, he might be so placed as to be able to secure financial assistance from state or national sources. The report was forwarded in due course to Governor Hancock and he in turn placed the matter before the Gentlemen of the Senate and the House of Representatives. "Though the island is situated in a foreign kingdom, yet it will be no less advantageous to the navigation of the United States". There the project seems to have been halted, nor does it appear how or when Governor Hancock's claim of ownership was extinguished. The opinion of the Committee that the project was one too great to be handled by any private organization was to gain ground, and when finally it was undertaken, a Provincial organization assumed the responsibility.

But if bona fide efforts at settlement were lacking, and if yet the necessity for providing some means for warning shipping of the dangers of the far reaching shoals did not bring about action, other forces were at work, the effect of which was soon to be felt. The island was gradually acquiring a reputation which year by year was becoming more sinister. Organized piracy may have been driven from, the seas, but there were yet groups of lawless seamen, prowling the deep for gain. Along many remote and isolated portions of the coastline, other groups, equally lawless, did not scruple at luring ships to their destruction for the loot of the cargo which might be obtained. Sable Island was known to be a place which lent itself to operations of this kind. A light displayed at night at any place along its shores meant to a passing mariner, either the riding light of a vessel safely moored or a shore light beckoning him to a secure anchorage. Woe betide the unlucky sailor if he so read the message, for once lured beyond a certain point, escape was almost impossible. A shipwrecked crew, which had succeeded in saving their lives and possibly some of their belongings, was ill able to protect either their lives or their belongings against the rapacities which were experiences common to such lawless groups. Even the bodies of the dead were not exempted from violation for the trinkets which might be found, and since it was more easy to rob the dead than the living, the line was not drawn at murder, if thereafter the end might be the more easily obtained. It became more and more bruited about that Sable Island lent itself to the exhibition of such practises. It is suggestive that when finally these considerations brought it about that permanent provisions were to be made for placing on the island a number of persons whose primary purpose it was to save lives and property, almost contemporaneously it became necessary to remove from the island some individuals whose presence had, it was thought, been actuated by motives which could little bear scrutiny. This was the experience of the year 1801 and from that date the second phase of the history of the island commences.

It begins with the action taken in the Nova Scotia Legislature in the year 1801. After providing for the removal of wreckers from the island, it arranged for the vote of $2,400.00 for the assistance of three families of entirely reputable persons to be kept permanently stationed at suitable places on the island for the care of property and the protection of life. A government Commission was appointed. James Morris was selected as the first Superintendent, at a salary, first of $240.00 a year, later increased to $400.00, for both himself and wife. Four men were employed, and an assistant in the person of Edward Hodgson, who, with his wife was to assume charge of one of the stations. The party sailed from Halifax on October 6, carrying supplies for the construction of a house and storehouse, what equipment was considered necessary, tools, a whaleboat and necessary provisions. The total amount estimated for the cost of this undertaking was $2,400.00. The party landed on the 13th, the supplies were put on shore and the vessel sailed for home. The supplies had been somewhat injured in the process of landing, and had it not been for finding bread in some of the wrecks which were found on the shore, the newcomers would have been in difficulties. However, construction was proceeded with as rapidly as possible, and by the 6th of November," a house was ready for occupancy. This was placed on the north side of the island, about five miles from its western end.

Near it was erected the flagstaff, and around it later clustered a little group of buildings, including a stable, a forge and a henhouse. There had been brought from Halifax a number of livestock, a bull and two cows, a boar and two sows, two goats, male and female, two rams, eight sheep and a horse.

About the center of the island there was, when Mr. Morris arrived, a house of small size, and the erection of one to be occupied by Mr. Hodgson at the eastern end of the island was arranged for. No provision was then made for

250

a lighthouse, but flagstaffs were placed at several points.

So began the first attempt at the rehabilitation of the island. Each succeeding year has added somewhat to the efficiency of the life saving work being carried on, contributing at the same time somewhat more of ease and convenience to the lots of those who have engaged themselves in the life saving effort.

It has not been an uninteresting story, that of what the years have brought in the many which have elapsed since the establishment of the first life saving station. It is almost impossible to estimate how many persons have profited, how many have been assisted. The list of known wrecks since that time mounts into the hundreds, the list of the saved into the thousands. If there have been periods of feast, there have also been periods of famine, when with two hundred or more persons added to the number of those habitually to be provided for,—those cast upon its shores but for whom transportation to the mainland could not be arranged,—it was necessary to slaughter for food the livestock or even the horses which roamed at large. If there have been deaths there have been births. If there have been storms, times when it appeared as if all the elements were conspiring to remove completely all vestiges of shelter or even the island itself, there also have been periods of calm, when the sea, without a ripple, melted imperceptibly into the sky at the far off horizon. If there have been periods of toil, periods when efforts almost superhuman were necessary, if many before whose feet death was yawning were to be brought in safety across the wide strip of surging waters which lay between their doomed ship and the wave wracked shore, there also have been periods of rest and calm with little to mark the doings of one day from that of the next. If there have been periods of tragedy, when the sea gave up its dead, there have been incidents of a lighter vein. It has been told that on one occasion a member of the island staff, desperate for the companionship which the island could not afford him, took one of the small dories and singlehanded rowed the entire distance to the mainland and the company he craved. If there have been periods in the clear sharp frost of winter when the surrounding sea smoked as would a caldron, there have been periods when the forms of the distant sand dunes were blurred from the heat waves arising from the scorching sands. If there have been incidents of sadness, as there were being borne to their last resting place the bodies of unknown unfortunates cast upon its sands, there have been times of grateful rejoicing as saved and saviours mingled their thanks, the ones for the fact of their salvation, the others for the knowledge that they had been the instruments of that salvation.

It was during the presence of Mr. Morris as Superintendent that efforts were made to place on the islands a number of animals of kinds not before represented. It was found that neither sheep nor goats thrived and increased in numbers. The objection to the presence of pigs can be understood, and though a number have been kept, an attempt is made to keep them near the stations. No attempt is now made to keep cattle beyond the number which can be made use of by the different households and for their use as work animals. English rabbits have been set free, and are still to be found. Some years ago rats which had come ashore from vessels stranded on the bars increased to such numbers as to make efforts at their extermination necessary, especially as they had almost brought about the disappearance of the rabbits. Cats were therefore set at large. but these became so destructive to the rabbits and so numerous and wild as to become a nuisance. An unlooked for factor is the extent to which occasional visiting snowy owls have attacked the small game which has been .introduced.

Near the end of Mr. Morris' tenure of office there were sixteen persons living on the island and connected with the establishment, of whom more than half were women and children. On his death in the year 1809, the 'second in charge, Mr. Edward Hodgson, was placed in charge of the whole station.

That, among the vessels which have come to grief on the Sable Island bars. so many have been naval vessels, either British or foreign, is something little looked for or expected.

It was the wreck of the British war vessels, the *Princess Amelia* in 1797, and the *Francis* in 1799, every man of the latter vessel perishing, which had so crystallized public opinion as to lead to the establishment on the island of the life-saving precautions. During Mr. Hodgson's tenure of the position, a French man-of-war, the *L'Africaine*, was one of these which met with disaster. It was indeed fortunate that eventually every man from this vessel was brought on shore, the boats from the station being used, as those of the vessel itself has been lost or destroyed in the storm. The French Government indicated its appreciation for the care given these two hundred men and for their rescue by sending a gold cup filled with gold coin for the men of the rescuing crew and a medal for the Superintendent.

Dying in 1830, Mr. Hodgson was succeeded in the position by Captain Joseph Darby, who had for a number of years been more or less in touch with the work of the station in his capacity as captain of the vessel which had been used in conveying stores and supplies to the island from Halifax. His reports for the fourteen years after accepting the position give an idea of the work which the crew of the island had been called upon to do. Thirteen ships, twelve brigs and eight schooners had been lost, and one ship with passengers had been assisted in getting clear after having grounded on one of the bars. Five hundred and eighty seamen and passengers had been brought ashore from wrecks, in many cases with their baggage, though in a number of instances the vessels had become total losses. In other instances the value of the salvaged goods and materials from the wrecks had amounted to many thousands of pounds. There had been shipped ashore as produce from the island two hundred and fourteen horses, ninety-one barrels of oil, seventy-one barrels of skins as well as other commodities. They had raised nearly four thousand bushels of vegetables, thirteen thousand six hundred pounds of pork, and twenty-seven thousand pounds of beef. They had manufactured one hundred and thirty thousand shingles from lumber cast ashore from timber-laden vessels, twenty-eight thousand feet of boards, much of which had been used in construction on the island, and collected four hundred cords of wood. They had built in all about thirty-six buildings, houses, storehouses, shelters, barns and outbuildings, had built one small vessel in which a number of visits had been made to Halifax and a number of boats of various sizes. Before his tenure of office was completed the number of persons who had been saved had increased to seven hundred and thirteen.

The extent to which he himself is responsible for a condition which was brought to the public attention during his presence on the island can not now be known but that it did exist was all too evident. The island was almost inaccessible, except for the occasional visits of vessels engaged in bringing supplies, and it is quite easy to understand that inaccessibility might be remembered by persons in whose families were members whom it was desired for a time or even permanently to have removed from public observation. The restrictions against the presence of liquor on the island were quite strict. The island was therefore a place very suitable for the temporary marooning of individuals for whom liquor was interdicted. This, however, was a rather minor matter, but not so was the practise of sending persons to the island who were suffering from mental defect or disease, and whose families desired no longer to be troubled with their continued presence in the home. To some extent this was due to the fact that there was not in the Province of Nova Scotia at that time suitable accommodation for these unfortunates, and, due to this fact, the custom had developed of farming out certain individuals of low grade mentality to farmers or other persons who were willing to give them some sort of maintenance for their keep. It being difficult at times to get persons to work in such an isolated place, the practice had developed of accepting some of these to help in the routine duties of the island. One regrets the fact that about the end of Captain Darby's term of office, it became necessary to insist that the Commission appointed to look after the affairs of the island should no longer tolerate the continuation of such a heartless practice.

Captain Matthew D. McKenna succeeded Captain Darby in 1844. It is interesting to see a description of the establishment at about this time. The main station was on the north side of the island about five miles from the west end, the site now being far out on the bar and covered by the sea. It consisted of a dwelling-place for the superintendent and some of the men. There was a large building for the purpose of sheltering wrecked seamen, and a warehouse for the storage of goods taken from the wrecks. There was a barn and stable, forge and carpenter's shop, an oil house and other outbuildings. Here, also, was a tall flagstaff with an observatory at a height of one hundred and twenty feet. Nine miles away to the east was a dwelling house occupied by one or more families, with a barn and here also was a flagstaff. Five miles still farther to the east much the same set of structures was duplicated. On the south side of the island was a house, unoccupied, and kept continually ready for immediate use by any person seeking it in need. The door was never locked, there were provisions in readiness, and materials for making a fire were always immediately accessible, with instructions as to the distance and direction of the main station. Another such building was to be found at the extreme eastern end of the island. A system of patrols covered the whole island, one patrolman meeting his neighbor at some intermediate point, so that the whole shoreline was subject to examination. Especially after storms was such a patrol a necessity.

What with this, the primary purpose of the staff, there were and are many other things to be done. The farm work and the care of the stock and horses, fencing, painting and repair of the buildings, gathering the crops, the care and repair of the boats, the keeping of supplies at the various outstations, picking the cranberries which are to be found in large numbers, the catching of fish on those days when it is fit to leave the shore, the killing of seals or game are mentioned in the report as being some of the things at which the force, then twelve in number, were continually engaged.

Of all the projects proposed for the development of the island economically, what seems the most bizarre dated from about this time. It was based upon the belief that the sands of the island were heavily auriferous. About the year 1847, gold had been discovered in the washings of sand from some of the beaches near Halifax. Several persons, headed by John Campbell and R. G. Fraser, convinced themselves that the Sable Island sands showed the presence of gold in such quantities, as to make its recovery a profitable venture. They succeeded in getting a vessel and the needed equipment and even the required personnel, and, were it not for the paternalism of the Nova Scotia Government, which, skeptical of the success of the project, imposed very onerous conditions on those asking for prospecting licenses, a start would have been made. This was the period when Mr. Howe himself was so sure that gold was not to be found in the Province that the advice he gave to a prospector asking for a license, was to "go home and mend his old shoes". When, a few years later, gold was actually found, the Government reversed its attitude and backed Mr. Campbell up in his prospecting endeavors. The Revenue cutler, Daring, was placed at Mr. Campbell's disposal. Three times it made an attempt to land the gold hunters on the island, meeting with failure in each attempt. Then the matter was allowed to drop, and if there is more gold to be found in the Sable Island sands than there is in the sands of any other Nova Scotia beach, the fact has up to the present escaped detection.

The experiences which the staff of the island has had with visitors have been quite large and varied. This applies both in respect of those who have been brought ashore from wrecks and of those who, out of curiosity or other motives, have spent some time as guests of the management. In respect of the former, some have expressed gratitude and thankfulness for the assistance which they have received, and when opportunity offered have not been slow in evidencing these feelings by actions which proved their sincerity. It is rather strange to report, however, that some have acted in an entirely different manner, and that it has been necessary on some occasions for the staff to have to request Halifax for aid against some members of unruly shipwrecked crews who have become mutinous and threatening. Some of those of the other class have not so acted as to make themselves welcome, especially some visitors from some of the fishing vessels who have taken time from their labor to see, often, what damage they could do to property or what equipment they could remove.

There was, however, one visitor who made a short stay on the island during Mr. McKenna's superintendency whose presence will always be remembered with gratitude and thanks. This was the visit of Miss Dorothea Lynde Dix, made in the year 1853. Miss Dix had occasion to visit the Province in connection with her interest in the establishment of suitable institutions for the care of the insane, a work to which she had devoted her life. It so happened that one of the members of the Provincial Commission responsible for the conduct of affairs on the island was also greatly interested in removing from the Province the stigma under which it had long remained in connection with the care of the mentally ill, for whom little or no provision had yet been made. She determined to see for herself the condition of those unfortunates whose friends had brought about their detention on the island in the desire to have them removed from the circle of their families. She remained on the island but two days, but during that time saw personally an incident which proved to her the value of the life saving service. A schooner of 152 tons, the *Guide*, of London from New York on her way to Labrador, running under full sail struck a bar on the inner side of the island. Through the efforts of the men of the station, the crew were brought safely ashore, though in the excitement the captain of the vessel became so maniacally insane that it was necessary for him to be bound hand and foot in order to carry him away from his vessel which he was determined not to leave. A special trip had to be made to the wreck by the life

254

saving crew before he could be secured, all the others having been safely landed before.

The incident so impressed Miss Dix that on her return to the States she set herself to the task of supplementing the life saving equipment by procuring for the island a number of lifeboats of a build more suitable for that particular work than were any which had yet been placed there. She secured the promise of four such boats, one named the *Victoria*, being obtained from generous minded citizens of Boston; another, the *Grace Darling*, being donated in Philadelphia, and the others, the *Reliance* and the *Samaritan*, being given by persons of the city of New York. In addition to these boats, there were also provided mortars for throwing life lines from the beach, cables, trucks and harnesses. The boats were the most modern metallic boats which could be secured.

The Boston boat, the *Victoria*, was sent to Halifax in November of the same year, to await the arrival of the others and then to be forwarded to the island. These left New York about the same time, but the vessel in which they were being carried was wrecked near Yarmouth. One of the boats was lost, carried off by the sea during the wreck and the others were so badly damaged that they had to be returned for repairs. It was not till November of the following year that two of them, the *Victoria* and the *Reliance*, were actually taken to the island, and placed in their respective stations, the *Victoria* on the south side of the island, and the *Reliance* at the main station.

Just fifteen days after their receipt, a ship, the *Arcadia*, of Warren, Maine, from Antwerp, with a full cargo, one hundred and forty-seven passengers, and a crew of twenty-one men, went ashore on the east bar at 6 P.M. There was a dense fog and a strong southeast gale. The information was not received at the station till the following morning, the wreck being twenty or more miles from help. All next day in the storm the work of rescue proceeded, but in spite of all their efforts in the gale only eight trips could be made to the wreck. It was not till the following morning that the last of the passengers and crew were landed, all safe after eighteen trips of the boat. The following night the ship was completely broken up in the raging seas, only a few packages of cargo being saved. It was the opinion of all concerned that without these boats few or none of the passengers or crew would have been saved. Is it a wonder that Miss Dix's timely visit to the island was considered as providential?

It can be understood that, especially when there were no other means of communicating with the land than by sailing vessels, it was not at times a very easy matter, either to send supplies to the island from the mainland or to ship produce from the island. Nor was it easy at times to send to the mainland the passengers and crews of wrecked vessels, many having to remain on the island for months at a time. On many occasions, vessels carrying supplies had to visit the island a number of times, returning to Halifax in the intervals, before being able fully to unload. It is a matter of record that one such supply vessel which left Halifax was blown so far from her course that her first port of call was Antigua in the West Indies, having lost three men in the vain attempt to land and there being left but two to navigate the vessel in the storm. On another occasion, at a somewhat later date, a vessel bound from the island to Halifax was lost with all hands, no one yet knowing where or how. The use of steamers instead of sailing vessels does much to offset this difficulty, but until recently there have been no methods of enabling immediate reports of the

255

needs of the members of the staff to be sent ashore. Carrier pigeons have been used to send messages ashore but with only qualified success.

Mr. McKenna left the island on September 5, 1855. The number of persons whose lives were considered to have been saved during his superintendency was over five hundred. The value of the produce and of goods or effects from wrecks had amounted during that time to about $60,000.00. He was succeeded in office by Mr. Philip Dodd, whose tenure of office lasted till 1873. There were during it some especially noteworthy incidents.

Confederation having become effective in the year 1867, the responsibility for the maintenance of the Station passed from the Province to the Federal government, the Department of Marine and Fisheries being thereafter placed in full control of its destinies. One of the first things undertaken was the consideration of further safeguarding the navigation of the coastal waters by the construction of lighthouses, if now these were considered likely to serve their intended purposes.

This matter had for years been considered. It was not only the cost of these which had prevented action. Those best acquainted with the conditions, aware that the danger from the outlying bars extended far beyond the area over which the lights then available could reach, knowing that, in the presence of the prevailing fogs lights might be blanketed so effectively that they would be capable of little service, and afraid, moreover, that mariners, seeing the light or lights might, instead of shunning them, actually be drawn towards them, in the event of them being mistaken for other shore lights, had decided against their being placed on the island. Much the same argument was presented in connection with the plan of placing fog horns or other mechanical means of warning seamen from the dangerous shoals. The radius of no such appliance could reach to what were perhaps the most dangerous points, and mariners, seeking to find and pick them up, might be lured into danger, where otherwise they would be sure to attempt to give the place a wide berth.

It had been the considered opinion of Mr. Cunard, then head of the Provincial Lighthouse Commission, that any benefit to some which might result from the installation of lights might be more than offset by the dangers into which they might lead other craft, and in this opinion no less a person than Captain Darby himself, who was one of the members of the life saving crew, concurred. The other side of the argument was vigorously contested by Joseph Howe and Captain Bayfield. Howe had visited the island in the year 1850, and thus had some personal knowledge of the conditions which were to be met. It is not an unreasonable deduction that out of this personal knowledge came the inspiration for the poem,—one of his best known—which has the Island for its subject. We may also deduce that his support went very unreservedly and whole heartedly to the newly appointed Minister of Marine and Fisheries, Mr. Mitchel, when after Confederation, it was announced that lighthouses were to be built.

The programme called for two lights, one to be placed at each end of the island, the total cost of both being about $80,000.00. The west end light, 98 feet in height, was a revolving light, visible about seventeen miles, with three flashes of half a minute, and then a cessation of light for a minute and a half. The east end light is a fixed light, visible 18 miles, placed in a building 86 feet in height. Constructed in 1873, the erosion of the western end of the island has been so great that it became necessary to move it a mile to the

256

eastward in 1883, and again to move it two miles eastward in 1888. It is perhaps worthy of remark that the installation of the lights has not been followed by such a diminution in the number of wrecks as to prove that the arguments above referred to were entirely fallacious.

The addition of the lights brought about a number of changes and among others was the increase in the staffs necessary for the maintenance of the two services. In the year 1894, there were in all five stations. The main station was about four miles from the west end of the island and here was the Superintendent and six men. The west end lighthouse was cared for by the lighthouse keeper and his assistant. The central station, about the middle of the island, was staffed by two boatmen. At the foot of the lake was the fourth station, also with two boatmen. The east end light was cared for by the lighthouse keeper and assistant, and here, also, two boatmen were stationed. In addition there were always on duty two or three others, making a total of about eighteen men. With their families, the total number of persons on the island was about fifty.

The present phase in the story of the island has been brought about as the result of achievements won far from its limited confines, the achievements of the scientist and the inventor. The replacement of the vessel dependent only on its sails for propulsion, by mechanically driven craft has removed the lee shore dangers, always the dread of any mariner. Even the fishing vessels, many of which are now equipped with auxiliary power, have found the means of escaping quickly and surely from any area of danger into which they may have ventured in the quest for a catch. Improved methods of sounding have enabled vessels more easily to make themselves aware of their positions on the sea, and the proximity of danger. Radio has provided instant communication, not only with the base on the shore, but with the vessel cautiously feeling its way through fog and mist and storm for a landfall, or threading its way along the sea lanes. Weather reports of increasing accuracy which forecast for even the tiniest fishing hamlets the coming of gales or storms give timely warning to the little and sometimes too venturesome craft, sending them scurrying for shelter as birds before a harrying hawk.

Ceaselessly the vessels pass, lumbering freighters, bound to or from the Gulf of St. Lawrence, deeply laden or riding high, with propellors viciously flailing, clumsy tankers or whalebacks, trim liners, shuttling backwards and forwards across the Atlantic, sleek and speedy fishing schooners, with topmasts housed as they move from bank to bank in quest of the moving schools of fish, perhaps with every spar or stack sharply etched against the horizon, perhaps betraying their presence only by rapidly dissolving wisps of smoke moving slowly at the extreme limit of vision. Safely they pass, in the long summer days when the tiny wavelets sparkle in the sunlight, in the sombre and grey days of winter, when the snow squalls of a howling northeaster blot out the sea and the sky, or when the fog banks roll, deep and impenetrable, over a smooth and oily sea. Unconcernedly they pass, as if little aware of the expenditure of treasure and lives which has bought for them their safety and has relieved them from the exaction of a toll, the heaviest and most grievous of any taken along the whole Atlantic seaboard. Rarely, indeed, from all that passing throng, do the far-reaching sandbars, insatiable as ever though they be, now succeed in claiming their prey.

257

It is little to be wondered at, if, in connection with this place of sinister reputation, whose first mention in history was associated with the story of an incident of privation and suffering, capable of arousing the most sluggish imagination, and whose name is rarely mentioned except in reminiscence of some story of suffering, hardship or death, there have not been told stories of the unusual, the weird or the uncanny. One of these goes back to the times of De LaRoche and his convict colonists.

It is said that among the number who were in his vessel, a vessel so tiny, that as one of the crew has left on record, it was possible for him to wash himself in the sea by stooping over from the main deck, was a Franciscan monk who had undertaken to carry the gospel to the New World. When De LaRoche sailed away, endeavoring to find a place for settlement on the mainland, this monk elected to remain on the island with the convicts. Among these, the scourings of French prisons, left on the island without leadership and authority, and shortly appreciating that they had been left to their fates, discord and strife developed, resulting at last in the division of the few who escaped into two groups, defined as the bad and the less bad, in absence of other qualifications. Throughout it all, the efforts of the monk to restore harmony for the common benefit was maintained, and he, as none other earned the respect and the liking of both groups. When after many weary years help at last came, this man would not leave the island. He had left France on his mission to the New World, and did not consider himself discharged of his obligation, then assumed. He had learned how to maintain himself even in the presence of conditions almost unsupportable, and considered that the fact that he had been able to exist proved divine intervention, which divine intervention he trusted for guidance and support in the future. At his own insistence, therefore, he remained on the island, where he is said to have lived in solitude for a number of years. It was vouchsafed for him to be of assistance to a number of persons who, even in those times when ships were not frequently found in those waters, were for a time unwilling visitors and whom he assisted till such time as a means of escape had been found. Rately, he had other visitants, persons who made their way thither in their hunt for seals and walrus. There he died, alone. Is it to be wondered at that still, when the wind brings the fog wisps swirling around the sand dunes, dim glimpses are seen of the black robed priest searching for persons who might profit from the assistance he might be able to give them?

Another story is much more frequently referred to in the literature of the Province. It dates from times much more recent, but a few years before the establishment of the relief station was decided upon. In fact, it may have had some part to play in the events which brought about that service, since one of the reasons for its establishment was the spread of rumors of ghoulish treatment of the dead or even the destruction of the living, by persons who had made the island their headquarters, drawn thitherward by the stories of the numerous wrecks.

About the end of the eighteenth century a naval vessel bringing to Halifax a number of army officers for duty at that station, some recruits for the regiments there on duty, and some women, the wives both of officers and men, went ashore on the island and became a total loss, all on board perishing.

Among the wives of the officers was a Mrs. Copeland, the wife of a regimental medical officer, who had already spent some time in the city and was well known by many in the social circles of which she was a member. She had been home on a visit and was returning to the station where her husband was on duty. The vessel not arriving when expected, the authorities in Halifax, thinking that she might have met disaster at Sable Island, but knowing little definitely, sent an officer down to the island in order to see if there had recently been a wreck on its shores. The name of the officer was Captain Torrens. As the story goes, his vessel herself came to grief, but the crew escaped to shore, where they set themselves to examine the island, while awaiting relief.

One day, while the crew of the vessel were staying at some shelter on one end of the island, Captain Torrens undertook to walk towards the other end, looking for evidences of any parties which might have been cast ashore. Night coming on, he went to a building which he had noticed, intending to pass the night there. When he opened the door of the building he saw a woman, dressed in a long flowing garment, which looked as if it had recently been wet. She said nothing, but held out towards him her hands, a finger of which had been hacked off, with the blood still running. She made her way past him and escaped from the building, on which he followed but soon lost her. On returning to the hut, again Captain Torrens saw the form, v/ith the bleeding hand, and then he recognized her as Mrs. Copeland, whom he well knew. He called her by name, and asked her if she had been killed and her rings taken. She nodded assent. He then said that he would do everything in his power to see that the persons who had injured her would be brought to justice, and immediately the form vanished.

On his return to Halifax, Captain Torrens set himself to carry into effect his promise. He received some information respecting a family, a member of which might have been concerned in the incident, as he was known to have visited the island on several occasions. Torrens made the acquaintance of the family, in the guise of a fisherman, occupying himself in fishing in a well known trout stream near by, and eventually heard from some member of the family, that they had had in their possession a ring, said to have been procured on Sable Island. He then succeeded in locating the ring, in the store of a pawnbroker, where it had been placed by someone connected with the family. Finally he secured it. It was at once recognized as Mrs. Copeland's ring, an old family heirloom well known by persons who had long been acquainted with the owner.

This story, given wide publicity, was a factor, either in the establishment of the relief station or in the continuance of its support, during the early years, when there was danger of that support being withdrawn. The death of the unfortunate Mrs. Copeland, which took place when the Francis was lost with every one of her crew and passengers, was the basis on which fantasy and imagination have woven this gruesome tale.

Another of these tales carries us back to the times of the Restoration of the Monarchy after the death of Cromwell. Quite determined efforts were then made to apprehend and bring to justice those who by vote or more direct action had been concerned in what was now considered to be the martyrdom of King Charles. It was known that some of these persons had succeeded in finding asylum in the New World and the literature of the period refers frequently to the attempts being made by the home authorities to prod the colonial governments into taking more effective measures for the apprehension of the fugitives. As a rule, these efforts met with little response, but, according to the legend, one of the so-called Regicides, distrustful of his ability to escape vengeance otherwise, sought the seclusion of Sable Island for his protection. He is supposed to have remained on Sable Island for some years and to have died there. According to the legend, he had succeeded in hiding during his lifetime all connection with those whom vengeance was now seeking out, and he was regarded only as an eccentric who had renounced the haunts of man for reasons quite different from the actual ones. Only after his death were these true reasons revealed. Now, each year on the 30th of January, the date of the King's death, the troubled shade of this man makes its appearance, clad, not in the garments he usually wore when alive, but in his old Cromwellian garb, his face partially hidden under his old steeple crowned hat. With his bright and shining sword in his hand he wanders along the dreary beaches and sand dunes, singing his old Cromwellian chants, which can be heard even above the roar of a tempest. Long though is the winter night, throughout it the search goes on, the search to evade the inescapable punishment incurred when violent hands were laid upon the Lord's anointed.

Farewell, Dark Isle.   The Muse must spread her wings
    To seek for brighter themes in scenes more fair.
Too happy if the strain she strove to sing
    Shall warn the sailor of thy deadly snare.
Would that the Gods but hear her fervent prayer
    The fate of famed Atlantis should be thine.
No longer crouching in thy dangerous lair,
    But sunk far down beneath the whelming brine.
Known but to History's page, or in the poet's line.
                  —J. HOWE.

Genealogies

Commencing a number of years ago, an attempt was made to determine how many of the arriving Loyalists remained on or in the vicinity of their holdings. From the examination then made, these genealogical records were compiled. It will be seen that the percentage of those who remained varied greatly in the different units. Some groups, given unsatisfactory locations, lost heavily by deaths or were forced quickly to seek sites more promising or offering greater degrees of comfort.

As genealogical records these records are quite incomplete. The compilation was done from church entries, cemetery inscriptions and private family records, and the whole forms little more than a framework on which more complete genealogies may in the future be compiled.

It will be noted that there are few or no records later than 1916.

The Pre-Loyalist Settlers of Guysborough

BIGSBY

Bigsby (Bixby), Daniel. He was born in 1723 at Chelmsford, Massachusetts and died (froze to death 19 Feb. 1788 at Birch Island, Guysborough Harbour), aged 65. He settled first at the Intervale but later moved to Guysborough village. His wife was Catherine Spawlding. Catherine Bigsby (presumably his daughter) was born at Chedabucto in 1778 and married Benjamin Godfrey 31 Dec. 1801.

SMITH

Smith, David. No record has been found of this man. An interesting speculation is whether this was the Rev. David Smith, the Presbyterian minister who was one of the first ministers of that denomination in the Province. Another speculation is concerning the identification of this David Smith with the person of the same name to whom Joseph Hadley gave a deed for one acre of land in 1784. Was that acre the old cemetery which was on the Hadley lot?

Editor's Note: Almost certainly this was the Captain David Smith who lost his life on the ice while hunting seals at Port Hood Island in Feb. 1789. He was from Truro, Cape Cod, Massachusetts as was his wife Rebecca Lombard. He left seven children and another was born posthumously.

The lot referred to was less than a half an acre (100' x 130') which Joseph Hadley sold to David Smith 3 Nov. 1784 and is located on McCaul's Island close to the head of Pompey Cove, where the long pebbly beach at the mouth of Guysborough Harbour meets the land. Perhaps the greater mystery is why he paid 20 pounds for it when 100 acre lots could be purchased for 3 or 4 pounds? This suggests there was a house on it. The 1783 survey map of Chedabucto done just before the arrival of the Loyalists shows three houses clustered around Pompey Cove on McCaul's Island at this time. Perhaps it is one of these houses he purchased from Captain Hadley.

CALLAHANS.

According to the wording of the grant giving them lands, there were two brothers, Robert and William, but records refer to other members of the family, Edward, John, Ann and Elizabeth. The births of two children to Edward and Margaret are recorded, Michael, born May 11, 1789, and Margaret, born Mar. 26, 1793. No other record has been found of John. Ann Callahan was married to George Whooton, and Elizabeth, who may have been Robert's daughter by a former marriage, was married to John Cook. Robert, in 1782, married William Hadley's widow, being her third husband.

Family

1. Robert.

2. Edward.

3. William.

4. Ann

5. Elizabeth.

1. Robert Callahan. No record of family.

2. Edward Callahan. Married Margaret. Births of two children recorded.

3. William Callahan married Diana Hadley.

Family.

6. William Robert. Born 11 Nov. 1784.

William Callahan was drowned in Canso about the time his son was born, and the widow married John Morgan.

4. Ann Callahan married George Whooton 4 Aug. 1789.

5. Elizabeth Callahan married John Cook 22 May 1801.

6. William Robert Callahan married first Eleanor.

Family.

7. Margaret Eleanor. Born 7 Oct. 1807.

He married second Mary Henderson 26 Dec. 1810.

8. Lucina. Born 18 Oct. 1811.

9. Alexander. Born 29 Mar. 1814.

10. William. Born 3 July 1816.

11. Diana. Born 12 May 1818.

12. Elizabeth Ann. Born 5 Nov. 1819.

13. Hannah Maria. Born 13 Mar. 1826.

14. John Henry. Born 4 Aug. 1828.

15. Archibald. Born 23 Oct. 1830.

16. Frances. Born 20 Oct. 1833.

17. Thomas Cutler. Born 4 Feb. 1836.

18. Mary.

7. Margaret Eleanor Callahan. No record.

8. Lucina Callahan married J. Cody.

9. Alexander Callahan married first Ruth Lawson 9 Feb. 1847 and after her death Jane Henderson in 1854.

Family.

19. Stanley. Born 27 June 1848.

20. Shannon.

21. John.

22. Lydia.

23. Burton. Born 4 May 1865.

24. Mary.   Born 15 Sept. 1866.

25. Martha Elizabeth.   Born 27 Oct. 1868.

26. Reuben.

27. Irad.

10. William Callahan moved to Maine, where the family now resides.

11. Diana Callahan married John Hadley 21 Apr. 1840.

12. Elizabeth Ann Callahan married John Morgan 8 May 1841.

13. Hannah Maria Callahan married Thomas Strople.

14. John Henry Callahan married Mary Scranton 1856.

Family.

28. Sophia Ann Scranton.   Born 28 Feb. 1857.

29. William Alexander.   Born 18 Nov. 1859.

30. Thomas.

31. John James.   Born 22 Jan. 1866.

15.   Archibald Callahan married Ann Hall 3 Aug. 1859.

Family.

32. William.

33. Clara.

34. Edmund.   Born 16 Feb. 1866.

35. Thomas.   Born 11 Feb. 1868.

36. Watson.   Born 25 May 1870.

16. Frances Callahan was not married.

17. Thomas Cutler Callahan married Harriet Harty 19 Jan. 1870.

Family.

37. Minnie.

38. William.

39. Edward.

40. Charles.

41. Howard.

42. Clement.

43. Harry.

18.   Mary Callahan married William Hadley 11 Jan. 1848.

COOKS.

It is said that some members of this family had been living in Chedabucto as early as 1772. However, Winthrop, the son of Elias, Junior, was born in the United States in 1776, according to an entry on his death certificate. The family is said to have come from Beverley, Mass. As can be told from the records, the family consisted of the father, Elias, and seven children. No reference has been found to the wife of this Elias. Several of his sons were married at the time the records commence, so that there were already persons of three generations living in the place. Elias Cook, the father, died on Mar. 29, 1809, aged 85, his birth therefore occurring in 1724.

Family.

2, Elias. Born 1745.

3. John. Born 1752.

4. Edward. Born 1752.

5. Benjamin. Born 1765.

6. Elizabeth.

7. Mary.

8. James.

2. Elias Cook, born in 1745, died 25 Aug. 1797. Wife's name, Ann Haskoll 27 Nov. 1769.   Married in Beverley, Mass.

Family.

9. Elias. Bapt. 16 Dec. 1770.

10. Stephen. Bapt. Oct. 23, 1774 (In Beverley, Mass.)

11. Winthrop. Born 1776 (In U.S.A.)

12. Edmund. Bapt. 8 Oct. 1780.

13. Ambrose.

14. Lydia.

15. Samuel. Born 11 July 1784.

16. Ann. Born 5 July 1788.

3. John Cook, born in 1752, died 2 Feb. 1840. Name of first wife, Eliza.

Family.

17. Sarah. Born 22 June 1786.

18. Godfrey.

19. John. Born 8 Jan. 1789.

20. Nathaniel Tobin.

21. J Mary Maria. Bapt. 15 May 1796 (Twins).

22. Edward. Born June 1798.

He married second Elizabeth Callahan, 22 May 1801.
She was born in 1782 and died 2 Oct. 1843.

Family.

23. William Edward.   Born 12 June 1802.

24. Lydia.   Born 8 Feb. 1804.

25. Diana.   Born 14 Apr. 1809.

26. Susannah Horton.   Born 14 Dec. 1811.

27. John Godfrey Peart.   Born 11 July 1818.

28. Ruth.

4. Edward Cook, born in 1752, died 16 Aug. 1846. Married Elizabeth

Family.

29. Elizabeth Ann.   Born 15 Feb. 1812.

5. Benjamin Cook, born in 1765, died 18 Feb. 1833.
He married first Philomela Hull 4 Mar. 1787.
She was born in 1769 and died 16 May 1809.

Family.

30. Elias.   Born 8 Sept. 1788.

31. Moses.   Born 8 July 1793.

32. William Francis.   Born 4 Feb. 1796.

33. Mary Elizabeth.   Born 23 Jan. 1798.

34. Sarah Amelia.   Born 4 Mar. 1803.

He married second Lucy Cameron 31 Aug. 1810.

Family.

35. Benjamin.   Bapt. 12 Jan. 1812.

36, James William.   Born 20 Nov. 1812.

37. William Cameron.   Born 5 May 1815.

38. Maria.

39. Caroline.

40. Wentworth.

41. Joseph Henry.

42. Charles.

6. Elizabeth Cook married John Wheaton 15 May 1796.

7. Mary Cook married William Foster 6 Jan. 1791.

8. James Cook married Beda.

Family.

43. Susannah.   Born 4 July 1797.

44. Lydia.   Born 8 Oct. 1799.

45. William.

Beda Cook, widow, married second John Conrad Demas, 8 Aug. 1802, and third David O'Brien.

9. Elias Cook.   Married Deborah Godfrey 7 Nov. 1791.

Family.

46. Gideon Godfrey.   Born 16 Oct. 1792.

47. Elias.   Born 27 Apr. 1795.

48. Mary Ann.   Born 20 Sept. 1797.

49. Elias.   Born 20 Mar. 1803.

50. Ann.   Born 20 Oct. 1805.

51. Godfrey Milner.   Born 15 Mar. 1812.

52. Stephen.   Born 9 July 1814.

53. Elias Henry.   Born 24 Nov. 1816.

54. William.   Born 10 Sept. 1822.

10. Stephen Cook, born in 1770, died in 1844. Married Sarah Demas, 1800.

Family.

55. Demas.   Born 11 May 1801.

11. Winthrop Cook, born 1776, died 23 Sept. 1867.

Married Lydia Cleeves.   She died 2 Jan. 1873.

Family.

56. Edmund Cleeves.   Born 28 Oct. 1804.

57. Rebecca Cleeves.   Born 9 Oct. 1806.

58. John.   Born 7 June 1808.

59. Samuel.   Born 8 Apr. 1809.

60. Lydia.   Born 4 June 1811.

61. John.   Born 14 Oct. 1813.

62. Winthrop.   Born 28 Feb. 1818.

63. James.   Born 13 Oct. 1820.

12. Edmund Cook.   Married Elizabeth

Family.

64. Sarah Demas.   Born 19 Jan. 1819.

65. Demas Samuel.   Born 22 Nov. 1825.

66. William Owen Heffernan.   Born 19 Aug. 1827.

67. Mary Ann.   Born 6 Apr. 1831.

68. John Joseph Marshall.   Bapt. 14 May 1832.

69. Mary Jane.   Born 28 July 1844.

This family moved to Country Harbour, where the children were baptised.

13. Ambrose Cook.   Married Eleanor Bixby.

Family.

70. Harriet.   Born 26 Mar. 1803.

71. Eleanor.   Born 5 Oct. 1805.

72. Mary.   Born 7 Nov. 1808.

73. Ann.   Born 4 June 1811.

74. Deborah Godfrey.   Born 28 Oct. 1814.

75. Sarah.

14. Lydia Cook married William Horton 2 Oct. 1791.

15. Samuel Cook.   No record.

16. Ann Cook married Matthew Hutcheson 17 Apr. 1806.

17. Sarah Cook.   No record.

18. Godfrey Cook.   Married Amelia.

Family.

76. George William Henry.   Born 2 May 1812.

77. Nathaniel James.   Born 31 Oct. 1814.

78. John Francis.   Born 16 June 1820.

79. Edward Freeman.   Born 20 Nov. 1822.

80. Child.   Bapt. 29 July 1827.

81. Henry Hopkins.   Born 29 Aug. 1828.

19. John Cook, born 8 Jan. 1789, died 5 Feb. 1875.

Married Mary Cameron 6 Dec. 1819. (She was a sister of Lucy Cameron, Benjamin's second wife.)

Family.

82. Louisa.

83. Edward.

84. William.

85. Henry.

86. Benjamin.

87. Godfrey.

88. Eliza

(These are not in order of birth, and there may have been more)

20. Nathaniel Tobin Cook. No record.

21. Mary Maria Cook married Mr. Gerry. She died 22 Feb. 1875.

22. Edward Cook probably died young.

23. William Edward Cook married Eleanor Cook. (No. 71.) 3 Jan. 1826.

Family.

89. Moses. Born 22 Oct. 1826.

90. George.

91. Lydia.

92. Maria

93. Frank.

94. William.

95. Amelia.

96. Sarah. Born 1840.

97. John C. Born 1843.

24. Lydia Cook married a Mr. Mason of Country Harbour.

25. Diana Cook married James Gorman.

26. Susannah Horton Cook married William McAllister.

27. John Godfrey Peart Cook married Sarah Cook 12 Oct. 1841. (She was probably No. 75.)

Family.

98. Mary Ann. Born 21 Jan. 1843.

No record has been found of others in this family.

28. Ruth Cook married Daniel Lawlor.

29. Elizabeth Ann Cook married Patrick Sheehan 26 Jan. 1851.

30. Elias Cook, born 8 Sept. 1788, died 5 Sept. 1870. Married Anna Horton 3 Jan. 1811. She was born 23 Apr. 1794, died 1895.

Family.

99. John James Hyde. Born 14 Apr. 1812.

100. Philomela. Born Oct. 1814.

101. Benjamin. Born 3 Dec. 1816.

102. Elias William. Born 18 Aug. 1819.

103. Moses. Born 19 Dec. 1823.

104. Sophia Margaret. Born 27 Feb. 1826.

105. Arthur McNutt. Born 7 Jan. 1833.

106. Sarah Maria. Born 10 Aug. 1834.

107. William Francis.

108. Zipporah M.

31. Moses Cook. Married Ann Foster 26 Jan. 1816.

Family.

109. Philomela. Born 21 Jan. 1817.

110. William Foster. Born 11 Feb. 1820.

111. Moses. Born 19 Sept. 1821.

112. Eliza.

113. Moses James. Born 1 Dec. 1826.

114. Maria Jane.

115. Mary Randall. Born 19 Oct. 1830.

32. William Francis Cook, born 4 Feb. 1796, died 6 Apr. 1882..
Married Eliza Cunningham 5 May 1822.
She was born 20 Jan. 1802, died 3 Jan.1850.

Family.

116. Eliza. Born 1 Sept. 1823.

117. Thomas Cutler. Born 28 Aug. 1828.

118. Ruth Amelia Webb. Born 11 Aug. 1830.

119. Harriet Amelia. Born 15 Apr. 1833.

120. Francis Cranswick. Born 12 Nov. 1835.

121. John Cunningham. Born 6 Dec. 1837.

122. Sophia Grace. Born 19 Jan. 1840.

123. James Randall. Born 21 Feb. 1843.

33. Mary Elizabeth Cook married James Randall 25 Jan. 1818.

34. Sarah Amelia Cook married John Jost 5 Dec. 1820.

35. Benjamin Cook died unmarried.

36. James William Cook married Sarah Ann Bears 5 Jan. 1841.

Family.

124. Abraham Whitman. Born 9 Oct. 1841.

125. John Spearwater. Born 5 June 1843.

126. Isaac.   Born 16 Jan. 1845.

127. Joseph.   Born 20 Aug. 1846.

128. Letitia.   Born 28 Aug. 1848.

129. James.   Born 14 May 1851.

130. Alfred.   Born 20 Oct. 1854.

131. Charles.   Born 4 Feb. 1857.

132. Francis.   Born 11 July 1860. This family moved to P.E.I.

37. William Cameron Cook, born 5 May 1815, died 6 Sept. 1866.
Married Sarah Esther McAllister 25 January 1844.
She was born 24 Sept. 1827, died 21 Nov. 1922.

Family

133. Charles Albert.   Born 24 Feb. 1845.

134. John Henry.   Born 11 Nov. 1846.

135. Herbert W.   Born 30 Jan. 1849.

136. Joseph C.   Born 4 May 1851.

137. Barlow M.   Born 9 Aug. 1853.

138. Caroline.   Born 4 Dec. 1855.

139. Minnie.   Born 2 Dec. 1858.

140. Sadie A.   Born 2 Apr. 1860.

141. Emma.   Born 15 June 1864.

142. Esther.   Born 20 Aug. 1866.

38. Maria Cook married James Horton 4 Mar. 1841.

39. Caroline Cook married William Freeman of Liverpool, N. S.

40. Wentworth Cook married and has a family living in New York.

41. Joseph Henry Cook married a Miss Freeman and lives in Queens County, N. S. (A son, Dr. Snow Cook, lives in Gloucester.)

42. Charles Cook.   No record.

43. Susannah Cook.   No record.

44. Lydia Cook married John Mason 21 Dec. 1819.

45. William Cook married first Margaret Whitman 4 Jan. 1827.

Family.

143. Child.   Born 19 Oct. 1827.

144. Hannah.   Born 5 Sept. 1829.

He married second Bertha Godfrey 21 Mar. 1832.

145. Benjamin Godfrey. Born 17 Mar. 1836.

146. Caroline Elizabeth. Born 22 Dec. 1834.

147. William. (After the death of William Cook, his widow married Benjamin Gerry.)

46. Gideon Godfrey Cook married Elizabeth Major 11 Jan. 1820.

Family.

148. William. Born 10 Sept. 1822.

149. Elias. Born 20 Sept. 1824.

150. Thomas Horton. Born 22 Sept. 1826.

No other records have been obtained of this family.

47. Elias Cook is said to have died young.

48. Mary Ann Cook married James B. Richardson 3 Aug. 1820.

49. Elias Cook married Catherine Gerry 9 Feb. 1831.

Family.

151. George Archibald. Born 22 Jan. 1832.

152. Mary Gerry. Born 16 Apr. 1839.

153. Daniel Gerry. Born 16 Mar. 1841.

154. Elias Henry. Born 11 Oct. 1844.

155. Gideon. Born 22 Nov. 1846.

No other records have been obtained of this family.

50. Ann Cook married Robert F. Rule 13 Nov. 1832.

51 to 54. No records have been obtained.

55. Demas Cook born 11 May 1801, died 13 Apr. 1856. He married Ann Russell 21 Jan. 1824. She was born 1806, died 15 April 1881.

Family.

156. William Alexander. Born 29 Jan. 1825.

157. Frank Demas. Born 1 July 1827.

158. Sarah Ann. Born 24 Dec. 1829.

159. Elizabeth Jane. Born 27 Jan. 1831.

160. James Brown. Born 31 Mar. 1833.

161. Emmeline Marshall. Born 12 Dec. 1835.

162. Stephen Marshall. Born 11 Apr. 1839.

163. Susan M. Born 4 Sept. 1841.

164. Thomas R. Born 18 Oct. 1843.

165. Christopher C. Born 28 Dec. 1846.

166. Joseph Demmick.   Born 24 Dec. 1849.

56. Edmund Cleeves Cook married Eliza Marrs.

Family.

167. Joseph Charles.

168. Lydia Euphemia.

57. Rebecca Cleeves Cook.   No record.

58. John Cook.   No record.

59. Samuel Cook Married Elizabeth Haines 26 Jan. 1837.

Family.

169. Elizabeth White.   Born 2 Feb. 1838.

170. Desire.   Born 16 Oct. 1844.

171. Lucinda.

172. Sophia Matilda.

60. Lydia Cook.   No record.

61. John Cook.   No record.

62. Winthrop Cook married Sarah Ann.

Family.

173. Abram Jordan.

63. James Cook married Charlotte Eve 9 Apr. 1845.

Family.

174. Edward James.

175. Gideon.

176. Sarah Ann.

177. Elisha.

64. to 69. No records.

70. Harriet Cook was not married.

71. Eleanor Cook married William Edward Cook (No. 23) 3 Jan. 1826

72. Mary Cook.   No record.

73. Ann Cook.   No record.

74. Deborah Godfrey Cook married John G. Gratto 7 July 1840.

75. Sarah Cook married John Cook (No. 27)   12 Oct. 1841.

76. to 81. No records.

82. Louisa Cook married Charles Gosbee 28 Jan. 1845.

85. Henry Cook is said to have died young.

89. Moses Cook married Jane McIntyre.

Family.

178. Clarence.

179. Loring.

180. Frank.

181. Carrie.

182. Grace.

183. Lottie.

90. George Cook married in the States.

Family.

184. John.

91. Lydia Cook married Fritz Harvey.

92. Maria Cook married Nathaniel Withim.

93. Frank Cook died aged 19 years.

94. William Cook died young.

95. Amelia Cook married Michael Harty.

96. Sarah Cock married John Coffin.

97. John C. Cook married Amelia Edson Cook. (No. 195.)

Family.

185. Florence.

186. Cordelia.

187. Lome.

188. Victoria.

99. John James Hyde Cook married Maria Cook, widow of his brother William

Francis No. 107. No record of a family.

100. Philomela Cook married John Peart 3 Aug. 1837.

101. Benjamin Cook married Ann MacKenzie.

Family.

189. George Washington, born 29 Dec. 1846.

190. Jeremiah.

191. Robert C.

192. Sarah Jane.

193. Elias.

194. Benjamin.

195. Amelia Edson.

196. Annie.

197. Susan.

102. Elias William Cook married Mary Ellen Brodie.

Family.

198. Charles Edward, born 31 Oct. 1850.

105. Arthur Mc Nutt Cook married in the United States.

106. Sarah Maria Cook married in the United States.

107. William Francis Cook married Lavinia Maria Toby 8 July 1854.

Family.

199. Odessa Lavina Jost, born 21 Aug. 1857.

200. Caroline Matilda, born 28 Feb. 1859.

201. Cordelia Edson, born 5 Nov. 1860.

202. Harriet Rebecca, bapt. 25 Feb. 1862.

108. Zipporah M. Cook married John A. Steele 20 Sept. 1853.

109. Philomela Cook married George Edmund Scott 11 Feb. 1834.

110. William Foster Cook died 8 June 1820,

111. Moses Cook died 20 Feb. 1823.

112. Eliza Cook was not married.

113. Moses James Cook died young.

114. Maria Jane Cook married Charles Bigsby 1 Feb. 1855.

115. Mary Randall Cook married James Sutherland 19 Jan. 1853.

116. Eliza Cook married Jairus Hart 11 Feb. 1846.

117. Thomas Cutler Cook, born 28 Aug. 1828, died 12 Nov. 1898.
Married Emma Bigelow 5 Jan. 1860. She was born 1839,
died 5 Sept. 1899.

Family.

203. Sarah. Born 20 Apr. 1862.

204. Frank Bigelow.   Born 6 May 1863.

205. Sophia Pamela.   Born 15 Oct. 1865.

206. William James Coleman.   Born 15 July 1867.

207. Emma Harriet Cook.   Born 15 Oct. 1869.

208. George Cunningham.   Born 10 May 1871.

209. Maria Norris. Born 31 Oct. 1873.

210. Lavinia Whitman. Born 13 Jan. 1876.

211. Edna Corinna. Born 22 Sept. 1879.

212. Thomas Whitman. Born 10 Sept. 1882.

118. Ruth Amelia Webb Cook died 26 July 1831, unmarried.

119. Harriet Amelia Cook died 18 July 1851.

120. Francis Cranswick Cook married first Sarah Alice Fuller, 14 Oct. 1864.

Family.

213. Lila Alice Euphemia, born 8 Jan. 1866.

214. Hartley.

215. Aubrey.

216. Estella.

He married second Elizabeth Catherine Wylde 21 Aug. 1878.

Family.

217. Evelyn.

218. Genevieve.

121. John Cunningham Cook was drowned unmarried.

122. Sophia Grace Cook married William Coleman.

123. James Randall Cook married Margaret Nichols.

This family lived in Bayfield, N. S.

124. Abraham Whitman Cook married Ellen MacDonald 6 Oct. 1864.

Family.

219. Francis Isaac. Born 4 Mar. 1865.

220. Abraham Whitman. Born 24 Mar. 1867.

221. Donald McDonald. Born 11 June 1868.

222. James William. Born 5 Jan. 1871.

223. Angus. Born 6 Aug. 1872.

224. Wellington Dixon. Born 1 Sept. 1874.

225. Isabella. Born 3 Mar. 1876.

226. Alfred Henry. Born 6 Jan. 1878.

227. Joseph. Born 22 May 1879.

125. John Spearwater Cook died 26 June 1853.

126. Isaac Cook married Susanna Bears, 7 Apr. 1870.

Family.

228. Benjamin.   Born 13 Feb. 1871.

229. Daniel James.   Born 22 Oct. 1872.

230. David Albert.   Born 13 Apr. 1874.

231. Mary Elizabeth.   Born 13 June 1876.

232. John.   Born 26 June 1879.

233. David.   Born 31 July 1881.

127. Joseph Cook died 25 Jan. 1852.

128. Letitia Cook married Donald McLeod 4 Feb. 1875.

129. James Cook married Flora McQuarrie 20 Feb. 1875.

Family.

234. Sarah Ann.   Born 23 Dec. 1875.

235. John.   Born 26 Dec. 1877.

236. Margaret Ellen.   Born 18 Nov. 1880.

237. Mary Letitia.   Born 2 Oct. 1882.

130. Alfred Cook married Hannah Campbell 13 Apr. 1881.

Family.

238. Charles Hector.   Born 15 Mar. 1882.

133. Charles Albert Cook was not married.

134. John Henry Cook married first Annie McDonald 27 Sept. 1876.

Family.

239. Ethel.   Born 6 July 1879.

240. Mabel.   Born 25 Sept. 1884.

241. Clarence.   Born 9 Feb. 1887.

242. Murray.   Born 21 Aug. 1888.

He married second Jane Carr, 9 Apr. 1901.

Family.

243. Albert H.   Born 18 Apr. 1902.

135. Herbert W. Cook married Isabelle Carson.

Family.

244. Cora Belle.   Born 20 Aug. 1882.

245. Laura Mildred.   Born 23 Feb. 1884.

136. Joseph C. Cook married Frances Morgan.

Family.

246. William.   Born 16 Oct. 1877.

247. Esther.   Born 28 Mar. 1880.

137. Barlow M. Cook married Nellie Rhodes.

Family.

248. Hattie.   Born 9 May 1884.

249. Albert.   Born 12 July 1887.

138. Caroline Cook married Thomas Cook.

139. Minnie Cook married Charles B. Dow.

140. Sadie A. Cook was not married.

141. Emma Cook married Frank Orcutt.

142. Esther Cook married Frank Grader.

144. Hannah Cook married James Porter 16 July 1868.

GODFREYS

The Godfreys were a family who belonged to the group coming from Liverpool. The family consisted of the father, Benjamin and a number of children. The first name of Benjamin's wife was Bethiah, her full name has not been found. Benjamin Godfrey died 26 Mar. 1805, aged 67 years.

Family.

1.   Matthea.

2.   Deborah.

3.   Ruth.

4.   Benjamin.

5.   Gideon.

6.   Hannah.

7.   Frances.

8.   John.

These are not in order of birth, and there may have been more.

1.   Matthea Godfrey died 21 Jan. 1791, aged 21 years.

2.   Deborah Godfrey married Elias Cook, 20 Dec. 1791.

3.   Ruth Godfrey married John McKeough 6 Oct. 1799.

4.   Benjamin Godfrey married Catherine Bigsby 31 Dec. 1801.

Family.

9.   John William Nixon.   Born 5 Oct. 1805.

10.   Joseph.   Born 12 Oct. 1807.

11.   Alicia Eliza.   Born 16 Mar. 1810.

279

12. Bertha.

13. Benjamin. Benjamin Godfrey died 28 Oct. 1818.

5. Gideon Godfrey married Cynthia Toby 16 June 1808.

Family.

14. Elizabeth.

6. Hannah Godfrey married William Sealey 1784.

15. Uriah. Born 7 Mar. 1785.

William Sealey, his wife and child, together with the nurse, were all drowned on 22 Oct. 1785, near the mouth of the harbour, while on their way to Church.

7. Frances Godfrey married Jairus Hart 31 Dec. 1795.

8. John Godfrey married Ruth Hadley. She was a daughter of Joseph Hadley, another of the Liverpool settlers. According to the Liverpool records, he died on a voyage from Barcelona. There was a family, but no reference has been found to them in Chedabucto.

9. John William Nixon Godfrey married Ruth Ann Scott, 9 Jan. 1827.

Family.

16. Ann Muller. Born 14 Jan. 1828.

17. Frances Maria, bapt. 22 Jan. 1833.

18. Benjamin. Born 23 Jan. 1835.

19. Sarah Ann. Born 18 July 1837.

20. William Benjamin Scott, bapt. 12 Apr. 1840.

21. Edward Cummings. Born 4 Jan. 1842.

22. Ruth Lucretia. Born 18 July 1844.

23. B. Jane. Born 9 Aug. 1846.

24. John Joseph Peart. Born 21 Mar. 1849.

25. Charles David. Born 25 June 1851.

11. Alicia Eliza Godfrey married George Spanks 3 Apr. 1845.

12. Bertha Godfrey married William Cook 21 Mar. 1834.

13. Benjamin Godfrey married Sarah Gerry 25 Nov. 1843.

26. Agnes O. married J. H. A. Peart.

27. Esther. Died unmarried 10 Oct. 1906.

14. Elizabeth Godfrey married first a Mr. Spanks.

She married second John Sangster 9 Oct. 1877.

No other records of this family have been found. The last descendant bearing the Godfrey name died a number of years ago.

HADLEYS

These were others of the Liverpool, Nova Scotia group. **Editor's note:** Joseph Hadley was born Nov. 24, 1724 in Gloucester, Maine, the son of John Hadley and Hanna Lowe. He removed to Liverpool, NS in 1763 from Rhode Island, where at least one of their six children was born from his first wife Ruth. Joseph Hadley moved his family to Chedabucto in 1768 though it seems likely he and perhaps his son John were in residence at least during the fishing season a few years earlier. His land grant was large, 1,500 acres including a long expanse of some of the most desirable water frontage within the harbour. Following the death of his first wife Ruth, born 1724, died 1790, aged 66 years, he married the widow Esther Atwater 8 Aug. 1791. She died Oct. 14th, 1807, aged 72. Joseph Hadley himself died in 1801 and is buried on the old family property in Manchester now known as McCaul's Island.

Family.

1. John
2. Ruth.
3. Diana.
4. Hannah.
5. Joseph.
6. Henry.

These are probably not in order of birth. There may have been more, but of others no records have been found.

1. John was married to Elizabeth Young. He was lost at sea returning to Liverpool, NS from Chedabcuto in 1767. Elizabeth Young married second Simeon Perkins of Shelburne.

2. Ruth Hadley was married to John Godfrey. He died on a voyage

   from Barcelona. His widow resided in Liverpool, and may have been married there a second time.

3. Diana Hadley married first William Callahan, who was drowned at Canso, after which she married John Morgan.

4. Hannah Hadley married William Campbell 5 June 1785. He was a member of one of the Loyalist Regiments, and after a most distinguished career, became the Chief Justice of Upper Canada, and was knighted. The

   records of the births of several children, born to the couple before he had moved away from Chedabucto, are to be found.

5. Joseph Hadley married Helen or Eleanor Abbott 20 Mar. 1785. She was born in 1764 and died 31 Jan. 1837.

   Family.

   7. Joseph Godfrey Hadley. Born 21 Feb. 1786.
   8. George Henry. Born 28 Nov. 1789.
   9. William. Born 15 Jan. 1792.
   10. John. Born 14 Aug. 1794.

11. Ruth. Born Sept. 1796.

12. Eleanor. Bapt. 22 Mar. 1799.

13. Daughter. Born 1800.

6. Henry Hadley married first Mary.

Family.

14. John. Born 18 Aug. 1784.

15. Sutia. Born 25 Dec. 1786.

Mary Hadley died 18 Feb. 1787.   He married second Marianne.

Family.

16. Ruth Godfrey. Born 18 Oct. 1796.

17. Child. Bapt. Mar. 1799.

18. Harriet Elizabeth. Born 8 July 1800.

19. Henry Alexander Mortimer. Born 22 July 1804.

20. Catherine.

7. Joseph Godfrey Hadley born 21 Feb. 1786, died 10 July 1854.
Married Judith Lawson 9 Feb. 1808.

Family.

21. William. Born 13 Jan. 1811.

22. George. Born 2 Apr. 1812.

23. Elizabeth. Born Aug. 1815.

24. Thomas. Brn 17 May 1820.

25. Eleanor. Born 20 Mar. 1S22.

26. John. Born 15 Feb. 1825.

27. Henry. Born 10 Apr. 1827.

28. Joseph John. Born 18 Apr. 1830.

29. Sarah.

8. George Henry Hadley, born 28 Nov. 1789.Married Elizabeth Collier 5 Jan.
1815.

Family.

30. Child. Bapt. 22 Feb. 1818.

31. Joseph Henry. Born 20 Dec. 1819.

32. George Thomas. Born 20 June 1822.

33. John Collier. Born 22 Dec. 1827.

34. Ruth Elizabeth. Born 28 Nov. 1830.

35. William.　Born 1 Apr. 1833.

36. James John.　Born 23 Dec. 1837.

9. William Hadley, born 15 Jan. 1792. Married Sarah Peart Hart 21 Mar. 1816.

Family.

37. John Henry.　Bapt. 22 Feb. 1818.

38. Joseph.　Born 27 Nov. 1819.

39. James.　Born 17 Feb. 1821.

40. William.　Born 25 Apr. 1822.

41. William.　Born 28 Oct. 1824.

42. Godfrey.　Born 26 Nov. 1827.

43. Jairus.　Born 10 Oct. 1829.

44. Thomas Harty.　Born 30 Dec. 1830.

45. Elizabeth.　Born 15 Dec. 1832.

46. Robert Cooney.　Born 27 May 1838.

10. John Hadley born 14 Aug. 1794, died 15 May 1876.

Married Lydia Hart 27 Mar. 1821.

Family.

47. Joseph.　Born 30 Dec. 1821.

48. Sarah Maria.　Born 24 Nov. 1822.

49. John Henry.　Born 24 June 1824.

50. Child.　Born 12 Nov. 1826.

51. Catherine Maria.　Born 9 June 1828.

52. Eleanor Abbott.　Born 13 Oct. 1830.

53. Sarah.　Born Jan. 1833.

54. Sarah Harriet Shreve.　Born 17 Apr. 1839.

55. Frances Jane.

56, William.

12. Eleanor Hadley married Donald McGregor 26 Jan. 1819.

13. Daughter born in 1800 died 2 July 1813.

20. Catherine Hadley married Thomas Harty 28 May 1810.

21. William Hadley born 13 Jan. 1811. Married Jane Carter 23 Apr. 1833.

Family.

57. Sarah Elizabeth.　Born 12 Oct. 1835.

58. Eleanor.　Born 27 Apr. 1837.

59. Judith Ann. Born 3 Feb. 1839.

60. Eleanor Jane. Born 3 Feb. 1841.

61. Naomi. Born 21 Jan. 1843.

62. Catherine. Born 14 May 1845.

63. William Henry. Born 2 Feb. 1847.

64. John Bruce.

65. George.

66. Joseph Godfrey.

22. George Hadley born 2 Apr. 1812.

Married Elizabeth Amelia Church 8 Apr. 1839.

Family.

67. Sarah Ann. Born 27 July 1840.

68. Catherine Judith. Born 19 Oct. 1841.

69. Mary. Born 11 Mar. 1844.

70. John Henry. Born 3 Sept. 1847.

71. Mark Abner. Born 16 Jan. 1857.

72. Abram Hattie. Born 19 Feb. 1860.

73. Robert

74. Joseph.

75. Amelia.

23. Elizabeth Hadley married John Martin 21 Feb. 1837.

24. Thomas Hadley married Frances Jane No. 54, daughter of John and Lydia Hadley.

Family.

76. Kate. Born 3 Sept. 1858.

77. Eva Mary. Born 30 Sept. 1859.

78. Ellen Maria Milligan. Born 19 Aug. 1861.

79. Irad Alex. Born 11 Sept. 1863.

80. Alfred.

81. Carrie.

82. Wesley.

83. Charles.

25. Eleanor Hadley married James Grant 15 Mar. 1841.

28. Joseph John Hadley married Sophia Carr 15 July 1839.

Family.

84. Mary Jane. Born 16 Oct. 1840.

85. Joseph John. Born 23 Aug. 1842.

86. George. Born 25 May 1844.

87. James B. Born 3 Aug. 1846.

88. Thomas.

89. Godfrey.

90. Robert.

91. Hiram.

92. Elizabeth.

29. Sarah Hadley married James Hattie 1838.

37. John Henry Hadley married Diana Calahan 21 Apr. 1840.

Family.

93. Mary Ann. Born 25 Nov. 1841.

94. William Henry. Born 29 Jan. 1844

95. John Godfrey. Born 2 Mar. 1849.

96. Sarah Maria. Born 29 Sept. 1850.

97. Levi. Born 22 July 1855.

98. Elizabeth Ann.

38. Joseph Hadley married Isabella Logan Harty 28 Jan. 1844.

Family.

99. William Godfrey. Born 29 Nov. 1844.

100. James Edward. Born 28 Mar. 1847.

101. Joseph Allison. Born 31 Mar. 1851.

102. Martha Elizabeth. Born 2 Apr. 1853.

103. Levi Havelock. Born 4 Aug. 1859.

104. Isabella Frances. Born 26 Mar. 1862.

105. Josephine Maria.

39. James Hadley is said to have died young.

40. William Hadley died young.

41. William Hadley married Mary Callahan.

Family.

106. Isabella. Born 29 Feb. 1854.

107. Frances Maria. Born 12 Jan. 1849.

108. Mary. Bapt. 23 May 1851.

After the death of William Hadley, his widow married a Mr. Buckley.

42. Godfrey Hadley married Mary Renton.

Family.

109. Sarah E. Born Oct. 1851,

110. Thomas Henry. Born 13 Apr. 1853.

111. Charles Archibald. Born 26 Oct. 1855.

112. Albert. Born 9 Aug. 1856.

113. Caroline Alma. Born 8 Jan. 1858.

114. Mary Jane. Born 25 Mar. 1860.

115. Button J. Born Sept, 1862.

116. James Edward. Born 27 Oct. 1864.

117. Annie Born Nov. 1868.

118. Guy Ellerton. Born 12 Nov. 1870.

43. Jairus Hadley married Sarah Ehler.

Family.

119. Stewart. Born 26 Mar. 1851.

120. Hannah. Born 21 Jan. 1853.

121. Donald Ehler. Born 21 Mar. 1854.

122. Ida Alice. Born 9 June 1856.

123. Lydia Elizabeth. Born 22 Oct. 1859.

124. Jairus Levi Hart. Born 16 July 1860.

125. Eliza Jane. Born 25 Sept. 1862.

126. Joseph William. Born 30 June 1864.

127. Sarah Ami. Born 16 Oct. 1866.

128. Daniel Christopher. Born 12 Oct. 1868.

129. Mary J. Born 24 Sept. 1870.

130. Ernestine. Born 23 Sept. 1874.

44. Thomas Harty married Jane Renton 7 Oct. 1856.

Family.

131. Kate.

132. Ernest.

133. Alfred.

134. Bessie Jane.

135. Lillian.

136. Eva.

137. Cora.

45. Elizabeth Hadley married Robert Carter.

46. Robert Cooney Hadley married Jane Ferguson.

Family.

138. James

139. Jairus.

140. Isabel Maggie,　Born 3 Oct. 1863.

141. William Cranswick.　Born 6 Oct. 1865.

142. Sarah Maria Peart.　Born 5 Oct. 1870.

143. Lucretia.

144. Joseph Albert.　Born 1866.

47. Joseph Hadley married Judith Hadley No. 58, 1860.

Family.

145. Esther.

146. Ella.

147. Isabel.　Born 1 Nov. 1865.

148. Burton.

149. John Cranswick.　Born 4 Oct. 1870.

150. Walter.

151. Albert Hooper.　Born 8 Jan. 1873.

152. Nettie.

153. Joseph.　4 Apr. 1876.

48. Sarah Maria Hadley married Robert Carter 17 Jan. 1843.

49. John Henry Hadley married Sarah Morgan 2 Feb. 1853.

Family.

154. John Wesley.　Born 20 June 1861.

155. Reuben.

156. Osbourne Wallace.　Born 2 Sept. 1873.

157. Levi.

158. Eliza.

51. Catherine Maria Hadley married Isaac L. Myers 31 Dec. 1850.

52. Eleanor Abbot Hadley married Lothrop Myers. (Second wife).

53. Sarah Hadley died 17 June 1837.

287

54. Sarah Harriet Shreve Hadley married James Henry Myers 8 Jan. 1861.

55. Frances Jane Hadley married Thomas Hadley. No. 23.

56. William Hadley married Anne Jane McKay 1848.

Family.

159. Alexander.

160. Lydia.

161. Margaret.

162. Sarah Ann.

163. Ruth.

164. Victoria.

165. Esther.

166. Ida.

167. Henrietta.

168. Francis.

169. William Edmund.   Born 6 Dec. 1870.

(These may not be in order of birth, though William Edmund was the youngest.)

57. Sarah Elizabeth Hadley married Alex Durah.

59. Judith Hadley married Joseph Hadley.   No. 46.

60. Eleanor Jane Hadley married Cyrus Parks.

64. John Bruce Hadley married a Miss Carter.

65. George Hadley married Matilda Carrogan.

66. Joseph Godfrey Hadley married Elizabeth Carrogan, 18 Dec. 1876.

67. Sarah Ann Hadley married John Porper 1865,

68. Catherine Judith Hadley married Zimri Carter.

69. Mary Hadley married George Hadley.

70. John Henry Hadley never married.

71. Mark Abner Hadley married a Miss Welsh.

72. Abram Hattie Hadley married Margaret Bruce.

73. Robert Hadley married Catherine Welsh.

74. Joseph Hadley never married.

75. Amelia Hadley married Miss Carr.

78. Ellen Maria Milligan Hadley married Alex Grant 1 Aug. 1882.

80. Alfred Hadley married a Miss Grant.

82. Wesley Hadley married a Miss Strople.

84. Mary Jane Hadley married John Alex Carr 14 Dec. 1869.

85. Joseph John Hadley married first Eliza Hadley 28 Jan. 1880. He married second a Miss Carr.

86. George Hadley married Mary Hadley.

87. James B. Hadley married Zilpah Grant.

88. Thomas Hadley married a Miss Cummings.

92. Elizabeth Hadley married William Grant 5 Nov. 1878.

94. William Henry Hadley married Sarah Maria Lumsden 23 Mar. 1866.

95. John Godfrey Hadley married Annie Munro 21 Dec. 1878.

96. Sarah Maria Hadley married Reuben Ehler.

98. Elizabeth Ann Hadley married Joseph Christopher Morgan 24 Sept. 1872.

99. William Godfrey Hadley married Mary Eliza Grant 27 Feb. 1879.

100. James Edward Hadley married M. E. H. Russel 2 Jan. 1870.

104. Isabella Frances Hadley married A. J. O. Maguire 19 July 6, 1882.

105. Josephine Maria Hadley married John Scott.

106. Isabella Hadley married Archibald McDonald 13 July 1869.

107. Frances M. Hadley .married Hercules Hewitt 16 Oct. 1867.

108. Mary Hadley married John Barry.

110. Thomas Henry Hadley married Jeannette E. Myers 11 Jan. 1881,

111. Charles Archibald Hadley married first Christina Jane Myers 22 Dec. 1880, second Esther Hadley No. 163.

114. Mary Jane Hadley was drowned 22 Aug. 1876.

HORTONS.

There were seven sons and daughters in the family which Isaiah Horton and his wife brought from Pictou, and the number was increased after their arrival by the birth of another son. Isaiah Horton married Anna Cleaves. Tradition claims his pro-revolutionary views enraged the newly arrived ultra loyal Highlanders from whom he hid in a hay stack for fear of his life.

Family.

1. Isaiah.

2. Stutely.

3. William.

4. Mary.

5. George.

6. Ann.

7. Hezekiah.

8. Charles. Born 2 Dec. 1785.

(The above is probably not in order of birth, though Isaiah was the eldest, followed by Stutely, and Charles was the youngest.)

1. Isaiah Horton married Zippora Hyde 15 Apr. 1793.

Family.

9. Ann. Born 23 Apr. 1794.

10. Sarah. Born 24 Mar. 1798.

11. John. Born 7 May 1800.

12. Zippora Cynthia. Born 6 June 1803.

13. Mary Bailey. Born 31 Oct. 1805.

14. Susannah Maria. Born 31 Jan. 1808.

15. William Isaiah. Born 2 Jan. 1810.

16. Ruth Amelia. Born 14 Feb. 1812.

17. James Alexander. Born 31 Apr. 1814.

18. Charles. Born 2 Oct. 1816.

19. Philomela. Born 12 Sept. 1819.

20. Isaiah.

21. Humphrey.

2. Stutely Horton married Hannah Fisher of Stewiacke.

Family.

22. William.

23. Isaiah.

24. Robert.

25. Alexander.

26. James.

27. John.

28. Samuel.

29. Elizabeth.

30. Ann.

3. William Horton married Lydia Cook 2 Oct. 1790.

Family.

31. William. Born 31 Jan. 1792.

32. Ambrose. Born 28 Oct. 1793.

33. George.   Born 25 Oct. 1795.

34. Hannah Cleeves.   Born 25 Aug. 1801.

35. John Stephen.   Born 25 July 1799.

36. Mary.   Born 24 Aug. 1809.

37. James Edward.   Born 24 June 1812.

38. Sarah Dorcas.   Born 15 May 1814.

39. Lydia.

40. Priscilla.

41. Thomas.

4. Mary Horton married Thomas Jones 21 Jan. 1794.

5. George Horton married first Susannah Langille 18 June 1803. She died 28 Dec. 1827. He married second Elizabeth MacKenzie 3 Feb. 1829.

Family.   (All by second wife.)

42. Susan Elizabeth.   Born 6 Nov. 1829.

43. George Washington.   Born 7 Jan. 1831.

44. Edward F..G.

45. Hezekiah.   Born 24 Feb. 1833.

46. Steven.

47. Charles.

48. Sarah.

6. Ann Horton married Benjamin Critchett 23 June 1785.

7. Hezekiah Horton married Mary Macintosh.

Family.

49. Elizabeth.   Born 19 June 1813.

8. Charles Horton married Sarah Scott 18 Jan. 1810.

Family.

50. Ruth Godfrey.   Born 5 Nov. 1810.

51. Ann Elizabeth.   Born 18 Jan. 1813.

52. Thomas Jones.   Born 14 Feb. 1815.

9. Ann Horton married Elias Cook 3 Jan. 1811.

10. Sarah Horton married James Brown 4 Jan. 1814.

11. John Horton married Margaret Bruce 27 Dec. 1827.

Family.

53. Elizabeth Ann.   Born 14 Jan. 1829.

54. Catherine.

12. Zippora Cynthia Horton married Alexander Horton.

13. Mary Bailey Horton married Thomas James Dickie 17 Apr. 1832.

14. Susannah Maria Horton married John George Cunningham 2 Sept. 1832.

15. William Isaiah Horton was lost at sea, unmarried.

16. Ruth Amelia Horton married George Jones 30 Dec. 1834.

17. James Alexander Horton married Lucy Maria Cook 4 Mar. 1841. This family, in which there were a number of children, moved to River John.

18. Charles Horton married Eliza Henline 16 Jan. 1837.

Family.

55. Sarah Elizabeth.   Born 25 Oct. 1837.

56. William Cranswick.   Born 4 Dec. 1839.

57. Charles.

58. Zippora Ann.   Bapt. 25 June 1844.

59. Frances.   Born 30 Dec. 1845.

60. Isaiah Washington.   Born 26 Dec. 1847.

61. Emmeline Amelia.

62. George Archibald.

63. Thomas James.   Born 31 Jan. 1855.

64. Freeman.

65. Mahala.

19. Philomela Horton was not married.

20. Isaiah Horton married Hannah Bears 8 Jan. 1811.

Family.

66. Isaiah Alexander.   Born 14 Jan. 1812.

67. David Bears.   Born 25 Oct. 1814.

21. Humphrey Horton married first Elizabeth Cook 10 Jan. 1826,,
She died 11 Mar. 1827. He married second Jane Jones 14 July 1829.

Family.

68. Zippora.

69. Mary Elizabeth.   Born 7 May 1833.

70. Mary.

71. Thomas.

72. Jane Isabella.   Born 25 Sept. 1838.

73. Alexander McNutt.   Born 27 Oct. 1839.

74. Wentworth Taylor.   Born 5 Oct. 1842.

75. Lavinia Ann. Born 31 May 1844.

76. Maria Esther.

77. Mary Elizabeth. Born 4 Oct. 1847.

22. William Horton married Elizabeth Myers 10 May 1810.

Family.

78. Mary. Born 26 Apr. 1811.

79. Elizabeth Catherine. Born 8 May 1813.

80. Hannah. Born 10 Mar. 1815.

81. Isaac John. Born 22 Apr. 1817.

82. Susan Margaret. Born 9 May 1819.

83. Joseph.

84. Stutely.

85. David Whitford.

86. Esther.

23. Isaiah Horton married Hannah Myers.

Family.

87. David.

88. John.

89. Alexander.

90. James.

91. Hezekiah.

92. Jane.

93. Rebecca.

94. Thankful.

95. Child.

24. Robert Horton married Zippora Jones 23 Dec. 1816.

Family.

96. Thomas.

97. Elizabeth Whitman. Born 20 Apr. 1820.

98. George.

99. Moses.

100. John.

101. Mary.

102. Hannah.

103. Catherine.

104. Albert.   Born 14 Jan. 1841.

Robert Horton died 15 July 1872, aged 82.

25. Alexander Horton married first Mary Myers 11 Mar. 1817.

Family.

105. James Thomas.   Born 6 Feb. 1818.

He married second Zippora Cynthia Horton.

Family.

106. Samuel.

107. John.

108. Isabella Smith.   Born 22 Sept. 1832.

(There were probably more in this family, which moved to Halifax.)

26. James Horton married a Miss Keller.

Family.

109. Samuel.

110. James.

(There were more in this family, which moved to Cumberland County.)

28. Samuel Horton married Nancy Watson.

Family.

111. William.

(This family moved to Musquodoboit.)

29. Elizabeth Horton married Alexander Kent.

30. Ann Horton married a Mr. Parker.

31. William Horton married Hannah Ryder 26 Jan. 1813.

Family.

112. George Henry.   Born 21 Jan. 1814.

113. William Mariner.   Born 27 May 1819.

114. Ambrose Cleeves)

115. Valentine.   )   Twins. Born 11 Oct. 1824.

116. Nancy.   Born 27 Nov. 1830.

32. Ambrose Horton married Dorothy Ryder 27 Dec. 1814.

Family.

117. Lydia.   Born 6 Nov. 1815.

Ambrose Horton died 14 Sept. 1873. Dorothy Horton died 18 May 1860.

33. George Horton married Mary Whitman.

No Family.

34. Hannah Cleeves Horton married William Cook.

35. John Stephen Horton married Elizabeth Russell 31 July 1823..

Family.

118. Susan.

119. Reuben.

120. Sarah Jane.

121. Ann.

122. James.

123. John.

124. Thomas.

125. Elizabeth.

126. Lydia Maria.

37. James Edward Horton married Mary Ann Gammon 15 Dec. 1836.

Family.

127. William Archibald.   Born 19 May 1838.

128. Ambrose.   Born 11 Jan. 1840.

129. Naomi Caroline.   Born 27 Dec. 1841.

130. Mary.

131. Lucina Maria.   Born 5 Mar. 1844.

132. Jeremiah J.   Born 8 Sept. 1847.

133. Eleanor Jane.   Born 2 Jan. 1854.

134. Hezekiah H.   )

135. Mahala Jemima.)   Twins.   Born 1 Jan. 1856.

136. George Whitfield.   Born 10 June 1858.

137. Thomas Henry.   Born 27 Aug. 1860.

138. Sydney Smith.   Born 10 Dec. 1864.

139. Eliza Dorcas.

38. Sarah Dorcas Horton married John Bigsby 21 Aug. 1839.

39. Lydia Horton married Robert Burns 13 July 1828.

41. Thomas Horton married Mary Cook 19 Jan. 1830.

Family.

140. Charity.

141. Esther.

142. Lydia.

143. Eleanor.

42. Susan Elizabeth Horton married Edward Jenkins.

43. George Washington Horton married Esther Horton 26 Mar. 1855.

44. Edward F. G. Horton married Mary Ann Kaizer 23 Aug. 1870. (The family moved to Port Beckerton.)

45. Hezekiah Horton married Caroline Jones 22 Dec. 1857.

46. Steven Horton married Miss Johnson,

47. Charles Horton married a Miss Kelly.

50. Ruth Godfrey Horton married Dan. Bigsby 26 Apr. 1831.

51. Ann Elizabeth Horton married Thomas Simpson 7 Jan. 1840.

52. Thomas Jones Horton was not married.

53. Elizabeth Arm Horton married Abraham Bigsby Jan., 1849.

54. Catherine Horton married Cribben Grant.

56. William Cranswick Horton married Matilda Shaw 13 Feb. 1868. (He died soon after, and the widow married Robert Digdon.)

58. Zippora Ann Horton married Elijah Rogers 15 Dec. 1863.

59. Frances Horton married Daniel Atkins 1 Dec. 1866.

61. Emmeline Amelia Horton married George Washington Cook 26 June 1868.

62. George Archibald Horton married Ellen Maloney 3 Feb. 1873.

65. Mahala Horton married John E. Grant 3 Oct. 1881.

73. Alexander McNutt Horton married first Ellen Diana Morgan 29 Dec. 1879. He married second Mrs. Porper, widow.

76. Maria Esther Horton married William Nickerson 29 Dec. 1879.

77. Mary Elizabeth Horton died 21 Jan. 1866.

78. Mary Horton married Godfrey Hart 18 Dec. 1834.

79. Elizabeth Catherine Horton married John Digdon 9 Mar. 1837.

81. Isaac John Horton married Eliza Gammon 29 Dec. 1840.

82. Susan Margaret Horton married Thomas Horton.

83. Joseph Horton married Elizabeth Pyle 2 Mar. 1856.

Family.

(1) Esther; (2) Hurd; (3) Katherine; (4) Havelock; (5) Alonzo; (6) Ada; (7) Stanley; (8) Minnie.

84. Stutely Horton married Maria Publicover.

85. David Whitford Horton married Lavinia Caroline Ehler 26 Apr. 1859.

86. Esther Horton married Arthur Ehler.

88. John Horton married a Miss Bears of Canso.

92. Jane Horton married Asa Cahoon.

93. Rebecca Horton married a Mr. Baker in the States.

94. Thankful Horton married a Mr. Bears.

96. Thomas Horton married Susan Margaret Horton.

97. Elizabeth Whitman Horton married George Whitman 19 Jan. 1847.

100. John Horton married Ann Kirby and moved to the States.

101. Mary Horton married. Isaac Archibald.

102. Hannah Horton married first John Morgan 7 Jan. 1868. She married second Charles I. Graves 15 May 1876.

103. Catherine Horton married Joseph Fifield.

104. Albert Horton married Mary Ann Lavinia Peart, 1868.

117. Lydia Horton married William Jeffers.

118. Susan Horton married James Campbell.

119. Reuben Horton married Jane Spanks 30 July 1874.

126. Lydia Maria Horton married John Tyrrel Cross 26 Mar. 1874.

127. William Archibald Horton married a Miss Kirby.

128. Ambrose Horton married Margaret L. Nickerson 30 Mar. 1867.

130. Mary Horton married William Hanson.

133. Eleanor Jane Horton married William Spanks 13 Apr. 1876.

134. Hezekiah H. Horton married Rebecca Smith 19 May 1878,

139. Eliza Dorcas Horton married W. D. Gillie 29 Dec. 1868.

140. Charity Horton married Elias Spanks 30 Dec. 1858.

141. Esther Horton married George W. Horton.

JOHN INGERSOL.

Although the name of this man is found on the grant to the old settlers, no other record has been found, either of him or of his family. It is possible, however, that the Lake named on the old maps as Ingersol's lake may have been called after him.

PEARTS.

Though only Godfrey Peart is named in the grant, there appears to have been two persons of that family name, who, it may be assumed, were brothers. These were

Godfrey and John Peart. The name of Thomas Peart has been found in the Canso records, dating from a time fifteen or twenty years previous to the settling of Guysborough. This Thomas may have been a connection, possibly the father of the two. John Peart married Cassandra Crockery 24 Dec. 1789, and died of Scarlet Fever 5 May 1804, aged 39. His widow married Hugh Miller 3 Apr. 1808. No record has been found of any family born to John Peart. Godfrey Peart's wife was Sarah Godfrey, a widow. This establishes some connection with the Pearts and the group of Liverpool settlers.

Family.

1. John Godfrey. Born 3 Oct. 1786.

2. Thomas. Born 6 June 1788.

Godfrey Peart died 10 Apr. 1831. Sarah Peart died 16 Sept. 1842, aged 88 years.

1. John Godfrey Peart married Maria W. Nixon 24 May 1807.

Family.

3. William Nixon. Born 12 May 1808.

4. John Godfrey. Bapt. 11 Nov. 1810.

5. Mary Patterson. Bapt. 14 Feb. 1813.

6. Godfrey. Born 14 Apr. 1815.

7. Maria William Nixon. Born 28 Aug. 1817.

8. Sarah Elizabeth. Born 27 Dec. 1819.

9. Harriet. Born 10 Dec. 1822.

10. Thomas Henry Inch. Born 18 Apr. 1825.

11. Harriet Isabella Marshall. Born 9 Nov. 1827.

12. Nixon Jones. Born 13 Feb. 1831.

2. Thomas Peart married Marianne Cribben 11 Feb. 1810.

Family.

13. Godfrey. Bapt. 5 May 1811.

14. Thomas Cribben. Born 26 Feb. 1113.

15. Lucinda Ann. Born 19 Aug. 1815.

16. John William. Born 26 May 1818.

17. Sarah Elizabeth. Born 6 Oct. 1820.

18. Cynthia Esther. Born 3 July 1823.

19. Maria Lavinia Inch. Born 16 Mar. 1828.

20. William W. Bapt. 4 Apr. 1831.

21. Henrietta Heinhaugh. Born 1834.

22. Frances Maria. Born 12 Oct. 1839.

Thomas Peart died 1 Sept. 1868. Marianne Peart died 19 May 1869, aged

78.

3. William Nixon Peart died 14 June 1810.

4. John Godfrey Peart is said to have died young.

5. Mary Patterson Peart married Thomas Foster 1854.

6. Godfrey Peart died in Gloucester, unmaarried.

9. Harriet Peart died 19 Oct. 1827.

10. Thomas Henry Inch Peart last heard of as a sailor, unmarried.

11. Harriet Isabella Marshall Peart died 17 Mar. 1837.

13. Godfrey Peart married Martha Isabella Scott.

Family

23. Mariaanne Lavinia. Born 1 Dec. 1835

24. William Scott. Born 5 June 1837

25. Caleb Henry Godfrey Shreve. Born 1 Oct. 1839.

26. Archibald Morrison. Born 3 Nov. 1841.

27. Charles Wallace. Born 12 Oct. 1843.

28. James Henry Albert. Born 24 Nov. 1845.

29. Jedediah Gordon. Born 5 apr. 1848.

30. Victoria Maria. Born 2 Dec. 1850.

31. Stewart Campbell. Born 14 Sept. 1853.

14. Thomas Cribben Peart married Frances Scott 13 Sept. 1836.

Family

32. Thomas Lemuel Cutler. Born 23 Jan. 1838.

33. Emma Maria. Born 15 Mar. 1840.

34. Stewart Campbell. Born 29 Mar. 1842.

35. Jane Ann. Bapt. 10 Nov. 1844.

36. Joseph Shannon. Born 4 Oct. 1846.

37. Edward Caritte. Born 8 Sept. 1848.

38. Louisa Clark. Born 6 Oct. 1850.

39. Alexander William. Born 25 Aug. 1852.

40. Julia Harriet. Born 2 Feb. 1855.

41. Ada May. Born 31 Oct. 1857.

15. Lucinda Ann Peart married John Heinhaugh 6 May 1834.

16. John William Peart married Philomela Cook 3 Aug. 1837.

Family

42. William Henry.

43. John James Cook. Born 4 June 1840.

44. Lucretia Ann. Born 28 Jan. 1842.

45. Mary Ann Lavinia. @9 Oct. 1844.

46. Elias Cook. Born 9 Nov. 1846.

47. Marshall.

48. Edward.

49. Emma.

50. Annie

17. Sarah Elizabeth Peart married E. H. Francheville 14 Feb. 1843.

18. Cynthia Esther Peart married Charles S. Scott 11 Jan. 1843.

19. Maria Lavinia Inch Peart died Aug. 1829.

20. William W. Peart died 15 Mar. 1837.

21. Henrietta Heinhaugh Peart married first Anthony Donald McKenzie 27 Jan. 1858. He died 1 Oct. 1861. The widow married Joseph Lee Martin 8 May 1865.

22. Frances Maria Peart died 10 Aug. 1859.

23. Marianne Lavinia Peart married Judson Bixby.

24. William Scott Peart married Mary Peddy 1 Jan. 1868.

25. Caleb Henry G. S. Peart married first Rebecca Brodie 9 Oct. 1867. He married second Lydia Ann Rheinold 25 Nov. 1884.

26. Archibald Morrison Peart married Margaret Ehler 12 Feb. 1873.

27. Charles Wallace Peart married Hattie A. Cook 16 Jan. 1872.

28. James H. A. Peart married Agnes O. Godfrey 16 Feb. 1876.

30. Victoria Maria Peart married John James Peart 6 Aug. 1873.

33. Emma Maria Peart married Charles S. Macintosh 22 Apr. 1879.

35. Jane Ann Peart married George Gilbert.

37. Edward Carritte Peart married Mary A. Cunningham 19 Feb. 1879.

38. Louisa Clark Peart married Charles Elliot.

42. William Henry Peart married Ida Alice Hadley 12 Dec. 1875.'

43. John James Cook Peart married Victoria Maria Peart.

44. Lucretia Ann Peart married first James A. Steele. She married second Albert Phelps.

45. Mary Ann Lavinia Peart married Albert Horton.

47. Marshall Peart married Maria Penny 24 Dec. 1873.

49. Emma Peart married David Russell Grant 22 Nov. 1870.

50. Annie Peart married Mr. Beals

TOBY

The Toby family consisted of the father Nathaniel, born in Sandwich Barnstable, Maine, June 30, 1721 and one son, Samuel. No record has been found of the date of Nathaniel Toby's death. He married Elizabeth Hopkins, Oct. 12, 1756 at Chatham, Barnstable, Massachusetts. His wife died 8 Apr. 1816, aged 95 years. Her father died in Barrington, NS, 1742. The Tobys were without a doubt settlers who had moved to Guysborough from Liverpool, NS. Nathaniel Toby's family consisted of,—

1. Samuel Toby, who married Elizabeth Whiteford 24 Nov. 1784.

Family.

  2. Cynthia. Born 4 June 1786.

  3. Elijah. Born 27 Aug. 1788.

  4. Diziah. Born 17 June 1791.

  5. Lydia. Born 6 Oct. 1792.

  6. William. Bapt. 15 May 1796.

  7. Joseph. Born 16 July 1798.

  8. Eliza.

2. Cynthia Toby married Gideon Godfrey 16 June 1808.

4. Diziah Toby died 11 Dec. 1792.

5. Lydia Toby married James Nickerson 8 Mar. 1813. 7.

7. Joseph Toby married Ruth Murphy 5 Jan. 1823.

Family.

  9. Ann Rebecca. Born 29 Nov. 1823.

  10. Elisha William. Born 12 Feb. 1826.

  11. Margaret Elizabeth. Born 22 July 1828.

  12. Thomas Harvey. Born 8 Jan. 1831.

  13. John Smith. Born 21 Dec. 1832.

  14. Lavinia Maria. Born 29 July 1835.

8. Eliza Toby married James Wheaton 23 Dec. 1835.

9. Ann Rebecca Toby married Henry Gosbie 11 Jan. 1848.

10. Elisha William Toby married Jane Harty, a widow, 21 Dec. 1875. Her maiden name was Morgan.

11. Margaret Elizabeth Toby died in 1840.

12. Thomas Harvey Toby was drowned in 1850.

13. John Smith Toby married Adelaide Augusta Scott 29 Jan. 1867.
14. Lavinia Maria Toby married William Francis Cook 8 July 1854.

THE DUKE OF CUMBERLAND'S REGIMENT
(MONTAGUE CORPS.)

	Town Lot		Rear Lands	
	Div.	Block	Number	Acres
*Ambrose John				100
Armsworthy Baptist	SE	I	19	100
*Barrett Robert. Ensign	SE	E	15	500
*Boswell William	SE	H	5	100
*Bradley David	SE	B	6	
*Brickstock Roger				100
*Brooks Timothy	SE	L	2	100
*Brown George	SE	B	2	100
*Brownley Robert	SE	H	14	100
Brownrigg Richard F. Capt	SE	N	3	850
Bruce George	SE	C	1	100
*Bryam John	SE	I	20	100
Bundy James	SE	G	18	100
*Carney Cornelius	SE	H	18	100
*Carney William	SE	I	14	
*Clark Lewis	SE	G	8	100
*Clements John	SE	I	7	100
*Connors Nathaniel	SE	F	3	100
*Coppard John	SE	L	8	100
Cowan John	SE	K	4	200
Critchett Benjamine	SE	F	2	200
*Cunningham Ralph. Capt	SE	N	1	900
Davis Zachariah	SE	B	11	100
*Deyenish George	SE	B	8	
*Douglas Randall				100
Driver Henry	SE	B	12	100
Dunaway John				200
*Essex David				100
Everige Isaac	SE	G	13	100

*Fielder Charles	SE	F	17	100
Flick John	SE	G	6	100
*Franklin Esom	SE	L	7	
Fraser Charles	SE	G	12	100
*Friend Ulrich	SE	K	8	100
Fryer William	SE	M	9	100
Gardner John	SE	C	2	100
*Glasgow Walter	SE	I	8	100
Goodwin Edward	SE	H	3	100
*Haddon John	SE	G	1	100
Hanagan Henry	SE	G	17	100
Hanagan Patrick	SE	H	2	100
Harboon William				350
Harden John	SE	C	8	100
*Harragan Jeremiah	SE	I	18	100
Harrel Peter	SE	K	3	350
Harris James	SE	C	11	100
Heffernan Edmund	SE	H	16	100
*Henry Harry				100
Hewin John	SE	F	12	200
Hines George	SE	K	5	200
*Hines Peter	SE	L	1	100
Homan Conrad	SE	A	12	250
*Homan Conrad Jr	SE	D	7	100
*Hoop John	SE	H	8	
Hopkins John	SE	F	19	100
Horsford, James	SE	I	17	300
*Jewell Samuel	SE	M	2	100
*Johnson Reuben	SE	B	7	200
Jones Thomas	SE	G	10	100
*Jones Stephen	SE	M	4	250
*Kennedy Isaac	SE	B	10	100
Laird James	SE	C	7	100
Lewis David	SE	C	9	100

*Lewis William	SE	F	2	100
*Litten Abel				100
McAlleese John	SE	I	12	100
McCaffree Edward	SE	B	1	100
*McCathry Daniel	SE	L	3	200
McCarthy William	SE	L	10	100
*McDonald Angus. Lieut	SE	L	5	600
McGee Oliver	SE	G	14	150
*McKay William	SE	C	6	100
McKeel Nathaniel	SE	L	6	100
McPherson James. Doctor	SE	K	1	600
*Main Samuel	SE	H	4	100
*Markham Robert	SE	F	14	100
Matthews Bryan	SE	F	7	100
Meighan Brian. Lieut	SE	K	7	600
Montague Lord	SE	N	4	
Murphy John	SE	I	4	100
*Murphy Miles	SE	F	3	100
*Nelson Jesse	SE	I	15	100
*Nouse Philip	SE	I	6	100
Oliver Samuel	SE	M	7	100
Parnell Abraham	SE	H	9	100
Parsons William	SE	C	5	100
*Pendlebury Marmaduke	SE	G	19	100
*Penrise Edward	SE	I	2	100
*Pierce William	SE	F	18	100
*Porter John	SE	G	16	100
Pringle John	SE	H	12	200
Pushee Nathaniel	SE	K	10	200
*Reed Edward	SE	G	5	100
*Reid John	SE	H	7	
*Rheideker Cutlip	SE	C	3	100
*Rhoads Matthew	SE	G	9	100
*Robertson Andrew	SE	B	5	100

Rogers Eli	SE	K	9	100
*Rogers William	SE	M	3	100
Russell Major	SE	F	13	200
*Sarriet Samuel	SE	G	3	100
Sellars Daniel	SE	G	7	100
Shanks John	SE	H	10	100
*Shearin William	SE	F	20	100
*Showers Thomas	SE	C	10	100
*Smtih Frederick	SE	H	17	100
*Spain William	SE	H	20	100
*Stanton James	SE	F	6	100
*Studhaven Barnabas	SE	B	4	100
Symonds Gideon	SE	I	10	150
Taylor James	SE	I	16	100
*Taylor William	SE	B	9	200
*Thompson, Samuel	SE	F	4	100
Tilley Lewis	SE	F	9	100
Upton John	SE	G	15	100
*Weatherhead John. (Weatherford)	SE	I	5	200
*Weller Philip				100
*Whelan William	SE	G	11	100
White Gideon. Capt	SE	N	2	850
Whitman George	SE	M	1	100
*Whit Isom	SW	N	8	100
*Whit John	SE	I	13	
*Williams, Daniel				
*Williams Zephaniah	SE	H	1	100
*Willoughby David	SE	C	2	100
*Willson John	SE	G	2	100
*Wishart James	SE	H	19	100

(Concerning those persons whose names are marked with a star (*) few or no records have been found.)

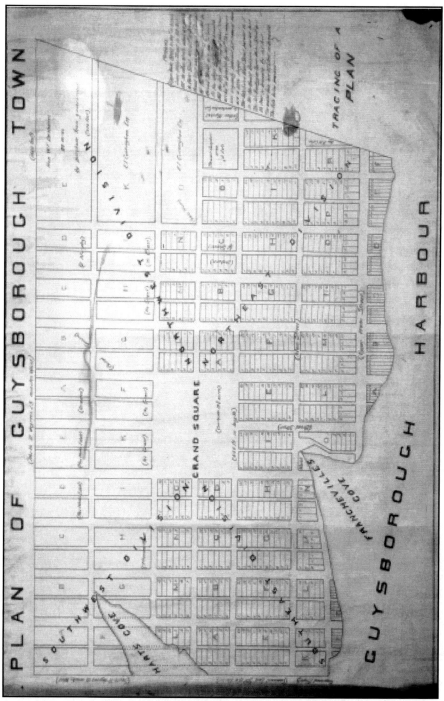

Original town plan of Guysborough by the Dept. of the Army and Navy

Women.

Mrs. McDonald.   Mrs. Cunningham
Mrs. Harrill.   Mrs. Horsford.
Mrs. Jones.   Mrs. Harbourn
Mrs. Ambrose.   Mrs. Symonds
Mrs. McGee.

Children Over Ten.

Chloe Harrill.   Elinor Wall Horsford
Betsey Ambrose.

Children Under Ten.

Ann Harrill.   Daniel McAdams.

Servants

Henry Thomas.   Toby Wheeler

Charles Boagan.   John Murphy

Mary Boagan.   John Adams

Three to Capt. Brownrigg.   Three to Capt. Cunningham

John McCoy.   Robert Harris

Duncan McLennan.   Diana

Three to Capt. Browning   Two to Doctor McPherson.

Armsworthy, Baptist. Married Mary Mass 15 Apr. 1793

Family.

1. Mary. Bapt. 11 Oct. 1796.
2. Abram.   Born 11 June 1797.
3. Ann.   Born 18 Apr. 1803.
4. Catherine.   Born 19 Sept. 1808.
5. William George.   Born 1 Apr. 1811.
6. Joseph.
7. George.
8. Martha.
9. James.

1. Mary Armsworthy married John O'Neil 5 Dec. 1815.

2. Abram Armsworthy.   No record.
3. Ann Armsworthy married David Griffin 27 Dec. 1830.

   (It was a boy of this family who was stabbed and killed at Cook's Cove.)
4. Cadierine Armsworthy married Robert Burns 28 Oct. 1830.
5. William George Armsworthy.   No record.
6. Joseph Armsworthy married Catherine George 21 Jan. 1834.

   Family.

   10. Abigail.   Born 4 Oct. 1836.

   11. Harriet.   Born 15 Mar. 1838.

   12. Margaret Ann.   Born 31 Oct. 1839.

   13. Joan Elizabeth.   Born 16 Apr. 1841.

   14. Eleanor Caroline.   Born 3 Oct. 1342.

   15. Isaac Levi.   Born 3 Apr. 1844.

   16. Joseph.   Born 9 Jan. 1846.

   17. Mary.

7. George Armsworthy married Mary E. Ryter 26 July 1837.

   Family.

   18. Arm Elizabeth.   Born 19 Oct. 1839.

   19. John Henry.   Born 15 May 1839.

   Mary E. Armsworthy died 20 May 1839.

   George Armsworthy married second, Ann Gray Henderson, 14 July 1840.

   Family.

   20. John Henry.   Born 26 Mar. 1843.

   21. Victoria Caroline.   Born 12 May 1845.

   22. Thomas Abraham.   Born 25 Oct. 1847.

   23. George Christopher.   Born 23 June 1850.

   24. James Alexander.   Born 21 Sept. 1852.

   25. Eleanor Catherine.   Born 14 Aug. 1854.

   26. Elizabeth Emmeline.   Born 26 Apr. 1859.

   27. Elsie Melissa.   Born 1 May 1868.

8. Martha Armsworthy married James Johnson 11 May 1842.
9. James Armsworthy married Hannah Silsy Boutiler.

   Family.

   28. George William.   Born 9 Aug. 1830.

   29. Caroline.   Born 10 May 1836.

30. Elizabeth. Born 6 May 1838.

31. Eleanor. Born 30 June 1839.

32. Hannah. Born 26 Feb. 1841.

33. Nancy. Born 3 Aug. 1842.

34. Sarah Jane. Born 6 June 1844.

35. Jane Abigail. Born 30 Nov. 1846.

36. Margaret. Born 21 Apr. 1832.

37. Hannah Silsy. Born 14 Aug. 1834.

(Mrs. James Armsworthy was 105 years old at the time of her death.)

10. Abigail Armsworthy married Christian Greencorn.

12. Margaret Ann Armsworthy married John George 7 May 1867.

13. Joan Elizabeth Armsworthy married John Manuel.

15. Isaac Levi Armsworthy married Susan Ann Cox 28 June 1870.

16. Joseph Armsworthy married Janet Ehler.

17. Mary Armsworthy married James Snow.

18. Ann Elizabeth Armsworthy died 1 Dec. 1856.

19. John Henry Armsworthy died in infancy.

21. Victoria Caroline Armsworthy married James Henry Meade 21 June 1869.

Brownrigg, Captain Richard F. He moved to Mirimachi. There is a reference to him in the Winslow Papers.

Bruce, George. This may be a mistake in the roll, or he may have gone by the name of James Bruce. James Bruce married Catherine Cadel 30 Jan. 1798.

Family.

1. Richard Samuel. Born 7 Sept. 1802.

2. Margaret Jane. Born 5 Nov. 1804.

3. Christopher. Born 1801.

4. John.

James Bruce was killed by a falling tree, 28 Mar. 1805, aged 40.

His widow married second, a Mr. Kilfyle.

1. Richard Samuel Bruce married Margaret Morgan 19 Feb. 1828. She died 16 Nov. 1875, aged 69.

Family.

5. James Christopher. Born 20 June 1829.

6. Charles Joseph. Born 20 Feb. 1833.

7. Robert Harvey. Born 24 Feb. 1835.

8. Catherine. Born 3 Aug. 1840.

9. Sarah Ann. Born 30 Aug. 1843.

10. Esther. Born 9 Oct. 1845.

11. Margaret Ellen.

2. Margaret Jane Bruce married John Horton 27 Dec. 1827.

3. Christopher Bruce married Abigail McKeough 25 Jan. 1827. Died 14 Apr. 1867.

Family.

12. William Moir. Born 4 Feb. 1831.

13. John Wesley. Born 12 Dec. 1832.

14. Christopher Langille. Born 11 Dec. 1S34.

15. Sarah Francis. Born 3 Oct. 1837.

16. Alexander William McLeod. Born 6 Aug. 1839.

17. John Godfrey. Born 18 July 1841.

18. Ruth Maria. Born 4 Sept. 1843.

19. John Joseph Marshall. Born 9 Jan. 1847.

20. Thomas Godfrey.

21. James Richard.

4. John Bruce married Caroline Scott 20 Mar. 1827.

Family.

22. William Wallace. Born 18 Nov. 1831.

23. Ruth Maria. Born 15 Oct. 1833.

24. John Joseph. Born 13 Oct. 1835.

25. James Robert Cooney. Born 9 Dec. 1838.

26. Mary Jane. Born 11 Mar. 1842.

27. George Christopher. Born 13 Apr. 1844.

28. Sarah Sophia.

5. James Christopher Bruce married Mary Moir McKeough 2 Feb. 1859. There was no family. He was a sea captain, and with his father-in-law and his brother-in-law was lost at sea, his vessel not being heard from.

6. Charles Joseph Bruce married Lydia Simpson McKeough 8 Feb. I860..

Family.

29. Anna Margaret. Born 28 Nov. 1860.

30. William Henry. Born 30 Oct. 1863.

31. Louisa Caroline. Born 10 Jan. 1873.

7. Robert Harvey Bruce died young.

311

8. Catherine Bruce married Mr. Hollier.

9. Sarah Ann Bruce married in the States.

10. Esther Bruce married Charles Cunningham.

11. Margaret Ellen Bruce married Josiah Hart 17 July 1858.

12. William Moir Bruce married Miss Fisk.

13. John Wesley Bruce married Hannah Fox, 1865.

Family.

    32. Abigaile McKay. Born 15 Dec. 1867.

    33. Alexander.

    34. William.

    35. Eldridge.

    36. Lila.

14. Christopher Langille Bruce married Sophia Henderson 8 Aug. 1864. She died 16 Feb. 1869.

Family.

    37. Norman.

    38. Abigail. Born 4 June 1865.

    39. Lydia Adeline. Born 3 Oct. 1866.

    40. Christopher. Born 15 Dec. 1868.

15. Sarah Francis Bruce married Ithiel Hull 4 Jan. 1871.

20. Thomas Godfrey Bruce married Mary Jane Whitman 7 Nov. 1866.

21. James Richard Bruce married Margaret Lipsett 24 Mar. 1857.

22. William Wallace Bruce married Maria Whitman 25 Dec. 1855.

23. Ruth Maria Bruce married Jeremiah Lyle.

24. John Joseph Bruce married Esther Bixby.

25. James Robert Cooney Bruce married Christina Stewart.

26. Mary Jane Bruce married Richard W. Cunningham.

28. Sarah Sophia Bruce married J. P. O'Brien 13 Jan. 1853 (She was the oldest of the family).

Bundy, James. Died 12 Aug. 1807, aged 55. No other record.

Cowan, John. Wife's name Mary.

Family.

    Mary Arm. Born Dec. 1796.

    John William. Born 12 Nov. 1799.

    Jane Catherine. Born 28 Feb. 1801.

There are no other records of this family.

Critchett, Benjamin.   He married Ann Horton 23 June 1785.

Family.

    1. William.   Born 23 Sept. 1786.

    2. Rachel.   Born 31 Jan. 1788.

    3. Anna.

    4. Benjamin.

1. William Critchett died 23 Mar. 1787.

2. Rachel Critchett married John Bigsby 4 Feb. 1806.

3. Anna Critchett married William Spanks 5 Dec. 1809.

4. Benjamin Critchett married Susan Stewart 3 Jan. 1837.

Davis, Zachariah married Hannah Reynolds 1 Apr. 1792.

Family.

    1. Sally.   Born 23 Apr. 1793.

    2. Susannah.

    3. Sarah.

2. Susannah Davis married Henry King 21 Dec. 1816.

3. Sarah Davis married George Taylor 8 Dec. 1814.

Driver, Henry. He sold his woodland in 1785. No other record.

Dunaway, John. He was drowned 2 Sept. 1785.

Everige, Isaac. His town lots were sold by Ralph Cunningham in 1788.

Flick, John. His woodland was sold by Lewis Hulsman in 1786.

Fraser, Charles.   He sold his town lot in 1786. His woodland was sold by Ralph Cunningham in 1788.

Fryer, William. He gave away his lot of woodland to L. Hulsman in 1785.

Gardner, John B. He died 17 June 1809, aged 40.

Glasgow, Walter. Moved to Antigonish about 1788.

Goodwin, Edward. His wife's name was Hannah. There is record of one child, Sarah, born 20 Nov. 1792.

Hannagan, Henry. Sold his woodland in 1785.

Hannagan, Patrick. He sold his land in 1786.

Harboon, William. His wife accompanied him to the settlement. His lands were sold for taxes in 1800, he having been absent since 1794.

Harden, John. He sold all lands in 1785.

Harrell, Peter. The name also appears as Harod, Harold or Harrill. Wife's name, Elizabeth.

Family.

    1. Joseph. Born 27 Aug. 1784.

    2. Lewis. Born 15 Dec. 1786.

    3. Margaret.

    4. James.

    5. Chloe.

    6. Ann.

1. Joseph Harrell must have been one of the first white children born in the settlement. He married Elizabeth North 23 Jan. 1803.

Family.

    7 Lewis. Born 4 Jan. 1805.

2. Lewis Harrell married Elizabeth

Family.

    8. Sarah. Born 10 Oct. 1812.

    9. James. Born 6 May 1816.

    10. Elizabeth. Born 22 Sept. 1819.

    11. Richard. Born 6 Apr. 1822.

    12. Peter. Born 23 Aug. 1826.

    13. Mary Jane. Born 19 July 1831.

3. Margaret Harrell married John Darrow 31 Aug. 1819.

4. James Harrell married Margaret Whittendale 29 Jan. 1826.

Of Chloe and Ann there is no record beyond their names on the register.

Harris, James. He died 12 May 1851, aged 94.

Heffernan, Edmund. He died 25 Oct. 1807, aged about 40.

Hewin, John. All lands sold by Miles Murphy in 1794.

Hines, George. All lands sold in 1785.

Homan, Conrad. In Halifax in 1789, selling his lands.

Hopkins, John. Gave power of Attorney to sell lands in 1785.

Horsford, Jonas, or James. Wife's name Tiley. There is record of one child, Margaret, born 3 Feb. 1795. The name of one child is also on the roll.

Jones, Thomas. Married Mary Horton 21 Jan. 1794. **Editor's note:** He was a native of Wales and a drummer who was a disbanded soldier at the age of 14. Thomas was killed by a falling tree and buried on his property at Cook's Cove.

Family.

1. Zipporah.
2. Anna.
3. John.
4. Elizabeth.
5. Susan.
6. Jane.
7. George.
8. Thomas.
9. Mary.
10. Sarah.

1. Zipporah Jones married Robert Horton 23 Dec. 1816.
2. Anna Jones married William Jenkins 3 Jan. 1815.
3. John Jones married Catherine Whitman 28 Aug. 1821.

Family.

11. Hannah.
12. William.
13. Mary.
14. Zipporah.
15. Sarah.
16. John.
17. Caroline.
18. Margaret.
19. Ann. Born 28 Jan. 1838.
20. Sophia. Born 28 Feb. 1840.
21. George Whitman. Born 13 Feb. 1844.
23. Charles. Born 2 Feb. 1846.

4. Elizabeth Jones married Eli Rogers 8 Jan. 1822.
5. Susan Jones married Lemuel Scott 2 Jan. 1827.
6. Jane Jones married Humphrey Horton.
7. George Jones married Ruth Amelia Horton 30 Sept. 1834.

Family.

24. Almira. Born 21 Dec. 1835.
25. Zipporah Jane. Born 1 Jan. 1838.
26. Susannah Cooney. Born 7 Dec. 1839.

27. Philomela.   Born 9 Oct. 1841.

28. James Alexander Horton.   Born 22 Dec. 1843.

29. Ruth Maria. Born 21 Jan. 1846.

30. Levi.

31. James.

8. Thomas Jones married Mary Ann Spanks.

Family.

32. Mary.

33. Thomas.

34. Martha.

35. Charles.

36. Benjamin.

37. William.

38. Stuteley.

39. Harriet.

40. Jane.

41. Esther)

42. Eliza.)   Twins.

43. Moses.

44. Aaron.

45. Annie.

9. Mary Jones married John Jamieson.

10. Sarah Jones married George Spanks 22 July 1834.

11. Hannah Jones married Benjamin Spanks.

12. William Jones married Jane Spanks.

Family.

46. Harriet.

47. Jane.

48. Alfred Frank. Born 2 Jan. 1856.

49. Jerry.

13. Mary Jones married John Spanks 24 Jan. 1854.

14. Zipporah Jones married Charles Spanks.

15. Sarah Jones married William MacDonald.

16. John Jones married Caroline Sangster 27 Dec. 1859.

Family.

      50. Cordelia.

      51. Josephine.

      52. Blanchard.

(Three others said to have died young.)

17. Caroline Jones married Hezekiah Horton 22 Dec. 1857.

18. Margaret Jones was not married.

19. Ann Jones was not married.

20. Sophia Jones married a Mr. McKenzie of Liverpool.

21. George Whitman Jones married Susan Spanks 23 Dec. 1873.

22. Alexander Jones was not married.

23. Charles Jones was not married.

24 to 31. This family moved away.

32. Mary Jones married a Mr. Palmer.

33. Thomas Jones married Annie Strople, 1865. (There is a family, living in Roachvale.)

34. Martha Jones married Bldridge Gerry.

35. Charles Jones married Mary Elizabeth Bedford, 1864.

36. Benjamin Jones married Ann Spanks, 1865.

Family.

      53. Benjamin.

      54. Annie.

      55. Irene.

37. William Jones. No record.

38. Stuteley Jones. No record.

39. Harriet Jones. No record.

40. Jane Jones. No family. Married and living in New Glasgow,

41. Esther Jones married Freeman Gerry.

42. Eliza Jones married Frank Gerry.

43. Moses Jones married ? MacDonald.

44. Aaron Jones. No record.

45. Annie Jones. No record.

46. Harriet Jones married Arthur W. Morgan 23 Jan. 1883.

47. Jane Jones married Charles Morgan.

48. Alfred Frank Jones married Philomela Adelaide Strople 3 June 1876.

Family.

      56. Charles A.

317

57. William.

58. William Percy.

59. Alfred F.

60. Hattie May.

61. Bessie May.

62. Joseph Murray.

63. Olive Jane.

64. Minnie Clare.

65. Lindsay A.

49. Jerry Jones married Ada Strople.   (There were seven children.)

50. Cordelia Jones married Fletcher Hurst.

51. Josephine Jones married Frank Cook.

52. Blanchard Jones married Hattie May Jones.

Lewis, David. Married Margaret Valentine 11 Mar. 1785. His lands were sold in 1787.

Meighan, Brian. He was married to Letitia Wheaton 30 Aug. 1790, by a J.P., according to the Town Clerk's Book. In 1793 his address was Antigonish, There is a memorial from him to the Provincial Government," but he was not living in Manchester.

Montagu, Lord. He was given a town lot, but apparently no other land was laid off for him, possibly because of his death. His armorial bearings are in St. Paul's Church in Halifax.

Murphy, John.   Wife's name, Elizabeth.

Family.

Mary.   Born 11 Mar. 1791.

Catherine.   Born 10 Jan. 1790.

Elizabeth.   Born 13 Sept. 1792.   Died 27 May 1804.

William.   Born 5 Jan. 1795.

Jane.   Born 15 July 1800.   Died 30 May 1804.

McAleese, John. Married Catherine Henline, widow, 20 Feb. 1804. He died 20 Sept. 1810. No other record.

McCaffree, Edward. He died 10 June 1809, aged 60 years. No record of any family.

McCarthy, William. Some William McCarthy, widower, married Sarah Petrie, widow, on 6 May 1802. There was one child, born 8 Dec. 1803, the child being named John.

McGee, Oliver.   Wife's name, Elizabeth.

Family.

Esther.   Born 17 Jan. 1785.

Oliver. Born 11 Apr. 1787.

Ann. Born 4 Feb. 179?.

Elizabeth. Born 1793.

Francis Henry. Born 1795.

Catherine. Born July 1797.

Charlotte. Bapt. 1805.

McKeel, Nathaniel. He married Rebecca Merriam 29 May 1788.

Family.

Joseph. Born 5 June 1789. There is no other record.

McPherson, James, Dr. Wife's name, Anna.

Family.

Elizabeth. Born 5 May 1785.

Mary. Born 6 Nov. 1786.

Isabella. Born 22 Apr. 1788.

Ann. Born 7 Apr. 1790.

John. Born 15 Nov. 1791.

It has not been possible to connect up the families of McPhersons now living in the County, with the old regimental surgeon.   No other record has been found of this family.

Oliver, Samuel. Married Mary Aikins 27 Apr. 1789.

Family.

Lydia. Born 29 Nov. 1790.

Abigail Submit. Born 15 Aug. 1794.

Mary Ann. Bapt. 16 July 1798.

Richard Samuel. Born Oct. 1799.

Elizabeth Caroline. Born 1802.

Eleanor. Born 22 July 1803. .

John Ryan. Born 1 Apr. 1805.

Lydia Oliver married William Davis 20 Jan. 1806.

Mary Ann Oliver married James Smith 19 Sept. 1825.

Parnell, Abraham. Wife's name, Margaret.

Family.

William.   Born 3 June 1787.

Elizabeth.   Born 23 Feb. 179?.

Mary Ann.   Born 20 Dec. 1792.

No other record has been found of this family.

Pearson (Parsons), William.   Married Mary Hanshel, widow, 26 Sept. 1790. No other record has been found.

Pringle, John.   Drowned in 1805, aged 67.   No other record.

Pushee, Nathan.   **Editor's note:** Born at Lunenburg, Massachusetts in 1758, he fought for the Americans but was captured by the British in 1780.   He later fought for the British in Jamaica (where he wouldn't have to fight fellow Americans) and later received pensions from both sides.   This is the ancestor of the Pushees of Antigonish and Mulgrave.   He early moved to Antigonish.

Reynolds, Thomas.   Married Rebecca King Jan. 1792.

Family.

Mary.   Born 13 Mar. 1793.

Frances.   Born 9 Feb. 1795.

Rebecca.   Born 25 Mar. 1799.

Rebecca Reynolds married Andrew Nelson 17 Sept. 1817

Rheideker, Cutlip.   No record.

Rogers, Eli.   Wife's name, Hannah.

Family.

Jacob.   Born 1798.

Eli.   Born 10 Oct. 1800.

Jacob married first.   He married second, Susan Do-rt 18 Feb. 1868.

Eli Rogers married Rachel.

Family.

Sarah.   Born 13 Mar. 1807.

Russell, Major.   Married Mary Bell 8 May 1797.

Family.

John.   Bapt. 12 Feb. 1799.

Ann.

Elizabeth.

John Russell.   No record.

Ann Russeil married Demas Cook 24 Jan. 1824.

Elizabeth Russell married John Horton 31 July 1823.

Sellars, Daniel. Married Margaret Key Sept. 1797.
Daniel Sellars died 15 July 1848, aged 90.
Margaret Sellars died 30 May 1848, aged 72.

Family.
1. Mary.   Born 6 Feb. 1799.
2. Donald.   Born 22 May 1803.
3. Eleanor Jane.   Born 2 Nov. 1804.
4. Peter.   Born 8 Sept. 1807.
5. Grace.   Born 28 Dec. 1808.
6. Mary Jane.   Born 25 July 1813.
7. James.   Born 1815.
8. John Archibald.   Born 17 June 1816.
9. Malcolm.   Born 26 Oct. 1821.
10. Margaret.
11. Isabella.

2. Donald Sellars married Isabella Bears 7 Dec. 1826.

Family.
12. Margaret.   Born 21 Sept. 1827.
13. Donald.   Born 31 Dec. 1829.
14. Charles Malcolm.   Born 8 Nov. 1837.

3. Eleanor Jane Sellars married William David 16 Jan. 1827
4. Peter Sellars died 15 Nov. 1807.
7. James Sellars married Isabella Hughes 15 Jan. 1833.

Family.
15. Donald Francis. Born 5 Oct. 1837.
16. Sarah Jane.   Born 11 Feb. 1840.
17. Malcolm.   Born 19 Dec. 1844.
18. John James.   Born 12 Oct. 1833.

James Sellars died 9 July 1847, aged 32.
8. John Archibald Sellars died 17 June 1825.
9. Malcolm Sellars married Isabella Archibald 11 Nov. 1845.
10. Margaret Sellars married Donald Ferguson 18 Jan. 1825.
11. Isabella Sellars married Thomas Ferguson 5 June 1833.

12. Margaret Sellars married William Torey 20 Aug. 1855.

14. Charles Malcolm Sellars married Elizabeth Caritte 18 Nov. 1873.

Family.

19. Frederick Edward. Born 7 Dec. 1875.

20. Kate Henrietta. Born 28 Apr. 1878.

Shanks, John. Married Mary O'Brien 28 Oct. 1785. No other record.

Taylor, James. Wife's name, Ann.

Family.

Margaret. Born 12 Oct. 1795.

James John. Born 5 Nov. 1796.

James Taylor was drowned 4 Nov. 1796, the widow then marrying James Bixby 1 Mar. 1797.

Tilley, Lewis. Wife's name Elizabeth.

Family.

Eugenia. Born 18 Dec. 1791.

Elizabeth. Born 8 Jan. 1799. No other records.

Upton, John. Wife's name, Mary or Polly.

Family.

Abigail. Born 7 Feb. 1794.

James. Born 18 Jan. 1796.

Robert. Bapt. 2 Mar. 1802.

Joseph. Born 26 Feb. 1804. No other records.

White, Capt. Gideon. No record of his having been in the settlement. This is the Gideon White whose descendants now live at Shelburne.

Whitman, George. Married Esther Atwater 13 Mar. 1788.

Family.

1. Lothrop. Born 29 May 1789.

2. Rufus. Born 8 June 1791.

3. Christian Frederick. Born 17 May 1793.

4. William Henry. Born 19 Aug. 1795.

5. George. Born 9 Aug. 1797.

6. Ann Catherine. Born 5 Aug. 1799.

7. Thomas Cutler.   Born 2 Apr. 1803.

8. Ira Atwater.   Born 14 May 1805.

9. Esther.   Born 24 Apr. 1807.

10. Sabina Eliza.   Born 8 May 1809.

11. Annabelle Caroline.   Born 26 Dec. 1811.

12. Julia Lucina.   Born 27 Oct. 1813.

He married second, Margaret Irwin, widow, 8 Sept. 1814.

Family.

13. Francis Irwin.   Born 10 Dec. 1815.

14. Abraham Berry.   Born 22 Nov. 1817.

15. George.   Born 20 Jan. 1820.

16. Murdock Campbell.   Bern 15 Dec. 1822.

17. Child.   Bapt. 27 Nov. 1825.

18. Catherine.   Born 27 June 1827.

19. Margaret Maria.   Born 13 Sept. 1829.

1. Lothrop Whitman married Warburton Campbell 17 Jan. 1811.

Family.

20. George.   Born 3 Nov. 1811.

21. Murdock.   Born 5 May 1813.

22. James Mitchell.   B orn 10 Nov. 1814.

23. Esther Lavinia.   Born 7 May 1816.

24. Warb urton Louisa.   Born 28 Dec. 1818.

25. Margaret Adams.   Born 18 July 1821.

26. Christopher Frederick.   Born 30 Jan. 1824.

2. Rufus Whitman married Margaret Kergan 2 Feb. 1813.

Family.

27. Esther Ann.   Born 10 Jan. 1814.

28. Edward William.   Born 9 Oct. 1815.

29. George Rufus.   Born 10 Dec. 1817.

30. Christian.   Born 31 Oct. 1819.

31. Priscilla.

32. Lothrop Christian.   Born 11 Oct. 1825.

33. Margaret.   Born 26 Jan. 1828.

34. Maria.

Rufus Whitman was killed accidentally 7 Apr. 1830.

5. George Whitman died May 1817.

6. Ann Catherine married James McPherson 26 Mar. 1816.

7. Thomas Cutler Whitman married Diana Morgan 13 Mar. 1827.

8. Ira Atwater Whitman married Alice Ross 12 Feb. 1828.

Family.

35. Ann Isabella. Born 14 Sept. 1832.

36. Margaret Jane. Born 1 May 1834.

37. Sarah Diana. Born 24 Feb. 1836.

38. William Cranswick. Born 20 Jan. 1839.

39. Lothrop Ira. Born 14 Mar. 1841.
Married Maria McKeough 2 Jan. 1867.

40. Elsie Caroline. Born 7 Sept. 1844.

41. Mary Jane. Born 1 Sept. 1846.
Married Thomas Godfrey Bruce 7 Nov. 1866. 9.

9. Esther Whitman married Robert Irwin 3 June 1828. 10.

10. Sabina Whitman married Charles B. Cunningham 1 Oct. 1839.

16. Murdock Campbell Whitman married Margaret McPhie 26 July 1870.

Family.

William. Born 4 Jan. 1872.

20. George Whitman died 30 Apr. 1813.

21. Murdock Whitman married Catherine Leary 11 Jan. 1848.

22. James Mitchell Whitman married Mary Ann O'Brien 25 Jan. 1853.

25. Margaret Adams Whitman married James Daniel McKay 27 Feb. 1845.

27. Esther Ann Whitman married John McKay 30 July 1833.

28. Edward William Whitman married Panthea Henderson. He died 13 May 1867.

Family.

Esther Ella. Born 7 Mar. 1865.

29. George R. Whitman married Sarah M. Cunningham, 1856.

Family.

Susan Maria. Born 30 Aug. 1868.

30. Christian Bruce died young.

34. Maria Whitman married William Wallace Bruce.

Williams, Daniel. Married Margaret Sartorius 15 Apr. 1799.

Family.

1. Elizabeth. Born 14 Jan. 1802.

2. Abigail. Born 15 Sept. 1803.

3. Valentine. Born Dec. 1805.

4. Donald (Daniel). Born 4 Apr. 1808.

5. William Henry. Born 17 Dec. 1814.

6. Margaret. Born 11 May 1817.

7. Jacob. Born 9 Jan. 1813.

Daniel Williams, widower, married Martha Greencorn 21 June 1825.

Family.

8. Peter. Born 10 Dec. 1827.

9. Marianne Eliza. Born 15 Nov. 1828.

1. Elizabeth Williams married Michael Murphy 20 Nov. 1824.

2. Abigail Williams married John George 11 Jan. 1825.

3. Valentine Williams married Elizabeth

Family.

10. Abigail Eliza. Born 11 Feb. 1831.

11. Mary Jane. Born 11 Mar. 1832.

12. Margaret Ann. Born 6 Oct. 1836.

13. Simon Peter. Born 29 Dec. 1838.

14. Albert Enos. Born 2 Oct. 1842.

15. Valentine George. Born 26 Oct. 1844,

16. Valentine Jacob. Born 1850.

Valentine Williams, widower, married Jane Gratto, widow, 2 Dec. 1855.

4. Donald (Daniel) Williams married Sophia Stewart 23 Sept. 1834.

Family.

17. John Alexander. Born 7 Mar. 1838.

18. Jacob Samuel. Born 10 Mar. 1840.

19. Margaret Ann. Born 5 Feb. 1843.

20. William Henry. Born 5 June 1845.

21. Daniel P. Married Almira Sceles 1 Jan. 1872.

5. William Henry Williams married Dorothy George.

Family.

22. Peter. Married Mary Anna Jamieson 24 Jan. 1871.

23. Henry. Married Janet Rogers 23 Jan. 1872.

24. Angeline. Married William Levi George 17 Aug. 1868.

6. Margaret Williams married Henry George.

12. Margaret Ann Williams married Charles Dont 21 Mar. 1871.

13. Simon Williams married Alice Walsh 9 Jan. 1871.

16. Valentine Jacob Williams married Abigail Stiles 24 Jan. 1871.

20. William Henry married Margaret Catherine Ryter 12 Feb. 1873.

Williams, Zephaniah. **Editor's note:** He was a native of St. Mary's County, Maryland. Moved to Antigonish in 1788 and married Ann Scott of Truro. Williams Point was named in his honour.

THE ASSOCIATED DEPARTMENTS OF THE ARMY AND NAVY

Many of the persons making up this group were among the last to leave New York. There were many in it who had not been members of line Regiments. Some (as for example, Thomas Cutler) had been named in the Massachusetts Banishment Act. The 71st and the 22nd Regiment were represented, although how many there were from each unit it is now difficult to say. Nor can it be told how many had been in distinctively Loyalist units, such as the Tarleton or British Legion. The name implied, too, that naval personnel were included, as well as members of the land forces and the staffs, so that it was a heterogeneous grouping of persons who had little but their need in common.

| | | | | Other Lands | |
	Div.	Block	No.	Front	Back
Adams, James	NE	H	7	30	70
*Addison, Thomas	NE	G	5	30	70
Aikins, Samuel	NE	H	11	87	262
Allis, John	NE	N	14	30	70
Anderson, Robert	NE	P	14	37 ½	112
Anderson, Thomas	NE	E	18	50	150
*Baker, Adam	NE	K	5	37 ½	112
*Baxter, Thomas	SE	H	13		
*Belchery, William	NE	I	12	30	70
*Black, Ralph	NE	L	6	30	70
Boggs, James Dr	SE	O	5	216	684
*Bollan, James	NE	O	5	30	70
*Bowers, Martin	NE	A	6	30	70
Bowie, James	NE	F	12	30	70
Bristow, Edward (Bristoc)	NE	P	15	37 ½	112
*Brogan, Solomon	NE	G	4	30	70
Brown, Aaron	NE	N	20	37 ½	112
*Brown, William ..	NE	G	11	50	150
Brown-Hulme, William	NE	R	5		
*Calder, David	NE	G	1	30	70
*Campbell, Colin Major	NE	K	12	240	760
Campbell, John	NE	K	19	30	70
Campbell, Murdock	NE	K	14	50	150
Campbell William	NE	O	13	120	380
Carr, Robert	NE	M	4	50	150

*Christie, William	NE	H	3	30	70
*Clarke, John	NE	P	16	120	380
*Cleary, William	NE	A	5	30	70
Cogill, Daniel	NE	L	14	75	225
Coombs, Thomas	NE	A	2	37 ½	112
*Coward, Benjamin	NE	N	10	50	150
Creamer, Henry	NE	O	12	37 ½	112
Crescine, John (Gresham)	NE	N	17	37 ½	112
*Crofts, Benjamin	NE	O	3	30	70
Crowdis, David	NE	F	8	30	70
Cummings, Alexander	NE	F	11	62 ½	187
Curtis, John	NE	O	16	168	532
Cutler, Thomas	NE	N	5	144	456
David, William	NE	H	5	30	70
Davis, John	NE	N	12	75	225
*Davis, William	NE	L	2	37 ½	112
Davison, James	NE	L	7	30	70
*Day, James				30	70
Demas, John Conrad	NE	K	3	50	150
*Derry, Adam	NE	F	5	30	70
Desson, William	NE	F	3	30	70
*Dewhurst, John__	NE	O	9	62 ½	187
*Diel, Joseph				30	70
*Dixon, Francis	NE	E	20	75	225
Doggett, Abner	NE	N	6		
*Donally, Barney	NE	O	14	30	70
*Dracy, Thomas	NE	H	13	30	70
*Drysdale, Dennis	NE	L	19	30	70
*Dryer, William	NE	M	3	30	70
*Dunbar, Alexander	NE	M	19	30	70
*Dunbar, William	NE	F	1	50	150
Elliot, Benjamin	SE	M	5		
*Elmsley, Alex	NE	G	15	30	70
*Farr, William	NE	G	17	30	70
Featherstone, Francis	NE	A	3	30	70

Name					
*Fenn, Thomas	SW	l	12		
Ferguson, Alex	NE	p	18	75	225
Field, Stephen	NE	G	10	87 ½	262
Fitzpatrick, John	NE	N	19	62 ½	187
Fiva, Anthony	NE	L	9	87 ½	262
*Fletcher, William	NE	L	50	150	
*Flynn, Michael			30	70	
Forkell, Jasper	NE	G	14	50	150
*Forrest, William				30	70
*Forst, Abram	SE	H	11		
Foster, William	NE	L	12	62 ½	187
*Fotheringham, George				30	70
*Foxe, John	NE	G	3	75	225
Fraser, William	NE	L	18	37 ½	112
*Garlock, Michael	NE	E	19	30	70
Gibson, William	NE	M	15	168	532
*Goodman, William	NE	K	2	30	70
Graham, William, Capt	SE	E	11		
Grant, William, Capt	NE	L	4	112 ½	337
*Gray, Archibald	NE	L	8	30	70
*Grayson, Samuel	NE	L	8	30	70
*Grimn, James	SE	M	6		
Griffin, John	NE	P	1	30	70
*Grimes, Robert	NE	E	7	30	70
Graham, John	NE	L	13	30	70
Grant, John	NE	O	4	216	684
Grant, Samuel	NE	N	2	75	225
*Hanrung, John	SE	E	1		
*Hammon, John	NE	E	16	30	70
*Harris, Samuel	NE	E	7	30	70
Heintzshel, Christopher	NE	I	15	37 ½	112
Henderson, Alex	NE	I	16	30	70
Henderson, James	NE	M	11	131	419
Henline, George	NE	E	3	50	150
*Henry, Edward	NE	F	17	37 ½	112

*Hepburn, William	SE	K	6		
*Herswell, George (Haswell)	NE	F	4	30	70
*Hollingsworth, Henry				50	150
Hubbill, Nathan	NE	N	11	179	571
Hughes, Hugh	NE	L	3	179	571
Hughes, Owen	NE	M	5	30	70
Hurley, Patrick	NE	P	8	62 ½	187
*Hyde, James	NE	R	3		
Imlay, James	NE	L	17		
Irvine, Francis	NE	M	10	62 ½	187
*James, Thomas	NE	I	1	30	70
*Jarvis, Henry	NE	N	15	37 ½	112
*Johnson, David	SE	A	1		
*Johnson, John	NE	I	20	30	70
*Johnson, Thomas	NE	K	8	30	70
Jones, Henry	NE	P	20	62 ½	187
*Jones, Malachi	NE	A	4	30	70
*Junks, Johannes				30	70
*Kelly, Thomas	SE	L	9		
*Kennebaugh, Charles	SE	M	8		
*Kenslough, Charles	SE	E	14		
*Kent, William	NE	F	6	30	70
Kergan, Edward	NE	O	7	30	70
*Kerr, John	NE	M	17	30	70
Key, James				100	300
*Lank, Edward	NE	I	2		
*Lawson, David	NE	R	1	30	70
Lawson, William	NE	P	2	37 ½	112
*LeBean, jean	NE	P	11	30	70
*Lovell, Joseph	NE	K	20	30	70
Lowrie, Robert	NE	H	10	50	150
Martin, Gregory	NE	O	20	30	70
*Maxwell, Orlando	NE	M	8	30	70
Meade, Samuel	NE	P	5	30	70
*Miller, John	NE	I	13	30	70

Name					
Mills, Robert	NE	E	2	63 ½	187
Moor," James	NE	P	13	37 ½	112
Morris, Richard	NE	M	13		
*Mortown, James				50	150
Munro, John	NE	I	11	30	70
Murdock, James	NE	R	7	30	70
Murphy, Michael	NE	O	1	37 ½	112
*Murray, Alex	NE	I	14	30	70
Molleson, Robert, Col	NE	E	1	264	836
*McDonald, Alex				30	70
*McDonald, James	NE	N	8	30	70
*McDonald, James	NE	I	19	30	70
*McDonald, John	NE	G	12	3 7 ½	262
*McDonald, John	NE	N	1	30	70
*McDonald, Neil	NE	P	12	125	325
McDougall, Alex	NE	P	10	50	150
McGill, James	NE	H	6	30	70
McGregor, Peter	NE	N	7	50	150
*McIntosh, Duncan	NE	P	4	30	70
Mcintosh, William	NE	E	4	30	70
McIntyre, Malcolm, 71st	NE	O	8	30	70
Mcintosh, Malcolm, Pilot	NE	O	10	50	150
*McArthur, Samuel	NE	I	18	50	150
McKay, James	NE	K	15	50	150
McKay, Angus	NE	M	7	30	70
McKay, John, 22nd	NE	F	16	30	70
McKay, John, 71st				30	70
McKay, Alex	NE	H	9	30	70
McKenzie, Alex	NE	R	2	30	70
McKenzie, Donald	NE	F	15	30	70
McKenzie, James	NE	F	10	50	150
McLeod, Alex	NE	H	14	30	70
McLeod, Donald	NE	K	6	30	70
McNair, Colin	NE	K	17	50	150
McNair, William	NE	K	17	50	150

McNeil, Andrew	NE	G	2	30	70
McPherson, Evan				30	70
McPherson, Paul	NE	I	17	50	150
Nash, John	NE	M	2	112 ½	337
Nash, Anne				25	75
*Nicholson, Anne					100
*Oat, Michael				30	70
Pearson, Robert	NE	N	5	50	150
Pyle, Steven	NE	O	11	50	150
Patten, Patrick	NE	P	19	62 ½	187
Perm, Richard	NE	R	9	50	200
*Read, Alexander				30	70
*Read, Thomas			30	70	
Read, William	NE	K	10		
*Rhoney, James	NE	P	17	30	70
*Rice, Thomas	NE	M	20	30	70
Robertson, Duncan	NE	G	9	37 ½	112
Rochford, Thomas	NE	K	9	30	70
*Ross, George	NE	H	12	50	150
Ross, Donald	NE	E	8	30	70
*Rutherford, Peter	NE	G	6	30	70
Sangster, Joseph	NE	O	17	75	225
Sceles, Thomas	NE	G	7		
*Schmaltz, Ernest	NE	K	18	50	150
*Selick, Charles (Selig)	NE	A	1	62 ½	187
*Shaffer, John	NE	O	6	50	150
Shaw, Evan	NE	L	16	62 ½	187
*Shaw, William	NE	N	13		
*Simms, James				30	70
*Simpson, James	NE	K	16		
Simpson, William	NE	G	8	30	70
*Skeles, Henry	NE	L	10	30	70
*Sloughman, Jeremiah	NE	M	14	30	70
*Smith, Herman	NE	G	16	30	70
*Smith, John	NE	M	6	50	150

Spanks, George	NE	E	17	30	70
*Sparks, Richard	NE	O	15	30	70
*Stamper, John	NE	L	11	37 ½	112
*Stark, Peter	NE	P	6	144	456
*Stewart, James	NE	R	6	62 ½	187
*Stewart, John	NE	L	20	155	495
*Stewart, John, 71st Regt. (Stuart)	NE	E	9	131	419
*Stoker, John	NE	N	3	30	70
*Strahan, George	NE	N	18	87 ½	262
Sutherland, William	NE	F	20		
Tanner, Isaac	NE	P	9	100	300
Taylor, John	NE	R	8	30	70
*Telford, James	NE	P	7	37 ½	42
*Thompson, Samuel	SE	F	4	30	70
*Thurston, Joseph	NE	F	9	37 ½	112
Torey, James	NE	K	13	30	70
*Tree, George	NE	N	16	37 ½	112
Thompson, William	NE	M	9		
*Tullock, Alexander	NE	E	10	50	150
*Waggoner, Simon	NE	M	12	30	70
*Waldburgh, William	SE	C	4	50	150
*Walling, John (Whalen)	NE	O	19	30	70
*Wardlow, Andrew	NE	F	14	30	70
*Wardlow, William	NE	I	8	50	150
*Warrington, Henry	NE	I	4	30	70
*Weeks, Andrew				30	70
Welsh, Matthew	NE	R	4	30	70
*White, Thomas	NE	O	18	30	70
Whitman, William	NE	E	15	30	70
*Wiliiams, James	NE	O	2	30	70
*Williams, Philip	NE	M	I	30	70
Wilson, Francis	NE	R	10	37 ½	112
Wilson, John	NE	L	30	70	
Wilson, Samuel	NE	E	6	37 ½	112
*Wooley, John	NE	F	2	20	70

*Wyatt, James	NE	G	13	120	380
*Whittendale, Christopher	SE	E	17		

Little or no record has been found of any person whose name is marked with a star (*).

Adams, James. The names of a woman or children, so called, are not on the roll. Wife's name, Susan. One child John, born 11 Sept. 1789. James Adams died in 1789 or 1790 and his wife married Donald McLeod.

Aikins, Samuel. The name of his wife, Elizabeth, and two children, Robert and Elizabeth, under ten, are on the roll. He is said to have been of Lowland Scotch descent. Wife's name, Elizabeth.

Family.

1. Robert.
2. John.   Born 14 Aug. 1786.
3. Eliza.   )
4. Samuel.) Twins.   Born 17 Nov. 1788.
5. William.   Born 4 July 1797.
6. Jane.
7. Mary.

Samuel Aikins died 20 Dec. 1826.

1. Robert Aikins married Margaret Miller 31 Dec. 1811.

Family.

8. Samuel.   Born 3 May 1813.
9. Sophia Margaret.   Born 20 June 1815.
10. John.   Born 10 Apr. 1817.
11. Hugh.   Born 9 June 1819.
12. Sarah.   Born 14 July 1821.
13. William.   Born 21 Oct. 1823.
14. Elizabeth Mary.   Born 16 Feb. 1826.
15. Margaret Sophia.   Born 23 Mar. 1831.
16. James.
17. Emma.
18. Mary.

Margaret Miller Aikins was born 1 Sept. 1794 and died 8 Feb. 1834.

2. John Aikins married first Mary Fraser 7 Feb. 1809.

Family.

19. Alexander.   Born 12 Nov. 1809.

20. Samuel. Born 6 May 1811.

21. Isabella Ann. Born 17 Sept. 1812.

22. Elizabeth Jane. Born 7 Oct. 1814.

23. Margery. Born 14 Oct. 1816.

24. Charlotte. Born 10 Apr. 1818.

25. Christie Ann Cummings. Born 17 Mar. 1822.

26. William Fraser. Born 31 May 1824.

27. Robert. Born 30 May 1826.

28. Child. Bapt. 10 June 1828.

29. Mary. Born 13 Feb. 1832.

He married second Catherine Campbell 3 Sept. 1839.

Family.

30. John Murdock. Born 26 May 1841.

31. James Lothrop. Born 14 Aug. 1842.

32. Ann Campbell. Born 10 June 1844.

Catherine Campbell Aikins was born 21 Oct. 1801 and died in 1896.

3. Eliza Aikins married William Nash 1 Oct. 1799.

4. Samuel Aikins married Margaret Davidson 29 Dec. 1818. She was born 17 Nov. 1788.

Family.

33. Elizabeth Jane. Born 20 Sept. 1820.

34. John Robert. Born 20 Sept. 1822.

35. James. Born 22 Jan. 1826.

36. Margaret. Born 27 Aug. 1827.

37. Samuel. Born 9 Aug. 1829.

38. William Thomas. Born 12 Aug. 1831.

39. Jane Honour. Born 25 Mar. 1834.

40. Robert Charles. Born 26 Aug. 1836.

41. James Alexander. Born 15 Feb. 1839.

42. Thomas Hugh. Born 3 Apr. 1845.

43. Ellen.

44. Sarah Sophia. Born 2 June 1848.

Samuel Aikins died 3 June 1855.

5. William Aikins married Mary Davidson, sister of brother's wife, 19 Jan. 1826. She was born 15 Oct. 1805.

Family.

45. James Davidson. Born 1827.

46. ?   Born 7 Apr. 1828.

47. William. Born 19 Mar. 1830.

48. James Alexander. Born 10 Apr. 1834.

49. ? Born 11 Apr. 1832.

6. Jane Aikins married Thomas Hugh 25 Jan. 1810.

7. Mary Aikins married Samuel Oliver 27 Apr. 1789.

8. Samuel Aikins married Mary Ann Graham 2 Feb. 1836.

Family.

50. Robert Miller. Born 15 Jan. 1837.

51. Margaret. Born 21 Dec. 1840.

52. Mary Ann. Born 12 Oct. 1847.

53. Emma Caroline. Born 8 Sept. 1849.

54. Samuel Charles. Born 5 June 1856.

55. Mary Isabella. Born 11 Aug. 1861.

56. Elizabeth.

9. Sophia Margaret Aikins married William Thomas Aikins.

10. John Aikins married Delia Randall.

12. Sarah Aikins married John Matthew Ferguson.

15. Margaret Sophia Aikins married John Murdock Aikins.

17. Emma Aikins married James Ferguson.

18. Mary Aikins married Samuel Hughes.

20. Samuel Aikins married Sarah McKay 23 June 1841. She was born
    3 Feb. 1819.

Family.

57. Mary Ann. Born 28 Mar. 1842.

58. Edward Cummings. Born 15 Mar. 1844.

59. Isabella. Born 9 Aug. 1849.

60. William Alexander. Born 31 Aug. 1851.

61. Esther. Born 14 Apr. 1855.

62. Charlotte Maria. Born 15 June 1859.

63. Martha Agnes. Born 19 Nov. 1863.

21. Isabella Ann Aikins married Thomas MacKenzie 24 Jan. 1832.

22. Elizabeth Jane Aikins married David Martin 16 Dec. 1837.

25. Christie Ann Cummings Aitkins married a Mr. Clewbine.

26. William Fraser Aikins moved to Australia.

27. Robert Aikins married Hannah Ehler 19 Dec. 1854.

Family.

    64. Lydia Susannah.　Born 13 Feb. 1857.

    65. Mary Catherine.　Born 11 Apr. 1863.

    66. John.

    67. William O.

    68. Edward E.

28. Child baptised 10 June 1828 is said to have died young.

30. John Murdock Aikins married first Margaret Sophia Aikins No. 15 3 Aug. 1863.

Family.

    69. Robert Cranswick.　Born 12 Nov. 1864.

    70. Samuel John.　Born 3 Sept. 1865.

    71. Annie Laura.　Born 18 Jan. 1867.

There were others in the family and he married a second time.

34. John Robert Aikins moved to Ontario and married.

36. Margaret Aikins married Alexander Ferguson 20 Mar. 1855.

37. Samuel Aikins moved to Idaho and married.

38. William Thomas Aikins married Sophia Margaret Aikins 22 July 1856.

Family.

Mary Ellen.　Born 24 May 1857.

This family afterwards moved to Idaho.

40. Robert Charles Aikins moved to Idaho.

41. James Alexander Aikins married and moved to Ontario.

53. Emma Caroline Aikins married James M. Ferguson 2 June 1870.

56. Elizabeth Aikins married Trios. William Ferguson 6 Feb. 1872.

59. Isabella Aikins married John Cranswick Ferguson 3 Nov. 1870.

62. Charlotte Maria Aikins married William A. Ferguson.

Allis (or Ellis) John. His woodlands were sold under power of attorney in 1786. There is no record of any family.

Anderson, Robert. Woodland sold under power of attorney in 1786. There is the name of a woman, Lucy, who may have been his wife, on the roll, but no other record has been found.

Anderson, Thomas. The name of his wife, Margaret, and one child Sarah, are on the roll.　Thomas Anderson died 11 Nov. 1842 aged 97.

Family.

1. Sarah.
2. Catherine. Born 20 Dec. 1784.
3. Mary. Born 7 Dec. 1786.
4. Ann. Born 17 Feb. 1789.
5. Thomas. Born 1790.
6. William.
7. John. Born 3 Oct. 1797.
8. Susannah. Born 12 Mar. 1803.
9. Elizabeth. Born 24 Apr. 1807.

1. Sarah Anderson married Alexander Shaw 15 Jan. 1800.
2. Catherine Anderson. No record.
3. Mary Anderson died 17 Jan. 1844.
4. Ann Anderson married Alexander McPherson 4 May 1809.
5. Thomas Anderson died 7 Nov. 1822.
6. William Anderson married first Jane Sutherland 26 Feb. 1824.

Family.

10. William Sutherland. Born 5 Dec. 1824.
11. Thomas. Born 23 Oct. 1826.
12. Elizabeth. Born 17 Dec. 1831.
13. Daniel. Born 7 Nov. 1828.

Jane Sutherland Anderson died 14 Jan. 1837.

William Anderson married second Elizabeth Grant 8 May 1839.

14. John. Born 12 July 1840.
15. Jane. Born 7 Nov. 1841.
16. James. Born 8 May 1843.

7. John Anderson married Mary Leet 16 Dec. 1824.

Family.

17. Mary Jane. Born 23 Mar. 1826.
18. Margaret Elizabeth. Born 1828.
19. Sarah Ann. Born 18 Feb. 1830.
20. Thomas. Born 18 Feb. 1832.
21. John. Born 14 Oct. 1833.

8. Susannah Anderson married William McKay 30 Dec. 1819.
9. Elizabeth Anderson died 14 Feb. 1808.

Boggs, James Dr. There is no record of his having been any time in the settlement, though he was given both a town lot and woodland. His woodland totalled 900 acres all told. He moved to Halifax, where he was given a position as surgeon to the Military forces, and where his descendants are yet to be found. No women or children of that name are on the roll.

Bowie Sr., James. **Editor's note:** Blacksmith with the 76th Regiment of Foot (MacDonald Highlanders). He joined the regiment in 1777 at Paisley, Scotland, where he was born in 1751. Discharged at New York, 1783 after being released as a POW (captured at Yorktown). He married Margaret Desson 28 Nov. 1788, daughter of William Desson. Assembled a farm at Havendale on the Milford Haven River after selling his Dept. of Army and Navy back lot on the north side of the said river (Bowie's Point, at the narrows where the natural gas pipeline crosses the river) and purchasing lots 80 (1815), 81 (1791), 82 and 83 (1788) and 84 (1810) on the south side of the same river. Being a blacksmith, he preferred this side of the river due to the Guysborough to Antigonish road being built here in 1788.

Family

1. William. Born 28 Mar. 1790.
2. Isabel. Born 24 May 1791.
3. James Jr. Born 26 June 1794.
4. George Sr., Born 4 Aug. 1797.

James Bowie Sr., died 2 Mar. 1836, aged 85.

1. William Bowie drowned in 1811.
2. Isabel married James Bears 23 Mar. 1813.

   She married second Donald Sellars 7 Dec. 1826 (Daniel).
3. James Bowie Jr. married Elizabeth Crescine 23 Sept. 1826. Moved to Antigonish by 1836.

Family.

5. George. Born 3 July 1827.
6. Hannah Sophia. Born 10 Mar. 1829.
7. Mary.
8. John C.

4. George Bowie Sr., married Margaret Desson (born 1808). Inherited farm at Havendale on the Milford Haven River in 1836 on the death of his father James Bowie Sr.

Family.

9. George Jr., Born 1839
10. Margaret.
11. Isabel
12. William.
13. Joseph.

14. Mary. Born 1851

15. Jane.

16. James. Born 1857

5. George Bowie married Clarissa McDonald, 26 July 1853. He worked at the old grist/shingle mill on Fraser's Brook and lived back of it on the original Guysborough to Antigonish road.

Family

17. Mary. Born 1854

18. Margaret Elizabeth

19. Caroline. Born 1871

8. John Bowie married Catherine Mahoney

Family

20. William Alfred

21. John James

22. Mary

23. Samuel

24. George Frances

9. George Bowie Jr. married Mary Long 26 Jan. 1875 (she died Sept. 4, 1920). Inherited the farm at Havendale in 1882 on the death of his father George Bowie Sr.

Family

25. William Joseph Born 15 Dec. 1876. Died 1902.

26. Ernest George   Born 1882

Ernest inherited the farm at Havendale in 1912 and it is still in the possession of the Bowie family to the present day.

Bristow (Bristoc or Bristol) Edward. The name of his wife Mary is on the roll. One child Elizabeth was born 29 Oct. 1786, who married George Luddington 6 May 1808. Mary Bristow, widow, married William David 8 Oct. 1789.

Brown, Aaron. He died 28 Nov. 1816, aged 70 years. No other record has been found.

Brown-Hulme, William. During the first years of the new settlement, this man occupied a prominent place. He was Sheriff for some years, and was part owner of the first saw and grist mill erected. In 1801 he was in Middlesex, England, and a deed of date 1804 gives his residence as Halifax, N. S. The unit with which he came has not been identified. Several children were born to him and his wife Jane, during their stay in Guysborough.

Family

1. William.   Born 10 May 1786.

2. Marianne Delaney.   Born 25 May 1787. Died 1789.

340

3. Mary Jane Brewer.   Born 4 Aug. 1788.

4. John Lyon.   Born 23 Sept. 1790.

5. Joseph Richard.   Born 19 June 1793.

Campbell, John. He married first Mary MacKenzie 14 Feb. 1799. She died 26 Apr. 1813, aged about 40. He married second Jane McCallum 31 Aug. 1814.

Family.

1. John James.   Born 14 Feb. 1816.

2. Mary Jane.   Born 12 Aug. 1817.

3. Archie John.   Bapt. 22 Oct. 1820.

Jane McCallum died 11 Feb. 1838 aged 48.

Campbell, Murdock. His wife's first name was Warburton, and is not on the roll.

Family.

1. Margaret.   Born 26 July 1786.

2. Warburton.   Born 30 May 1788.

3. John.   Born 12 May 1790.

4. Donald.   Born 12 May 1794.

5. James.   Born 20 Aug. 1797.

6. Catherine.   Born 21 Oct. 1801.

7. Ann.   Born 9 Jan. 1804.

8. Murdock.   Born 19 July 1807.

Murdock Campbell died 16 Aug. 1807, aged 49. Warburton Campbell died 21 Apr. 1852, aged 87. i.

1. Margaret Campbell married Francis Irvine 14 Jan. 1808.

2. Warburton Campbell married Lothrop Whitman 17 Jan. 1811.

3. John Campbell married Jane Cummings 17 Apr. 1827.

5. James Campbell married Margaret Anderson 30 Dec. 1824.

Family.

9. Warburton. Bapt. 4 dec. 1825

10. Thomas. Born 1 June 1827

11. Margaret Maria. Born 20 July 1829

12. Murdoch. Bapt. 22 June 1832.

13. Catherine Jane.   Born 20 Aug. 1837.

14. James.   Born 25 June 1840.

15. Daniel William.   Born 22 Nov. 1845.

16. Elizabeth.

6. Catherine Campbell married John Aikins 3 Sept. 1839. (She was his second wife.)

7. Ann Campbell died 2 Aug. 1838.

8. Murdock Campbell married Isabella Fraser 8 Mar. 1838.

Family.

17. Josephine.

18. Maria.

19. Warburton Harriet.   Born 17 Dec. 1841.

20. Margaret Ann.   Born 20 Oct. 1842.

21. Esther Maria.   Born 19 Apr. 1845.

22. Wentworth.   Born 18 Aug. 1849.

23. Lavinia.

24. Jessie.

25. Cranswick.

9. Warburton Campbell married Jacob Jarvis.

12. Murdock Campbell married Mary Ann Barry.

13. Catherine Jane Campbell married John Irvine.

14. James Campbell married Mary Susannah Horton 7 Dec. 1870.

15. Daniel William Campbell married Emma McLean.

17. Josephine Campbell married Samuel Nickerson Crescine.

19. Warburton Harriet Campbell married in the States.

22. Wentworth Campbell was not married.

23. Lavinia Campbell married Mr. Dangerfield.

Campbell, William, afterwards Sir William Campbell, and Chief Justice of Upper Canada. He married Hannah Hadley in 1785.

Family.

1. Christianna.   Born 20 Dec. 1785.

2. Alexander.   )   Born 7 Jan. 1788.

3. William Joseph.) Twins. Born 7 Jan. 1788.

4. Elizabeth.   Born 15 Dec. 1789.

5. Mary Ann. Born 23 Aug. 1794.

6. Catherine.

Carr, Robert B. His wife's name was Margaret. Her name is not on the roll of women.

Family

1. Mary.   Born 12 Nov. 1784.

2. Robert.   Born 8 Feb. 1787.

3. Katherine.   Born 17 Oct. 1789.

4. George.   Born 5 June 1791.

5. John.   Born 9 Dec. 1793.

6. Henry.   Born 2 July 1796.

7. James.   Born 23 Jan. 1800.

8. Peter.   Born 24 Aug. 1803.

Robert B. Carr died 21 Jan. 1823, aged 67. His wife died 10 Mar. 1840, aged about 81.

1. Mary Carr.   No record.

2. Robert Carr married Mary Jamieson 24 Jan. 1813.

Family.

9. James William.   Born 25 Jan. 1814.

10. Mary Jane.   Born 5 Jan. 1817.

11. Charlotte.   Born 8 Apr. 1819.

12. Robert Henry.   Born 22 Dec. 1820.

13. James William.   Born 10 Feb. 1823.

14. Ann.   Born 26 May 1827.

15. George Joseph.   Born 22 June 1829.

16. Catherine Jane.   Born 24 Apr. 1832.

17. Robena (Rowena).   Born 23 Apr. 1833.

18. Janet.

19. Mary Ann.

4. George Carr married Mary Porper 28 Dec. 1815.

Family.

20. Sophia.   Born 16 July 1817.

21. William Frederick.   Born 12 Apr. 1819.

22. Mary Jane.   Born 4 Feb. 1825.

23. George.   Bapt. 24 Dec. 1827.

23. Elizabeth Maria.   Born 31 Oct. 1829.

24. John James.   Born 18 Mar. 1832.

5. John Carr married Catherine Carter 9 Jan. 1821.

Family.

26. Mary.   Born 26 Feb. 1822.

27. Robert.   Born 19 Dec. 1823.

28. George Henry.   Born 24 May 1827.

29. Mary Jane.   Born 2 Nov. 1828.

30. John Bruce.   Bora 14 Oct. 1830.

31. James Henry.   Born 30 Mar. 1832.

32. Sarah Elizabeth.   Born 11 Jan. 1837.

33. Peter.

34. William.   Born 24 Apr. 1839.

35. Levi.   Born 8 Oct. 1841.

36. Margaret Eleanor.   Born 17 Oct. 1843.

37. Caroline Maria.   Born 7 Dec. 1846.

38. Zimn.

39. Colin.

6.   Henry Carr married Margery McMaster 3 Apr. 1826.

Family.

40. James.   Born 6 Oct. 1827.

41. John Alexander.   Born 23 June 1830.

42. George.   Born 5 Sept. 1832.

43. Robert.

44. William Cummings.   Born 26 May 1839.

45. Ann Margaret.   Born 13 July 1842.

46. Mary.   Born 9 June 1845.

Henry Carr died 9 Oct. 1868.

Margery McMaster Carr died 29 Sept. 1878.

7.   James Carr married Janet Jamieson 9 Apr. 1827.

Family.

47. John Henry.   Born 22 Nov. 1828.

48. Charlotte Jane.   Born 3 Apr. 1832.

49. William Alexander.   Born 19 Jan. 1837.

50. Catherine Sophia.   Born June 1839.

51. Charity Esther.   Born 4 Dec. 1845.

52. Mary Ann.

53. Robert.

8.   Peter Carr married Mary DeLochan 17 Apr. 1827.

Family.

54. John Henry.　Born 6 Dec. 1827.

55. Nancy.　Born 25 Feb. 1831.

56. Marianne.　Born 19 Oct. 1832.

57. Catherine.

58. Sophia Margaret.　Born 12 Jan. 1337.

59. Thomas.　Born 12 July 1842.

60. Hannah.　Born 13 Oct. 1844.

61. Robert B.　Born 28 Sept. 1839.

9. James William Carr died Jan. 1823.

12. Robert Henry Carr married Mary Ferguson 6 Jan. 1846.

13. James William Carr married Jane McKenzie 8 Jan. 1851.

14. Ann Carr married James Grant.

15. George Joseph Carr married Sarah Simpson 4 Jan. 1870.

16. Catherine Jane Carr married James Ly'e 3 Jan. 1848.

17. Robena Carr married James Henry Carr No. 31.

18. Janet Carr married John Carter 7 Feb. 1848.

19. Mary Ann Carr married Alexander Grant.

20. Sophia Carr married Joseph John Hadiey 12 July 1840.

21. William Frederick Carr married Miss Eleanor Kelly 8 Dec. 1846.

22. Mary Jane Carr married ? Grady.

24. Elizabeth Maria Carr married Henry Hadiey.

25. John James Carr married Miss Grady.

26. Mary Carr married David Porper 2 Feb. 1841.

27. Robert Carr died 3 Dec. 1850.

28. George Henry Carr married Catherine Carr No. 57.

29. Mary Jane Carr died young.

30. John Bruce Carr married Miss Morris.

31. James Henry Carr married Rowena Carr (Robena) No. 17.

32. Sarah Elizabeth Carr married in the States.

34. William Carr married Miss Morris.

36. Margaret Eleanor Carr married William Whelan.

37. Caroline Maria Carr married in the States.

38. Zimri Carr married in the States.

39. Colin Carr married in the States.

41. John Alexander Carr married Mary Jane Hadiey 14 Dec. 1869.

42. George Carr married Miss Stearns.

45. Ann Margaret Carr married Thomas Mackintosh.

47. John Henry Carr died 7 Feb. 1840.

48. Charlotte Jane Carr married Joseph Ehler 30 Dec. 1850.

51. Charity Esther Can married Charles Gosbie.

52. Mary Ann Carr married George Ehler.

54. John Henry Carr married Miss Frances Myers 27 July 1859.

56. Marianne Carr married Mr. Grady.

57. Catherine Carr married George Henry Carr No. 28.

58. Sophia Margaret Carr married George Carter.

60. Hannah Carr married Pat Keay.

61. Robert B. Carr married Margaret Kelly 13 Feb. 1870.

Chapman, Amos.   He was one of the surveying party who laid off the lands. He had no woodland, and sold his town lot in 1787.

Cogill, Dan.   The name of his wife, Margaret, is on the roll, with those of three children, John, William and Catherine.

Family.

    1. John.

    2. William.

    3. Catherine.

    4. Ann.   Born 21 May 1786.

    5. Margaret.   Born 24 May 1788.

    6. Alexander.   Born 24 Dec. 1790.

    7. Ann.   Born 29 Jan. 1793.

    8. Daniel.   Born 13 Sept. 1794.

3. Catherine Cogill married Thomas Brown 30 Dec. 1799.

6. Alexander Cogill married Ann.

Family.

    9. Catherine.   Born 10 July 1817.

8. Daniel Cogill married Elizabeth.

Family.

    10. John William.   Born 8 June 1816.

    11. Margaret Jane.   Born 8 Aug. 1819.

    12. Donald.   Born 31 May 1821.

13. Robert. Born 26 May 1828.

14. Catherine Ann. Bapt. 10 Oct. 1832.

15. Mary Jane. Born 17 Apr. 1835.

9. Catherine Cogill. No record.

10. John Cogill married Isabella Wilson 9 Mar. 1841.

Family.

16. Alexander. Born 12 Dec. 1841.

17. Melissa Ann. Born 29 May 1844.

18. William McKeough. Born 8 Aug. 1846.

19. Elizabeth. Born 1 Dec. 1848.

20. John Godfrey. Born 28 July 1851.

21. Hugh Charles. Born 28 Apr. 1854.

22. Donald. Born 18 Sept. 1856.

There are no records of these except of #13, Robert Cogill, who died 25 Mar. 1829, of #19, Elizabeth, who died 15 Nov. 1873, and of #21, Hugh Charles, who died 11 Oct. 1876. The last of the name moved away from the county many years ago.

Coombs, Thomas. Wife's name Margaret or Martha. There was one child, Ann or Nancy born 2 Sept. 1784. Thomas Coombs died 21 Aug. 1817, aged about 60. No other record.

Cramer, Henry. **Editor's note:** His wife died 7 Sept. 1818. He died 8 May 1838, aged 80. Progenitor of the many Creamers in Philips Harbour

Family

1. Henry Creamer Jr. Born 1817, died 1895.

1. Henry Creamer Jr. Married Hanna Sceles (1817 - 1917) on 22 Sept. 1838.

Family

2. George (1845 - 1935)

3. Catherine. Born 1848

4. John. Born 1850

5. Nancy. Born 1853

6. Robert. (1857 - 1920)

7. David. (1861 - 1952)

Crescine, John. (This name also appears some times as Gresham.) He married Hannah Sower 27 July 1784.

Family.

347

1. William.   Born 27 June 1790.
2. John.   Born 23 May 1792.
3. Mary.   Born 21 May 1794.
4. George.   Born 8 Aug. 1796.
5. Ann.   Born 9 Nov. 1798.
6. Margaret.   Born 1801.
7. Elizabeth.   Born 13 Sept. 1803.
8. Hannah.   Born 28 Apr. 1806.
9. Margaret.   Born 12 Dec. 1809.

John Crescine died 30 Mar. 1816.   Hannah Sower Crescine died 11 Apr. 1858, aged 92.

1. William Crescine married Margaret Smith 23 Jan. 1822.

Family.

10. George James.   Born 18 Jan. 1823.
11. Margaret.   Born 3 Mar. 1827.
12. Ann Dora.   Born 5 Feb. 1829.
13. William Joseph.   Born. 11 May 1831.
14. John Alexander.   Bapt. 15 Sept. 1833.
15. Samuel Nickerson.   Born 6 Sept. 1839.

2. John Crescine married Margaret Imlay 27 Aug. 1815.

Family.

16. John William.   Born 24 June 1816.
17. Mary Jane.   Born 21 May 1818.
18. Margaret.   Born 31 Jan. 1821.

John Crescine died 10 July 1829. Margaret Imlay Crescine died 18 Dec. 1833. (She was a widow when married by Crescine, her first name being Cassells.)

3. Mary Crescine married Jesse Nickerson 31 Jan. 1815.
4. George Crescine never married.
5. Ann Crescine married Charles Morgan 23 Mar. 1819.
6. Margaret Crescine died 15 July 1808.
7. Elizabeth Crescine married James Bowie 28 Sept. 1826.
8. Hannah Crescine married William Pyle 27 Jan. 1829.
9. Margaret Crescine married first, James Shaw 17 Jan. 1850, and second, Godfrey Hart.
10. George James Crescine married Elizabeth C. Roberts 28 Oct. 1840.

Family.

    19. Margaret Ann.   Born 3 Feb. 1851.

    20. John William.

    21. George A.   Born 9 May 1855.

    22. James Joseph.

    23. Elizabeth Rebecca.   Born 23 Feb. 1861.

    24. Sarah Jane.   Born 2 Sept. 1865.

11. Margaret Crescine married Mr. Griffiths.

12. Ann Dora never married.

13. William Joseph married Sarah Bears.

14. John Alexander Crescine married Rebecca Ann Roberts, sister of brother's wife, 20 Sept. 1857.

Family.

    25. James Alexander,   Born 14 Sept. 1859.

    26. Lydia Sophia.   Born 8 Apr. 1861.

    27. William Joseph.   Born 23 June 1863.

    28. Martha Ann.

    29. Margaret Catherine.   Born 19 Apr. 1869.

    30. William.

    31. Rebecca.

15. Samuel Nickerson Crescine married Josephine Campbell 30 Jan. 1867.

Family.

    32. Alonzo Harrison.   Born 22 Feb. 1868.

    33. Samuel Cranswick.   Born 20 Sept. 186?.

16. John William Crescine.   No record.

17. Mary Jane Crescine.   No record.

18. Margaret Crescine married Oliver P. Leet 22 Jan. 1840.

19. Margaret Ann Crescine married William Imlay.

20. John William Crescine married Martha Ann Davie.

21. George A. Crescine married Annie Jarvis.

22. James Joseph Crescine married Sarah Victoria Imlay 27 Sept. 1881.

23. Elizabeth Rebecca Crescine married Thaddeus Leet.

24. Sarah Jane Crescine married John Godfrey Hart 6 Dec. 1886.

25. James Alexander Crescine married Maria Jane Jarvis 1 Aug. 1881.

26. Lydia Sophia Crescine married George Sceles.

28. Martha Ann Crescine married first, John Ross, and second, George L.

Nickerson.

29. Margaret Catherine Crescine married John Myers.

Crowdis, David. He died 8 Nov. 1813. There are no other records, but there was a family. This, intermarried with the Harts and Ingrams and Hulls, formed the settlers who moved from Manchester to the vicinity of Margaree, where many descendants are still to be found.

Cummings, Alexander. He was of Scotch descent, and the number of acres drawn by him, 250, was double that given a private. He married first, Katherine McMaster, who died 12 Dec. 1784.

Family.

1. George. Born 2 Dec. 1784.

He married second, May Fraser (widow of William Fraser) 28 Jan. 1790.

Family.

2. Christina. Born 11 Oct. 1790.

3. Hugh. Born 7 Mar. 1793.

4. Jane. Born 22 Apr. 1795.

5. John. Born 12 Mar. 1797.

6. Alexander. Born 1798.

7. Dugald Edward. Born 29 Mar. 1803.

He died 11 Dec. 1818.

1. George Cummings married Hannah Henderson 24 Mar. 1818.

Family.

8. Catherine. Bapt. 25 July 1819.

9. Lucina Margery. Born 23 Jan. 1821.

10. Alexander. Born 10 Mar. 1823.

11. Hugh. Born 1 June 1828.

12. Mary Isabella. Born 23 July 1830.

13. George Robert. Born 23 Sept. 1838.

14. Margaret Elizabeth. Born 1 Dec. 1841.

15. Edward.

16. John.

17. Christina.

2. Christina Cummings married John Fox 4 Aug. 1823.

3. Hugh Cummings died unmarried 23 Apr. 1858.

4. Jane Cummings married John Campbell 17 Apr. 1827.

5. John Cummings married Lorain Margaret McMaster 10 July 1849,

Family.

18. Mary Isabella.   Born May 1850.

19. Robert Molleson Cutler.   Born 2 Dec. 1851.

20. Margery Christina.   Born 28 Oct. 1853.

21. George Duncan.

22. Ida Victoria.

23. Ann.

24. John Alexander.

25. Frederick Darin.

6. Alexander Cummings married Charlotte McMaster 19 Dec. 1848.

Family.

26. Experience Margaret.   Born 2 Nov. 1849.

27. Dugald.   Born 11 Jan. 1851.

28. Alexander McLaughlin.   Born 16 Jan. 1852.

29. Margery Jane.

30. George William.

7. Dugald Edward Cummings died 19 June 1841.   Unmarried.

8. Catherine Cummings married John McMaster.

9. Lucina Margery Cummings married Thomas McKay. (She was his second wife.)

10. Alexander Cummings married Mary Porper.

12. Mary Isabella Cummings married Frederick Uloth. (She was his fourth wife.)

17. Christina Cummings married John McMaster.

18. Mary Isabella Cummings married first, a Mr. Gross, and second, a Mr. Teeter.

19. Robert Molleson Cutler Cummings married a Miss England.

20. Margery Christina Cummings married a Mr. Gerringer.

21. George Duncan Cummings married in the States.

22. Ida Victoria Cummings married a Mr. Rugg.

23. Ann Cummings married a Mr. Cook.

24. John Alexander Cummings married Jane McMaster.

25. Frederick Darin Cummings married Lila Abigail Bruce.

30. George William Cummings was drowned at sea, unmarried.

(Alexander Cummings and his wife Charlotte, the parents of these last five, were burned to death on 11 Nov. 1861, both being buried the same day.)

The Cummings and McMasters were closely connected by marriage, Alexander Cummings' wife being a sister of John McMaster. Other Cummings came from Scotland.

James Cummings married Mary Foster 19 Nov. 1812.

Family.

1. Peter Ball.
2. Ann Foster.   Born 5 Oct. 1815.
3. William.   Born 28 May 1818.
4. James Foster.   Born Jan. 1831.
5. John.   Born 20 Feb. 1824.
6. Mary.   Born 2 Dec. 1826.
7. Isabel.
8. Mary Jane. Born 1 Dec. 1830. Mary Foster Cummings died 2 Dec. 1830.

1. Peter Ball Cummings died 1 July 1814.
2. Ann Foster Cummings married Elias Hutcheson 27 June 1836.
3. William Cummings married Catherine Henderson 24 Dec. 1856.
4. James Foster Cummings died 5 June 1822.
5. John Cummings married Mary Henderson.
6. Mary Cummings died 15 Dec. 1826.
7. Isabel Cummings married David James Williams 13 Dec. 1882.
8. Mary Jane Cummings married George H. Ryter 13 Dec. 1882.

Curtis, John. His wife, Theodosia, was on the roll of women, and a son, John William Henry, born 13 Oct. 1783.   No other record.

Cutler, Thomas. **Editor's note:** Born in Lexington, Maine, 8 Feb. 1752. He was a graduate of Yale University and a lawyer whose actions as an officer in a Loyalist regiment caused him to be proscribed. That is, his property was confiscated and he could not return on pain of death. Popularly known as 'King' Cutler, this man occupied for many years a most prominent place in the County. He married Elizabeth Goldsbury 3 Mar. 1783.

Family.

1. Robert Molleson.   Born 9 Oct. 1784.
2. Harriet Elizabeth.   Born 15 Sept. 1787.
3. Elizabeth Armstrong.   Born 13 Mar. 1790.
4. Caroline Priscilla.   Born 13 Feb. 1792.
5. Maria Sophia.   Born 25 Sept. 1798.

Thomas Cutler died Feb. 1837, aged 84. Elizabeth Goldsbury Cutler died 17 Nov. 1832.   There were other Cutlers and Goldsburys among the Loyalists arriving in Nova Scotia, but the connection has not been established.

1. Robert Molleson Cutler married Sophia Reynolds 2 Dec. 1809.

Family.

   6. Elizabeth Mary.   Born 11 Nov. 1810.

   7. Sophia Olivia.   Born 25 May 1812.

   8. Harriet Ballaine.   Born 2 Oct. 1814.

   9. Thomas.   Born 29 Sept. 1816.

   10. Robert.   Born 6 Sept. 1819.

   11. William Reynolds.   Born 3 Nov. 1822.

   12. Frances Jane.   Born 6 June 1828.

   13. Caroline Horton.   Born 27 Mar. 1832.

Robert Molleson Cutler died 2 May 1883.   Sophia Reynolds Cutler died 8 Sept. 1849.

2. Harriet Elizabeth Cutler married first, John Ballaine 24 Dec. 1806. She married second. Robert Hartshorne 21 Mar. 1816, John Ballaine drowned in Halifax. Robert Hartshorne died 24 Mar. 1851. Harriet Elizabeth Hartshorne died 7 Feb.1847.

3. Elizabeth Armstrong Cutler married a Mr, Jones of Halifax.

4. Caroline Priscilla Cutler married Duncan McColl 16 Nov. 1814.

5. Maria Sophia Cutler married William F. DesBarres 19 July 1825.

6. Elizabeth Mary Cutler married Murdock MacLean 7 Jan. 1839.

7. Sophia Olivia Cutler married James Marshall 29 Sept. 1847.

8. Harriet Ballaine Cutler married Francis Collins 3 Sept. 1853.

9. Thomas Cutler left no issue.

10. Robert Cutler married Eleanor Carritte 7 Jan. 1852.

Family.

   14. Henrietta Sophia.   Born 25 Sept. 1852.

   15. Thomas Mattox.   Born 17 Feb. 1854.

   16. Kate Carritte.   Born 8 Nov. 1856.

   17. Edward Molleson.   Born 26 Mar. 1858.

   18. Frances Collins.   Born 15 May 1864.

   19. Robert M.   Born 7 May 1862.

   20. Infant. Born 1866. Died 1 Nov. 1866, aged 6 months.

11. William Reynolds Cutler married Mary Hubert.

Family.

   21. William Owen.   Born 16 Oct. 1853.

22. Florence Ida. Born 25 Nov. 1855.

23. Melville Fixott. Born 11 Mar. 1863.

24. D'Auvergne Hubert. Born 27 June 1865.

25. Clement Gordon. Born 25 Nov. 1868.

26. Henry Cline. Born 27 Dec. 1870.

27. Laura Ann. Born 30 Apr. 1872.

12. Frances Jane Cutler married Henry George Farish.

13. Caroline Horton Cutler married William LeVisconte (a father of Confederation) 1 Nov. 1855.

15. Thomas Mattox Cutler died 7 Feb. 1911.

18. Frances Collins Cutler died 7 Sept. 1865.

21. William Owen Cutler married Martha Annie Crichton who died 21 Aug. 1893. He married second, Christina Isabella Crichton.

22. Florence Ida Cutler married William H. Paint.

23. Melville Fixott Cutler married Isabella Woodill.

24. DAuvergne Hubert Cutler married Elizabeth Crichton.

25. Clement Gordon Cutler married Florence Ida Crichton.

26. Henry Cline Cutler died young.

27. Laura Ann Cutler died young.

David, William. Married Mary Bristow, widow 8 Oct. 1789.

Family.

1. William. Born 17 Sept. 1790.

2. Ann. Born 6 Feb. 1794.

3. Joseph D. Born 15 Oct. 1796.

4. John. Born 1 Sept. 1799.

William David, Senior, died 6 Feb. 1807, aged 62.

1. William David married Eleanor Sellars 16 Jan. 1827.

Family.

5. William Sellars. Born 12 Nov. 1827.

6. Margaret Isabella. Born 4 Jan. 1830.

7. James Alexander. Born 27 Apr. 1831.

8. Sarah Jane. Born Nov. 1832.

9. Mary Eleanor. Born 18 Sept. 1834.

10. Eliza Abigail. Born 7 Apr. 1836.

11. Charles Malcolm. Born 24 Feb. 1838.

12. Lydia Ann Hartley.   Born 10 Nov. 1839.

13. Sophia Harriet Shreve.   Born 4 June 1842.

14. Frances Martha Caroline.   Born 22 Sept. 1844.

4. John David married Margaret Ehler 4 Jan. 1827.

Davis, John. He died in 1804. His wife's name was Mary, and there was one son William, born 17 Nov. 1785. This son married Lydia Oliver 20 Jan. 1806, and there was one child Elizabeth Mary born 1 May 1816. No other records have been found.

Davison, James.   His wife's name was Allison ?

Family

1. Eneith.   Born 17 Sept. 1797.

2. Alexander.   Born 2 Apr. 1799.

3. Helen Whitecross.   Born 19 May, 1804.

4. Elizabeth Vess.   Born 26 Jan. 1807.

Of these Elizabeth Vess Davison married Thomas Sceles 8 Apr. 1828, and Alexander Davison married Susan Honor MacKenzie 17 Apr. 1827. It has not been possible to connect this family with the records of the many Davisons, who almost without exception moved to Ontario, about the same time as the Hughes and Aikins. These Davisons were the families of John, Alexander and William.

Demas, John Conrad. He died in 1817. His wife's name was Susannah, and there was one child, Hitte, born 24 Apr. 1785. Mother and child died in June of the same year, and the widower married Biddy Cook, widow, on 8 Aug. 1802. After the death of Demas, she married David O'Brien.

Desson, William. There are records of several Dessons, said to have been descendants of William. One, Margaret, married James Bowie 28 Nov., 1789, and a son, William, had a number of children, William, Isabella, Margaret, John, Jane and Alice. Of these Margaret Desson married George Bowie.

Doggett, Abner. His wife, Rebecca, died 9 Dec. 1784. He sold his town lot in 1785 and there is no later record.

Elliott, Benjamin. He died 9 Dec. 1846, aged 93. His wife's name was Elizabeth.   She died Nov. 1818. His occupation is recorded as being a vintner.

Family

Elizabeth.   Born 9 Dec. 1786.

William E.   Born 17 Dec. 1791.

Catherine.   Born 10 Nov. 1793.

John.   Born 20 Jan. 1796.

Harriet.   Born 22 Aug. 1788.

Of these, Elizabeth married William Atwater 12 Feb. 1812, and Harriet married James Grady 14 Jan. 1809.

355

Featherstone, Francis. Died 2 Dec. 1830. No other records.

Ferguson, Alexander. The name of his wife, Christine, is on the roll, with two children, Duncan and Mary, both under ten.

Family.

Alexander Ferguson married first Christine MacDonald.

Family.

1. Duncan.
2. Mary. Born 1782.
3. John. Born 2 Jan. 1787.
4. James .)
5. Alexander.) Twins. Born 15 Jan. 1789.
6. William. Born 4 Sept. 1792.
7. Peter. Born 24 Aug. 1794. 8.
8 & 9. Twins. (Names or dates not known.)

He married second Honour Hierlihy 3rd Jan. 1800.

10. Donald. Born 19 July 1802.
11. Jennet. Born 22 Sept. 1803.
12. Thomas. Born 19 Jan. 1806.
13. Margaret. Born 27 May 1808.
14. James.
15. John Collins. Born 24 Sept. 1812.
16. Alexander. Born 7 Sept. 1814.

(It will be seen that in the two families, many of the names are the same.)

Alexander Ferguson died 27 Oct. 1814, aged 56.

Honour Ferguson died 9 June 1865, aged 84.

2. Mary Ferguson married first Christopher Wittendale 9 Apr. 1801. She married second Alexander Grant 10 July 1808. 6. William Ferguson married Isabella Key13 Mar. 1817.

Family.

17. Mary. Born 24 Oct. 1821.
18. Gracie Ann.
19. Christina.
20. Alexander.
21. James.
22. Margaret. Born 1829.
23. William Smith, Born 13 Feb. 1834.

24. Jane Sophia.   Born 9 Jan. 1832.

It is said that only two of the family by the first wife remained in Nova Scotia. They were all sailors, and little is known of them after leaving home.

10. Donald Ferguson married Margaret Sellars 18 Jan. 1825.

Family.

25. James Key.   Born 25 Feb. 1826.

26. Donald Sellars.   Born 25 Dec. 1826.

27. Honor Eleanor.   Born 31 Aug. 1828.

28. Alexander.   Born 27 June 1830.

29. John.   Born 19 Apr. 1832.

30. Thomas.   Born 15 Jan. 1834.

31. James Malcolm.   Born 14 Oct. 1835.

32. William.   Born 10 Aug. 1837.

33. Margaret Ann.   Born 19 July 1839.

34. Isabella Jane.   Born 4 Aug. 1841.

35. Peter.   Born 8 July 1843.

11. Jennet F Ferguson married Isabella Sellars, sister of brother's wife 5 Jan. 1833.

Family.

36. James William.   Born 6 Dec. 1833.

37. John Matthew.   Born 6 Nov. 1835.

38. Donald (Daniel).   Born 21 Nov. 1837.

39. Margaret.   Born 8 Feb. 1840.

40. Jennet.   Born 28 Apr. 1842.

41. Honora Ann.   Born 27 Oct. 1844.

42. William.

43. Mary Eleanor.   Born 19 Jan. 1847.

44. Alexander MacLeod.   Born 24 Sept. 1849.

45. Caleb.

46. Joseph Bunting.   Born 20 Oct. 1861.

13. Margaret Ferguson married William Graham 28 Feb. 1832.

14. James Ferguson married Sarah Jane Hughes 17 Feb. 1835.

Family.

47. Honora.   Born 26 Nov. 1835.

48. Thomas William.   Born 14 Aug. 1837.

357

49. Alexander. Born 18 June 1840.

50. James. Born 13 Feb. 1842.

51. John Cranswick.

52. Donald Buckley. Born 24 Aug. 1847.

53. William Aikins. Born 17 Sept. 1850.

54. Margaret Jane Narraway. Born 16 Mar. 1855..

Sarah Jane Ferguson died 10 Dec. 1866 age 54.

16. Alexander Ferguson moved to the States and married there.

17. Mary Ferguson married Robert H. Carr 6 Jan. 1846.

18. Grace Ann Ferguson married Elisha At water.

19. Christina Ferguson died unmarried.

20. Alexander Ferguson married Margaret Aikins 20 Mar. 1855.

Family.

55. Esther Jane. Born 21 Jan. 1854.

56. William Fenwick. Born 12 May 1857.

57. Christina Ann. Born 31 Aug. 1859.

58. Samuel Milligan. Born 27 July 1861.

59. Alexander Grant. Born 25 Dec. 1863.

22. Margaret Ferguson died 20 Dec. 1864.

23. William Smith Ferguson moved to Ontario, where he married.

24. Jane Sophia Ferguson married Robert Cooney Hadley.

26. Donald Sellars Ferguson married Mary Caroline Key (Keay) 20 July 1852.

Family.

60. James Alfred. Born 3 Feb. 1855.

61. Eleanor Jane. Born 16 Mar. 1869.

62. Wesley Beales. Born 22 Oct. 1856.

63. Mary Louisa. Born 27 Oct. 1863.

64. Margaret.

65. Heber.

66. Isabella M. Born 17 June 1867.

67. Harriet Maria. Born 3 Nov. 1872.

28. Alexander Ferguson married Mary Elizabeth McKenzie 24 Oct. 1854.

Family.

68. James Isaiah Milligan.

69. Elizabeth Ann. Twins. Born 25 Mar. 1862.

70. Margaret A.   Born 6 Feb. 1868.

71. Stanley.   Born 15 Mar. 1872.

30. Thomas Ferguson moved to the States and married.

31. James Malcolm Fergusion married Emma Caroline Aikins 2 June 1870.

33. Margaret Ann Ferguson married Asa Stropel. (His second wife).

34. Isabella Jane Ferguson married Asa Stropel.   (His first wife).

36. James William Ferguson married Caroline Lucinda Ross 27 Mar. 1860.

Family.

72. Esther Margaret. Born 23 Feb. 1861.

73. Rebessa. Born 17 Feb. 1864.

74. Richard Smith

75. Emma. Born 13 Nov. 1866.

76. William. Born 11 Aug. 1872.

37. John Matthew Ferguson married first Sarah Ross 15 Dec. 1866. He married second Sarah Aikins.

Family

77. Catherine Maria. Born 9 April 1868

78. Maggie G. Born 18 March 1872.

46. Joseph Bunting Ferguson married Mary Louisa Ferguson.

47. Honora Ferguson married Robert Kirk Torey 31 Dec. 1861

48. Thomas William Ferguson married first Mary Ann Aikins. He married second Elizabeth Aikins 6 Feb. 1872.

Family

Mary E. Born 14 Oct. 1872

49. Alexander Ferguson married Ann Martin 3 April 1864.

51. John Cranswick Ferguson married Isabel Aikins 3 Nov. 1870

52. Donal Buckley Ferguson married in the States.

53. William Aikins Ferguson married Charlotte Aikins.

54. Margaret Jane Narraway Ferguson never married.

Field, Stephen. Wife's name Margaret

Family

Ann. Born 6 Jan. 1790.

Stephen. Born 8 Feb. 1794.

Margaret Field died 7 Nov. 1826, aged 70 years. Stephen Field died 7 March, 1830.

Fitzpatrick, John. Wife's name Helen, Nelly or Eleanor.

Family

> Elizabeth. Born 3 May 1774
>
> Hannah. Born 27 Dec. 1779
>
> Ann. Born 3 Aug. 1784.
>
> Bridget. Born 24 July 1791 (Died Nov. 17, 1791.)

John Fitzpatrick froze to death 16 Feb. 1808, aged 88 years.

Fiva, Anthony. Wife's name Anna. There is a birth record of one child Anthony B., born 7 Feb. 1786. Fiva was Deputy Sheriff for some time but did not remain long in the settlement. The names of Fanny, Kitty, James and George are on the roll of children.

Forkell, Jasper. Wife's name Mary.

Family

> Katherine. Born 17 Nov. 1785.
>
> William. Bora 7 Feb. 1788.

Mary Forkell, widow, married George Spanks 3 Jan. 1792.

Katherine Forkell married John George Stropel 16 Jan. 1806.

Foster, William. Married Mary Cook 6 Jan. 1791.

Family.

> 1. Mary. Born 21 Feb. 1792.
>
> 2. John. Born 5 Oct. 1793.
>
> 3. Sarah. Born 3 Oct. 1795.
>
> 4. Ann. Born 9 Oct. 1796.
>
> 5. Elizabeth. Born 15 Nov. 1800.
>
> 6. William Nixon. Born 28 Apr. 1803.
>
> 7. Elias. Born 11 Sept. 1805.
>
> 8. James. Born 5 Dec. 1807.
>
> 9. Thomas. Born 13 May 1810.

William Foster died 10 Jan. 1833. Mary Cook Foster died 29 June 1825, aged 53.

1. Mary Foster married James Cummings 19 Nov. 1812.

4. Ann Foster married Moses Cook 25 Jan. 1816.

7. Elias Foster married Elizabeth Hugh 15 Feb. 1831.

Family.

> 10. William Thomas. Born 12 Dec. 1831.

11. Mary Jane. Born 7 Apr. 1834.

12. Elias. Born 7 July 1836.

13. James Francis. Born 20 July 1840.

14. Ann Cook. Born 12 Nov. 1842.

15. Charles Shreve. Born 16 July 1846.

16. Moses Cook. Born 6 Jan. 1850.

8. James Foster married Mary Eleanor Harty 12 Dec. 1830.

Family.

17. Michael Harty. Born 7 Dec. 1833.

James Foster died 25 Dec. 1833. Mary Eleanor Harty Foster married second, Matthew Hutcheson 24 Aug. 1836.

9. Thomas Foster married May (Mary) Ann Peart 25 May 1854. He died 29 March 1873.

10. William Thomas Foster married Lydia Henderson. He died 1875. She died 25 June 1926.

Family.

18. William Thomas. Born 27 Apr. 1857.

19. James Alexander. Born 17 Dec. 1858.

20. Maria Nixon. Born 7 Mar. 1862.

21. Maud Isabella. Born 25 July 1865.

22. Bessie.

Fraser, William. Wife's name Marjory.

Family.

1. John. Born 1778.

2. Elizabeth.

3. Alexander. Born 31 Dec. 1784.

4. Mary.

5. Isabel. Born 21 July 1788.

William Fraser was drowned 29 June 1788. His widow married second,

Alexander Cummings. John Fraser married Margaret ?

Family.

6. Marianne. Born 9 Apr. 1806.

7. Alexander Archibald. Born 4 Mar. 1808.

8. Isabella. Born 25 Dec. 1810.

9. Margery. Born 28 Feb. 1814.

361

10. Simon James. Born 2 Jan. 1816.

11. Hugh William. Born 25 Feb. 1818.

12. Catherine Elizabeth. Born 17 Nov. 1823.

13. John Walter. Born 29 Aug. 1829.

14. Margery Eleanor. Born 2 Apr. 1831.

2. Elizabeth Fraser married George Lowrie 10 Apr. 1810.

3. Alexander Fraser married Ann Diggedon 2 Jan. 1816.

4. Mary Fraser married John Aikins 7 Feb. 1809.

5. Isabel Fraser married John Sangster 4 July 1805.

6. Marianne Fraser. No record.

7. Alexander Archibald Fraser married Elizabeth Wilson 15 Jan. 1839.

8. Isabella Fraser married Murdock Campbell 8 Mar. 1838.

9. Margery Fraser married James Leet 23 Feb. 1841.

10. Simon James Fraser. No record.

11. Hugh William Fraser married Esther Ehler 10 Feb. 1846.

Gibson, William. Wife's name Ann. There are records of four children, all born prior to 1788.

Graham, William Capt. Captain Graham was an officer of the 22nd Regiment, and a prominent Mason, in the regimental Masonic Lodge. His name is to be seen on a demit given to William Grant from the Lodge. He moved to Ontario, where his death took place. The families of Grahams at present living in the County are descended from another stock. Wife's name Unis Elizabeth.

Family.

1. William.

2. Adam.)

3. Peter.)   Twins.

4. Margaret.

5. Jane.

Captain William Graham died in 1813 and his wife died in 1814.

1. William Graham died unmarried in 1825.

4. Margaret Graham married James Edminson.

5. Jane Graham married Thomas Coates.

Grant, William Captain. He was also a member of the 22nd Regiment, and a very prominent man in the new settlement. A most interesting document is still in existence in the family records, it being the demit from the Regimental Lodge of the regiment in which he was a member, and which is one of the oldest Masonic relics of the Province. The demit, written on lambskin, is still in perfect condition, the writing legible and the ink not faded, while to it is attached the seal of the Lodge, in almost perfect condition. It reads as follows,—

"And the Light shineth in Darkness and the Darkness comprehendeth it not.

We, the Master, Wardens and Secretary of the Moriah Lodge No. 133 in His Majesty's 22nd Regiment of Foot on the Registry of Scotland do hereby certify that our trusty and well beloved brother William Grant was entered, passed and raised a Master Mason, is a Past Master, and a Royal Arch Excellent Mason, and as such we recommend him to all regular Lodges and worthy brothers to whom these presents shall come.   Greeting.

Given under our hands and the seal of our Lodge in the Lodge room this 24th day of August 1783, in Masonry 5783. Staten Island."

Signed,	Signed,
Charles Cardiff,	Peter Taylor, G.M.
Secretary.	William Grant, S.W.
	Patrick Finnigan, J.W.

Captain Grant did not lose interest in Masonry after his removal to Nova Scotia, and was the first Master of old Temple Lodge, formed in Manchester shortly after the arrival of the settlers. The name of his wife Martha is on the roll of women and also the name of Mrs. John Grant, presumably a widow.

Among the children are to be found the names of James, J. A., Ann and Catherine, over the age of ten, while under ten are Mary, Robert, Martha, Betsy, Samuel and two Johns. At least one of the Johns and Martha were of the family of Captain William Grant. Other children were born in Guysborough. The family appears to have consisted of the following.

Family.

1. John. Born 1782.

2. Martha.

3. Isobel. Born 4 Dec. 1785.

4. Mary. Born 2 Feb. 1788.

5. William. Born 12 Feb. 1790.

6. Barbara. Born 5 July 1792.

7. Donald. Born 2 Aug. 1794.

Captain Grant married second, Submit Leet, 9 June 1801.

8. Elizabeth Jane. Born 5 May, 1802.

9. James. Born 9 Dec. 1803.

Submit Leet Grant, widow, married later Ebenezer Partridge 5 July 1804.

William Grant died 12 April 1804, aged 55.

1. John Grant married Cynthia Cribben 2 Feb. 1804.

Family.

10. Martha Lucinda Rattray.   Born 2 Feb. 1804.

11. Cynthia.   Born 2 Mar. 1806.

12. John William Cribben.   Born 25 Nov. 1807.

13. Thomas.   Born 19 Aug. 1809.

14. William.   Bapt. 5 May 1811.

15. James Henry.   Born 26 Mar. 1815.

16. George.   Bapt. 7 Mar. 1817.

17. John William.   Born 4 Feb. 1819.

18. Alexander.   Born 1 Jan. 1821.

19. Angus Owen.   Born 10 Aug. 1822.

20. Edward Wallace.   Born 15 Apr. 1825.

21. Robert Bruce.   Born Dec. 1827.

John Grant died 2 June 1830.   Cynthia Grant died 30 Jan. 1842.

2. Martha Grant married Michael Harty 9 Dec. 1802.

4. Mary Grant married Abijah Scott 6 Feb. 1810.

5. William Grant married Catherine Martin.

Family.

22. Abijah Alexander.   Born 20 Dec. 1822.

23. Kenneth.   Born 1 Dec. 1824.

24. Michael.   Born 3 Oct. 1829.

25. Robert Hartshorne.   Born 6 June 1830.

26. John James.   Born 20 Oct. 1832.

27. Sarah Elizabeth.   Born 12 Oct. 1835.

(There were said to be a family of twelve all told, eight sons and four daughters. The entire family moved to Prince Edward Island.)

7. Donald Grant. No record beyond the fact of his death on 19 Oct. 1847.

9. James Grant married Sophia Grant 8 Feb. 1832.

Family.

28. James Joseph.   Born 2 June 1836.

29. William Henry.   Born 13 Feb. 1838.

30. Robert.   Born 18 Apr. 1840.

31. George Whittendale.   Born 11 Dec. 1841.

364

32. John. Born 23 Aug. 1844.

33. James. Born 26 Dec. 1846.

34. Margaret Jane. Born 19 May 1848.

35. Charles Shreve. Born 7 Sept. 1849.

36. Submit. Born 20 July 1851.

37. Richard Smith. Born 1 Sept. 1854.

10. Martha Lucinda Rattray Grant married William Imlay 8 Mar. 1827,

11. Cynthia Grant married William Roberts 20 Jan. 1831.

12. John William Cribben Grant married first   ?   Sloan.

Family. (None by first wife).

He married second Rebecca Dennis 7 May 1845.

38. Joseph.

He married third   ?   Horton, John's daughter.

39. Owen.

40. Bruce

41. Margaret.

42. Prim.

13. Thomas Grant married Mary Dennis.

Family.

43. Robert Bruce. Born 12 Sept. 1839.

44. Thomas Gribben. Born 22 Jan. 1841.

45. Theodore Russell. Born 11 Mar. 1843.

46. George Y.

47. Elizabeth.

48. Caroline.

49. Edward.

14. William Grant married Jane Dennis 14 Mar. 1833.

Family.

50. Alice. Born 29 Apr. 1834.

51. Alexander William MacLeod. Born 5 Nov. 1840.

52. Robert Henry. Born 8 July 1843.

53. William Lewis. Born 6 July 1848.

54. Wallace.

He married second Christina Torey 8 June 1853.

55. Cynthia Jane. Born 12 June 1854.

56. William Henry.   Born 25 Dec. 1855.

57. John Edmund.   Born 10 Aug. 1857.

16. George Grant died 8 Mar. 1817.

17. John William Grant married Anne Dennis 14 Mar. 1833. (Four brothers of this family thus married four sisters.)

Family.

58. William Dennis.   Born 13 Jan. 1834.

59. Charles Warren.   Born 10 Dec. 1840.

60. Elizabeth Isabella Morrison. Bapt. 15 Oct. 1843.   Married Wm. Hutcheson Jan. 4, 1864.

61. John Warren.   Born 25 Nov. 1845.

62. Charles Wallace.   Born 18 Apr. 1848.

63. Cynthia Ann Augusta.   Born 17 Mar. 1850.

64. Lewis Alexander. Born 23 Oct. 1852.

65. Emma Louise.   Born 4 Nov. 1855.

66. Annie.

There are a number of other families of Grants, most of whom are descended from an Alexander Grant, whose wife was Mary Whittendale, a widow, who was before marriage Mary Ferguson. Alexander Grant was born in 1771.

Family.

1. Alexander Ferguson.   Born 7 July 1809.

2. Sophia.   Born 27 May 1811.

3. Lewis William.   Born 8 May 1813.

4. James John.   Born 3 May 1815.

5. Robert.   Born 16 Aug. 1819.

Of the above:—

Alexander Ferguson Grant married Mary Ann Carr.

Sophia Grant married James Grant 8 Feb. 1832.

Lewis William Grant married Martha Church 19 Apr. 1839.

James John Grant married Eleanor Hadley 15 Mar. 1841.

Robert Grant married Bridget Brennan 26 Jan. 1847.

There were in all cases large families, many of the records of which are to be found. It has not been possible to connect this Alexander Grant with Captain William Grant.

Griffin, John. He married Jane Scott 3 Jan. 1799, and Elizabeth Harrod on 30

March 1802.   No other record has been found.

Heintzshel, (Hansel) Christopher. Wife's name, Kitty or Catherine. One child, Hannah, was on the roll over ten, and one child, George William, was born 6 Aug. 1787.   No other record.

Henderson, Alexander.   Married Lucina Luddington 16 Aug. 1791.

Family.

1. Mary.   Born 30 May 1792.
2. John.   Born 29 Mar. 1794.
3. Archibald.   Born 24 Apr. 1796.
4. Hannah.   Born 16 Apr. 1798.
5. Alexander Gregor.   Born 5 Nov. 1800.
6. Alexander Hugh.   Born 4 Dec. 1804.
7. Donald.   Born 4 Apr. 1805.
8. William.   Born 29 Jan. 1808.
9. James.   Born 9 Mar. 1810.
10. Miriam Ann.   Born 5 May 1812.
11. Allan.   Born 17 June 1816.

1. Mary Henderson married W. Callahan 26 Dec. 1810.
2. John Henderson married Margery McKay 5 Mar. 1816.

Family

12. Nancy Jane.   Born 27 May 1817.
13. May Elsie.   Born 11 Apr. 1819.
14. Lucina Margaret.   Born 16 Dec. 1821.
15. Panthea.   Born 2 May 1824.
16. Sarah Cornelia.   Born 12 June 1826.
17. John Donald.   Born 16 June 1828.
18. Margery Ann.   Born 14 Nov. 1830.
19. Alexander.   Born 26 Feb. 1833.
20. Thomas.   Born 28 Aug. 1836.

3. Archibald Henderson married Lydia Moss Myers 23 Apr. 1818.

Family.

21. Charles William.   Born 13 May 1820.
22. Panthea.   Born 16 Jan. 1822.
23. Sarah Margery.   Born 7 Jan. 1827.
24. Alexander.   Born 4 Nov. ~1828.
25. Elizabeth Ann.   Born 31 July 1837.

26. Irad Myers.   Born Sept. 1839.

27. Sophia Scranton.   Born 9 Feb. 1842.

28. Tyrus Hart Henderson.   Married Joanna O. Gorman.

Lydia Moss Myers Henderson died 6 Apr. 1847, aged 50.

4. Hannah Henderson married George Cummings 24 Mar. 1818.

5. Alexander Gregor Henderson died 25 June 1802.

6. Alexander Hugh Henderson married Isabella Shaw 3 Nov. 1825.

Family.

29. Mary.   Born 1 Aug. 1828.

30. Lucina.   Born 24 July 1830.

31. Sarah Margaret.   Born 13 Dec. 1826.

7. Donald Henderson married Marcy Andrews 20 Jan. 1829.

Family.

32. Lydia Jane.   Born 28 Nov. 1829.

8. William Henderson married Nancy Patterson 11 June 1830.

Family.

33. John Patterson.   Born 12 Jan. 1832.

34. Alexander.   Born 9 Aug. 1833.

35. William Wallace.   Born 27 Dec. 1834.

36. Ann Jane.   Born 24 July 1836.

37. James Joseph.   Born 28 Oct. 1837.

38. Robert.   Born 24 Sept. 1840.

39. Allen.   Born 15 May 1842.

40. Harriet Maria.   Born 29 Aug. 1843.

41. Lucina Ann.   Born 9 Apr. 1844.

42. Elizabeth.   Born 24 Mar. 1851.

Henline, George. His wife, Katherine, is on the roll with two children, Matty (Martha) and Kitty (Catherine), both under ten years of age.

Family.

1. Martha.

2. Catherine.

3. Elizabeth.   Born 22 Apr. 1786.

4. Hannah Wilhelmina.   Born 23 Jan. 1789.

5. George.   Born 7 Oct. 1793.

6. Christian Lavers.   Born 8 Aug. 1795.

7. William. Born 14 Mar. 1798.

George Henline died 22 Feb. 1804 and his widow married Simon Waggoner 23 Apr. 1805.

1. Martha Henline married George Rogers 22 Feb. 1803.
2. Catherine Henline married Joseph Stringer 21 Feb. 1804.
3. Elizabeth Henline married John Patheram 27 Apr. 1812.
4. Hannah Wilhelmina Henline died 4 May 1791.
7. William Henline married Francis Jane Diggedon.

Family.

8. George William.   Born 2 Apr. 1827.
9. Hannah.   Born 28 Mar. 1829.
10. Leonard Francis.   Born 9 Mar. 1837.
11. Charlotte.
12. Ann.

Hubbill, Nathan. This was the first name on the grant. He married Honor Hierlihy 10 Nov. 1786.

Family.

Elizabeth.   Born 27 Aug. 1787.

James.   Born 1 June 1790.

Mary Newton.   Born 31 Mar. 1792.

He returned to Connecticut where he married his second wife in 1790. His tombstone identifies him as "Lieutenant Colonel" in the service of "his Brittanic Majesty".

Hughes, Hugh.   His wife, Sarah, is on the roll, with two children, Thomas and John, both under ten years of age. Hugh Hughes died in May, 1815, and Sarah Hughes apparently on the 9th of May, 1836.

Family.

1. John.
2. Thomas.

1. John Hughes married Mary Power 18 Sept. 1809. This family moved to Ontario, and from one of the sons, Sir Sam Hughes was descended.
2. Thomas Hughes married Jane Aikins 25 Jan. 1810.

Family.

3. Sarah Jane.   Born 31 Oct. 1812.
4. Isabella Ann.   Born 10 May 1814.
5. Thomas Hugh.   Born 22 Oct. 1816.

6. John Hugh Anthony. Born 22 Oct. 1818.

7. Elizabeth Sarah.

8. Mary Jane. Born 20 Mar. 1822.

Thomas Hughes died 20 Mar. 1860, aged 77.

3. Sarah Jane Hughes married James Ferguson 17 Apr. 1835.

4. Isabella Ann Hughes married James Sellars 15 Jan. 1833.

5. Thomas Hugh Hughes married Janet Knowles 16 May 1839.

Family.

9. Nancy Eleanor. Born 1 Oct. 1840.

Janet Knowles Hughes died Dec. 1841, aged 32 years.

Thomas Hughes married second, Ellen McDonald.

10. Mary Jane. Born 25 July 1846.

11. Hugh. Born 1 Oct. 1847. He married Jane Rumley 27 Dec. 1871.

12. Ann. Born 23 Jan. 1851.

13. John. Born 15 Apr. 1852.

14. Samuel. Born 15 July 1855.

7. Elizabeth Sarah Hughes married Elias Foster 15 Feb. 1831.

8. Mary Jane Hughes. No record.

Hughes, Owen. This man is said to have moved to Prince Edward Island. It is possible that he was a son of Hugh Hughes, though nothing has been found which would point to that conclusion.

Hurley, Patrick. Wife's name, Margaret.

Family.

Nancy. Born 11 Aug. 1784.

Mary. Born 9 Oct. 1790.

Margaret. Born 1 May 1793.

No other records have been found.

Imlay, James. Married Margaret Cassels 4 Dec. 1797.

Family.

1. Margaret. Born 12 Apr. 1802.

2. William. Born 3 Feb. 1804.

3. James. Born 1 Mar. 1806.

4. Alexander. Born May 1808.

5. George. Born 27 Apr. 1812.

6. John.

7. Ann.

James Imlay died 11 March 1813. His widow married John Crescine 27 Aug. 1815.

1. Margaret Imlay married Thomas Hall 15 Mar. 1821.

2. William Imlay married Martha Grant 8 Mar. 1827.

Family.

    8. Cynthia Elizabeth Grant.   Born 13 Dec. 1827.

    9. Maria Ann Lavinia.   Born 28 Oct. 1829.

  10. Martha Margaret.   Born 6 Aug. 1831.

  11. Harriet Jane.   Born 13 July 1835.

  12. Isabella Morrison.   Born 28 Feb. 1837.

  13. Caroline Cribben.   Born 9 Mar. 1839.

  14. Ann Brown.   Born 27 Jan. 1841.

  15. Charles Shreve.   Born 24 May 1843.

3. James Imlay married Christina MacDonald 29 Apr. 1845.

4. Alexander Imlay died 29 May 1809.

6. John Imlay married Jane Mason 1 Oct. 1826.

Family.

  16. Mary Jane Cassels.   Born 1 Sept. 1827.

  17. Margaret.   Born 22 Aug. 1829.

  18. Catherine.   Born 22 Sept. 1831.

  19. ? Bapt. 20 Dec. 1833.

  20. Sarah Elizabeth.   Born 2 May 1837.

  21. Rosina Caroline.   Born 13 June 1839.

  22. Martha Caroline.   Born 10 Nov. 1841.

  23. Eliza Christina.   Born 31 Aug. 1844.

7. Ann Imlay married Hibbert MacPherson 18 Dec. 1828.

Irvine, Francis. It would seem that this man was married twice, though no record of the first marriage has been found.

Family.

1. Daniel.

2. Robert.

He married Margaret Campbell 14 Jan. 1808.

3. Elizabeth.   Born 14 May 1809.

4. John Whitman.   Born 19 May 1811.

5. Warburton.   Born 7 Jan. 1814.

Francis Irvine died in 1814 and his widow married second, George; Whitman 8 Sept. 1814.

1. Daniel Irvine married Elizabeth
>
> Family,
>
> 6. Daniel.   Born 17 Sept. 1808.
>
> 7. Thomas Archibald.   Born 17 Mar. 1812.
>
> 8. Robert.   Born 16 Aug. 1813.
>
> 9. Richard.   Born 11 Dec. 1815. 10.
>
> 10. Henry.   Born 12 Dec. 1818.

2. Robert Irvine married Esther Whitman 3 Jan. 1828.
>
> Family.
>
> 11. George Whitman.   Born 19 Apr. 1829.
>
> 12. Jane.   Born 5 Mar. 1831.
>
> 13. Robert Daniel.   Born 28 Apr. 1833.

3. Elizabeth Irvine married John L. Hart 8 Mar. 1831.

4. John Whitman Irvine married Marjory Leet 20 June 1848.
>
> Family.
>
> 14. Francis.   Born 1 May 1849.
>
> 15. Margaret Eleanor.   Born 5 Feb. 1852.

John Whitman Irvine married second, Jane Campbell 2 Jan, 1855.
>
> Family.
>
> 16. Emmeline Jane.   Born 9 Apr. 1860.
>
> 17. Sapporina.   Born 27 May 1862.
>
> 18. Warburton Augusta.   Born 10 Sept. 1865.

5. Warburton Irvine married John Ehler 5 July 1848.

6. Daniel Irvine married Sophia Ann Baker 3 Mar. 1835.
>
> Family.
>
> 19. Margaret Elizabeth.   Born 19 June 1841.
>
> 20. Sarah Maria.   Born 15 Jan. 1843.
>
> 21. Thomas William.   Born 10 Nov. 1844.

Jones, Henry.   Married Jane Bowden 18 July 1786.
>
> Family.
>
> 1. Edward.   Born 15 Jan. 1788.

2. Elizabeth.   Born 31 Jan. 1790.

George.   Born 1794. Henry Jones died 10 Dec. 1816, aged 67 years.

No other record has been found.

Kergan, Edward.   Married Margaret Sangster, widow of Joseph Sangster 26 Oct. 1786.   (It is possible that this name is that now spelled Carrogan.)

Key (Keay), James.   Wife's name, Grizel, which is on the roll with those of two children, Jane and Nelly.

Family.

1. Jane.
2. Nellie.
3. Mary.   Born 28 Apr. 1786.
4. Grizel.   Born 10 June 1789.
5. Ann.   Born 1 Apr. 1792.
6. Isabel.   Born 8 June 1794.
7. James Alexander.   Born 9 Mar. 1797.

James Key died Oct. 1819.   Grizel Key died 11 May 1846, aged 96.

1. Jane Key married John Graham 20 Jan. 1802.
3. Mary Key married Luman Atwater 29 Dec. 1808.
4. Grizell (Grace) Key married Peter McChesney 15 June 1815.
6. Isabel Key married William Ferguson 13 Mar. 1817.
7. James Alexander Key married Isabella McPherson 4 Feb. 1823.

Family

8. Grace Jane.   Born 2 Dec. 1823.
9. James.   Born 28 June 1825.
10. Isabella Margaret.   Born 26 Mar. 1827.
11. Mary Caroline.   Born 19 Feb. 1829.
12. John Alexander.   Bapt. 1 Apr. 1831.
13. Eliza Ann.   Born 28 Apr. 1833.
14. Charles Thomas.   Born 10 July 1838.
15. Peter Heber.   Born 28 Mar. 1841.

Lawson, William.   The name of his wife, Martha, is on the roll of women.

Family.

1. Isaac.   Born 1 Apr. 1785 or 1786.

2. Judith. Born 26 Oct. 1787.

3. Jane. Born 10 Mar. 1791.

4. William. Born 9 Sept. 1793.

5. Elizabeth. Born 11 Dec. 1795.

William Lawson died 19 June 1817, aged 58. Martha Lawson died 30 June 1830.

1. Isaac Lawson married Jane Torey 11 Dec. 1805.

Family.

6. Christine. Born 12 Oct. 1806.

2. Judith Lawson married J. G. Hadley 3 Feb. 1808.

3. Jane Lawson married William Johnson 20 July 1808.

4. William Lawson married Mary Scott 11 Feb. 1819.

Family.

7. Martha Elizabeth. Born 6 May 1820.

8. Ruth Ann. Born 21 Oct. 1821.

9. Sarah. Bapt. 25 Jan. 1824.

10. Abijah Scott. Born 26 Oct. 1826.

11. Mary Jane. Born 20 Dec. 1830.

12. John Joseph. Born 23 May 1839.

13. William.

6. Christine Lawson married Abner Myers 7 Feb. 1826.

7. Martha Elizabeth Lawson married Joseph Rogers 2 Feb. 1843.

8. Ruth Ann Lawson married Alexander Callahan 9 Feb. 1847.

9. Sarah Lawson married David Leary 4 July 1847.

13. William Lawson married ? McDaniels.

Lowrie, Robert. His wife's name was Elizabeth.

Family.

1. Andrew. Born 22 Apr. 1786.

2. Janet. Born 26 June 1788.

3. Peggy. Born 5 Jan. 1791.

4. Nancy. Born 7 Sept. 1793.

5. Robert. Born 11 Sept. 1795.

1. Andrew Lowrie married Jemina ?

Family.

6. Robert. Born 28 Feb. 1815.

7. James.   Born 7 Jan. 1819.

8. Andrew.   Bapt. 28 May 1821.

9. Mary Jane.   Born 10 Feb. 1823.

10. Charlotte.   Born 18 May 1825.

11. Elizabeth Nancy.   Born 19 Mar. 1830.

12. Charles.   Born 5 Aug. 1832.

13. William.   Born 31 Jan. 1835.

14. John.   Born 12 Aug. 1837.

15. Josiah.   Born 10 Apr. 1841.

Martin, Gregory.   No record, except that of his death 3 Sept. 1808.

Mead, Samuel.   Married Hannah Fitzpatrick 1 Jan. 1795.

Family.

1. Elinor.   Born 9 July 1797.

2. William.   Born July 1799..

He married second, Susannah Smith 8 June 1802.

Family.

3. Mary Ann.   Born 3 Nov. 1810.

4. James Abraham.   Born 4 Mar. 1815.

5. Samuel Lewis.   Born 11 May 1817.

2. William Mead married Dorothy Rider 27 May 1845.   (Second wife.)

Mills, Robert. Had returned to New York in 1788, selling his property in Guysborough. There are records of two children, born before his arrival in Guysborough.

Morris, Richard.   Wife's name, Margaret.

Family.

1. Richard I. (or J.)   Born 6 Jan. 1783.

2. Edward John.   Born 30 Jan. 1785.

3. Thomas.   Born 9 Feb. 1787.

4. Edward.   Born 15 May 1789.

5. Jane Isabella Lucretia.   Born 28 May 1793.

   Also possibly

6. Guy.

1. Richard I. Morris married Margaret.

Family.

7. Richard Thomas. Born 19 June 1812.

8. Margaret Jane. Born 16 Aug. 1813.

9. Daniel. Born 11 July 1814.

10. Christopher Whittingdale. Born 21 Sept. 1815.

11. Christina Elizabeth. Born 24 Nov. 1816.

12. Thomas James. Born 24 Apr. 1818.

13. William Archibald. Born 16 Jan. 1820.

14. Catherine Lucretia. Born 16 Feb. 1825.

15. Mary Ann. Born 1 June 1823.

16. Sarah Lucretia. Born 27 May 1826.

17. Matthew Irvin. Born 2 Mar. 1828.

18. Jane Martha. Born 10 July 1829.

19. Rhoda Rebecca. Born 9 Mar. 1831.

20. Harriet Amelia. Born 26 Nov. 1832.

21. Lydia Lavinia. Born 25 July 1832.

22. Cynthia Sophia. Born 22 Dec. 1836.

23. Edward J.

2. Edward John Morris died 1 July 1788.

3. Thomas Morris married Janet Torey 19 Jan. 1808.

Family.

24. Christine. Born 25 Jan. 1809.

25. Margaret Ann. Born 8 Mar. 1814.

26. Jane Bridget. Born 29 Sept. 1816.

27. Thomas. Born 15 June 1824.

28. Christie. Born 4 Oct. 1826.

4. Edward Morris married Elizabeth Elms 11 Apr. 1810.

Family.

29. Richard James. Born 4 Nov. 1813.

30. Maddison. Born 25 Oct. 1815.

31. Mary. Born 7 May 1817.

32. Margaret. Born 7 Aug. 1819.

5. Jane Isabella Lucretia Morris. No record.

6. Guy Morris married Sybella E. Leggett 15 July 1807.

Family.

33. James Guy. Born 21 Apr. 1808.

34. Maria Frances Ann.   Born 12 Feb. 1810.

7. Richard Thomas Morris is said to have died in Philadelphia.

8. Margaret Jane Morris married Charles Morgan 1 Mar. 1836.

10. Christopher Whittingdale Morris died 3 Apr. 1832.

12. Thomas James Morris died 13 Feb. 1819.

14. Catherine Lucretia Morris married ? Barney.

15. Mary Ann Morris died 28 July 1847.

16. Sarah Lucretia Morris died 14 July 1840.

17. Matthias Irvin Morris married ? Kenney.

18. Jane Martha Morris married Samuel Kenney 12 Aug. 1852.

20. Harriet Amelia Morris married ? Marin.

21. Lydia Lavinia Morris married John Luddington.

22. Cynthia Sophia Morris married ? Ferguson.

23. Edward J. Morris married M. A. Aikins.

Family.

35. George Shepherd.   Born 7 Mar. 1845.

36. William Henry.   Born 29 July 1847.

37. Margaret Jane.   Born 6 Mar. 1855.

38. George Albert.   Born 30 Sept. 1857.

39. Alfred Ernest.   Born 28 Sept. 1863.

40. Edward Christopher.   Born 6 Dec. 1864.

41. Emma.

42. Richard.

24. Christine Morris died 19 June 1820.

25. Margaret Ann Morris died 1 July 1816.

26. Jane Bridger Morris married Robert Irvin 15 Feb. 1843.

28. Christie Morris died 17 Nov. 1827.

30. Maddison Morris married Catherine McCowan 9 Jan. 1844.

Family.

43. Mary Jane.   Born 26 Oct. 1853.

44. John Frederick.   Born 14 Oct. 1857.

45. William Obed.   Born 15 Apr. 1859.

46. Amelia Milligan.   Bapt. 21 July 1862.

The above record of the Morris family is very incomplete. It has not been possible to connect this family with the family of Morris, who for so many years acted as Provincial surveyors. The older Morris, was however, a surveyor,

377

and did the surveying for the settlers. To two of his children, very young in years, were given lots of land. The records refer to many others of the name whose definite places in the families cannot be fixed.

Munro, John.   Married Elizabeth McGregor.

Family.

1. Christina.   Born 17 Nov. 1801.
2. Jane.   Born 23 May 1803.
3. Peter Alexander.   Born 17 Feb. 1805.
4. Lewis William.   Born 28 Feb. 1807.

Elizabeth McGregor Munro died 5 Mar. 1807.

1. Christina Munro married Donald McKenzie 4 Aug. 1824.
3. Peter Alexander Munro married Mary Decoff 27 Jan. 1829.

Murdock, James.   Married Ann Campbell 20 Mar. 1804.

Family.

1. Mary Campbell.   Born 11 Feb. 1805.
2. John.   Born 17 Nov. 1808.
3. James.   Born 1 July 1810.
4. Dugald William.   Born 23 Dec. 1811.
5. Jane.   Born 3 Mar. 1814.
6. Nancy Eleanor.   Born 21 June 1818.

Murphy, Michael.   Married Margaret Taylor 25 Feb. 1784.

Family.

1. Katherine.   Born 4 Feb. 1785.
2. Thomas.   Born 25 Aug. 1786.

No other records have been found.

McDonald. There was an Alexander, apparently two James, two Johns, and a Nathaniel or Neil McDonald in the unit. It has been impossible to follow the individual families.

MacDougall, Alexander. Wife's name, Margaret. One child was born Margaret, on the 5th of Nov., 1784.   No other record.

McGill, James. There is apparently the record of the death of this man on the 5th of June, 1812, which is the only record.

McGregor, Peter.   Married Elizabeth Fitzpatrick 4 Feb. 1794.

Family.
1. Daniel (Donald). Born 19 Sept. 1795.
2. Alexander.

Elizabeth Fitzpatrick McGregor married John Munro 8 Mar. 1801.
1. Daniel (Donald) McGregor married first, Eleanor Hadley 26 Jan. 1819.
Family.
3. Eleanor. Born 25 Mar. 1822.
4. Eliza. Bapt. 1 Mar. 1828.
5. Joseph Sentell. Born 19 Aug. 1831.
6. Ruth Amelia Hadley. Born 10 Nov. 1833.

Daniel (Donald) McGregor married second, Panthea Simpson.
2. Alexander McGregor married Mary Margaret Leggett 30 Nov. 1817.
3. Eleanor McGregor married H. R. Cunningham 4 Oct. 1842.
4. Eliza McGregor married James A. Tory.
6. Ruth Amelia Hadley McGregor married ? Stirling.

Daniel (Donald) McGregor married (third ?), Annie Brodie.

Macintosh, William.   Married Miriam Luddington 22 Nov. 1798.
Family.
Daniel. Born 8 Sept. 1799.
Jared. Born 26 Sept. 1801.
Jane. Born 15 Mar. 1803.

Miriam Macintosh married second, William McDonald 14 May 1811.
William Macintosh had been killed by a falling tree 30 Nov. 1804.
Of the family, Jane Macintosh married John Stewart 23 Feb. 1830.

MacIntyre, Malcolm. There were two of this name, and no record has been found, except that one of them married Leviath Knowles, a widow, 5 Nov. 1784. One of the Malcolms was named as a "Pilot," the other belonged to the 71st Regiment.

McKay, Alexander. It has been impossible to follow the McKays, McPhersons, McNairs, and McKenzies, though there are many records.

Nash, Ann.   Married Alex McKay 21 Nov. 1789.

Nash, John. Wife's name, Bridget, whose name is on the roll. There is also the name of one child, Robert, under ten. Few records have been found of the family. A William Nash, the relationship to John not being known, married Elizabeth Aikins 1 Oct. 1799. Many of the family moved to Ontario.

Nixon, William.   Wife's name, Ann. He was a prominent merchant whose place of business was close to Fort Point at the entrance to Guysborough Harbour.

Family.

1. William. Born 1778.
2. Ann. Born 25 June 1787.
3. Maria. Born 14 Jan. 1790.
4. Elizabeth. Born 1793.
5. Mary.

1. William Nixon was drowned 21 July 1789.
2. Ann Nixon died 16 May 1793.
3. Maria Nixon married John G. Peart 24 May 1806.
4. Elizabeth Nixon died 11 May 1794.
5. Mary Nixon married first, a Mr. Patterson and second, Dr. Inch. Dr. Inch was killed 28 Jan. 1828.

Patton, Patrick. Married Margaret Brown. He was the first school master.

Family.

Mary. Born 30 May 1790.

James Key. Born 24 Sept. 1791. Died 14 Nov. 1791.

David. Born 17 Nov. 1792. Died Dec. 1792.

Margaret. Born 3 Mar. 1794.

Patrick Patton died 29 June 1816. Margaret Brown Patton died 19 Feb. 1833. No other records.

Pearson, Robert. Married widow, Mary Sceles 5 Sept. 1784 He died in Oct, 1821 and his widow on 19 Jan. 1832. No other records.

Penn, Richard. Wife's name, Martha. There was one child, John Henry, born 21 Aug. 1786, but no other records.

Pyle, Steven. Married Mary MacKenzie 25 Nov. 1785. No family by this first wife. He married second, Elizabeth Hull 10 Nov. 1797,

Family.

1. James George. Born 20 May 1803.
2. Moses Hull. Born 28 Jan. 1805.
3. Stephen. Born 3 May 1808.
4. Mary Amelia. Born 17 July 1812.
5. James. Born 16 Aug. 1824.
6. Samuel.
7. William.

4. Mary Amelia Pyle married Lothrop F. Myers 14 Feb. 1837.

6. Samuel Pyle married Rebecca Boles 12 Jan. 1843.
7. William Pyle married Hannah Crescine 27 Jan. 1829. Died 4 Feb. 1867.

Robertson, Duncan.   Wife's name, Christina.

Family.

George Peter.   Born 20 Jan. 1786.

He married second, Ann Fitzpatrick 22 May 1801.

Family.

John.   Born 18 Nov. 1810.

There are no other records.

Ross, Donald.   Wife's name, Ann.

Family.

1. Margaret.   Born 27 Sept. 1794.
2. Richard.   Born 1 Dec. 1795.
3. Ann.   Born 1 Mar. 1800.
4. Elsie.   Born 3 May 1802.
5. Bridget Jane.   Born 30 May 1807
6. Isabella.   Born 16 Mar. 1809.
7. Mary.   Born 6 Sept. 1811.
8. Sarah Mehitabel.
9. Hugh.
10. John.
11. George.

Ann Ross died 17 Oct. 1813.

1. Margaret Ross married Henry Morgan 27 Jan. 1817.
2. Richard Ross married Catherine Bears 4 Feb. 1833.

Family.

12. Donald Joseph.   Born 13 Dec. 1833.
13. Caroline Lucina.   Born 24 Aug. 1837
14. Esther Ann Rogers.   Born 15 June 1839.
    Married William W. Simpson 1865.
15. Sarah Catherine.   Born 23 July 1844. Married John Ferguson.
16. Richard Smith.   Born 10 May 1850.

3. Ann Ross married Thomas Godfrey Hart 15 Feb. 1825.

4. Elsie Ross married I. A. Whitman 12 Feb. 1828.

5. Bridget Jane Ross married Charles Myers 18 Feb. 1833.

6. Isabella Ross married Jairus Hart 22 July 1834.

7. Mary Ross married John William Peart Hart 1 Dec. 1836.

   (Three sisters of this family thus married three Hart brothers.)

8. Sarah Mehitabel Ross married Charles Edward Morgan 3 Feb. 1851.

9. Hugh Ross married Isabel MacKenzie 25 Apr. 1826.

10. John Ross married Elizabeth Bears 6 Mar. 1827.

Family.

17. George Bears.   Born 4 Feb. 1832.

18. Ann Isabella.   Born 28 Mar. 1834.

19. John Henry.   Bern 26 May 1836.

20. Elizabeth Jane.   Born 30 Sept. 1838.

21. Richard.   Born 29 Aug. 1840.

22. Catherine.   Born 1 June 1842.

23. William Smith.   Bapt. 8 Oct. 1844.

24. Caleb James.   Bapt. 9 Aug. 1846.

25. Mary Amelia.   Born I Mar. 1851.

11. George Ross married Mary Ann

Family.

26. Richard James.   Born 31 May 1840.

12. Donald Joseph Ross married Susanna Ehler 30 Apr. 1857.

13. Caroline Lucina Ross married James William Ferguson 27 Mar. 1860.

Sangster, Joseph.   Wife's name, Margaret.

Family.

1. James.

2. John.

3. Wiliiam.   Born 7 Mar. 1785.

Joseph Sangster was drowned in that year and his widow married Edward Kergan 26 Oct. 1786.

1. James Sangster married Eunice Leet 22 Dec. 1799.

Family.

4. John.   Born 12 Jan. 1804.

5. Joseph Andrew.   Born 26 Mar. 1809.

6. Margaret Jane. Bapt. 4 Aug. 1811.

7. Eunice Catherine. Born 21 June 1813.

8. Mary Elizabeth.

9. James.

10. William.

2. John Sangster married Isabella Fraser 5 Feb. 1804.

Family.

11. Isabella Mehitabel. Born 21 Jane 1805.

12. Michael. Born 7 Oct. 1807.

3. William Sangster married Lucretia Leet 26 Jan. 1804.

Family.

13. Joseph. Born 2 Nov. 1804.

14. Edward. Born 11 Feb. 1806.

15. William. Bapt. 20 Sept. 1807.

16. Margaret. Born 11 Apr. 1809.

17. Submit. Born 5 July 1812.

18. Andrew. Born 20 Mar. 1815.

19. John.

4. John Sangster married first, Mary Maria Jefferies 2 Dec. 1834, and second, Elizabeth Spanks, widow, 9 Oct. 1877.

Family.

20. Caroline. Born 29 Mar. 1836.

21. Margaret Jane.

22. Frances Maria.)

23. Mary Elizabeth.) Twins. Born 23 Nov. 1840.

5. Joseph Andrew Sangster married Frances Gammon.

Family.

24. Mary Ann. Born 13 Feb. 1838.

25. James William Ullitz. Born 15 Aug. 1842.

26. Eunica Lavinia. Born 29 Dec. 1844.

27. Joseph Alexander. Born 5 Feb. 1848.

28. John Charles. Born 27 Sept. 1850.

6. Margaret Jane Sangster married Charles Nickerson.

7. Eunice Catherine Sangster married first, David Nickerson 17 Jan. 1832. She married second, John E. Miller 11 Dec. 1838.

8. Mary Elizabeth Sangster married James Gillie 5 Jan. 1842.

9. James Sangster married first, Margaret Ann Nickerson 5 Jan. 1842.

                           Family.

    29. James William.   Born 18 June 1844.

    30. Mary Sophia.   Born 20 Sept. 1845.

He married second, Submit Sangster (No. 48.)

                           Family.

    31. Townshend.

    32. Wellington.

    33. Hiram.

    34. Nettie.

    35. ?

    36. Ira.

10. William Sangster married Maria Hull, 1856.

                           Family.

    37. David James. Born 29 Oct. 1857.

    38. John Henry Cranswick.   Born 25 Dec. 1862.

    39. Elizabeth Hooper.   Born 12 June 1866.

13.   Joseph Sangster married Mary Patterson 9 Dec. 1824.

                           Family.

    40. William James.   Born 6 Sept. 1825.

    41. John Patterson.   Born 19 July 1827.

    42. Jane.   Born 5 Oct. 1831.

    43. Lucre.

    44. Mary Ann.

    45. Alice.

    46. Margaret.

    47. Joseph.

    48. Submit.

    49. Andrew T.

    50. Eunice.

    51. Robert.

    52. Frances.

16.   Margaret Sangster married William Luddington.

18.   Andrew Sangster married Ann Jane Henderson 21 Nov. 1837.

                           Family.

53. Lucretia Sarah.   Born 3 Sept. 1839.

54. John Joseph.   Born 20 Jan. 1841.

55. William.

56. Adam.

57. Margery.)

58. Eunice.) Twins.

59. Michael.

60. Jane.

61. Alexander.

62. Olivia.

20. Caroline Sangster married John Jones 27 Dec. 1859.

21. Margaret Jane Sangster married Thomas H. Hull 18 Jan. 1866.

29. James W. Sangster married Sarah O'Hara.

30. Mary Sangster married first, Robert Sangster, and second, Levi Sponagle.

31. Townshend Sangster married Laura Sponagle.

32. Wellington Sangster married Stella Dimock.

33. Hiram Sangster married   ? MacKenzie.

34. Nettie Sangster married Thomas Gillie.

39. Elizabeth Hooper Sangster married Wallace Sangster.

40. William James Sangster married Sarah Henderson.

41. John Patterson Sangster married Elizabeth Ann Nickerson 24 Aug. 1854.

Sceles, Thomas. He married Phoebe West 12 Mar. 1792.

Family.

1. Mary.   Born 26 Jan. 1794.

2. Elizabeth.   Born 12 Aug. 1795.

3. Thomas.   Born 8 Aug. 1801.

4. John.   Born 19 Dec. 1802.

5. Robert Henry.   Born 22 May 1805.

6. David.   Born 11 June 1812.

7. Susan Dean.   Born 12 Aug. 1814.

8. Hannah.   Born 13 Apr. 1817.

9. George.   Born 18 Mar. 1810.

10. Ann.

11. William.

Phoebe West Sceles died 5 Dec. 1856, aged 85.

3. Thomas Sceles married Elizabeth Davidson 8 Apr. 1828.

Family.

12. James. Born 8 Jan. 1829.

13. William Thomas. Born 22 Feb. 1831.

14. Elsie Eleanor. Born 12 Aug. 1835.

15. Robert Cutler. Born 8 Mar. 1838.

16. Elsie Watt.   )

17. George Crescine.) Twins. Born 14 Sept. 1840.

18. Elizabeth Sarah. Born 16 July 1843.

19. Mary Jane. Born 27 Feb. 1847.

20. Alexander. Born 29 Aug. 1850.

Thomas Sceles died 25 May 1854, aged 53.

4. John Sceles married Mary Lamb, widow, 5 Oct. 1825.

Family.

21. John David. Born 10 Oct. 1826.

22. Mary Ann Catherine. Born 21 July 1838.

5. Robert Henry Sceles married Elizabeth Hart 6 Dec. 1831.

Family.

23. John Hurst. Born 10 Nov. 1833.

24. George Crescine. Born 27 Feb. 1836.

25. Mary. Born 15 Jan. 1839.

26. Elizabeth. Born 5 Mar. 1841.

27. Almira. Born 24 Mar. 1843.

7. Susan Dean Sceles married Levin Hurst 26 Dec. 1843.

8. Hannah Sceles married Henry Creamer 22 Sept. 1838.

10. Ann Sceles married William Rheinold 14 Dec. 1819.

11. William Sceles married Eleanor Davidson 20 Dec. 1836.

Family.

28. Elsie Elizabeth. Born 25 May 1837.

29. Thomas Alexander. Born 13 Nov. 1840.

30. William. Born 13 May 1844.

31. James William Davidson. Born 28 Dec. 1845.

Shaw, Evan.   He was married when he arrived in the settlement, his wife's name being May.

Family.

1. Isobel.   Born 29 Apr. 1785.
2. Margaret.   Born 31 Mar. 1787.
3. William.   Born 24 June 1789.
4. James.   Born 25 Mar. 1792.
5. James.   Born 10 June 1794.
6. Alexander.

Evan Shaw died in May 1812.   His wife died 6 May 1826.

2. Margaret Shaw married John Fraser 4 July 1805.
3. William Shaw married Ann McKay 30 Mar. 1813.

Family.

7. Isabella.   Born 22 Feb. 1814.
8. Christie Sophia.   Born July 1821.
9. William.   Born 14 Sept. 1823.
10. William Owen.   Born 10 Feb. 1824.
11. Elizabeth.   Born 24 Dec. 1826.
12. John. Henry.   Born 14 Jan. 1829.
13. Abigail Sarah.   Born 16 Feb. 1831.
14. Joseph William Smith.   Born 19 May 1834.

5. James Shaw married Elizabeth Welsh, widow 22 Mar. 1819.

Family.

15. Margaret Jane.   Born 31 Oct. 1820.
16. Elizabeth Sophia.   Born 6 Mar. 1822.
17. Mary Jane.   Born 14 Mar. 1824.
18. ?   Born 18 Oct. 1826.
19. Sarah Maria.   Born 12 June 1828.
20. ?   Bapt. 14 Oct. 1832.

James Shaw, widower, married Margaret Crescine 17 Jan. 1850.
He died 25 Jan. 1858, and his widow married a Godfrey.

6. Alexander Shaw married Sarah

Family.

21. Janet.   Born 17 Apr. 1812.
22. Elizabeth.   Born 28 May 1814.
23. Catherine Jane.   Born 28 June 1816.

387

24. Eleanor. Born 25 Apr. 1819.

25. Evan Thomas. Born 5 Apr. 1821.

26. Mary Ann. Born 9 Apr. 1806.

27. Sarah. Born 27 Feb. 1810.

28. Isabella. Born 3 May 1804.

29. Margaret Elizabeth. Born 2 Aug. 1808.

30. Alexander. Born 2 Mar. 1824.

Simpson, William. Married Lydia Hart 13 July 1796. His wife died 29 March 1871, aged 96.

Family

1. William. Born 13 Apr. 1800.

2. Lydia Ann. Born 8 Aug. 1802.

3. Henry Hart. Born 2 Sept. 1804.4.

4. Panthea. Born 12 Oct. 1806.

5. Margaret. Born 12 Mar. 1809.

6. John Ballain. Born 4 July 1813.

7. Thomas. Born 23 Apr. 1815.

8. Martha Caroline. Born 9 Apr. 1818.

9. Ann.

1. William Simpson married Sarah Boles 23 Jan. 1830.

Family.

10. Rebecca. Born 3 Dec. 1830.

11. Lydia.

12. William. Born 3 Nov. 1833.

13. Sarah.

14. Eliza. Born 1 Apr. 1837.

15. Robert Boles. Born 19 Oct. 1838.

16. Albert. Born 25 June 1840.

17. Charles Shreve. Born 3 June 1842.

18. John Joseph. Born 3 Apr. 1844.

19. Victoria. Born 31 Jan. 1846.

20. Henry.

21. Ann.

2. Lydia Ann Simpson married David Scranton 23 Mar. 1824.

4. Panthea Simpson married Donald McGregor.

5. Margaret Simpson married ? Crowdis.

6. John Ballain Simpson married Mary Darin. She died 10 Sept. 1866, aged 51.

7. Thomas Simpson married Ann Horton 7 Jan. 1840.

8. Martha Caroline Simpson married ? Wylde.

9. Ann Simpson married John McKeough 28 June 1834.

10. Rebecca Simpson married David Scranton 1865.

11. Lydia Simpson married John McPherson 1852.

12. William Simpson married Abigail Brymer.

13. Sarah Simpson married George Joseph Carr 4 Jan. 1870.

16. Albert Simpson married first, Caroline Bears 26 June 1869. He married second, Hattie Ross.

17. Charles Shreve Simpson married Emma Hart.

18. John Joseph Simpson was not married.

19. Victoria Simpson married Donald Myers 1868.

20. Henry Simpson married Cynthia Grant.

Spanks, George.   There seems to have been at least two boys, one of whom, George, married Mary Forkell Jan. 3 1792, and the other, William, who married Anna Critchett on Dec. 5, 1809.   There are many records, which makes it impossible to disentangle.

Tanner, Isaac. Married to Mary Myers, widow of George Myers. There is record of a family.

Torey, James. Wife's name, Christiana or Christine Kirke. She died Jan. 12, 1807, aged 60 years.

Family.

1. Alexander B. Born 17 Mar. 1786.

2. Jane. Born 2 Nov. 1787.

3. Jenet. Born 21 Dec. 1789.

4. James. Born 5 Apr. 1791.

5. Henry. Born 18 Feb. 1794.

6. John. Born 2 Sept. 1796.

James Torey married second, Christine Chisholm 22 June 1808.

1. Alexander B. Torey died 30 July 1790.

2. Jane Torey married Isaac Lawson 11 Dec. 1805.

3. Jenet Torey married Thomas J. Morris 19 Jan. 1808.

4. James Torey married Elizabeth McKenzie 18 Dec. 1816.

He died 28 Aug. 1877.   She died 5 Feb. 1879.

Family.

7. James Alexander.   Born 26 July 1818.

8. John Henry.   Bapt. 22 Apr. 1821.

9. Christina.

10. James Alexander.   Born 13 Dec. 1822.

11. John Henry.   Born 19 June 1824.

12. Alexander George.   Born 14 Feb. 1828.

13. George Isaiah.   Born 13 Apr. 1830.

14. Child.   Born 16 May 1832.

15. Jane.   Born 4 July 1837.

16. Elizabeth.

17. William,

(Probably not in order of birth.)

5. Henry Torey married Ann Dieckhoff 13 Feb. 1816. She died 12 Apr. 1874.

Family.

18. Christine Eleanor.   Born 28 Nov. 1816.

19. Jane Isabella.   Born 21 June 1819.

20. James A.   Born 9 Aug. 1823.

21. Marianne.   Born 23 Nov. 1825.

22. Janet Amelia.   Born 3 June 1830.

23. John William.   Born 9 Apr. 1833.

24. Robert Kirk.   Born 3 June 1838.

25. Joseph.   Born 24 Oct. 1840.

26. Elizabeth.

27. Henry.

10. James Alexander Torey married Elizabeth MacGregor.

11. John Henry Torey married Elizabeth Brymer.

12. Alexander George Torey married Sarah Whitman.

13. George Isaiah Torey married Mary MacPherson.

16. Elizabeth Torey married William Fred MacDonald.

17. William Torey married Margaret Sellars.

18. Christine Eleanor Torey married Isaac Andrews.

19. Jane Isabella Torey married David Andrews.

20. James A. Torey married Ann Ross Morgan.

21. Marianne Torey married John Lipsitt.

23. John William Torey married Sarah Hull.

24. Robert Kirk Torey married Honora Ferguson.

25. Joseph Torey married Catherine Letitia Kirby.

26. Elizabeth. Torey married Isaiah Brown.

27. Henry Torey married a Miss Morgan.

Welsh, Matthew. No family, though married. This is the individual who left his estate to the use of the schools of the community. He was a blacksmith.

Whitman, William.   Married Anna Firtla 8 Apr. 1799.

Family.

1. Catherine.   Born 29 Dec. 1801.

2. Mary.   Born 10 Oct. 1803.

3. Margaret.   Born 25 Sept. 1805.

4. Phoebe.   Born 13 Sept. 1807.

5. Hannah.   Born 3 May 1812.

6. Ann.   Born 12 June 1814.

7. Priscilla.   Born 10 Oct. 1816.

8. George William.   Born 2 Mar. 1810.

9. Ira.

10. Rufus.

1. Catherine Whitman married John Jones 28 Aug. 1821.

2. Mary Whitman married George Horton 15 Jan. 1822.

3. Margaret Whitman married William Cook 4 Jan. 1827.

8. George Whitman married Elizabeth Horton 19 Jan. 1847.

9. Ira Whitman married Elsie Ross.

10. Rufus Whitman married Margaret Kergan.

Wilson, Francis. Wife's name, Rebecca. There was one son, John, who married Margaret Hall 13 Oct. 1808.

Willson, Samuel.   Died 4 Dec. 1810, aged about 80 years.   No other record.

Whittendale, Christopher. Married Mary Ferguson 9 Apr. 1801. There were two children, George and Margaret Catherine. George married Caroline Carter; Margaret married James Harrol.

LAND GRANTS OF
THE SIXTIETH REGIMENT — ROYAL AMERICANS

	Name	Town Lots Block Letter	Lot Number	Other Lands Lot Number	Acres
1.	*Bayne, Alex	E	19	30	250
2.	*Bush, John Godfrey	A	6	45	250
3.	*Brush, Jacob (Ludovic)	E	20	51	250
4.	Bedford, Levin	—	—	26	250
5.	*Brown, John	D	3	53	100
6.	*Boyer, John	—	—	—	—
7.	*Christ, George	D	11	—	—
8.	*Chapman, William	—	—	—	—
9.	Deickhoff, Herman	E	8	24	200
10.	Deiterich, Adam (Dederick)	—	—	56	300
11	Dort, Valentine	E	6	31	200
12.	*Derr (Durr), John	B	3	50	100
13.	*Esbach, Gottfrey	D	4	7	250
14.	Elar (Ehler), John	E	2	8	200
15.	*Fleisher, Conrad	I	1	15	150
16.	*Fener, Joseph	—	—	57	100
17.	Fricke, Augustus	N	6	21	600
18	*Goldman, Christian	E	9	49	200
19.	*Gunn, John	M	8	14	300
20.	Greencorn, Ludovic (Krinkhorn)	A	8	29	300
21.	Greencorn, Ludovic	—	—	25	100
22.	Greencorn, Adam	—	—	23	100
23.	*Gleigh, Martin	—	—	41	100
24.	*Goyonally, David	—	—	—	—
25.	George (Gurgon), Justice (Justus)	E	7	13	100
26.	*Heskell, John	—	—	—	—
27.	*Henning, John	E	1	—	—
28.	Hurst, Samuel	E	3	20	300
29	*Hounsheil, John	N	7	16	150
30.	*Homan, Conrad, Sr	A	12	10	250

393

31	*Homan, Conrad, Jr	D	7	22	100
32.	*Hull, Henry	—	—	40	200
33.	*Hartman, Joshua (Joseph)	E	10	34	200
34.	*Hulsman, Ludovic (Lewis)	O	1	59	250
35.	*Innes (?), Henry	—	—	—	—
36.	Jamieson, John	D	1	39	300
37.	Joppe (Joppy), Ludovic	A	10	46	250
38.	*Johnstone, David	A	1	—	—
39.	*Jones, John	—	—	—	—
40.	*Linton, John	—	—	—	—
41.	Lowry (Laurie), James	—	—	4	300
42.	*Merryweather, Thomas	—	—	—	—
43.	Muller, Christian	O	3	38	250
44.	Meyer (Myers), Ferdinand	M	5	6	100
45.	Meyer, George	D	12	9	100
46.	*Meyer, Charles	—	—	3	100
47.	*Munn (Mann), John	E	18	17	100
48.	*Mills, John	—	—	—	—
49.	*Nutt, Daniel	D	6	42	100
50.	*Orphenius, William	D	8	2	100
51.	*Pope, Joshua	—	—	—	—
52.	*Pape (Papa), Frederick	A	7	19	150
53.	*Patch, Frederick	A	3	43	200
54.	*Rumple, William	—	—	12	250
55.	Reuter (Ryder), Henry	D	10	33	300
56.	Rheinhold (Rhynold), Casper.—		—	5	300
57.	*Rhoeden, Moritz	A	5	32	250
58.	*Range, Joseph	—	—	35	100
59.	*Ryan, John	—	—	37	150
60.	*Richardson, John	—	—	—	—
61.	*Shoenwise, John	M	9	48	100
62.	Sneider, John, Sr	A	11	11	100
63.	*Sneider, Christian	A	9	1	200
64.	Sartorius, Valentin (Valentine)	A	4	58	200
65.	Stropel, George	N	5	18	300
66.	*Sealy, Lieut	—	—	—	—
67.	*Stafford, Oliver	F	5	28	350
68.	Sneider, John, Jr	I	3	27	100

69. *Sartorius, Ludovic	—	—	36	100
70. *Taylor, James	I	16	47	250
71. Uloth, Adam	O	2	54	300
72. *Wendell, Peter	D	5	55	250
73. *Wick, Henry	D	5	55	250
74. *Wright, John	—	—	—	—
75. *Willis, Richard	—	—	—	—
76. *Wendell, Christian	—	—	52	200

The names were taken from a copy of the Muster Roll taken at Halifax, July 17, 1784. The apportionments of lands were taken from the Town Clerk's Book. Apparently Christian Wendell's name had been omitted from the Roll or the copy of it. The Muster Master notes that neither John Linton nor John Jones were present at the muster either at Halifax or Chedabucto..

(Concerning those marked with a (*), little or no record has been found.)

Women.

Mrs. Sealy	Alithea Fricke
Catherine Uloth	Unity Muller
Maria Gunn	Anne Bayne
Anne Hulsman	Charlotte Jamieson
Maria Hounshell	Maria Goyonally
Elinora Bush	Elizabeth Fener
Maria Stropel	Maria Stafford
Eliza Sartorius	Dorothy Reuter
Maria Brush	Esther
Maria Pope	Ann Ryan
Catherine Rhoeden	Maria Wick
Eliza Dort	Ann Rheinhold
Eliza Deitrick	Ann Fleisher
Ann Taylor	Henrietta Lowry
Maria Esbach	Maria Merryweather
Maria Roemple	Elizabeth Hurst
Elizabeth Greencorn	Jane Joppy

Children Under Ten Years of Age.

Augustus Uloth	George Stropel
Grace Stafford	Maria Stafford
Ludovic Sartorius	Maria Reuter
Jacob Greencorn	John Hurst
Elizabeth Hurst	Sarah Hurst
Elinora Deitrick	Eliza Merryweather

Children Over Ten Years of Age. These numbered 7, but the names are not given.

Servants.

Martha Gottfrey	Joshua Veal
James May	Lucretia Sowell

The total number of names on the Muster Roll was as follows:—

Names of Men. (See alphabetical List)	76
Women	34
Children under Ten	12
Children over Ten	7
Servants	4
Total	133

These were mustered at Halifax by William Shaw, Muster Master, on the 17th of July, 1784.

Bedford, Levin.   Name of wife, Esther.

Family.

1. William.   Born 23 June 1785.
2. Esther.   Born 31 Oct. 1787.
3. George.   Born 1789.
4. John.   Born 2 Feb. 1790.
5. Mary.
6. Levin.   Born 23 Feb. 1794.
7. Elizabeth.   Born 24 Aug. 1795.
8. Eliza.   Bora 25 March 1798.
9. Mileath.   Born 25 Apr. 1800.

1. William Bedford married Ann Hurst 27 Nov. 1806.
2. Esther Bedford married John Hurst 22 May 1804.
3. George Bedford died 16 Oct. 1792.
4. John Bedford.   No record.

5. Mary Bedford married William Dort 7 May 1809.
6. Levin Bedford married Charlotte Delaney 11 Dec. 1833.

Family.

    10. Levin.   Born 5 Feb. 1837.
    11. William.   Born 16 Feb. 1839.
    12. Jane Catherine.   Born 8 June 1841.
    13. Mary Elizabeth.   Born 31 Oct. 1843. Married Charles E. Jones.
    14. Catherine Nancy.   Born 14 Feb. 1850.

7. Elizabeth Bedford married George Myers 30 Aug. 1814.
9. Mileath Bedford married Jacob Rogers 18 Jan. 1819.

Brush (Brusch), Jacob (Ludovic).   He was the father-in-law of Henry Reuter and Valintine Sartorius. Both daughters named their first sons in his honour. His place of origin was Eberbach, Beden/Wurltenberg.

Dederick, Adam. This name is found spelt in a number of ways. The name of his wife, Elizabeth, is on the muster roll. There are records of two children.

    Eleanor.   Born 8 June 1784.

    Mary.   Born 6 Mar. 1787.

Deickhoff, Herman.   This name has been much corrupted. Married Elizabeth Marshall 27 June 1791.

Family.

    1. Elizabeth.   Born 20 Aug. 1793.

    2. Ann.   Bapt. 21 Aug. 1796.

    3. Mary.   Born 30 Mar. 1800.

    4. Gasehe.   Born 30 Mar. 1803.

    5. Samuel.   Born 13 July 1805.

    6. Mary.   Born 9 May 1807.

    7. James Herman.   Born 26 Mar. 1809.

    8. Sarah.   Born 31 Mar. 1813.

    9. Otto Joachim.   Born 13 Apr. 1815.

    10. Edward Thomas.   Born 10 Apr. 1817.

    11. Ann.

    12. Susannah.

    13. John.

    14. Isabella.

Herman Deickhoff died 10 Feb. 1839, aged 88. His wife died 20 Nov. 1831.

1. Elizabeth Deickhoff married John Feltmate 31 Dec. 1811.
4. Gasehe Deickhoff died 19 May 1810.

5. Samuel Deickhoff married Hannah Strople 24 Apr. 1832. He died 11 Jan. 1874.

Family.

15. Elizabeth. Born 10 Oct. 1837.

16. John Edward. Born 20 Mar. 1840.

Married Minnie Whitman (widow) 10 Apr. 1882.

17. William Albert. Born 14 Dec. 1842. Married Mary Jane Carroll 5 Feb.1872.

18. Mary Ann. Born 29 Aug. 1845.

19. Thomas James. Born 1 Aug. 1848.

20. Samuel Herman. Born 9 Jan. 1852.

21. Maria Caroline. Born 12 Dec. 1857.

6. Mary Deickhoff married Peter Munro 27 Jan. 1829.

7. James Herman Deickhoff married Jane Grey Henderson.

Family.

22. Catherine Elizabeth.

23. Charles Levi.

24. Emmeline Lavinia.

11. Ann Deickhoff married Henry Torey 13 Feb. 1816.

12. Susannah Deickhoff married Asa MacKenzie 1 Jan. 1817.

13. John Deickhoff married Isabella Grey Henderson 17 Dec. 1833.

14. Isabella Deickhoff married Casper Rheinold 8 May 1843.

Dort, Valentine. Married Elizabeth Keisel.

Family.

1. Christian. Born 25 Feb. 1785.

2. Valentine. Born 29 July 1789.

3. Ann. Born 7 June 1792.

4. Sarah. Born 15 May 1800.

5. Thomas. Born 25 Mar. 1803.

6. Elizabeth. Born 5 Nov. 1808.

7. William.

8. Peter. Born 1794.

1. Christian Dort married Elizabeth Sartorius 25 Aug, 1805.

Family.

9. Valentine. Born 2 Nov. 1806.

10. Mary Ann. Born 1 Dec. 1811.

11. Elizabeth. Born 31 July 1813.

12. Abigail. Born 12 Dec. 1815.

13. Margaret. Born 17 Aug. 1817.

14. Catherine. Born 5 Oct. 1819.

15. Christopher. Born 8 Nov. 1823.

He married second, Elizabeth Ryder 8 June 1824.

16. Christian. Born 19 Nov. 1828.

He married third Ann Gammon 18 Dec. 1845.

2. Valentine Dort married Eve Sneider 18 Dec. 1813.
His wife died 9 July 1871.

Family.

17. Elizabeth. Born 26 July 1815.

18. John Valentine. Born 23 Aug. 1817.

19. Abigail. Born 14 Sept. 1819.

20. Susannah. Born 18 Feb. 1822.

21. William James. Born 23 Sept. 1824.

22. Marianne. Born 18 May 1828.

23. Catherine Susannah. Born 15 June 1829.

24. Margaret. Born 27 Jan. 1831.

25. ? Bapt. 15 Sept. 1833.

26. Ann Catherine. Born 6 Feb. 1838.

27. Thomas Charles. Born 30 Mar. 1840.

3. Ann Dort married John Greencorn 2 May 1815.

4. Sarah Dort married Christian Sneider 23 Mar. 1818.

5. Thomas Dort married Ann Rhynold 15 Sept. 1834.

Family.

28. Phoebe Eliza. Born 9 Oct. 1836.

29. Phoebe Elizabeth. Born 30 Nov. 1838.

30. Eliza Selina. Born 27 Mar. 1841.

31. Phoebe Caroline Amelia. Born 16 Aug. 1843.

32. Isabella Matilda. Born 9 Dec. 1846.

33. William Levi. Born 13 Oct. 1853.
Married Mary Elizabeth Dort 6Oct.1880.

34. George Alexander. Born 24 May 1857.

7. William Dort married first Mary Bedford 7 May 1809. (She died in giving birth to twins, the three being buried together.) He married second, Barbara Webber 9 Mar. 1813.

Family.

35. Marianne. Born 20 Dec. 1814.

36. Elizabeth. Born 10 Mar. 1816.

37. Sarah. Born 27 Sept. 1817.

38. Jared. Born 27 June 1819.

39. Valentine. Born 27 Jan. 1821.

40. Janet. Born 5 Dec. 1822.

41. William. Born 15 Oct. 1824.

42. John W.

43. Christian.

44. Philip William. Born 14 Nov. 1830.

8. Peter Dort married Susannah Sneider 22 Dec. 1817. He died 7 Dec. 1869.

Family.

45. John David. Born 17 Nov. 1819.

46. Elizabeth. Born 27 Apr. 1821.

47. Susanna. Born 27 June 1823.

48. Peter Valentine. Born 2 Jan 1827.

49. James. Bapt. 14 July 1833.

50. Christopher. Born 27 Feb. 1840.

51. Joseph. Born 6 Dec. 1842.

52. Margaret.

53. Mack.

54. Ann Betsy.

Susannah Dort, Peter's wife died 5 April 1878 aged 85.

9. Valentine Dort married first Charity.

Family.

56. Margaret Ann. Born 7 Feb. 1837.

57. Charity Elizabeth. Born 22 Jan. 1839.

He married second Elizabeth I. McKay 21 April 1840. He married third Kitty Shaughnessy.

58. Ira married Charity Caroline Jamieson 6 Sept. 1882.

10. Mary Ann Dort married John Sneider 24 Aug. 1840.

12. Abigail Dort married Martin George 6 Dec. 1836.

13. Margaret Dort married J. P. McVie 12 Dec. 1837.

14. Catherine Dort married William Feltmate 25 Jan. 1841.

16. Christian Dort married Annie Neale (or O'Neil) 1857.
    Caroline.   Born 28 Sept. 1868.

17. Elizabeth Dort married Matthew Brown.

18. John Valentine Dort married Zipporah Brown 1 Feb. 1842.

Family.

59. Joseph Henry.   Born 24 Jan. 1843.

60. Martha or Matilda.   Born 29 Oct. 1844.

61. Susan Elizabeth. Born 9 Aug. 1853. Married William Burton Silver 19 Jan. 1881.

62. John James.   Born 16 May 1855. He married second Ann Strider 2 Jan. 1864.

63. William Henry.   Born 1864.

64. Hezekiah.   Born 2 May 1867.

65. Edmund Franklin.   Born 25 May 1871.

20. Susannah Dort married Jacob Rogers 18 Feb. 1868.

21. William James Dort married Esther Bedford 26 Dec. 1865.

27. Thomas Charles Dort married Martha Jane George 23 Jan. 1866.

29. Phoebe Elizabeth Dort married Isaac Greencorn 14 Feb. 1860.

41. William Dort married Abigail Williams 8 Jan. 1850.

Family.

Barbara.   Born 1850.

Albert William.   Born 4 May 1855.

William Dort died 25 May 1860.

Abigail Dort married second Christian Dort 18 Jan. 1872.

42. John W. Dort married Esther Shrider 11 Jan. 1851.

Family.

Harriet Eleanor.   Born 17 June 1855.

John Charles.   Born 5 Nov. 1858.

George Whitfield.   Born 18 Feb. 1861.

James William Havelock.   Born 9 Apr. 1863.

Arthur O.   Born 14 May 1868.

Wesley.

Eliza Letitia.   Married George Shrider 27 Mar. 1875.

43. Christian Dort married Adelaide George 19 Dec. 1854.

Family.

James Christopher. Born 18 Feb. 1856.

Henry Augustus. Born 17 May 1858.

John Jacob. Born 10 July 1861.

Letitia Elizabeth. Born 25 Sept. 1870.

44. Philip William Dort married Ellen George 2 Dec. 1856.

Family.

Mary Elizabeth. Born 1857.

William Alexander. Born 31 Oct. 1863.

Barbara Ellen. Born 31 Dec. 1870.

45. John David Dort married Elizabeth Shrider 9 Feb. 1851.

Family.

Susan Ann. Born 5 Feb. 1852.

John James. Born 3 Dec. 1853.

Emma Eliza. Born 21 Apr. 1855.

George Levi. Born 16 Mar. 1857.

Melissa Elizabeth. Born 9 Feb. 1859.

David Alonzo. Born 22 Aug. 1862.

Charles Frederick. Born 6 Feb. 1867.

49. James Dort married Charity Catherine Delaney 26 Apr. 1856.

Family.

Patrick James. Born 6 Feb. 1857.

Pamela Ann. Born 1 June 1859.

Helena Elizabeth. Born 13 May 1861.

William Alonzo. Born 6 Nov. 1864.

Almira Jane. Born 10 Mar. 1871.

50. Chistopher (Christian) Dort married Abigail Dort 18 Jan. 1872, widow.

52. Margaret Dort married Thomas Godfrey Dort.

60. Martha M. married Thos. George Jarvis 6 Oct. 1874.

60a Sarah Dort married Joseph Dimock Luddington 16 Nov. 1870.

Ehler (Elar) John. The name is spelt in a variety of ways on the rolls of the Regiment. He is said to have been a miller by trade. His wife's name was Catherine.

Family.

1. Christian Philip. Born 14 Dec. 1790.

2. John James.   Born 12 Dec. 1792.

3. Daniel Ludovic.   Born 2 Nov. 1795.

4. Margaret.   Born 6 Mar. 1810.

After the death of her first husband Catherine Ehler married Hugh Miller 9 June 1829.

1. Christian Philip Ehler married Abigail Sartorius 16 July 1811.

Family.

5. Catherine.   Born Apr. 1812.

6. John.   Born 19 Dec. 1813.

7. Abigail.   Born 8 Jan. 1819.

8. Elizabeth.   Born 24 Dec. 1819.

2. John James Ehler married Catherine Myers 2 July 1815.

Family.

9. James David.   Born 18 Sept. 1817.

10. Joseph Daniel.   Born 18 Oct. 1818.

11. John Christian Miller.   Bapt. 27 June 1821.

12. William Alexander.   Born 12 Oct. 1822.

13. Christian Arthur.   Born 5 Oct. 1824.

14. Mary Catherine.   Born 31 Jan. 1828.

15. David Samuel.   Born 9 Dec. 1829.

16. George Frederick.   Born 27 Feb. 1831.

17. Margaret Elizabeth.   Born 2 Dec. 1831.

18. Adam Ferdinand.   Born 1 May 1833.

19. Matthew Henry.   Born 14 Apr. 1835.

20. Levi Nathaniel.   Born 18 Apr. 1837.

21. Lavinia.   Born 20 Mar. 1840.

22. Harriet Jane.   Born 16 Aug. 1841.

23. Enos Robert.   Born 22 July 1843.

He married second Warburton Irvine 5 July 1848.

24. Catherine.

25. Margaret C.

26. Violetta Ann.   Born 9 Sept. 1856.

27. James Mitchell Smith.   Born 31 May 1860.

28. Frank.

3. Daniel Ludovic Ehler married Hannah Perrin.

29. Mary Catherine. Born 9 Dec. 1820.

30. Abraham. Born 6 Sept. 1825.

31. Isaac. Born 3 May 1827.

32. Jacob. Born 24 July 1829.

33. Sarah. Born 26 Apr. 1831.

34. Susan. Born 7 Apr. 1833.

35. Lydia. Born 1 May 1835.

36. Daniel Born 28 Dec. 1836.

37. Elizabeth Catherine. Born 20 Dec. 1840.

38. Esther.

39. Hannah.

4. Margaret Ehler married John David 4 Jan. 1827.

5. Catherine Ehler married Zimri Carter 21 Dec. 1830.

6. John Ehler married Ann Hurst 1835.

Family.

40. John James. Born 3 Apr. 1837.

41. Christian Levi. Born 12 July 1839.

42. Esther Ann. Born 20 Jan. 1842.

7. Abigail Ehler married John Uloth 15 Jan. 1839.

10. Joseph Daniel Ehler married Charlotte Jane Carr 30 Dec. 1850.

Family.

43. John James. Born 11 Nov. 1853.

44. Joseph Alexander. Born 25- Feb. 1856.

45. James David. Born 16 May 1858.

46. Janet Catherine. Born 3 Apr. 1862.

47. Charity Elizabeth. Born 8 July 1864.

48. Mary Ann. Born 18 June 1868.

49. Esther A. M. Born 20 Apr. 1870.

50. William Levi Buckley. Born 3 May 1874.

11. John Christian Ehler married Catherine Henderson 10 Dec. 1844.

Family.

51. Martha Jane.

52. Matilda.

53. Eliza.

404

54. John W.

He married second Jane Henderson.

12. William Alexander Ehler married Elizabeth Jamieson 24 May 1849.

Family.

55. Abigail Eleanor.   Born 24 Feb. 1850.

56. David James.   Born 31 July 1852.

57. William A.   Born 9 Dec. 1854.

58. Lydia Catherine.   Born 5 Feb. 1857.

59. Robert Levi.   Born 27 June 1858.

60. Robert Enos.   Born 3 June 1861.

61. John Joseph Forsythe.   Born 19 Feb. 1864.

62. Harriet Elizabeth.   Born 1 July 1866.

63. Eliza Eimira.   Born 21 May 1869.

13. Christian Arthur Ehler married Esther Horton.

Family.

64. Reuben Alfred.   Born 31 July 1853.

65. Elizabeth Catherine.

66. Josephine L.

67. Elizabeth Ann.   Born 3 Dec. 1859.

68. David S. F.   Born 15 Apr. 1861.

69. John H.   Born 23 May 1864.

70. William Arthur.   Born 25 May 1867.

71. Martha Catherine.   Born 17 Apr. 1869.

72. Hannah Odessa.   Born 4 July 1872.

14. Mary Catherine Ehler married George Tanner 16 Jan. 1855.

16. George Frederick Ehler married Mary Ann Carr.

Family.

73. Janet Catherine.

74. Abram Rufus.

75. Martha Jane.

76. Laura.

17. Margaret Elizabeth Ehler married George MacKenzie.

18. Adam Ferdinand Ehler married Angeline Munro.

Family.

77. James.

78. Minnie.

79. Bessie.

21. Lavinia Ehler married David Horton.

22. Harriet Jane Ehler married John James Ehler 20 Jan. 1861.

23. Enos Robert Ehler married Isabel MacKenzie.

24. Catherine Ehler married Robert J. Jamieson 27 Apr. 1870.

25. Margaret C. Ehler married Archibald Peart 12 Feb. 1873.

26. Violetta Ann Ehler married Daniel Cogle.

33. Sarah Ehler married Jairus Hadley.

35. Lydia Ehler married Thomas MacDonald.

36. Daniel Ehler married Lydia Ann Myers 1869.

38. Esther Ehler married Hugh William Fraser 10 Feb. 1846.

39. Hannah Ehler married Robert Aikins.

40. John James Ehler married Harriet Jane Ehler 20 Jan. 1861.

Family.

80. Christian David.

81. Edmund.

82. John Charles.

83. Catherine Esther.

84. Annie. Born 5 Sept. 1868.

85. Georgina.

86. William Edmund.

87. Henrietta.

88. Minnie L.

89. Margaret.

90. Ernest Arthur.

91. Alonzo Lamont.

41. Christian Levi Ehler married Eliza Jane Jamieson 17 Sept. 1868.

Family.

92. John.

93. William Everett.

94. Nettie.

95. Gertrude.

96. Levi C.

97. Celia.

42. Esther Ann Ehler married George D. Jamieson.

43. John James Ehler married Mary Ryter.

Family.

98. Charity Catherine.

99. Wallace.

100. Joseph.

101. Charles.

102. Mary.

103. Louise.

104. Alice   Winifred.)

105. Lois Annie.)   Twins.

106. Margaret Olga.

107. James William.

108. John Austin.

109. Harry Everett.

44. Joseph Alexander Ehler married Lizzie McInnis.

45. James David Ehler married a widow, Mrs. Dago.

46. Janet Catherine Ehler married a Mr. MacFarlane.

51. Martha Jane Ehler married John C. Jamieson 22 Dec. 1869.

52. Matilda Ehler married Moses Scott 1864.

53. Eliza Ehler married David Bernard.

54. John W. married Eliza Jane Armsworthy 10 May 1880.

55. Abigail Eleanor Ehler married Valentine Jacob Williams 24 Jan. 1871.

56. David James Ehler married Elizabeth C. Tanner 12 Dec. 1880.

Family.

110. William Levi.   Born 23 July 1882.

111. Margaret Lavinia.

112. George Robert.   Born 9 Dec. 1884.

113. James David.   Born 30 Nov. 1887.

114. Charles Angus.   Born 8 July 1890.

115. Freeman Havelock. Born 14 July 1892.

116. Mary Elizabeth.   Born 7 Dec. 1894.

117. Lewis Stanley.   Born 24 Mar. 1898.

118. Margaret Ethel.   Born 13 Sept. 1899.

119. Albert Frederick.   Born 1 Feb. 1903.

58. Lydia Catherine Ehler married John William Williams.
60. Robert Enos Ehler married Elizabeth H. Jamieson.

Family.

    120. James Arthur. Born 3 June 1890.

    121. Robert Leslie. Born 15 Sept. 1895.

    122. Ida Blanche. Born 5 Apr. 1898.

    123. Margaret Marion. Born 20 Apr. 1907.

61. John James Forsythe Ehler married Catherine Kennedy.

Family.

    124. Charles Wilfred. Born 13 Sept. 1901.

    125. Janet Catherine. Born 22 July 1904.

    126. Anna Mary. Born 21 May 1907.

    127. Harriet Mabel. Born 23 Oct. 1909.

    128. Margaret Winifred. Born 4 July 1911.

62. Harriet Elizabeth Ehler married William Kennedy.
63. Eliza Elmira Ehler married Enos Dort.
64. Reuben Alfred Ehler married Sarah Hadley.
67. Elizabeth Ann Ehler married a Mr. Lacey.
72. Janet Catherine Ehler married Joseph Armstrong.
79. Hannah Odessa Ehler married George Smith.
80. Christian David Ehler married Maria Porper.
82. John Charles Ehler married Ernestine Hadley.
83. Catherine Esther Ehler married William Publicover.
84. Annie Ehler married Andrew Munro.
85. Georgina Ehler married Otto Feltmate.
86. William Edmund Ehler married Elizabeth A. Williams.
87. Henrietta Ehler married Alfred Munro.
88. Minnie L. Ehler married Walter Anderson.
92. Margaret Ehler married James Daniels.
93. William Everett Ehler married Leonora Hendsbee.
97. Levi C. Ehler married Maud C. Hendsbee.
98. Charity Catherine Ehler married a Mr. Flynn.
99. Wallace Ehler married Florence McIsaac.
102. Mary Ehler married Ernest Scranton.

Fricke, Augustus. The first records of Christ Church were in the copper plate writing of Augustus Fricke. He was the first clerk of the Vestry. In addition he had many other offices at different times, being a Justice of the Peace, Deputy Sheriff, etc. He was in Guysborough as late as 1795. The rolls of the Regiment contain the name of his wife Alithea. Two children were born to them in Guysborough.

John George. Born 30 Oct. 1784.

Elizabeth. Born 12 Aug. 1786.

George, Justus. There are many corruptions of this name, which indeed seems originally to have been Gurgon or Jurgon. Also, Justice is sometimes used for Justus. It has been in the form given, that is, George, for many years. Justus George married Mary Ryder 24 Nov. 1795.

Family.

1. John. Born 6 Oct. 1796.
2. Mary. Born Sept. 1798.
3. Elizabeth. Born 2 Feb. 1804.
4. Henry. Born 19 June 1806.
5. Margaret. Born 28 Apr. 1808.
6. Dorothy. Born 21 Apr. 1811.
7. Marianne. Born 14 Nov. 1814.
8. Catherine. Born 9 Aug. 1817.
9. Valentine. Born 24 May 1820.
10. Thomas James. Born 11 Nov. 1825.
11. Martin.
12. Peter.

After the death of Justus George his wife married a Mr. Garland.

1. John George married Abigail Williams 11 Jan. 1825. She was born in 1803 and died 29 Apr. 1879.

Family.

13. Valentine. Born 13 Mar. 1826.
14. Elizabeth.
15. John. Born 10 Dec. 1828.
16. Daniel. Born 1830.
17. Eleanor. Born 24 Apr. 1838.
18. Jacob.
19. Martha Jane. Born 15 Dec. 1843.
20. Lydia.

21. Margaret.

2. Mary George married William Greencorn.

3. Elizabeth George married William Fitzgerald.

4. Henry George married Margaret Williams.   He died 4 Apr. 1871.

Family.

22. Abigail Eliza. Born 28 Apr. 1836.

23. Abigail Eliza. Born 3 May 1839.

24. Henry. Born 27 Sept. 1840.

25. Almira Catherine. Born 19 May 1842.

26. John Jacob. Born 6 May 1844.

27. Almira Catherine.   Born 9 July 1846.

28. Alexander David.   Born 24 Jan. 1850.

29. Alexander James. Born 15 Dec. 1851.

30. Simon Peter.   Born 25 Dec. 1851.

31. Margaret Elizabeth. Born 24 June 1859.

32. Harriet Letitia.   Born 23 July 1861.

5. Margaret George married James Harrigan 24 Nov. 1830.

6. Dorothy George married Henry Williams.

7. Marianne George married William Greencorn 8 Dec. 1831.

8. Catherine George married Joseph Armsworthy 21 Jan. 1834.

9. Valentine George married Ellen Ryan.

Family.

33. Mary Ann.

34. Joseph. Born 14 Apr. 1843.

35. Annie. Born 11 May 1845.

36. Catherine.   Born 2 Apr. 1850.

37. Elizabeth.   Born 18 Aug. 1852.

38. Abigail. Born 13 Jan. 1856.

39. John. Born 12 Aug. 1858.

40. Thomas. Born 9 May 1860.

41. Ellen. Born 14 July 1861.

42. Bridget. Born 6 June 1865.

10. Thomas James George married Annie Jamieson 1 Aug. 1852.

Family.

43. Rachel Catherine. Born 27 Aug. 1853.

44. Eleanor Elizabeth. Born 20 Aug. 1855.

11. Martin George married Abigail Dort 6 Dec. 1836.

Family.

45. Alexander Valentine. Born 1 Aug. 1838.

46. Christopher. Born 2 Feb. 1840.

47. Enos.

48. Phoebe.

49. Elizabeth.

12. Peter George married Charlotte Richardson 18 May 1828.

Family.

50. Ann. Born 26 May 1829.

51. Mary. Born Jan. 1830.

52. Peter. Born Jan. 1832.

53. Caroline Esther. Born 3 May 1836.

54. John. Born 19 July 1838.

55. Catherine. Born 14 Sept. 1840.

56. William Levi. Born 17" Oct. 1842.

57. Mary. Born 3 Oct. 1844.

58. Eliza. Born 8 March 1847.

59. Charlotte Elizabeth. Born 23 March 1850.

60. Margaret Jane. Born 29 May 1852.

13. Valentine George married Elizabeth Sneider 9 Mar. 1851.

Family.

61. James Valentine. Born 17 Dec. 1852.

62. Elizabeth Ann. Born June 1854.

63. Ephraim. Born 19 Apr. 1856.

64. John Charles. Born Apr. 1859.

65. Mary Abigail. Born 29 Dec. 1864.

66. Henry Augustus. Born 27 Mar. 1863.

67. Margaret Jane. Born 4 Apr. 1869.

68. Cecelia.

69. Lila.

15. John George married Margaret Armsworthy 7 May 1867.

Family.

    70. Martha Jane.

    71. Joseph. Born 22 July 1869.

    72. Martha Jane. Born 3 Nov. 1870.

16. Daniel George married first Rebecca Sceles 4 July 1852.

Family.

    73. Abigail Eliza. Born 25 Dec. 1853.

    74. Sophia Jane. Born 23 May 1855.

    75. Mary Elizabeth. Born 21 July 1857.

    76. John Levi. Born 22 May 1859.

    77. Mary Harriet. Born 18 Oct. 1861.

    78. Daniel S.

After the death of his first wife he married a widow named Price, 22 Jan. 1882. No family.

17. Eleanor George married Philip Dort.

18. Jacob George married first Mary George (No. 57) 23 Jan. 1872.

Family.

    79. Martin.

    80. Jacob.

    81. Currie.

He married second, Mary Ann Richardson.

19. Martha Jane George married Thomas Charles Dort 23 Jan. 1866.

20. Lydia or Adelaide George married Christian Dort 19 Dec. 1854.

21. Margaret George married Robert G. Jamieson 28 Mar. 1854.

23. Abigail Eliza George married first John Worth 17 Jan. 1860. She married second ? MacKenzie.

26. John Jacob George married first Margaret Jamieson. He married second, Margaret McVie.

27. Almira Catherine George married David Sneider 15 Jan. 1868.

30. Simon Peter George married Martha Armsworthy 19 Dec. 1881.

31. Margaret Elizabeth George married Robert Jamieson.

32. Harriet Letitia George married Henry George (No. 66.)

33. Mary Ann George married Arthur Keefe 19 Feb. 1873.

34. Joseph George married Hannah Elizabeth Ryter 13 Jan. 1876.

35. Annie George married Edward Doherty.

36. Catherine George married Thomas Greene.

37. Elizabeth George married Christopher Murphy 20 Jan. 1875.

38. Abigail George married Albert Dort.

39. John George married Mary Ann Jamieson.

40. Thomas George married Margaret Richards.

41. Ellen George married John Hines.

42. Bridget George married James Dort.

43. Rachel George married Levi Andrew Luddington 22 May 1875.

44. Eleanor Elizabeth George married B. Gerry.

45. Alexander Valentine George married Mary Jane Necoles.

46. Christopher George married Eliza Necoles.

47. Enos George married Ann Phelan.

48. Phoebe George married William Necoles.

49. Elizabeth George married William Carrigan.

50. Ann George married James McDuff 28 Aug. 1855.

52. Peter George married Sarah McDuff.

53. Caroline Esther George married Theodore Gerroir.

54. John George married Elizabeth Ann Marshall 25 June 1865.

56. William Levi George married first Angelina Williams. He married second, Widow Munro.

57. Mary George married Jacob George (No. 18.)

58. Eliza George married Joseph Uloth 8 Feb. 1867.

60. Margaret Jane George married John Samuel Uloth 13 Feb. 1871.

62. Elizabeth Ann George married ? Johnson.

63. Ephraim George married Janet Catherine Jamieson 17 Jan. 1882.

64. John Charles George married Abigail Jamieson.

65. Mary Abigail George married Robert Jamieson.

66. Henry Augustus George married Harriet Letitia George (No. 32.)

67. Margaret Jane George married James Doiron.

68. Cecelia George married Stewart Spanks.

73. Abigail Eliza George married Christopher Armsworthy 28 Jan. 1873.

74. Sophia Jane George married Reuben Munro.

75. Mary Elizabeth George married ? Crooks.

76. John Levi George married Emmeline Armsworthy.

78. Daniel S. George married Theresa Duncan.

Greencorn. The names of three Greencorns were on the roll of the Regiment, and there was one woman Elizabeth, and one child Jacob. No record has been found of Adam Greencorn. The name is probably a corruption of Krinkhorn. Unless one of those named Ludovic later took the name Nicholas, it is impossible to trace them. The large number of the name now living can be traced to a John Greencorn, whose wife was said to have been Mary Ryder. The relation of this John to those named on the roll can not be traced.

Hurst, Samuel. His wife's name, Elizabeth, is on the roll of the Regiment.

Family.

1. John.   Born 1781.

2. Hannah.   Born 2 Feb. 1785.

3. Mary.   Born 18 Mar. 1787.

4. Ann.   Born 13 May 1789.

5. Sophia.   Born 4 July 1793.

6. Lydia.   Born June 1796.

7. Susannah.

8. Elizabeth.

9. Sarah.

1. John Hurst married Mary Bedford 22 May 1804. He died 11 Sept. 1857.

Family.

10. Elizabeth.   Born 31 Oct. 1806.

11. Esther.   Born 17 Oct. 1809.

12. John.   Born 9 Nov. 1810.

13. Mary.   Born 26 Apr. 1814.

14. Ann.   Born 7 June 1817.

15. Laban (Levin).   Born 5 Dec. 1819.

16. Samuel.   Born 14 Sept. 1823.

17. William.   Born 25 May 1826.

18. Mahala.   Born 1 Jan. 1830.

19. Sarah.   Born 6 May 1836.

2. Hannah Hurst.   No record.

3. Mary Hurst married Stephen Diggedon 20 June 1809.

4. Ann Hurst married William Bedford 27 Nov. 1806.

5. Sophia Hurst married John Antoin Selv 5 Aug. 1811.

6. Lydia Hurst married Frederick Rhynold.

7. Susannah Hurst married John Nowland, Jr. 16 Nov. 1802..

8. Elizabeth Hurst married Samuel Deickhoff.

9. Sarah Hurst married John Hyde 13 Dec. 1797.

10. Elizabeth Hurst married Robert Sceles.

11. Esther Hurst married Elisha Demings.

12. John Hurst married Rachel Almira McPherson 14 Oct. 1833.

> Family.
>
> 20. Evan McPherson. Born 13 July 1834.
>
> 21. Eliza McPherson. Born 16 June 1836.
>
> 22. John Laban. Born 20 Dec. 1840.
>
> 23. Eliza Esther. Born 29 Nov. 1842.
>
> 24. Mary Mahala. Born 8 Apr. 1845.
>
> 25. Samuel Alexander. Bora 17 Sept. 1848.
>
> 26. Margaret Ann. Born 12 July 1851.
>
> 27. George William. Born 9 Jan. 1854.
>
> 28. Sarah Almira. Born 24 May 1856.

13. Mary Hurst married William Meades.

14. Ann Hurst married John Ehler 1835.

15. Laban (Levin) Hurst married Susan Sceles 26 Dec. 1843.

> Family.
>
> 29. Mary Elizabeth. Born 27 Jan. 1846.
>
> 30. John Robert. Born 12 Oct. 1848.
>
> 31. William McPherson. Born 22 Apr. 1851.
>
> 32. Margery Eleanor. Born 3 June 1854.
>
> 33. George Laban. Born 29 Aug. 1857.

16. Samuel Hurst married Diana Smith.

> Family.
>
> 34. George. Born 20 Mar. 1855.
>
> 35. Mary Isabella. Born 25 Aug. 1863.
>
> 36. Samuel. Born 6 Mar. 1864.
>
> 37. John B. Bapt. 21 Aug. 1866.
>
> 38. Eliza Olivia Gertrude. Born 15 Nov. 1872.
>
> 39. Evan McPherson. Married Maria Feltmate 15 Oct. 1881.

40. William E.   Married Eunice Weeks 4 Dec. 1880.

41. Jeremiah.

17. William Hurst married Bridget O'Donnell.

Family.

42. Mary.

43. Esther.

44. Bridget Ann.

18. Mahala Hurst married Thomas Carter.

19. Sarah Hurst married William Dobson 16 Jan. 1861.

20. Evan McPherson Hurst married Mary Jane Smith 1856.

21. John Laban Hurst married Matilda Horton 2 July 1863.

22. Eliza Esther Hurst married Thomas Henderson 14 Jan. 1873.

23. Mary Mahala Hurst married William Rhynold 5 Jan. 1871.

25. Samuel Alexander Hurst married Eliza Jane Diggedon 1 June 1868.

28. Sarah Almira Hurst married Enos Goodwin.

30. John Robert Hurst married first Adelaide Self 9 Feb. 1875. He married second Jane Lelacheur.

34. George Hurst married Margaret McDonald.

35. Mary Isabella Hurst married John McKenzie.

36. Samuel Hurst married Margaret Parker.

Jamieson, John. It is said that John Jamieson was attached to the regiment in some kind of instructional capacity. He was for many years very prominent in the community, and was the direct cause for three of his brothers, Kenneth, Hugh and Robert, coming to Nova Scotia from their home in Scotland. He died 17 Jan. 1842, aged 81. John Jamieson married Charlotte Morrison.

Family.

1. Robert. Born 9 Jan. 1785.

2. Jane. Born 30 July 1788.

3. Charity. Born 9 Jan. 1790.

4. Mary Elizabeth. Born 9 Oct. 1792.

5. Catherine. Born 4 May 1795.

6. John. Born 5 Mar. 1798.

7. Charlotte. Born 23 Nov. 1800.

8. Alexander. Born 16 Sept. 1803.

9. Jennet. Born 23 Feb. 1806.

10. Charlotte. Born 6 Jan. 1809.

11. William Alexander. Born 25 Feb. 1811.

1. Robert Jamieson married Ann Langille 6 Jan. 1807.

Family.

12. John. Born 23 Oct. 1807.

13. Robert Lee. Born 13 Mar. 1809.

14. Mary Ann. Born 6 Nov. 1810.

15. George. Born 10 Oct. 1812.

16. Susan Catherine. Born 2 Mar. 1815.

17. Charity. Born 22 July 1817.

18. David. Born 29 Jan. 1820.

After the death of Robert Jamieson, his widow married Kenneth Jamieson, who was her first husband's uncle.

2. Jane Jamieson married Patrick Delaney 6 Jan. 1807.

3. Charity Jamieson married Daniel Atkins 19 Dec. 1814.

4. Mary Elizabeth Jamieson married Robert Carr 24 Jan. 1813.

5. Catherine Jamieson married Henry Rider 2 Dec. 1815.

6. John Jamieson married Mary Jones 10 Feb. 1824.

Family.

19. Mary. Born 17 Mar. 1826.

20. John Patterson. Born 29 Oct. 1831.

21. Charlotte.

He married second Hannah Elizabeth Kirby 6 Dec. 1832.

Family.

22. Martha Elizabeth. Born 25 Dec. 1833.

23. John Charles. Born 3 May 1836.

24. William Alexander. Born 11 Feb. 1838.

25. David Robert. Born 7 Apr. 1840.

26. John Charles. Born 13 Feb. 1842.

27. Eunice Letitia. Born 9 Feb. 1844.

28. Joseph Thomas. Born 12 June 1845.

29. Eliza Jane.

30. Janet Wallace. Born 29 Apr. 1847.

9. Jennet Jamieson married James Carr 9 Mar. 1827.

12. John Jamieson married Mary Neal 24 Jan. 1844.

Family.

31. John James. Born 5 Dec. 1844.

32. Eliza Jane. Born 13 Sept. 1846.

33. Mary Ann. Born 11 Aug. 1847.

34. Margaret Elizabeth. Born 26 July 1849.

35. Eliza Jane. Born 8 Aug. 1851.

36. Nancy Jane. Born 15 Aug. 1853.

37. William David. Born 27 June 1855.

38. Robert George. Born 1 Apr. 1857.

39. Alexander. Born 31 July 1859.

40. Charity Caroline. Born 29 Aug. 1861.

41. Janet Almira. Born 5 Nov. 1863.

42. Charlotte Catherine. Born 4 Feb. 1866.

43. Eliza Abigail. Born 1 Aug. 1868.

14. Mary Ann Jamieson married John Kirby 9 Jan. 1833.

15. George Jamieson married Caroline Myers 9 Jan. 1834.

Family.

44. Robert James. Born 14 Sept. 1834.

45. George David. Born 26 June 1836.

46. Mary Ann. Born 12 Apr. 1836.

47. Charlotte Elizabeth. Born 13 Dec. 1842.

48. Charity.

49. Janet Caroline. Born 25 Feb. 1849.

17. Charity Jamieson married Valentine Dort.

19. Mary Jamieson married Charles W. Taylor.

20. John Patterson Jamieson married Janet E. Delaney 20 Sept. 1859. He died 17 Sept. 1871.

Family.

50. William Alexander. Born 26 Nov. 1860.

51. John Patrick. Born 25 Mar. 1863.

52. Harriet L. Born 5 Dec. 1865.

53. Armenia Jane. Born 18 Apr. 1867.

54. Joseph Thomas. Born 20 Sept. 1870.

418

He married second, Nancy Shrider (widow)   11 Aug. 1874.

21. Charlotte Jamieson married John Myers 10 Mar. 1846.

22. Martha Elizabeth Jamieson married W. G. Scott 1 Feb. 1855.

26. John Charles Jamieson married Martha Ehler 22 Dec. 1869.

27. Eunice Letitia Jamieson married Thorndyke Whitney 3 Apr. 1867.

29. Eliza Jane Jamieson married Christian Ehler 17 Sept. 1868.

30. Janet Wallace Jamieson married first, John Kirby, and second Thomas Whitney.

31. John James Jamieson married Mary Ann Jamieson (No. 46) 4 Feb. 1876.

32. Eliza Jane Jamieson died unmarried.

33. Mary Ann Jamieson married Peter Williams 24 Jan. 1871.

34. Margaret Elizabeth Jamieson married John Jacob George 25 Jan. 1871.

36. Nancy Jane Jamieson married Sidney Grover.

37. William David Jamieson married Elizabeth Shrader 29 Jan. 1880.

39. Alexander Jamieson married Cynthia Feltmate.

40. Charity Caroline Jamieson married Ira Dort 6 Sept. 1882.

41. Janet Almira Jamieson married ? Hendsbee.

42. Charlotte Catherine Jamieson married William Peart.

44. Robert James Jamieson married Catherine Ehler.

45. George David Jamieson married Esther Ehler 16 Jan. 1867.

46. Mary Ann Jamieson married (No. 31) John James Jamieson 4 Feb. 1876.

47. Charlotte Elizabeth Jamieson married Philip Webber 29 Apr. 1868.

48. Charity Jamieson married James J. Gammon.

Joppe (or Joppy), Ludovic. His wife, Jane, accompanied him. No reference to any family has been found. Nor has there been found the dates of death of either Joppy or his wife. For a number of years he attended to the medical needs of the community, though it is possible that he was not a physician. It is said that he is buried in the private burying ground on the old Hadley (now Porter) place across the harbour.

Lowry (or Laurie), James. According to the Church Records, his wife's name was Lettie. The regimental rolls refer to her as Henrietta. There are records of two children.

George.   Born 29 Jan. 1785.

John Ernest James.   Born 1789.

George Lowry married Elizabeth Fraser 10 Apr. 1810, and there are records of at least two children.

Muller, Christian. His wife was Ann Francheville, the marriage taking place in Halifax before the Regiment went to Chedabucto. There was no family. He died in March 1841, aged 90 years, and she died 2 Aug. 1846, aged 82.

Myers, Charles. There were three persons named Myers - Charles, Ferdinand and George. Their relationship, if any existed, has not been determined. Charles Myers married Panthea Hart.

Family.

1. Lydia Moss. Born 1 Jan. 1797.
2. Abigail. Born 6 Apr. 1799.
3. Charles. Born 8 Oct. 1801.
4. Ferdinand. Born 16 Feb. 1812.
5. Ithiel. Born 17 Nov. 1813.
6. Irad. Born 8 June 1816.
7. Abner. Born 1800.
8. Lothrop.

1. Lydia Moss Myers married Archibald Henderson 23 Apr. 1818.
3. Charles Myers married Bridget Jane Ross 18 Feb. 1833.

Family.

9. Panthea.
10. Daniel Josiah.
11. Charles.

7. Abner Myers married Christina Lawson 7 Feb. 1825.
   He died 9 July 1874, and his wife died 2 Dec. 1870.

Family.

12. Charles William. Born Dec. 1826.
13. Isaac. Born 20 July 1828.
14. Panthea. Born 2 July 1829.
15. Abner. Born 5 June 1831.
16. Joseph. Born 5 June 1833.
17. James Henry. Born 27 Apr. 1835.
18. Jane Lawson. Born 14 May 1837.
19. Irad Ferdinand. Born 27 Aug. 1839.
20. Christina. Born 23 Mar. 1842.

8. Lothrop Myers married Mary Pyle 14 Feb. 1836.

Family.

21. Philomela. Born 30 Aug. 1837.

22. Panthea Jane. Born 31 May 1839.

23. Elizabeth. Born 11 Mar. 1842.

24. Caroline. Born 25 May 1844.

25. Lothrop James. Born 25 Apr. 1846.

26. Amelia.

27. Irad William.

He married second Ellen Hadiey.

Family.

28. John.

29. Hartley.

9. Panthea Myers married Francis Brown.

10. Daniel Josiah Myers married Victoria Simpson 23 Dec. 1868.

Family.

Charles Howard. Born 18 Apr. 1870.

Laura Theresa. Born 18 Dec. 1872.

13. Isaac Myers married Catherine Maria Hadley 31 Dec. 1850.

Family.

30. Martha Maria. Born 10 Jan. 1852.

31. John Henry. Born 13 Dec. 1855.

32. Abner Smith. Bapt. 22 Mar. 1857.

33. Christina Jane. Born 18 May 1859.

34. Margaret Frances. Born 19 Sept. 1861.

35. Joseph Hemmeon. Born 15 Sept. 1863.

36. Sarah.

37. Panthea. Born 20 Jan. 1867.

38. Isaac Thurlow. Born 4 Oct. 1870.

14. Panthea Myers married a Mr. Rogers in Gloucester.

15. Abner Myers married Margaret McKeough 1 Aug. 1855. He died 15 Apr. 1866. His widow married William O'Brien 27 Feb. 1868.

Family.

39. Christy Ann. Born 19 Apr. 1857.

40. John J. McKeough. Born 1 Apr. 1859.

41. Irad.

42. Maria Emma.   Born 9 Oct. 1863.

43. Lillian Maria.   Born 6 Dec. 1865.

16. Joseph Myers died young.

17. James Henry Myers married Sarah Hadiey, 1859.

22. Panthea Jane Myers married ? Mackintosh.

23. Elizabeth Myers married Charles Hart.

25. Lothrop James Myers married Sarah Partridge.

26. Amelia Myers married Andrew Hall.

27. Irad William Myers married Catherine Amelia McKay 9 Jan. 1877.

28. John Myers married Margaret Crescine.

30. Martha Maria Myers married a Mr. Hicks.

31. John Henry Myers married Caroline Jemima O'Hara 12 Jan. 1881.

32. Abner Myers married Sarah McMaster.

33. Christina Jane Myers married Charles Hadley 22 Dec. 1880.

35. Joseph Hemmeon Myers married a Miss Gosbee.

37. Panthea Myers married a Mr. Huse in Lowell, Mass.

39. Christy Ann Myers married Heber Keay.

40. John J. McKeough Myers married Margery McMaster.
    After his death she married Thomas Hadley.

41. Irad Myers married Kate Penny.

42. Maria Emma Myers married John A. MacMaster.

43. Lillian Myers married John Ellis MacMaster. After his death she married Hugh Cummings.

Myers, Ferdinand.   He married Mary Langille 9 Aug. 1790.

Family.

1. Elizabeth.   Born 23 June 1791.

2. George Adam.   Born 8 Aug. 1793.

3. Mary.   Born 12 Dec. 1795.

4. Catherine.   Born 18 Feb. 1798.

5. Margaret.   Born 25 Dec. 1799.

6. John Ferdinand.   Born 19 Feb. 1804.

7. David Lee Robert.   Born 19 Oct. 1805.

1. Elizabeth Myers married William Horton 10 May 1810.

2. George Adam Myers married Elizabeth Bedford 30 Aug. 1814.

Family.

    8. Levin John. Born 4 July 1815.

    9. John Ferdinand. Born 7 Apr. 1817.

  10. Mary Esther. Born 18 July 1818.

  11. William Adam. Born 19 Dec. 1825.

  12. George.

  13. Enos. Born 1823. Died 31 Mar. 1867.

3. Mary Myers married Alexander Horton 11 Mar. 1817.

4. Catherine Myers married John Ehler.

6. John Ferdinand Myers married first Martha Kirby, second Charlotte Jamieson.

12. George Myers married Sarah Dobson 11 June 1851.

Myers, Charles. He married Mary Rheinholt 4 Apr. 1802.

Family.

1. Anna. Born 24 Mar. 1803.

2. Charles. Born 8 Apr. 1806.

3. Elizabeth. Born 27 Sept. 1807.

4. Caroline Susannah. Born 7 Mar. 1811.

Reuter, Henry. This name appears in a number of spellings, and is now Rider, Ryder or Ryter. He was married previous to his arrival at Chedabucto, his wife's name being Dorothy, and there was one child, Maria. In a letter sent home to Siegen, Westphalia, Reuter tells of his marriage, the birth and death of his first child (Jacob, named for his father-in-law Jacob Busch), the birth of Maria and his hopes for a future in Nova Scotia.

Family.

1. Maria.

2. Hannah. Born 15 July 1786.

3. Elizabeth. Born 6 Feb. 1789.

4. John Henry. Born 14 Mar. 1792.

5. Dorothy. Born 4 Mar. 1794.

6. Margaret. Born 7 Sept. 1796.

7. Kitty. Born 1 Mar. 1799.

8. Valentine. Born 14 May 1801.

9. Abigail. Born 20 Jan. 1803.

10. Susan.

11. Alexander.

2. Hannah Ryder married William Horton 26 Jan. 1813.

3. Elizabeth Ryter married Christian Dort 8 Jan. 1824.

4. John Henry Ryter married Catherine Jamieson 5 Dec. 1815.

Family.

12. Mary Elizabeth. Born 17 Mar. 1818.

13. Valentine. Born 8 Mar. 1820.

14. Dorothy. Born 19 May 1822.

15. Charlotte. Born 3 Aug. 1825.

16. Abigail. Born 26 Jan. 1830.

17. Margaret. Born 9 Apr. 1832.

5. Dorothy Ryter married Ambrose Horton 27 Dec. 1814.

7. Kitty Ryter married John Dort 21 Dec. 1824.

9. Abigail Ryter married Patrick Connell 13 July 1830.

10. Susan Ryter married John McDonald 23 Aug. 1825.

11. Alexander Ryter married Catherine Connell, a daughter of Patrick Connell's by a former wife.

Family.

18. William.

19. Thomas.

20. Mary.

21. Ludlow.

22. Eliza.

12. Mary Elizabeth Ryter married George Armsworthy 26 July 1837.

13. Valentine Ryter married Ann Henline 15 Jan. 1847. He died 8 Feb. 1872.

Family.

23. George Henry. Born 27 Jan. 1848.

24. Margaret Catherine. Born 4 Mar. 1849.

25. Hannah Eliza. Born 23 May 1854.

26. John Valentine. Born 1 Jan. 1856.

27. Freeman Fraser. Born 14 Mar. 1861.

28. Levi.

29. Letitia.

14. Dorothy Ryter married William Meads 27 May 1845.

15. Charlotte Ryter married John Munro.

16. Abigail Ryter married Anthony Rheinold 23 Dec. 1875.

18. William Ryter married Jane Knowlan.

20. Mary Ryter married John James Ehler.

Rheinhold, Casper (or John Casper). This name has been much corrupted and is usually now spelt Rhynold. The name of his wife Ann is on the Roll of the Regiment. She was Ann Lowry, sister of James Lowry, battalion mate of Casper. He married her during his storm forced stay at Falmouth, England. Adam Uloth, also of the Regiment, acted as witness to the marriage. It is interesting that the two brothers-in-law drew joining 300 acre lots at Peasbrook and no town lots.

Family

1. Mary. Born 19 Feb. 1785.

2. Ann. Born 7 Sept. 1787.

3. Elizabeth. Born 13 Dec. 1788.

4. William Frederick. Born 31 Aug. 1790.

5. Jasper. Born 13 Aug. 1795.

6. Susannah. Bapt. 23 Aug. 1796.

7. John Gleason. Born 1 July 1798.

8. William. Born 29 Oct. 1799.

9. Frederick.

1. Mary Rheinhold married first George Myers 4 April 1802, and after his death married George Tanner 5 Dec. 1814. She died 7 Jan. 1870.

2. Ann Rheinhold married James Harrigan 2 Aug. 1802. She died 7 Jan. 1870.

3. Elizabeth Rheinhold married Louis Uloth 14 Aug. 1809. Died 10 Feb. 1870.

   (The record tell of these three sisters who were all residents of Cole Harbour and who died within a month of each other.)

4. William Frederick Rheinhold married Anna Sceles 14 Dec. 1819.

6. Susannah Rheinhold married George Shrader 2 Jan. 1815.

7. John Gleason Rheinhold married Catherine MacKenzie 2 Nov. 1816.

Family

10. Nancy Eleanor. Born 12 Aug. 1818.

9. Frederick Rheinhold married Lydia Hurst. She died 19 Dec. 1871.

Family

11. Casper John. Born 28 Dec. 1814.

12. William. Born 23 April 1835. Married Mary Mahala Hurst.

13. George Tanner. Born 27 May 1830.

14. Frederick. Born 29 April 1838.

15. Anthony. Born 27 Nov. 1841. He married first, Abigail Ryder 23 Dec. 1875. Second wife, Esther snow 22 Jan. 1874.

16. Lydia Ann. Born 19 Sept. 1844.

11. Casper John Rheinhold married Isabella Decoff 8 May 1843.

Family

17. Esther Catherine. Born 4 Dec. 1844.

18. Nancy Jane. Born 10 Oct. 1846.

19. Mary Elizabeth. Born 5 July 1850.

20. Alexander. Born 1853, married Abigail Nowlan 10 May 1873.

Sartorius, Valentine (Walter). His wife's name was Eliza, and they were married on their arrival in Chedabucto. She was the second daughter of Jacob Brusch (Busch) and the younger sister of Dorothy Reuter. There was one child under ten years of age, Ludovic.

Family.

1. Ludovic.

2. Jacob.

3. Elizabeth. Born 19 Sept. 1788.

4. Abigail. Born 11 July 1791 (Posthumous).

Valentine Sartorius died in 1791. His wife married second Peter Wendell.

2. Jacob Sartorius married Elizabeth Feltmate 18 July 1809.

Family.

5. Jacob Valentine. Born 6 Sept. 1810.

6. Jacob. Born 2 Jan. 1813.

7. Mary Elizabeth. Born 28 Oct. 1815.

8. James Crawford. Born 1 Apr. 1818.

3. Elizabeth Sartorius married Christian Dort 25 Aug. 1806.

4. Abigail Sartorius married Christian Ehler 16 July 1811.

Sneider, John, Junior. His wife's name was Elizabeth.

Family.

1. Christian. Born 11 July 1794.

2. Eve. Born 13 Aug. 1797.

3. Susanna. Born 22 Sept. 1799.

4. Elizabeth. Born 18 Feb. 1801.

5. John David. Born 17 Dec. 1806.

6. Catherine. Born 11 Mar. 1803.

Elizabeth Sneider, widow, married James McVeigh 4 Sept. 1811.

1. Christian Sneider married Sarah Dort 23 Mar. 1818.

Family.

7. John George. Born 17 Jan. 1820.

8. Elizabeth. Bapt. 18 July 1822.

9. Christian. Born 5 Oct. 1822.

10. Margaret. Born 14 Aug. 1824.

11. James Valentine. Born 24 Nov. 1826.

12. Sarah. Born 20 Feb. 1829.

13. Jacob. Born 4 Dec. 1830.

14. Elizabeth. Born Apr. 1833.

15. Sarah Susanna. Born 29 Nov. 1836.

16. David. Born 26 May 1839.

17. Catherine. Born 29 Apr. 1841.

18. William Charles. Born 10 July 1843.

19. James Joseph. Born 9 Apr. 1846.

20. Abigail.

2. Eve Sneider married Valentine Dort 18 Dec. 1813.

3. Susanna Sneider married Peter Dort 20 Dec. 1817.

4. Elizabeth Sneider married Edward Dobbins 22 Mar. 1819.

5. John David Sneider married Mary or Marianne Dort 24 Aug. 1830.

Family.

21. Elizabeth Ann. Born 25 Nov. 1832. He died 28 Apr. 1839.

9. Christian Sneider married Mary Ann Connell, widow, 2 May 1853.

10. Margaret Sneider married Robert Cox 10 Nov. 1846.

11. James Valentine Sneider married a Miss Mosher.

12. Sarah Sneider married a Mr. Bennett.

14. Elizabeth Sneider married Valentine George 9 Dec. 1851.

15. Sarah Susanna Sneider married John Sneider.

16. David Sneider married Catherine George 15 Jan. 1868.

17. Catherine Sneider married Henry Bohn or Bond 29 July 1856.

18. William Charles Sneider married a Miss Brown.

20. Abigail Sneider married Frank Bohn or Bond.

(This is by no means a complete record. The name has now become corrupted to Snyder.)

Stafford, Oliver. His wife's name was Mary and one child, Katherine, was born 5 June 1785. There is no other record.

Stropel (or Strople), George. His wife's name was Mary or Maria, the latter being that which appears on the Roll of the Regiment. The name of one child, George, also appears on the Roll. The father was drowned in May 1814.

Family.

1. George. Born 1783.
2. William. Born 14 March 1786.

1. George Strople, also called John George Strople, married Catherine Furtel Jan. 16, 1806. She died 24 May 1873, aged 89.

Family.

3. Mary. Born 28 Feb. 1807.
4. Catherine. Born 6 Dec. 1809.
5. Hannah. Born 12 Sept. 1813.
6. John George. Born 2 Oct. 1815.
7. William Henry. Born 13 Oct. 1819.
8. Catherine Ann. Born 7 June 1822.
9. George William. Bapt. 22 July 1822.
10. Thomas Robert. Born 1 Feb. 1827.

2. William Strople married Esther Atwater 26 Aug. 1807.

Family.

11. George Henry. Born 15 Oct. 1808.
12. Sarah Amelia. Born 28 Oct. 1810.
13. Rufus William. Born 27 Mar. 1813.
14. Elisha Randall. Born 14 July 1815.
15. James William. Born 22 Feb. 1818.
16. John Alexander. Born 17 Sept. 1820.
17. William Alexander. Bapt. 22 Oct. 1820.
18. Joseph Luman. Born Feb. 1824.
19. Marianne Annabelle. Born 13 July 1828.
20. Esther. Born 28 Oct. 1833.

3. Mary Strople married David Bowles 29 Oct. 1829.
5. Hannah Strople married Samuel Decoff 24 Apr. 1832.

6. John George Strople married Mary Elizabeth Henderson 20 Dec. 1842.

Family.

21. John Henry.

22. George Robert.

23. Philomela Adelaide.   Born 2 Apr. 1853.

24. Elida Lucinda.   Born 23 Feb. 1865.

25. Ada.

26. Marjory.

27. Ann.

28. Mary.

(The above are not in order of birth, Marjory being the eldest of the family.)

7. William Henry Strople married Hannah MacKenzie 15 Jan. 1839.

Family.

29, George Henry.   Born 16 Dec. 1839.

30. Asa MacKenzie.   Born 19 Apr. 1841.

31. Elisha William.   Born 2 Apr. 1843.

32. Mary Annabel.   Born 26 Oct. 1845.

33. Susan Elizabeth.   Born 20 Apr. 1848.

34. John Alexander.   Born 22 Aug. 1850.

35. James Robert.   Born 27 Feb. 1853.

36. Ann Delilah.   Born 5 Mar. 1855.

37. Donald Joseph.   Born 11 Apr. 1857.

8. Catherine Ann Strople married John D. Henderson 13 Dec. 1853.

10. Thomas Robert Strople married Hannah Maria Callahan. She died 30 Mar. 1865.

Family.

38. Caroline.

11. George Henry Strople married Grace Bowles 31 May 1832. He died 15 June 1870.

Family.

39. William.   Born 12 Nov. 1838.

40. Robert Bowles.   Born 8 Jan. 1841.

41. George Henry.   Born 29 May 1843.

42. John Alexander.   Born 3 Mar. 1846.

43. Harriet Grace. Born 6 June 1851.

44. Rebecca.

14. Elisha Randall Strople married Ruth Cunningham.

15. James William Strople married Harriet Simons.

16. John Alexander Strople married Jane Giles.

19. Marianna Annabella Strople married Joseph Randall.

21. John Henry Strople married Elizabeth Aikins, widow, 9 Dec. 1871.

22. George Robert Strople married Charity Jane Aikins 9 Dec. 1873.

23. Philomela Adelaide Strople married Alfred Frank Jones 3 June 1876.

24. Elida Lucinda Strople died 25 Feb. 1865.

25. Ada Strople married Jerry Jones.

26. Marjory Strople.   No record.

27. Ann Strople.   No record.

28. Mary Strople.   No record.

29. George Henry Strople married Ann MacDonnell 18 June 1865.

Family.

45. George H.   Born 17 Dec. 1867.

46. Grace.   Born 8 Mar. 1870.

47. Blanche Harriet)

48. Eveline.   ) Twins.   Born 20 July 1872.

49. Preston.   Born 4 Sept. 1875.

30. Asa MacKenzie Strople married Mary Ferguson Grant.
She died Jan. 19, 1866.

Family.

50. Mary H.   Born 13 Jan. 1866.

He married second, Jane Ferguson 25 Jan. 1867.

Family.

51. Daniel F.   Born 4 Apr. 1868.

52. Ann Abigail.

53. Hannah Maria.   Born 29 July 1876.

He married third, Margaret Ann Ferguson 14 Jan. 1881.

31. Elisha William Strople married Sarah Sophia Grant 1865.

Family.

54. Lewis Havelock.   Born 17 Apr. 1867.

32. Mary Annabel Strople married Thomas Johnson.

33. Susan Elizabeth Strople married Peter Lawson.

34. John Alexander Strople married Elizabeth Morris 1872.

Family.

55. Clara. Born 15 Sept. 1876.

35. James Robert Strople married Mary Eliza Lipsett 28 Sept. 1875.

36. Ann Delilah Strople married James Robert Andrews 17 Aug. 1875.

37. Donald Joseph Strople. No record.

38. Caroline Strople married Steven Myers 24 Apr. 1882.

39. William Strople. No record.

40. Robert Bowles Strople. No record.

41. George Henry Strople. No record.

42. John Alexander Strople married Carrie Redmond 23 Jan. 1875.

43. Harriet Grace Strople married Henry Stephen MacPherson 24 April 1875.

Uloth, Adam. He was married on his arrival in Chedabucto, and there was one child, Louis (Lewis) born in 1780. There is no record of other children. His wife's name, according to the roll of the Regiment, was Catherine.

Family.

1. Lewis. Born 1780.

1. Lewis Uloth married Elizabeth Rheinhold 14 Aug. 1809.

Family.

2. Adam Casper. Born 1 Apr. 1813.

3. John James. Born 24 May 1815.

4. Eliza Jane. Born 23 Apr. 1817.

5. Frederick. Born 15 Oct. 1819.

6. George.

7. Amelia Ann. Born 2 Nov. 1831.

2. Adam Casper Uloth married Grace Feltmate 14 Jan. 1838.

Family.

8. Adam Casper. Born 30 Nov. 1838.

9. Elizabeth Ann. Born 20 Nov. 1840.

10. Sarah Jane. Born 15 Aug. 1842.

11. John Samuel. Born 1849.

12. Susanna Maria. Born 12 Aug. 1856.

13. Joseph.

14. James.

15. Mary Elizabeth.

16. Martha.

3. John James Uloth married Abigail Ehler 15 Jan. 1839.   She died 24 May 1875. No family.

4. Eliza Jane Uloth married Stephen Diggedon.

5. Frederick Uloth married first Elizabeth Luddington 30 Jan. 1842.

Family.

17. Mary Ann.   Born 2 Feb. 1843.

18. Emmeline Elizabeth.

19. William.

20. Henry Allen.

21. George.

22. John James.

He married second, Mary Ann Sangster, who died 15 Oct. 1872.

Family.

23. Adam Casper.   Born 4 Dec. 1860.

24. Caroline.

He married third, Mary Gray Henderson 12 May 1873.

Family.

25. Esther.

He married fourth, Mary Isabella Cummings.

6. George Uloth married Ann or Nancy Harrigan 30 Jan. 1843.

Family.

26. Eliza Sophia.   Born 12 Jan. 1844.

27. Abigail.

28. Maria.

29. Phoebe Elizabeth.   Born 25 Apr. 1849.

30. Albert.

31. Mary Drucilla.

32. George Adam.   Born 5 Oct. 1856.

33. Lewis.

7. Amelia Ann Uloth married Samuel Feltmate.

9. Elizabeth Ann Uloth married John Fitzgerald.

10. Sarah Jane Uloth married Andrew Haley.

11. John Samuel Uloth married Margaret Jane George 13 Feb. 1871.

Family.

    34. Lola Belle.

    35. Minnie.

    36. Bessie.

    37. Albert.

13. Joseph Uloth married Eliza George 8 Feb. 1867.   No family.

14. James Uloth married Mahala Duncan 10 Jan. 1872.

Family.

    38. Abraham.

15. Mary Elizabeth Uloth married Samuel Feltmate 9 May 1849.

16, Martha Uloth married Edward Munro 24 Oct. 1871.

17. Mary Ann Uloth married William Munro.

18. Emmeline Elizabeth Uloth, who died 5 Mar. 1868, married William George Myers 3 Jan. 1868.

19. William Uloth married Frances Sangster 22 May 1874.

Family.

    39. Leonora.

    40. Lilla.

    41. Bertha.

    42. Milton G.

    43. Nina.

20. Henry Uloth married first, Elizabeth Ann Webber 10 Jan. 1877, and second, Mary Jane Fitzgerald.

Family.

    44. Martha.

    45. Richard.

    46. Frederick.

    47. Covert.

22. John James Uloth married Lavinia Caroline Webber 11 Oct. 1880.

Family.

    48. William F.

    49. Charles.

    50. Walter.

    51. Gilbert.

23. Adam Casper Uloth married Elizabeth Dort.

52. Lewis.

53. Leslie.

54. Cleveland.

55. Sylvester.

25. Esther Uloth married William M. Munro.

27. Abigail Uloth married Thomas A. Grover 27 Oct. 1866.

28. Maria Uloth married George O'Neill 12 Feb. 1873.

30. Phoebe Elizabeth Uloth married E. C. Lumsden 28 Mar. 1872.

31. Mary Drucilla Uloth married Jeremiah Freeman Lumsden 1 Jan. 1876.

32. George Adam Uloth married Catherine Williams 21 Feb. 1876.

Family.

56. Edward,

57. Albert.

35. Minnie Uloth married Thurlow Munro.

37. Bessie Uloth married Henry Williams.

38. Abraham Uloth married Charity Fanning.

39. Leonora Uloth married George Manthorn.

40. Lilla Uloth married Rev. F. P. Dresser.

41. Bertha Uloth married Charles Clarke.

42. Milton G. Uloth married Alice O'Hara.

43. Nina Uloth married Tupper Davison.

44. Martha Uloth married Havelock Munro.

45. Richard Uloth married a Miss Knowlan.

46. Frederick Uloth married Winifred Munro.

SAINT AUGUSTINE SETTLERS.

	Acres		Acres
*Agnew, Elizabeth	100	North, Thomas	150
*Barnell, William (Barnett)	100	*Ogilvie, John	100
*Beazley, Jacob	100	*Ogilvie, Peter	100
*Bird, Robert (Byrd)	100	*Panton, Timothy	150
Campbell, George	100	*Pinkney, George	100
Carter, Joseph	400	Proctor, Benjamin	150
*Cook, Ralph	150	Proctor, James	150
*Dorsey, George	100	Read, William	300
Fox, Thomas	100	Reeves, James	100
*Fryermouth, Adam	250	Reynolds, Ann	350
George, William	100	*Robson, Andrew	100
*Gottney, Isaac	100	Rogers, Joseph	450
Higgins, William	350	Scott, Samuel	300
Hunt, Matterson	350	*Sloane, Robert	100
Johns, Henry (Jones)	250	*Smith, Samuel	100
*King, George	300	*Smith, Thomas	100
*King, John	100	*Snellock, Thomas	100
*King, Sterling	100	*Spangs, George	100
Lyle, James	250	*Todd, John	450
*Magee, James	100	*Tucker, William	100
Martin, David	100	*Walsh, David (Welsh)	100
Matterson, John	150	*Wilkins, Abraham	100
*Mayer, William	400	*Willson, John	100
*McDonald, Archibald	250		
*McNeighton, Alexander	200		

(Concerning those marked with a (*) little or no record has been found. None of these received a town plot.)

Agnew, Elizabeth. No record beyond that of her arrival in the settlement.
Beazley, Jacob. No record.
Carter, Joseph. His wife's name was Rhoda or Rosamond.

Family.

1. Richard. Born in 1771.

2. Susanna. Born 18 Dec. 1778.

3. Joseph.

4. George Bruce. Born 9 Oct. 1786.

5. Sarah. Born 22 Oct. 1789.

6. Lydia. Born 30 Apr. 1792.

7. Temperance.

8. John.

9. Robert.

10. Elizabeth.

1. Richard Carter died 20 Jan. 1848, aged 77. Wife's name, Bridget.

Family.

11. Joseph. Born 10 Aug. 1795.

12. Edward. Bapt. 15 Apr. 1799.

13. Richard Woodson. Born 20 June 1806.

14. Richard. Born 4 June 1808.

15. John.

2. Susanna Carter married David Martin.

3. Joseph Carter married Esther ?

Family.

16. Richard. Born 4 July 1805.

17. Robert. Born 8 Oct. 1817.

4. George Bruce Carter married Sarah ?

Family.

18. Elizabeth. Born 20 Jan. 1802.

19. George Bruce. Born 5 Aug. 1803.

20. James. Born 17 Dec. 1804.

21. Catherine. Born 17 Apr. 1806.

22. Mary Caroline. Born 29 Nov. 1811.

23. Robert. Born 3 May 1813.

24. John. Born 28 May 1818.

25. Naomi. Born 10 Oct. 1820.

26. Lydia Rebecca. Born 11 Dec. 1827.

27. Zimri.

28. Patrick.

29. Maria.

30. Levi.

(There were 19 children in all in this family. Robert, John and Zimri were drowned in the August Gale of 1873.)

5. Sarah Carter.   No record.

6. Lydia Carter married James Lyle.

7. Temperance Carter married James Reeves.

8. John Carter married Elizabeth Snow 13 Jan. 1822.

Family.

Thomas William. Born 27 Oct. 1824.

Susanna Catherine Eleanor. Born 30 Oct. 1822.

James Henry. Born 27 Dec. 1826.

Married second, Mary Ann   ?

Maria. Born 18 Aug. 1837.

James. Born 4 Sept. 1839.

Sarah Bridget. Born 27 Sept. 1841.

Mary Ann. Born 25 Dec. 1843.

Elizabeth Catherine. Born 27 Jan. 1846.

9. Robert Carter married Mary   ?

Family.

31. Margaret Jane. Born 7 Aug. 1827.

32. Marianne. Born 17 Oct. 1829.

33. John. Born 26 Dec. 1831.

34. Sarah Rebecca. Born 12 Aug. 1836.

35. James. Born 23 Aug. 1823.

36. Robert Bruce. Born 12 Feb. 1839.

37. George Richard. Born 1 Dec. 1844.

38. Alexander.

14. Richard Carter married Elizabeth Bigsby.

Family.

39. George William. Born 25 Apr. 1829.

40. Richard Henry. Born 14 Apr. 1837.

41. James Edmund or Edward. Born 22 May 1839.

42. Eliza Jane. Born 18 Nov. 1841. Died 26 Dec. 1847.

43. Rachel Ann. Born 30 Apr. 1844.

44. Alexander. Born 13 Nov. 1846.

15. John Carter married Mary Maguire.

Family.

    45. Maria. Born 18 Aug. 1837.

    46. James. Born 4 Sept. 1839.

    47. Sarah Bridget. Born 27 Sept. 1841.

    48. Mary Ann. Born 25 Dec. 1843.

    49. Elizabeth Catherine. Born 27 Jan. 1846.

18. Elizabeth Carter married Thomas Johnson 4 Feb. 1828.

20. James Carter married Effy Matterson 14 Aug. 1829.

Family.

    50. Sarah Jane. Born 27 Aug. 1830.

    51. Daniel. Born 11 Mar. 1832.

21. Catherine Carter married John Carr.

22. Mary Caroline Carter married George Whittendale.

23. Robert Carter married Sarah Hadley.

24. John Carter married Janet Carr 7 Feb. 1848.

27. Zimri Carter married Catherine Ehler 21 Dec. 1830.

Family.

    52. John James. Born 30 Nov. 1837.

    53. Robert Daniel. Born 5 Feb. 1840.

    54. Zimri Patrick. Born 2 May 1841.

    55. Levi. Born 31 Jan. 1843.

    56. Elizabeth Rebecca. Born 26 Sept. 1846.

30. Levi Carter married Susan Martin 16 Feb. 1857.

Fox, Thomas. Wife's name Elizabeth.

Family.

    1. Thomas.

    2. John.

    3. Alexander.

    4. Charles.

    5. Robert.

    6. Philip. Born 30 June 1807.

    7. Jane.

1. Thomas Fox. No record.

2. John Fox married Christina Cummings 4 Aug. 1823.

Family.

      8. Margery Elizabeth.   Born 7 Oct. 1824.

      9. Christina McMullen.   Born 19 Apr. 1829.

   10. Isabella Jane.   Born 26 Feb. 1831.

   11. Alexander.   Born 19 May 1826.

   12. Hannah.

3. Alexander Fox married Mary McMullen.

Family.

   13. William.   Born 2 Oct. 1835.

   14. Rebecca Miriam.   Born 21 Sept. 1837.

   15. Elizabeth Jane.   Born 23 Oct. 1840.

   16. John James.   Born 14 Sept. 1842.

   17. Martha Pamela.   Bapt. 31 Aug. 1845.

   18. Robert.

   19. Philip,

 4. Charles Fox married ?   McLean.

 6. Philip Fox married

 7. Jane Fox married John Carew.

 8. Margaret Elizabeth Fox married Dave McMaster.

10. Isabella Jane Fox married ?   Wilkinson.

12. Hannah Fox married John Wesley Bruce, 1865.

George, William.   Married Africa Rogers.

Family.

   1. William. Born 3 Feb. 1795.

   2. Farriby.   Born 22 Dec. 1797.

   3. Joseph.   Born 6 Mar. 1798.

   4. Mary.   Born 11 July 1801.

   5. Thomas.   Born 17 Nov. 1803.

   6. Needham.   Born 29 Oct. 1805.

No other records of this family have been found.

Higgins, William. His wife's name was Hannah. They were married on their arrival in the settlement, and there were two children, James and Reuben over the age of ten, and one, Sarah, under ten.

Family.

1. James.
2. Reuben.
3. John.
4. Eleanor.
5. Mary.
6. Sarah.
7. Henry. Born 3 Apr. 1796.

Hunt, Matterson. Wife's name Anne, and there were two children, Thomas and James over ten, and two, Jennet and Sarah, under ten, when they arrived in the settlement.

Family.

1. Thomas.
2. James.
3. Jennet.   Married Bryan Rogers 5 Jan. 1792.
4. Sarah.
5. Hezekiah.   Born 24 Mar. 1790.
6. William.   Born 16 June 1787.
7. Elizabeth.   Born 19 Nov. 1793.

2. James Hunt married Temperance   ?

Family.

8. Margaret.   Born 26 Jan. 1793.
9. Lydia.   Born 17 Nov. 1795.

Johns, Henry. In some places the name is given as Jones. The name of his wife was Charity or Ann.   There was one child George, under ten.

Family.

1. George.
2. Sarah.   Born 20 July 1786.
3. Lydia.   Born 1 Dec. 1788.

Lyle, James.   Wife's name, Elizabeth.

Family.

1. Agnes.
2. James.
3. David.   All Bapt. 23 Aug. 1789.

Elizabeth Lyle, widow, married John Grant 17 Aug. 1792.

1. Agnes Lyle.   No record.
2. James Lyle married Lydia Carter.

Family.

    4. Elizabeth Agnes.   Born 6 Feb. 1812.
    5. Susanna.   Born 1 Aug. 1814.
    6. Maria.   Born 22 Nov. 1816.
    7. David.   Born 22 Mar. 1819.
    8. James.   Bapt. 28 May 1821.
    9. Caroline.   Born 18 Oct. 1823.
    10. Rhoda.   Born 6 Feb. 1826.
    11. Jeremiah Woods.   Born 29 Apr. 1828.
    12. Margaret.   Born 13 July 1830.
    13. John.   Born 31 July 1832.

3. David Lyle.   Married Ann Parks.

Family.

    14. Pamela.   Born 14 Feb. 1819.
    15. William.   Bapt. 28 May 1821.
    16. David.   Born 14 Feb. 1829.
    17. Daniel.   Born 29 Feb. 1832.
    18. Joseph.   Born 26 July 1837.

4. Elizabeth Agnes Lyle married Jesse Anderson 6 Mar. 1837.
5. Susanna Lyle married   ?   Butterworth.
7. David Lyle married Susannah Proctor 31 Dec. 1844.

Family.

    19. Harriet Wilhelmina.   Born 7 Sept. 1845.
    20. Joseph Bruce.   Born 24 May 1847.
    21. James.
    22. David.
    23. Alexander.

8. James Lyle married Nancy Carr 3 Jan. 1848.

Family.

    24. Jeremiah.   Died unmarried.
    25. Freeman.   Married Jane Martin.
    26. Joseph.   Unmarried.

27. George.   Unmarried.

28. Maria.   Married George Martin.

29. Mamie.   Married J. Gordon Peart.

30. Lettie.   Married Henry Reeves.

31. Margaret.   Married Alexander Reeves.

32. Robert.   Died young.

33. Adeline.   Died young.

9. Caroline Lyle married Demas Hutcheson 29 Dec. 1845.

11. Jeremiah Lyle married Ruth Bruce.

Family.

34. Bruce.

35.   ?

12. Margaret Lyle married John Maguire.

13. John Lyle married Ann Whitman.

18. Joseph Lyle married Elizabeth Bouche.

Family.

36. Nancy.   Married Rufus Garrogan.

37. Annie.   Died young.

38. William.   Died unmarried.

39. James.   Died unmarried.

40. Lydia.   Unmarried.

Martin, David.   Married Susanna Carter.

Family.

1. Agnes.   Born 2 Aug. 1793.

2. Alexander.   Born 30 Aug. 1795.

3. David.   Born 23 Jan. 1798.

4. Joseph.   Born 13 Aug. 1800.

5. William.   Born 23 Mar. 1803.

6. William.   Born 5 Feb. 1805.

7. James Bruce.   Born 4 Oct. 1808.

8. Eliza.   Born 12 Oct. 1811.

9. John George.   Born 7 June 1814.

10. Thomas Carew.   Born 27 Apr. 1818.

1. Agnes Martin married John Smith 28 Jan. 1817.

2. Alexander Martin married first Marianne

Family.

    11. David Alexander.   Born 10 Aug. 1824.

    12. Mary Jane.   Born 24 Nov. 1826.

He married second, Amelia Crittenden.

Family.

    13. Alexander.   Born 17 Apr. 1830.

    14. David.   Born 17 Nov. 1831.

    15. Ann Wilmot.   Born 21 Nov. 1835.

3. David Martin married Elizabeth Jane Aikins 16 Dec. 1837.

Family.

    16. John. Born 24 Oct. 1838.

    17. Ann. Born 31 Aug. 1840.

    18. David Alexander.   Born 17 Aug. 1842.

4. Joseph Martin married Marianne Hart 27 Jan. 1829.

Family.

    19. William Wallace.   Born 27 Nov. 1829.

    20. David Bruce.   Born 23 Nov. 1830.

    21. Margaret Eliza.   Born 8 Mar. 1832.

    22. Joseph Lee.   Born 26 Oct. 1833.

    23. Susan.   Born Mar. 1835.

    24. Lydia Elizabeth.   Born 3 Nov. 1837.

    25. Robert Alexander.   Born 11 Oct. 1839.

6. William Martin married Mary Eleanor Carrogan 27 Dec. 1832.

Family.

    26. Catherine.   Born 14 Mar. 1834.

    27. David Thomas.   Born 26 Jan. 1836.

    28. William Henry.   Born 16 Jan. 1838.

    29. Edward James.   Born 11 Oct. 1840.

    30. Alexander.   Born 19 Apr. 1843.

    31. Alexander Joseph.   Born 10 Nov. 1845.

    32. Thomas.

7. James Bruce Martin married Martha Harty.

Family.

    33. Martha Elizabeth.   Born 10 Apr. 1836.

34. Agnes.   Born 24 Apr. 1839.

35. Mary Eleanor.   Born 15 Apr. 1841.

36. Caroline Ann.   Born 12 Jan. 1843.

37. Susan Catherine.   Born 24 Apr. 1847.

9.   John George Martin married first Elizabeth Hadley 21 Feb. 1837.

Family.

38. Susanna Jane.   Born 7 May 1838.

39. Eleanor Eliza.   Born 16 May 1840.

40. Joseph John.   Born 26 Aug. 1842.

41. George Bruce Carter.   Born 3 Dec. 1844.

42. James Henry.   Born 18 Nov. 1847.

He married second, Mary Lowrie.

43. William.

44. Louisa.

45. John.

46. Adeline Amelia.   Born 17 Mar. 1866.

47. David Wesley.   Born 26 Sept. 1870.

17.   Ann Martin married Alexander Ferguson.

18.   David Alexander Martin married Jane Mundell.

Family.

48. Margaret.

49. Joseph.

50. Edward.

20.   David Bruce Martin married Abigail Carter.   No Family.

21.   Margaret Eliza Martin married James Wilkinson.

22.   Joseph Lee Martin married Henrietta (Peart) MacKenzie 8 May 1865

Family.

51. Minnie.

52. Joseph.

53. Laura.

54. C. Victoria.

55. Eugenia.

23.   Susan Martin married Levi Carter 16 Feb. 1857.

24.   Lydia Martin married William O'Brien.

25.   Robert Alexander Martin married Mary McKeough.

Family.

56. Anna.

57. Hattie.

58. Bertha.

59. Vincent.

60. Eva.

28. William Henry Martin married Harriet McPherson.

Family.

61. Jane.

62. Howard.

32. Thomas Martin married Jane McPherson.

Family.

63. Hattie.

64. Ada.

65. Addison.

35. Mary Eleanor Martin married Augustus Cunningham.

38. Susanna Jane Martin married Johnathan Gabriel.

39. Eleanor Eliza Martin married Edward Welsh.

40. Joseph John Martin married Mary Ann Carr.

Family.

66. Ethel.

67. James.

68. Mabel.

69. Oscar.

70. Lester.

41. George Bruce Martin married first Maria Lyle.

Family.

71. Waldo.

72. James.

He married second, Ann Cushin.

44. Louisa Martin married Alexander Jamieson.

46. Adeline Martin married Frederick Reeves.

Matterson, John. His wife, Elizabeth, is named on the roll of women.

Family.

William. Born 6 Apr. 1787.

Lucy. Born 22 Mar. 1790.

John Frederick. Born 22 Sept. 1792.

Peyton. Born 13 Sept. 1794.

Henry. Born 17 Aug. 1796.

Effy, who married James Carter 14 Aug. 1829.

North, Thomas. Wife's name Milly or Emily.

Family.

Elizabeth. Born 29 Jan. 1786.

James. Born 24 June 1788.

John. Bapt. 20 Oct 1796.

Proctor, Benjamin. Wife's name Eliza.

Family.

Mary. Born 15 Oct. 1785.

Nathan. Born 22 Oct. 1787.

James Shadwell. Born 1 Apr. 1789.

William. Born 27 July 1792.

Elizabeth. Born 2 July 1794.

Benjamin. Born 10 July 1796.

Proctor, James or John. Wife's name Helena.

Family

Robert. Born 2 Dec. 1792.

James. Born 5 Nov. 1794.

Farriby. Born 12 Sept. 1796.

Read, William. (The name is also spelled Reid.) Wife's name Agnes, and the names of three children under ten are on the roll, Jennet, Mary and William. John and Samuel were born after their arrival in the settlement.

Reeves, James. Married Temperance Carter.

Family.

1. John. Born 2 May 1791.

2. Elizabeth. Born 25 June 1794.

3. Nancy. Born 13 Aug. 1796.

446

4. Rhoda. Born Sept. 1798.

5. James. Born 11 Apr. 1800.

6. Susanna. Born 13 May 1803.

7. Temperance. Born 18 Oct. 1805.

8. Richard. Born 27 Sept. 1807.

9. Sarah. Born 17 May 1811.

10. William. Born 6 Nov. 1813.

11. George. Born 9 Apr. 1818.

12. Margaret. Born 26 Jan. 1793.

13. Lydia. Born 1795.

1. John Reeves married Ann.

Family.

14. James Rutherford. Born 4 Oct. 1811.

5. James Reeves. Wife's name Evelina.

Family.

15. James. Born 30 Nov. 1823.

16. Edward. Born 31 Aug. 1826.

17. Sarah. Born 23 July 1827.

18. Evelina. Born 6 July 1829.

19. John. Born 15 Sept. 1831.

20. George Owen. Born 30 Apr. 1835.

21. Caleb Henry. Born 3 June 1838.

22. Elizabeth Elvina. Born 1 Feb. 1841.

23. William Wallace. Born 9 Apr. 1843.

24. Charles Otis. Born 10 Dec. 1845.

8. Richard Reeves married Mary Anderson 30 Dec. 1830.

Family.

25. Hannah. Born 31 Nov. 1831.

26. James Adam. Born 22 Aug. 1835.

27. Robert Joseph. Born 10 Nov. 1837.

28. Richard John. Born 15 Nov. 1839.

29. Jesse William. Born 23 May 1842.

30. Thomas Johnson. Born 9 Sept. 1845.

11. George Reeves married Mary Flynn 28 Jan. 1845.

Reynolds, Ann. She was apparently a widow with two sons Stephen and Thomas, whose names are not on the roll of children, together with Mary and Ann, listed as above the age of ten, and Hannah, below ten.

Stephen Reynolds married Mary Strahan Oct. 22, 1800.

Family.

Elizabeth. Born 2 Sept. 1801.

Anna. Born 17 Nov. 1802.

Thomas Reynolds married Rebecca King Jan. 1792.

Family.

Mary. Born 13 Mar. 1793.

Frances. Born 9 Feb. 1795.

Rebecca. Born 25 Mar. 1799.

Hannah Reynolds married Zachariah Davis 1 April 1792.

Rogers, Joseph. His wife's name on the roll is Ferreby, and there were three children oven ten, Bryan, Needham and Africa. There was probably a George born later, and there are births of two children to Joseph and Abigail Rogers in the record, so Joseph was probably married a second time.

Family.

1. Bryan.

2. Needham.

3. Africa.

4. George.

5. Joseph. Born 10 Sept. 1793.

6. Needham. Born 3 Sept. 1796.

1. Bryan Rogers married Jennet Hunt 5 Jan. 1792.

Family.

7. Isaac. Born 29 Mar. 1794.

8. Anna. Born 10 Jan. 1797.

9. William. Born 9 June 1798.

10. Matterson. Born 30 Nov. 1799.

11. George Shepherd, Born 9 Feb. 1802.

12. Thomas. Born 4 Apr. 1804.

13. Bryan. Born 13 July 1806.

14. Farriby. Born 4 July 1808.

15. Jennet. Born 26 Sept. 1811.

He married second, Christie Stewart 4 Sept. 1827.

16. Margaret Jane. Born 4 Oct. 1828.

17. Christian. Born 27 May 1831.

3. Africa Rogers married William George.

4. George Rogers married Mattine ?

Family.

18. George. Born 24 May 1807.

19. Henry. Born 5 Mar. 1809.

7. Isaac Rogers married Marianne ?

Family.

20. Matilda. Born 28 Aug. 1829.

21. Madison Charles. Born 18 Mar. 1836.

8. Anna Rogers married Thomas Cochrane.

9. William Rogers married Temperance Carter 10 Dec. 1828.

Family.

22. William. Born 9 Nov. 1829.

23. Bridget. Born Feb. 1832.

24. Marianne. Born 13 Dec. 1833.

25. William. Born 10 May 1836.

26. John Madison. Born 15 Oct. 1838.

27. George Shepherd. Born 20 Sept. 1840.

28. Richard. Born 12 Aug. 1843.

29. Catherine Jane. Born 5 Sept. 1845.

12.   Thomas Rogers married Janet McNair 21 Nov. 1828.

Family.

30. Thomas. Born 4 July 1837.

31. John William. Born 29 May 1842.

13. Bryan Rogers married Mary Anne ?

Family.

32. Charlotte Elizabeth. Born 22 May 1847.

14. Farriby (or Ferribe) Rogers married Stephen Maguire 28 Nov. 1839.

Scott, Samuel. His wife's name was Mary and there were three children when they arrived in the settlement.

Family.

Janet. Born 1771.

William.

John.   Born   1781.

Samuel.   Born 4 Oct. 1784.

Mary.   Born 10 Nov. 1786.

Wheaton.   Born 16 Nov. 1789.

Josiah.   Born 15 Dec. 1792.

Rebecca.   Born 12 Sept. 1794.

William.   Born 14 Sept. 1796.

Jemima.   Born 27 Aug. 1798.

Zilpah.   Born 29 May 1801.

Of these there is record only of Wheaton, and his wife Mary, who had two children, Samuel born in 1842, who later married Emmeline Jane Carr, and Joseph, born 5 Sept. 1844.

Andrews., Aaron. Born in Wallingford, Connecticut circa 1762, he was the son of Denizen Andrews and Abigail Whiting and grand son of Samuel and Abigail Andrews. Married Ann Charlotte Grant 26 Sept. 1793.

Family.

Julie Ann. Born 30 June 1794.

John Dennison. Born 18 Dec, 1795.

Nina.)

Oliver.) Twins. Born 25 Jan. 1797.

James Francis Grant. Born 13 Jan. 1799.

Julie Ann Andrews married Lawrence Publicover 25 Dec. 1817. (There may have been other members of this family, which can not be traced farther. It is thought they all moved away.)

Andrews, Isaac. He was the son of Elon and Sarah Andrews of Wallingford, Connecticut and was born 8 March 1762. He was also the grandson of Samuel Andrews, a clergyman who had been involved in encouraging emigration from Connecticut. Isaac and Aaron were first cousins. Married Lydia Potter.

Family.

1. Jane.)

2, Ann.) Twins. Born 12 Aug. 1794 or 1795.

3. Moses. Born 1 Apr. 1797.

4. Lydia. Bapt. 23 June 1799.

5. Phoebe. Born 29 May 1802.

6. Sarah. Born 11 Mar. 1804.

7. Abigail Hannah. Born 25 Apr. 1806.

8. Lydia. Born 4 May 1808.

9. Mercy. Born 25 Apr. 1810.

10. Isaac. Born 14 Feb. 1812.

11. David.

12. Aaron.

1. Jane Andrews married Rev. Sanuel Darin 19 Oct. 1815.

5. Phoebe Andrews married John George Loach 11 Nov. 1819.

6. Sarah Andrews married James Brown.

8. Lydia Andrews married Thomas Reynolds 17 June 1833.

9. Mercy Andrews married Donald Henderson 20 Jan. 1829. 10.

10. Isaac Andrews married Christina Torey 31 Jan. 1837.

Family.

 13. Anne Elizabeth. Born 25 Dec. 1837.

 14. Eunice Talbert. Born 10 Oct. 1839.

 15. Henry Torey. Born 8 June 1843.

 16. Margaret Jemima. Born 7 Feb. 1846.

 17. James Buckley. Born 23 Sept. 1848.

After the death of her first husband Christina Andrews married Dennison Atwater. All the family by her first husband are said to have moved to the States.)

11. David Andrews married Jane Isabella Torey.

Family.

 18. Henry Reuben. Born 12 Nov. 1840

 19. James Robert. Born 25 Aug. 1842.

 20. Isaac Lawson. Born 22 Mar. 1844.

 21. Mary Eleanor. Born 1 June 1848.

 22. David Albert. Born 5 Apr. 1853.

 23. Charles Joseph Born 7 Apr. 1857.

 24. Obadiah. Born 8 Nov. 1859.

 25. Janet.

 26. Anne Jane.

 27. George.

12. . Aaron Andrews married Amelia Langley.

Family.

 28. Thomas John Beech. Born 22 July 1826.

 29. John Henry.)

 30. David Lawrence.) Twins. Born 10 Mar. 1837.

 31. Aaron Samuel. Born 10 May 1840.

 32. Edwin Jeremiah. Born 23 Dec. 1842.

 33. Nancy Margaret. Born 11 July 1845.

18. Henry Reuben Andrews married Janet Amelia Wheaton 1 Jan. 1867.

19. James Robert Andrews married Anne Strople 17 Aug. 1875.

20. Isaac Lawson Andrews married Mary C. Sullivan 3 Dec. 1872.

21. Mary Eleanor married Mr. Peterson.

25. Janet Andrews married Eldridge Gerry.

26. Anne Jane Andrews married Mr. Cornpton.

27. George Andrews married Harriet Gosbee.

Atwater.

Ira Atwater and William Atwater, Jr., both of whom are named in the Hallowell Grant, were sons of William Atwater. William Atwater, Sr., was the son of Phineas Atwater and Mary Ward. Two other sons, Rufus and Ward also moved to Nova Scotia. Phineas Atwater was the son of John Atwater and Abigail Mansfield. John Atwater, born 1 Nov. 1654, was the sixth child and the third son of David Atwater and Damaris Sayre. David Atwater was one of the first settlers of New Haven, Conn., and was born in Royton in Lenham, Kent, England. His descent can be traced to Thomas Atwater of Royton, who died in 1484.

William Atwater, Sr., was born in 1730 and married 3 Jan. 1754 to Esther Turtle, who was born 10 Feb. 1736. William Atwater died within a few years after his arrival in Guysborough, and his widow married Joseph Hadley, 8 Aug. 1791. She died 14 Oct. 1807.

Family.

1. Rufus.   Born 29 Nov. 1754.

2. Luman.   Born 8 Feb. 1757.

3. William.   Born 16 Feb. 1759.

4 . Abel Ward.   Born 1761.

5. Chloe.   Born 21 Sept. 1763.

6. Ira.   Born 21 June 1765.

7. Asenath.   Born 30 Oct. 1768.

8. Esther.   Born 4 Oct. 1771.

1. Rufus Atwater married Mary Tuttle 18 Dec. 1777. He was killed by a falling tree 26 Apr. 1790. His widow married Elisha Randall 23 Aug. 1792, and died 13 July 1822.

Family.

9. Sabina.   Born in U.S.A.

10. Luman.   Born in U.S.A.

11. Adolphus.   Born in U.S.A.

12. William.   Born 28 Nov. 1785.

13. Esther.   Born 23 Dec. 1789.

2. Luman Atwater died 9 Sept. 1795.

3. William Atwater married Esther or Sarah Esther Andrews.

Family.

14. Sabina.   Born 6 Apr. 1787.

15. Alvarous.   Born 15 Aug. 1789.

16. Abner.   Born 29 Oct. 1791.

17. Dennison Andrews.   Born 10 Nov. 1795.

18. Ward.   Bapt. June 1798.

19. Charlotte Ann.   Born 12 Mar. 1803.

20. Asenath.

21. Abigail.

22. John.

23. Joseph.

4. Abel Ward Atwater died 15 Mar. 1823. If he accompanied his father to Nova Scotia, he at least remained here but a short time.

5. Chloe Atwater married John Clark.

6. Ira Atwater apparently returned to Yalesville, Conn., and has not been traced.

8. Esther Atwater married George Whitman 13 Mar. 1788.

9. Sabina Atwater married John Dunn 9 Feb. 1797. She married second, Morgan Connor 1 Apr. 1799.

10. Luman Atwater married Mary Key 20 Dec. 1808.

Family.

24. Elisha.   Born 11 Jan. 1813.

25. James George.   Born 1 Nov. 1814.

26. Elisha Matthew.   Born 3 Apr. 1817.

27. Elizabeth Jane.   Born 15 Feb. 1819.

28. Luman.   Born 19 Aug. 1824.

29. David Graham.   Born 12 Mar. 1828.

11. Adolphus Atwater married Sarah   ?

Family.

30. Rufus William.   Born 20 May 1811.

31. Margaret Ann.   Born 2 Jan. 1812.

32. Eunice.   Born 28 May 1816.

33. Rufus William.   Born 28 Nov. 1818.

34. Adolphus.   Born 9 Aug. 1821.

35. Joseph Adolphus.   Born 7 June 1824.

36. Mary Eliza.   Born 26 July 1826.

12. William Atwater married Elizabeth Elliott 13 Feb. 1812. She died 16 Sept. 1818. His second wife was Catherine Babson.

Family.

37. Rufus William.   Born 1813.

38. James Randall.   Born 7 Jan. 1816.

39. William.

40. William Collins.   Born Nov. 1825.

41. Joseph.   Born Nov. 1825.

42. Joseph Babson.   Born Nov. 1827.

43. Constant Loyal Tuttle.   Born 29 Sept. 1830.

44. Mary Ann.   Born 18 Sept. 1832.

13. Esther Atwater married William Strople 26 Aug. 1807.

14. Sabina Atwater married John Kergill McKeen 29 Oct. 1808.

15. Alvarous Atwater married Margaret McKay 23 Feb. 1813. He died
1 July 1867.   She died 17 Dec. 1868.

Family.

45. James William.   Born 30 Jan. 1814.

46. John.   Born 17 June 1816.

47. Alvarous.   Born 8 Mar. 1818.

48. Amelia Eleanor.   Born 19 Apr. 1820.

49. Thomas Harvey.   Born 23 Dec. 1823.

50. William Rufus.   Born 13 July 1828.

51. Elizabeth Jane.   Born 21 Sept. 1831.

52. Joseph Daniel.   Born 28 Mar. 1834.

53. Charles Alvarous.   Born 21 May 1837.

54. Margaret.   Bapt. 11 June 1826.

17. Dennison Andrews Atwater married Christina Andrews, widow of
Isaac Andrews. He died 15 June 1867.

Family.

55. William Abner.   Born 19 June 1854.

18. Ward Atwater married Mary Ann Bigelow 20 Jan. 1825.

Family.

56. Charlotte Ann.   Born 9 Sept. 1831.

57. William Bigelow.   Born 3 Aug. 1832.

58. James.   Born 3 June 1835.

59. Joseph.   Born 7 May 1837.

19. Charlotte Ann Atwater married Joseph Hart 31 Jan. 1826.

20. Asenath Atwater married Henry Baker 13 Aug. 1806.

21. Abigail Atwater married Angus McKay 30 Aug. 1814.

26. Elisha Matthew Atwater married Grace   ?

Family.

60. William.   Born 1844.

(There were probably others.)

38. James Randall Atwater married Mary Jane Boles 9 May 1844.

Family.

    61. Robert William. Born 9 June 1845.

    62. Elisha Randall. Born 25 Oct. 1846.

    63. Charles James.

    64. Samuel Joshua.

    65. John Cogswell.

    66. Rebecca Boles.

    67. Frederick Potter.

    68. Frederick Babson.

    69. Rollo Everett.

    70. Mansfield.

45. James William Atwater died 2 Apr. 1866.

48. Amelia Eleanor Atwater married James Lewis Whitman 17 Feb. 1846.

50. William Rufus Atwater married Mary Gretna 1852.

Family.

    71. James. Born 8 May 1865.

    72. Abner Hart. Born 25 Apr. 1867.

(There are a number of others in this family.)

51. Elizabeth Jane Atwater married John George Leet 29 Dec. 1870.

53. Charles Alvarous Atwater married Almira Torey 4 Feb. 1868.

Family.

    73. Joseph A. Born 15 Jan. 1869.

    74. Charles A. Born 27 May 1872.

    75. John H. Born 21 Oct. 1870.

    76. Elizabeth J. Born 3 Nov. 1874.

    77. Emma A. Born 14 Aug. 1876.

    78. Margaret A. Born 22 Aug. 1878.

    79. James H. Born 6 Apr. 1883.

    80. Monson. Born 14 Nov. 1886.

    81. Sarah A. Born 30 Aug. 1889.

55. William Abner Atwater married Emma Gray Davidson 25 Dec. 1873. He moved to the States.

59. Joseph Atwater married Sabina. There was a family of four daughters and three sons. This family lived at Bayfield.

Bryant, Gideon. No record has been found of this man or of any family.

Hart., Josiah. He was born 22 Feb. 1741 and was the fifth son of Nathaniel Hart and Martha Lee. Nathaniel Hart, born 19 June 1702, was the eldest son of Hawkins Hart and Sarah Roys. Hawkins Hart, born in 1677, was the eldest son of Capt. Thomas Hart and Ruth Hawkins. Capt. Thomas Hart, born in 1644. was the third son and youngest child of Stephen Hart, who came from Braintree, Essex, England, to Massachusetts Bay about 1632. The date of Josiah Hart's death is not known, nor the date of his wife's birth. She died 25 Dec. 1809.

Family.

1. Rama. Born 26 June 1766.
2. Joseph. Born 20 July 1767.
3. Jairus. Born 17 Feb. 1769.
4. Irad. Born 2 Jan. 1771.
5. Tyrus. Born 13 Jan. 1773.
6. Panthea. Born 10 June 1775.
7. Lydia. Born 19 Apr. 1777.
8. Lee. Born 23 Aug. 1779.
9. Ithiel. Born 17 Dec. 1782.

1. Rama Hart is supposed to have died young.
2. Joseph Hart is supposed to have returned to the States, and his descendants have not been traced.
3. Jairus Hart married Frances Godfrey 31 Dec. 1795. After his death, the widow married a Mr. Oates.

Family.

10. Sarah Peart. Born 13 Apr. 1797.
11. Josias. Bapt. 1799.
12. Thomas Godfrey. Born 31 Oct. 1803.
13. Elizabeth Hopkins. Born 27 Oct. 1805.
14. Frances Ann. Born 18 Feb. 1807.
15. Godfrey Peart. Born 1 Sept. 1809.
16. Jairus. Born 15 Dec. 1811.
17. John William Peart. Bapt. 1815.
18. Ruth. Bapt. 1816.
19. Esther Maria. Born 25 Apr. 1817.
20. Marianne. Born 28 Aug. 1819.
21. Martha Maria. Born 29 Aug. 1822.

4. Irad Hart married first Armenia Ingram 3 July 1797. After the death of his first wife, he married Sarah Shaw, widow. The family are all by the first wife. Armenia Hart died 1 Nov. 1828.

22. Sarah. Born 22 Sept. 1798.

23. Lorain Maria. Born 15 Apr. 1800.

24. Panthea. Born 8 Mar. 18*02.

25. Josiah.)

26. Hezekiah.) Twins. Born 8 Feb. 1804.

27. Irad. Born 4 Feb. 1806.

28. Ithiel. Born 24 Dec. 1807.

29. William. Born 26 March 1810.

30. John. Born 10 Sept. 1814.

31. Joseph. Born 10 Sept. 1814.

32. Mark. Born 7 May 1816.

33. Armenia. Born 27 June 1818.

Irad Hart moved to Margaree with his family, and to him a great many of the Harts of the island of Cape Breton owe their descent.

5. Tyrus Hart married Martha Ingram. He died 30 July 1828. She died 25 May 1826.

Family.

34. Joseph. Born 28 Sept. 1801.

35. William. Born 11 Feb. 1803.

36. Tyrus. Born 20 Sept. 1804.

37. Martha. Born 10 Aug. 1805.

38. Sarah. Born 10 Feb. 1808.

39. Jacob Stiles. Born 8 June 1809.

40. Lydia. Born 16 Oct. 1812.

41. Elizabeth. Born 27 Sept. 1813.

42. Harriet. Born 7 Oct. l815.

43. Maria. Born 18 July 1817.

44. Jairus. Bora 31 Mar. 1819.

45. Reuben. Born 16 Aug. 1821.

46. Lavinia. Born 18 May 1823.

47. Levi. Born 18 May 1826.

6. Panthea Hart married Charles Myers.

7. Lydia Hart married William Simpson 13 July 1796.

8. Lee Hart married Margaret Langille 7 Mar. 1803. She died 22 Feb. 1872, aged 87 years.

Family.

48. John.　Born 27 Oct. 1805.

49. Mary Ann Eve.　Born 13 Oct. 1808.

50. Ithiel.　Born 25 Feb. 1811.

51. Lydia Margaret.　Born 28 Jan. 1813.

52. Joseph Lee.　Born 1 Oct. 1816.

53. Robert Alexander.　Born 29 Apr. 1819.

9. Ithiel Hart was killed by lightning 27 Oct. 1807, unmarried.

10. Sarah Peart Hart married William Hadley 21 Mar. 1816.

11. Josiah (or Josias) Hart married Sarah Arnold, daughter of John and Naomi Arnold 5 Feb. 1822.　He died 2 Jan. 1873.

Family.

54. Marianne.　Born 22 Jan. 1823.

55. Tyrus.　Born 1 Jan. 1827.

56. William.　Born 15 Mar. 1829.

57. Margaret.　Born 4 Apr. 1831.

58. Henry.　Born 25 Oct. 1836.

59. Eliza Abigail.)

60. Sarah Smith.) Twins.　Born 24 Aug. 1842.

61. John Henry.

62. Josiah.

63. Charles W.

64. Frances M.

12. Thomas Godfrey Hart married Ann Ross, daughter of Donald and Ann Ross 5 Feb. 1825.

Family.

65. Ann Elizabeth.　Born 3 Oct. 1826.

66. Frances Maria.　Born 7 May 1828.

67. Martha Armenia.　Born 15 Jan. 1830.

68. Margaret Jane.　Born 24 Feb. 1832.

69. John Godfrey.　Born 1846.

70. William H.

71. Hannah Maria.

13. Elizabeth Hopkins Hart married Josiah Hooper 29 Jan. 1828.

14. Frances Ann Hart married James Hull 10 Mar. 1829.

15. Godfrey Peart Hart married Mary Ann Horton 18 Dec. 1834.

Family.

   74. Elizabeth. Bapt. 22 Mar. 1837.

   75. Frances Maria. Born 24 Nov. 1838.

   76. Hannah.

   77. William.

   78. Susan.

   79. John G.

   80. James.

16. Jairus Hart married Isabel Ross, daughter of Donald and Ann Ross.

Family.

   81. Maria. Born 4 May 1834.

(There were probably others. This family moved to Arichat and has not been traced.)

17. John William Peart Hart married Mary Ross, daughter of Donald and Ann Ross 1 Dec. 1836. (This family moved to Boston, where there are said to be descendants.)

18. Ruth Hart married David Hull 21 May 1833. There were eight children from the marriage. After the death of the first husband, the widow married a Mr. Cochrane, who died very shortly after the marriage. She then married Jesse Nickerson, one child being the result of the union.

19. Esther Maria Hart married John Walsh.

(In the above family, three brothers (Harts) married three sisters (Ross) and two sisters (Harts) married two brothers (Hulls).

22. Sarah Hart married John Crowdis.

(Fourteen children were born of this marriage.)

24. Panthea Hart married Mark Crowdis.

25. Josiah Hart married Mary Amelia Hull 12 Oct. 1828.

Family.

   82. John Hezekiah. Born 24 May 1830.

   83. Joseph Henry. Born 28 Jan. 1832.

   84. William F. Born 11 Apr. 1834.

   85. Frederick D. Born 3 June 1836.

   86. Charles Myers. Born 23 Aug. 1838.

   87. Charles Myers. Born 12 Mar. 1840.

   88. Irad.

   89. James.

   90. Eliza.

91. Rhoda Ann.

92. Eliza.   )

93. Freeman.) Twins.   Born Oct. 1853.

27. Irad Hart married Isabel Taylor, widow.

Family.

94. Lorena.

95. Charles.

(This family moved to California.)

29. William Hart married Harriet Ross 9 May 1835.

Family.

96. William Edmund.   Born 6 Mar. 1836.

97. Armenia Victoria.   Born 29 Mar. 1838.

98. Lydia.   Born 21 June 1840.

99. Eliza.   Born 17 Sept. 1842.

100. Albert Judson.   Born 29 Dec. 1844.

101. Phoebe.   Born 9 Sept. 1846.

102. Elizabeth.   Born 7 Aug. 1848.

103. Priscilla Ann.   Born 14 Dec. 1850.

104. Sarah Panthea.   Born 20 May 1853.

105. Harriet.   Born 28 Dec. 1856.

William Hart died 28 Aug. 1874. Harriet (Ross) Hart died 18 Feb. 1903. She was born 18 Mar. 1810.

30. John Hart died 31 Oct. 1828.

(The three brothers, Hezekiah, Ithiel and John, with the mother died within a day of each other of typhus fever, and were buried the same day.)

31. Joseph Hart married Maria Ingram.

Family.

106. Jacob S.

107. Albert.

32. Mark Hart married Lydia Ann Scranton.   She died 4 Feb. 1904.

Family.

108. Henry Ithiel.   Born 19 Nov. 1843.

109. Lydia Adeline.   Born 10 July 1845.

110. David John Osbert.   Born 25 Apr. 1847.

111. Armenia Melinda.   Born 4 Sept. 1849.

461

112. Mark Alfred.   Born 14 June 1852.

113. Ethelbert.   Born 20 Oct. 1854.

114. Una Sophia.   Born 4 July 1856.

115. Sarah Edith.   Born 25 Apr. 1859.

116. John O.   Born 25 Dec. 1860.

117. Anetta E.   Born 1862.

118. Alma L.   Born 1865.

33. Armenia Hart married Stiles Ingram.

34. Joseph Hart married Charlotte Atwater 31 Jan. 1826. He died 30 Jan. 1890.

Family.

119. Martha.   Born 19 Dec. 1826.

120. Tyrus.   Born 28 Oct. 1828.

121. William.   Born 23 Aug. 1830.

122. Joseph.   Born 1 Oct. 1832.

123. James R.   Born 25 Oct. 1834.

124. Thomas Davies.   Born 31 May 1837.

125. Sarah.   Born 30 Sept. 1839.

126. Abner.   Born 12 Apr. 1841.

127. Maria Annabelle.   Born 2 Nov. 1843.

35. William Hart married Letitia Whitman 30 June 1831. He died 4 Nov. 1889.

Family.

128. William Henry.   Born 24 Aug. 1832.

129. James Edward.   Born 5 Oct. 1834.

130. Alfred Whitman.   Born 5 Feb. 1837.

131. Abraham Whitman.   Born 1 Feb. 1840.

132. Charles Harrington.   Born 30 Oct. 1841.

133. Letitia Ann.   Born 12 Feb. 1843.

134. Carrie Maria.   Born 25 Nov. 1845.

135. George N. Wilberforce.   Born 6 June 1847.

136. Charlotte C.   Born 26 Aug. 1849.

137. Lewis E.   Born 4 Mar. 1853.

36. Tyrus Hart married Arabella MacIntosh 31 Dec. 1832.

Family.

138. James Henry D.   Born 6 Oct. 1833.

462

139. Henry Tyrus.   Born 16 Sept. 1834.

140. Christopher Cranswick.   Bapt. 11 Dec. 1835.

141. Charles William Webb.   Bapt. 20 Sept. 1837.

142. Reuben Whitman.   Born 19 Nov. 1838.

143. Alex. William McLeod.   Born 8 Aug. 1840.

144. Edward Caritte.   Born 23 Aug. 1842.

145. Lavinia Ann Maria.   Born 26 Mar. 1845.

146. Clement Carvossah.   Born 7 Sept. 1848.

   Married Miss Hattie ?   Son, Frank.

37. Martha Hart married Spinney Whitman 3 July 1830.   She died 2 July 1878.

38. Sarah Hart married Rev. William Smith 22 Aug. 1833.   She died 27 June 1838. She was the grandmother of Vincent Massey, first Canadian born Governor General of Canada and his brother Raymond Massey, the prominent actor.

39. Jacob Stiles Hart married Emmeline Marshall 14 Aug. 1838.   She was born 28 Apr. 1819 and died 22 June 1886. He died 25 Sept,1890
   Family.

   147. Edith Georgina.   Born 27 July 1840.

   148. Gordon Joseph.   Born 13 Dec. 1841.

   149. Emmeline Roselia.   Born 19 July 1842.

   150. James Marshall.   Born 2 May 1845.

   151. John Inglis.   Born 9 Dec. 1846.

   152. Cora St. Clair.   Born 5 Dec. 1848.

   153. William Lang Black.   Born 12 Feb. 1850. 1851.

   154. Sarah.   Born 16 Mar.

   155. Eliza Campbell.

   156. Stiles Canrobert.   Born 8 May 1855.

   157. Sydney Jarvis.   Born 28 Jan. 1857.

40. Lydia Hart died Oct. 1812.

41. Elizabeth Hart married William Grant Scott 16 Feb. 1841. She died 25 Nov. 1905.

42. Harriet Hart married Christopher Jost 4 Sept. 1837. She died 9 Feb. 1896.

43. Maria Hart married George Michael Cunningham. She died 24 Jan. 1885.

44. Jairus Hart married Eliza Cook 11 Feb. 1846. No family. He died 26 Oct. 1906.

45. Reuben Hart married Grace Cunningham.   He died 29 Jan. 1907.
   Family.

   158. John George.   Born 24 Dec. 1852.

   159. George Reuben.   Born 14 Aug. 1854.

46. Lavinia Hart married Abram N. Whitman 20 Mar. 1841. She died 26

463

Jan. 1905.

47. Levi Hart married Jane Deborah Whitman 6 Nov. 1852. He died Dec. 1907.

Family.

160. Havelock McColl. Born 5 Nov. 1857.

161. Frederick Walter. Born 3 Apr. 1861.

162. Arthur Lee. Born 18 June 1864.

163. Eugenis. Born 21 Sept. 1867.

164. Maud Maria. Born 11 Nov. 1878.

48. John Hart married Elizabeth Irwin 8 Mar. 1830.

Family.

165. James Lee. Born 1832.

166. Joseph. Born 20 Dec. 1833.

167. John Francis. Born 27 Feb. 1836.

168. Adeline Elizabeth. Born 20 Mar. 1838.

169. Melissa Maria. Born 29 Sept. 1840.

49. Mary Ann Eve Hart married Joseph Martin 27 Jan. 1829.

51. Lydia Margaret Hart married John Alexander Steel, 31 March 1834. After her death he married Zippora Cook.

52. Joseph Lee Hart married Rebecca Smith 7 Jan. 1840.

Family.

170. Margaret Matilda. Born 16 Jan. 1841.

171. Agnes Susannah. Born 7 Apr. 1843.

172. Mary Ann. Born 11 Feb. 1845.

173. Joseph Lee. Born 27 Nov. 1847.

174. Frances Esther. Born 29 July 1853.

175. Elizabeth Steele. Born 16 Aug. 1854.

176. Lydia.

177. Parker.

53. Robert Alexander Hart married Jane Smith, sister of brother's wife, 4 Feb. 1845.

Family.

178. Levi Smith. Born 16 Mar. 1848.

179. Maria Alma. Born 25 Dec. 1856.

180. Alexanna Ada. Born 19 Oct. 1860.

181. Agnes Adelina. Born 3 July 1863.

182. Emma.

183. John S.

184. Alfred.

185. Lydia Ann.

186. Walter.

58. Henry Hart married Margaret Morgan 4 Aug. 1863.

Family.

187. Isaiah Frederick. Born 4 Jan. 1867.

188. Margaret. Born 6 Aug. 1868.

189. William Wallace. Born 18 Oct. 1874.

190. Alice. Born 17 Jan. 1876.

59. Eliza Abigail Hart married Judson Mackintosh.

61. John Henry Hart married first Sarah Whooton. She died 31 Mar. 1868. He married second, Christie Ann Brymer 24 Mar. 1869. All the family were by the first wife.

Family.

191. John.

192. Sarah.

193. Ruth.

194. Maria.

195. Esther.

196. Lydia.

197. Ada.

198. Josiah. Born 1861.

62. Josiah Hart married Margaret Ellen Bruce 17 July 1858.

Family.

199. Henry Bruce. Born 31 Mar. 1859.

200. James Josiah. Born 4 Dec. 1860.

201. Ida Anzenetta. Born 6 Mar. 1862.

202. Margaret. Born 13 Sept. 1865.

203. Stanley.

204. Bessie.

206. Richard Harvey. 10 June 1867.

63. Charles W. Hart married Elizabeth Myers 1864.

Family.

207. Reuben. Born 23 Sept. 1866.

208. Irad William. Born 15 June 1872.

209. Alonzo.

210. Josiah.

There were a number of children in this family. The graves of a number of children are to be found in an old cemetery on the Strait Road.

64. Frances M. Hart married Charles Whooton 23 Dec. 1852.

74. Elizabeth Hart married James M. Gammon 24 Sept. 1861.

75. Frances Maria Hart married Levi P. Mackintosh 7 May 1867.

76. Hannah Hart married a Mr. Rogers.

77. William Hart married a Miss Whitman and moved to Cape Cod.

79. John G. Hart married first Sarah Hadley in 1873. After her death he married Sarah Jane Crescine 6 Dec. 1886.

Family.

211. Mary. Born 6 Feb. 1875.

212. William. Born 7 Jan. 1876.

119. Martha Hart married George Wells Tuttle 30 Sept. 1854. She died 18 March 1899. He was born 9 Aug. 1823 and died 23 Apr. 1900.

122. Joseph Hart married Emma Woodill. There was no family. He died 19 March 1880.

123. James R. Hart married Emmeline Shaw Robinson 16 Jan. 1865. He died 8 Oct. 1918.   She died June 1919.
Family.
213. Joseph William.   B orn 19 Nov. 1865.
214. Anna Robinson.   Born 1867.
215. Ingram Thornton.   Born 23 Dec. 1869.
216. Harold Renton.
217. Grace.   Born 10 Jan.   1877.

124. Thomas Davies Hart married Charlotte Jane Dixon. He died 12 July 1923.
Family.
218. Charlotte Elizabeth,   Born 4 July 1864.
219. Joseph Arthur Thornton.   Born 28 Nov. 1866.
220. Sarah Lippington.   Born 25 Aug, 1868.
221. Louisa Helena.   Born 6 June 1870.
222. Mary Laura Eugenia.   Born 13 Nov. 1871.
223. Edward Reuben Kenniard.   Born 21 Jan. 1874.
224. Alice Maria.   Born 26 Oct. 1875.
225. Frederick William.   Born 7 Sept. 1877.
226. Lillian Maud Dixon.   Born 8 Apr. 1879.
227. Cecelia May.   Born 13 Apr. 1882.
228. Emmeline.   Born 25 Sept. 1883.

126. Abner Hart married Mary Ann Hutcheson 14 July 1864.
Family.
229. Harrison L.   Born 19 Apr. 1865.
230. Annie Emma Woodill.   Born 24 Feb. 1867.
231. Sarah Alicia.   Born 14 Oct. 1869.
232. Laurie Bligh.   Born 8 Oct. 1871.
233. William Arthur.   Born 4 Mar. 1874.
234. Walter Joseph.   Born 26 Jan. 1876.
235. Francis Cyril.   Born 15 Jan. 1878.
236. Charlotte Maria.   Born 22 July 1880.
237. Mary Elizabeth.   Born 19 July 1882.
238. Hedley Abner.   Born 31 Aug. 1885.

127. Maria Annabelle Hart married Rev. W. Purvis. She died 10 Mar. 1897.

128. William Henry Hart married Kate Coppin 17 June 1854. No family.

129. James Edward Hart married Harriet E. Cunningham 24 Dec. 1857. She is the author of the book *History of the County of Guysborough.*
Family.
239. Edward Francis.   Born 20 Oct. 1861.
240. Clarence William.   Born 10 Apr. 1866.

130. Alfred Whitman Hart married Mary Narraway 23 Feb. 1861.

131. Abraham Whitman Hart married Maria W. Cunningham 10 Feb. 1863.

Family.

241. Aubrey.

242. Guy Carleton. Born 24 Feb. 1865.

243. Percy William Edward. Born 27 Jan. 1870.

133. Letitia Ann Hart married William F. DesBarries 24 May 1866.

136. Charlotte C. Hart married Leonard C. Harrington 11 July 1868.

137. Lewis B. Hart married Lucinda Hutcheson 14 Dec. 1881.

Hawley, Matthew. Referred to as Captain Hawley, he was the son of Obadiah Hawley of Stratford, Connecticut. "Removed to Nova Scotia 30 May 1773", he was at Chedabucto several years before moving to Port Hood Island. He was the progenitor of the Hawleys of Inverness County.

Hulls. The Hulls arriving with the Hallowell Grant settlers were the father, Moses, and three children of whom records are found. There may have been others of the family who remained in Connecticut. Moses Hull did not long remain in the land of his adoption, but returned, and his death took place soon after. He is said to have been drowned. No record has been found of his wife, and he may have been a widower at the time of his arrival in Nova Scotia.

Family.

1. Samuel.

2. Elizabeth.

3. Philomela.

1. Samuel Hull married Sarah Ingram.

Family.

4. Samuel Ingram. Born 16 Sept. 1796.

5. John.

6. Hezekiah. Born 30 Apr. 1800.

7. James. Born 12 Apr. 1802.

8. Moses. Born 21 Mar. 1804.

9. David. Bora 26 Oct. 1806.

10. Mary Amelia. Born 14 July 1809.

11. Elizabeth Martha. Born 15 Apr. 1812.

12. Harriet. Born 11 Feb. 1815.

2. Elizabeth Hull married Stephen Pyle 10 Nov. 1787.

3. Philomela Hull married Benjamin Cook 4 Mar. 1787.

4. Samuel Ingram Hull married Hannah Arnold 16 Jan. 1816

Family.

13. John Moses. Born 22 Jan. 1818.

14. Samuel. Born 20 May 1820.

There were other children, apparently at least three. This family moved to Cape Breton, where it is said that descendants are still to be found.

5. John Hull died in Boston, said to have been single. He is said to

have been a Baptist minister.

6. Hezekiah Hull married Elizabeth Bigelow.

Family.

15. Mary Alice.
16. John Prior.
17. Judson.
18. Jane.

There were others in this family. Hezekiah also was a Baptist minister, and there is said to be descendants in New York.

7. James Hull married Frances Hart 10 Mar. 1829.

Family.

19. John. Born 8 Jan. 1830.
20. William. Born 8 Aug. 1831.
21. James. Born 1 June 1833.
22. Sarah Jane. Born June 1836.
23. Jairus Harding.
24. Ithiel Hart. Born 19 Oct. 1842.
25. Annie.
26. Frederick.

8. Moses Hull married a Miss MacDonald in Cape Breton. This family also moved to Cape Breton, and there is said to be descendants near Baddeck.

9. David Hull married Ruth Hart, sister of brother's wife 21 May 1833.

Family.

27. Frances Maria. Born 25 June 1834.
28. Samuel. Born 1 May 1836.
29. Joseph (or Josiah).
30. Thomas Henry.)
31. John Godfrey.) Twins. Born 23 Dec. 1841.
32. James Christopher. Born 3 May 1843.
33. Jairus Hart. Born 8 Nov. 1845.
34. Elizabeth Abigail Buckley. Born 5 July 1848.

After the death of David Hull, his widow married a Mr. Cochrane who was drowned very soon after their marriage. She then married Jesse Nickerson.

10. Mary Amelia Hull married Jairus Hart, said to have been a Congregational minister.

11. Elizabeth Martha (or Margaret) Hull married James Willis 12 July 1831.

19. John Hull married Rebecca Boles. This family moved Gloucester. There is said to have been one son, Herbert.

20. William Hull married Lavinia Lumsden. There is a large family, living in Manchester.

21. James Hull married Katherine O'Brien, widow. Her name before marriage was Livingstone. No family.

468

22. Sarah Jane Hull married John Torey 1859.

23. Jairus Harding Hull married Mary Livingstone, sister of his brother's wife, in 1863. There is said to have been a large family in Boston, where they moved.

24. Ithiel Hart Hull married Sarah Bruce 4 Jan. 1871. These also moved to Gloucester. No family.

25. Annie Hull married a Mr. Green, in Gloucester.

27. Frances Maria Hull married William Sangster 1856.

28. Samuel Hull married Margaret Sangster.

29. Josiah Hull married Frances Mason 17 Sept. 1868.

30. Thomas Henry Hull married Margaret Sangster.

31. John Godfrey Hull married Margaret Ann Wright 27 May 1874.

34. Elizabeth Aibigail Hull married Michael Gillie.

Leet, Andrew. With Andrew Leet and his wife came a family of at least five children, of whom there are some records, and one child was born after their arrival in Nova Scotia. It is somewhat of a coincidence that not only was there both a Leet and a Scranton in this little migration, but that the names of both families were connected in old correspondence respecting with the regicides, Whalley and Goffe, who had sought asylum in the new world. At that time, the latter half of the 17th century, a William Leet was Governor of Connecticut and a Scranton also filled the same position at another time. Andrew Leet died 16 Feb. 1808, aged 79 years. Andrew Leet was born in Guilford, Connecticut where he married first Esther Blatchey 12 May 1763. A letter still in the family tells that he left for Chedabucto in the spring of 1773 but returned to Guilford where he married second Submit Crockett. She died 4 Oct. 1804, aged 50 years. It is not clear where they resided between 1773 and 1785, but it may have been at the Guysborough Intervale.

Family.

1. Jabez (Jarret).
2. Andrew.
3. Submit.
4. Lucretia.
5. Huldah.   Born 6 May 1788.
6. John.

These are not in order of birth and there may have been more.

1. Jabez (Jarret) Leet married Margaret McPherson 7 Dec. 1800, daughter of Paul MacPherson. She died 28 May 1873, aged 93.

Family.

7. Andrew.   Born 9 Apr. 1802.
8. John.   Born 6 July 1804.
9. William.   Born 14 July 1806.
10. Oliver Paul.   Born 25 May 1808.

Jabez Leet died in Oct. 1814 and his widow married John MacDonald 13 Dec. 1815.

2. Andrew Leet married Mary MacPherson 7 Dec. 1800. She was born in Inverness, Scotland in 1782 and died 29 May 1873. She

469

was the daughter of Paul MacPherson. Andrew Leet died 16 Jan. 1865, aged 89, and the record says that he was born in Connecticut.

Family.

    11. Submit. Born 14 Apr. 1802.
    12. Joanna. Born 18 Feb. 1804.
    13. Mary. Born 19 June 1807.
    14. Margaret. Born 3 June 1809.
    15. Andrew. Born 7 May 1811.
    16. Cassandra. Born 9 Mar. 1813.
    17. James Augustus. Born 9 Apr. 1815.
    18. John Zadia. Born 9 July 1817.
    19. Isabella. Born 9 May 1820.
    20. Harriet. Born 22 July 1823.
    21. Alexander Tyrus. Born 15 Feb. 1826.
    22. Jannah.

3. Submit Leet married William Grant 9 June 1801.
4. Lucretia Leet married William Sangster 26 Jan. 1804.
6. John Leet. No record. This may be an incorrect entry in the record.
7. Andrew Leet married Margaret Bears 22 Nov. 1832.

Family.

    23. John George. Born 6 Sept. 1836.
    24. Mary Jane. Born 23 Dec. 1838.
    25. Isabel Sarah. Born 11 Dec. 1840.
    26. William Henry. Born 27 May 1842.
    27. Margaret Abigail. Born 28 Oct. 1844.
    28. Harriet Sophia. Born 4 June 1847.
    29. Elizabeth Caroline. Born 25 Dec. 1850.
    30. Martha Elizabeth. Born 9 Apr. 1855.
    31. James. Born 1835.

11. Submit Leet married Rory MacDonald.
13. Mary Leet married John Anderson 10 Dec. 1824.
14. Margaret Leet married Philip Dorey 7 May 1829.
15. Andrew Leet married Margaret Sellars.
16. Cassandra Leet married Henry Varley 27 Feb. 1832.
17. James Augustus Leet married Marjory Fraser 23 Feb. 1841.
18. John Zadia married Abigail McKay. No family.
22. Jannah Leet married Elizabeth Jane Atwater 29 Dec. 1870.
23. John George Leet married Elizabeth Jane Atwater 29 Dec. 1870.
24. Mary Jane Leet married Donald MacKenzie.
26. William Henry Leet married Anastasia Wallace, 1873.
27. Margaret Abigail Leet was married in the States.
29. Elizabeth Caroline married James Whitman.
31. James Leet married Judy Grant 11 Jan. 1871.

470

Merriam, Ebenezer. No record has been found of this man.

Munson., Mansfield. There is little record of this man to be found. There is the record of the birth of a child, Mary, born 3 Sept. 1787. His wife's name was apparently Sue or Sui. He was the son of Walter and Mable below.

Munson, Walter. Born 25 Dec. 1773 in North Haven, Connecticut, he was the son of Obadiah and Hanna Booth Munson. Married Mable Mansfield on 19 June 176?.

Scranton, David. He was the second son of Abraham Scranton and Beulah Seward, both of Durham, Conn. Abraham was the sixth child of Samuel Scranton and Elizabeth Bishop, of Guilford, Conn. Samuel Scranton was the son of Thomas, who was the son of John, who was the first white settler in Guilford, Conn., having moved there from Guilford, England, in 1639. He was twice married, his first wife, Phoebe Curtis of Durham, died before he moved to Nova Scotia. His second wife, Lorain Strong, and his oldest child, Sarah, accompanied him to Nova Scotia. .He died 5 March 1838. He was born 27 Oct. 1751. Lorain Scranton died 8 Nov. 1839. All children from 2nd wife.

Family.

1. Sarah. Born 11 Aug. 1786.
2. Nancy. Born 26 Feb. 1788.
3. Thomas Strong. Born 17 June 1789.
4. Beulah. Born 7 Mar. 1791.
5. Henry. Born 11 Nov. 1793.
6. Lois Experience. Born 12 July 1795.
7. David. Born 10 Oct. 1797.
8. Henry.)
9. Thomas Henry.) Twins. Born 26 Feb. 1802.

At the time of his death, four of his ten children, thirty-four of his thirty-nine grandchildren and thirty-two of his thirty-five great grandchildren, born before his death, were living.

1. Sarah Scranton married John McMaster 20 Sept. 1808.
2. Nancy Scranton married Allen Livingstone 28 Apr. 1812.
3. Thomas Strong Scranton died of smallpox Jan. 1801.
6. Lois Experience Scranton married George McMaster, brother of sister's husband.
7. David Scranton married Lydia Ann Simpson 23 Apr. 1824.

Family.

10. Lydia Ann. Born 9 Jan. 1825.
11. William Frederick. Born 2 July 1827.
12. Henry Allen. Born 10 Nov. 1838.
13. Sophia Caroline. Born 12 Feb. 1840.
14. David. Born 17 Sept. 1843.
15. Osbert. Born 12 Nov. 1844.
16. Sarah Maria. Born 17 July 1847.

9. Thomas Henry Scranton married Sophia Ann Porper 18 Dec. 1827. He died 8 July 1873. She died 30 Mar. 1868.

Family.
17. David.　Born 4 Nov. 1828.
18. Mary Jane.　Born 24 July 1830.
19. Wallace Frederick Porper.　Born 18 Apr. 1833.
10. Lydia Scranton married Mark Hart.
11. William Frederick Scranton married Sarah Crowdis 30 Oct. 1849.
Family.
20. William Clarence.　Born 29 Oct. 1851.
21. Sarah Olivia.　Born 4 Oct. 1853.
22. Frederick.
After the death of his first wife he married Sarah Philips.
12. Henry Allen Scranton married Angie Smart.
This family moved to the States.
16. Sarah Maria Scranton married Abram Alexander.
17. David Scranton married Rebecca Simpson 4 July 1865.
Family.
23. Thomas Henry.　Born 22 Nov. 1868.
24. W. Fenwick.　Born 5 Oct. 1866.
25. Stewart.
18. Mary Jane Scranton married John Callahan.
19. William Frederick Scranton married Ann Jane Lipsitt 23 June 1870.　No family.

Stillman, Willis.　No record has been found of this man.

Yale, Theophilus.　Little record has been found of him, except those connected with the birth of three children. He was a close connection of the founder of Yale University. Born in 1759, son of Theophilus and Azubah DeWolf Yale, he died at St. Andrews, New Brunswick in 1805. His wife was Sarah Andrews. The children were:

1. Miles.　Born 22 Oct. 1786.
2. Joseph.　Born 25 Apr. 1791.
3. Sarah.　Born 1 Apr. 1793,

474

478

327

480

484

485

487